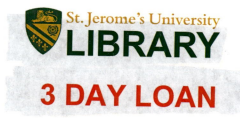

THEODICY

An Annotated Bibliography on the Problem of Evil
1960-1991

BARRY L. WHITNEY

Related Publications

Analytic Philosophy of Religion: A Bibliography 1940-1996
    Robert G. Wolf, Editor
    ISBN 0-912632-61-5
    Published in 1998

50 Years of Events: An Annotated Bibliography 1947 to 1997
    Roberto Casati & Achille C. Varzi, Editors
    ISBN 0-912632-66-6
    Published in 1997

Thomas Aquinas: International Bibliography, 1977-1990
    Richard Ingardia, Editor
    ISBN 0-912632-92-5
    Published in 1993

Published by the Philosophy Documentation Center
Bowling Green State University
Bowling Green, OH 43403-0189 USA

Phone: **419-372-2419**
Fax: **419-372-6987**
e-mail: **pdc@mailserver.bgsu.edu**
web site: **http://www.bgsu.edu/pdc**

ISBN 1-889680-01-X

Dedication

To my children,

Christopher Jón Whitney
Matthew Pétur Whitney
Barbara Lára Margrét Whitney

My three bright lights in a world too often overwhelmed by anguish and suffering. May you find the strength and wisdom to overcome the adversities which inevitably will come to you, as to all.

Contents

Preface (to the 1998 edition)

> Apart from it [the religious vision], human life is a flash of occasional enjoyments lighting up a mass of pain and misery, a bagatelle of transient experience. (Alfred North Whitehead, *Science and the Modern World,* 192)

I am grateful to Dr. George Leaman, Director of The Philosophy Documentation Center for publishing the new edition of this bibliography, first published in 1993 by Garland Publishing, Inc., New York. The text is unchanged except for some modifications and updating of the introductions to the chapters and appendices. I've also modified some of the annotations and added some new ones. It is too early to publish an updated version of the bibliography, one which extends the items beyond the 1991-1992 date of the first edition. Nonetheless, this remains the first and only extended annotated bibliography on the "theodicy" issue. Theodicy, of course, otherwise referred to as "the problem of evil," is the attempt to reconcile belief in God, particularly the western monotheistic God, with the world's suffering. I am confident that this book will continue to be an indispensable aid to scholars and students working in the field. As I note in the introductory chapter, there may be no more important and timely theological/philosophical issue than the theodicy issue. The number of publications in the past thirty-five years has continued to multiply significantly.

I have utilized various data bases, including the American Theological Library Association's *Religion Indexes I and II*, the Philosophy Documentation Center's *Philosopher's Index*, *Religious and Theological Abstracts*, and University Microfilms' *Dissertations Abstracts International*. While none of these data bases offers a complete listing of the items on theodicy, the combination of these lists and various footnoted references have resulted in as complete a bibliographical listing as exists within a single volume, and the only extended annotated bibliography on the topic. I cannot claim that the listings are fully comprehensive, but it was my goal to be as comprehensive as possible.

Despite this optimistic hope that the labors of the past few years will be beneficial, a note of cautious humility is in order. Anyone who is familiar with the research and organization involved in constructing a substantial bibliography will, I am certain, be empathetic to the inhibiting nature of the task. For those who have not attempted this particular kind of task, I can only ask for understanding. The construction of a extensive bibliography is, by the very nature of the task, a thankless one, a task doomed ultimately to fail *if* the bibliographer has illusions of seeking to be fully comprehensive. The theodicy issue is an immensely complex issue and one which has virtually endless peripheral sub-themes. Indeed, as noted more fully in *Chapter One*, the issue's related themes encompass much of the enterprise known as "theology"—the divine attributes, free will, miracles, heaven and hell, eschatology, sin, and so on. One can strive toward the ideal of comprehensiveness, but this goal quickly sinks to a morbid, yet realistic pragmatism at best, and a wistful despair at worst: it becomes apparent that the task is far greater than any one person, and group of people, even if armed with the latest in computer technology, CD-ROM data bases, and "on-line" access to several hundreds of thousands of potential entries. It becomes all-too-apparent that the scope of the task must be limited to within manageable means. Even if one could do the impossible and include all of the relevant items, the result would be a text of unmanageable complexity, length, to say nothing of the cost. Difficult decisions had to be made about what is central to the book's theme and what is peripheral. What is central to one scholar often may be deemed peripheral by another. There are, of course, seminal items and basic publications which obviously belong in the listings, but there are far more items which could be listed or delegated to peripheral status. Among the risks a bibliographer takes is that of offending other scholars who have produced first class publications on the topic at hand, but who may find their work missing from this text or relegated to appendices. Despite the constant attempt to seek both comprehensiveness and objectivity, the end result reflects the background and perspective of the bibliographer more so than one would wish. There is also the losing battle against time: with each new month, relevant new items are published and quickly incorporated into the bibliography. At some stage, the decision must be made that no further new items can be entered.

I acknowledge, with gratitude, the significant research grant funding from the Canadian government: the Social Sciences and Humanities Research Grant awarded to me (1988–1990) has been an indispensable aid in completing this book within a reasonable time. Research funding from the University of Windsor is also appreciated, as well as the administrative and sabbatical leaves granted to me in the fall semesters of 1989 and 1990, respectively. It was during these periods of release from teaching and administrative duties that the bulk of work on this project was completed. I am grateful also to former University of Windsor Academic Vice-President Gordon Wood, for permitting me to resign as Head of my department in order to find more time for the completion of this and other pressing research obligations.

To *Norris Clarke, S.J.* (Fordham University) I am particularly grateful for his support of this bibliographical project in its initial stages. To *David Griffin* (School of Theology at Claremont and Claremont Graduate School), for whom I have the deepest respect as one of the foremost theologians on the contemporary scene and as a supportive and cherished colleague, I am grateful for his interest and encouragement in this project and for his positive evaluations of my previous books on the theodicy issue, *What Are They Saying About God and Evil?* (Paulist, 1989) and *Evil and the Process God* (Mellen, 1985). To *John Hick* (Claremont and Birmingham), *John Cobb* (School of Theology at Claremont and Claremont Graduate School), *Richard Creel* (Ithaca College), *Robert Mesle* (Graceland College), *Philip Devenish* (Divinity School, University of Chicago), and many others, I am grateful for the kind words they have written about my previous publications on theodicy and in process theology and philosophy. To *John C. Robertson, Jr.* (McMaster University), in particular, I am indebted for having introduced me to the writings of Alfred North Whitehead and Charles E. Hartshorne. From process thought, I have gained invaluable insights into life and into the rewards of philosophical theology. Process metaphysics has revealed to me the aesthetic meaning of life, the fundamental rightness of it all, and the possibilities for hope and goodness amid and despite the inevitable suffering and anguish we must endure, the bagatelle of human misery and woe. It has been a distinct privilege to have been able to know *Charles Hartshorne* (University of Texas) as a great and humane human being as well as a great philosopher. I am indebted also to *Lewis S. Ford* (Old Dominion University) for his continued interest and assistance in my career and in me as a unique human being. I am grateful to *Ian Weeks* (Australia's Deakin

University) for introducing me to the theodicy issue and analytical thinking so long ago when I was a graduate student at McMaster University.

While I have spent long hours collecting, organizing, reading and annotating the hundreds of publications entered in this bibliography, some of my former graduate students have aided me in the drudgery of photocopying articles and chapters and in collecting and ordering hundreds of books and articles through the University of Windsor's Inter-Library Loan service. Among those who participated in this manual labour with enthusiasm were *Wayne Harter* (1987), *Carolyn Whelan* (1988), *Ruth Lavery* (1989), *John MacDonald* (1990), *Barbara Delisle* (1991) and my son, *Christopher Whitney* (1992).

While this is a book about human suffering, it is appropriate to include such an acknowledgement which affirms life. Despite the suffering, amid all the sorrow and misery that humans beings bring to one another and the suffering which comes from an amoral and impersonal nature, there is joy and hope and beauty to be found in the world—in friendships and in the love of one's children. Mystical writings speak of the "peace which passes all understanding," of the unity and hope that permeates all life. Despite the suffering and anguish we must all endure, there is opportunity for the experience of such positive affirmations of life. I rejoice particularly in the lives of my children, *Christopher Jón Whitney*, *Matthew Pétur Whitney*, and *Barbara Lára Margrét Whitney*. While their world was ravaged and we have been separated by hundreds of miles since work on this book began in 1987, my love for them and their love in return has always been the foundation of my hope and inspiration. I hope that all that is good in me will live on and grow in them. All that is not so good in me and in my life, I hope, will not be a burden to them.

That the universe is friendly is, as Einstein recognized, the most important human question and to experience it as such is perhaps the most important means of coping with suffering. That the universe imparts to us a sense of fundamental rightness, without which all else would be merely pain and misery, is a truth Whitehead acknowledged and one which we all ought to seek and appropriate.

Barry L. Whitney
University of Windsor
7 September 1997

Chapter 1

Introduction

This is the first and only extended annotated bibliography of publications on the significant and increasingly prominent theological/philosophical issue of "*theodicy*," the so-called "*problem of evil*." Such a bibliography obviously is long overdue.[1] If there is a more pressing and contentious issue faced by contemporary theologians, I am uncertain what it could be. It would be easy to refer virtually to scores of publications that assign to the theodicy issue its fundamentally central role among the issues facing contemporary theologians and philosophers of religion. Considering this, the fact that there has been a renewed scholarly interest in theodicy and an ever-increasing compilation of publications is itself long overdue. The theological community has been complacent about the theodicy issue for far too long, due largely to the dominance of the Augustinian influence (see below). Yet, the past thirty years has seen an explosion of publications on the problem of reconciling God and suffering, and the number of publications continues to multiply annually at an astounding pace.

Interest in the theodicy issue slowly is permeating into the public sphere as well. The cover story of *Time*, June 10, 1991, entitled "Evil," (written by Lance Morrow) reflects this fact, as does the phenomenon of Rabbi Harold Kushner's best selling book, *When Bad Things Happen to Good People*. Over three million copies in several languages have been sold. Process theologian David Griffin and Kushner appeared on Dan Rather's *CBS Evening News* (January 4, 1983) in response to the controversy occasioned by Kushner's book and the flurry of letters resulting from a *Los Angeles Times* article on "Process Theology: God's Power Over Evil Questioned?" (October 19, 1982).[2] Many writers other than Kushner, of course, have written about theodicy on a popular level; they have done so in response to the increasing need of the general populace to come to terms with the suffering in the world and its very real threat to belief in God. Traditional Judaeo-Christianity has not answered the question satisfactorily, especially for this post-holocaust age. Kushner's book, which is in fact a version of process theology, challenged the traditional doctrine of divine power as the cause of all things, of all goods and evils. The fact that this book and its thesis have had such an astonishing influence attests to the deep dissatisfaction with traditional understandings of God and the problem of suffering. Not only professional theologians and philosophers of religion, but the general populace seeks new insights into the issue of suffering and, in particular, its relationship to God.

The fact that there has been no detailed, annotated and comprehensive bibliographical resource to guide scholars, student researchers, and the general populace through the unimaginably large amount of material available is baffling.[3] This book seeks to ameliorate this situation as much as possible by providing an informed account of the most important publications in the field. I cannot claim that this present bibliography is fully comprehensive, since (as discussed below) the overwhelming number of items and related issues frustrates any attempt at total comprehensiveness. I have included, nevertheless, the publications I consider to be the most relevant and important in the contemporary discussions. The goal of this bibliography was the idealistic one of including everything that is relevant and excluding (or relegating to appendices) those items that are related but not as central to the main issues. A fuller explanation of this methodology and selection criteria follows.

I   Methodology and Selection Criteria

This book was intended originally to complement my 1989 book, *What Are They Saying About God and Evil?* (Mahwah, NJ: Paulist Press; available now from the author in an undated version, 1998), and my 1985 book, *Evil and the Process God* (Lewiston, NY: Edwin Mellen Press). While the latter book focuses on process theodicy, it provides (as does the Paulist book) an overview of the various contemporary options and major thinkers who have discussed the theodicy issue. The present bibliography presents these options in a different format and includes references, obviously, to far more writers and positions. Some may have wished that this present bibliography contained more critical assessment. I would agree with them, but the insertion of my critical commentaries not only would have intruded upon an objective presentation of the material but would have resulted in a much lengthier and far more complex volume. The present bibliography permits the authors to speak for themselves—through my summaries of their main arguments and conclusions—and allows the researcher to draw his or her own conclusions without the distraction of my critical assessments. The publication of a companion volume of substantial critical essays is planned, as well as periodic updates of new items to supplement this present bibliography.

When I began to investigate in an academic and systematic manner the various articles, books, book chapters, reviews and dissertations on the theodicy problem as long ago as 1972, I was astonished to discover that there was an almost unmanageable mass of literature. The number of publications in the English language during the past 30 years approaches several thousand, and if publications in other languages and, more particularly, if related issues were included, the number would be in the tens of thousands. As such, I have had to limit the items included in this bibliography to those that focus directly on, and contribute significantly to, the current philosophical and theological issues on the theodicy issue. Book reviews are not included, with the exceptions of a selected few that are significant "review articles," written by or about major writers who have contributed notably to the theodicy issue. The bibliography is limited to items in English, including English translations from other languages. The items listed have been published from 1960 to 1990, with the exception of some significant items written before 1960 and some 1991 and 1992 items I was able to include before the manuscript was sent to the original publisher (Garland).

I am aware that any selective process is somewhat of a subjective decision, but I submit that selectiveness was not only necessary but an informed decision, made with as much objectivity as possible.[4] The goal was to omit nothing that is relevant, to include nothing that is irrelevant, and to present the material clearly and accurately. The task has been complicated by the fact that there are so many related items: the enormous literature on the *holocaust*, the interminable and fascinating literature on *divine attributes* (omnipotence, omniscience, immutability, etc.), the *free will—determinism issue*, the related themes concerning divine *providence*, the issue of *sin* and *original sin*, the *biblical writings* on suffering and divine righteousness (including the massive literature on the *Book of Job*), and countless other aspects of theological thought. These related items are germane in one way or another to the discussion of theodicy. Yet, obviously, a complete annotated listing which included these related issues would be hopelessly long and unavoidably complex. As such, I have included what I consider the most relevant of these related items (approximately 2,600 items, many of which are annotated) in appendices and in lists at the ends of each chapter. The remaining annotated items (approximately 1,500 items) are those which have been published in the past thirty years (and more particularly, the past twenty years), those which focus on the problem of evil in the most creative and efficacious manner.

The material is organized into six annotated chapters and five appendices. The annotated chapters are as follows: *Chapter 2*, "Free Will Theodicy," lists items on the free will solution and defense, as well as relevant publications on divine omnipotence and omniscience; *Chapter 3*, "Best Possible World Theodicy," lists items about the best possible world and the greater good defense, as well as references to the debates about "Middle Knowledge" and other related issues; *Chapter 4*, "Natural Evil Theodicy," lists publications about the problem of natural or physical evil, and includes references to the related problem of animal suffering; *Chapter 5*, "Hick's Irenaean Theodicy," lists publications by and about John Hick, whose theodicy has presented a clear alternative to traditional Augustinian theodicy; *Chapter 6*, "Process Theodicy," lists the relevant publications about process theodicy, an even more radical alternative to traditional Augustinian theodicy, and lists also items on related issues, the question of divine power in particular; and *Chapter 7*, "Other Philosophical Theodicies," is subdivided into various sections: proponents of theism, opponents of theism, various critical discussions, the question of God and the Good, and related publications.

Items relegated to the five appendices are as follows: *Appendix A*, "Biblical Theodicy"; *Appendix B*, "Historical Theodicy," including Thomism—for which many of the items are annotated; *Appendix C*, "Suffering of God Theodicy"; *Appendix D*, "Miscellaneous Publications," sub-divided into several sections; and *Appendix E*, "Dissertations."

I have referred already to the justification for this categorization and division of the material, but let me elaborate. As an informed theodicist, having researched and published in this area since the mid-1970s and having read with care over 4,000 of the relevant publications since that time, I have made the decision that the items annotated in the six chapters are more central to the current debates and to a profitable advancement of the issue than the items assigned to the appendices and non-annotated lists at the end of the chapters. The choice I faced was to include these peripheral items in appendices and in lists at the end of the chapters or omit them entirely. I chose the former, with the support of Garland's senior editor, since these items are the most relevant of the thousands of items peripheral to the contemporary discussions on theodicy. It goes without saying, I presume, that these items are important in their own right. My point is that they are not as central to the current philosophical and analytical theological debates focused upon in this bibliography's six annotated chapters. There will likely be a difference of opinion about some of these, but this is the unavoidable result of the subjectivity of the author, despite the idealistic goal of objectivity.

Appendix A is a case in point: biblical scholars, with very few exceptions, have not entered into the theological and philosophical debates as much as we might have wished. Their publications include countless hundreds of items on *The Book of Job*, as well as innumerable discussions on questions of divine justice, the suffering servant, divine sovereignty, etc. These discussions obviously are important, but only a relatively small handful of biblical scholars has related such discussions directly to the contemporary debates on the theodicy question *per se*.

Appendix B may be more contentious. Some readers may object to the relegation of discussions of historical writers (most particularly Augustine, Aquinas, Hume, and Leibniz) to an appendix. Yet these items, in my opinion, are of a different order than the annotated items included in the six chapters. Historical figures certainly have made significant contributions to theodicy, but are no longer considered central in the majority of the contemporary philosophical discussions. The influence of Augustine and Hume is still pervasive, of course, and Roman Catholic writers continue to refer directly and explicitly to the writings of Thomas Aquinas as the key to unlocking the theodicy mystery. To acknowledge these facts, I have not merely listed the relevant items on historical theodicy but annotated many of the entries. Thomistic writers have continued to exploit and develop what I refer to as the Augustinian—Thomistic theodicy. In my opinion, these publications (in general, at least) provide little advancement of the contemporary debates; they have only fleeting association with the contemporary, "mainstream" philosophical and theological issues being discussed. Indeed, they are far more theological (in a conservative sense) than the philosophical emphasis in the publications listed in the annotated chapters. I endorse fully John Hick's point that "Augustine's theodicy has continued substantially unchanged with the Roman Catholic Church to the present day. It was adopted also by the Protestant Reformers of the sixteenth-century and has been virtually unquestioned as Protestant doctrine until within approximately the last 100 years."[5] Indeed, Augustine's theodicy has persisted through the centuries, as Hick notes, not "because it is an inherently satisfying response to the mystery of evil, but because the Christian mind was for so long content to refrain from examining it critically."[6] John Hick's theodicy—and much more so, Whiteheadian-Hartshornean process metaphysics and its radical new vision of God, has awakened many of us from our Augustinian slumber.

Appendix C is included since the "suffering of God" theme has become one of the most important new aspects of the contemporary debates in theodicy. The theology of the suffering of God has had a variety of sources, but perhaps none so pervasive as the writings of process philosophers and theologians who deny the omnipotent power ascribed to the more traditional theism espoused by Christian theology.

Appendix D lists in several sub-sections almost 1,300 related, yet peripheral publications. These items include such topics as *Sin, Pain, Satan*, the *Holocaust* and *Jewish Theodicy, Providence, Theodicy in Literature, Women and Theodicy, Non-Christian Theodicy*, and a large number of *Miscellaneous Publications* that contain not only general writings and surveys but also important perspectives on *Existential Coping* and some of the *Ethical Aspects* of the theodicy issue. The lists are selective, although every effort has been made to include the most important and relevant items, important in their own right (as is the case with all the items contained in the non-annotated lists).

Appendix E, finally, arguably is not peripheral, since by their very nature dissertations contain references to and discussions of issues being debated in contemporary publications. Not all of these items, for various reasons, are worthy of publication, however, and this has been a factor in acknowledging these writings, but without annotations.

Before turning to a brief discussion of the theodicy issue in its historical and contemporary setting, and before outlining the content of the annotated chapters, there are some other methodological and procedural points to which I wish to draw attention.[7]

I have not cross-listed any of the items. Each entry is listed only once and assigned a single item number, although at least several hundred of the entries easily could have been entered many times in various places throughout the bibliography. This lack of cross-listing may be seen as a problem to some researchers, but my decision was based largely on the attempt to keep the present book within manageable page-limits. I have sought to compensate for the lack of duplicate listings of items by referring within the annotations to the related items.

Other considerations are relevant not only to the choice of items that have been annotated but to the varying lengths and nature of the annotations. I have referred above to the fact that my task was to include in the annotated chapters all the writings that contribute in a creative and significant manner to the current theological and philosophical debates in the published literature. I have included some items that are somewhat peripheral because they have been written by scholars who have made significant contributions to the theodicy issue. With respect to the length of the annotations and the format, I have focused upon the main theses of the individual items and, more particularly, on the item's contributions to the theodicy issue. The length of the annotations does not reflect necessarily the importance of the items; this was not the sole nor even the most central consideration. More relevant to the length of individual annotations was the complexity of the argumentation and the avoidance of undue repetition.

II   The Theological Problem of Evil

The problem of suffering is the greatest threat to belief in God.[8] As such, it is the responsibility of theologians and philosophers of religion to seek intelligible explanations for the reason(s) God permits evil. This is not to say that the issue can be fully comprehended by finite human minds, but to dispense with rational investigation in the name of blind faith would be irresponsible and would contradict the very essence of theology (*theos* = "God" + *logos* = "reason"), as rational thinking about God, "faith seeking understanding," as Augustine put it so long ago. Some would argue, I would note, that the issue cannot be settled rationally and that the attempt to do so borders on impiety and human arrogance. Yet, if this indeed were the case, all theological activity would be such, since theology is the active search for rational understanding of religious doctrines and beliefs. Basing one's beliefs and one's faith in biblical texts or traditional church teachings may seem to some to be the only acceptable approach, but the biblical writings do not contain systematic theodicies and the past centuries of biblical criticism have revealed the human hand in these writings, despite these writings supposedly being divinely inspired. Denominational dogma, likewise, betrays a human hand and formulations of religious doctrines that are conditioned by the presuppositions and world views of the formulators.

[a] The Faith Solution and Rational Solutions

The "faith solution" appeals to faith as the ultimate (and only legitimate) solution to the theodicy issue: God has given or permits the evil and suffering we must endure for good reasons, it is held, reasons that are beyond complete human comprehension. I concede that this appeal to faith and the mystery of divine action as the bases for a resolution of the problem of evil may have the positive value of giving comfort to the sufferer and a reassurance that the suffering has a meaning and purpose. The faith solution offers to suffering people and to intellectuals writing about the issue an alluring and simple solution: all things, it is believed, are in the hands of God and beyond human understanding. With this belief, evil supposedly is to be endured in the faith that its source is in God's providential plan. If the sufferer believes that the evil has a divinely ordained or divinely condoned meaning, any suffering most likely can be endured. Perhaps the evil is a test of faith, or a means to bring us to greater goods, or divine punishment or discipline. Perhaps the evil is the result of evil powers. These explanations and others have been proposed in the biblical writings and repeated throughout the Christian centuries. The basic premise has been that God is in control (despite human free will) and that the perfect world envisaged and created by God has been destroyed by the fall of Adam and Eve.

But there are some serious negative consequences of such a position. Not only can the faith solution result in an abdication of reason and rational inquiry, it can lead to an abandonment of human responsibility for evil and suffering. Belief that all things are in the hands of God and beyond human comprehension and human control, moreover, can lead to fatalism and despair, an attitude that we have no control over our lives and, hence, no responsibility to seek to overcome the suffering and anguish of the poor and destitute.

The premise upon which the faith solution is based (noted above) is no longer prevalent outside conservative circles—Thomism and evangelical Protestantism, and the general populace with its popular theology, largely untouched by academic theological discussions. The religious world view has been challenged by the rise of the scientific paradigm as a naturalistic alternative: the world is explained in terms of physics and chemistry, as the product of blind and random evolution. Belief in God has been questioned on many fronts and is no longer assumed by many, nor assumed easily by the many who continue to believe in an all-loving and all-powerful God. Biblical criticism and "demythologizing" have shed light on the human hand in the scriptures and in denominational dogmas. In the contemporary world, the problem of evil has become an argument against God's existence, a situation which is of unparalleled urgency for theistic apologists. In the contemporary world, which has been witness to a new and overwhelming symbol of evil, the Nazi holocaust, belief in the traditional God of Judaeo-Christianity, a God who controls all worldly affairs with loving providence is—to say the least—no longer as indisputable nor as certain as it once was to the eyes of faith or certainly to the eyes of rational theological investigation. Serious theological attention to the problem of evil is required, and the past thirty years has witnessed this welcomed phenomenon.

There are two major approaches by which the problem of evil is addressed: it can be faced existentially or theoretically/philosophically. The latter seeks to understand evil and its relationship to God, to seek explanations that are intellectually tenable as well as pragmatically appealing. The free will defense, theodicies of natural evil, Hick's Irenaean theodicy, the process theodicies, and assorted other motifs are examples. The existential approach focuses upon the sufferer and practical means to cope with and to overcome the suffering. The emphasis is not upon understanding and explanation, but with the everyday struggles against evil. This aspect of the theodicy issue appeals more directly to the general populace, of course, since the theoretical approach is far more intellectually demanding, esoteric and increasingly sophisticated in its argumentation. The major existential writings are listed in *Appendix D*. These publications are important in their own right, yet peripheral to the theoretical writings annotated in the chapters.

I wish to note that while I readily concede that existential coping is not only a significant aspect of the theodicy issue but a human necessity, I suggest that without some rational underpinning, some viable theodicy, coping can be seriously hindered by poor or non-existent explanations for the suffering with which we seek to cope. I contend that we can cope better if we have some understanding of the reasons for the evil and suffering which affects us. I reject the argument (used, for example, by Kushner and a host of others) that the sufferer wants consolation rather than explanation. Both are necessary, and the latter can be an indispensable aid to the former. To believe in naïve, uninformed, and unquestioning faith that afflictions have been caused by God for a good reason (unknown to human beings) may indeed sustain the sufferer in the midst of crisis; yet, such a faith may find that it has a breaking point and that the human mind is driven toward a more mature and critical faith which seeks rational understanding of the suffering and its relationship to God. Faith, indeed, seeks understanding, and while the *Book of Job* reminds us that Wisdom lies in God alone, the light of that wisdom shines also, I feel certain, in human beings, however dimly.

My hope is that the intellectual activities of professional theologians and philosophers (which seek to formulate rational explanations for suffering and its relationship to God) will become more accessible to the general masses. To speak in terms which are meaningful to the non-professional populace has, of course, been the challenge of professional theologians and philosophers for centuries, as it is in other disciplines, notably science. Yet the incredible reaction to Kushner's book shows how hungry common people are for new ways to understand and cope with the suffering we all endure. Kushner's book lacks intellectual rigor, of course, and deliberately so: he wrote it for the non-professional, for the sufferer who seeks consolation. Similar books by Philip Yancey and Burton Cooper (and several dozens of others) have not gained the attention of the public as much as Kushner's book has, but some of them may be more adept in bridging the gap between the intellectual and existential perspectives. One reviewer of my 1989 book, *What Are They Saying About God and Evil?* (currently available, as noted above, only from the author in an updated edition, 1998), has suggested that this book in fact has bridged the gap (where Kushner's did not) between theoretical theodicies and the non-professional public. I certainly hope this might prove to be the case, although the book was not written as an existential coping aid, but rather as a means by which a sufferer can gain informed rational insight into his or her suffering and use that insight to cope better with the suffering.

[b] Contemporary Theodicies

After several centuries of accepting in near unanimity the Augustinian solution (adopted by Aquinas and the Protestant Reformers), the past decades have produced radically different ways to address the issues. John Hick's Irenaean theodicy *(Chapter 5)* has been one major option that challenges many of the premises of the more traditional theodicy. The process theodicies, developed from the writings of Alfred North Whitehead and Charles Hartshorne, have been an even more radical option, rejecting and redefining the traditional doctrine of divine power and other supposed attributes of God *(Chapter 6)*. There have been a variety of other theological and philosophical writings focused upon the free will defense *(Chapter 2)*, the best possible world theodicy *(Chapter 3)*, and the problem of physical evil *(Chapter 4)*. The discussions in the 1960s and 1970s focused on the "logical" problem of evil, but more recent discussions are directed more toward the "evidential" problem and the question of gratuitous evil.[9] The logical problem centered upon the famous triad of (alleged) logically inconsistent propositions: God is omnipotent; God is omnibenevolent; and yet evil exists. Atheists (or, more generally, sceptics) argued that theists had to make the impossible choice between denying the reality of evil or denying the attributes and the existence of God. Theists, in turn, denied that there was any logical inconsistency between the defined attributes of God and the existence of evil. Alvin Plantinga's response to John Mackie's famous challenge may have resolved this version of the theodicy problem (see below).

Both atheists and theists have recognized increasingly that the logical problem is inadequate to settle the issue. Debate now centers upon the inductive, evidential issue concerning the amount of evil in the world and whether this evil counts as decisive evidence against God's existence. Current debates also address the related problem of gratuitous evil: some evil indeed may be compatible with God's existence as an all-powerful and all-good creator, but is there not too much meaningless evil to permit belief in God as justified?

Both the logical and the evidential versions of the problem of evil are discussed throughout the annotated chapters, although *Chapter 7* in particular considers the discussions most explicitly. I wish to note that it is often difficult to distinguish between the logical and evidential versions in the writings of many of the advocates and opponents of theism. The distinction, as such, is somewhat artificial, but it is helpful as one means by which to categorize and organize the myriad of items that have been published. My alternative has been to organize the material (in *Chapter 7*) into proponents/defenders of God vis-à-vis evil, opponents/sceptics, and various related issues which have been discussed in the literature of the past three decades.

[c] Moral and Physical Evil

Discussions of the problem of evil generally consider the problem as at least two distinct, though related, problems: "moral evil," and "natural evil" or "physical evil." Moral evil is defined as evil caused deliberately (or, perhaps at times, unintentionally) by human beings. Moral evil includes such vices as the greed, hatred, contempt, deceit, and the countless other means by which we mutually torment each other as well as wreak havoc on ourselves and on non-human creatures and the environment. Many writers have suggested that moral evil is the cause of most human suffering: Augustine believed that moral evil is the result of the misuse of human freedom and that *all* evil is moral evil—or, more precisely, that all evil is moral evil or its consequence: physical evil. The latter was understood by him as divine punishment for moral evil. More recently, C.S. Lewis estimated that four-fifths of the world's evil is the result of human wickedness. I would suggest that the figure is even higher: *most* of the evil and suffering seems to be caused by human beings. The issue then becomes: does human responsibility for moral evil conflict with or contradict the understanding we have of divine causative power? *Chapter 2* and *Chapter 3* focus on moral evil. They address the contentious free will defense, the leading candidate to explain moral evil. Alvin Plantinga's free will defense employs a "best possible world" ontology (see *Chapter 3*), and as such, this theme has been greatly influential in the contemporary discussions.

Although most of the world's evil may be moral evil, physical evil is real ("genuine," rather than merely "apparent") and, as a major aspect of the theodicy issue, likewise demands an explanation. *Chapter 4* annotates the major publications that address this issue, focusing upon the theodicies of Richard Swinburne, Bruce Reichenbach, and Austin Farrer, among others. The chapter includes a list of writings on a closely related issue: animal suffering. There are, I wish to note, many other significant contributions to natural evil theodicy, contributions that are listed in other chapters: the process theodicies, Hick's theodicy, Plantinga's theodicy, to name just a few. The same applies to the moral evil issue. Process theodicy claims to have a free will defense of moral (and physical) evil that is far more valid than past versions, but discussion of the process version of the free will defense and its discussions of moral and physical evil are contained in *Chapter 6*. Hick's theodicy, likewise, explains moral evil in terms of the free will defense, but this discussion and his justification of natural evil are contained mostly in *Chapter 5*, rather than in the chapters on the free will defense and natural evil *(Chapter 4)*. There is, as such, a problem of sorts with the lack of cross-referencing; but (as noted above), to have cross-listed virtually hundreds of items would have expanded the size and complexity of this book very significantly. The index, I trust, and references within the annotations to the relevant texts, provides an acceptable option. As noted above, each publication is listed only once and has been assigned only one item number.

Notes

1. The American Theological Library Association had available for a short time a "special bibliography" on "Theodicy, Suffering, Good and Evil." The first was edited by G.F. Dickerson in 1981; the second was edited by Tom Davis in 1987. While neither is available, I had access to the draft version of the Davis edition, for which I am very grateful. The ATLA data list covers several hundred theological journals *(Religion Index I)* as well as books and multi-authored publications *(Religion Index II)*. I am also grateful for the data list of philosophical publications provided by the Philosophy Documentation Center which publishes *The Philosopher's Index*. The selected articles abstracted in *Religious and Theological Abstracts* was also helpful as a data source, among others. For dissertations, I made use of the University Microfilms data base and *Dissertations Abstracts International*. I have selected the relevant items from these data bases and supplemented them with footnoted and bibliographical references I have found in numerous publications.

2. As I was preparing this manuscript for press, Paul Galloway, feature writer for *The Chicago Tribune*, interviewed Plantinga, Hick, as well as myself for a feature article about "evil." The recent mass murders in Milwaukee occasioned this article.

3. The data bases acknowledged in note 1 are the sole exceptions, and none of the lists is comprehensive of the relevant items. The listings vary significantly in the quality of the annotations when there are annotations. It is interesting to note that David Griffin, an eminent process theologian and influential writer on the theodicy issue, made reference in his review of Arthur McGill's *Suffering: A Test of Theological Method*, stating that he (Griffin) had been unaware of this book, first published in 1968 (reissued in 1982). Griffin notes: "My own reflection on the problem of evil and divine power would have been greatly enriched by McGill's ideas." One wonders how much the published debates on the theodicy issue would have been altered if a comprehensive bibliography had been available. Certainly, much needless repetition would have been avoided and articles written in apparent ignorance of relevant items presumably would have been modified.

4. David Griffin, in his *Evil Revisited*, has been kind enough to refer to my work in theodicy as earning me the status of "fast becoming the world's authority on the problem of evil." I am especially grateful for this aculeate since Griffin is among the world's most important theologians and has done very significant work on the theodicy issue. I am grateful also to John Hick's positive evaluation on my 1989 Paulist book, *What Are They Saying About God and Evil?* and his complimentary comments about the first edition of this present bibliography (1993). Hick's classic book, *Evil and the God of Love*, has had a major influence on the theodicy issue. My study of process theodicy, *Evil and the Process God*, is indebted to the writings of Charles Hartshorne and Alfred North Whitehead, the insights of whom (together with David Griffin's elaborations) have been revolutionary for the theodicy issue.

5. John Hick, *Evil and the God of Love*, 246.

6. John Hick, *Evil and the God of Love*, 61.

7. In the interests of consistency, I have spelled the word "defense" throughout with an "s" rather than with a "c." The actual spelling in the publications varied between the two.

8. Aquinas noted that the problem of evil and the problems associated with proving God's existence were the main challenges to belief in God. I would add that among the other serious threats to belief in God is the rise of science in the past three centuries. Science defines the world purely naturalistically (without reference to God or anything supernatural or spiritual). Its world view is based on physics and chemistry; there is no reference to God or divine teleology.

9. Since the publication of the first edition of this present bibliography in 1993, a very significant collection of essays on the "evidential" problem of evil has been published: *The Evidential Problem of Evil*, edited by Daniel Howard-Synder (Bloomington, IN: Indiana University Press, 1996). Many of the essays are new. The authors are William Rowe, Paul Draper, Richard Swinburne, Eleonore Stump, Alvin Plantinga, William

Alston, Stephen Wykstra, Peter van Inwagen, Paul Draper, Bruce Russell, Richard Gale, and Daniel Howard-Synder. Another significant book published in early 1998 is David O'Connor's *God and Inscrutable Evil* (Lanham, MD: Rowman and Littlefield). O'Connor discusses both the logical and evidential problems of evil, dealing with the issue largely from the perspective of natural gratuitous evil.

Chapter 2

Free Will Theodicy

This chapter lists and annotates publications which focus on the free will solution to the problem of evil. Alvin Plantinga has made an important distinction between a free will *defense* and a free will *theodicy*, and while this distinction has been much discussed in the literature (see below), the free will theodicy generally has been referred to as "the free will defense."[1] Philosophers and theologians have, for several hundred years, attributed moral evil to the misuse and abuse of free will by human beings, be it intentional or unintentional or the necessity of "double effect."[2] There has been, however, a significant resurgence of interest in this strategy during the past few decades. While I find the observation of *George Schlesinger* to be somewhat of an exaggeration (that "the free will defense has been subject to a greater amount of discussion by analytic philosophers, in the last 25 years or so, than have the rest of the solutions put together"),[3] the free will defense/theodicy undeniably has been exceptionally influential and the subject of an impressive theological/philosophical mass of literature. The writings of *Alvin Plantinga* and his commentators, in particular, have dominated during the past two decades, a fact clearly reflected in the annotated section of this chapter and in the annotated section of the following chapter *(Best Possible World Theodicy)*. Since Plantinga's free will defense employs a "best possible world" ontology,[4] many of the items listed in *Chapter 3* are interrelated with many of the items listed in this present chapter, particularly as they concern discussions of Plantinga's writings.

The publications listed at the end of the annotated section in this present chapter, I wish to note, are listed because they are pertinent to the free will theodicy. They discuss, for example, the (re)defining and reconciling of the divine attributes—omnipotence and omniscience in particular—with human free will. *John Mackie's* seminal article, "Evil and Omnipotence" *(Mind* 64 [1955]), established this link clearly. This article and related publications became a major impetus in the growing literature centered on the issue of God's power, human freedom and their relevance for the theodicy issue. *Antony Flew's* highly influential article, "Divine Omniscience and Human Freedom" *(New Essays in Philosophical Theology*, edited by Flew and Alasdair MacIntyre, SCM, 1955*)*, should also be cited for its significant role in the renewed interest in the free will defense. Plantinga has credited Flew with coining the term, "free will defense," and has acknowledged that he (Plantinga) first encountered the defense through the writings of Mackie and Flew.[5] The Flew-MacIntyre volume, moreover, can be credited as having been one of the most significant influences toward the reinstatement of philosophy of religion as a legitimate philosophical and theological discipline.

The free will defense, of course, has been a central feature of theodicy since at least the time of *Augustine*.[6] There is, as far as I can ascertain, no explanation for moral evil other than that of the misuse of human free will. A possible exception would be the attribution of moral evil to the "fall" of Adam and Eve. Yet, the vast majority of philosophers and theologians who fill the annotated chapters of this bibliography do not base rational theodicy upon the Adamic myth. This remains one of the issues which separates analytic philosophers of religion from more conservative writers who are more literal in their interpretation of the Judaeo–Christian teachings. There is no doubt that confessional perspectives, which consider issues such as original sin, the fall, heaven and hell, Christology, etc., shed a different light on the theodicy issue than does purely rational, analytic philosophical attempts to come to terms with the problem. The two perspectives, nevertheless are interlinked somewhat: the confessional perspective contributes existential and concrete reality to the often arid philosophical analyses, while the latter, of course, contributes precision and analytic argumentation to an otherwise potentially blind and rationally uninformed confessional stance. The present bibliography focuses upon the philosophical publications, yet lists hundreds of theological and existential publications in *Appendix D*.

Historically, *Augustine* exploited (indeed, originated) the free will explanation as the central feature of his theodicy, arguing that all evil is the result of human free will.[7] Augustine, to be sure, leaned heavily toward a theological determinism and a conception of divine omnipotence which seems to render creaturely freedom problematic. The fact that major theological and philosophical writers followed Augustine's lead, nonetheless, is a matter of history. *Aquinas* and his significant number of disciples, for example, argued that God acted as the "primary cause" of all human action, but relegated to human beings the power of "secondary" causation. This is one means by which Aquinas argued for genuine freedom, and as such, found an explanation for moral evil. Yet the distinction between these two types of causation has been rejected as meaningless by later writers—process philosophers, in particular.[8] (See the Thomistic section in *Appendix B* and the criticisms by process writers *(Chapter 6).*

A fundamental question addressed by the analytic philosophical writings on free will has been that of determining whether or not such free will is compatible with divine omnipotence and omniscience. There is a massive literature on the "free will—determinism" debate, not all of which could not be included in this chapter. I *have* included those publications which deal most significantly with the free will issue as it relates to the theodicy question.

While *Austin Farrer* and, more recently, *Alvin Plantinga* are perhaps the foremost defenders of the free will argument, and while Farrer's free will defense has been cited as among the most significant works on the issue,[9] he did not exploit this defense in his theodicy. Plantinga *has* done so, and a significant number of publications have focused on Plantinga's work. He is widely recognized as among the most significant of contemporary contributors to the discussions on the problem of evil.[10] Plantinga's work, indeed, is seminal. His book, *God and Other Minds* (1967), has been cited as "the most important contribution to the philosophy of religion that has appeared in several decades."[11] He followed this with *God, Freedom and Evil* (1974) and *The Nature of Necessity* (1974), as well as a number of articles which not only clarify and defend his free will defense, but argue related points: that belief in the existence of God is rational and "basic," that the ontological proof for God's existence is valid, etc.

As noted above, while proponents of the free will defense or a free will theodicy generally assume that free will is of such significance that it outweighs the evil free will produces, there are significant criticisms of the free will solution in the writings of philosophers like *John Mackie, H.J. McCloskey, Antony Flew, Michael Martin, Peter Hare* and *Edward Madden*, among many others. It was John Mackie and Antony Flew who initiated the contemporary flurry of publications and interest in the free will defense, a phenomenon which has continued unabated for the past four decades.[12] Their logical challenge seems to have been met, but the evidential problem remains (see *Chapter 7*).

A significant number of the publications listed in this chapter, and a large number in the following chapter, center upon the writings of *Alvin Plantinga*. He has distinguished his free will *defense* from free will *theodicy*. A "defense" does *not* attempt, as does a "theodicy," to explain the existence of evil; it is a defense against the arguments which hold there is a logical inconsistency in the propositions that God is omnipotent and wholly good, and that evil exists. A defense at best tells us what reasons God might possibly have for not preventing evil. According to Plantinga, such possible reasons need not be *true*; they need only be *possible*—a position which has been criticized by many writers: is a defense enough, or do we not need a theodicy as well?

Plantinga claims that the heart of the free will defense is to find a proposition which is consistent with the propositions just stated (God as omnipotent and omnibenevolent exists, and evil exists). The proposition to which Plantinga refers would show that it is possible that God could not have created a world containing moral good (or *as much* moral good as this world contains) without creating a world which also contains moral evil. Plantinga appeals to the idea of "trans-world depravity" as the proposition needed to explain why God could not actualize a world in which people are significantly free and yet never do wrong. "Every essence suffers from trans-world depravity,"[13] a proposition which need not be *true*, but merely *possible*. Plantinga argues that it is *possible* that God could *not* have created a universe wherein creatures act always for good. Against the compatibilist objection (Mackie and Flew, etc.) that God could have created free creatures and could have caused them somehow never to do anything wrong without contradicting their freedom, Plantinga assumes an incompatibilist view: freedom as incompatible with determinism. He rejects the view that an omnipotent God could have created any possible world, including a world with moral good but with no moral evil. Thinking otherwise, Plantinga argues, was "Leibniz's lapse," repeated by countless others.

This brings Plantinga to the complex and much discussed issue of "middle knowledge," the listings for which are entered in the following chapter. The sixteenth century Jesuit theologian, *Luis de Molina*, espoused this view;[14] namely, that God knows what every possible free creature would do freely in every situation in which that creature could act freely. Such knowledge is referred to as "middle knowledge," since it falls between God's knowledge of the actual and the possible, and between God's knowledge of necessary truths and truths God causes to be true.[15] (See *Chapter 3*).

I wish to point out that while a great proportion of the contemporary discussions of the free will defense and free will theodicy have been centered on Plantinga's writings, there certainly are many other significant publications which relegate central importance to free will theodicy. This chapter lists references to versions (and discussions) of the free will defense, for example, by *Stephen Davis*, *William Wainwright*, *George Wall*, *Keith Yandell*, among others. The free will solution, moreover, is not confined to this chapter, since it is an important aspect of most theodicies and an aspect of many of the critical discussions about theodicy. Process theologians and philosophers, for example, argue that the theistic vision of Whitehead and Hartshorne results in a viable free will defense (see *Chapter 6*), whereas the traditional free will defense is an invalid "hybrid" version at best.[16] For process theists, the argument (used by many) that the traditional God has all the power—unilateral power,[17] but refuses to use it, renders God responsible for the evil which free creatures generate. Process writers *(Charles Hartshorne, John Cobb, David Griffin, Lewis Ford, Barry Whitney*, and others) extend the free will defense to account for both natural and moral evil, on the basis that all of reality necesarily has some varying degree of creativity and, hence, the potential for evil results as well as good results from free (creative) actions. (See *Chapter 6).*

John Hick's influential Irenaean theodicy, moreover, employs a combination of free will theodicy with his "soul-making" vision. Hick argues that God could not create creatures who were both free and good. Freedom, he argues, has evolved in the process of evolution and only slowly are human creatures learning how best to use that free will for good ("soul-making"—see *Chapter 5).*

The following annotated pu blications are among the most important contemporary contributions to the free will solution, both as a defense and a theodicy. The items listed in the final section of the chapter are included because of their importance to the on-going debates on the free will issue.

Notes

1.   For some relevant dissertations on the free will theodicy, see *Appendix E.* Among the most important are the following: Peter Horban, *God, Evil, and the Metaphysics of Freedom: An Evaluation of the Free Will Defense of Alvin Plantinga* (University of Western Ontario, 1979); Stephen Joseph, *The Problem of Evil: An Examination of Classical and Contemporary Attempts at Philosophical Theodicy—With Special Refer- ence and Attention to the Free Will Defense* (University of Pennsylvania, 1979); Paul Sauer, *The Incompatibility of Foreknowledge and Freedom and Some Consequences Stemming Therefrom if Moral Responsibility is Assumed* (Syracuse University, 1991); James Sennet, *Modality, Probability and Rationality: A Critical Examination of Alvin Plantinga's Philosophy* (University of Nebraska, 1990); Mark Whitten, *An Affirmation of the Ockhamist Explanation of the Compatibility of Divine Foreknowledge and Human Freedom* (Baylor University, 1989); Paul Davis, *The Cheap Trick of Compatibilism and Why the Problem of Free Will Won't Go Away* (University of Edinburgh, 1989); etc.

2.   The free choice of one person for some good end can have undesirable effects for other people.

3.   George Schlesinger, *New Perspectives on Old-Time Religion* (Oxford: Oxford Unver- sity Press, 1988), 42.

4.   Plantinga uses the idea of "possible persons" in *God and Other Minds* (Cornell Univer- sity Press, 1967; reprinted, 1990), and the "possible worlds and essences" theme in other works, *Nature of Necessity* (Oxford University Press, 1974), etc. See his com- ments in *Alvin Plantinga (Profiles, Volume 5),* edited by James Tomberlin and Peter van Inwagen (Boston: Reidel, 1985), 47.

5.   *Alvin Plantinga (Profiles, Volume 5),* 41.

6.   See, for example, the informative overview by Theodore Kondoleon, "The Free Will Defense: New and Old," *Thomist* 47 (1983).

7.   Actually, as noted in the text, Augustine argues that while *moral evil* is the result of human free will, *physical evil* is God's just punishment for moral evil.

8.   See the seminal work of David Griffin, *God, Power and Evil* (Westminster, 1976; reissued by University Press of America, 1990). Griffin discusses the traditional theodicies of major figures: Augustine, Aquinas, Leibniz, Spinoza, Luther, Calvin, Barth, John Hick, James Ross, as well as others like Fackenheim and Brunner, Personal Idealism and Greek and the biblical theodicies. He critiques these theodicies from the perspective of Whiteheadian- Hartshornean process theodicy. In a more recent work, *Evil Revisited* (State University of New York Press, 1991), Griffin expands upon and defends his position against the major published criticisms his work has elicited. These two books, combined with Griffin's chapter and defense of his theodicy in *Encountering Evil,* edited by Stephen Davis (John Knox Press, 1981) form a trilogy of publications on theodicy which, while supplemented

by other important publications by Griffin, constitute a major achievement. I consider them to be as important as the work of John Hick and Alvin Plantinga on theodicy, among a select number of others.

9. For Farrer's publications, see *Chapter 4*. The statement cited is from Brian Hebblethwaite, "Austin Farrer's Concept of Divine Providence," *Theology* 14 (1970), 541-551.

10. See Robert M. Adams, "Plantinga and the Problem of Evil," *Alvin Plantinga (Profiles, Volume 5)*, 225.

11. William Rowe, "God and Others Minds," *Noûs* 3 (1969), 259.

12. Among the most useful and recent books—and bibliographical lists—on the topics discussed in this chapter and the next is *Moral Responsibility*, edited by John Martin Fischer (Ithaca: Cornell University Press, 1986). Fischer's contributions to the issue are particularly informative and insightful. Another useful book—and its bibliography— is *The Dilemma of Freedom and Foreknowledge*, edited by Linda Trinkaus Zagzebski (New York: Oxford University Press, 1991).

13. Plantinga, *The Nature of Necessity, Chapter 9*.

14. Robert Adams, in "Middle Knowledge and the Problem of Evil." *American Philosophical Quarterly* 14 (1977), 109-117, suggests that Molina may have coined the term, "middle knowledge." The context was the fierce controversy which erupted in the 1580s between the Jesuits and Dominicans (eg: Diego Alvarez) about the relationship between God's grace and human freedom. While the Dominicans seemed to believe that God controls human events by causal control, Luis de Molina and others (Francisco Suárez, etc.) argued that God, rather, caused circumstances in which God knew we would freely act in accord with the divine plan.

15. For one of the more accessible introductory discussions of this concept, see William Lane Craig's *The Only Wise God* (Grand Rapids: Baker Book House, 1987), *Chapter 12*.

16. See David Griffin's *God, Power and Evil*, and *Evil Revisited*.

17. The issue, to be sure, is contentious. Process philosophers, in particular, have criticized the traditional conception of divine power, while Thomistic and conservative Protestant thinkers have defended the traditional view. The issue of determining the nature and extent of divine power is of critical concern for theodicy.

I   Free Will Theodicy

1.   Ackerman, Robert. "An Alternative Free Will Defense." *Religious Studies* 18 (1982): 365-372.

   Argues for the validity of the free will defense on grounds that are philosophically more appealing and more compatible with the biblical record than Plantinga's version (*God, Freedom and Evil* [#109]). Ackerman argues for a "theory of computability" and in particular the result from this theory known as "the insolvability of the (general) halting problem for Turing Machines." He concludes that it was not possible for God to survey all possible histories of all possible worlds in order to determine which one to actualize. God must re-enter history to make corrections for possibly unforeseen developments.

2.   Adams, Marilyn McCord. "Is the Existence of God a 'Hard' Fact?" *Philosophical Review* 76 (1967): 492-503.

   Response to Pike's "Divine Omniscience and Voluntary Action" [#96]. Adams contends that we should distinguish hard facts (facts about the past that *do not* include facts about the future) and soft facts (facts about the past that *do* include facts about the future). Only the latter can be altered.

3.   Alston, William P. "Divine Foreknowledge and Alternative Conceptions of Human Freedom." *International Journal for Philosophy of Religion* 21 (1985): 19-32.

   Response to Pike's "Divine Omniscience and Voluntary Action" [#96]. Alston contends that Plantinga's argument relies on the conditional conception of power (freedom) as used by Hume and Schlick. He recasts Plantinga's defense of the proposition ("It was within Jones's power at T2 to do something such that if he had done it, then God would not have held the belief that in fact he did hold") as a defense of the position that power-to-do-otherwise is compatible with causal determinism. Alston claims this argument is at least as strong as Plantinga's argument that power-to-do-otherwise is compatible with divine foreknowledge. [See Pike's response, "Alston on Plantinga and Soft Theological Determinism" [#102].]

4.   Anderson, Susan. "Plantinga and the Free Will Defense." *Pacific Philosophical Quarterly* 62 (1981): 274-281.

   Rejects Plantinga's free will defense. Anderson argues that God could take away our freedom when it will be used for sin. [See Basinger's response, "Anderson on Plantinga: A Response" [#12].]

5.   Anglin, William S. *Free Will and the Christian Faith.* Oxford: Clarendon Press, 1990.

   Defends the compatibility of traditional theism and libertarianism. He argues for the free will defense and privation account of (moral) evil, and defends divine goodness by the principle of double effect. Natural evils lead to greater goods.

6.   Barnhart, Joe E. "God, Evil and Suffering: Two Versions of Classical Theism." *Religion and the Challenge of Philosophy.* Totawa, NJ: Littlefield, Adams and Co., 1975: 111-133.

An exposition of the Calvinist (and Muslim) reconciliation of free will and divine power as predetermining, and the Arminian (alternative) view of divine providence.

7.   ——. "Theodicy and the Free Will Defense: Response to Plantinga and Flew." *Religious Studies* 13 (1977): 439-453.

Examines the controversy between Flew and Plantinga. Criticizes Plantinga's views (as representative of orthodox Christianity) as having serious flaws and undesirable implications. Plantinga, for example, insists on a doctrine of free will that makes it possible that some human actions are not causally determined; yet his shifting to the distinctions between fettered and unfettered, rather than determined and undetermined, does not overcome Flew's denial that there are undetermined human actions and choices. Plantinga does not grasp the primary meaning of freedom and free will as these terms are used by Flew ("Divine Omnipotence and Human Freedom" [#45]). Barnhart criticizes also Plantinga's views on hell and Satan. [See also Barnhart's "God, Genes, and Chance," *Existence of God*. Edited by John R. Jacobson and Robert Lloyd Mitchell. New York and Toronto, ON: Edwin Mellen Press, 1988, 183-197.]

8.   Basinger, David. "Human Freedom and Divine Omnipotence: Some New Thoughts on an Old Problem." *Religious Studies* 15 (1979): 491-510.

Proposes that God's control can accomplish its ends only in a very general sense. God cannot ensure that states of affairs, with respect to which human agents are significantly free, will always come about in the manner desired by God. Basinger argues that this view is inconsistent with various popular Christian tenets, and that these tenets must be modified.

9.   ——. "Christian Theism and the Free Will Defense." *Sophia* 19 (1980): 20-33.

Argues that the free will defense is of little apologetic value for orthodox Christianity, since there is a fundamental incompatibility between the concept of divine omnipotence implicit in orthodox Christianity and the concept implicit in the free will defense. God's goodness is preserved, but at the expense of God's specific sovereignty (omnipotence). Basinger rejects Wainwright's opposite conclusions ("Christian Theism and the Free Will Defense" [#154]), that the orthodox concept of divine sovereignty is compatible with the view of God set forth in the free will defense.

10.   ——. "Plantinga's 'Free-Will Defense' as a Challenge to Orthodox Theism." *American Journal of Theology and Philosophy* 3 (1982): 35-41.

Argues that Plantinga's free will defense (*The Nature of Necessity* [#110]) implies a strong case against the self-consistency of the orthodox theism he defends. To affirm a coherent concept of God, the orthodox theist must turn to some form of libertarianism or compatibilism. Basinger argues that Plantinga's defense gives philosophical support to the concept of God affirmed by process theists.

11.   ——. "Determinism and Evil: Some Clarifications." *Australasian Journal of Philosophy* 60 (1982): 163-164.

Refutes Martin Davies's claim ("Determinism and Evil" [#31]) that if causal determinism is true, it is far from clear that the mere existence of moral evil provides an argument against God's existence. Davies cannot show that there is compatibility between a deterministic world and the existence of God and evil.

12. ———. "Anderson on Plantinga: A Response." *Philosophy Research Archives* 8 (1982/1983): 315-320.

     Refutes Anderson's critique of Plantinga's free will defense ("Plantinga and the Free Will Defense" [#4]), claiming that her arguments (God could take away human freedom when it is foreseen that such freedom will be used for sin, and that Plantinga has failed to produce a theodicy) misinterpret Plantinga's position.

13. ———. "Omniscience and Deliberation: A Response to Reichenbach." *International Journal for Philosophy of Religion* 20 (1986): 169-172.

     Argues against Reichenbach's distinction between deliberate and non-deliberate actions ("Omniscience and Deliberation" [#306]) to resolve the tension between divine omniscience and divine intentional action.

14. Basinger, David, and Randall Basinger. "In the Image of Man Create They God: A Challenge." *Scottish Journal of Theology* 34 (1981): 97-107.

     Contends that Christian theists frequently utilize two basic propositions in an inconsistent and arbitrary manner: that God creates human agents such that they have free will with respect to certain actions and, therefore, are morally responsible for them; and that God is an omniscient, wholly good being who is omnipotently in control over all existent states of affairs. The Basingers argue that there is no acceptable philosophical/theological basis for such selectivity and, as such, many theists are guilty of a theology of convenience.

15. ———. "Divine Omnipotence: Plantinga Vs. Griffin." *Process Studies* 11 (1981): 11-24.

     Argues that both process theists (Griffin) and classical theists (Plantinga) are wrong in their criticism of the other's position: process theists wrongly reject the classical doctrine of divine omnipotence for rendering the problem of evil insoluble, while classical theists wrongly reject process theism for solving the problem of evil at the expense of divine omnipotence. [See Plantinga's response, "Reply to the Basingers on Divine Omnipotence" [#113]; and Griffin's response in *Evil Revisited* [#873].]

16. ———. "Divine Determinateness and the Free Will Defense: Some Clarifications." *Philosophy Research Archives* 8 (1982/1983): 531-534.

     Responds to Paulsen's claim ("Divine Determinateness and the Free Will Defense" [#94]), that the free will defense cannot hold that God has an eternally determinate nature since God could not be considered morally good with such a nature, given the developmental concept of morality. Basinger rejects the latter aspect of this claim and holds that even were it the case for humans, it need not be the case for God.

17. ———. "Inerrancy, Dictation and the Free Will Defense." *Evangelical Quarterly* 55 (1983): 177-180.

     The free will defense seems at odds with the inerrancy teaching which holds that God's dictation to the biblical writers was divinely controlled. The free will defense implies the possibility of errors in recording God's word.

18. ———. "Inerrancy and Free Will: Some Further Thoughts." *Evangelical Quarterly* 58 (1986): 351-354.

Response to Geisler's critique ("Inerrancy and Free Will: A Reply to the Brothers Basinger" [#53]) of the Basingers's article, "Inerrancy, Dictation and the Free Will Defense" [#17]. David and Randall Basinger point out misunderstandings of their argument by Geisler and challenge his belief in both a best of all possible worlds theodicy and the affirmation of a free will theodicy: the two views are inconsistent.

19.   Bennett, Philip W. "Evil, God and the Free Will Defense." *Australasian Journal of Philosophy* 51 (1973): 39-50.

Refutes Plantinga's version of the free will defense (*God and Other Minds* [#107]) and argues that both rational theodicies and atheistic refutations fail to understand the nature of religious belief. Both wrongly assume that God's existence is open to proof or disproof and that belief in God is open to and in need of justification.

20.   Boër, Steven E. "The Irrelevance of the Free Will Defense." *Analysis* 38 (1978): 110-112.

Reforms the free will defense, claiming that it exonerated God only for *allowing* us to do evil but not for *actually* doing evil. He argues that Plantinga's free will defense does not show that the evil consequences of evil choices are compatible with theism, since God could have created a world in which such consequences would always be prevented by coincident miracles. The free will defense, then, is irrelevant to the problem of moral evils in its most serious form: the problem of natural evil. [See Dilley's response, "Is the Free Will Defense Irrelevant?" [#35].]

21.   Botterill, G. "Falsification and the Existence of God: A Discussion of Plantinga's Free Will Defense." *Philosophical Quarterly* 27 (1977): 114-134.

Proposes several objections to Plantinga's free will defense (*The Nature of Necessity* [#110]), objections he claims argue decisively against it. Plantinga has not shown that the auxiliary propositions (added by Plantinga to the analysis of the problem of evil) are not just *possible* but *true* as well.

22.   Brümmer, Vincent. "Paul Helm on God and the Approval of Sin." *Religious Studies* 20 (1984): 223-226.

Response to Paul Helm's refutation ("God and the Approval of Sin" [#1397]) of Brümmer's "Divine Impeccability" [#1385]. Helm confuses abilities and tendencies, supposing that if God has the ability to deviate, it follows that God has the tendency sometimes to deviate. Brümmer rejects also Helm's claim that if the free will defense succeeds, his (Brümmer's) thesis fails, and *vice versa*. He argues that his thesis is identical to the free will defense: only if God has the ability to deviate from the divine character can God be a personal agent who freely does not deviate. To reject this is to reject the free will defense, as Helm does. Brümmer concludes that Helm has not shown how to ascribe significant personal agency to God (Yahweh) and yet deny to God the ability to deviate from the divine character.

23.   Burch, Robert F. "The Defense from Plenitude Against the Problem of Evil." *International Journal for Philosophy of Religion* 12 (1981): 29-37.

Defends the Augustinian argument from plenitude and contends that it is both plausible in itself and superior to Plantinga's free will defense (*The Nature of*

Necessity [#110] and *God, Freedom and Evil* [#109]), in some respects. Burch claims that it is better that there is a world where free agents do go wrong rather than a world without free agents. He agrees with John Mackie's well-known critique of the free will defense ("Evil and Omnipotence" [#1217]), that God could have created creatures with free will, none of whom could have gone morally wrong: angels were created as such. The defense from plenitude denies Mackie's other claim, that it is better for God to create a world containing only free creatures who do *not* go wrong than to create a world of free creatures who *do* go wrong.

24.   Burgess-Jackson, Keith. "Free Will, Omnipotence and the Problem of Evil." *American Journal of Theology and Philosophy* 9 (1988): 175-185.

Holds that the theist cannot solve the problem of evil by limiting God to that which is "logically possible" or by adopting an "actual-choice" conception of free will.

25.   Chernoff, Fred. "The Obstinance of Evil." *Mind* 89 (1980): 269-273.

Refutes Plantinga's free will defense (*The Nature of Necessity* [#110]). Chernoff's argument is that Plantinga wrongly dismisses as trivially false the claim that God's perfect goodness prevents God from bringing about a world containing moral evil. He argues also that Plantinga's free will defense begs a central task of the defense in *assuming* (rather than *proving*) God's goodness and the divine actualization of a world are consistent with God's omnipotence and trans-world depravity.

26.   Clifford, Paul. "Omnipotence and the Problem of Evil." *Journal of Religion* 41 (1961): 118-128.

As Paul Tillich proposed in *Love, Power and Justice* (London: Oxford University Press, 1954), the power of God is not the capacity to do anything or to control all things, but the expression of the divine perfection. God is found amid suffering (the Book of Job), in the passion and death of Jesus, and in the midst of our own suffering.

27.   Cobb, Jeffrey. "Determinism, Affirmation, and Free Choice." *Southern Journal of Philosophy* 24 (1986): 9-16.

Critique of the argument that determinism is self-refuting, contained in *Free Choice: A Self-Referential Argument*, by Joseph M. Boyle, Germain Grisez and Olaf Tollefsen (Notre Dame, IN: University of Notre Dame Press, 1976).

28.   Cooper, K.J. "Here We Go Again: Pike Vs. Plantinga on the Problem of Evil." *International Journal for Philosophy of Religion* 14 (1983): 107-116.

Defends Plantinga's free will defense (*God, Freedom and Evil* [#109] and *The Nature of Necessity* [#110]) against Pike's argument ("Plantinga on Free Will and Evil" [#100]), that God could have created morally good creatures who always act for good. God cannot actualize a contradictory state of affairs. Pike's 1979 arguments versus Plantinga are essentially the same as those he raised first in his 1966 exchange with Plantinga. The new element, Pike's "over-power" theme, succumbs to the same misunderstandings of Plantinga's position as his former arguments. Pike rejects Plantinga's premise that it is not within the power of an omnipotent God to create a world containing only moral good (with no moral evil).

29.   Coughlan, Michael J. "Moral Evil Without Consequences." *Analysis* 39 (1979): 58-60.

Refutes Boër's argument that the free will defense is irrelevant to theodicy, since God could have created a world in which agents made morally reprehensible choices but in which these choices (or intentions) never resulted in evil consequences ("The Irrelevance of the Free Will Defense" [#20]). One cannot be described as trying to do something that one must know from experience is impossible. There seems to be no way in which an agent in this reformed world of Boër's could require a concept of evil.

30.   ——. "In Defense of Free Will Theodicy." *Religious Studies* 23 (1987): 543-554.

Defends the relevance of the free will defense against Boër ("The Irrelevance of the Free Will Defense" [#20]). Coughlan argues that free will theodicy demands no more than that good *on the whole* outweighs evil *on the whole*.

31.   Davies, Martin. "Determinism and Evil." *Australasian Journal of Philosophy* 58 (1980): 116-127.

Holds that evil does not provide an argument against God's existence, even if causal determinism were true. Causal determinism cannot count against divine benevolence unless some alternative total set-up would be more valuable. [See Basinger's response, "Determinism and Evil: Some Clarifications" [#11].]

32.   Davis, Stephen T. "A Defense of the Free Will Defense." *Religious Studies* 18 (1972): 335-343.

Rejects Mackie's claim ("Evil and Omnipotence" [#1217]), that an omnipotent being is required to create the state of affairs of all human beings always freely choosing good. It is logically impossible to ask of God to have created humans such that it is guaranteed that we always choose the good. The definition of divine omnipotence (contra Aquinas) must be modified to hold that God can create any *logically possible* state of affairs, rather than *any* state of affairs (Aquinas).

33.   ——. "Free Will and Evil" and "Response." *Encountering Evil*. Edited by Stephen Davis. Atlanta, GA: John Knox Press, 1981: 69-83, 92-99.

Defends a version of the free will defense. While this is not the best of all possible worlds, the amount of evil in the end will be outweighed by the good that will exist, and this favorable balance was obtainable by God in no other way. Davis rejects Mackie's claim ("Evil and Omnipotence" [#1217]), that God could have created free moral agents who always freely choose the good. He accepts, moreover, Plantinga's argument that natural evil could possibly be caused by Satan. That the amount of evil in the world is cost-effective is known only by God and by believers in faith. [Critiques by Sontag, Griffin, Roth and Hick follow in the text, 83-92.]

34.   ——. *Logic and the Nature of God*. Grand Rapids, MI: Eerdmans, 1983.

Seeks to provide a defense of the concept of God that is inherently Christian (according to Davis's evangelical perspective). He defends the view of God as omnipotent, loving (it is impossible for God to do evil), omniscient, immutable, etc. *Chapter 7* ("Evil") distinguishes between the logical and the emotive problems of evil. He defends also the free will defense. This chapter follows closely the wording in Davis's "Free Will and Evil" [#33]. *Chapter 2* ("Omniscience") is a revised version of his "Divine Omniscience and Human Freedom" (*Christian Scholar's Review* 9 [1980]).

35.   Dilley, Frank B. "Is the Free Will Defense Irrelevant?" *Religious Studies* 18 (1982): 355-364.

Refutes Boër's attempt to reform the free will defense ("The Irrelevance of the Free Will Defense" [#20]). Boër's argument is that God, in giving creatures free will, should have intervened with coincident miracles to prevent any evil that resulted; this makes the free will defense irrelevant, since that defense requires only the opportunity to try, not the opportunity to succeed in acting freely. Dilley argues that Boër's idea of coincident miracles would require drastic revisions in natural laws and would prevent creatures from being cognitively free with respect to God. Dilley refutes also McKim's attempt ("Worlds Without Evil" [#87]) to defend Boër against the attacks of Coughlan ("Moral Evil Without Consequences" [#29]).

36.   ———. "A Modified Flew Attack on the Free Will Defense." *Southern Journal of Philosophy* 20 (1982): 25-34.

Refutes McKim's critique ("Worlds Without Evil" [#87]) of his (Dilley's) arguments ("Is the Free Will Defense Irrelevant?" [#35]) against Boër ("The Irrelevance of the Free Will Defense" [#20]). He rejects McKim's revision of Boër's proposal, that God allows us to do some harm while yet limiting the amount of harm we can do. McKim cannot define the limits.

37.   ———. "The Free Will Defense and Worlds Without Moral Evil." *International Journal for Philosophy of Religion* 21 (1990): 1-15.

Response to McKim's attempts ("Worlds Without Evil" [#87]) to overcome the alleged defects in Boër's argument ("The Irrelevance of the Free Will Defense" [#20]). He argues that McKim's proposed modification of Boër's argument undermines, rather than strengthens, the argument.

38.   Dore, Clement. "Plantinga on the Free Will Defense." *Review of Metaphysics* 25 (1971): 690-706.

Response to Plantinga's free will defense (*God and Other Minds* [#107]). Plantinga's solution as to why God does not instantiate only free and perfect possible people needs to be supplemented by Dore's answer to this question. God is not to be blamed for not having prevented the creation of beings whose freedom to fail was foreseen by God.

39.   Evans, J.N. "LaFollette on Plantinga's Free Will Defense." *International Journal for Philosophy of Religion* 14 (1983), 117-122.

Refutes LaFollette's argument against Plantinga ("Plantinga on the Free Will Defense" [#79]), that the *possibility* of transworld depravity entails its *necessity*. LaFollette misconceived Plantinga's argument by mistakenly translating possible world terminology to modal terminology.

40.   Feinberg, John S. "'And the Atheist Shall Lie Down with the Calvinist': Atheism, Calvinism, and the Free Will Defense." *Trinity Journal* 1 (1980): 142-152.

Argues that the atheist and the Calvinist share a common commitment to compatibilism and that both atheists and Calvinists must reject the free will defense, since it is committed to an incompatibilist view of freedom. [See Wall's response, "A New Solution to an Old Problem" [#155]. See also Feinberg's *Theologies and Evil, Chapter 4* [#1088].]

41.   ——. "God Ordains All Things." *Predestination and Free Will: Four Views of Divine Sovereignty and Human Freedom.* Edited by Randall and David Basinger. Downers Grove, IL: InterVarsity Press, 1986: 17-43.

Defends a view of specific sovereignty (theological determinism) and compatibilism. [Responses by Geisler, Reichenbach and Pinnock follow in the text, 45-60].

42.   ——. "Divine Causality and Evil." Symposium: Divine and Human Action. *Christian Scholar's Review* 16 (1987): 383-404.

Defends a view of soft determinism (compatibilism) as a response to Mavrodes' "Is There Anything Which God Does Not Do?" [#86]. Feinberg distinguishes between God acting directly (as in creation out of nothing) and acting through mediators. This is the meaning, he contends, of scriptural references to divine action (for example, the hardening of Pharaoh's heart). He argues for a form of divine determinism that does not rule out human freedom. [See the response by Mavrodes following in the text, "A Reply to Professors Feinberg and Pinnock" [see #86].]

43.   Felder, D.W. "Disanalogies in Plantinga's Argument Regarding the Rationality of Theism." *Journal for the Scientific Study of Religion* 10 (1971): 200-207.

Rejects Plantinga's argument (*God and Other Minds* [#107]) that belief in God is rational. Certain propositions regarding the nature of evil must be believed for the teleological argument to be valid, propositions which atheists reject.

44.   Fischer, John Martin. "Van Inwagen on Free Will." *Philosophical Quarterly* 36 (1986): 252-260.

Argues that there are gaps in Peter van Inwagen's argument for incompatibilism (*An Essay on Free Will* [#150]; "A Formal Approach to the Free Will Problem" [#329]; and "The Incompatibility of Free Will and Determinism" [#330]). Van Inwagen's argument (that the performing of a certain act that would require a law of nature to be violated rules out the possibility of a human agent performing the act) is a questionable and misleading premise. The premise could be denied, for example, for reasons entirely apart from any consideration of the relationship between our powers and natural laws.

45.   Flew, Antony G.N. "Divine Omnipotence and Human Freedom." *Hibbert Journal* 53 (1955): 135-144.

Expanded version of Flew's chapter of the same title in Antony Flew and Alasdair MacIntyre (editors), *New Essays in Philosophical Theology* (London: SCM, 1955, 141-169). Flew argues that God could have created human beings who always freely do what is right. There is no contradiction between divine causation and human freedom. If the theist denies this, the theist must abandon belief in an omnipotent God.

46.   ———. "Compatibilism, Free Will and God." *Philosophy* 48 (1973): 231-244. [A revised version is published as "The Free Will Defense" in Flew's *God, Freedom and Immortality*, 81-99 [#225]].

Rejects Plantinga's free will defense in *God and Other Minds* [#107]. Aquinas, Leibniz, Luther and Calvin, as compatibilists, held that creation is totally dependent upon God, while humans can act without constraint (freely). Flew argues that a free will defense based on either a compatibilist or libertarian view of free will must fail. He contends that Plantinga's understanding of free action is defective, supposing it to be incompatible with actions, beings, and events which are causally determined. He argues also that Plantinga is mistaken both in regarding the dispute over the proper use of "free" as merely verbal and holding that the dispute can be avoided by defining "unfettered" to mean both free, in Flew's sense, and also causally determined.

47.   Flint, Thomas P. "Divine Sovereignty and the Free Will Defense." *Sophia* 23 (1984): 41-52.

Refutes Basinger's claim in "Christian Theism and the Free Will Defense" [#9], that orthodox Christianity's understanding of divine sovereignty is incompatible with the free will defense. Flint argues that the free will defense need not assume God would create the best possible world, the most valuable state of affairs.

48.   Freeman, David. "On God and Evil." *God and the Good*. Edited by Clifton Orlebeke and Lewis Smedes. Grand Rapids, MI: Eerdmans, 1975: 174-180.

Argues that evil can be understood only on the *assumption* of God's existence. Evil has a moral meaning only if a God with moral will and judgement exists. To deny God's existence is to deny the existence of evil as a moral category.

49.   Gales, Richard. M. "Freedom Versus Unsurpassable Greatness." *International Journal for Philosophy of Religion* 23 (1988): 65-75.

Refutes Plantinga's new version of the ontological proof. The property of unsurpassable greatness (necessary being and maximum excellence) cannot be instantiated, since it is incompatible with various possible properties; for example, a world in which all people always freely do wrong.

50.   Gallois, Andre. "Van Inwagen on Free Will and Determinism." *Philosophical Studies* 32 (1977): 99-105.

Response to van Inwagen's attempts to demonstrate the incompatibility of one historically important variety of determinism with the claim that some actions are freely performed ("The Incompatibility of Responsibility and Determinism" [#151]). Gallois agrees with van Inwagen that a determinism framed in terms of causal laws excludes freedom of action; yet he argues that van Inwagen's argument to this conclusion is inadequate.

51.   Gan, Barry L. "Plantinga's Transworld Depravity: It's Got Possibilities." *International Journal for Philosophy of Religion* 13 (1982): 169-177.

Refutes LaFollette's critique ("Plantinga on the Free Will Defense" [#79]) of Plantinga's free will defense. Gan claims Plantinga's argument was misunderstood or misconstrued. LaFollette, for example, wrongly attributes to Plantinga the claim that it was not in fact in God's power to create a world containing moral good but not moral evil. Plantinga's claim, rather, is that it is *possible* that such is the case.

52. Geisler, Norman L. "Man's Destiny: Free or Forced?" *Christian Scholar's Review* 9 (1979): 99-109.

Critiques three views of human nature and freedom: Skinner's behaviorism, Hick's universalism, and Edwards's Calvinism. Geisler proposes an alternative view, based on C.S. Lewis's writings, a view he (Geisler) defends as neither Calvinistic, Armenian, nor Pelagian. [Brief responses by Norman Wenneberg (a discussion of Geisler's doctrine of hell) and Dewey Hoitenga (a discussion of Geisler's critique of Jonathan Edwards) follow the Geisler text.]

53. ———. "Inerrancy and Free Will: A Reply to the Brothers Basinger." *Evangelical Quarterly* 57 (1985): 349-353.

Response to Randall and David Basinger's contention ("Inerrancy, Dictation and the Free Will Defense" [#17]), that divine control and human freedom cannot be reconciled. Geisler argues that since human beings can at times speak without error, it is not contradictory to think the biblical writers could do so, and that they could do so freely.

54. ———. "God Knows All Things." *Predestination and Free Will: Four Views of Divine Sovereignty and Human Freedom.* Edited by Randall and David Basinger. Downers Grove, IL: InterVarsity Press, 1986: 61-84.

Argues for the self-deterministic view of human freedom against objections to the indeterminist view. His conjunction of theological determinism and human self-determinism is a mystery which, while not contrary to reason, goes beyond reason. [Responses by Feinberg, Reichenbach and Pinnock follow in the text, 85-98.]

55. ———. "Is Inerrancy Incompatible with the Free Will Defense?" *Evangelical Quarterly* 62 (1990): 175-178.

Response to David and Randall Basinger's "Inerrancy and Free Will: Some Further Thoughts" [#18]. Geisler argues that the Basingers have overlooked the distinction between guaranteeing results *by force* and guaranteeing results *without coercion.* Beneath the inability to see the compatibility of inerrancy and free will is the challengeable premise that the only way for God to guarantee a result is to control human choices totally. This overlooks the possibility that God can guarantee an inerrant book by omniscience alone, as well as by persuasive grace. Only those who reject divine omniscience (process philosophers) have the problem shared by the Basingers in accepting inerrancy.

56. Griffin, David R. "Critique [of Davis]." *Encountering Evil.* Edited by Stephen Davis. Atlanta, GA: John Knox Press, 1981: 87-89.

Rejects Davis's appeal ("Free Will and Evil" [#33]) to the end of history to justify the evils that now exist. His position mistakenly holds, for example, that moral evil has instrumental value in the good it obtains, thereby denying it as genuine evil. [See Davis's response, following in the text.]

57.   Gutting, Gary. "Is Ross's God the God of Religion?" *Journal of Philosophy* 55 (1980): 630.

Response to Ross's "Creation" [#129]. Gutting rejects Ross's definition of omnipotence (that God's effective willing is logically equivalent to the obtaining of every state of affairs), and rejects Ross's defense of divine immutability as atemporality. [See also Gutting's *Religious Belief and Religious Scepticism*. Notre Dame, IN: University of Notre Dame Press, 1982].

58.   Hall, Ronald L. "Responsibility and Intention: Reflections on the Problem of God's Will and Human Suffering." *Religious Studies* 15 (1979): 142-151.

Develops John Sibler's distinction between "voluntary" and "status" responsibility ("Being and Doing: A Study of Status Responsibility and Voluntary Responsibility" (*The Anatomy of Knowledge*. Edited by Marjorie Grene. Amherst, MA: University of Massachusetts Press, 1969, 165-216) to clarify the relationship between responsibility and intention, between God's intentions (God's will) and human suffering. Hall denies the dilemma that evil is either the result of God's will or that it occurs randomly, by chance, or by necessity. God is responsible for suffering in the sense of being the creator ("status responsibility") but not in the sense of "doing" it ("voluntary responsibility").

59.   Hasker, William S. "Foreknowledge and Necessity." *Faith and Philosophy* 2 (1985): 121-157.

Presents the case for the incompatibility of divine omniscience and human freedom, and responds to the most recent arguments of compatibilists. Hasker poses the dilemma that either we give up the traditional view of omniscience (that God has foreknowledge of future events) or we commit ourselves to the dubious view that we can alter the past. [See Reichenbach's response, "Hasker on Omniscience" [#125].]

60.   Hebblethwaite, Brian L. "Some Reflections on Predestination, Providence and Divine Foreknowledge." *Religious Studies* 15 (1979): 433-448.

Holds that God does not know or determine the future, as traditionally held. Such a view would render God responsible for evil. Hebblethwaite insists that the freedom of human beings must be taken seriously. As such, divine providence cannot be seen as predetermining all things. The world is genuinely open and we are responsible for evils, God being responsible only in the sense of making such a world in which there are free creatures.

61.   Hedenius, Ingemar. "Disproofs of God's Existence?" *Personalist* 52 (1971): 23-43.

Critiques the concepts of divine omnipotence, divine omniscience, the belief in afterlife compensation for suffering, and the view that freedom compensates all evil states of affairs. On the basis of this critique, Hedenius rejects Plantinga's arguments (*God and Other Minds* [#107]) for God's existence.

62.   Helm, Paul. "God and Free Will." *Sophia* 13 (1974): 16-19.

Discusses some aspects of Plantinga's free will defense (*God and Other Minds* [#107]). Helm argues that there is a stalemate in the debate between Plantinga and Mackie: Plantinga does not accept Mackie's view of omnipotence but, rather, a view that does not regard control as essential. Thus, instead of showing that it is possible for God to instantiate possible human beings who always do what is right, Plantinga shows that the question of whether or not an omnipotent God can instantiate such possible persons does not arise—on his definition of omnipotence.

63.   ———. "Divine Foreknowledge and Facts." *Canadian Journal of Philosophy* 4 (1974): 305-315.

Response to Anthony Kenny's "Divine Foreknowledge and Human Freedom" [#461], which argued that what God foreknows is necessary. This article is a response also to Pike's "Divine Omniscience and Voluntary Action" [#96] and to Marilyn McCord Adams's response to Pike's "Is the Existence of God a 'Hard' Fact?" [#2]. Helm rejects Adams's distinction between hard and soft facts. He concludes that attempts to show the consistency in a temporal but omniscient God and human freedom imply that the theist must restrict the notion of omniscience more seriously than many traditional theists would allow.

64.   ———. "Timelessness and Foreknowledge." *Mind* 84 (1975): 516-527.

Defends the coherence of divine omniscience against A.N. Prior ("The Formalities of Omniscience" [#299] and *Past, Present and Future* [#300]); William C. Kneale ("Eternity and Sempiternity," *Proceedings of the Aristotelian Society* [1968/1969], 223-238); Norman Kretzmann ("Omniscience and Immutability" [#261]; and Kenny ("Divine Foreknowledge and Human Freedom" [#461]. Helm concludes that divine foreknowledge implies fatalism. What God knows is necessary and, as such, there cannot be free will even if God's knowledge of human actions is timeless. [See also William Kneale's "Time and Eternity in Theology," *Proceedings of the Aristotelian Society* 61 (1960/1961), 87-108.]

65.   ———. "Foreknowledge and Possibility." *Canadian Journal of Philosophy* 6 (1976): 731-734.

Refutation of Holt's argument for the compatibility of divine foreknowledge and freedom ("Foreknowledge and the Necessity of the Past" [#69]) against Helm's critique of similar arguments ("Divine Foreknowledge and Facts" [#63]). Helm contends that Holt's distinction between hard and soft facts is irrelevant to the discussion. Holt's argument, that Helm has not distinguished between "possibility for" and "possibility that," rests on an equivocation on the term "can." He concludes that Holt has not shown that a person has the power to bring it about that God does not know what a person will do. The further question of whether, if God had that power, God *knows* that the person will do "x" or God only has the *belief* that the person will do "x," is not a problem.

66.   ———. "Theism and Freedom." *Neue Zeitschrift für Systematische Theologie und Religionsphilosophie* 21 (1979): 139-149.

Argues against Flew ("Compatibilism, Free Will and God" [#46], "Divine Omnipotence and Human Freedom" [#45], *God and Philosophy* [#223], etc.), that the same considerations which lead him to defend the compatibilism between human freedom and determinism are, if sufficient, also sufficient to uphold the compatibilism between human freedom and theistic creation. [See also Helm's more recent, *Eternal God*. Oxford: Oxford University Press, 1988.]

67.   Hick, John. "Critique [of Davis]." *Encountering Evil*. Edited by Stephen Davis. Atlanta, GA: John Knox Press, 1981: 86-87.

Stephen Davis ("Free Will and Evil" [#33]) has modified the traditional Augustinian account for the origin of evil in humans by holding (as does Hick's Irenaean theo-dicy) that the first creatures were spiritually immature. Hick contends, however, that Davis also should have argued (as does Hick) that the first creatures were morally imperfect. Davis's appeal, moreover, to Satan as the cause of natural evils is totally lacking in plausibility, and his separation of theodicy into philosophical and emotive problems is invalid. [See Davis's response, following in the text.]

68.   Hoitenga, Dewey J. "Logic and the Problem of Evil." *American Philosophical Quarterly* 4 (1967): 114-126.

Critiques the "higher good defense" versus Pike (*God and Evil* [#1156]). Theists, in providing for the justification of evil in the higher good, provide also for the necessity (inevitability) of evil. Hoitenga argues that the issue between sceptics and theists is not about the consistency or inconsistency of propositions, but about the meaning of the term "good." There are, he argues, two incompatible views of the nature of goodness: the *incompatibility* view (the opposition of good and evil is absolute) and the compatibility view (good often depends on evil, etc.). He rejects free will theodicy (a version of the higher good defense) on several grounds, and agrees with Mackie and Flew (contra Plantinga) that free will and infallible moral perfection in human beings is not incompatible. He identifies four views of the relationship between freedom and divine causation: [1] incompatibility (Mackie), [2] compatibility (Augustine, Aquinas, Leibniz, Descartes), [3] incompatibility of good and evil, yet compatibility of free will and determinism (Flew), and [4] the incompatibility of free will and determinism, yet the compatibility of good and evil (Hick, Plantinga). Hoitenga concludes that the sceptic can support the claim that theistic beliefs are self-contradictory only if the incompatibility meanings of the key terms are held; likewise, the theist can defend the consistency of belief in God only if the compatibility meanings of the key terms are held (versus Hick, Plantinga, and others).

69.   Holt, Dennis C. "Foreknowledge and the Necessity of the Past." *Canadian Journal of Philosophy* 6 (1976): 721-734.

Response to Helm's defense of a traditional argument for the incompatibility of foreknowledge and free will ("Divine Foreknowledge and Facts" [#63]) against attempts of Anthony Kenny ("Divine Foreknowledge and Human Freedom" [#461]) and others to provide a reconciliation. Holt proposes a reconciliationist argument similar to Kenny's but not susceptible to Helm's criticism. Helm, for example, has not distinguished between "possibility for" and "possibility that." It is possible for one to do other than "x" even though it is *not* possible that one *can* do otherwise. [See Helm's response, "Foreknowledge and Possibility" [#65].]

70.   Hudson, William D. "An Attempt to Defend Theism." *Philosophy* 39 (1964): 18-28.

Refutes the arguments of Flew ("Divine Omnipotence and Human Freedom" [#45]) and Mackie ("Evil and Omnipotence" [#1217]): it makes no sense to talk of human freedom unless human selves have an existence that is independent of God and at least some human acts are made independently of God's power. Hudson admits that human free will is inconsistent with the doctrine of God as a necessary being, yet rejects Pontifex's attempt to reconcile the two ("The Question of Evil" [#1920]). He rejects the doctrine of God as a necessary being and contends that this rejection surrenders nothing that is essential to theism. A proper understanding of omnipotence is to see that the all-powerfulness of God is all-power in goodness. [See also Hudson's *The Philosophical Approach to Religion*. London: Macmillan, 1974.]

71.   Kane, G. Stanley. "The Free Will Defense Defended." *New Scholasticism* 50 (1976): 435-446.

Refutes the argument (McCloskey, Hare and Madden) that God could have created free beings with the disposition or bias to act freely (always) for right action. Kane argues that critics assume that the factors which influence the choices made by human beings have not changed appreciably; yet the doctrine of original sin tells us that once moral evil was first introduced into the world, the moral nature of human beings was affected for the worst. Perhaps God gave the earliest human beings a strong disposition to do what was right and the introduction of moral evil and its proliferation changed this situation drastically.

72.   Keller, James A. "The Basingers on Divine Omnipotence: A Further Point." *Process Studies* 12 (1982): 23-25.

David and Randall Basinger have argued ("Divine Omnipotence: Plantinga Vs. Griffin" [#15]) that the process theist's understanding of omnipotence has great advantages over the God of classical theism. Keller agrees and argues that classical theists cannot deal adequately with the natural order without accepting the view that God cannot create without a limitation of divine power. Beings are self-creative, as process thought holds.

73.   Knox, John, Jr. "A.C. Ewing—A Critical Survey of Ewing's Recent Work." *Religious Studies* 11 (1975): 229-255.

Critique of various aspects of A.C. Ewing's theology, as represented in Ewing's posthumous book, *Value and Reality: The Philosophical Case for Theism* [#1085]. Indeterminism is essential for theism, yet Ewing has not established the theory of indeterminism nor shown it is consistent with human responsibility. Ewing is open to the charge that the denial of complete determinism by the past admits that chance factors enter into the decision-making. Knox contends that this rules out responsibility.

74.   Kondoleon, Theodore J. "Moral Evil and the Existence of God: A Reply." *New Scholasticism* 47 (1973): 366-374.

Rejects Oakes's argument ("Actualities, Possibilities, and Free-Will Theodicy" [#91]), that divine goodness is not refuted by moral evil. Kondoleon argues a Thomistic answer to the question about the divine permission of evil: moral evil is permitted for the sake of some good end, and our failure to attain our proper ends accentuates our complete dependency upon God. He argues also against

Walter's argument ("Are Actualities Prior to Possibilities?" [#160]), rejecting the view that moral agents must be able to sin: God, as a moral agent, does not sin.

75.   ———. "The Free Will Defense: New and Old." *Thomist* 47 (1983): 1-42.

Refutes Plantinga's free will defense (*The Nature of Necessity*, *Chapter 9* [#110]; *God, Freedom and Evil* [#109]), contending that its implicit theory of "middle knowledge" assumes something is knowable that is intrinsically unknowable. He argues that Aquinas offered a better version of the free will argument: Aquinas has demonstrated that evil is not incompatible with God's existence (contra the arguments of McCloskey, *God and Evil* [#1235]). [See also Kondoleon's "More on the Free Will Defense," *Thomist* 47 (1983), 1-42.]

76.   Kraemer, Eric, and Hardy Jones. "Freedom and the Problem of Evil." *Philosophical Topics* 13 (1985): 33-49.

Refutes Plantinga's free will defense of theism (*God, Freedom and Evil* [#109]). Kraemer argues that Plantinga has not met Philo's objections, and that Plantinga cannot consistently appeal both to ignorance in response to the various problems of evil, and claim to have conclusive evidence that certain plans of actions are for the worst or best. The appeal to human free will is insufficient to salvage rational theism.

77.   Kroon, Frederick W. "Plantinga on God, Freedom, and Evil." *International Journal for Philosophy of Religion* 12 (1981): 75-96.

Contends that Plantinga's consistency proof for God (*God, Freedom, and Evil* [#109]) fails to demonstrate it was not possible for God to actualize worlds without evil. While a superficially similar consistency proof in Plantinga's *The Nature of Necessity* [#110] is more successful, Kroon argues that there are various reasons for being dissatisfied with consistency proofs which categorically rule out the possibility that God could have brought about any actual state of affairs. There is a certain lack of generality in Plantinga's consistency proofs, and Plantinga's uncompromising incompatibilism is a weakness.

78.   La Croix, Richard R. "Unjustified Evil and God's Choice." *Sophia* 13 (1974): 20-28.

Refutes Plantinga's claim (*God and Other Minds* [#107]), that there is a set of logically true propositions or propositions which are essential to theism, propositions which render belief in God contradictory. Plantinga's search for such propositions is too restrictive. The free will defense misses the point: the options God faced were more than [1] to create a world with evil or [2] to create a world without evil. If God could not create a world without evil, God ought not to have created at all. [See Wall's response, "Why Plantinga Must Move from Defense to Theodicy" [#159].]

79.   LaFollette, Hugh. "Plantinga on the Free Will Defense." *International Journal for Philosophy of Religion* 11 (1980): 123-132.

Refutes Plantinga's version of the free will defense (*God, Freedom and Evil* [#109]. Plantinga has failed to produce an example of at least one logically possible world which God cannot actualize. Plantinga needs to show there are no ppossible worlds that contain moral good but no moral evil, but he confuses possibility with *conceivability*: his argument amounts to "it is logically possible that, it is logically necessary that, all possible humans suffer from transworld depravity." [See responses by Gan, "Plantinga's Transworld Depravity: It's Got Possibilities" [#51]; and Evans, "LaFollette on Plantinga's Free Will Defense"[#39]].]

80.   Lehe, Robert T. "God's Perfection and Freedom: A Reply to Morriston." *Faith and Philosophy* 3 (1986): 319-323.

Response to Morriston's argument ("Is God 'Significantly Free'?" [#88]), that Plantinga's free will defense is incompatible with his version of the ontological argument. Morriston's critique is based on a faulty conception of God's perfection—that God has moral obligations which are not discharged in some possible world, and of divine freedom—God's freely performing an action entails there are possible worlds in which God does not perform it.

81.   Lomasky, Loren E. "Are Compatibilism and the Free Will Defense Compatible?" *Personalist* 56 (1975): 385-388.

Defends Plantinga's free will defense against Flew's critique ("Compatibilism, Free Will and God" [#46]). Lomasky argues that Plantinga's understanding of free action is not deviant in supposing free actions are incompatible with actions which are causally determined. Flew's agnosticism concerning the occurrence of uncaused actions does not strike a mortal blow to Plantinga's free will defense. Flew's rejection of Plantinga's use of "unfettered" action is less able to fend off Flew's critique, yet Plantinga's argument would work (against Flew's critique) if the word "unmanipulated" were substituted for unfettered.

82.   Lovin, Keith. "Free Will and Moral Evil." *Rice University Studies* 61 (1974): 45-57.

Contends that Plantinga has not given a cogent refutation of compatibilism. Plantinga's free will defense (*God, Freedom and Evil* [#109], *The Nature of Necessity* [#110]) requires freedom of an indeterministic sort. But there are good reasons for rejecting such a view. Plantinga has not, as such, resolved the alleged contradiction between a morally perfect God and the world's evil.

83.   ——. "Plantinga's Puddle." *Southwestern Philosophical Studies* 4 (1979): 103-108.

While Leibniz had a lapse in claiming that God could have created any possible world and in claiming that the existent world is "the best of all possible worlds, "Lovin argues that Plantinga's attempt (*God, Freedom and Evil* [#109], *The Nature of Necessity* [#110]) to remedy this lapse entails a notion of freedom that has disastrous implications for moral understanding: it renders incompatible morally available actions and actions that result from causal or influencing factors. Plantinga's use of Satan is unsubstantiated and ineffective: either God is to blame for creating devils or God should have restricted their free actions.

84.   MacIntyre, Alasdair C. *Difficulties in Christian Belief*. London: SCM Press, 1959.

The first four chapters discuss some fallacious solutions to the problem of evil and argue for a free will solution to theodicy. MacIntyre defends his solution against various objections. He holds that God restrains the divine power in order to permit human freedom.

85.   Mavrodes, George I. "Some Recent Philosophical Theology." *Review of Meta-physics* 85 (1970): 82-111.

       Refutes Ross's theodicy (*Philosophical Theology* [#1163]), and criticizes an aspect of Plantinga's theodicy (*God and Other Minds* [#107]). With respect to the latter, Mavrodes holds that Plantinga has not shown that human beings have the sort of freedom he (Plantinga) discusses in relation to theodicy, and that Plantinga's failure to explain evil or provide a justification for it (a "theodicy" rather than merely a "defense") stops short of what is required.

86.   ——. "Is There Anything Which God Does Not Do?" *Christian Scholar's Review* 16 (1987): 383-393.

       Symposium on "Divine and Human Action" that employs, as a paradigm case, the biblical text of God hardening the Pharaoh's heart. Mavrodes offers four models to explain how God can act in an event and how the same event can be a free human act. [See responses in the Symposium by Feinberg [#42] and Pinnock [#105], and Mavrodes response, following in the text, "A Reply to Professors Feinberg and Pinnock": Mavrodes rejects Feinberg's soft determinism.]

87.   McKim, Robert. "Worlds Without Evil." *International Journal for Philosophy of Religion* 15 (1984): 161-170.

       Defends and develops Boër's argument ("The Irrelevance of the Free Will Defense" [#20]) against objections by Coughlan ("Moral Evil without Consequences" [#29]) and Dilley ("A Modified Flew Attack on the Free Will Defense" [#36]), that Plantinga's free will defense results in the view that God cannot create creatures who are free and who never make morally wrong choices, yet that God can prevent the consequences of such choices. McKim argues that the *amount* of evil cannot be accounted for by Plantinga. [See Coughlan's response, "The Free Will Defense and Natural Evil" [#551].]

88.   Morriston, Wesley. "Is God 'Significantly Free'?" *Faith and Philosophy* 2 (1985): 257-264.

       Holds that Plantinga's version of the ontological proof (*God, Freedom and Evil* [#109], *The Nature of Necessity*, Chapters 9 and 10 [#110]), when seen in light of his free will defense, results in the position that God is not free to choose between good and evil and, as such, that God is not "good" in the moral sense of this word. The presuppositions of the free will defense entail that moral goodness cannot be an essential property of any person; yet the premises of the ontological argument entail that moral goodness is an essential property of at least one being: God. Morriston suggests a revised version of the ontological argument that can save the free will defense. This revision exacts a heavy toll: God is not morally perfect in the actual world. [See response by Lehe, "God's Perfection and Freedom: A Reply to Morriston" [#80], and Morriston's "Pike and Hoffman on Divine Foreknowledge and Human Freedom," *Philosophy Research Archives* 8 (1982/1983), 521-530. In this article, Morriston argues that Hoffman's attack ("Pike on Possible Worlds, Divine Foreknowledge, and Human Freedom" [#380]) on Pike's view of divine power ("Divine Foreknowledge, Human Freedom, and Possible Worlds" [#397] can be refuted).]

89.   Murphree, Wallace A. "Can Theism Survive Without the Devil?" *Religious Studies* 21 (1985): 231-244.

Contends that since Plantinga's free will defense (*God, Freedom and Evil* [#109] is the only defense acceptable to common sense, the devil's existence (which is used in Plantinga's defense as a possible explanation for natural evil) must also be accepted by common sense.

90.   Myers, C. Mason. "Free Will and the Problem of Evil." *Religious Studies* 23 (1987): 289-294.

Argues that neither the soft determinist nor the libertarian can regard consistently an omniscient and omnipotent creator to be free from blame for choices which are seemingly evil, unless we maintain the radical "agatheistic" theory— that no human choice is evil in the sense that some alternative choice would have been better. Yet this agatheistic view is incompatible with ordinary moral judgments. The libertarian has no advantage over the soft determinist in solving the problem of evil: both can solve it only by regarding ordinary distinctions between good and seemingly bad choices as illusory.

91.   Oakes, Robert A. "Actualities, Possibilities, and Free Will Theodicy." *New Scholasticism* 46 (1972): 191-201.

Defends the free will against Mackie ("Evil and Omnipotence" [#1217]) and Wallace Matson (*The Existence of God* [#1317]): both argued that the free will theodicist is wrong in supposing that because wrong choices are possible, it follows that wrong choices will actually be made. Oakes clarifies the epistemic ordering of actualities and possibilities, and argues that we cannot know wrong choices are possible in the absence of their actuality. Since moral choice involves awareness of the possibility of choosing wrongly, the realization of moral freedom cannot take place independently of the actuality of some moral evil. Thus, he defends theism against the charge that the divine permission of moral evil contradicts the concept of an omnipotent and omnibenevolent God. [See Walter's response, "Are Actualities Prior to Possibilities?" [#160]; and Kondoleon's response, "Moral Evil and the Existence of God: A Reply" [#74].]

92.   ——. "Actualities and Possibilities Once Again." *New Scholasticism* 47 (1973): 113-116.

Response to Walter's critique ("Are Actualities Prior to Possibilities?" [#160]) of Oakes's "Actualities, Possibilities, and Free-Will Theodicy" [#91]. Oakes defends his thesis that we cannot know anything is factually *possible* without knowing of any case of its *actuality*. Walter is mistaken in assuming that direct experience is the way of coming to know the actual. No such classical empiricist assumption is necessary; the dispute between rationalism and empiricism concerns the correct method for arriving at knowledge of actuality, while the principle Oakes defends is neutral, essentially, with respect to this issue. [See also Oakes, "Temporality and Divinity: An Analytic Hurdle," *Sophia* 31 (1992), 11-26.]

93.   ——. "God, Evil, and Professor Ross." *Philosophy and Phenomenological Research* 35 (1974): 261-267.

Rejects Ross's claim (*Philosophical Theology* [#1163]), that God's causal necessity and sufficiency for all events exonerates creatures of moral responsibility. If this were true, there would be no moral evil in the world for which God could be responsible. Oakes argues that the locus of moral responsibility would change, but it does not follow that the world would be bereft of moral evil: God would be the sole cause of it. [Ross rejects Oakes's criticism of him in Oakes, "Classical Theism and Pantheism: A Victory for Process Theism?" [see #130].]

94.   Paulsen, David L. "Divine Determinateness and the Free Will Defense." *Analysis* 41 (1981): 150-153.

Argues that one cannot hold that God has an eternally determinate nature and that the free will defense is an adequate response to the problem of evil. Paulsen argues that both Tennant (*Philosophical Theology*, *Volume 2* [#605]) and Hick (*Evil and the God of Love* [#750]) have incoherent responses to the critique of the free will defense (that God could have created a world with both freedom and no moral evil). Both Tennant and Hick have an understanding of God as having an eternally immutable, morally determinate nature. This is inconsistent with their view that moral goods are earned by creatures through a developmental process. [See response by David and Randall Basinger, "Divine Determinateness and the Free Will Defense: Some Clarifications" [#16].]

95.   Penelhum, Terence. *Religion and Rationality: An Introduction to the Philosophy of Religion*. New York: Random House, 1971.

Two of the twenty-five chapters address the problem of evil (*Chapter 16*, "The Problem of Evil: Some Traditional Defenses"; and *Chapter 17*, "The Problem of Evil: The Free Will Defense"). Penelhum argues that the theist is committed to some form of the free will defense. Against Pike ("Hume on Evil" [#1157]), Penelhum holds that we cannot be agnostic about the general reasons God may have for allowing evil.

96.   Pike, Nelson. "Divine Omniscience and Voluntary Action." *Philosophical Review* 74 (1965): 27-46.

Argues that if God exists and is essentially omniscient as well as everlasting, no one has power at any time to do other than what one actually does. [See also *Chapter 4* of Pike's *God and Timelessness* [#99], and responses by Adams, "Is the Existence of God a 'Hard' Fact?" [#2]; Alston, "Divine Foreknowledge and Alternative Conceptions of Human Freedom" [#3]; and Pike's reply, "Alston on Plantinga and Soft Theological Determinism" [#102].]

97.   ——. "Plantinga on the Free Will Defense: A Reply." *Journal of Philosophy* 63 (1966): 93-104.

Response to Plantinga's "The Free Will Defense" [#106]. Pike contends that Plantinga's critique of Mackie and Flew is unsuccessful. He examines Plantinga's two meanings of "possible persons" performing free and morally wrong actions. Neither definition answers the critique of Flew and Mackie: they ask how an omnipotent, omniscient and all-good God could instantiate possible persons as subsets of sets including the property "freely-performs-at-least-one-morally-wrong-action," rather than as subsets of sets including the property "freely-performs-only-right-actions." [See Plantinga's response, "Pike and Possible Persons" [#398].]

98.   ——. "Omnipotence and God's Ability to Sin." *American Philosophical Quarterly* 6 (1969): 208-216.

Offers a solution to the problem of omnipotence and impeccability. "God" is a descriptive expression, not a proper name, and its meaning is that God is omnipotent and perfectly good. If God sinned or did evil, God would not be God. [See response by Gellman, "Omnipotence and Impeccability" [#1096].]

99.   ———. *God and Timelessness.* New York: Schoken Books, 1970.

Chapter 4 ("Timelessness, Foreknowledge and Free Will," an earlier version of which was published as "Divine Omniscience and Voluntary Action" [#96]) contains Pike's thesis (contra Plantinga) that no human action is free, if God exists and is everlastingly omniscient. Pike shows that other attributes of God are inconsistent with timelessness. He concludes that the doctrine of timelessness has no place in Christian theism.

100.   ———. "Plantinga on Free Will and Evil." *Religious Studies* 15 (1979): 449-473.

Examines Plantinga's defense ("The Free Will Defense" [#106]) and Adams's critique ("Middle Knowledge and the Problem of Evil" [#445]) of free will theodicy and its "possible worlds" ontology. That God is omnipotent, omniscient and perfectly good does not entail that any free creatures created by God always do what is right (contra Mackie). Plantinga's argument—that an omnipotent and omniscient God is unable to create a world containing free creatures who always do what is right—is invalid. The argument requires a revised version of trans-world depravity. Yet this leads, in turn, to an absurd result. Pike argues that Augustine's free will theodicy is more promising than Plantinga's version.

101.   ———. "Over-Power and God's Responsibility for Sin." *The Existence and Nature of God.* Edited by Alfred J. Freddoso. Notre Dame, IN: University of Notre Dame Press, 1983: 11-35.

Argues against the view of Urban and Walton ("Freedom within Omnipotence," *The Power of God* [#165]); Flew (*God and Philosophy* [#223]); and David Griffin's process theodicy (*God, Power and Evil* [#861]), that the traditional Christian understanding of divine power implies God has all the power, such that there is no power (freedom) in creatures. Pike argues that God has delegated power to creatures. He develops a concept of "over-power" to argue that there can be creaturely freedom within the scope of divine omnipotence. Over-power is power to completely determine which powers are possessed by others. He considers the theodicies of Aquinas and Augustine regarding divine power and creaturely freedom, concluding that future efforts in theodicy must not assume that God is not responsible for the freely performed actions of creatures.

102.   ———. "Alston on Plantinga and Soft Theological Determinism." *International Journal for Philosophy of Religion* 27 (1990): 17-40.

Challenges Alston's thesis ("Divine Foreknowledge and Alternative Conceptions of Human Freedom" [#3]) regarding Plantinga's claim that divine foreknowledge is compatible with human freedom. Alston holds that Plantinga's argument is best understood as relying on the conditional conception of power employed by such historical figures as Hume and Schlick. Pike agrees with Alston that Plantinga's argument for the compatibility of divine foreknowledge and human freedom (in his *God, Freedom, and Evil* [#109]) turns on a conception of power not articulated in the text. Yet Pike argues that the conception in question is not the one Alston supposes. Alston's soft deterministic reading of Plantinga is not correct.

103.   Pinches, Charles. "Christian Pacifism and Theodicy: The Free Will Defense in the Thought of John H. Yoder." *Modern Theology* 5 (1989): 239-255.

Constructs a theodicy based on a free will defense and which uses Yoder's pacifism, a theodicy not susceptible to Surin's critique (*Theology and the Problem of Evil* [#1364] of ahistorical abstraction in the contemporary theodicies of Hick, Plantinga and Swinburne. Yoder re-theologizes the free will defense to focus on its historical (versus rationalistic) aspect. God is actively engaging evil. His pacifism is an account of Christianity's God as essentially non-coercive. While more convincing than other positions, this position has its own problems: Yoder's theodicy cannot provide a future resolution to the problem of suffering, since he has defined God's action as pacifism and emphasized human free will. His belief in a hell also has various problematic aspects. [For relevant Yoder references, see *The Original Revolution*. Scottdale, PA: Herald Press, 1971; *He Came Preaching Peace*. Scottdale, PA: Herald Press, 1985.]

104.   Pinnock, Clark. "God Limits His Knowledge." *Predestination and Free Will: Four Views of Divine Sovereignty and Human Freedom*. Edited by Randall and David Basinger. Downers Grove, IL: InterVarsity Press, 1986: 141-162.

Challenges the conventional view of divine power and knowledge: both attributes must be limited to secure a strong account of human freedom. God can bring about the divine will, nevertheless, since God can anticipate the obstructions creatures create and can respond accordingly. [Responses by Reichenbach, Feinberg, and Geisler follow in the text, 163-177.]

105.   ——. "A Comment on 'Is There Anything Which God Does Not Do?' A Symposium on Divine and Human Action." *Christian Scholar's Review* 16 (1987): 384-404.

Response to Mavrodes, "Is There Anything Which God Cannot Do?" [#86]. Pinnock agrees that the problem of divine causation is problematic. [See Pinnock's "God Limits His Knowledge" [#104].]

106.   Plantinga, Alvin. "The Free Will Defense." *Philosophy in America*. Edited by Max Black. Allen and Unwin, 1965: 204-220. [Reprinted in Plantinga's *God and Other Minds*].

Restates his free will defense in response to various challenges: Flew's "Divine Omnipotence and Human Freedom" [#45]; Mackie's "Evil and Omnipotence" [#1217]; and McCloskey "God and Evil" [#1231]. Plantinga refines and expands the arguments in *The Nature of Necessity* [#110] and *God, Freedom, and Evil* [#109].

107.   ——. *God and Other Minds: A Study of the Rational Justification of Belief in God*. Ithaca, NY: Cornell University Press, 1967. Reprinted, 1990.

Exploration of the rationality of belief in the existence of God. *Part II* contains an expanded version of "The Free Will Defense" [#106] and a consideration of verificationism and the paradox of omnipotence. Plantinga discusses and rejects various arguments offered by atheologians to demonstrate that theism is logically incoherent. Atheologians have not produced a proposition which is necessary or essential to theism, a proposition which, when combined with the triad of propositions (God is all-powerful, God is all-loving and evil exists) supposedly renders theism invalid.

108. ———. "The Incompatibility of Freedom with Determinism: A Reply." *Philosophical Forum* 3 (1970): 141-148.

Response to Tomberlin's contention ("Plantinga's Puzzles About God and Other Minds" [#147]), that Plantinga's free will defense, commenting on Flew's "Divine Omnipotence and Human Freedom" [#45], is invalid. Plantinga argues that Tomberlin has not shown that freedom and causal determinism are compatible. It is possible that some actions are both free and causally determined, yet this does not entail that it is possible that all actions are such.

109. ———. *God, Freedom and Evil*. New York: Harper and Row, 1974.

A simplified version of *The Nature of Necessity* [#110]. The one exception (addition) is that Plantinga considers the compatibility of divine foreknowledge and human freedom, arguing that they are mutually compatible.

110. ———. *The Nature of Necessity*. New York: Oxford University Press, 1974.

A systematic treatment of modality. *Chapter 4* explains the concept of possible worlds; *Chapter 9* deals with the problem of evil, an expanded and refined version of his "The Free Will Defense" [#106].

111. ———. "Existence, Necessity and God." *New Scholasticism* 50 (1976): 61-72.

Response to Purtill's "Plantinga, Necessity and God" [#119]. Plantinga refutes various criticisms levied by Purtill, including the claim that he (Plantinga) has confused *probability* with *likelihood*.

112. ———. "The Probabilistic Argument from Evil." *Philosophical Studies* 35 (1979): 1-53.

Surveys current theories of probability, and argues that none of them can establish the existence of God as improbable, given the evil in the world.

113. ———. "Reply to the Basingers on Divine Omnipotence." *Process Studies* 11 (1981): 25-29.

Both the Basinger brothers ("Plantinga Vs. Griffin" [#15]) and David Griffin (*God, Power and Evil* [#861]), as well as many others, have complained that Plantinga's appeal to Satan is implausible. Plantinga argues that the credibility of his appeal to Satan is irrelevant for the viability of his free will defense. He agrees with the Basingers that he rejects what Griffin defines as "I-omnipotence." [See Griffin's response in *Evil Revisited* [#873].]

114. ———. "Self-Profile" and "Replies." *Alvin Plantinga (Profiles, Volume 5)*. Edited by James E. Tomberlin and Peter van Inwagen. Dordrecht and Boston, MA: Reidel, 1985: 3-97, 313-398.

Plantinga outlines his contributions to theodicy (36-54), noting the relevant primary texts where the various aspects of his argument are published. He clarifies some of the major points that were unclear in his original arguments. Plantinga claims that his free will defense *assumes* there are counterfactuals of freedom but that it *does not assume* God has middle knowledge. He notes that the arguments against the logical incompatibility of theistic claims about God and evil are no longer as central to the debates as is the question of the existence of God being improbable or unlikely vis-à-vis evil; hence, his refutation of probabilistic arguments. Plantinga also replies to Robert Adams's chapter in this book, "Plantinga on the Problem of Evil," 371-382 [#446]. [The book contains Plantinga's annotated bibliography of his own publications to 1983 (399-404).]

115.   ———. "Is Theism Really a Miracle?" *Faith and Philosophy* 3 (1986): 109-134.

Response to Mackie's *The Miracle of Theism* [#1220]. He contends that Mackie confuses a *defense* with a *theodicy*. Mackie's critique of Plantinga's free will defense (*The Nature of Necessity* [#110]) fails, and his rejection of Plantinga's concept of transworld depravity is confused.

116.   ———. "On Ockham's Way Out." *Faith and Philosophy* 3 (1986): 235-269.

Presents two traditional arguments for the incompatibility of divine foreknowledge and human freedom, and partially endorses Ockham's response to the second (the argument from the necessity of the past). Only propositions strictly about the past are accidentally necessary; past propositions about God's knowledge of the future are not strictly about the past. [Reprinted in *The Concept of God*. Edited by Thomas V. Morris. Oxford: Oxford University Press, 1987.]

117.   ———. "God, Evil and the Metaphysics of Freedom." *The Problem of Evil*. Edited by Marilyn McCord Adams and Robert Merrihew Adams. New York: Oxford University Press, 1990: 83-109.

Reprinted from *Chapter 9* of *The Nature of Necessity* [#110].

118.   Purtill, Richard L. "Walton on Power and Evil." *International Journal for Philosophy of Religion* 6 (1975): 163-166.

Refutes Walton's claim ("Language, God and Evil" [#162]), that God's responsibility for evil is unclear in light of basic theological views. There is ambiguity in Walton's argument, for example, between God being the *sufficient* cause and the *necessary* cause of every state of affairs. Walton's "power stalemate principle" likewise is problematic. [See Walton's response, "Purtill on Power and Evil" [#164].]

119.   ———. "Plantinga, Necessity, and God." *New Scholasticism* 50 (1976): 46-60.

Critiques Plantinga's *The Nature of Necessity* [#110], including his defense of theistic beliefs (as unprovable) as too modest. Plantinga confuses *probability* with *likelihood*. Since the existence of evil or the amount of evil does not disconfirm the complete theistic hypothesis, which includes the existence of God and the existence of freedom, Purtill holds that it does not disconfirm the existence of God. [See Plantinga's response, "Existence, Necessity and God" [#111].]

120.   ———. "Flew and the Free Will Defense." *Religious Studies* 13 (1977): 477-483.

Rejects Flew's arguments against the free will defense ("Compatibilism, Free Will and God" [#46]). Libertarian free will is incompatible with the view of creatures as dependent upon God as sustaining cause.

121.   Quinn, Philip L. "Divine Foreknowledge and Divine Freedom." *International Journal for Philosophy of Religion* 9 (1978): 219-240.

Refutes La Croix's claim ("Omniprescience and Divine Determinism" [#269]), that divine foreknowledge and divine freedom are inconsistent. Quinn rejects La Croix's contention that God cannot make decisions about what God will do at a later time and that, as such, there is no divine freedom. He contends, for example, that this argument depends upon a premise that neither follows from the doctrine of divine everlasting omniprescience (despite La Croix's argument that it does) and that it is not a necessary truth in itself.

122.   ———. "Plantinga on Foreknowledge and Freedom." *Alvin Plantinga (Profiles, Volume 5)*. Edited by James E. Tomberlin and Peter van Inwagen. New York: Reidel, 1985: 271-287.

Evaluations of Pike's arguments in "Divine Omniscience and Voluntary Action" [#96] and in "Divine Foreknowledge, Human Freedom and Possible Worlds" [#397], for the consistency of divine foreknowledge and the claim that some human actions are voluntary. Quinn evaluates also Plantinga's arguments to the contrary, in *God, Freedom and Evil* [#109]. Quinn argues that Plantinga is correct in his negative assessment of Pike's arguments. [See Plantinga's reply, *Alvin Plantinga (Profiles, Volume 5)*, 384-385 [#114].]

123.   Ratzsch, Del. "Tomberlin and McGuinness on Plantinga's Free Will Defense." *International Journal for Philosophy of Religion* 12 (1981): 235-244.

Rejects the critique of Tomberlin and McGuinness ("God, Evil, and the Free Will Defense" [#148]) of Plantinga's free will defense (in "Which Worlds Could God Have Created?" [#400] and *The Nature of Necessity* [#110]). Ratzsch argues that Tomberlin and McGuinness have missed many of Plantinga's key insights and have put forth a number of invalid arguments and unsupported premises.

124.   Reichenbach, Bruce R. "God Limits His Power." *Predestination and Free Will: Four Views of Divine Sovereignty and Human Freedom*. Edited by Randall and David Basinger. Downers Grove, IL: InterVarsity Press, 1986: 99-124.

Argues that the more freedom God grants creatures, the less control God has over us. [Responses by Feinberg, Geisler, and Pinnock follow in the text, 125-140.]

125.   ———. "Hasker on Omniscience." *Faith and Philosophy* 4 (1987): 86-92.

Refutes Hasker's argument for the incompatibilism of divine omniscience and human freedom ("Foreknowledge and Necessity" [#59]). Hasker's argument rests on an equivocation between *bringing about* and *altering* the past. Only the former is invoked by those who think omniscience is incompatible with freedom. Reichenbach claims to escape Hasker's proposed dilemma, that we either give up the traditional notion of divine omniscience or commit ourselves to the dubious belief that we can alter the past. Reichenbach argues that we can freely bring about the future and the past by our actions, because God's beliefs about our actions are conditioned by our actions. His conclusion is that the compatibilist is not impaled on either of the horns of Hasker's dilemma.

126.   ———. "Evil and a Reformed View of God." *International Journal for Philosophy of Religion* 24 (1988): 67-88.

Reformed theologians cannot resort to the libertarian defense from evil, since they are committed to the compatibilist position. Reichenbach argues against the reformed theologians' rejection of God being able to create better beings. There are no moral grounds for supporting the concept of the "fortunate fall" over creatures who remained innocent.

127.   Rice, Richard. *The Openness of God: The Relationship of Divine ForeKnowledge and Human Free Will.* Nashville, TN and Washington, DC: Review and Harold Publishing Association, 1980.

Argues against the conventional Christian view of God's relation to the world, and that God experiences the events of the world as they happen, rather than "all at once" in some timeless, eternal perception. Rice contends that God does not know the future in all its details. This view has biblical support as well as the support of religious experience. God is not responsible for evil only if (as Rice argues) God created a world wherein evil *could* exist, but the possibility of which was not definite. Otherwise (as in Hick's theodicy), evil would be part of God's original plan, implying that evil is not really evil. God is responsible for the *possibility* of evil (as in process theology, though this is not mentioned by Rice), but God is not responsible for its actual *occurrence*, this being the result, rather, of human choices. [See the critique by Gruenler, *The Inexhaustible God* [#877].]

128.   Richman, Robert J. "Plantinga, God, and (Yet) Other Minds."*Australasian Journal of Philosophy* 50 (1972): 40-54.

Challenges Plantinga's arguments in *God and Other Minds* [#107], including the claim that belief in God is not incompatible with evil. Richman contends that Plantinga's suggestion that the problem of evil is not a problem for the theist rests on the implicit assumption that free will is in fact an explanation (and justification) for God's permitting evil in the world.

129.   Ross, James F. "Creation." *Journal of Philosophy* 77 (1980): 614-629.

Contends that the definition of divine omnipotence implies that God determines which is to be the actual world among possible worlds. Ross argues also that human freedom and divine causation are compatible, and that God's creation of the actual world required no change in God (as Aquinas also held). [See response by Gutting, "Is Ross's God the God of Religion?" [#57].]

130.   ———. "Creation II." *The Existence and Nature of God.* Edited by Alfred J. Freddoso. Notre Dame, IN: University of Notre Dame Press, 1983: 115-142.

Further clarifies his view of divine power (see previous entry). Ross rejects various criticisms (David Griffin, *God, Power and Evil* [#861]; Robert Oakes, "Classical Theism and Pantheism: A Victory for Process Theism?" *Religious Studies* 13 [1977], 167-173; etc.), critiques which hold that since—according to Ross—God creates various effects that are metaphysically dependent on them, Ross supposedly is arguing that created things are non-metaphorically a kind of dreaming or imagining. Ross denies this and denies the critics' conclusion that creatures would not be free. He rejects as pernicious also Plantinga's and others' use of "possible worlds" ontology: this misunderstands God's creative causation. The only causality exerted by God as creator is to cause "being."

131.   Roth, John K. "Critique [of Davis]." *Encountering Evil*. Edited by Stephen Davis. Atlanta, GA: John Knox Press, 1981: 89-92.

Holds that Davis's theodicy ("Free Will and Evil" [#33]) leads to too many unresolved questions to be convincing. The amount of evil, for example, its cost-effectiveness, is inadequately explained. [See Davis's response, following in the text.]

132.   Rowe, William L. "God and Other Minds." *Noûs* 3 (1969): 259-284.

Response to Plantinga's *God and Other Minds* [#107]. In the section on the free will defense, Rowe argues that Plantinga's shift from the free will defense to "the unfettered will" counters Flew's attack only by substantially weakening another point in the defense. Plantinga's original argument (contra Mackie's attack on the free will theodicy), that the proposition—God can instantiate possible persons containing the property of always freely doing what is right is contingent—is valid. Yet, Mackie's argument does not require this premise. Mackie's premise is that if God is omnipotent, God can instantiate possible persons containing the property of always freely doing what is right. Plantinga shows that the consequent of this proposition is contingent, but *not* that the proposition itself is contingent. Rowe concludes that there must be a clearer definition of the proposition that God is omnipotent before we can conclude that Plantinga has refuted the critiques of Mackie and others.

133.   Runzo, Joseph. "Omniscience and Freedom for Evil." *International Journal for Philosophy of Religion* 12 (1981): 131-148.

Argues that divine omniscience is compatible with human free will. This issue is logically interdependent upon the free will defense as an attempted theodicy. God cannot foreknow the truth of any propositions referring to future contingent states of affairs. Yet there is not anything here to know and, as such, there is no lacking in divine omniscience. God is not morally reprehensible for actual human moral evil, then, even if there would be a high preponderance of moral evil over good: God could not have foreknown this.

134.   Russell, John M. "Davis's Free Will Defense: An Exposition and Critique." *Encounter* 47 (1986): 245-256.

Maintains that various problems militate against the validity of Stephen Davis's free will defense ("Free Will and Evil" [#33]), mostly stemming from the concept of divine omnipotence. Russell holds that since, for example, God foreknew our evil decisions and yet created the conditions under which they would occur, Davis's God is responsible for evil, since God's knowledge is necessary.

135.   Settle, T.W. "A Prolegomenon to Intellectually Honest Theology." *Philosophical Forum* 1 (1968): 136-170.

A section on theodicy argues against the attacks of Flew ("Divine Omnipotence and Human Freedom" [#45]) and Mackie ("Evil and Omnipotence" [#1217]) on the free will defense, and then argues that, if heaven is assumed, the free will defense is defeated "in advance." Settle asks: if there are free human beings in heaven who are guaranteed to make good choices, why was this state not created by God in the first place?

136.   Silvester, H. *Arguing with God: A Christian Examination of the Problem of Evil*. Downers Grove, IL: InterVarsity Press, 1971.

Defends the free will defense but rejects Hick's criticisms of it in the Augustinian format (*Evil and the God of Love* [#750]). God ordains all and yet we are responsible ("First Order Approval" and "Second Order Approval"). Divine power was limited so that we could be free. As for natural evils, Hick is cited approvingly, noting that natural evils are not as serious as often made out: such evils serve as a backdrop for human life, the crown of creation, and are greatly mitigated by following God's commands. The only final justification is universal salvation.

137.   Slote, Michael. "Selective Necessity and the Free Will Problem." *Journal of Philosophy* 77 (1982): 5-24.

Examines a new form of the argument for the incompatibility of free will and determinism in Carl Ginet ("Might We Have No Choice?" [#236]); James Lamb ("On a Proof of Incompatibilism" [#273]); Peter van Inwagen ("The Incompatibility of Responsibility and Determinism" [#151]); and David Wiggins ("Towards a Reasonable Libertarianism" [#345]). Slote contends that these new arguments remedy glaring deficiencies in previous defenses of incompatibilism, yet suffer important weaknesses because of insufficient attention to a kind of necessity ("selective necessity") that is prevalent in ordinary thought about the world.

138.   Sontag, Frederick E. "Critique [of Davis]." *Encountering Evil*. Edited by Stephen Davis. Atlanta, GA: John Knox Press, 1981: 83-85.

Refutes Stephen Davis's free will defense ("Free Will and Evil" [#33]) on several grounds. Davis's assumption that his free will defense presumes that this is the best possible world begs the question: there is little to justify this claim. Davis's God is not free, since God is bound by Davis's restrictions in being able to attain ends in no other way. Davis's appeal to Satan as the cause of natural evils is unjustified, and Davis does not deal adequately with the core problem—the *amount* of evil in the world. [See Davis's response, following in the text.]

139.   Steen, John W. "The Problem of Evil: Ethical Considerations." *Canadian Journal of Theology* 11 (1965): 255-264.

Rejects the incompatibilistic view of freedom and supports a deterministic account, the latter being compatible with divine omnipotence. Steen argues that theists place so high a value on freedom (as justifying evil) that they beg the question as to whether this is the best of all possible worlds. He contends that total *goodness* is better than total *freedom*, and that God could have given us abilities we do not have—to do good, replacing abilities we do have, abilities for doing evil.

140.   Sterba, James P. "God, Plantinga and a Better World." *International Journal for Philosophy of Religion* 7 (1976): 446-451.

Responds to various arguments of (unnamed) critics of Plantinga's free will defense, concerning mainly the criticism that Plantinga has not supported his assumptions that freedom requires indeterminism, and that an indeterministic world is better than any deterministic world. Sterba argues for the validity of

Plantinga's premises. It is logically possible that indeterminism holds with respect to free actions which are morally evil. [Plantinga's references cited include his *God, Freedom and Evil* [#109]; *The Nature of Necessity*, *Chapter 9* [#110]; and *God and Other Minds*, *Chapters 5 and 6* [#107].]

141. Steuer, Axel D. "Once More on the Free Will Defense." *Religious Studies* 10 (1974): 301-311.

Argues that Mackie offered two distinct (yet related) criticisms of the free will defense ("Evil and Omnipotence" [#1217]), but that the relationship between the two has been unnoticed by Plantinga ("The Free Will Defense" [#106]) and by Davis ("A Defense of the Free Will Defense" [#32]). Steuer concludes that both of Mackie's criticisms—an omnipotent being would be capable of creating free beings who would always choose the good, and an omnipotent being would be capable of asserting total control over the wills of human beings—can be answered by pointing out that these criticisms assume that an omnipotent being would be required to engage in activity that cannot be logically performed. He resolves Mackie's paradox of omnipotence by arguing that it does not compromise God's omnipotence to hold that God creates beings with self-control.

142. ——. "The Freedom and God and Human Freedom." *Scottish Journal of Theology* 36 (1983): 163-180.

Argues that, contrary to much of western philosophical and theological thought, there is no fundamental conflict between divine freedom and human freedom. He contends that it is possible to reconcile divine omnipotence and divine omniscience with human freedom, and he denies divine foreknowledge of human free actions.

143. Suttle, Bruce B. "On God Tolerating Evil." *Sophia* 26 (1987): 53-54.

Rejects McGrath's criticisms ("Evil and the Existence of a Finite God" [#1320]) of Mackie, that theodicy can be resolved only if divine omnipotence or goodness is rejected. He argues that McGrath ignores the conditions necessary to tolerate evil.

144. Talbott, Thomas B. "On the Divine Nature and the Nature of Divine Freedom." *Faith and Philosophy* 5 (1988): 3-24.

Defends the view that God's power to act is not limited by the divine essential properties. He argues that divine freedom and the kind of human freedom required by the free will defense is the same kind of freedom: action determined by their own respective characters and natures.

145. Tannous, Alfif I. "Order and Disorder: Thermodynamics, Creation, and Values." *Zygon, Journal of Religion and Science* 20 (1985): 445-450.

Response to several articles, including Russell's "Entropy and Evil" [#315]. Tannous argues that Russell and the general trend of Christian thought has misunderstood the nature and meaning of evil: there is no evil in physical nature. All concepts are creations of the human mind and, as such, must be open to modification and repudiation as our knowledge continues to accumulate. The source of evil is the abuse of human freedom—any act that abuses creative freedom in humans and in nature.

146.   Thomas, George F. "The Problem of Evil." *Philosophy and Religious Belief.*
        New York: Scribner, 1970: 220-258.

        Argues that Augustine's privation view is misleading and overly optimistic, and
        that Leibniz's "best possible world" is based on questionable premises. He
        questions Tennant's view of natural evil as too anthropocentric, yet sees natural
        evils as incidental effects in the regular workings of the natural order and
        necessary for the evolution of life and the moral development of humans.
        Critics of the free will defense (Mackie, Flew, McCloskey) have rendered the
        problem of moral evil uncertain, yet Thomas holds that moral evil is the price
        paid for freedom.

147.   Tomberlin, James E. "Plantinga's Puzzles About God and Other Minds."
        Philosophical Forum 2 (1969): 372-375.

        Rejects Plantinga's argument ("The Free Will Defense" [#106]), that an action
        cannot be both causally determined and free. [See Plantinga's response, "The
        Incompatibility of Freedom with Determinism: A Reply" [#108].]

148.   Tomberlin, James E., and Frank McGuinness. "God, Evil, and the Free Will
        Defense." *Religious Studies* 13 (1977): 455-475.

        A consideration of Rowe's critique ("God and Other Minds" [#132]) of Plan-
        tinga. The authors argue that the free will defense can be defended. Yet, they
        propose an argument which refutes the free will defense. The free will defense
        requires that the proposition—that there is some A-property F such that God
        causally brings it about that F is instantiated—is false. Tomberlin and McGuin-
        ness argue that it is not false. [See response by Ratzsch, "Tomberlin and
        McGuinness on Plantinga's Free Will Defense" [#123].]

149.   Vanauken, Sheldon. "God's Will: Reflections on the Problem of Pain." *The
        Intellectuals Speak Out About God.* Edited by Roy A. Varghese. Chicago, IL:
        Regnery Gateway, 1984: 355-362.

        Maintains that the reason for evil is the free will of creatures: God cannot
        simultaneously give us freedom and yet determine our actions.

150.   Van Inwagen, Peter. *An Essay on Free Will.* New York: Oxford University
        Press, 1983.

        Argues for three versions of a basic argument for incompatibilism, the "conse-
        quence argument." He rejects the compatibilist arguments and holds that free
        will is genuine. Since free will is incompatible with causal determinism, causal
        determinism does not hold. [See response by Fischer, "Van Inwagen on Free
        Will" [#44].]

151.   ——. "The Incompatibility of Responsibility and Determinism." *Moral Re-
        sponsibility.* Edited by John Martin Fischer. Ithaca, NY: Cornell University
        Press, 1986: 241-250.

        Contends that free will and determinism are incompatible, contra Plantinga,
        Chisholm, Anscombe and others. [See responses by Michael Slote, "Selective
        Necessity and the Free Will Problem" [#137], and John Martin Fischer, "Intro-
        duction: Responsibility and Freedom" [#216].]

152. Wachterhauser, Brice R. "The Problem of Evil and Moral Scepticism." *International Journal for Philosophy of Religion* 17 (1985): 167-174.

     Holds that the logical coherence of classical theism can be defended by the free will defense and the argument from divine omniscience and human finitude, but only at the cost of moral scepticism. Clear and undeniable cases of morally unjustifiable evils are construed as merely apparently unjustifiable evils from some moral point of view. Basic evils cannot be justified, however, from any moral perspective. The necessary condition for having a moral perspective demands that certain evils are recognized as unjustifiable from any moral perspective. If classical theists reject this moral scepticism, then they must show that there are cases of morally unjustifiable evil; yet this would undermine the logical coherence of theism.

153. Wainwright, William L. "Freedom and Omnipotence." *Noûs* 2 (1968): 293-301.

     Contends that Plantinga ("The Free Will Defense" [#106]) is correct in holding that it is not incompatible with divine omnipotence that God cannot determine the free actions of other agents. Wainwright argues that Plantinga's God is omnipotent despite being limited by the contingent fact that free persons, contingently created as such, are indeed free. Plantinga's free will defense implies that God is prevented from realizing the divine purpose by limiting facts which God has not created directly. Yet this does not contradict divine omnipotence, since it does not appear to be logically possible that there is a being freer from restrictions than God is. God need not have created free creatures.

154. ———. "Christian Theism and the Free Will Defense: A Problem." *International Journal for Philosophy of Religion* 7 (1975): 243-250.

     Argues that classical theism holds irreconcilably both that God is a moral agent and that God is unable to sin. As such, Wainwright maintains that a basic premise of the free will defense is jeopardized. Rather than arguing that God's permission of evil is necessary if there are to be moral agents, and that the existence of moral agents is a good, Wainwright suggests a modified version of the free will defense: God's permission of moral evil is necessary if there are to be moral agents who are not essentially good, and that the existence of such agents is a good. This version overcomes the major incoherence in classical theism; yet it is not as attractive a free will defense as the traditional version.

155. Wall, George B. "A New Solution to an Old Problem." *Religious Studies* 15 (1979): 511-530.

     Proposes a solution to the problem of evil which offers a free will *theodicy*, rather than a free will *defense*. [See Plantinga, "The Free Will Defense" [#106].] God's experiment with freedom had to ensure that freedom be given the best chance possible to become autonomously responsible; natural evil helps serve this function more so than moral evil would alone.

156. Wallace, Gerald. "The Problems of Moral and Physical Evil." *Philosophy* 46 (1971): 349-351.

     By examining some similarities between moral and physical evils, Wallace disputes the assumption that the free will defense and the thesis that physical evils are logically necessary conditions for certain moral virtues and vices are, in fact, compatible.

157. Walls, Jerry L. "The Free Will Defense, Calvinism, Wesley and the Goodness of God." *Christian Scholar's Review* 13 (1984): 19-33.

Assesses Feinberg's argument ("'And the Atheist Shall Lie Down with the Calvinist': Atheism, Calvinism, and the Free Will Defense" [#40]), that both atheists and Calvinists must reject the free will defense because of their common commitment to compatibilism. Walls discusses how free will theologians and Calvinists differ: Calvinism is committed to *compatibilism*; free will theologians to *incompatibilism*. He argues for the incompatibilist doctrine on the grounds that Calvinists offer no good reasons why God determines so many to do evil only to condemn them to damnation. Wesley maintained God's goodness and denied that God could determine some of us to choose evil; Calvinism holds to divine determinism and is unclear as to how such a God can be good.

158. ———. "A Fable of Foreknowledge and Freedom." *Philosophy* 62 (1987): 67-75.

Argues the case for reconciling human freedom and divine foreknowledge. If God's purpose is that we have the freedom to develop morally, then God cannot intervene to give us foresight of future events without undermining that purpose.

159. ———. "Why Plantinga Must Move From Defense to Theodicy." *Philosophy and Phenomenological Research* 51 (1991): 375-378.

While Plantinga has insisted that his free will defense is not a theodicy, Walls argues that it follows from Plantinga's belief—that God is perfectly good, omnipotent and omniscient—that creatures are free "in fact." Plantinga, as such, has moved from a *defense* to a *theodicy*.

160. Walter, Edward. "Are Actualities Prior to Possibilities?" *New Scholasticism* 46 (1972): 202-209.

Refutes Oakes's exoneration of God (*contra* Mackie's seminal, "Evil and Omnipotence" [#1217], and Matson, "An Introduction to Omniscience" [#282]) for permitting a world with evil, since (Oakes contends) the knowledge of the possibility of evil can be acquired only if evil is experienced ("Actualities, Possibilities and Free-Will Theodicy" [#91]). Walter objects that actualities are epistemologically prior to possibilities and finds fault with Oakes's definition of "persons." He questions whether freedom can be bestowed on humans by a God who has given us our abilities and limitations as well as the environmental maze. Since God gave us our gifts and deficiencies, we cannot be free in the sense of being morally responsible for adhering to God's commands. Thus, God could have prevented the possibility and the actuality of moral evil without sacrificing human freedom.

161. Walton, Douglas. "Modalities in the Free Will Defense." *Religious Studies* 10 (1974): 325-331.

Contends that Plantinga's free will defense can be clarified and improved by precise syntactical statements of key assumptions. Walton considers Davis's argument ("A Defense of the Free Will Defense" [#32]), that "x is 0" is incompatible with "x can be either 0 or not-0." This is so, according to Walton, only if one assumes "a deviant alethic modal logic."

162. ———. "Language, God and Evil." *International Journal for Philosophy of Religion* 6 (1975): 154-162.

Formulates some basic assumptions of the free will defense by constructing a formal base language, a theological dialectic. The expressions, sentences, axioms and rules of religious discourse concerning the problem of evil must be set out clearly in such language in order that theologians and atheologians can isolate areas of disagreement. He examines the "Power Stalemate Principle" and Plantinga's "First and Second Principles" (in Plantinga's *The Nature of Necessity* [#110]).

163.   ——. "Principles of Interpersonal Agency in the Free Will Defense." *Bijdragen* 37 (1976): 36-46.

Argues that Plantinga's free will defense can be strengthened by clear syntactical statement and semantic analysis of the underlying principles at the basis of disagreement between theists and atheists.

164.   ——. "Purtill on Power and Evil." *International Journal for Philosophy of Religion* 8 (1977): 263-267.

Response to Purtill's critique ("Walton on Power and Evil" [#118]) of Walton's "Language, God and Evil" [#162]. The "Power Stalemate Principle" requires an idea of control as *full* control, yet Purtill suggests that all control is really *partial*.

165.   Walton, Douglas, and Linwood Urban. "Freedom within Omnipotence." *The Power of God: Evil and Omnipotence*. Edited by Linwood Urban and Douglas Walton. Oxford: Oxford University Press, 1977: 192-213.

Contend that attempts to combine consistently the notion of God's omnipotence (taken to mean the power to determine every outcome) with the notion of human freedom cannot succeed. Walton proposes an alternative conception of omnipotence. If God has created a world, parts of which are governed by chance, then God cannot determine the outcomes of these chance events. God has given us freedom and cannot intervene to determine outcomes, as long as the acts are free. Critics of this proposal, who might suggest that an omnipotent being must be able to control every outcome, must hold paradoxically that an omnipotent being could not create a world governed by chance or by human freedom. Walton and Urban argue against Mackie's position ("Omnipotence" [#1218]), that there is a rational way to choose between two conceptions of omnipotence: a God who can limit itself by creating worlds in which God has either complete control or only partial control. The latter is a greater control. [See also some of Walton's other discussions of divine omnipotence and their relevance for theodicy: "Some Theorems of Fitch on Omnipotence" [#336]; and "The Omnipotence Paradox" [#335]; etc.]

166.   Watson, S. Youree. "The Other Face of Evil." *Essays in Morality and Ethics*. Edited by James Gaffney. New York: Paulist Press, 1980: 3-28.

Contends that free choice is between incommensurable goods; that pain is the condition for moral growth; and he attempts to justify the suffering of children.

167.   Wierenga, Edward R. *The Nature of God: An Inquiry into Divine Attributes*. Ithaca, NY: Cornell University Press, 1989.

Discusses several issues, all of which are relevant to theodicy: divine *omnipotence*—using Plantinga's distinction between strong and weak actualization;

omniscience—God knows the truth of every true proposition; divine *foreknow-ledge* and *free will*—rejects accidental necessity, past truths about future events; *middle knowledge*—God's middle knowledge is compatible with human free-dom only if God "weakly" actualizes a possible world; *counterfactuals of freedom*—the free will defense requires that some counterfactuals are possibly true, eternity, timelessness, immutability, divine benevolence; and defends *the divine command theory* of the source of morality.

168.   Wilson, Kenneth. *Making Sense of It: An Essay in Philosophical Theology*. London: Epworth Press, 1973.

Chapter 8 ("Evil") defends the free will defense against several criticisms, mainly Flew's seminal, "Divine Omnipotence and Human Freedom" [#45]. The final resolution of the problem of evil is in Christ, the perfection of creation.

169.   Windt, Peter Y. "Plantinga's Unfortunate God." *Philosophical Studies* 24 (1973): 335-342.

Refutes Plantinga's argument ("The Free Will Defense" [#106]), that while it is logically possible that morally perfect people exist, circumstances still might arise in which God would be unable to create any of them; thus, since a world with free people and evil is better than a world with no evil and no freedom, the mere existence of evil cannot be regarded as inconsistent with God's exis-tence. Windt argues that Plantinga's argument, if correct, is strong evidence *against*, rather than evidence *for*, the claim that an omnipotent, omniscient and wholly good God exists. That which Plantinga's God can create is partly a matter of fortune, and this contradicts divine omnipotence.

170.   Yandell, Keith E. "Logic and the Problem of Evil: A Response to Hoitenga." *God, Man, and Religion*. Edited by Keith Yandell. New York: McGraw-Hill, 1973: 351-364. [see #1189–#1194 for other Yandell items.]

Refutes Hoitenga's critique of the free will defense ("Logic and the Problem of Evil" [#68]). Yandell argues that Hoitenga has not shown any inconsistency between ordinary moral experience or moral belief and the compatibility of good and evil. Nor has Hoitenga defended his contention that human goodness is an inappropriate model on which to understand divine goodness.

171.   ——. "The Problem of Evil." *Philosophical Topics* 12 (1981): 7-38.

Argues that it is illegitimate to limit God's omnipotence in order to seek to resolve the problem of evil. Yandell defends a version of the free will defense similar to Plantinga's against Nelson Pike's objections ("Plantinga on Free Will and Evil" [#100], and "Plantinga on the Free Will Defense: A Reply" [#97]).

172.   Young, Robert. *Freedom, Responsibility and God*. London: Macmillan, 1975.

Chapter 14 (201-222) discusses Plantinga's free will defense in "The Free Will Defense" [#106]. If one assumes a libertarian concept of freedom, Plantinga's defense is valid; if one assumes a compatibilist view of freedom, God could create worlds in which free beings never act badly. Yet these worlds would not be better than the actual world.

173. ——. "Omnipotence and Compatibilism." *Philosophia* 6 (1976): 49-67.

Examines the possibilities for a compatibilist theist, in comparison with libertarians, to demonstrate that it is impossible for human beings to be made such that we freely do what is right on all occasions. It is impossible to construct a compatibilist version of the free will defense.

174. Zeis, John, and Jonathan Jacobs. "Omnipotence and Concurrence." *International Journal for Philosophy of Religion* 14 (1983): 17-23.

Propose an understanding of omnipotence which clarifies the problem of evil. The authors argue that God's effective choice of the actual world is not distributive or closed. As such, God's congruence with the free actions of creatures is possible. In choosing an actual world, God does not choose a conjunction by individually choosing each one of the components of that conjunction. God chooses the conjunction as a whole. [See also John Zeis, "To Hell with Freedom," *Sophia* 25 (1986), 41-48.]

II Related Publications on Freedom and Omnipotence [Selected]

175. Alston, William P. "Divine and Human Action." *Divine and Human Action*. Edited by Thomas V. Morris. Ithaca, NY: Cornell University Press, 1988: 257-280.

176. ——. *Divine Nature and Human Language*. Ithaca, NY: Cornell University Press, 1989. [See also Alston's "The Inductive Argument from Evil and the Humean Cognitive Condition." *Philosophical Perspectives* 5 (1991), 29-67.]

177. Anglin, William S. "Can God Create A Being He Cannot Control?" *Analysis* 40 (1980): 220-223.

178. Beckerman, Wilfred. "The Problem of Judging Evil." *The Times* (London), December 17, 1986: 18. [See also Beckerman's contribution to *The Times* (London), February 7, 1987, 8.]

179. Bertocci, Peter A. "Free Will, the Creativity of God, and Order." *Current Philosophical Issues: Essays in Honor of Curt John Ducassé*. Edited by Frederick C. Dommeyer. Springfield, IL: C.C. Thomas, 1966: 213-235.

180. Boh, Ivan. "Divine Omnipotence in the Early *Sentences*." *Divine Omniscience and Omnipotence in Medieval Philosophy*. Edited by Tamar Rudavsky. Dordrecht and Boston, MA: Reidel, 1985: 185-212.

181. Bonifacio, Armando F. "On Capacity Limiting Statements." *Mind* 74 (1965): 87-88.

182. Brown, Robert. "Divine Omnipotence, Immutability, Aseity and Human Free Will." *Religious Studies* 27 (1991): 285-295. [If God's timeless omniscience is compatible with human free will, then it is incoherent to hold that such a God is immutable and *a se* as well as omniscient.]

183. Cargile, James. "On Omnipotence." *Noûs* 1 (1967): 201-205.

184.   Carr, Craig L. "Coercion and Freedom." *American Philosophical Quarterly* 25 (1988): 59-67.

185.   Carter, W.R. "Impeccability Revisited." *Analysis* 45 (1985): 52-55.

186.   Chan, Stephen. *Fate, Logic and Time*. New Haven, CT: Yale University Press, 1967.

187.   Chisholm, Roderick. "He Could Have Done Otherwise." *The Nature of Human Action*. Edited by Myles Brand. Glenview, IL: Scott, Foresman, 1970.

188.   Clark, Gordon H. *Religion, Reason and Revelation*. Philadelphia, PA: Presbyterian and Reformed Publishing Company, 1961. [Argues against the free will defense as a solution to theodicy: free will does not resolve God of responsibility for evil.]

189.   Collins, Anthony. *Determinism and Free Will*. The Hague, Netherlands: Martinus Nijhoff, 1976.

190.   Cook, Robert R. "God, Time and Freedom." *Religious Studies* 23 (1987): 81-94.

191.   ———. "Divine Foreknowledge: Some Philosophical Issues." *Vox Evangelica* 20 (1990): 57-72.

192.   Courtenay, William J. "The Dialectic of Omnipotence in the High and Late Middle Ages." *Divine Omniscience and Omnipotence in Medieval Philosophy*. Edited by Tamar Rudavsky. Dordrecht and Boston, MA: Reidel, 1985: 243-270.

193.   Cowan, Joseph L. "The Paradox of Omnipotence." *Analysis* 25 (1965): 102-108. [See also Cowan's "The Paradox of Omnipotence Revisited," *Canadian Journal of Philosophy* 4 (1974), 435-445.]

194.   Craig, William Lane. *The Only Wise God: The Compatibility of Divine Foreknowledge and Human Freedom*. Grand Rapids, MI: Baker, 1987. [Defense of the compatibility of divine foreknowledge and human freedom. The final chapter contains an introduction to the "middle knowledge" concept and its relevance to theodicy.]

195.   ———. "Boethius on Theological Fatalism." *Ephemerides Theologicae Lovanienses* 64 (1988): 324-347.

196.   ———. "Tachyons, Time Travel, and Divine Omniscience." *Journal of Philosophy* 86 (1988): 135-150.

197.   ———. "'Nice Soft Facts': Fischer on Foreknowledge." *Religious Studies* 25 (1989): 235-246.

198.   ———. "Purtill on Fatalism and Truth." *Faith and Philosophy* 7 (1990): 229-234. [See Purtill's "Foreknowledge and Fatalism" [#302].]

199.   Davis, Charles, and Vaughn R. McKim. "Temporal Modalities and the Future." *Notre Dame Journal of Symbolic Logic* 17 (1976): 233-238.

200.   Davis, Stephen T. "Divine Omniscience and Human Freedom." *Religious Studies* 15 (1979): 303-316.

201.   DeRose, Keith. "Plantinga, Presumption, Possibility, and the Problem of Evil." *Canadian Journal of Philosophy* 21 (1991): 497-512.

202. Double, Richard. "Meta-Compatibilism." *American Philosophical Quarterly* 25 (1988): 323-329. [See also his "Determinism and the Experience of Freedom," *Pacific Philosophical Quarterly* 72 (1991), 1-8.]

203. Ducassé, Curt John. "The Problem of Evil." *A Philosophical Scrutiny of Religion*. New York: Ronald Press Company, 1953: 352-379.

204. Edwards, Jonathan. *Freedom of the Will*. Indianapolis, IN and New York: Bobbs-Merrill, 1969.

205. Ehring, Douglas. "Causal Asymmetry." *Journal of Philosophy* 79 (1982): 761-774.

206. Ellis, R. "God and 'Action'." *Religious Studies* 22 (1988): 463-481.

207. Elphinstone, Andrew. *Freedom, Suffering and Love*. London: SCM Press, 1976.

208. Engstrom, Stephen. "Conditional Autonomy." *Philosophy and Phenomenological Research* 49 (1988): 435-453.

209. Falk, A. "Some Modal Confusions in Compatibilism." *American Philosophical Quarterly* 18 (1981): 141-148.

210. Feldman, Seymour. "The Binding of Isaac: A Test-Case of Divine Foreknowledge." *Divine Omniscience and Omnipotence in Medieval Philosophy*. Edited by Tamar Rudavsky. Dordrecht and Boston, MA: Reidel, 1985: 105-134.

211. Fischer, John Martin. "Responsibility and Control." *Journal of Philosophy* 79 (1982): 24-40.

212. ———. "Incompatibilism." *Philosophical Studies* 43 (1983): 127-137. [Argues against Peter van Inwagen's modal argument for the validity of incompatibilism [see #330].]

213. ———. "Freedom and Foreknowledge." *Philosophical Review* 92 (1983): 67-79.

214. ———. "Ockhamism." *Philosophical Review* 94 (1985): 67-79.

215. ———. "Pike's Ockhamism." *Analysis* 46 (1986): 57-63.

216. ———. "Introduction: Responsibility and Freedom." *Moral Responsibility*. Edited by John Martin Fischer. Ithaca, NY: Cornell University Press, 1986: 9-61. [This book contains a bibliographical list of recent items on freedom and determinism, compatibilism, incompatibilism, possible worlds, etc.]

217. ———. "Power Necessity." *Philosophical Topics* 14 (1986): 77-91. [Argues that Slote's explanation of the purported failure of power necessity ("Selective Necessity and the Free-Will Problem" [#137]) to obey the main modal principle is inadequate.]

218. ———. "Hard-Type Soft Facts." *Philosophical Review* 95 (1986): 591-601.

219. ———. "Freedom and Actuality." *Divine and Human Action*. Edited by Thomas V. Morris. Ithaca, NY: Cornell University Press, 1988: 236-256.

220. ———. "Freedom and Miracles." *Noûs* 22 (1988): 235-252.

221. ———. "Soft Facts and Harsh Realities: A Response to William Craig." *Religious Studies* 27 (1991): 523-539. [See Craig's "'Nice Soft Facts': Fischer on Foreknowledge" [#197].]

222. Fitch, Frederick. "A Logical Analysis of Some Value Concepts." *Journal of Symbolic Logic* 28 (1963): 135-142.

223. Flew, Antony G.N. *God and Philosophy*. London: Hutchinson, 1966.

224. ———. "The Presumption of Atheism." *Canadian Journal of Philosophy* 2 (1972): 29-46. [Reprinted in Flew's *God, Freedom and Immortality*. Buffalo, NY: Prometheus Press, 1984, 13-30.]

225. ———. *The Presumption of Atheism*. London: Elek Books: Pemberton Publishing Co., 1976. Republished as *God, Freedom and Immortality*. [#224]

226. ———. "The Philosophy of Freedom." *Journal of Liberal Religion* 9 (1989): 69-80.

227. Flint, Thomas P., and Alfred J. Freddoso. "Maximal Power." *The Existence and Nature of God*. Edited by Alfred J. Freddoso. Notre Dame, IN: University of Notre Dame Press, 1983: 81-113. [Also published in *The Concept of God*, edited by Thomas V. Morris. Oxford: Oxford University Press, 1987.]

228. ———. "The Problem of Divine Freedom." *American Philosophical Quarterly* 20 (1983): 255-264.

229. Foley, Richard. "Compatibilism and Control Over the Past." *Analysis* 39 (1979): 70-74.

230. ———. "Reply to van Inwagen." *Analysis* 40 (1980): 101-103.

231. Frankfurt, Harry G. "The Logic of Omnipotence." *Philosophical Review* 73 (1964): 262-263.

232. ———. "Alternative Possibilities and Moral Responsibility." *Journal of Philosophy* 66 (1969): 829-839.

233. Geach, Peter T. "Omnipotence." *Philosophy* 48 (1973): 7-20. [Rejects four doctrines of omnipotence. See response by J. Harrison, "Geach on God's Alleged Ability to do Evil" [#246].]

234. Gellman, Jerome. "The Paradox of Omnipotence and Perfection." *Sophia* 14 (1975): 31-39.

235. Gendin, Sidney. "Omnidoing." *Sophia* 6 (1967): 17-22.

236. Ginet, Carl. "Might We Have No Choice?" *Freedom and Determinism*. Edited by Keith Lehrer. New York: Random House, 1966: 87-104.

237. ———. "Can the Will be Caused?" *Philosophical Review* 75 (1966): 49-55.

238. ———. "In Defense of Incompatibilism." *Philosophical Studies* 44 (1983): 391-400.

239. Godbey, John W. "The Incompatibility of Omnipotence and Omniscience." *Analysis* 34 (1973): 62.

240. Gorsuch, Richard L., and Craig S. Smith. "Attributions of Responsibility to God: An Interaction of Religious Beliefs and Outcomes." *Journal for the Scientific Study of Religion* 22 (1983): 340-353.

241. Grave, Selwin A. "On Evil and Omnipotence." *Mind* 65 (1956): 259-262.

242. Gregory, Donald R. "Divine Omnipresence and Literary Creativity: Has La Croix Shown their Incompatibility?" *Religious Studies* 18 (1982): 77-80.

243. Grim, Patrick. "Some Neglected Problems of Omniscience." *American Philosophical Quarterly* 20 (1983): 265-276.

244. ———. "Against Omniscience: The Case from Essential Indexicals." *Noûs* 14 (1985): 265-266.

245. Habgood, John. "Man's Freedom with Responsibility." *The Times* (London), January 12, 1987: 12.

246. Harrison, Jonathan. "Geach on God's Alleged Ability to do Evil." *Philosophy* 51 (1976): 208-215. [Refutes Peter Geach's arguments ("Omnipotence" [#233]) against four views of divine omnipotence. Geach has confused a *necessitas consequentiae* with a *necessitas consequentis*: Geach confuses "It is necessary that, if God has promised A, God will perform A" (a *necessitas consequentiae*) with "If God has promised A, it is necessary that God will perform A" (a *necessitas consequentiae*). Harrison rejects also Geach's substitution of God's power as *almighty* for God's power as *omnipotent*.]

247. Helm, Paul. "God and Whatever Comes to Pass." *Religious Studies* 14 (1978): 315-323. [Argues against Geach's argument, "The Future," *New Blackfriars* 64 (1973), that the future is indeterminate. Helm supports the view that the future is determinate.]

248. ———. "On Theological Fatalism Again." *Philosophical Quarterly* 24 (1974): 360-362.

249. ———. "Fatalism Once More." *Philosophical Quarterly* 25 (1975): 289-296.

250. ———. "Omnipotence and Change." *Philosophy* 51 (1976): 454-461.

251. ———. "Omniscience and Eternity." *The Aristotelian Society Supplementary Volume* 63 (1989).

252. Hill, David K. "Can God be Infinite?" *Journal of West Virginia Philosophical Society* 3 (1976): 17-20. [Claims to have refuted the free will defense: God would allow only evils necessary for the realization of greater goods.]

253. Horgan, Terence. "Compatibilism and the Consequence Argument." *Philosophical Studies* 47 (1985): 339-356. [Critique of van Inwagen's arguments for the compatibility of freedom and causal determinism [see #150 and #330].]

254. Hudson, James L. "Schlesinger and the Newcomb Problem." *Australasian Journal of Philosophy* 57 (1979): 145-156.

255. Iseminger, Gary. "Foreknowledge and Necessity." *Midwest Studies in Philosophy*. Morris, MN: University of Minnesota Press, 1976: 5-12.

256. Kapitan, Tomis. "Can God Make Up His Mind?" *International Journal for Philosophy of Religion* 15 (1984): 37-47.

257. ———. "Deliberation and the Presumption of Open Alternatives." *Philosophical Quarterly* 36 (1986): 230-251.

258. ———. "Doxastic Freedom: A Compatibilist Alternative." *American Philosophical Quarterly* 26 (1989): 31-42.

259. ———. "Agency and Omniscience." *Religious Studies* 27 (1991): 105-120. [See also Kapitan's "Ability and Cognition: A Defense of Compatibility." *Philosophical Studies* 63 (1991), 231-243.]

260. Kiernan-Lewis, Delmas. "Not Over Yet: Prior's 'Thank Goodness' Argument." *Philosophy* 66 (1991): 241-243. [See Arthur Prior, "Thank Goodness That's Over" [#298].]

261. Kretzmann, Norman."Omniscience and Immutability," *Journal of Philosophy* 63 (1966): 409-421.

262. Kretzmann, Norman, and Eleonore Stump. "Eternity." *Journal of Philosophy* 79 (1981): 429-458. [Reprinted in *The Concept of God*. Edited by Thomas V. Morris. Oxford: Oxford University Press, 1987.]

263. Kuntz, Paul G. "The Sense and Nonsense of Omnipotence: What Does it Mean to Say 'With God All Things Are Possible'?" *Proceedings of the Seventh Inter-American Congress of Philosophy*, Canadian Philosophical Association, 1967: 122-131.

264. ———. "The Sense and Nonsense of Omnipotence." *Religious Studies* 4 (1968): 525-538.

265. Kvanvig, Jonathan L. "Unknowable Truths and the Doctrine of Omniscience." *Journal of the American Academy of Religion* 62 (1989): 485-507.

266. ———. *The Possibility of an All-Knowing God*. New York, NY: St. Martin's Press, 1986.

267. Lachs, John. "Professor Prior on Omniscience," *Philosophy* 38 (1963): 361-364. [See also Lachs, "God's Actions and Nature's Ways," *Idealistic Studies* 3 (1973), 223-228. See Arthur Prior's "The Formalities of Omniscience" [#299]].

268. La Croix, Richard. "Omnipotence, Omniscience and Necessity." *Analysis* 34 (1973): 63-64.

269. ———. "Omniprescience and Divine Determinism." *Religious Studies* 12 (1976): 365-381.

270. ———. "The Impossibility of Defining 'Omnipotence'." *Philosophical Studies* 32 (1977): 181-190.

271. ———. "Failing to Define Omnipotence." *Philosophical Studies* 34 (1979): 311-315.

272. Lackey, Douglas P. "A New Disproof of the Compatibility of Foreknowledge and Free Choice." *Religious Studies* 10 (1974): 313-318. [See also Lackey's "Divine Omniscience and Human Privacy," *Philosophy Research Archives* 10 (1984/1985), 383-392.]

273. Lamb, James. "On a Proof of Incompatibilism." *Philosophical Review* 86 (1977): 20-35.

274. Levin, Bernard. "The Evil Some Men Do Is Born Within Them." *The Times* (London), November 23, 1986: 16.

275. ———. "Programmed to Choose." *The Times* (London), January 20, 1987: 14.

276. Lucas, John R. *The Freedom of the Will*. Oxford: Oxford University Press, 1970.

277. ———. *The Future*. Cambridge: Blackwell, 1989.

278. Mackie, John. "The Direction of Causality." *Philosophical Review* 75 (1966): 441-456.

279. Macquarrie, John. "Divine Omnipotence." *Proceedings of the Seventh Inter-American Congress of Philosophy*, Canadian Philosophical Association, 1967: 132-137.

280. Mann, William E. "Ross on Omnipotence." *International Journal for Philosophy of Religion* 8 (1977): 142-147.

281. ———. "God's Freedom, Human Freedom, and God's Responsibility for Sin." *Divine and Human Action*. Edited by Thomas V. Morris. Ithaca, NY: Cornell University Press, 1988: 182-210.

282. Matson, Wallace I. "An Introduction to Omniscience." *Analysis* 28 (1968): 8-12.

283. Mavrodes, George I. "Some Puzzles Concerning Omnipotence." *Philosophical Review* 72 (1963): 221-223.

284. ———. "Aristotelian Necessity and Freedom." *Midwest Studies in Philosophy* 1. Edited by Peter French, Theodore Euhling, and Howard Wettstein. Minneapolis, MN: University of Minnesota Press, 1976.

285. ———. "Defining Omnipotence." *Philosophical Studies* 32 (1977): 191-202. [See also Joshua Hoffman's "Mavrodes on Defining Omnipotence." *Philosophical Studies* 35 (1979), 311-313.]

286. ———. "Is the Past Unpreventable?" *Faith and Philosophy* 1 (1984): 131-146.

287. Mellor, D.H. *Real Time*. Cambridge, MA: Cambridge University Press, 1981.

288. Moonan, Lawrence. "On Dispensing with Omnipotence." *Ephemerides Theologicae Lovanienses* 65 (1989): 60-80.

289. Morris, Thomas V. "Perfection and Power." *International Journal for Philosophy of Religion* 20 (1986): 165-168.

290. ———. *Our Idea of God: An Introduction to Philosophical Theology*. Notre Dame, IN: University of Notre Dame Press, 1991. [See also Morris's "Duty and Divine Goodness," *American Philosophical Quarterly* 21 (1984), 261-268. Reprinted in *The Concept of God*. Edited by Thomas V. Morris. Oxford: Oxford University Press, 1987.]

291. Normore, Calvin G. "Divine Omniscience, Omnipotence, and Future Contingents: An Overview." *Divine Omniscience and Omnipotence in Medieval Philosophy*. Edited by Tamar Rudavsky. Dordrecht and Boston, MA: Reidel, 1985: 3-22.

292. ———. "Future Contingents." *Cambridge History of Later Medieval Philosophy*. Edited by Norman Kretzmann, Anthony Kenny, and Jan Pinbog. Cambridge, MA: Cambridge University Press, 1982.

293. Ockham, William. *Predestination, God's Foreknowledge and Future Contingents*. Translated by Marilyn McCord Adams and Norman Kretzmann. [See also Marilyn McCord Adams's massive 2 volume, 1402 page study of Ockham: *William Ockham*. Notre Dame, IN: University of Notre Dame Press, 1987. For a critical review of McCord Adams's boom, see Martin Tweedale, "Critical Notice," *Canadian Journal of Philosophy* 21 (1991), 211-244.]

294. Pike, Nelson. "Of God and Freedom: A Rejoinder [to John Saunders, "Of God and Freedom]" [#317], *Philosophical Review* 75 (1966): 369-379. [See also Pike's

"Fischer on Freedom and Foreknowledge," *Philosophical Review* 93 (1984), 599-614.]

295. Plantinga, Alvin. *Does God Have a Nature?* Aquinas Lecture. Milwaukee, WI: Marquette University Press, 1980.

296. Pradham, Sudhir Chandra. "The Problem of Evil and Human Freedom." *Indian Philosophical Quarterly* 13 (1986): 15-24.

297. Prior, Arthur N. *Time and Modality.* Oxford: Oxford University Press, 1957.

298. ——. "Thank Goodness That's Over." *Philosophy* 34 (1959): 12-17. [See response by Kiernan-Lewis, "Not Over Yet: Prior's 'Thank Goodness' Argument" [#260].]

299. ——. "The Formalities of Omniscience." *Philosophy* 37 (1962): 114-129.

300. ——. *Past, Present and Future.* Oxford: Clarendon Press, 1967.

301. Puccetti, Roland. "Is Omniscience Possible?" *Australasian Journal of Philosophy* 41 (1963): 92-93.

302. Purtill, Richard. "Foreknowledge and Fatalism." *Religious Studies* 10 (1974): 319-324.

303. Quinn, Philip L. "Divine Causation, Continuous Creation and Human Action." *The Existence and Nature of God.* Edited by Alfred J. Freddoso. Notre Dame, IN: University of Notre Dame Press, 1983: 55-80.

304. Ramsey, Ian T. "The Paradox of Omnipotence." *Mind* 65 (1956): 263-266.

305. Reichenbach, Bruce. "Mavrodes on Omnipotence." *Philosophical Studies* 36 (1980): 211-214. [See also Mavrodes, "Some Puzzles Concerning Omnipotence" [#283].]

306. ——. "Omniscience and Deliberation." *International Journal for Philosophy of Religion* 16 (1984): 225-236.

307. Roderey, Nicholas. *The Way of Power.* New York: Philosophical Library, 1969.

308. Rosenkrantz, Gary, and Joshua Hoffman. "What an Omnipotent Agent Can Do." *International Journal for Philosophy of Religion* 11 (1980): 1-19.

309. ——. "On Divine Foreknowledge and Human Freedom." *Philosophical Studies* 37 (1980): 289-296.

310. ——. "Hard and Soft Facts." *Philosophical Review* 93 (1984): 149-156.

311. Rosenthal, David M. "The Necessity of Foreknowledge." *Midwest Studies in Philosophy, Volume 1.* Edited by Peter French, Theodore Uehling, and Howard Wettstein. Minneapolis, MN: University of Minnesota Press, 1976: 22-25.

312. Rosenthal, Gilbert S. "Omnipotence, Omniscience and a Finite God." *Judaism* 39 (1990): 55-72.

313. Rowe, William L. "On Divine Foreknowledge and Human Freedom: A Reply." *Philosophical Studies* 37 (1980): 429-430 [see #309.]

314. Russell, Paul. "Causation, Compulsion, and Compatibilism." *American Philosophical Quarterly* 25 (1988): 313-321.

315. Russell, Robert John. "Entropy and Evil." *Zygon, Journal of Religion and Science* 19 (1984): 449-468.

316. ———. "The Physics of David Bohm and its Relevance for Theology." *Zygon, Journal of Religion and Science* 20 (1985): 135-158.

317. Saunders, John T. "Of God and Freedom." *Philosophical Review* 75 (1966): 219-225. [See also Saunders, "The Temptations of 'Powerlessness'." *American Philosophical Quarterly* 25 (1968), 104-107.]

318. Savage, C. Wade. "The Paradox of the Stone." *Philosophical Review* 72 (1963): 221-223.

319. Schlesinger, George N. "The Unpredictability of Free Choices." *British Journal for the Philosophy of Science* 25 (1974): 209-221.

320. ———. "An Important Difference Between People and Mindless Machines." *Australasian Journal of Philosophy* 54 (1976): 205-212.

321. ———. "Perfect Diagnosticians and Incompetent Predictors." *Australasian Journal of Philosophy* 54 (1976): 221-230.

322. Slote, Michael. "Is Belief in God Justified?" *Journal of Philosophy* 67 (1970): 31-45. [See also Slote's *Goods and Virtues*. Oxford: Clarendon Press, 1983.]

323. Smilansky, Saul. "The Contrariety of Compatibilist Positions." *Journal of Philosophical Research* 16 (1990/1991): 293-308.

324. Stenner, Alfred J. "A Paradox of Omniscience: Some Attempts at a Solution." *Faith and Philosophy* 6 (1989): 303-319.

325. Swinburne, Richard G. "Omnipotence." *American Philosophical Quarterly* 10 (1973): 231-237. [See Joshua Hoffman, "Swinburne on Omnipotence," *Sophia* 23 (1984), 36-40.]

326. Talbott, Thomas B. "On Divine Foreknowledge and Bringing about the Past." *Philosophy and Phenomenological Research* 47 (1986): 455-469.

327. Tomberlin, James E. "Is Belief in God Justified?" *Journal of Philosophy* 67 (1970): 31-38.

328. Urban, Linwood. "Was Luther a Thoroughgoing Determinist?" *Journal of Theological Studies* 22 (1971): 113-139.

329. Van Inwagen, Peter. "A Formal Approach to the Free Will Problem." *Theoria* 40 (1974): 9-22.

330. ———. "The Incompatibility of Free Will and Determinism." *Philosophical Studies* 30 (1975): 185-199.

331. ———. "Reply to Narveson's 'Compatibilism Defended'." *Philosophical Studies* 32 (1977): 89-98. [See Jan Narveson, "Compatibilism Defended," *Philosophical Studies* 32 (1977), 83-88.]

332. ———. "Compatibilism and the Burden of Proof." *Analysis* 40 (1980): 98-100.

333. ———. "The Place of Chance in a World Sustained by God." *Divine and Human Action*. Edited by Thomas V. Morris. Ithaca, NY: Cornell University Press, 1988: 211-235.

334. Wainwright, William J. "Divine Omnipotence: A Reply to Professors Kuntz ["The Sense and Nonsense of Omnipotence" [#263]] and Macquarrie ["Divine

Omnipotence" [#279]]. *Proceedings of the Seventh InterAmerican Congress of Philosophy*, Canadian Philosophical Association, 1967: 138-149.

335.   Walton, Douglas. "The Omnipotence Paradox." *Canadian Journal of Philosophy* 5 (1975): 705-715. [Reprinted in *The Power of God: Readings on Omnipotence and Evil*. Edited by Linwood Urban and Douglas Walton. New York: Oxford University Press, 1978, 153-164.]

336.   ——. "Some Theorems of Fitch on Omnipotence." *Sophia* 15 (1976): 20-27. [Reprinted in *The Power of God: Readings on Omnipotence and Evil*. Edited by Linwood Urban and Douglas Walton. New York: Oxford University Press, 1978, 182-191.]

337.   Wasserman, Gerhard D. *Brains and Reasoning*. London: MacMillan, 1974.

338.   ——. "Human Behaviour and Biology." *Dialectica* 37 (1983): 169-184.

339.   ——. "Morality and Determinism." *Philosophy* 63 (1988): 211-230.

340.   Waterlow, Sarah. "Backward Causation and Continuing." *Mind* 83 (1974): 372-387.

341.   Werner, Louis. "Some Omnipotent Beings." *Critica* 3 (1971): 55-69.

342.   Whitrow, G.J. *The Natural Philosophy of Time*. Oxford: Clarendon Press, 1980.

343.   Widerker, David. "A Problem for the Eternity Solution." *International Journal for Philosophy of Religion* 29 (1991): 87-95. [Contends that the eternalist approach to reconciling divine knowledge and human freedom, by placing God outside of time, fails.]

344.   Wierenga, Edward. "Omnipotence Defined." *Philosophy and Phenomenological Research* 43 (1983): 363-376.

345.   Wiggens, David. "Towards a Reasonable Libertarianism." *Essays on Freedom of Action*. Edited by Ted Honderich. London: Routledge and Kegan Paul, 1973: 31-61.

346.   Wiles, Maurice F. "Religious Authority and Divine Action." *Religious Studies* 7 (1971): 1-12. [See also Wiles, *Faith and the Mystery of God*. Philadelphia, PA: Fortress Press, 1982.]

347.   Wippel, John F. "Divine Knowledge, Divine Power and Human Freedom in Thomas Aquinas and Henry of Ghent." *Divine Omniscience and Omnipotence in Medieval Philosophy*. Edited by Tamar Rudavsky. Dordrecht and Boston, MA: Reidel, 1985: 213-244.

348.   Wolfe, Julian. "Omnipotence." *Canadian Journal of Philosophy* 1 (1971): 245-247.

349.   Wren-Lewis, John. "God and Chance." *Hibbert Journal* 57 (1959): 271-278.

Chapter 3

Best Possible World Theodicy

This chapter contains references to the contemporary debate about the "best possible world" theodicy,[1] in particular as it has been centered around *Alvin Plantinga's* free will defense (see *Chapter 2)*. As such, there is a direct relationship among many of the publications listed in this chapter and those listed in the previous chapter. There are also numerous references in this present chapter to other versions of best possible world theodicy; in particular, *George Schlesinger's* "greatest happiness solution" and *Keith Yandell's* "greater good defense."

As noted briefly in the introductory section to the preceding chapter, *Alvin Plantinga's* free will defense employs a "best possible world" ontology. Plantinga assumes that God has "middle knowledge," following the arguments of the sixteenth century theologian, *Luis de Molina*. This knowledge, supposedly possessed by God, is knowledge of what every possible creature would do in every situation in which that creatures could possibly have the occasion to act freely. This divine knowledge has been described in terms of *counterfactual conditional propositions*, or *counterfactuals of freedom*.[2] The question of "middle knowledge" is important in that it has direct relevance to the question as to whether God could have made free creatures who would always have freely done what is right.

Plantinga's solution to the logical problem of evil holds that God could not have actualized *each and every* possible world, as Leibniz mistakenly believed. If this were the case, this imperfect world would be designated the "best possible world," a conclusion to which Plantinga refers as "Leibniz's lapse." Plantinga holds that there are possible worlds which God cannot actualize. There may be, he concedes, possible worlds containing free creatures who always do what is right, but given the possibility of "trans-world depravity," with respect to a creature's essence, it is at least possible that there are worlds that God could not actualize—worlds without *moral evil*. Moreover, given the possibility of fallen angels, Plantinga contends that *natural evil* likewise may be unavoidable.

It is interesting that, after all the work he has done to employ the concepts of "middle knowledge" and "best possible world" theodicy as aspects of his free will defense, Plantinga quite recently has suggested that "an interesting project would be to develop in detail a version of the Free Will Defense that does not involve either middle knowledge or counterfactuals of freedom."[3] Plantinga is aware, no doubt, that the use of the concepts, "possible worlds" and "middle knowledge," has become a philosophical thicket; perhaps no philosophical problem has grown so profusely over the past 25 years, and none is so tangled.[4] The discussions have reopened the issue of the Leibnizian concept of the best possible world and related questions of divine omniscience and (fore)knowledge and the alleged compatibility or incompatibility with human freedom. All have important implications for the problem of evil. Contemporary defenders of the viability of divine "middle knowledge," besides Plantinga, include such writers as *James Tomberlin, Peter van Inwagen, Jonathan Kvanvig, William Craig, Richard Otte,* and *Edward Wierenga*. Among the major critics are *Robert Merrihew Adams, Anthony Kenny, James Felt, William Hasker,* and *David Hunt*.[5]

George Schlesinger's use of "best possible world" theodicy takes a different twist than does Plantinga's. Schlesinger is one of a very few theists who has claimed that the problem of evil can be solved. Few theologians and philosop1hers accept this apparently outrageous claim, but Schlesinger's solution has been hailed as "ingenious," "original" and "novel"; indeed, it has been cited (arguably) as "the most significant contribution to the problem of theodicy since Leibniz."[6] In short, his argument is that God cannot create a greatest state of happiness any more than there can be a greatest integer. Since "there is no prima facie case for saying that the greatest possibilities for happiness are finite, God's inability to create "the greatest state of happiness" cannot be used as decisive evidence against the existence of God. The amount of evil in the world is "entirely irrelevant, and cannot be introduced as evidence concerning the moral nature of God."[7]

Another version of "best possible world" theodicy is *Keith Yandell's* "greater good defense." For every evil that exists, he argues, there must be a morally sufficient reason why God permits it to exist. Yandell defends the claim that the existence of evil neither conclusively refutes nor provides strong evidence against theism. Some evils, he argues, are justified in as much as they provide opportunities for moral struggle and the overcoming of the evils. This does not mean, of course, that we must not seek to eliminate them.

The list of annotated publications which follows includes the most important contributions to the "best possible world" theodicy (for which there are many entries also in other chapters, notably *Chapter 7)*, the issue of "middle knowledge" and "counterfactuals of freedom." Related publications are listed at the end of the chapter.

Notes

1.   For some relevant dissertations, see *Appendix E*. Among the most pertinent are the following: Dennis Holden, *Ockhamism and the Divine Foreknowledge Problem* (University of California, 1988); Eric Ormsby, *An Islamic Version of Theodicy: The Dispute Over Al-Ghazali's 'Best of All Possible Worlds'"* (Princeton University, 1981); Patrick Wilson, *The Anthropic Cosmological Principle* (University of Notre Dame, 1989); and Charles Fink, *Conditionals* (University of Miami, 1988).

2.   See Robert M. Adams, "Plantinga and the Problem of Evil," *Alvin Plantinga (Profiles, Volume 5)*. Edited by James Tom berlin and Peter van Inwagen (Dordrecht: Reidel, 1985), 230.

3.   *Alvin Plantinga (Profiles, Volume 5)*, 50.

4.   The reference paraphrased here to James Felt, "Impossible Worlds" *(International Philosophical Quarterly* 23 [1983]), 251.

5.   Included in this chapter are some very informative discussions about the doctrine of the *best possible world* and discussions of the nature of the *middle knowledge* debates.

6.   George Schlesinger, "The Problem of Evil and the Problem of Suffering," *American Philosophical Quarterly* 1 (1964), 244-247.

7.   Schlesinger, "The Problem of Evil and the Problem of Suffering," 246.

I   Best Possible World Theodicy

350.   Adams, Robert Merrihew. "Must God Create the Best?" *Philosophical Review* 81 (1972): 317-332. [Reprinted in *The Concept of God*. Edited by Thomas V. Morris. Oxford: Oxford University Press, 1987.]

Argues that God need not create the best possible world. God's choice in creating a lesser world than the best possible is accounted for in terms of divine grace, inherent in the divine goodness. [See responses by Basinger, "In What Sense Must God Do His Best?" [#357]; Quinn, "Mustn't God Create the Best?" [#406]; Hasker, "Must God Do His Best?" [#378]; and Weinstock, "Must God Create the Best World?" [#440].]

351.   ———. "Theories of Actuality." *Noûs* 8 (1974): 211-231.

Analyses various theories of actuality: the divine choice theory; the indexical theory; the simple property theory; and the true-story theory of actuality. To avoid extreme realism in the concept of possible worlds, Adams proposes a reduction of possible worlds to propositions, to "world-stories." [See response by Robert Stalnaker, "Possible Worlds" [#432].]

352.   ———. "Existence, Self-Interest, and the Problem of Evil." *Noûs* 13 (1979): 53-65.

Argues that since it is good for us to exist, God has not wronged us by permitting evils to befall us. Evils are necessary for our existence and none of us would be who we are if the evils in human history had not been as they have been. God has seen to it that we have lives worth living, despite the evils.

353.   Barnhart, J.E. "Omnipotence, Evil and Moral Goodness." *The Personalist* 52 (1971): 107-110.

Against the critiques of Flew and Mackie, Smart has argued ("Omnipotence, Evil and Supermen" [#429]) that God could not create morally perfect creatures. Yet Barnhart draws the conclusion from this that God is not morally good unless God also faces temptations and conflicts. This contradicts the traditional doctrine of omnipotence and, hence, omnipotence is incompatible with divine moral goodness. He proposes that finite theism resolves this dilemma.

354.   Basinger, David. "Must God Create the Best Possible World? A Response." *International Philosophical Quarterly* 20 (1980): 339-341.

Refutes Reichenbach's claim ("Must God Create the Best Possible World?" [#409]), that the notion of best possible world is meaningless since there is an infinity of possible worlds. Basinger argues that God would have omniscient *a priori* knowledge of the best possible world. Human beings cannot claim to identify the upper limit in an infinite series of possible worlds, but God can. Moreover, he suggests that perhaps the series of possible worlds is not infinite, and insists that God would create the best world possible. [See Reichenbach's response, "Basinger on Reichenbach and the Best Possible World" [#410].]

355.   ———. "Divine Omniscience and the Best of All Possible Worlds." *Journal of Value Inquiry* 16 (1982): 143-148.

Argues that there is a fundamental incompatibility between Schlesinger's claim that there is no best possible world and the claim that God is omniscient. As such, the argument that an omniscient, omnipotent, and wholly good God is obligated only to create a world that is good, a world that has a net balance of good over evil, is invalid. [See Schlesinger's response, "The Problem of Evil," *Chapter 4* of his *New Perspectives on Old-Time Religion* [#423]. See also David Gordon's response, "Must God Identify the Best?" [see #455]].

356.   ———. "In What Sense Must God be Omnibenevolent?" *International Journal for Philosophy of Religion* 14 (1983): 3-15.

Argues that even if God cannot create a best possible world, God is obliged to maximize the quality of life for those beings which are created. As such, the evil that exists is either a *by-product* of other goods or *necessary* for goods. Basinger argues against Robert Adams's view ("Existence, Self-Interest and the Problem of Evil" [#352]), that God needed only to create beings whose lives are worth living *on the whole*, rather than having the maximum possible value. Basinger's position implies that theists must affirm either that all evil is non-gratuitous (a necessary condition for a greater good) or the unavoidable by-product of others goods, like freedom.

357.   ———. "In What Sense Must God Do His Best? A Response to Hasker." *International Journal for Philosophy of Religion* 18 (1985): 161-164.

Response to Hasker's rejoinder ("Must God Do His Best?" [#378]) to a previous article by Basinger ("In What Sense Must God Be Omnibenevolent?" [#356]) wherein he argued that God must maximize the quality of life in all worlds that are created. Basinger rejects Hasker's claim that this (Basinger's claim) is too demanding.

358.   Benditt, Theodore. "A Problem for Theodicists." *Philosophy* 50 (1975): 470-474.

Against the theists who holds that physical evils are necessary for there to be moral goods in the world, Benditt argues that a situation in which there is no evil and no expression of moral virtue is often (and usually) better than one in which there is both some evil and a resulting expression of moral virtue.

359.   Blumenfeld, David. "Is the Best Possible World Possible?" *Philosophical Review* 84 (1975): 163-177.

Defends Leibniz's conception of a best possible world against Plantinga's objection ("Which Worlds Could God Have Created?" [#400]). There are indications in Leibniz as to how he would have blocked the objection that it is paradoxical that God created a best possible world since experience contradicts this. Yet Leibniz's strategy contradicts God's freedom. Blumenfeld proposes an alternative argument for the conclusion that there is a best possible world, an argument that leads naturally from Leibniz's doctrine of the divine nature.

360.   Brecher, Robert. "Notes and Comments: Knowledge, Belief and the Sophisticated Theodicist." *Heythrop Journal* 17 (1976): 178-183.

Refutes the claim that an omniscient God would know that the value of the goods achieved in suffering outweigh the suffering. He rejects Dore's claim ("Do Theodicists Mean What They Say?" [#1076]), that while theodicists may *believe* the value of the ends served by suffering outweighs the suffering, God, in allowing suffering to occur, *knows* omnisciently that the ends outweigh the suffering. The best possible world and greater good defense require this—that the suffering is outweighed by the ends obtained by it. Dore has not succeeded in showing that God has no blame in acting in ways which, if the theodicist acted accordingly, would be blameworthy. [See also Brecher's "Knowledge, Belief and the Sophisticated Theodicist." *Heythrop Journal* 17 (1976), 178-183.]

361.   Burch, Robert F. "Plantinga and Leibniz's Lapse." *Analysis* 39 (1979): 24-29.

Rejects Plantinga's claim (*The Nature of Necessity* [#110], etc.) that Leibniz had a lapse in holding that God could have created any possible world in which God exists. Plantinga's claim begs the question by assuming the existence of a certain possible world which Leibniz would deny.

362.   Campbell, Richmond. "God, Evil and Humanity." *Sophia* 23 (1984): 21-34.

Holds that the argument from evil, which depends upon the assumption of a best possible world, is beset with difficulties. There may be an infinite hierarchy of better worlds with no best possible world; the best world (if it includes insignificant creaturely freedom) may not be something that can be created by a single being; the best world, if such is possible, may be something God may choose not to create, while acting consistently in perfect moral goodness. Campbell concludes with an argument from evil which determines *not* that there is no God, but that there is disbelief. He argues that basic beliefs held by religious people are incoherent.

363.   Chrzan, Keith. "Linear Programming and Utilitarian Theodicy." *International Journal for Philosophy of Religion* 20 (1986): 147-157.

Applies linear programming (a mathematical tool for modelling optimization problems) to the "best possible world" argument. Such programming exposes defects in theodicies and in implicit value judgments.

364.   ———. "The Irrelevance of the No Best Possible World Defense." *Philosophia* 17 (1987): 161-167.

Refutes all of the best possible world arguments, including Schlesinger's version (*Religion and the Scientific Method* [#418]. Chrzan contends that the argument from the "no best possible world" defense is irrelevant to the problem of evil. The most it can achieve is to excuse our world for not being the best possible; it cannot demonstrate that evil must exist in our world. He concludes with the dilemma: lacking a greater goods defense, the no best possible world argument is *irrelevant*; given a greater goods defense, the no greatest possible world argument would be *superfluous*.

365.   Coughlan, Michael J. "Must God Create Only the Best Possible World?" *Sophia* 26 (1987): 15-19.

Rejects the claim that God would create only a best possible world. He argues that God could create an infinite set of optimal worlds and that God still could create other worlds. The existence of our world, even if it is not the best world, is compatible with an omnipotent and omnibenevolent God who sought to create a best possible world.

366.   Erlandson, Douglas K., and Charles Sayward. "Is Heaven a Possible World?" *International Journal for Philosophy of Religion* 12 (1981): 55-58.

Contend that the three following propositions are inconsistent: [1] evil does not exist in heaven, [2] heaven is better than the present world, and [3] heaven is a possible world. If evil exists in heaven, it is not a possible world. If evil does not exist in heaven, then much of theodicy is jeopardized, since heaven would contain all that is good (free will, etc.) without the evil. The authors conclude that the theist should give up belief in heaven as a possible worrld.

367.   Felt, James W. "Impossible Worlds." *International Philosophical Quarterly* 23 (1983): 251-265.

Argues that the notion of best possible world is a metaphysical monstrosity. There are no *possible worlds* at all, none of metaphysical interest. Felt rejects the possible worlds ontology of David Lewis (*Counterfactuals* [#503]) and Nicholas Rescher, "The Ontology of the Possible," *Logic and Ontology* (Edited by Milton Munitz. New York: New York University Press, 1973). Felt rejects also Luis de Molina's and Leibniz's conditional possibilities (ways things would have been) and the view implicit in best possible worlds ontology that God knew what evils would occur in this world before it was created.

368.   ———. "God's Choice: Reflections on Evil in a Created World." *Faith and Philosophy* 1 (1984): 370-377.

Contends that God's choice in creating was not a Leibnizian calculated selection from among diverse particular possibilities, since there were none from which to choose. There was no determinate knowable history to know *prior* to God's creative act. Creating free creatures was a gamble and yet, as the history of redemption shows, it was ultimately assured a happy ending.

369.   Fine, Kit. "Plantinga on the Reduction of Possibilist Discourse." *Alvin Plantinga (Profiles, Volume 5)*. Edited by James E. Tomberlin and Peter van Inwagen. Dordrecht and Boston, MA: Reidel, 1985: 145-186.

Responds to Plantinga's defense of how possibilist discourse makes sense (*The Nature of Necessity* [#110]; "Actualism and Possible Worlds" [#401]; "De Essentia," *Essays on the Philosophy of Roderick M. Chisholm.* Edited by E. Sosa. Rodopi: Amsterdam, 1979, 101-121; and "On Existentialism," *Philosophical Studies* 44, 1-20). Fine criticizes (as circular, question-begging) Plantinga's reduction of possibilist discourse in which possible worlds and possible individuals give way to propositions and properties. She proposes an alternative explanation which escapes the problems Plantinga's reduction faces: a reduction in which reference to *possibles* becomes a modal matter of references to *actuals*. Fine's proposal does not presuppose possible individuals, does not use any kind of possible entity, and claims to be more economical in its ontology and assumptions than Plantinga's. [See Plantinga's response, *Alvin Plantinga (Profiles, Volume 5)*, 145-186 [#114].]

370.   Fitzpatrick, F.J. "The Onus of Proof in Arguments about the Problem of Evil." *Religious Studies* 17 (1981): 19-38.

Discusses Ahern's theodicy (*The Problem of Evil* [#1263]) and the greater good defense. Fitzpatrick contends that the onus of proof is on the atheist to produce grounds for rejecting the view that evils are justified by being necessary conditions for the attainment of ends which God intends to bring about. Neither theists nor atheists should assume that human beings can understand God's reasons for permitting evil. Thus, the problem of evil is a question-begging procedure, if it is used to establish atheism. Yet, theists cannot solve the problem of evil without demonstrating that God exists. Fitzpatrick defends the greater good defense versus Rowe, "The Problem of Evil and Some Varieties of Atheism" [#1246]; Martin, "Is Evil Evidence Against the Existence of God?" [#1227]; and Hare and Madden, "Evil and Inconclusiveness" [#1212]. [See O'Connor's response, "Theism, Evil and the Onus of Proof: Reply to F.J. Fitzpatrick" [#576].]

371.   Flew, Antony G.N. "Are Ninian Smart's Temptations Irresistible?" *Philosophy* 37 (1962): 57-60.

Contends that Smart ("Omnipotence, Evil and Supermen" [#429]) has not addressed his (Flew's) main point, that God could have arranged it that people always freely choose the right. [See Smart's response, "Probability" [#430].]

372.   ———. "Possibility, Creation and Temptation." *Personalist* 52 (1971): 111-113.

Expands upon Barnhart's response ("Omnipotence, Evil and Moral Goodness" [#353]) to Smart's argument, that God could not create a perfect world ("Omnipotence, Evil and Supermen" [#429]). Flew argues that there are other ways to make the argument *ad hominem* against Smart. Smart's definition of moral virtue logically presupposes temptation and a practical possibility of succumbing to it. As such, his blessed beings still must face temptations and be capable of sin, although they will not succumb to sin. Flew notes that this was his (Flew's) very claim against theism—that God could have arranged creation so that human beings would freely choose the right.

373.   Forrest, Peter. "The Problem of Evil: Two Neglected Defenses." *Sophia* 20 (1981): 49-54.

Puts forward two defenses against the problem of evil: the "all good possible worlds" defense and the "no best possible worlds" defense. Forrest argues that God could have created all possible good worlds and that there is no best possible world, no best "version." Theism can be defended against the philosophical problem of evil if the principle of perfectionism is rejected, without relying on the greater good defense or the free will defense.

374.   Garcia, Laura L. "A Response to the Modal Problem of Evil." *Faith and Philosophy* 1 (1984): 378-388.

Response to Theodore Guleserian's contention ("God and Possible Worlds: The Modal Problem of Evil" [#376]), that theists are mistaken in holding that God exists necessarily and has perfections essentially. The existence of such a being is logically incompatible with the truth that morally objectionable worlds are possible and, as such, the traditional view of God must be abandoned. Garcia defends the traditional doctrine of God (omnipotent, omniscient and morally perfect), and admits that this view of God is incompatible with the possibility of morally objectionable worlds. Yet, the modal problem of evil does not require the theist to surrender the traditional doctrine of God. The modal problem of evil holds that God would not create immoral worlds; since we can describe such worlds, they seem very possible.

375.   Goetz, Ronald. "The Divine Burden." *Christian Century* 95 (1978): 298-302.

Contends that since God wills to be involved in and has created the world in which even God cannot act in perfect blamelessness, God cannot avoid ultimate primordial culpability for human suffering. Seen in the light, Christ's death occurred not only for our sins, but on God's behalf. This understanding of the atonement grows out of—and yet also contradicts—aspects of Anselm's *satisaction theory* (Christ's death satisfied our debt to God).

376.   Guleserian, Theodore. "God and Possible Worlds: The Modal Problem of Evil." *Noûs* 17 (1983): 221-238.

Argues that either God does not have necessary existence (existence in every possible world) or God does not have one of the properties of being essentially omnipotent, omniscient or morally perfect. No being can be essentially morally perfect. Theists have exaggerated the virtues of God beyond those which God could possess. [See Garcia's response, "A Response to the Modal Problem of Evil" [#374].]

377.   Hare, Peter. "Review of George Schlesinger, *Religion and the Scientific Method*." *Metaphilosophy* 11 (1980): 292-295.

Rejects Schlesinger's proposed solution to theodicy [#418]. While Schlesinger's theodicy holds that there is no conceivable limit to the increase in a "degree of desirability of state" (DDS), Hare argues that God must be a in the state of the highest DDS. Schlesinger's dismissal of this and his view that God neither suffers nor enjoys is a *reductio ad absurdum* of his (Schlesinger's) own position. Hare concludes that Schlesinger's solution is not relevant to the Christian problem of evil. It undercuts some basic Christian tenets.

378.   Hasker, William S. "Must God Do His Best?" *International Journal for Philosophy of Religion* 16 (1984): 213-223.

Rejects Basinger's view ("In What Sense Must God Be Omnibenevolent?" [#356]), that God must do all that is possible to maximize our quality of life. Hasker argues that this demand, that God is morally required to create the best, is too strict and conflicts with the traditional belief that God acts graciously, as Adams has pointed out. [See Basinger's response, "In What Sense Must God Do His Best? A Response to Hasker" [#357].]

379.   ———. "The Hardness of the Past: A Reply to Reichenbach." *Faith and Philosophy* 4 (1987): 337-342.

Response to Reichenbach's refutation ("Hasker on Omniscience" [#125]) of Hasker's argument for the incompatibility of divine omniscience and human freedom ("Foreknowledge and Necessity" [#59]). Hasker rejects Reichenbach's understanding of power. It is neither the impossible power to alter the past nor the power to bring about past events that have already occurred. It is a power in which a person's powers normally remain more or less constant, while the possibilities of their being exercised come and go.

380.   Hoffman, Joshua. "Pike on Possible Worlds, Divine Foreknowledge, and Human Freedom." *Philosophical Review* 86 (1979): 433-442.

Defends Plantinga (*God, Freedom and Evil* [#109]) against Pike criticisms ("Divine Omniscience and Voluntary Action" [#96]). Hoffman argues that Pike's possible worlds analysis of human freedom is incorrect, and since his argument for incompatibilism relies on that analysis, his argument is unsound and his defense of incompatibilism is unsuccessful. [See Pike's response in

"Alston on Plantinga and Soft Theological Determinism" [#102]. See also Morriston's response, "Pike and Hoffman on Divine Foreknowledge and Human Freedom" [see #88]].

381. Kane, G. Stanley. "Theism and Evil." *Sophia* 9 (1970): 14-21.

Response to Yandell's greatest goods defense ("Ethics, Evils and Theism" [#441]). Kane holds that even if Yandell's arguments are valid, they do not overcome the problem of evil. Yandell's arguments, however, do not warrant his (Yandell's) conclusions. Theists must show that there is a plausible explanation for evil. The claim that evil is necessary for good is suspect. Theists must account for evil's origin, but the free will defense has not succeeded in showing this. [See Yandell's response in "Theism and Evil: A Reply" [#442].]

382. Khatchadourian, Haig. "God, Happiness and Evil." *Religious Studies* 2 (1967): 109-120.

Critiques Schlesinger's solution to theodicy ("The Problem of Evil and the Problem of Suffering" [#415]). He rejects the assumption that there is no upper limit to happiness, and that even if the assumption were to be granted, the problem of evil remains. He argues that more precision is needed in the definitions of basic terms used in Schlesinger's argument ("necessary suffering," "perfectly good," "finite/infinite possibilities for happiness"). Khatchadourian also rejects La Para's view ("Suffering, Happiness, Evil" [#385]), that God ought not to have created a world since there was no obligation on God to create and since every world is worse than some possible world.

383. King-Farlow, John. "Evil and Other Worlds." *Sophia* 6 (1967): 9-14.

Argues that a Christian version of reincarnation in Plato's "Myth of Er" may be developed vertically (a series of lives after death). This doctrine of *transmigration* may answer the question of gratuitous evils.

384. ———. "Evil: On Multiple Placings in Time and Space." *Sophia* 25 (1986): 44-46.

Argues for a version of reincarnation in Plato's "Myth of Er," with reference to a *horizontal* series and models. [In his "Evil and Other Worlds" [#383], he argued for this with reference to a *vertical* series of lives]. King-Farlow proposes that a soul may have many bodies or a body may have many souls. This would be another logical possibility or categorically possible world, which gives more reason—in a world like ours—to think of God as just. The question of evil and gratuitous evil, accordingly, is rendered less problematic.

385. La Para, Nicholas. "Suffering, Happiness, Evil." *Sophia* 4 (1965): 10-16.

Refutes Schlesinger's arguments ("The Problem of Evil and the Problem of Suffering" [#415]), that evil would exist in any world since there is no upper limit to goods: no matter how good the world might be, it could always be better. La Para argues that God should be morally concerned that the universe which has been created contains *more* suffering than others which were possible. [See Khatchadourian's response, "God, Happiness and Evil" [#382].]

386. Leslie, John. "The Best Possible World." *The Challenge of Religion Today: Essays on the Philosophy of Religion*. Edited by John King-Farlow. New York: Science History Publications, 1976.

Rejects various solutions to the theodicy issue (that the universe as a whole has immense goodness, etc.). Leslie employs the "B-theory of Time" that holds it is true now that past and future events are real or are in existence. This overcomes the logical contradiction in the idea of a best possible world that is developing historically and the question as to why God did not create the best possible world in the first place.

387. Lucey, Kenneth G. "Theism, Necessity and Invalidity." *Sophia* 25 (1986): 47-50.

Argues that theists who defend and employ the modal concept of God cannot argue that any argument for God's existence is invalid, since this would logically imply the denial of theism.

388. McHarry, John D. "A Theodicy." *Analysis* 38 (1978): 132-134.

Contends that the possibility of more than one actual world refutes (resolves) the problem of evil. This is not the best of all possible worlds; God has created multiple worlds, each of which is unique. If there is a best possible world, God need not have created our world as the best possible. [See Perkins's response, "McHarry's Theodicy: A Reply" [#396].]

389. McMahon, William E. "The Problem of Evil and the Possibility of a Better World." *Journal of Value Inquiry* 3 (1969): 81-90.

Maintains that anti-theists like Hume, Mackie and McCloskey have not shown that the notion of a better possible world is intelligible. McMahon argues that the notion may be *conceivable*, but that this does not mean it is *actual*. There is, moreover, no way to make an evaluative comparison between a best possible world and our own world. [See response by James King, "The Problem of Evil and the Meaning of Good" [#1400].]

390. Morris, Thomas V. "A Response to the Problems of Evil." *Philosophia* 14 (1984): 173-186.

After outlining and defending Schlesinger's theodicy against his critics (Shea, Hare, Wall, Rosenberg, Khatchadourian, Quinn, Dore, and J.B. Maund—see the latter's review of *Religion and the Scientific Method* [#418] in *Australasian Journal of Philosophy* 57 [1979], 170-171), Morris concedes that Schlesinger's theodicy, while rational and intriguing, is incomplete in the sense that he does not attempt even a partial explanation of *why* our world is as it is. Schlesinger shows only that there is no reason why it ought not to contain evils and suffering. [See Schlesinger's response, *New Perspectives on Old-Time Religion* [#423].]

391. Morriston, Wesley. "Is Plantinga's God Omnipotent?" *Sophia* 23 (1984): 45-57.

Defends Plantinga's argument (*God, Freedom and Evil* [#109], *The Nature of Necessity* [#110], etc.) that there are possible worlds that God could not have created. Yet Morriston argues that Plantinga's argument succeeds at the price of denying divine omnipotence. Plantinga's God is more like Plato's "demiurge" than the Judaeo-Christian God; Plantinga's God has to work with a stock of possible persons that have various dispositional properties, all of which limit divine power.

392.   Nozick, Robert. "Theological Explanation." *Ploughshares* 14 (1986): 151-166.

Argues that what prevents God from bringing into this world creatures with an infinite "degree of desirability of state" (DDS) is, as Schlesinger has argued, not that they might encroach upon the Divine, but rather logical barriers—like those that prevent God from picking the highest possible integer. Yet, as Nozick points out, if this is so, why did God create at all?

393.   O'Connor, David. "Schlesinger and the Morally Perfect Man." *Journal of Value Inquiry* 20 (1986): 245-249.

Refutes Schlesinger's claim that theodicy is a pseudo-problem ("Suffering and Evil" [#419], *Religion and the Scientific Method* [#418], and "The Problem of Evil and the Problem of Suffering" [#415]. Schlesinger's God is not morally good and, as such, the core of traditional theism is jeopardized. A finite being (the mythically perfect Aeatus, for example) could be imagined as constantly engaging in trying to raise everyone's "degree of desirability of state" and, given unlimited time, could do so. O'Connor argues that God would be less good than this finite mythical man. [See Schlesinger's responses in "The Moral Value of the Universe" [#422] and *New Perspectives on Old-Time Religion* [#423].]

394.   Olding, A. "Finite and Infinite Gods." *Sophia* 6 (1967): 3-7.

Responds to Mackie's suggestion ("Evil and Omnipotence" [#1217]), that a valid solution to theodicy may be obtained by modifying one of the propositions concerning the divine attributes. Olding argues that this yields an interesting consequence which, in turn, has implications for the view that God is not limited in any way. If God were limited in power and yet good and omniscient, God would have decided that creating this universe was more worthwhile, on the whole, than not creating it. God may have created, in fact, several possible universes which are worthwhile overall. Since God can create more than one world, it is to be expected that God has created many worlds and not just the best possible world. Indeed, since our world contains good, the fact that it is not the best world does not count against God's existence.

395.   Paterson, R.W.K. "Evil, Omniscience and Omnipotence." *Religious Studies* 15 (1979): 1-23.

Rejects various traditional theodicies, yet defends the view that God has created a balance of virtue and happiness (hence, explaining moral evil). He argues also that divine omnipotence cannot alter physical laws which are optimal for the greatest possible world, nor can immortality be assumed (hence, explaining natural evils). God, as Leibniz held, created the best possible world, and this implies that of all the worlds possible, God created that which contains the largest possible *surplus* of good. This in turn implies that God creates not just the best creatures, but less than good creatures as well. We have grounds to believe that each and every creature will, in the fullness of time, justify God's creation of good and evil creatures, since all creatures will be predominantly good. Divine omnipotence is not exhausted in the creation of flawless creatures, even if these were limitless.

396.   Perkins, R.K., Jr. "McHarry's Theodicy: A Reply." *Analysis* 40 (1980): 168-171.

Refutes McHarry's claim ("A Theodicy" [#388]), that, since there could be other worlds, the fact that our world is not the best possible cannot be used as an argument against the existence of God. Perkins rejects the claim that God has used up all variations of better possible worlds and, as such, could not have made our world better.

397.   Pike, Nelson. "Divine Foreknowledge, Human Freedom and Possible Worlds." *Philosophical Review* 86 (1977): 209-216.

Response to Plantinga's critique (*God, Freedom and Evil* [#109]) of Pike's argument ("Divine Omniscience and Voluntary Action" [#96]), that God does not exist if certain theological assumptions are accepted. Pike argues that Plantinga has not formulated the question correctly, that Plantinga has not taken account of the restrictions which must be respected if one is to employ a "possible worlds" analysis of what it is for something to be within one's power. [See Hoffman's response, "Pike on Possible Worlds, Divine Foreknowledge, and Human Freedom" [#380]. See also Basinger's response, "Divine Omniscience and Human Freedom: A 'Middle Knowledge' Perspective" [#447]; and Morriston's response, "Pike and Hoffman on Divine Foreknowledge and Human Freedom" [see #88].]

398.   Plantinga, Alvin. "Pike and Possible Persons." *Journal of Philosophy* 63 (1966): 105-108.

Response to Pike's "Plantinga on the Free Will Defense" [#97]. Plantinga rejects Pike's mistaken view in claiming that he (Plantinga) fails to see the distinction between *making someone do something* and *creating someone whom God knows in advance will do something*. He insists that this proposition is *contingent*, not *necessary* (as Pike seems to think): it is logically possible that God can instantiate every free possible person as the instantiation of a perfect possible person ("freely performs only right actions"), and it is logically possible that God cannot do so. It is contingent upon the free choices these possible persons would make.

399.   ———. "World and Essence." *Philosophical Review* 79 (1970): 461-492.

Argues that essence is a full-bodied concept and that for any property "P" and world "W," God knows whether or not someone has "P" in "W." God knows that a certain world has the distinction of being the actual world. Hence, God knows all the properties, accidental as well as essential, that a person in fact does have.

400.   ———. "Which Worlds Could God Have Created?" *Journal of Philosophy* 70 (1973): 539-552.

Contends that there are possible worlds which include free acts that an omnipotent God cannot create. Plantinga argues also that the problem of evil can be solved by showing there is no inconsistency in asserting both that an omnipotent, omniscient, and all-good God exists and that evil exists: God creates a world containing moral good and every creaturely essence suffers from "transworld depravity." [See responses by Rowe, "Plantinga on Possible Worlds and Evil" [#413]; and Adams, "Middle Knowledge" [#444].]

401.   ———. "Actualism and Possible Worlds." *Theoria* 42 (1976): 139-160.

Endorses Robert Adams's "actualism" ("Theories of Actuality" [#351]), the view that there neither are nor could be any nonexistent individuals. He sets out the essentials of an actualist conception of possible worlds.

402.　　———. "Possible Worlds." *Listener* 13 (1976): 604-605.

Popularized version (a published version of a radio discussion) of the meaning of possible worlds and its role in defending the compatibility of divine knowledge and human freedom.

403.　　———. "Tooley and Evil: A Reply." *Australasian Journal of Philosophy* 60 (1982): 66-75.

Refutes Tooley's charge (in "Alvin Plantinga and the Argument from Evil" [#435] and in his (Tooley's) review of *The Nature of Necessity* (*Australasian Journal of Philosophy* 59 [1981]), that Plantinga's defense is logically and philosophically weak. Tooley's contention, that Plantinga's argument is fallacious, is based on a confusion. Tooley's rejection of Plantinga's use of subjunctive conditionals as unsupportive is erroneous. Plantinga rejects Tooley's claims that he (Plantinga) has misemphasized the incompatibility thesis rather than the improbability argument from evil, and that the philosophers he cited as endorsing the incompatibility thesis (Mackie, McCloskey, Aiken) did not endorse it.

404.　　Platt, David. "God, Goodness and a Morally Perfect World." *Personalist* 46 (1965): 320-326.

Response to Brown's argument ("Religious Morality" [#1381]), that since God causes evil to exist, it is good to do so, or else "God" would not be "God." Platt argues that this is paradoxical and implausible, making it impossible to talk rationally about God. Brown is mistaken in assuming it is logically possible that God could have created a perfect world. The autonomy of decision-making guarantees that some conflict (evil) is always bound to arise. It follows that Brown is mistaken in thinking that Christianity can be falsified, since (Platt argues) it is meaningless to speak of a morally perfect world; yet only this could falsify Christianity.

405.　　Pollock, John L. "Plantinga on Possible Worlds." *Alvin Plantinga (Profiles, Volume 5)*. Edited by James E. Tomberlin and Peter van Inwagen. Dordrecht and Boston, MA: Reidel, 1985: 121-144.

While Plantinga's clarification of the notion of possible worlds (*The Nature of Necessity* [#110]) is the most sophisticated theory of possible worlds yet to be constructed, there remain various problems. The theory of serious actualism endorsed by Plantinga (that an object cannot have a property in a world in which it does not exist), for example, is either *false* or *uninteresting*. Actualism, moreover, the view that there is not anything that does not exist, is false (a position endorsed by Plantinga). [See also Pollock's *Knowledge and Justification*, Princeton, NJ: Princeton University Press, 1974. For Plantinga's response, see *Alvin Plantinga (Profiles, Volume 5)*, 313-329 [#114].]

406.　　Quinn, Michael S. "Mustn't God Create the Best?" *Journal of Critical Analysis* 5 (1973): 2-8.

Response to the argument of Robert Adams ("Must God Create the Best?" [#350]), that God need not create the best possible world, but only a world where the inhabitants are happy *as a whole*. Quinn argues that divine benevolence is understood as doing what is morally best and since God has not done so (for this world), God's benevolence is questioned.

407.   Quinn, Philip L. "God, Moral Perfection, and Possible Worlds." *God: The Contemporary Discussion*. Edited by Frederick Sontag and M. Darroll Bryant. New York: Rose of Sharon Press, 1982: 197-215.

Responds to the challenge of Robert Adams ("Must God Create the Best?" [#350]) to the Leibnizian philosophical tradition of supporting the doctrine of a best possible world.

408.   Ramberan, Osmond G. "God, Evil, and the Idea of a Perfect World." *Modern Schoolman* 53 (1976): 379-392.

Contends that the concept of a best possible world, a perfect world, is ambiguous and incompatible with morality, rationality, and creativity.

409.   Reichenbach, Bruce. "Must God Create the Best Possible World?" *International Philosophical Quarterly* 19 (1979): 203-212.

Maintains that the notion of a best possible world is meaningless, since for any world so designated, there would always be another that is better. Since God cannot do what is meaningless or impossible, it makes no sense to inquire whether God could create the best possible world. As such, failure to do so is not contradictory to God's possession of perfect goodness, omnipotence and omniscience. In reference to God's creation, the theist need only affirm (as in Genesis I) that it was good. [See response by Basinger, "Must God Create the Best Possible World? A Response" [#354]; and Reichenbach's reply to this response, "Basinger on Reichenbach and the Best Possible World" [#410].]

410.   ———. "Basinger on Reichenbach and the Best Possible World." *International Philosophical Quarterly* 20 (1980): 343-345.

Reaffirms his argument, against Basinger ("Must God Create the Best Possible World? A Response" [#354]), that there is no best possible world, since there are an infinite number of possible worlds. It is meaningless to claim that, as omniscient, God could know the upper limit of the infinite series of possible worlds. Reichenbach argues also that Basinger has not established his claim (against Reichenbach) that the notion of possible worlds is meaningful *to God*.

411.   Resnick, Lawrence. "God and the Best Possible World." *American Philosophical Quarterly* 10 (1973): 313-317.

Contends that God would necessarily create the best possible world, if God exists. He holds also that since God *does* exist necessarily, this is the best possible world and that worse ones are logically possible. Resnick argues that certain forms of classical theism, as such, are incoherent. His argument is that for God to be worthy of moral praise, there must be a choice between genuinely possible worlds.

412.   Rosenberg, Jay F. "The Problem of Evil Revisited." *Journal of Value Inquiry* 4 (1970): 212-218.

Agrees with Schlesinger ("The Problem of Evil and the Problem of Suffering" [#415], that we cannot stipulate the type of world God ought to create (a best possible world is a meaningless concept in the same way that a greatest integer is meaningless), yet he argues that we can stipulate what types of world a deity ought *not* to create: a world containing a gap between potential and actual happiness and a world in which intrinsic evils are present. Both of these, however, are what we find in our world. [See Schlesinger's response, "On the Possibility of the Best of All Possible Worlds" [#417].]

413. Rowe, William L. "Plantinga on Possible Worlds and Evil" (Abstract). *Journal of Philosophy* 70 (1973): 554-555.

Response to Plantinga's "Which Worlds Could God Have Created?" [#400]. Rowe contends that Plantinga's arguments—that there are possible worlds including free acts that an omnipotent God cannot create, and that there is no contradiction in asserting both that God exists and that evil exists—are not without controversy. Yet, if Plantinga's thesis of incompatibility is false, his arguments fail.

414. Schall, James V. "On the Scientific Eradication of Evil." *Communio* 6 (1979): 157-172.

Contends that evil is not to be explained away or removed, as some social ethicists believe. Evil cannot be eradicated, since it depends upon creaturely free will. The evil which exists is necessary in order that the best possible world be actualized, the world in which free creative choices exist. The sociological conclusion is that there is no political, psychological, economic, or social program that can eliminate every evil: all such plans make the world worse.

415. Schlesinger, George N. "The Problem of Evil and the Problem of Suffering." *American Philosophical Quarterly* 1 (1964): 244-247.

Argues, in this first statement of his solution to theodicy, that the amount of pain and suffering in the world is irrelevant and cannot be cited as evidence against the existence of the God of Christianity. God can no more create a world with the greatest happiness than God can create a greatest integer.

416. ———. "Omnipotence and Evil: An Incoherent Problem." *Sophia* 4 (1965): 21-24.

Response to La Para's "Suffering, Happiness, Evil" [#385]. Schlesinger rejects La Para's contention that God ought not to have created any universe, if all possible worlds contain evil. Schlesinger holds that if God had not created, God would be blameworthy for not doing what is most desirable (creating a world) and, paradoxically, since God has created the world, La Para does not see this as less desirable.

417. ———. "On the Possibility of the Best of All Possible Worlds." *Journal of Value Inquiry* 4 (1970): 229-232.

Response to the criticisms of Shea ("God, Evil, and Professor Schlesinger" [#428]); and Rosenberg ("The Problem of Evil Revisited" [#412]). Schlesinger rejects Shea's charge that it makes no difference whether the world is governed by an omnipotent and perfectly good being or by an absolutely powerful monster. Schlesinger also refutes Shea's claims regarding the relevance of Leibniz's solution. He dismisses Rosenberg's distinction between *sins of commission* and *sins of omission*: the distinction applies to humans, but not to God. He rejects Rosenberg's ethical rule that we must not allow a gap between *actual* and *potential* amounts of happiness.

418.   ——. *Religion and the Scientific Method*. Dordrecht and Boston, MA: Reidel
Publishing Company, 1977.

Part One ("The Problem of Evil") contains a more detailed and sophisticated
version of his earlier arguments for a solution to theodicy, first offered in 1964
("The Problem of Evil and the Problem of Suffering" [#415]). It contains also a
response to various critics: Hare and Madden, La Para, Rosenberg, and Shea.
Schlesinger refers favorably to Hick's soul-making theodicy. *Part Two* ("Free
Will, Men and Machines") discusses aspects of free will. The final section, *Part
Three* ("The Confirmation of Theism"), discusses Pascal, the verification prin-
ciple, miracles and evidence for theism.

419.   ——. "Suffering and Evil." *Contemporary Philosophy of Religion*. Edited by
Stephen M. Cahn and David Shatz. New York: Oxford University Press, 1982:
25-31.

Argues that it is logically impossible for God to grant us "a degree of desirability of state" higher than that which is inconceivable. It is, then, logically
impossible for God to fulfil what is required of the universal ethical principle (if
everything else is equal, we ought to increase the degree of desirability of the
state of another as much as possible), the principle to which mortals are bound.

420.   ——. *Metaphysics*. Oxford: Blackwell, 1983.

The section on theodicy (the first section of *Chapter Three*, "Theism and the
Scientific Method," 48-67) rejects the free will defense, contending that it is
false to claim it is logically impossible for God to create a genuinely free agent
and, at the same time, to predict with complete certainty all that agent's
actions. He defends a soul-making theodicy, a "virtuous response" theodicy.

421.   ——. "The Theological Implications of the Holocaust." *Philosophical Forum*
14 (1984/1985): 110-120.

Summarizes his (Schlesinger's) solution to the theodicy issue and responds to
objections by Morris ("A Response to the Problems of Evil" [#390]); and Shea
("God, Evil, and Professor Schlesinger" [#428]). Schlesinger affirms his arguments that God cannot do what is inconceivable, and that God cannot fulfil what
is required by the universal ethical principle (that we must increase the degree of
desirability of state as much as possible). Schlesinger rejects also the responses of
Rubenstein and Borowitz to the Holocaust (that there can be no religious meaning
in it). Schlesinger's theodicy attempts to provide such a meaning.

422.   ——. "The Moral Value of the Universe." *Journal of Value Inquiry* 22 (1988):
319-325.

Response to O'Connor's "Schlesinger and the Morally Perfect Man" [#393] and
to Nozicks's "Theological Explanation" [#392]. While O'Connor acknowledges
that numerous objections to the "degree of desirability of state" have been
disposed of convincingly, he proposes a novel line of attack. Schlesinger argues
that his more recent, more fuller and refined account of the "degree of
desirability of state" principle (*New Perspectives on Old-Time Religion* [#423]) can
answer O'Connor's criticisms. O'Connor notes that the "desirability of state"
solution eliminates the grounds for ascribing evil to God, but leaves us with the
problem of asking whether God is morally good. A finite man (Aeatus) may
work to promote the greatest good, while God does not, thereby rendering

Aeatus greater than God. Schlesinger's response to this is that God has created and sustains people like Aeatus, and remains, as such, the greatest being, morally good, and worthy of worship.

423.   ——. *New Perspectives on Old-Time Religion*. New York and Oxford: Oxford University Press, 1988.

Chapter 4 ("The Problem of Evil") updates and refines Schlesinger's theodicy. He responds also to various critics. Schlesinger holds that the various versions of the free will defense are unsuccessful and ineffective, although the defense has the merit of being based on a number of significant assumptions. Advocates of the free will defense have not explained adequately why God could not have prevented Hitler's atrocities by a limitless variety of psychological, physical or social factors. Schlesinger argues against the "virtuous response to suffering" argument (that no noble sentiment or act can be actualized unless there is pain and suffering), yet uses this theory as integral to his more complex theodicy. He responds to Swinburne's critique of the virtuous response solution ("The Problem of Evil" [#596]); to McCloskey's critique ("God and Evil" [#1231]); and to Hare and Madden's critique (*Evil and the Concept of God* [#1210]). He argues against the critics' assumption that God would want the maximum happiness and the minimum of suffering for all creatures. There is no greatest possible state, and no matter what level of happiness is attained, a greater is always possible. God cannot be faulted, then, for not creating this greatest state of happiness. Since such a state is logically impossible, it does not diminish God's omnipotence not to have actualized it. He defends this principle against the criticisms of Peter Hare ("Review of George Schlesinger, *Religion and the Scientific Method*" [#377]) and Winslow Shea ("God, Evil and Professor Schlesinger" [#428]), as well as against George Wall ("Other Worlds and the Comparison of Value" [#438]) and David Basinger ("Divine Omniscience and the Best of All Possible Worlds" [#355]). Schlesinger develops his theodicy's "degree of desirability of states" principle (DDS) further, to meet the objections of Thomas Morris ("A Response to the Problems of Evil" [#390]) and David O'Connor ("Schlesinger and the Morally Perfect Man" [#393]). Schlesinger rejects the latter's claim that a "morally perfect man" would be morally superior to God and the former's claim that Schlesinger's theodicy fails to provide religious solace. He rejects also the attempts to redefine God as less than all-powerful (Kushner, *When Bad Things Happen to Good People* [#1132], and Roger Crisp, "The Avoidance of the Problem of Evil: A Reply to McGrath" [#1282]).

424.   ——. "The Anthropic Principle." *Tradition* 23 (1988): 1-8.

Argues that since the "anthropic principle" holds that the laws of nature are as they must be to sustain human life, this implies someone (God) planned and willed such laws. This principle constitutes a major development in cosmology that puts the atheist on the defensive. Schlesinger also answers objections to the theistic conclusion. [See also Schlesinger's *Aspects of Time*. Indianapolis, IN: Hackett, 1980; and Schlesinger's more recent, *The Sweep of Probability*. Notre Dame, IN: University of Notre Dame Press, 1991].

425.   Schrader, David E. "Evil and the Best of Possible Worlds." *Sophia* 27 (1988): 24-37.

Critiques and then expands upon Plantinga's free will defense. Schrader argues that based on an analysis of the good, all possible worlds which are commensurable morally with the real world must have a considerable amount of evil, much like the present world. Likewise, natural evil is not a problem for theism if Schrader's non-utilitarian moral theory is accepted—acting *in reverence for* moral laws rather than *in accordance with* moral laws.

426.　Schuurman, H. "The Concept of a Strong Theodicy." *International Journal for Philosophy of Religion* 27 (1990): 63-85.

Examines the concept of a strong theodicy and distinguishes it from a weak theodicy. The former sees the purpose of theodicy as explaining why particular evils occur by giving God's morally sufficient reasons for permitting them. Schuurman argues that a strong theodicy is possible only if the actual world is either the best possible world or the best world God could actualize. He defends this so-called "perfectionist principle" against the view that the greater good principle can be the basis of a strong theodicy without the assumption that the actual world is in some sense the best.

427.　Sennett, James F. "God and Possible Worlds: On What There Must Be." *Southern Journal of Philosophy* 27 (1989): 285-297.

Defends Plantinga against the criticism by Charles Sayward ("God and Empty Terms" [#524]). Sayward argued that under the Kripkean semantics Plantinga endorses, the assignment of an extension to a predicate in a world does not entail the exemplification of that predicate in the world. Sennett contends that Plantinga has blocked this objection, yet proposes a better way to do so: there is no need to make the strong claim that no predicate has extension without exemplification, but only that *this particular predicate* has this. [See also Sennett's "The Free Will Defense and Determinism," *Faith and Philosophy* 9 (1991).]

428.　Shea, Winslow W. "God, Evil, and Professor Schlesinger." *Journal of Value Inquiry* 4 (1970): 219-228.

Refutes Schlesinger's argument regarding the denial of a greatest possible happiness ("The Problem of Evil and the Problem of Suffering" [#415] and "Omnipotence and Evil: An Incoherent Problem" [#416]). Shea argues that the concept is vague and that it seems logically possible for there to be an upper and lower limit to happiness, even if the series of states of possible happiness is infinite. Yet, granting Schlesinger's argument that there is no greatest state of happiness, what follows is that there is no best possible being, no God. Shea argues that Schlesinger's solution implies that it makes no difference what the state of the world's creatures is, since nothing can be done to bring anyone nearer to a state that could not be infinitely improved. Thus, there seem to be no obligations on God's goodness; the attribute has no meaning when applied to God. [See Schlesinger's response, "On the Possibility of the Best of all Possible Worlds" [#417].]

429.　Smart, Ninian. "Omnipotence, Evil and Supermen." *Philosophy* 36 (1961): 188-195. [Reprinted in Pike, editor, *God and Evil*. Englewood Cliffs, NJ: Prentice-Hall, 1964: 103-112].

Distinguishes the *compatibility thesis* (determinism and free will are compatible) from the *utopia thesis* (God could have made us wholly good). Smart argues against the possibility of a world in which there is no evil. He proposes and rejects as unconvincing four possible utopian worlds in which evil does not exist. None would permit meaningful human freedom. If there is a fifth option, a fifth utopian theory, Smart issues the challenge for it to be formulated.

430. ———. "Probability." *Philosophy* 37 (1962): 60.

Response to Flew's critique ("Are Ninian Smart's Temptations Irresistible?" [#371]). He rejects Flew's contention that God could have made us in such a manner that we always overcome temptations. Smart argues that if the struggle against temptations is unreal, the temptations have no value.

431. ———. *Philosophers and Religious Truth.* New York: Collier Books, 1969.

In *Chapter 6* ("F.R. Tennant and the Problem of Evil," 139-162), Smart proposes a theodicy based on Tennant's views—the evolutionary world and the denial of the Adamic myth as the historical basis of sin, etc. [see #605]. Moral evil is the necessary price of creativity, since God cannot create creatures with moral qualities. These must be achieved by the creature itself over time. The evolutionary struggle in which evil is unavoidable is better than a world of static perfection. The evolution of values implies a regularity in the cosmos which often conflicts with individual beings.

432. Stalnaker, Robert L. "Possible Worlds." *Noûs* 10 (1976): 65-75.

In dialogue with David Lewis (*Counterfactuals* [#503]) and Robert Adams ("Theories of Actuality" [#351]), Stalnaker defends a concept of possible worlds which rejects extreme realism but takes possible worlds seriously as irreducible entities. It also treats possible worlds as more than a convenient myth (John Mackie, *Truth, Probability and Paradox*, Oxford: Clarendon Press, 1973), but as less than universes which resemble our own. [See also Stalnaker's "A Theory of Conditionals," *American Philosophical Quarterly*, Monograph Series 2, 98-112, a work cited approvingly by Plantinga. Also relevant is Stalnaker's "A Defense of Conditional Excluded Middle," *Ifs*. Edited by Stalnaker, et al. Dordrecht and Boston, MA: Reidel, 1981.]

433. Stewart, Melville. "O Felix Culpa, Redemption, and the Greater Good Defense." *Sophia* 25 (1986): 18-31.

Argues that common to Plantinga's free will defense, Hick's soul-growth theodicy, and Yandell's growth-to-moral-maturity specification is the greater good defense. This defense contributes to a resolution of theodicy. The fall (evils and suffering) is necessary to bring about the greater good of redemption (*o felix culpa*). Stewart argues for an Augustinian, rather than Irenaean (Hickean), interpretation: some sort of a fall is necessary for the meaningfulness of redemption as a theological concept and to the possibility of redemption as a restorative act.

434. Strasser, Mark. "Leibniz, Plantinga, and the Test for Existence in Possible Worlds." *International Journal for Philosophy of Religion* 18 (1985): 153-159.

Rather than refuting Plantinga's ontological proof, Strasser argues that Tooley's proof (which establishes there is no being that has the characteristics often attributed to God ["Alvin Plantinga and the Argument from Evil" [#435]]) can be used by Plantinga to establish there is no possible world in which there is no being that has the characteristics often attributed to God. Strasser argues, accordingly, that there is need to amend the test by which we determine whether or not a property exists in some possible world. He adopts Leibniz's insight that a quality's not being self-contradictory is not a sufficient condition for its existence in some possible world.

435.   Tooley, Michael. "Alvin Plantinga and the Argument from Evil." *Australasian Journal of Philosophy* 58 (1980): 360-376.

Refutes various claims made by Plantinga (*The Nature of Necessity*, *Chapter 9* [#110]. Tooley contends that Plantinga is mistaken in focusing on the logical incompatibility version of the problem of evil; Plantinga is wrong to reject the thesis that any evil would be logically incompatible with God's existence; and Plantinga's attempt to show that evil does not count against God's existence fails. He concludes that Plantinga's discussion of the problem of evil is logically and philosophically weak. [See Plantinga's response, "Tooley and Evil: A Reply" [#403]; and Strasser's response to the Plantinga—Tooley debate, "Leibniz, Plantinga and the Test for Existence in Possible Worlds" [#434]. See also Peter van Inwagen's defense of Plantinga's trans-world depravity concept, "Plantinga on Trans-world Identity" [#436] against the criticisms of Tooley, in Tooley's "Critical Notice of *The Nature of Necessity*," *Journal of Philosophy* 74 (1977), 91-102.]

436.   Van Inwagen, Peter. "Plantinga on Trans-world Identity." *Alvin Plantinga (Profiles, Volume 5)*. Edited by James E. Tomberlin and Peter van Inwagen. Dordrecht and Boston, MA: Reidel, 1985: 101-120.

Defends Plantinga (*The Nature of Necessity*, *Chapter 4* [#110]) against confusions by Baruch A. Brody (*Identity and Essence*, Princeton, NJ: Princeton University Press, 1980) and Michael Tooley ("Critical Notice of *The Nature of Necessity* [see #435]), about Plantinga's theory of trans-world depravity. He contends that there is no "problem" of trans-world depravity. [See Plantinga's brief response, *Alvin Plantinga (Profiles, Volume 5)*, 313 [#114].]

437.   Wall, George B. "Heaven and A Wholly Good God." *Personalist* 58 (1977): 352-357.

Argues that belief in a heaven renders belief in a wholly good God suspect. A wholly good God would have made a world with less moral evil (less freedom) and less natural evil, a world like our image of heaven. Wall argues against the "Panglossian Principle" which holds it would have been logically impossible for a God to have created a world with as much value as this one, but less moral evil and less natural evil.

438.   ——. "Other Worlds and the Comparison of Value." *Sophia* 18 (1979): 10-19.

Maintains that the notion of a heaven is a serious obstacle for theism's defense of divine goodness. As noted in the previous entry, the "Panglossian Principle" holds that it would have been logically impossible for a God to have created a better world than this one. Yet, Wall argues that the notion of heaven is not logically impossible or unintelligible (contra Schlesinger), and that heavenly values and earthly values are not incommensurate with heaven, the higher value-state. Thus, Wall denies the assumption that it would have been logically impossible for God to have created a better world than this present world. [See response by Schlesinger in *New Perspectives on Old-Time Religion* [#423].]

439. Wei, Tan Tai. "The Question of a Cosmomorphic Utopia." *Personalist* 55 (1974): 401-406.

Argues against the view that God could have created a utopia of morally perfect creatures, and a world of creatures who could not choose evil or excessive evil. Human freedom would choose between various degrees of goodness.

440. Weinstock, Jerome A. "Must God Create the Best World?" *Sophia* 14 (1975): 32-39.

Response to Adams ("Must God Create the Best?" [#350]). Weinstock contends that it makes no sense to argue that divine grace is a reason for God to create a less than perfect world.

441. Yandell, Keith E. "Ethics, Evils and Theism." *Sophia* 8 (1969): 18-28.

Defends the claim that the existence of evil neither conclusively refutes nor provides strong evidence against theism. As such, it cannot be shown that evil is a conceptual problem for the theist. Yandell resolves the apparent paradox between holding that evils are justified and that we have an obligation to eliminate evils. Some evils are justified (for example) in as much as they provide opportunities for moral struggle and the overcoming of the evils. Such evils are justified; yet we must seek to eliminate them. [See response by Kane, "Theism and Evil" [#381], and Yandell's reply to Kane, "Theism and Evil: A Reply" [#442].]

442. ———. "Theism and Evil: A Reply." *Sophia* 11 (1972): 1-7.

Response to Kane ("Theism and Evil" [#381]), who contends that Yandell has not shown that evil is a conceptual problem for the theist. Yandell denies the paradoxes Kane purports to find in Yandell's arguments.

443. ———. "The Greater Good Defense." *Sophia* 13 (1974): 1-16.

Contends that theodicy must accept the greater good defense, that God has created the world as morally good. There is no equivocation on the term "good." The world as it is, is preferable to no world. The theist accepts God's goodness and providence and, hence, some version of the greater good defense: the theist may not understand fully the means, but trusts in the divine ends.

II Middle Knowledge and Counterfactuals

444. Adams, Robert Merrihew. "Middle Knowledge." *Journal of Philosophy* 70 (1973): 552-554.

Abstract of a paper presented at the American Philosophical Association, in response to Plantinga's "Which Worlds Could God Have Created?" [#400]. Adams contends that Plantinga's indeterministic position contradicts his support for the doctrine of middle knowledge.

445. ———. "Middle Knowledge and the Problem of Evil." *American Philosophical Quarterly* 14 (1977): 109-117.

A later version of his "Middle Knowledge" [#444]. He rejects attempts by Plantinga and others (Molina and Scarez) to show that God has middle knowledge, knowledge of what every possible indeterministically free creature would do freely in every situation in which it could possibly find itself. He argues that the propositions that are supposed to be known in middle knowledge cannot be true. Adams also answers objections to his denial of middle knowledge (including Plantinga's examples of it).

446.   ———. "Plantinga on the Problem of Evil." *Alvin Plantinga (Profiles, Volume 5)*. Edited by James Tomberlin and Peter van Inwagen. Dordrecht and Boston, MA: Reidel, 1985: 225-255.

Contends that Plantinga has solved the logical problem of evil by showing that there is no inconsistency in belief in God and the existence of evil. Adams, however, finds fault with Plantinga's use of middle knowledge and with Plantinga's defense against the probabilistic argument from evil. He questions how plausible Plantinga's claim is, that human actions would be morally worse on the whole if God did not permit as much evil as has actually been permitted. Plantinga has not explained adequately how God may have good reasons for permitting the evil that occurs. Plantinga suggests that a complete explanation is found in the overall balance of moral good and evil in the world, but Adams suggests that other considerations might provide a more plausible reason for the permission of some evils. [See Plantinga's reply, *Alvin Plantinga (Profiles, Volume 5)*, 371-382 [#114].]

447.   Basinger, David. "Divine Omniscience and Human Freedom: A 'Middle Knowledge' Perspective." *Faith and Philosophy* 1 (1984): 291-302.

Responds to Dennis Ahern's "Foreknowledge, Nelson Pike and Newcomb's Problem" (*Religious Studies* 15 [1979], 489-490); and to Pike's "Divine Foreknowledge, Human Freedom and Possible Worlds" [#397]. Basinger argues that while human freedom is compatible with divine omniscience (if what God knows about the future is contingent upon what we will in fact do), this knowledge can only be contingent if we can in some sense by our actions determine beliefs held by God in the past. Yet, Ahern and others argue that it is impossible for us in any sense by present actions to determine the past, to determine God's past beliefs about our actions. As such, if God is omniscient, we cannot be free. Against this, Basinger argues that, assuming God has middle knowledge, the fear of retrodetermination is not an adequate basis for questioning the compatibility of divine omniscience and human freedom.

448.   ———. "Middle Knowledge and Classical Christian Thought." *Religious Studies* 22 (1986): 407-422.

Contends that unless God has middle knowledge, creation of a world in which creatures have indeterministic freedom was a significant gamble. A God *without* middle knowledge (i.e., a God with either present knowledge or simple foreknowledge), would be a cosmic gambler. [See response by Gordon and Sadowsky, "Does Theism Need Middle Knowledge?" [#455]].

449.   ———. "Middle Knowledge and Human Freedom: Some Clarifications." *Faith and Philosophy* 4 (1987): 330-336.

Response to Hasker's critique of middle knowledge ("A Refutation of Middle Knowledge" [#457]). Basinger argues that Hasker has not shown that God *cannot* have middle knowledge (knowledge of what would in fact happen in every conceivable situation), such that human freedom is jeopardized. Hasker's argument, that all counterfactuals of freedom are incoherent, is unconvincing. [See Hasker's response, "Reply to Basinger on Power Entailment" [#458].]

450. ———. "Divine Knowledge and Divine Control: A Response to Gordon and Sadowsky." *Religious Studies* 26 (1990): 267-275.

Defends his argument and clarifies the issue ("Middle Knowledge and Classical Christian Thought" [#448]), that God has middle knowledge, against the critique of Gordon and Sadowsky ("Does Theism Need Middle Knowledge?" [#455]). Basinger rejects the critics' contention, attributed to Basinger, that a God with middle knowledge would have total control. A God with middle knowledge can avoid the label of cosmic gambler, not because such knowledge allows God to better control free creatures, but because God would know beforehand what the consequences of free choice will be in any given context.

451. ———. "Middle Knowledge and Divine Control: Some Clarifications." *International Journal for Philosophy of Religion* 30 (1991): 129-139.

Clarifies the relationship between middle knowledge and divine control, and concludes that middle knowledge is not the panacea assigned to it by theists, nor the liability portrayed by theological indeterminists. He contends that the claim of both sides is contentious, the claim that God's having middle knowledge gives God significant power over earthly events, including control over the indeterministically free choices of human beings. The providential capacities of a God of middle knowledge have been overstated by several scholars: David Gordon and James Sadowsky ("Does Theism Need Middle Knowledge?" [#455]); William Craig ("*The Only Wise God* [#194]); and William Hasker ("A Refutation of Middle Knowledge" [#457]).

452. Cook, Robert R. "God, Middle Knowledge and Alternative Worlds." *Evangelical Quarterly* 62 (1990): 293-310.

Overview and clarification of the middle knowledge debate, noting its historical roots and contemporary exponents. Cook argues that God knew all possible worlds and chose this one. He argues also that middle knowledge offers the evangelical theologians a middle way between Calvinism and Arminianism.

453. Craig, William L. "'No Other Name': A Middle Knowledge Perspective on the Exclusivity of Salvation Through Christ." *Faith and Philosophy* 6 (1989): 172-188.

Contends that there is no contradiction between God's having middle knowledge and certain persons' being damned. He notes the theological advantages and disadvantages of middle knowledge, and considers the question of the truth value of counterfactuals. Craig argues, to the contrary, that divine middle knowledge and damnation *are* compatible. [See response by David Hunt, "Middle Knowledge and the Soteriological Problem of Evil" [#460], and other discussions of middle knowledge by Craig; for example, in *The Only Wise God* [#194].]

454.   Davison, Scott A. "Foreknowledge, Middle Knowledge and 'Nearby Worlds'."
        International Journal for Philosophy of Religion 30 (1991): 29-44.

        Seeks to clarify the middle knowledge debate. Davison argues against the pos-
        sibility of God's foreknowledge of free events, and against God's possessing
        middle knowledge of free actions.

455.   Gordon, David, and James Sadowsky. "Does Theism Need Middle Know-
        ledge?" *Religious Studies* 22 (1989): 75-87.

        Response to Basinger's "Middle Knowledge and Classical Christian Thought"
        [#448]. Gordon and Sadowsky reject Basinger's contention that a God with simple
        foreknowledge is a cosmic gambler in a sense that a God with middle knowledge
        is not. [See Basinger's response, "Divine Knowledge and Divine Control: A
        Response to Gordon and Sadowsky" [#450]. See also David Gordon, "Must God
        Identify the Best?" *Journal of Value Inquiry* 19 (1985), 81-83, in response to
        Basinger's "Divine Omniscience and the Best of All Possible Worlds" [#355].]

456.   Halpin, John F. "The Miraculous Conception of Counterfactuals." *Philosophical
        Studies* 63 (1991): 271-290.

        Argues for the validity of a "miracle" theory of counterfactuals—see David
        Lewis, *Philosophical Papers* [#506]; Frank Jackson, "A Causal Theory of
        Counterfactuals" [#492]; Thomason and Gupta, "A Theory of Conditionals in the
        Context of Branching Time" [#532]. This view argues against various non-
        miraculous theories—see D. Nute, *Topics in Conditional Logic* [#514]; J. Pollock,
        "A Refined Theory of Counterfactuals" [#518]; J. Bennett, "Counterfactuals and
        Temporal Direction" [#471]; and P. Horwich, *Asymmetries in Time* (Cambridge,
        MA: MIT Press, 1976).

457.   Hasker, William S. "A Refutation of Middle Knowledge." *Noûs* 20 (1986):
        545-557.

        Challenges the validity of the concept of middle knowledge. If counterfactuals
        are true, they are not counterfactuals of freedom. On the other hand, if agents
        are genuinely free, there are no true counterfactuals which state what that agent
        would definitely do under various possible circumstances. As such, the doctrine
        of middle knowledge is untenable: there are no true counterfactuals of freedom.
        [See Basinger's response, "Middle Knowledge and Human Freedom: Some
        Clarifications" [#449]].

458.   ——. "Reply to Basinger on Power Entailment." *Faith and Philosophy* 5
        (1988): 87-90.

        Response to Basinger's "Middle Knowledge and Human Freedom: Some Clarifi-
        cations" [#449]. Hasker rejects Basinger's claim that his alternative principles (in
        support of middle knowledge) are equivalent to the ones employed by Hasker to
        refute middle knowledge.

459.   Hunt, David Paul. "Middle Knowledge: The 'Foreknowledge Defense'." *Faith
        and Philosophy* 7 (1990): 1-24.

        Clarifies the current debate over middle knowledge: see Adams ("Middle
        Knowledge and the Problem of Evil" [#445]); Hasker ("A Refutation of Middle
        Knowledge" [#457]); Kenny (*The God of the Philosophers* [#462]); and Hunt

("Middle Knowledge and the Soteriological Problem of Evil" [#460]), all of whom reject middle knowledge. They hold that they do not see what it would be for counterfactuals to be true (Adams), and who or what could bring it about that these propositions are true (Hasker). Among the defenders of middle knowledge noted by Hunt are the following: Plantinga (*The Nature of Necessity* [#110]); Kvanvig (*The Possibility of an All-Knowing God* [#266]); Otte ("A Defense of Middle Knowledge" [#464]); Craig (*The Only Wise God* [#194]); Freddoso ("Introduction" [#484]); Wierenga (*The Nature of God* [#167]); and Basinger ("Human Freedom and Divine Providence: Some New Thoughts on an Old Problem" [#8], "Divine Omniscience and Human Freedom: A 'Middle Knowledge' Perspective" [#447]), "Middle Knowledge and Classical Christian Thought" [#448]). Hunt rejects Plantinga's defense of middle knowledge and Basinger's statement that counterfactuals "simply are true" as adequate grounds for refusing the demand for a ground. Hunt responds to Otte's efforts [#464] to overcome this impasse by recognizing the futility of resolving the impasse, as stated, and seeking another way. Hunt rejects the assumption of Plantinga and Otte that counterfactuals of freedom share the same modal structure as future-factuals of freedom.

460. ———. "Middle Knowledge and the Soteriological Problem of Evil." *Religious Studies* 27 (1991): 3-26.

Rejects Craig's appeal to middle knowledge in arguing for a Molinist, Christian exclusivistic soteriology (*The Only Wise God* [#194]). Hunt argues that it is impossible both that the subjunctive conditionals toward which middle knowledge are directed are adequately "grounded," and that the responses expressed in their consequences are free in any sense that is compatible with determinism.

461. Kenny, Anthony. "Divine Foreknowledge and Human Freedom." *Aquinas: A Collection of Critical Essays.* Edited by Anthony Kenny. New York: Garden City, 1969: 255-270. [Also published in *Logical Analysis and Contemporary Theism.* Edited by John Donnelly. New York: Fordham University Press, 1972, 162-174.]

Defends (in a qualified manner) Aquinas's reconciliation of God's foreknowledge and human freedom. Yet Kenny argues that Aquinas's position is more of a denial of divine foreknowledge and omniscience than the reconciliation proposed. Aquinas's concept of a timeless eternity is radically incoherent. Kenny proposes an alternative argument to show the compatibility of divine foreknowledge and human freedom. [See Helm's response, "Divine Foreknowledge and Facts" [#63]. See also the recent response by Graham Oddie and Roy W. Perrett, "Simultaneity and God's Timelessness," *Sophia* 31 (1992), 123-127.]

462. ———. *The God of the Philosophers.* Oxford: Clarendon Press, 1979.

Chapter 5 (65-71) discusses Plantinga's free will defense and the best possible worlds ontology. Kenny contends that Plantinga's account of middle knowledge is incoherent and that this is so for the same reasons as those urged by the Dominicans in the sixteenth century against Molinism. He argues that in advance of the decision to create, God cannot know which of the relevant counterfactuals are true and that, as such, cannot know which worlds are in the divine power to actualize. The decision to create, accordingly, cannot be the wise one claimed by the Molinists. Kenny's conclusion is that the attempts to reconcile divine foreknowledge and the indeterminacy of human freedom fail. [Part of Kenny's book is published as "The Definition of Omnipotence," in *The Concept of God*. Edited by Thomas V. Morris. New York and Oxford: Oxford University Press, 1987.]

463. King-Farlow, John, and Francis Jeffrey Pelletier. "Pains Across Persons Across Possible Worlds." *Idealistic Studies* 7 (1977): 61-75.

Contend that Leibniz's view of possible worlds is more appropriate than Saul Kripke's view (*Naming and Necessity* [#497]). The authors find Kripke's notion of possible worlds is ontologically shallow. There is more to the notion of possible worlds, they insist, than counterfactuals. The notion of possible worlds should be approached by philosophers with more respect for traditional problems of ethics and metaphysics.

464. Otte, Richard. "A Defense of Middle Knowledge." *International Journal for Philosophy of Religion* 21 (1987): 161-169.

Refutes Robert Adams's rejection of the possibility of God having middle knowledge. Otte contends that middle knowledge is as possible as foreknowledge. [See response by Hunt, "Middle Knowledge: The 'Foreknowledge Defense'" [#459].]

465. Schlesinger, George N. "Critical Notice of Fred Wilson: *Laws and Other Worlds*." *Canadian Journal of Philosophy* 19 (1989): 155-160.

Disputes Wilson's rejection of possible world analysis of counterfactuals. [See Fred Wilson, *Laws and Other Worlds*. Dordrecht and Boston, MA: Reidel, 1986.]

466. Van Inwagen, Peter. "Indexicality and Actuality." *Philosophical Review* 89 (1980): 403-426.

Discusses David Lewis's thesis (*Counterfactuals* [#503], and in "Anselm and Actuality" [#502]), that the term "actual" is an indexical term, a term whose references varies depending on the context. He argues that this theory, original to Lewis, is stated ambiguously by him. Lewis is not consistent about talking of possible worlds as the "ways things could have been." Van Inwagen suggests the definition of possible worlds be amended from the "ways things could have been" to "possibilities" that are either realized or unrealized.

III.   Related Publications [Selected]

467. Adams, Robert Merrihew. "Critical Study: *The Nature of Necessity* (Alvin Plantinga)." *Noûs* 11 (1977): 175-190.

468. Austin, David F. "Plantinga on Actualism and Essences." *Philosophical Studies* 39 (1981): 35-42.

469. ———. "Plantinga's Theory of Proper Names." *Notre Dame Journal of Formal Logic* 24 (1983): 115-132.

470. Barrow, John D., and Frank J. Tipler. *The Anthropic Cosmological Principle*. Oxford and New York: Oxford University Press, 1988.

471. Bennett, J. "Counterfactuals and Temporal Direction." *Philosophical Review* 93 (1984): 57-91.

472. Blumenfeld, David. "On the Compossibility of the Divine Attributes." *Philosophical Studies* 34 (1978): 91-103. [Reprinted in *The Concept of God*. Edited by Thomas V. Morris. Oxford: Oxford University Press, 1987.]

473. Brody, Baruch A. "'*De Re* and *De Dicto*' Interpretations of Modal Logic as a Return to Aristotelian Essentialism." *Philosophia* 2 (1972): 117-136. [See also Brody's *Identity and Essence* [see #436].]

474. Camp, J. "Plantinga on *De Dicto* and *De Re*." *Noûs* 5 (1971): 215-226.

475. Carr, B.J., and M.J. Rees. "The Anthropic Principle and the Structure of the Physical World." *Nature* 28 (1979): 605-612.

476. Carter, Brandon. "Large Number Coincidences and the Anthropic Principle in Cosmology." *Confrontation of Cosmological Theories with Observable Data*. Edited by M.S. Longair. Dordrecht and Boston, MA: Reidel, 1974: 291-298.

476. Carter, W.R. "Plantinga on Disembodied Existence." *Philosophical Review* 81 (1972): 360-363.

478. ———. "On Relative Possibility." *Philosophia* 5 (1976): 489-498.

479. Chandler, Hugh S. "Plantinga and the Contingently Possible." *Analysis* 36 (1976): 106-109. [See response by Fumerton, "Chandler on the Contingently Possible" [#485].]

480. Craig, William L. "Julian Wolfe and Infinite Time." *International Journal for Philosophy of Religion* 11 (1980): 133-135.

481. ———. "Lest Anyone Should Fall: A Middle Knowledge Perspective on Perseverance and Apostolic Writings." *International Journal for Philosophy of Religion* 29 (1991): 65-74.

482. ———. "Middle Knowledge: A Calvinist—Arminian Rapprochement?" *The Grace of God*. Edited by Clark H. Pinnock. Grand Rapids, MI: Eerdmans, 1989.

483. ———. "God and Real Time." *Religious Studies* 27 (1991): 335-347. [Response to Padgett, "God and Time" [#516]. See reply by Padgett, "Can History Measure Eternity? A Reply to William Craig" [#517].]

484. Freddoso, Alfred J. "Introduction." *Luis de Molina: On Divine Foreknowledge: Part IV of the Concordia*. Ithaca, NY: Cornell University Press, 1986: 1-81. [See also Freddoso's *The Existence and Nature of God*. Notre Dame, IN: University of Notre Dame Press, 1983.]

485. Fumerton, R. "Chandler on the Contingently Possible." *Analysis* 36 (1976): 39-40. [Response to Chandler, "Plantinga and the Contingently Possible" [#479].]

486. Gean, W. "The Logical Connection Argument and *De Re* Necessity." *American Philosophical Quarterly* 12 (1975): 349-352.

487. Grover, Stephen. "Why Only the Best is Good Enough." *Analysis* 48 (1988): 224.

488. Halpin, John F. "Counterfactual Analysis: Can a Metalinguistic Theory Be Revitalized?" *Synthese* 81 (1989): 47-62.

489. Hasker, William S. "Concerning the Intelligibility of 'God is Timeless'." *New Scholasticism* 57 (1983): 170-193.

490. ———. *God, Time and Knowledge*. Ithaca, NY: Cornell University Press, 1989. [See also his *Metaphysics*. Downer's Grove, IL: InterVarsity Press, 1983. *Chapter Two* discusses theodicy and the free will defense.]

491. Heinaman, Robert. "Incompatibilism Without the Principle of Alternative Possibilities." *Australasian Journal of Philosophy* 64 (1986): 266-276.

492. Jackson, Frank. "A Causal Theory of Counterfactuals." *Australasian Journal of Philosophy* 55 (1977): 3-21.

493. Kenny, Anthony. *The Metaphysics of Mind*. New York and Oxford: Oxford University Press, 1989.

494. King-Farlow, John. "Precosmological Hypotheses." *Sophia* 3 (1965): 22-26. [To clarify talk about God as good, he argues that God should be described as a temporally eternal Person (as in the Bible), rather than as the timeless, immutable Being of Boethius and Aquinas.]

495. ———. "God and the Stone Paradox: Comment III," *Sophia* 10 (1971): 31-33. [See also the companion essays: David Londey, "God and the Stone Paradox: Comment I," *Sophia* 10 (1971), 23-25; and Barry Miller, "God and the Stone Paradox: Comment II," *Sophia* 10 (1971), 26-31.]

496. Kripke, Saul. "Naming and Necessity." *Semantics of Natural Language*. Edited by Donald Davidson and Gilbert Harman. Dordrecht and Boston, MA: Reidel, 1974: 253-255, 736-739.

497. ———. *Naming and Necessity*. Cambridge, MA: Harvard University Press, 1980. [Argues that we can stipulate certain counterfactual situations.]

498. Langton, Douglas C. *God's Willing Knowledge: The Influence of Scotus' Analysis of Omniscience*. University Park, PA: Pennsylvania State University Press, 1986.

499. Lefton, Brian. "Timelessness and Foreknowledge." *Philosophical Studies* 63 (1991): 309-325.

500. Leslie, John. "Anthropic Principle, World Ensemble, Design." *American Philosophical Quarterly* 19 (1982): 141-151.

501. ———. "The Scientific Weight of Anthropic and Teleological Principles." *Current Issues in Teleology*. Edited by N. Rescher. Lanham, MD: University Press of America, 1986.

502. Lewis, David. "Anselm and Actuality." *Noûs* 4 (1970): 175-188.

503. ———. *Counterfactuals*. Cambridge, MA: Harvard University Press, 1973.

504. ———. "Causation." *Journal of Philosophy* 70 (1973): 556-567. [Hume's two theories of causation present both the dominant view of causation (a causal succession is supposed to be a succession that instantiates a regularity) and a counterfactual analysis of causation among events (if the first object had not been, the second would never have existed). Lewis shows how this analysis distinguishes genuine causes from effects, epiphenomena, and preempted potential causes].

505. ———. "Counterfactual Dependence and Time's Arrow." *Noûs* 13 (1979): 455-476.

506. ———. *Philosophical Papers, II*. Oxford: Oxford University Press, 1986.

507. MacBaeth, Murray. "Omniscience and Eternity." *The Aristotelian Society Supplementary Volume* 63 (1989).

508. Mann, William E. "The Best of All Possible Worlds." *Being and Goodness*. Edited by Scott MacDonald. Ithaca, NY: Cornell University Press, 1991: 250-277. [See also Mann's "Simplicity and Immutability in God." *International Philosophical Quarterly* 23 (1983), 267-276. Reprinted in *The Concept of God*. Edited by Thomas V. Morris. Oxford: Oxford University Press, 1987.]

509. Mavrodes, George I. "How Does God Know the Things He Knows?" *Divine and Human Action*. Edited by Thomas V. Morris. Ithaca, NY: Cornell University Press, 1988: 345-361.

510. McMichael, Alan. "What Ought to Be." *Philosophical Studies* 38 (1980): 69-74.

511. ———. "A Problem for Actualism About Possible Worlds." *Philosophical Review* 82 (1983): 49-66.

512. Moore, A.W. "Possible Worlds and Diagonalization." *Australasian Journal of Philosophy* 44 (1984): 21-22.

513. Naylor, Margery Bedford. "A Note on David Lewis's Realism about Possible Worlds." *Analysis* 45 (1985): 28-29.

514. Nute, D. *Topics in Conditional Logic*. Dordrecht and Boston, MA: Reidel, 1980.

515. Otte, Richard. "A Theistic Conception of Probability." *Faith and Philosophy* 4 (1987): 427-444. [Also published in *Christian Theism and the Problems of Philosophy*. Edited by Michael D. Beaty. Notre Dame, IN: University of Notre Dame Press, 1990, 92-117.]

516. Padgett, Alan G. "God and Time." *Religious Studies* 25 (1989): 209-215. [See response by Craig, "God and Real Time" [#483].]

517. ———. "Can History Measure Eternity? A Reply to William Craig." *Religious Studies* 27 (1991): 333-335. [Response to Craig's "God and Real Time" [#483].]

518. Pollock, John L. "A Refined Theory of Counterfactuals." *Journal of Philosophical Logic* 10 (1981): 239-266. [See Pollock's *Foundations of Philosophical Semantics*. Princeton, NJ: Princeton University Press, 1984.]

519. Puccetti, Roland. "Before Creation." *Sophia* 3 (1964): 24-36. [See King-Farlow's response, "Precosmological Hypotheses" [#494].]

520. ———. "Mr. King-Farlow on Precosmological Goodness." *Sophia* 4 (1965): 25-27. [Response to King-Farlow's "Precosmological Hypotheses" [#494].]

521. Ratzsch, Del. "Nomo(theo)logical Necessity." *Christian Theism and the Problems of Philosophy*. Edited by Michael D. Beaty. Notre Dame, IN: University of Notre Dame Press, 1990: 184-207.

522. Richards, Tom. "The Worlds of David Lewis." *Australasian Journal of Philosophy* 53 (1975): 105-108.

523. Salmon, Nathan. "Impossible Worlds." *Australasian Journal of Philosophy* 44 (1983/1984): 114-117.

524.   Sayward, Charles. "God and Empty Terms." *International Journal for Philosophy of Religion* 18 (1985): 149-152.

525.   Stalnaker, Robert. "A Theory of Conditionals." *Studies in Logical Theory.* Edited by Nicholas Rescher. Oxford: Oxford University Press, 1968.

526.   Streveler, Paul. "The Problems of Future Contingents." *New Scholasticism* 47 (1973): 233-247.

527.   Stump, Eleonore. "Intellect, Will, and the Principle of Alternate Possibilities." *Christian Theism and the Problems of Philosophy*. Edited by Michael D. Beaty. Notre Dame, IN: University of Notre Dame Press, 1990: 254-285.

528.   Swinburne, Richard G. "Review of Plantinga, *The Nature of Necessity*." *Mind* 85 (1976): 131-134.

529.   Taylor, Richard. "The Problem of Future Contingency." *Philosophical Review* 66 (1957): 1-28.

530.   ———. "Fatalism." *Philosophical Review* 71 (1962): 56-66.

531.   ———. "Deliberation and Foreknowledge." *American Philosophical Quarterly* 1 (1964): 73-80.

532.   Thomason, R., and A. Gupta. "A Theory of Conditionals in the Context of Branching Time." *Philosophical Review* 89 (1980): 423-441.

533.   Tolhurst, W. "On the Alleged Inconsistency in Plantinga's Defense of Actualism." *Philosophical Studies* 41 (1982): 427-430.

534.   Tomberlin, James E. "A Correct Account of Essentialism?" *Critica* 4 (1970): 55-67.

535.   Vihvelin, Kadri. "Freedom, Necessity, and Laws of Nature as Relations Between Universals." *Australasian Journal of Philosophy* 68 (1990): 371-381.

536.   ———. "Freedom, Causation, and Counterfactuals." *Philosophical Studies* 64 (1991): 161-184.

537.   Viney, Donald Wayne. "God Only Knows? Hartshorne and the Mechanics of Omniscience." *Hartshorne, Process Philosophy and Theology*. Edited by Robert Kane and Stephen Phillips. Albany, NY: State University of New York Press, 1989: 71-90.

538.   White, Michael J. "Plantinga and the Actual World." *Analysis* 37 (1977): 97-104.

539.   Williams, C.J.F. "Knowing Good and Evil." *Philosophy* 66 (1991): 235-240.

540.   Zagzebski, Linda Trinkaus. "Divine Knowledge and Human Free Will." *Religious Studies* 21 (1985): 279-298.

541.   ———. "What if the Impossible Had Been Actual?" *Christian Theism and the Problems of Philosophy*. Edited by Michael D. Beaty. Notre Dame, IN: University of Notre Dame Press, 1990: 165-183.

542.   ———. *The Dilemma of Freedom and Foreknowledge*. New York and Oxford: Oxford University Press, 1991.

Chapter 4

Natural Evil Theodicy

The problem of *natural* or *physical* evil has been as difficult to resolve, if not more, as the problem of *moral* evil.[1] There has not been as much work on the former problem, yet besides the proposals found in process theodicies, in *John Hick's* Irenaean theodicy, and in other theodicies—like *Alvin Plantinga's*,[2] the theodicies of *Richard Swinburne* and *Bruce Reichenbach*, in particular, have been foremost among the attempts to construct theodicies of natural evil and respond to atheological arguments from the evidence of natural evil. Swinburne argues that natural evils are a necessary condition for human free will. Natural evils "are necessary if agents are to have the *knowledge* of how to bring about evil or prevent its occurrence, knowledge that they must have if they are to have a genuine choice between bringing about evil and bringing about good."[3] The "crux of the problem of evil," however, as Swinburne and most others are coming to recognize, is the *amount* of evil in the world. The question is whether God "has inflicted too much suffering on too many people (and animals) to give knowledge to others for the sake of the freedom of the latter."[4] Swinburne's response is that there are divinely imposed limits to the amount of suffering given to us. To those critics who argue that the limits are too wide, permitting too much evil, Swinburne responds that if there were fewer natural evils there would be less opportunity for us to exercise our free will.

While Swinburne's theodicy holds (controversially) that natural evils are the necessary prerequisite for freedom, Reichenbach's more modest claim is that the possibility of natural evil is inherent in the system of natural laws which are essential to support human life. He rejects the contention of atheological sceptics (*McCloskey, Mackie*, et al) that natural evil is more than sufficient ground for rejecting belief in God. McCloskey's argument is that God (if such a Being existed) could eliminate natural evils by miraculous intervention or by having created a very different world in the first place. To the former point, Reichenbach responds that divine interference in the world, if in fact it did occur, would destabilize the world to the extent that rationality would be jeopardized. In such a world, "there would be no necessary relation between phenomena, and in particular between cause and effect."[5] To McCloskey's second criticism, that God could have created a world with different laws in order to prevent or eliminate natural evils, Reichenbach's response is that "to introduce different natural laws would entail alteration of the objects governed by those laws." F.R. Tennant (in his 1928 book, *Philosophical Theology*) made this same point.

It is important to stress again that there have been other significant theodicies of natural evil, some of which are not listed in this chapter, but listed elsewhere. *John Hick's* Irenaean theodicy explains natural evil as a necessary environment for soul making *(Chapter 5)*; process writers *(David Griffin, John Cobb, myself, and others)* utilize a free will defense to account for all evil—natural and moral *(Chapter 6)*; *Alvin Plantinga* postulates the possibility of an evil power (Satan and demonic cohorts) as an explanation for natural evil, an explanation that need not be actual or even plausible. As a mere possibility, it refutes the supposed logical version of the atheistic protest *(Chapters 2 and 3)*. Others,[6] like Austin Farrer (included in this present chapter), have formulated influential theodicies of natural evil. Farrer has done seminal work also on the related issues of free will and divine providence.

Listed at the end of the chapter are selected writings on the related issue of *animal suffering*, an aspect of physical evil about which a large literature has been accumulating during the past two decades. Often, those who defend the goodness of God in theodicies minimalize nature and the importance of animal suffering. We have had an anthropocentric view of life, and environmentalists and others contend that the theodicies that reflect this bias are lacking in concern for animal suffering. The writings of *Peter Singer* and *Tom Regan* are among the most important of those listed below, both of whom defend animal (and other forms of non-human) rights with conviction. *Mary Midgley*, *John Feinberg*, and a host of others have made important contributions regarding the rights of animals. Others, needless to say, argue that the "animal rights" activists are arguing nonsense.

A fairly recent issue of *Newsweek* (December 26, 1988) contained a cover story entitled, "The Battle over Animal Rights: A Question of Suffering and Science." The article noted that at least 17 million animals are used in laboratory experiments each year in the United States and that the issue has now focused on whether the benefits outweigh the moral costs. Thousands of pigs were used to develop the CAT scan, rabbits to understand the rejection of organs, and so on. Is the suffering endured by such creatures worth the benefits to humans?[7] Slowly, this is becoming a serious consideration for the theodicy issue. Animal suffering and is also an aspect of the growing field of environmental ethics. The journals, *Environmental Ethics*, *Between Species*, among others, are recommended to the reader for further references.

Following is an annotated list of theodicies of natural evil and the discussions to which they have given rise, followed by a selected list of major writings on animal suffering, those which reflect most directly the implications for the theodicy issue.

Notes

1.   See *Appendix E* for relevant dissertations. Among them are the following: Brian Morley, *Swinburne's Inductive Argument for Theism* (Claremont Graduate School, 1991); Rosemary Rodd, *Biology, Ethics, Animals* (Open University, 1987); Floyd Ross, *Personalism and the Problem of Natural Evil* (Yale University, 1935); Mark Richardson, *Human Action and the Making of a Theist: A Study of Austin Farrer's Gifford Lectures* (Graduate Theological Union, 1991); George Lamore, *Theories of Natural Evil in the Thought of Henry Nelson Wieman, Edwin Lewis, and Paul Tillich* (Boston School of Theology, 1959); etc.

2.   Plantinga's interest in a "defense," rather than a "theodicy," affects his discussions of both natural and moral evil. As for the former, the *possibility* of its source in Satan is enough of a defense for Plantinga; yet many others insist that a theodicy is needed, a rational explanation for evils. See the discussions in *Chapters 2 and 3*.

3.   Richard Swinburne, *The Existence of God* (Oxford: Clarendon Press, 1969), 202-203.

4.   Swinburne, *The Existence of God*, 219.

5.   Bruce Reichenbach, *Evil and a Good God* (New York: Fordham University Press, 1982).

6.   This chapter includes defenses of Farrer's theodicy by Brian Hebblethwaite, as well as the caustic critiques of *Michael Martin* of the natural evil theodicies of Richard Swinburne and Bruce Reichenbach. Martin pursues the challenges put forth earlier by H.J. McCloskey. Also included are *David O'Connor's* criticisms of Swinburne's theodicy and his (O'Connor's) alternative theodicy, a version of the free will defense. Included in this chapter also are the relevant publications of Diogenes Allen, who offers a theodicy of natural evils, *Robert Jooharigan's* book-length treatment of natural evil, and many other important publications on the natural evil theme, including the 1991 article of *Quentlin Smith*, "An Atheological Argument from Evil and Natural Laws," which contributes critiques of the natural evil theodicies of Swinburne, Reichenbach, Hick, and Plantinga. Other publications on natural evil are scattered liberally throughout the annotated chapters, although the most directly focused publications on this sub-theme have been included in this present chapter.

7.   As I write this, the news reports speak of a protest against General Motors for killing thousands of animals in its tests of car safety. The number of incidents concerning animal mistreatment is becoming an issue of wide public awareness and concern.

I   Natural Evil Theodicy

543.   Allen, Diogenes. "Natural Evil and the Love of God." *Religious Studies* 16 (1980): 439-456.

Defends the position that suffering (natural evil) is a medium in and through which God's love can be experienced. Suffering teaches us that we are a very small part of the universe and that it is egotistical to ask for more good than is possible. Paradoxically, our self-centered response to suffering enables us to transcend our physical nature and realize our spirituality. Allen expands upon Simone Weil's point (see Weil's *The Need for Roots*, New York: Harper and Row, 1971; *Waiting on God* [see #3706], "The Love of God and Affliction," *On Science, Necessity and the Love of God* [#3707]), that in suffering and affliction, we have the most perfect contact with the love of God possible for human beings in this life. Allen argues that the acceptance of suffering as God's will transcends the suffering. Hick's soul-making theodicy lacks this dimension.

544.   ———. *Traces of God in a Frequently Hostile World*. Cambridge, MA: Cowley, 1980.

Argues that suffering and its acceptance leads to an awareness of our spirituality, as Allen has argued in various essays: "Suffering at the Hands of Nature" [#545]; "Natural Evil and the Love of God" [#543]; and "The Witness of Nature to God's Existence and Goodness" [#546].

545.   ———. "Suffering at the Hands of Nature." *Theology Today* 37 (1980/1981): 183-191.

Despite the suffering we endure from nature, Allen's position is that we must submit to God's rule. Through suffering, we experience divine love. Allen shows the relevance of Jesus's suffering for human suffering. This argument (and the example of the intense suffering of affliction described by Simone Weil) is made also in Allen's *Traces of God in a Frequently Hostile World* [#544] and in other essays. Jesus's victory over evil lies in the fact that he acquiesced to God's will. We too must acquiesce to God's will in our suffering.

546.   ———. "The Witness of Nature to God's Existence and Goodness." *Faith and Philosophy* 1 (1984): 27-43.

Seeks to show how the existence and order of nature functions as a witness to God's existence and goodness. Allen argues that pursuing the question as to whether or not the world is ultimate enables us to view nature as a witness to another reality and the possibility of receiving another witness, the Christian community. [See also Diogenes Allen's more recent essay on Farrer's theology, "Faith and the Recognition of God's Activity," in *Divine Action: Studies Inspired by the Philosophical Theology of Austin Farrer*. Edited by Brian Hebblethwaite and Edward Henderson. Edinburgh: T&T Clark, 1990. Allen's chapter concludes with a 51-page index of Farrer's main works. Also included in the book are relevant chapters by David Burrell, "How an Eternal God Acts in Time," Rodger Forsman, "'Double Agency' and Identifying Reference to God," and others.]

547.   Allen, Ronald J. "How We Respond to Natural Disaster." *Theology Today* 38 (1982): 458-464.

Contends that natural disasters are the result of the brokenness of creation and a sign of divine judgment, a call for people to reflect on their values and turn toward God.

548.   Aspensen, Steven S. "Reply to O'Connor's 'A Variation on the Free Will Defense'." *Faith and Philosophy* 6 (1989): 95-98.

Critique of David O'Connor's "A Variation on the Free Will Defense" [#579] in which he claimed that natural evil is necessary for free will, that natural evil is required for the possibility of a morally credible free choice. O'Connor's justification of the free will defense fails to meet an anticipated objection, that we could be moral without the property O'Connor calls "P," the property of being prone to choosing possible evils. An altered understanding of his definition of a morally credible free choice would not help, and if O'Connor's God's moral condition is different than our own, then it cannot be used as an example of "P" as unessential for human beings being moral.

549.   Beggiani, Seeley. "A Re-evaluation of the Problem of Evil." *American Ecclesiastical Review* 162 (1970): 173-185.

Argues that traditional Christian theodicy (Augustine, Thomas, the Scholastics, Journet) preserved divine omnipotence, but failed to offer an acceptable answer to the problem of physical evil. Beggiani favors the views of process thinkers (Teilhard and Hartshorne) for an explanation of physical evil and the need to reformulate the concept of divine omnipotence.

550.   Brand, Paul. "God's Astounding Laws of Nature." *Christianity Today* 23 (1978): 13-19.

From his position as a medical doctor, Brand answers questions from Philip Yancey in this published interview. The complexity of the universe is strong evidence for God, yet it is a God who is constantly creating and developing the skills of a creator, versus the traditional view of divine omnipotence. Physical pain is an essential mechanism for survival, and death is a natural process.

551.   Coughlan, Michael J. "The Free Will Defense and Natural Evil." *International Journal for Philosophy of Religion* 20 (1986): 92-108.

Presents a qualified defense of Swinburne's argument regarding the relationship between natural evil and moral evil (*The Existence of God* [#600]) against Moser's "Natural Evil and the Free Will Defense" [#574]. Coughlan responds also to McKim's "Worlds Without Evil" [#87]: he insists that one cannot acquire the ability to make moral choices without the experience of evil, without natural evils, and without the availability of moral evil.

552.   Cuppitt, Don. "Natural Evil." *Man and Nature.* Edited by H. Montefiore. London: Collins, 1975: 110-120.

Rejects the distinction (made by classical writers on the problem of evil in the eighteenth century) between three kinds of evil: metaphysical, moral and natural. Death and animal suffering, as prime examples, show that it is far from clear whether such things are evils at all, still less what kind of evil. Cuppitt seeks to use modern knowledge to amend the terms of the theodicy debate. He argues that we no longer see the corruptibility of nature as implying that something is wrong

with it. We have learned also to look at nature and at our idea of God historically: God built the universe from below and God will remain ambiguous until
the end of time.

553.   Curtis, Philip. "The Rational Theology of Austin Farrer." *Theology* 73 (1970):
        249-256.

        A critical overview of Farrer's work. [See Hebblethwaite's supplementary
        comments in "Austin Farrer's Concept of Divine Providence" [#562].]

554.   Eaton, Jeffrey C. *The Logic of Theism: An Analysis of the Thought of Austin
        Farrer*. Lanham, MD: University Press of America, 1980.

        Contains a brief exposition of Farrer's theodicy (93-110), a bibliography of
        Farrer's publications (191-200) and a selected bibliography of writings about
        Farrer (201-203).

555.   Farrer, Austin. *Love Almighty and Ills Unlimited: An Essay on Providence and
        Evil*. Garden City, NY: Doubleday, 1961.

        Farrer is concerned almost exclusively with the problem of natural evil, rather
        than with moral evil. He argues that the divine creation of creatures involves the
        interaction of different hierarchical systems, each operating according to its own
        nature. The result is an inevitably complex whole in which there are inevitable
        conflicts. God's hand is perfectly hidden, yet perceptible in the course of evolu-
        tion and in the particular course of history, especially the history of salvation.
        Not all the divine purposes can be realized in this world, and thus an eternal life
        is necessary.

556.   ———. *Saving Belief*. London: Hodder and Stoughton, 1964.

        The final two chapters summarize and clarify the arguments of *Love Almighty
        and Ills Unlimited* [#555]. Farrer describes different kinds of divine activity with
        respect to different levels of creatures. [See also Farrer's *Finite and Infinite*.
        Dacre: Westminster, 1943. Second edition, with revised preface, 1959. Also
        published by Macmillan and Humanities Press, 1966 and reissued by Seabury
        Press, 1979.]

557.   ———. *A Science of God?* London: Bles, 1966. Published in the United States
        of America as *God is Not Dead*. Moorehouse-Barlow, 1966.

        Reaffirms the basic points of his theodicy. Natural disasters, for example, are
        the result of God "making the world make itself." The will of divine provi-
        dence is hidden, but effective.

558.   ———. *Reflective Faith: Essays in Philosophical Theology*. London: SPCK
        Press, 1972 and Grand Rapids, MI: Eerdmans, 1974. [See also Farrer's *Faith
        and Speculation*. London: Adam and Charles Black, 1966.]

        In the chapter entitled "Grace and the Human Will," Farrer argues that divine
        grace and human free will are not competitors. God's action *in us* is experi-
        enced when we most fully embrace our true freedom. We must learn to submit
        ourselves freely to divine grace.

559.   ———. *The Freedom of the Will*. Gifford Lectures for 1957. London: Adam and
        Charles Black, 1958. Second edition, New York: Scribners, 1960.

A major philosophical refutation of determinism. Farrer explains how our will is a matter of rational choice over which we have control. He expounds upon the nature of voluntary action and the capacities of human beings to act freely. [See also Farrer's *Reflective Faith* [#558] and his "Free Will in Theology," *Dictionary of the History of Ideas*. New York: Scribner's, 1973-1974. Reprinted in *Interpretation and Belief*. Edited by C. Conti. London: SPCK Press, 1976, 186-201.]

560.   Ferré, Frederick. "Theodicy and the Status of Animals." *American Philosophical Quarterly* 23 (1986): 23-43.

Urges more consideration for animal suffering and less theological anthropocentrism. He notes that the free will defense does little for animal suffering.

561.   Ferré, Nels. *Reason in Religion*. London and Edinburgh. Thomas Nelson, 1963.

Chapter 14 ("Nature and the Problem of Evil," 236-282) defends God's creation of human beings and the inevitability of evil. Nature is the condition of human freedom, providing us with the opportunity for free choices and moral growth. [See also Ferré's much earlier publication, *Evil and the Christian Faith*. New York: Harper and Row, 1947, *Chapter 7*. Reprinted, New York: Books for Libraries Press, 1971.]

562.   Hebblethwaite, Brian L. "Austin Farrer's Concept of Divine Providence." *Theology* 14 (1970): 541-551.

Focuses upon that aspect of Farrer's work [see #555-559] which holds that God's causal agency operates in and through the world. Hebblethwaite describes Farrer's writings as the most direct, sustained and searching treatment of the problem of divine providence among modern theological writings.

563.   ———. "Providence and Divine Action." *Religious Studies* 14 (1978): 223-236.

Defends Austin Farrer's concept of divine agency [see #555-559], arguing that it is superior to the demythologizing approach which concedes too much to the positivist and historicist by insisting that God's act is located only at the tangential point of existential response to the preached word. He discusses Farrer's defense of the theory of primary and secondary causation. The implications for theodicy are noted: God acts within natural structures and does not override them, because of the necessity of a stable environment for the emergence and growth of free creatures.

564.   ———. "Freedom, Evil, Farrer." *New Blackfriars* 66 (1985): 178-187.

Argues that Farrer's theodicy [see #555-559] is more realistic and plausible than Plantinga's [see Chapters 2 and 3]. Both Farrer and Plantinga reject Mackie's compatibilism, but Farrer *argues* the case for libertarianism while Plantinga merely *assumes* it. Both Farrer and Plantinga reject Hick's concession to Mackie, that it is possible that a world of free creatures always acts well in a morally frictionless environment. Hebblethwaite argues that the best of Hick's Irenaean theodicy was already present in Farrer. [See also Hebblethwaite's earlier writings on Farrer, including "On Understanding What One Believes, *New Fire* 1 (1971), 11-15; and "The Doctrine of the Incarnation in the Thought of Austin Farrer," *New Fire* 4 (1977), 460-468.]

565.   Jones, W. Paul. "Evil and Creativity: Theodicy Re-Examined." *Religion in Life* 32 (1963): 521-533.

Contends that a reinterpretation of Genesis as an understanding of "human" evil does so at the expense of incapacitating Genesis as an explanation for physical evil. Jones argues that creation is incomplete and that redemption is not a restoration from finitude but from fallenness, in order to bring about the completion of creation.

566.   Jooharigan, Robert Badrik. *God and Natural Evil.* Bristol, England: Wyndham Hall Press, 1985.

Responds to Hume's critique from evil, using Hick's Irenaean themes [see Chapter Five]. He offers a cumulative theodicy of natural evils: such evils are necessary for the growth of morality and for commun ality (with others and with nature). He supports Hick's view of immortality as necessary for theodicy and intra-historical eschatology. He argues that just as there are many valuable qualities of personality and communality that cannot be realised without a struggle with evil, so too is this the case with respect to our relationships to God, our "theologicality." He concludes with a chapter on animal suffering.

567.   Loades, Ann. "Austin Farrer on *Love Almighty.*" *For God and Clarity.* Edited by J. Eaton and A. Loades. Allison Park, PA: Pickwick Publications, 1983: 93-110.

Presents an uncritical exposition of Farrer's theodicy, as expressed in his *Love Almighty and Ills Unlimited* [#555].

568.   Martin, Michael. "God, Satan and Natural Evil." *Sophia* 22 (1983): 43-45.

Argues that there are two theses held by Terence Penelhum (*Religion and Rationality* [#95]) which are contradictory and insoluble in the framework of Penelhum's theology: he identifies God as the only incorporeal being, and yet holds that natural evils may be due to the activities of fallen spirits (Satan). Satan, as such, must be corporeal or identical with God (as incorporeal). Martin contends that both conclusions are problematic.

569.   ———. "The Coherence of the Hypothesis of an Omnipotent, Omniscient, Free and Perfectly Evil Being." *International Journal for Philosophy of Religion* 17 (1985): 185-191.

Refutes Swinburne's contention (*The Existence of God* [#600]; *The Coherence of Theism* [#598]; etc.), that theism has a higher *a posteriori* probability than atheism. He argues that the proposition—that there is an omniscient, omnipotent, free and perfectly evil Being—rivals Swinburne's theistic hypothesis and has as much probability. Swinburne's reasons for rejecting the atheistic hypothesis as incoherent are mistaken.

570.   ———. "Reichenbach on Natural Evil." *Religious Studies* 24 (1988): 91-99.

Refutes Reichenbach's theodicy of natural evils (*Evil and a Good God* [#587]). Reichenbach's appeal to natural laws fails to offer an adequate basis for evils. There are other ways God could have arranged the world, other than the current natural laws. Reichenbach offers no morally sufficient reason why God did not actualise such a world. Martin rejects also Reichenbach's claim that a world of miracles (divine intervention) would be incompatible with rational decisions and moral choice. He repudiates Reichenbach's claim that a world operating only with statistical laws is impossible, and rejects as ambiguous his claim that statistical laws are based on the assumption of universal laws.

571.   McDaniel, Jay. "Land Ethics, Animal Rights and Process Theology." *Process Studies* 18 (1988): 88-102.

Holds that Peter Singer's "animal rights" argument [see #'s 726-733] conflicts with Aldo Leopold's land ethics (*A Sand Country Almanac*. New York: Oxford University Press, 1949), since the latter emphasises the rights of ecosystems and the former emphasizes the rights of individual organisms. The truths of both of these movements, however, (as well as Heidegger's writings and "the deep ecology movement") can be affirmed by a creative use of Whitehead's philosophy, as demonstrated by *The Liberation of Life: From Cell to Community*, by John Cobb and Charles Birch. Cambridge, MA: Cambridge University Press, 1981.

572.   McGrath, P.J. "Is There a Problem of Evil?" *Philosophical Quarterly* 39 (1989): 91-94.

Critique of O'Connor ("On the Problem of Evil's Not Being What It Seems" [#578]). He refutes O'Connor's argument that theistic explanations of quantified evil are circular, and the conclusion that there can be no quantified argument from natural evil. He rejects O'Connor's claim that the limitations of human reason can never devise a satisfactory criterion to distinguish evils that are incompatible with God from evils that are not. [See O'Connor's response, "On the Problem of Evil's Still Not Being What It Seems" [#581].]

573.   McLean, Murdith. "Residual Natural Evil and Anthropic Reasoning." *Religious Studies* 27 (1991): 173-188.

Starting with Tennant's explanation for natural evil (*Philosophical Theology, II* [#605]), that such evils are justified by being the logically inevitable outcome of that order necessary to produce the most morally estimable world (a view revived and reconsidered by Ninian Smart, *Philosophers and Religious Truth* [#431]), McLean applies the contributions of contemporary cosmological physics to explain better the concepts of residual (or gratuitous) evil. Tennant did not support two of his fundamental theories: all residual evil is the logically un-avoidable out- come of regularities that also work for the goods which make the world valuable, and the view that no set of regularities superior to those of this world could be devised with a preferable balance in production of goods over evils. Based on the anthropic principle (See John D. Barrow and Frank J. Tipler, *The Anthropic Cosmological Principle* [#470]), McLean argues for an "anthropic reasoning," aimed at determining what fundamental regularities and initial conditions must obtain in the universe (given its production of creatures such as ourselves), and whether any other combinations of regularities would suffice to produce the same or a similar result. McLean then argues that anthropic reasoning supports both of Tennant's unproven theories. [See also two more recent publications by Errol E. Harris on the philosophical implications of the anthropic principle: *Cosmos and Anthropos: A Philosophical Interpretation of the Anthropic Cosmological Principle*. Atlantic Highlands, NJ: Humanitties Press International, 1991; and *Cosmos and Theos: Ethical and*

Theological Implications of the Anthropic Cosmological Principle. Atlantic Highlands, NJ: Humanities Press International, 1992.]

574.   Moser, Paul K. "Natural Evil and the Free Will Defense: Reply to R.G. Swinburne, *The Existence of God.*" *International Journal for Philosophy of Religion* 15 (1984): 49-56.

Criticizes Swinburne's argument (*The Existence of God* [#600] and "Natural Evil" [#599]), that natural evil is *necessary* for knowledge of moral evil. Since knowing how to bring about moral evil with some action does not entail knowing that some action has evil consequences, and since this does not entail knowingly bringing about moral evil, Swinburne's argument is invalid. Moser argues also that the possibility that there could be a superhuman agent who gives us the knowledge needed undercuts Swinburne's basic assumption, that our knowledge of our past actions' consequences must come from inductive inference from our past experiences of evil. Moser proposes an alternative argument which improves upon Swinburne's, that *only some* morally responsible agents must acquire a concept of evil through the experience of natural evil.

575.   O'Connor, David. "Swinburne On Natural Evil." *Religious Studies* 19 (1983): 65-73.

Refutes Richard Swinburne's argument (*The Existence of God* [#600]) in defense of God despite natural evils. O'Connor argues that it was available to an omnibenevolent and omnipotent God to bring about a desirable state of affairs (a world of morally responsible people) by a less painful means than the present world of natural evils. As such, Swinburne's argument to the contrary is undercut. O'Connor argues for the viability of *the verbal knowledge option* dismissed by Swinburne.

576.   ———. "Theism, Evil and the Onus of Proof: Reply to F.J. Fitzpatrick." *Religious Studies* 19 (1983): 241-247.

In response to Fitzpatrick's "The Onus of Proof in Arguments About the Problem of Evil" [#370], O'Connor argues that the atheist can expect theism to justify its belief in God, if it holds that God has a reason, unknown to human beings, for permitting evil in the world.

577.   ———. "On Natural Evil's Being Necessary for Free Will." *Sophia* 24 (1985): 36-44.

Holds that natural evil is logically necessary for freedom of choice and that Swinburne's argument (*The Existence of God* [#600]) to the same conclusion is invalid, since God could have made available to us the requisite knowledge of evil affects of our choices and acts by implanting the needed data in our brains before birth.

578.   ———. "On the Problem of Evil's Not Being What It Seems." *Philosophical Quarterly* 37 (1987): 441-447.

Argues that both atheists and theists beg the question of theodicy, since noncircular arguments from quantified evil cannot be formulated and non-circular theistic explanations cannot be formulated. O'Connor contends that the "quantified problem of evil," the problem of showing that all evil is compatible with

God's existence, is circular. Human limitations are incapable of finding a solution to theodicy or in refuting God from the argument from evil. [See Mc-Grath's response, "Is There a Problem of Evil?" [#572].]

579. ——. "A Variation on the Free Will Defense." *Faith and Philosophy* 4 (1987): 160-167.

Argues that the standard formulation of the free will defense fails to establish that natural evil (defined as something inferior to what it might possibly have been) is a logically necessary precondition of free choice. God could have implanted in us the necessary knowledge needed for free choice, rather than require us to experience natural evil (contra Swinburne). O'Connor defends a variation of the free will defense, that natural evil is necessary for free choice: we have the property "P"; we are prone to choosing possible evils. He defends this variation against several objections. [See response by Aspensen, "Reply to O'Connor's 'A Variation on the Free Will Defense'" [#548].]

580. ——. "In Defense of Theoretical Theodicy." *Modern Theology* 5 (1988): 61-74.

Argues that Surin (*Theology and the Problem of Evil* [#1364]) fails to substantiate his claim that theoretical theodicy is inherently flawed. O'Connor argues that theoretical theodicy escapes Surin's attacks on it and that it is a worthy and valuable *philosophical-cum-theological* enterprise. He rejects Surin's claim that theoretical theodicy is subject-irrelevant to the *existential-cum-pastoral* problem of evil.

581. ——. "On the Problem of Evil's Still Not Being What It Seems." *Philosophical Quarterly* 40 (1990): 72-78.

Response to McGrath's critique ("Is There a Problem of Evil?" [#572]) of O'Connor's "On the Problem of Evil Not Being What it Seems" [#578]. He argues that McGrath misrepresents his position and that McGrath's attacks are invalid. O'Connor proposes a new argument for his relativist position, that there are no grounds for deciding between theism and atheism. He argues that the comparison of the state in which the world would be *if God existed* and *if God did not exist* cannot decide the issue for or against theism or atheism. [O'Connor has elaborated this argument in his "On Failing to Resolve Theism-Versus-Atheism Empirically," *Religious Studies* 27 (1991), 91-102.]

582. ——. "Swinburne on Natural Evil from Natural Processes." *International Journal for Philosophy of Religion* 30 (1991): 77-87.

Refutes Swinburne's argument (*The Existence of God* [#600] and "Knowledge from Experience, and the Problem of Evil" [#603]), that natural evils from natural processes are logically necessary for human beings to become morally mature and able to choose our own destinies. O'Connor argues that moral maturity and choice of destiny are possible *without* any such evils. [O'Connor's most recent publication on the problem of natural evil incorporates many of the items listed above: *God and Inscrutable Evil: In Defense of Theism and Atheism*. Lanham, MD: Rowman and Littlefield, 1998.]

583. Phillips, D.Z. "The Problem of Evil" and "Postscript." *Reason and Religion*. Edited by Stuart C. Brown. Ithaca, NY: Cornell University Press, 1977: 103-121, 134-139.

Summary and critique of Swinburne's theodicy (81-102). He rejects Swinburne's optimistic view ("The Problem of Evil" [#596]), that the world is a God-given setting in which human beings can exercise rational choices that determine the kind of people they become. This is *not* the world in which we live.

584. Reichenbach, Bruce R. "Natural Evils and Natural Law: A Theodicy for Natural Evils." *International Philosophical Quarterly* 16 (1976): 179-196. [A revised version is contained in his *Evil and a Good God* [#587].]

Contends that the two requirements which need to be met by theodicies of natural evil *can* be met. It is contradictory for God to intervene by violating natural laws. It is impossible to determine whether God has created the best possible world, since it cannot be determined whether or not this *is* the best possible world.

585. ———. "The Inductive Argument From Evil." *American Philosophical Quarterly* 17 (1980): 221-227. [A revised version is Reichenbach's *Evil and a Good God* [#587]].

Employs "Bayles' Theorum" to reconstruct the atheologian's thesis that it is improbable that God exists, given the amount of (natural) evil in the world. He refutes this inductive argument: the atheologians' evidence, for example, is inadequate and has excluded relevant counter-evidence (the theistic proofs), etc.

586. ———. "The Deductive Argument From Evil." *Sophia* 20 (1981): 25-42. [A revised version is contained in his *Evil and a Good God* [#587].]

Refutes the deductive argument (Mackie, "Evil and Omnipotence" [#1217]; McCloskey, *God and Evil* [#1235]), that the existence of evil *per se* is logically inconsistent with the existence of a good, omnipotent and omniscient God. The burden of proof is on the atheologian to show that the propositions are inconsistent. The atheologian has not shown it is a necessary truth that an omnipotent and omniscient being can eliminate every evil state of affairs without losing a greater good or producing a greater evil. [For a recent publication on McCloskey's challenge, see Charles T. Hughes. "Theism, Natural Evil, and Superior Worlds," *International Journal for Philosophy of Religion* 31 (1992), 45-61. Hughes rejects versions of an argument originally proposed by H.J. McCloskey concerning God's ability to change natural laws.]

587. ———. *Evil and a Good God*. New York: Fordham University Press, 1982.

Contains revised sections of five previously published articles: "Natural Evils and Natural Law" [#584]; Must God Create the Best Possible World?" [#409]; "The Deductive Argument from Evil" [#586]; "The Inductive Argument from Evil" [#585]; and "Why is God Good?" [#1412]. While the book focuses on physical evils, the chapter on moral evils challenges the thesis of Mackie ("Evil and Omnipotence" [#1217]) and McCloskey (*God and Evil* [#1235]), that God could bring it about that there are free agents who do not use their freedom for evil.

588. ———. "Evil and a Reformed View of God." *International Journal for Philosophy of Religion* 19 (1988): 67-85.

Contends that the compatibilist reformed theologian has not shown it was possible for God to create human beings with a more perfect nature, or that doing so would violate some fundamental principle of value.

589.   ———. "Fatalism and Freedom." *International Philosophical Quarterly* 28 (1988): 271-285.

Argues that God's goodness is compatible with evil and that divine foreknowledge provides the basis for God's actions. He maintains also that God has middle knowledge and that in certain cases can bring about the past. [see Chapter 3.]

590.   Rice, Stanley. "On the Problem of Apparent Evil in the Natural World." *Journal of the American Scientific Affiliation* 39 (1987): 150-157.

For biblical and biological reasons, Rice holds that the apparent evil in the natural world cannot be due to the fall of human beings (the Adamic fall). Natural evils are necessary for the functioning of the ecosystem as a whole, but only if individuals within species and species within ecosystems work for the common good. Yet, natural selection is a selfish process, thereby worsening the problem of evil: the unselfish love of God is contradicted by the selfishness of creatures. Rice proposes a metaphorical view of nature as a solution to the problem. The biblical approach to nature imposes metaphorical interpretations on nature.

591.   Sainsbury, R.M. "Benevolence and Evil." *Australasian Journal of Philosophy* 58 (1980): 128-134.

Rejects two versions of the atheological argument from natural evil: that God could eliminate all evil is false; and that God would not allow so much evil is false. Neither can be established. We have no reason for thinking that the nature of the actual world is other than optimal.

592.   Smith, Quentlin. "An Atheological Argument from Evil and Natural Laws." *International Journal for Philosophy of Religion* 29 (1991): 159-171.

Proposes an atheological argument—the "law of predation" is ultimately evil—that renders invalid the natural evil theodicies of George Schlesinger (*Religion and the Scientific Method* [#418]); Richard Swinburne (*The Existence of God* [#600]); John Hick (*Evil and the God of Love* [#750]); Bruce Reichenbach (*Evil and a Good God* [#587]); and Alvin Plantinga's defense ("The Probabilistic Argument from Evil [#112]). [Other related publications of Quentlin Smith include the following: "A Big Bang Cosmological Argument for God's Non-existence," *Faith and Philosophy* 9 (1992); "Atheism, Theism and the Big Bang Cosmology," *Australasian Journal of Philosophy* 69 (1991); "The Uncaused Beginning of the Universe," *Philosophy of Science* 55 (1988), 39-57.]

593.   Spencer, Bonnell. *God Who Dares to Be Man: Theology for Prayer and Suffering*. New York: Seabury Press, 1980.

Contends that natural evil is a misnomer: violent and destructive forces of nature are necessary elements in a universe of self-determining creatures. Human sin is the source of evil, the risk God took in giving us freedom. Yet, Spencer holds that God's persistent love will turn evils into goods. Theodicy, the attempt to judge and justify God in terms of human morals, is sinful. Spencer develops a theodicy based on process themes: God is not all-controlling power nor impassible; God has undergone a self-limitation, resulting in the origin of all evil; in Christ, God became human. [See Griffin's response in his review article on Spencer [#865].]

594. Straton, Douglas. "God, Freedom, and Pain." *Harvard Theological Review* 55 (1962): 143-159.

Explains the necessity of natural evil in the world. Such evils are due to the finitude and freedom of the natural process. Mutations are successful adaptations to a new situation within the environment. God risks these in creating or bringing forth a finite world of freely developing processes. Straton also argues that this is the "best possible world," the only world imaginable in which freedom is possible for creatures with a genuine moral nature.

595. Stump, Eleonore. "Knowledge, Freedom and the Problem of Evil." *International Journal for Philosophy of Religion* 14 (1983): 49-58.

Refutes Swinburne's claim (*The Existence of God* [#600]) that natural evil is necessary for knowledge of the consequences of our morally free actions. Stump proposes that God could communicate such knowledge in dreams which, over time, would be shown to be and accepted to be true. Such knowledge would not infringe on human freedom and it would obviate the need for natural evil. Swinburne's argument is circular: God is good to permit natural evils since natural evils produce knowledge to enable us to avoid natural evils.

596. Swinburne, Richard G. "The Problem of Evil." *Reason and Religion*. Edited by Stuart C. Brown. Ithaca, NY: Cornell University Press, 1977: 81-102.

Argues against the atheological argument from evil. He defends the free will defense as the explanation of moral evil and appeals to fallen angels as a cause of physical evil (as does Plantinga). God permits other physical evils as biological and psychological means of human character-development, not otherwise attainable. He argues that the existence of God is probable on generally accessible evidence. There are no evils that can serve a higher good, and there are no evils that make it improbable there is a God. Swinburne acknowledges that the crux of the problem of evil, nevertheless, is the *amount* of evil in the world. His response is that fewer natural evils would afford us fewer opportunities to exercise responsibility.

597. ———. "Postscript." *Reason and Religion*. Edited by Stuart C. Brown. Ithaca, NY: Cornell University Press, 1977: 129-133.

Responds to Phillips's critique, "The Problem of Evil" [#583] of his (Swinburne's) "The Problem of Evil" [#596]. Swinburne rejects the claim that some evil is pointless. God has created a world of free creatures capable both of great goods and terrible evils. The evils, nevertheless, lead to good ends, greater goods, often only known to God.

598. ———. *The Coherence of Theism*. Oxford: Clarendon Press, 1977.

Discusses the coherence of the divine attributes: free, omnipotent, omniscient, perfect goodness, eternal, immutable, and necessary. [See the review of Swinburne's book by Brian Davies: *New Blackfriars* 60 (1979), 76-83.]

599. ———. "Natural Evil." *American Philosophical Quarterly* 15 (1978): 295-301.

Argues that the free will defense is valid in providing an explanation for God's allowing moral evil. There must be natural evils if human beings are to have the knowledge needed to bring about moral evils. There must be natural evils if we are to have opportunity to bring about serious evils by actions or neglect and if all knowledge of the future is obtained by induction. God cannot give non-inductive knowledge (verbal knowledge) of the consequences of our actions.

600.   ———. *The Existence of God*. Oxford. The Clarendon Press, 1979. Second edition, 1991.

The second edition contains two new appendices, shortened versions of previously published papers. The first responds to Mackie's criticisms (*The Miracle of Theism* [#1220]); the second assesses the evidential force of recent scientific discoveries. *Chapter 11* ("The Problem of Evil," 200-224) is a reprinted version of Swinburne's "The Problem of Evil" [#596] in Stuart C. Brown's *Reason and Religion*, and Swinburne's "Natural Evil" [#599].

601.   ———. "A Theodicy of Heaven and Hell." *The Existence and Nature of God*. Edited by A. Freddoso. Notre Dame, IN: University of Notre Dame Press, 1983: 37-54.

Based on material used in his *Faith and Reason* (Oxford: Oxford University Press, 1981), Swinburne argues for the reality of heaven, and denies the possibility of hell as endless punishment. He concludes that it is compatible with God's goodness that some human beings might find themselves beyond the possibility of salvation, because it is compatible with the goodness of God to allow us to *choose* the sort of person we will be.

602.   ———. "Original Sinfulness." *Neue Zeitschrift* 27 (1985): 235-250.

Argues that there exists in human beings a "proneness" to sin that is transmitted genetically. This proneness is increased or decreased by the social environment. For sin to exist, there must be some moral beliefs.

603.   ———. "Knowledge from Experience, and the Problem of Evil." *The Rationality of Religious Belief*. Edited by William J. Abraham and Steven W. Holtzer. Oxford: Clarendon Press, 1987: 141-167.

Presents his argument for the compatibility of natural evil and God's existence, in response to various criticisms: O'Connor ("Swinburne on Natural Evil" [#575]); Stump ("Knowledge, Freedom and the Problem of Evil" [#595]); and Moser ("Natural Evil and the Free Will Defense" [#574]). Swinburne restates (in more precise form) his arguments from "Natural Evil"[#599] and *The Existence of God, Chapters 9-11* [#600]: natural evils are the major means by which we acquire practical and moral knowledge, knowledge which is essential in order for us to have a free and responsible choice of destiny. Moral knowledge could be given to us in a different way, but not the practical knowledge, not without a heavy cost in some other form of evil.

604.   ———. "Does Theism Need a Theodicy?" *Canadian Journal of Philosophy* 18 (1988): 287-311.

Contends that in the absence of strong evidence for the existence of God, the theist needs a theodicy with respect to those evils which seem to count against God's existence. Swinburne responds to Wykstra's argument that apparent evils do not count against theism ("The Humean Obstacle to Evidential Arguments from Suffering" [#1188]), and to Plantinga's criticisms ("The Probabilistic

Argument from Evil" [#112]) of his (Swinburne's) views in *The Existence of God* [#600]. Swinburne argues it is not enough to hold that God *may* be pursuing greater goods that are beyond our present comprehension; theism needs a *theodicy* to show that it is at least probable each known evil leads to goods.

605.   Tennant, Frederick R. *Philosophical Theology. Volume II.* Cambridge: Cambridge University Press, 1930. Reprinted, 1968.

Rejects pantheism and some theistic attempts to solve the problem of evil (evil as illusion, evil as an inadequate idea, evil as an appearance that would dissolve if we could see *sub specie aeternitatis*, etc.). He defends the notion of the best possible world as the most viable with respect to moral worth and instrumentality. The best world cannot be the most pleasurable since there must be moral agents. God stands "a hand-breadth off," allowing creaturely freedom room to grow. The best possible world (the evolutionary world) affords us the opportunity for the attainment of moral growth. Natural evil is not an accidental superfluity emerging out of the evolutionary process, but is essentially instrumental to organic progress. The physical order must be characterized by law and regularity, and this necessitates that suffering will occur.

606.   Wainwright, William J. "God and the Necessity of Physical Evil." *Sophia* 11 (1972): 16-19.

Refutes McCloskey's argument ("God and Evil" [#1231]), that the theistic belief that all physical evil is necessary for a greater good is incompatible with the theistic belief that the struggle against physical evil is morally legitimate. Wainwright rejects the view that the reduction of physical evil would reduce the total amount of good in the universe. [For a more recent critique of McCloskey's argument from natural evils, see Charles T. Curran, "Theism, Natural Evil, and Superior Possible Worlds," *International Journal for Philosophy of Religion* 31 (1992), 45-61.]

607.   Walker, Ian "The Problem of Evil and the Activity of God." *New Blackfriars* 63 (1982): 25-31.

Argues that presentations of the problem of evil entail certain notions of the way God has acted or failed to act. Walker has argued elsewhere ("Miracles and Coincidences" (*Sophia* 22 [1983], 15-28; "Miracles and Violations" (*International Journal for Philosophy of Religion* 13 [1982], 103-108) that there is no logical contradiction in holding two views about how God could prevent evils: God can intervene to contravene laws of nature, and apparently natural remissions of diseases can be construed as God's actions. Walker argues that there is no need to seek out divine reasons for events (diseases, etc.) which have natural causes, and he argues that attributing divine intervention to apparently natural healing is vacuous and problematic.

608.   Wijkman, Anders, and Lloyd Timberlake. *Natural Disasters: Acts of God or Acts of Man?* Philadelphia, PA: New Society Publishers, 1988.

Contends that so-called natural disasters can be understood to be increasingly caused by human beings. Droughts and floods are typical examples. Tropical windstorms may seem to be solely "acts of God," yet their destructive effects are increased by human acts of deforestation and inadequate communication systems. Likewise, earthquakes are more destructive in third world countries (as are all natural disasters), due to houses that are less adequately constructed than those in industrialized countries, and other such human factors.

609.   Wiles, Maurice F. "Farrer's Concept of Double Agency." *Theology* 84 (1981): 243-249.

Response to David Galilee ("Letter," *Theology* 78 [1975], 554-555), and Brian Hebblethwaite ("Providence and Divine Action" [#563]). Wiles argues that Farrer's concept of double agency does not succeed in reconciling divine and human agency. Since Farrer admits that we cannot know the modality of divine action, Wiles argues that we cannot then define its relation to our finite human acting. Farrer's concept of double agency is close to the biblical account, yet he does little to help us understand the biblical language. Farrer's understanding of divine agen- cy is so distantly analogical to our action that it is unconvincing. [See also Wiles's *God's Action in the World*. London, 1986, and Vincent Brümmer's critique of Wiles and Farrer, "Farrer, Wiles and the Causal Joint," *Modern Theology* 8 (1992), 1-14. Brümmer refutes the use of double agency in Farrer and Wiles, and proposes that the alternative view—God is the agent of human actions—is coherent, and does full justice to the integrity of human action.]

II   Publications on Animal Suffering [Selected]

610.   Adams, David, and Margaret Rose. "Evidence for Pain and Suffering in Other Animals." *Animal Experimentation: The Consensus Changes*. Edited by Gill Langley. New York: Chapman and Hall, 1989: 42-71.

611.   Amory, Cleveland. *Man Kind? Incredible War on Wildlife*. New York: Harper and Row, 1974.

612.   Barad, Judith. "The Possibility of Settling the Issue of Animal Suffering on Rational Grounds." *Between Species* 4 (1988): 251-254.

613.   Belaief, Lynne. *Toward a Whiteheadian Ethics*. Lanham, MD: University Press of America, 1984.

614.   Benson, John. "Duty and the Beast." *Philosophy* 53 (1978): 529-549.

615.   Betty, L. Stafford. "Making Sense of Animal Pain: An Environmental Theodicy." *Faith and Philosophy* 9 (1992): 65-85.

616.   Birch, Charles. *Nature and God*. Philadelphia, PA: Westminster Press, 1966. [See also Birch, *A Purpose for Everything: Religion in a Postmodern Worldview*. Mystic, CN: Twenty-Third Publications, 1990.]

617.   Birch, Charles, and John B. Cobb. *The Liberation of Life*. Denton, TX: Environmental Ethics Books, 1990.

618.   Bube, Paul C. *Ethics in John Cobb's Process Theology*. Atlanta, GA: Scholars Press, 1988.

619.   Callicott, J. Baird, "Animal Liberation: A Triangular Affair." *Environmental Ethics* 2 (1980): 311-338. [See also Callicott's "Animal Liberation and Environmental Ethics: Back Together Again." *In Defense of the Land Ethic: Essays*

in Environmental Philosophy. Albany, NY: State University of New York Press, 1988: 115-174].

620. Carruthers, Peter. "On the Possibility of 'Non-Conscious' Experience." *Journal of Philosophy* 86 (1989): 258-269.

621. Causey, Ann S. "On the Morality of Hunting." *Environmental Ethics* 11 (1989): 327-343.

622. Cauthen, Kenneth. *Process Ethics: A Constructive System*. New York and Toronto, ON: Edwin Mellen Press, 1984.

623. Cave, George P. "On the Irreplaceability of Animal Life." *Ethics and Animals* 3 (1982): 106-116.

624. ———. "Animals, Heidegger, and the Right to Life." *Environmental Ethics* 4 (1982): 249-254. [Cave's references to Martin Heidegger focus on Heidegger's *Being and Time*. Translated by John Macquarrie and Edward Robinson. New York: Harper and Row, 1962. Cave contends that Heidegger offered radical new interpretations of the "Being" of inanimate objects and of humans, but remained silent on the "Being" of non-human animals. Cave argues the case for non-human animals, using Heidegger's categories: while Heidegger's analysis seems to confer unique ontological status to human beings, much of the analysis can be extended to non-human animals.]

625. Clark, Stephen R.L. *The Moral Status of Animals*. Oxford: The Clarendon Press, 1977.

626. ———. "Animal Wrongs." *Analysis* 38 (1978): 147-149.

627. ———. "How to Calculate the Greater Good." *Animals' Rights—A Symposium*. Edited by David Patterson and Richard D. Ryder. London: Centaur Press, 1979: 96-105.

628. Cobb, John B. *Is It Too Late? A Theology of Ecology*. Beverly Hills, CA: Bruce, 1972.

629. ———. "Beyond Anthropocentrism in Ethics and Religion." *On the Fifth Day*. Edited by R. Morris and Michael Fox. Washington, DC: Acropolis Books, 1978: 137-153.

630. ———. "Process Theology and Environmental Crisis." *Journal of Religion* 60 (1980): 440-458.

631. ———. "Christian Existence in a World of Limits." *Environmental Ethics* 1 (1979): 149-158.

632. ———. *Matters of Life and Death*. Louisville, KY: Westminster/John Knox Press, 1991.

633. Day, David. *The Doomsday Book of Animals: A Natural History of Vanished Species*. New York: Viking Press, 1981.

634. Dennis, S., and R. Melzack. "Perspectives on Phylogenetic Evolution of Pain Expression." *Animal Pain: Perception and Alleviation*. Edited by R.L. Kitchell and H.H. Erickson. Bethesda, MD: American Physiological Society, 1983.

635. Devine, Philip E. "The Moral Basis of Vegetarianism." *Philosophy* 53 (1978): 481-505.

636.   Diamond, Cora. "Eating Meat and Eating People." *Philosophy* 53 (1978): 465-479.

637.   Dixon, Bernard. "Animal Liberation: Time for a New Approach." *Animals' Rights: A Symposium.* Edited by David Patterson and Richard D. Ryder. London: Centaur Press, 1979: 178-186.

638.   Dombrowski, Daniel A. *Hartshorne and the Metaphysics of Animal Rights.* Albany, NY: State University of New York Press, 1988.

639.   Donnelley, Strachan and Kathleen Nolan, editors. *Animals, Science and Ethics. Hastings Center Report,* 1990: 1-32.

640.   Ehrlich, Paul, and Anne Ehrlich. *Extinction: The Causes and Consequences of the Disappearance of Species.* New York: Random House, 1981.

641.   Feinberg, Joel. "Can Animals Have Rights?" *Animal Rights and Human Obligations.* Edited by Tom Regan and Peter Singer. Englewood Cliffs, NJ: Prentice-Hall, 1976.

642.   ———. "The Rights of Animals and Unborn Generations." *Philosophy and Environmental Crisis.* Edited by William T. Blackstone. Athens, GA: University of Georgia, 1974. [This book contains also essays by Eugene P. Odum, "Environmental Ethic and the Attitude Revolution"; William Blackstone, "Ethics and Ecology"; Charles Hartshorne, "The Environmental Results of Technology"; Walter H. O'Briant, "Man, Nature and the History of Philosophy"; Nicholas Rescher, "The Environmental Crisis and the Quality of Life"; etc.]

643.   Fern, Richard L. "Human Uniqueness as a Guide to Resolving Conflicts Between Animal and Human Interests." *Ethics and Animals* 2 (1981): 7-21.

644.   Fox, Michael Allen. *The Case for Animal Experimentation: An Evolutionary and Ethical Perspective.* Berkeley, CA: University of California Press, 1986.

645.   ———. "Animal Liberation: A Critique." *Ethics* 88 (1978): 106-118.

646.   ———. "Animal Suffering and Rights: A Reply to Singer and Regan." *Ethics* 88 (1978): 134-138.

647.   ———. "Animal Experimentation: A Philosopher's Changing Views." *Between Species* 3 (1987): 55-60.

648.   ———. "Animal Rights and Nature Liberation." *Animals' Rights—A Symposium.* Edited by David Patterson and Richard D. Ryder. London: Centaur Press, 1979: 48-60.

649.   Frey, Raymond G. "Animal Rights." *Analysis* 37 (1977): 186-189.

650.   ———. "What Has Sentiency to do with the Possession of Rights?" *Animals' Rights: A Symposium.* Edited by David Patterson and Richard D. Ryder. London: Centaur Press, 1979: 106-111.

651.   ———. *Interests and Rights: The Case Against Animals.* Oxford: Oxford University Press, 1980.

652.   ———. *Rights, Killing, and Suffering: Moral Vegetarianism and Applied Ethics.* Oxford: Blackwell, 1983.

653. ——. "Pain, Amelioration and the Choice of Tactics." *Morality in Practice*. Edited by James P. Sterba. Belmont, CA: Wadsworth, 1984. Second Edition 1988: 335-344.

654. ——. "Moral Standing, The Value of Lives, and Speciesism." *Between Species* 4 (1988): 191-201.

655. Godlovitch, Roslind. "Animals and Morals." *Philosophy* 46 (1971): 23-33.

656. Godlovitch, Stanley, and Roslind Godlovitch and John Harris, editors. *Animals, Men and Morals: An Inquiry into the Maltreatment of Non-Humans*. London: Gollancz, and New York: Taplinger, 1971.

657. Granberg-Michaelson, Welsey. *A Worldly Spirituality: The Call to Take Care of the Earth*. San Francisco, CA: Harper and Row, 1984.

658. Gray, James R. *Process Ethics*. Lanham, MD: University Press of America, 1983.

659. Griffin, Donald. *Animal Thinking*. Cambridge, MA: Harvard University Press, 1984.

660. Hall, Douglas. *Imaging God: Dominion as Stewardship*. Grand Rapids, MI: Eerdmans, 1986.

661. Harris, John. "Killing for Food." *Animals' Rights: A Symposium*. Edited by David Patterson and Richard D. Ryder. London: Centaur Press, 1979: 117-121.

662. Harrison, Peter. "Theodicy and Animal Pain." *Philosophy* 64 (1989): 79-92.

663. ——. "Do Animals Feel Pain?" *Philosophy* 66 (1991): 25-40.

664. Harrison, Ruth. *Animal Machines*. London: Stuart, 1964.

665. Hartshorne, Charles. *Born to Sing: A World Interpretation of Bird Song*. Bloomington, IN: Indiana University Press, 1973.

666. ——. "Foundations for a Humane Ethics: What Human Beings Have in Common with Other Higher Animals." *On the Fifth Day: Animal Rights and Human Ethics*. Washington, DC: Acropolis Books, 1978.

667. Haworth, Lawrence. "Rights, Wrongs and Animals." *Ethics* 88 (1978): 95-105.

668. James, Susan. "The Duty to Relieve Suffering." *Ethics* 92 (1982): 4-21.

669. Joad, C.E.M., and C.S. Lewis. "The Pains of Animals: A Problem in Theology." *God of the Docks: Essays on Theology and Ethics*. Edited by C.S. Lewis. Grand Rapids, MI: Eerdmans, 1970: *Chapter 20*. [Originally published in *Month* (1950), 95-104. Also published in *Animals and Christianity: A Book of Readings*. Edited by Tom Regan and Andrew Linzey. New York: Crossroad, 1990, 55-62].

670. Joranson, Philip N., and Ken Butigan. *Cry of the Environment: Rebuilding the Christian Creation Tradition*. Sante Fe, NM: Bear and Co., 1984.

671. Kaplan, Helmut B. "Do Animals Have Souls?" *Between Species* 7 (1991): 13-17.

672. Kingston, A. Richard. "Theodicy and Animal Welfare." *Theology* 70 (1967): 482-488. [Also published in *Animals and Christianity: A Book of Readings*. Edited by Tom Regan and Andrew Linzey. New York: Crossroad, 1990, 71-78].

673. Linzey, Andrew. "Animals," *The Westminster Dictionary of Christian Ethics*. Edited by James F. Childress and John Macquarrie. Philadelphia, PA: Westminster

Press, 1986: 28-33. [See also Linzey's *Christianity and the Rights of Animals*. New York: Crossroad, 1987].

674. Lockwood, Jeffrey. "Not to Harm a Fly: Our Ethical Obligations to Insects." *Between Species* 4 (1988): 204-211.

675. Lockwood, Michael. "Singer on Killing and the Preference for Life." *Inquiry* 22 (1979): 157-170.

676. Machan, Tibor R. "Some Doubts About Animal Rights." *Journal of Value Inquiry* 19 (1985): 73-76.

677. Mackie, John L. "The Law of the Jungle." *Philosophy* 53 (1978): 455-464.

678. Magel, C.R. *A Bibliography of Animal Rights and Related Matters*. Washington, DC: University Press of America, 1981.

679. Martin, Michael. "A Critique of Moral Vegetarianism." *Reason Papers* 3 (1976): 13-43.

680. Matthews, Gareth B. "Animals and the Unity of Psychology." *Philosophy* 53 (1978): 437-454.

681. McDaniel, Jay. "Physical Nature as Creative and Sentient." *Environmental Ethics* 5 (1983): 219-317.

682. ———. "A Feeling for the Organism: Christian Spirituality as Openness to Fellow Creatures." *Environmental Ethics* 8 (1986): 33-46.

683. ———. *Of God and Pelicans: A Theology of Reverence for Life*. Louisville, KY: Westminster/John Knox Press, 1989.

684. McFarland, David. "Pain." *The Oxford Companion to Animal Behaviour*. Edited by David McFarland. Oxford: Oxford University Press, 1981.

685. Merchant, Carolyn. *The Death of Nature: Women, Ecology, and the Scientific Revolution*. San Francisco, CA: Harper and Row, 1985.

686. Midgley, Mary. "Animals and the Problem of Evil." *Chapter 2* of *Beast and Man*. Edited by Mary Midgley. Ithaca, NY: Cornell University Press, 1978: 25-49.

687. ———. *Animals and Why They Matter*. New York: Penguin Books, 1983, and Athens, GA: University of Georgia Press, 1984.

688. ———. "Are You an Animal?" *Animal Experimentation: The Consensus Changes*. Edited by Gill Langley. New York: Chapman and Hall, 1989: 1-18.

689. Moltmann, Jürgen. *God in Creation: A New Theology of Creation and the Spirit of God*. San Francisco, CA: Harper and Row, 1985. Translated by Margaret Kohl.

690. Narveson, Jan. "Animal Rights." *Canadian Journal of Philosophy* 7 (1977): 161-178.

691. ———. "Animal Rights Revisited." *Morality in Practice*. Edited by James P. Sterba. Belmont, CA: Wadsworth, 1984. Second edition, 1988: 327-334.

692. Norman, Richard, and Leslie Pickering Francis. "Some Animals Are More Equal than Others." *Philosophy* 53 (1978): 507-527.

693.   Ost, D.E. "The Case Against Animal Rights." *Southern Journal of Philosophy* 24 (1986): 365-373.

694.   Paske, Gerald H. "Why Animals Have No Right to Life: A Response to Regan" [#702]. *Australasian Journal of Philosophy* 66 (1988): 512-516.

695.   Passmore, John. *Man's Responsibility for Nature*. London: Duckworth, 1974.

696.   Prigogine, Ilya, and Isabelle Strengers. *Order Out of Chaos: Man's New Dialog with Nature*. New York: Bantam Books, 1984.

697.   Putman, Daniel. "Tragedy and Nonhumans." *Environmental Ethics* 11 (1989): 345-353.

698.   Rachels, James. "Do Animals Have a Right to Liberty?" *Animal Rights and Human Obligations*. Edited by Tom Regan and Peter Singer. Englewood Cliffs, NJ: Prentice-Hall, 1976.

699.   ———. "On the Right Not to be Made to Suffer Gratuitously." *Canadian Journal of Philosophy* 10 (1980): 473-478.

700.   ———. "A Reply to VanDeVeer" [#740]. *Animal Rights and Human Obligations*. Edited by Peter Singer and Tom Regan. Englewood Cliffs, NJ: Prentice-Hall, 1976: 230-232.

701.   Regan, Tom. "The Moral Basis of Vegetarianism." *Canadian Journal of Philosophy* 5 (1975): 181-214.

702.   ———. "Do Animals Have a Right to Life?" *Animal Rights and Human Obligations*. Edited by Tom Regan and Peter Singer. Englewood Cliffs, NJ: Prentice-Hall, 1976.

703.   ———. "Narveson on Egoism and the Rights of Animals." *Canadian Journal of Philosophy* 7 (1977): 179-186.

704.   ———. "Fox's Critique of Animal Liberation." *Ethics* 88 (1978): 126-133. [see #645.]

705.   ———. "An Examination and Defense of One Argument Concerning Animal Rights." *Inquiry* 22 (1979): 189-219.

706.   ———. "Exploring the Idea of Animal Rights." *Animals' Rights—A Symposium*. Edited by David Patterson and Richard D. Ryder. London: Centaur Press, 1979: 73-86.

707.   ———. "Vegetarianism, Utilitarianism, and Animal Rights." *Philosophy and Public Affairs* 9 (1980): 305-324.

708.   ———. "Cruelty, Kindness, and Unnecessary Suffering." *Philosophy* 55 (1980): 532-541.

709.   ———. *All That Dwell Therein: Essays on Animals and Environmental Ethics*. Berkeley, CA: University of California Press, 1982.

710.   ———. "The Case for Animal Rights." *Morality in Practice*. Edited by James P. Sterba. Belmont, CA: Wadsworth, 1984. Second edition, 1988: 319-326.

711.   ———. "Ill-Gotten Gains." *Animal Experimentation: The Consensus Changes*. Edited by Gill Langley. New York: Chapman and Hall, 1989: 19-41.

712. Reynolds, Charles H. "Somatic Ethics: Joy and Adventure in the Embodied Moral Life." *John Cobb's Theology in Process*. Edited by David R. Griffin and Thomas J.J. Altizer. Philadelphia, PA: Westminster Press, 1977: 116-132.

713. Rickaby, Joseph. "Of the So-Called Rights of Animals." *Animal Rights and Human Responsibility*. Edited by Peter Singer and Tom Regan. Englewood Cliffs, NJ: Prentice-Hall, 1976: 173-178.

714. Rollin, Bernard E. *Animal Rights and Human Morality*. Buffalo, NY: Prometheus Press, 1981.

715. Rolston, Homes. "Values in Nature." *Environmental Ethics* 3 (1981): 113-128.

716. ———. "Are Values in Nature Subjective or Objective?" *Environmental Ethics* 4 (1982): 125-151.

717. ———. *Philosophy Gone Wild: Essays in Environmental Ethics*. Buffalo, NY: Prometheus Press, 1986.

718. ———. *Science and Religion: A Critical Survey*. New York: Random House, 1987. [See also Rolston's *Environmental Ethics: Duties to and Values in the Natural World*. Philadelphia, PA: Temple University Press, 1988.]

719. Rowan, Andrew, and David De Grazia. "Pain, Suffering, and Anxiety in Animals and Humans." *Theoretical Medicine* 12 (1991): 193-211.

720. Ryder, Richard Douley. *Victims of Science: The Use of Animals in Research*. London: Davis-Poynter, 1975.

721. ———. "Speciesism in the Laboratory." *In Defense of Animals*. Edited by Peter Singer. San Francisco, CA: Harper and Row, 1979: 25-42.

722. ———. "The Structure Against Speciesism." *Animals' Rights: A Symposium*. Edited by David Patterson and Richard D. Ryder. London: Centaur Press, 1979: 3-14.

723. Santmire, H. Paul. *The Travail of Nature: The Ambiguous Ecological Promise of Christian Theology*. Philadelphia, PA: Fortress Press, 1985.

724. Sapontzis, Steve F. "Predation." *Ethics and Animals* 5 (1984): 27-38.

725. ———. "Everyday Morality and Animal Rights." *Between Species* 4 (1987): 107-127.

726. Singer, Peter. "Animal Liberation." *The New York Review of Books*. April 5, 1973: 17.

727. ———. "All Animals are Equal." *Animal Rights and Human Obligations*. Edited by Tom Regan and Peter Singer. Englewood Cliffs, NJ: Prentice-Hall, 1976. [Collection of essays about animal rights from the Old Testament to the present.]

728. ———. *Animal Liberation: A New Ethics for Our Treatment of Animals*. New York: The New York Review, 1975.

729. ———. "The Parable of the Fox and the Unliberated Animals." *Ethics* 88 (1978): 122.

730. ———. "Killing Humans and Killing Animals." *Inquiry* 22 (1979): 145-156.

731. ———. Editor. *In Defense of Animals*. New York: Blackwell, 1985.

732.   ——. "All Animals are Equal." *Morality in Practice*. Edited by James P. Sterba. Belmont, CA: Wadsworth, 1984. Second edition, 1988: 307-318.

733.   ——. "Comment on Frey's 'Moral Standing, The Value of Lives, and Speciesism'" [#654]. *Between Species* 4 (1988): 202-203.

734.   Sperling, Susan. *Animal Liberators: Research and Morality*. Berkeley, CA: University of California Press, 1988.

735.   Stafford, Tim. "Animal Lib." *Christianity Today* 28 (1990): 19-23.

736.   Stone, Christopher. "Should Trees Have Standing? Toward Legal Rights for Natural Objects." *Southern California Law Review* 45 (1972): 450-501.

737.   Stubbs, Anne C. "Morality and Our Treatment of Animals." *Philosophical Studies* 27 (1980): 29-39.

738.   Thomas, Lewis. *The Lives of a Cell: Notes of a Biology Watcher*. New York: Viking Press, 1974.

739.   Turner, E.S. *All Heaven in a Rage*. London: Michael Joseph, 1964. [Documents events the history of the fight against cruelty to animals in Britain.]

740.   Van De Veer, Donald. "Defending Animals by Appeals to Rights." *Animal Rights and Human Obligations*. Edited by Peter Singer and Tom Regan. Englewood Cliffs, NJ: Prentice-Hall, 1976: 224-229. [See the response by James Rachels, "A Reply to Van De Veer," 230-232 [#700]. See also Van De Veer's "Animal Suffering." *Canadian Journal of Philosophy* 10 (1980), 463-471.]

741.   Vitali, Theodore R. "Sports Hunting: Moral or Immoral?" *Environmental Ethics* 12 (1990): 69-82.

742.   Warren, Karen. "Feminism and Ecology: Making Connections." *Environmental Ethics* 9 (1987): 3-20.

743.   Warren, Mary Ann. "Rights of the Nonhuman World." *Environmental Philosophy*. Edited by Robert Elliot and Arran Gare. University Park, PA: State University of Pennsylvania Press, 1983: 109-134.

744.   Wennberg, Robert. "Animal Suffering and the Problem of Evil." *Christian Scholar's Review* 21 (1991): 120-140.

745.   Wenz, Peter S. "Civil Liberties and Cruelty to Animals." *Philosophical Forum* 19 (1988): 309-316.

746.   Willard, L. Duane. "About Animals 'Having' Rights." *Journal of Value Inquiry* 16 (1982): 177-187.

747.   Wilson, Edmund. *Sociobiology: The New Synthesis*. Cambridge, MA: Harvard University Press, 1975. [Contains extensive bibliography.]

748.   Zimmerman, Michael E. "Feminism, Deep Ecology, and Environmental Ethics." *Environmental Ethics* 9 (1987): 21-44. [See also Zimmerman, "Toward a Heideggerian Ethos for Radical Environmentalism," *Environmental Ethics* 5 (1983), 99-131.]

Chapter 5

Hick's Irenaean Theodicy

The theodicy of John Hick has been a major influence on philosophical and theological writings since the appearance of his classic, *Evil and the God of Love*, in 1966.[1] The references to Hick's publications *(Section I)* and to the discussions they have evoked *(Section II)* are restricted to those which deal directly with Hick's theodicy. I should note (again) that *this bibliography has not cross-listed items*; if this had been done and all of the publications which make reference to Hick's theodicy, for example, had been listed in this chapter as well as in other chapters, this chapter would be considerably larger by several hundred items and the bibliography would have been increased significantly in length. It is an understatement of significant proportions to note that references to Hick's writings virtually permeate the literature on theodicy during the past two decades. Whether or not one accepts Hick's theodicy, all must acknowledge that, like Mackie and Flew three decades ago, Hick's work is seminal and has revitalized and redefined the theodicy issue.[2] In a poor paraphrase of Kant, I would suggest that Hick has awakened many of us from our Augustinan slumber. Perhaps more accurately, it has been Alfred North Whitehead who has awaken us, although Hick's Irenaean theodicy has been highly influential. My own awakening had begun in graduate school in 1972, with the discovery of the writings of Whitehead and Hartshorne and the process philosophy and theology they induced. Hick's theodicy has many similarities with process theodicy, although Hick's few assessments of process theodicy have attacked its supposed "elitism" and its "finite God." Process thinkers find Hick's God far too traditional, in the sense that Hick's God is conceived as having *all* the power, even though this power is never used to supersede the freedom of creatures. The process God does *not* have all the power, since creatures—*as such*—have some power ("creativity"), however infinitesimal *(see Chapter 6)*.[3]

Hick's theodicy, which utilizes and develops insights from the writings of St. Irenaeus (c. 130-202), constitutes the first clearly defined alternative to the traditional Augustinian—Thomistic theodicy which has dominated western Christian theodicy. Hick himself acknowledged the nineteenth century theologian, Friedrick Schleiermacher, as the first to turn from the Augustinian theodicy.[4] Hick, however, was the first to develop the alternative "Irenaean" theodicy systematically. He has astutely pointed out that the Augustinian theodicy "is so familiar that it is commonly thought of as *the* Christian view of ... [humans] and ... [our] sinful plight."[5] Yet, due largely to Hick's influence, it is now common parlance to refer to both Augustinian and Irenaean theodicies (as well as process theodicy) as the "major types" of theodicies. Hick argues that God could not create creatures who were both perfect and free—at least, with respect to God. "In order to be a person, exercising some measure of genuine freedom," he explains, "the creature must be brought into existence, not in the immediate divine presence, but at a 'distance' from God."[6] In response to the celebrated criticisms of *John Mackie* and *Antony Flew*, who argued that God could have created us as morally perfect and also as free creatures who could have used that freedom solely for good, Hick's position is that virtues hard won by moral agents are "intrinsically more valuable" than virtues created within us ready made."[7] Hick concedes to Mackie and Flew, in other words, that God could have created us as morally perfect and free, but (like Ninian Smart, and others) Hick makes the value judgment that such a creation would be of less intrinsic worth than a creation in which we freely worked out our moral perfection (soul-making). In a somewhat different context, Hick elaborates: to be free to choose our actions with respect to other creatures would not necessarily rule out a divine determinism of our acts, but to be free with respect to God would rule out such a divine causative force—if that freedom is to have any real value to God. Many critics have found this too much of a concession to Mackie and Flew.[8]

It is by means of the Irenaean—Schleiermacherian hypothesis that God created an imperfect creation (in contradistinction to Augustinian theodicy's perfect creation which inexplicably went wrong with the "fall" of Adam, Hick argues for the validity of a *free will defense* as a solution to the problem of *moral evil*.[9] The Augustinian—Thomistic version of the free will defense, Hick argues, is *morally*, *logically* and *scientifically* objectionable,[10] whereas his version of a free will defense escapes these problems; it is not muddled with the traditional views of the Adamic myth of the "fall" (taken more or less literally as the source of all evil), predestination, divine causative power, and original sin. Process philosophers and theologians, in their criticisms of Hick, to be sure, argue that Hick's God is still the traditional omnipotent God who could, but will not, take away some or all of the world's evil. As such, Hick's free will defense is but a "hybrid free will defense,"[11] since Hick's God is still responsible for the world's evil and, as such, could have disallowed these evils. Hick, in turn, has argued against what he considers to be the "limited" God proposed by process theism as an alternative, and he has suggested that there are good reasons why God has not and will not intervene intermittently to overwhelm human free will, even though he insists that God could do so.

The solution to *physical evil*, according to Hick,[12] is that such evil serves as the environment for human soul-making. In a world devoid both of dangers to be avoided and rewards to be won, there could be no soul-making. The world, despite its imperfection (indeed, because of them) is "perfect" in the sense that it is a perfect environment for human beings to develop spiritual qualities.

Animal suffering is part of this harsh environment, and a prime example of physical evil.[13] Many critics of Hick's theodicy have found him far too distanced from the plight of animals and condemned his theodicy as too egocentric, a charge which could apply (I would suggest) to most of traditional theodicy. Hick is aware of this criticism and has responded to it, as he has to many other criticisms of his theodicy. To the charge, for example, that there is too much *gratuitous evil* in the world for theists to justify belief in God—the criticism which Hick admits is the most difficult to answer[14]—Hick responds that the lack of gratuitous evil would be an even greater problem. If good and evil were rewarded and punished in this world in direct proportion to the action of moral agents, there would be no gratuitous evil; yet, the entire soul-making process would be jeopardized and the basis of morality undercut: we would act for good ends because of the guaranteed reward, rather than for the sake of goodness.[15]

Hick proposes a *universal salvation* for all people. Such will be gained in an immortal *post mortem* world wherein God's efforts to urge us to create our spiritual characters will continue endlessly until the task is accomplished.[16] Hick's writings on "eschatological verification" and his study of immortality beliefs in various cultures and religions are relevant to this aspect of his theodicy. Some critics regard the appeal to heaven as inappropriate for a rational theodicy,[17] yet it is essential for Hick's theodicy, since God's creation of an imperfect world can be justified only if there is universal salvation for the imperfect creatures who must struggle and suffer on the road to spiritual perfection.

Hick's theodicy has been cited by numerous opponents and critics. One of the earliest of these critics was *Stanley Kane*, whose critique is answered in the second edition of Hick's *Evil and the God of Love* (1978). Included also is a recent book-length critique of Hick by Robert Mesle, *John Hick's Theodicy* (St. Martin's Press, 1991), a publication that conveniently contains both a reprinted portion of one of Hick's clearest statements of his theodicy (originally published in *Encountering Evil*, edited by Stephen Davis), and Hick's informative response to Mesle's criticisms. Included also is *Evil and the Mystics' God*, the published version of Michael Stoeber's dissertation (University of Toronto Press, 1992). The critical articles by *Stanley Kane, Roland Puccetti, Keith Ward, Peter Hare* and *Edward Madden, Frederick Sontag, John Roth, Stephen Davis, David Griffin*, and others, are annotated in this chapter. Other references to Hick's theodicy are scattered liberally throughout the other annotated chapters.[18]

Notes

1. For some of the most relevant dissertations on Hick's theodicy, see *Appendix E*. See, in particular, Myra Beth Macke, *John Hick's Theodicy* (Duke, 1980); Robert Rainwater, *The Theodicy of John Hick* (Southern Baptist, 1980); Douglas Geivett, *A Critical Evaluation of John Hick's Theodicy in Defense of the Augustinian Tradition* (MA Thesis, Gonzaga University, 1985) and his *The Logic of the Problem of Evil* (University of Southern California, 1991); Jay Robinson, *Personal Eschatology: An Analysis of Contemporary Christian Interpretations* (Southern Baptist Theological Union, 1990); Joseph Thanavelil Kurian, *Language, Faith and Meaning: A Critical Study of John Hick's Philosophy of Religion: Towards a Metaphysical Approach to Philosophical Theology* (Pontificia Universitas Gregorian, 1990); etc.

2. The work of *Alvin Plantinga* on the free will defense is also seminal. So too is the work of process theologian, *David Griffin*. Citing an author as "seminal" is not to be done lightly. The select number of others who qualify for this distinction are found in the annotated sections of this bibliography.

3. Hick's work in theology has been seminal on a number of fronts besides theodicy: his eschatological verification theory, for example, and his work on the general status of religious belief; his important work on immortality theories; and his most recent work in world religions and defining the nature of religion as such; etc.

4. See Hick's *Evil and the God of Love*. Second edition (San Francisco, CA: Harper and Row, 1978), *Chapter 10*.

5. John Hick, *Evil and the God of Love*, 202.

6. John Hick, "An Irenaean Theodicy," *Encountering Evil*. Edited by Stephen Davis (Atlanta, GA: John Knox Press, 1981), 43.

7. Hick, "An Irenaean Theodicy," 44.

8. See, for example, David Griffin's critique of Hick in *God, Power and Evil* (Philadelphia, PA: Westminster, 1976 and Lanham, MD: University Press of America, 1990) and *Evil Revisited* (Albany, NY: State University of New York Press, 1991). Hick's discussions of Mackie and Flew are found in *Evil and the God of Love*, 265-279; and in his "An Irenaean Theodicy," 43-44. Ninian Smart, in "Omnipotence, Evil and Supermen," *Philosophy* (1961), argues that the proposition that "'God might have created men wholly good' is without intelligible content." Hick approves of Smart's attack on the "Utopia thesis" (the

claim that humans could have been created wholly good): see *Evil and the God of Love*, 269-270.

9.   See Hick, *Evil and the God of Love*, *Chapter 13*, "Moral Evil"; and his "An Irenaean Theodicy," 41-45; etc.

10.   Hick's argument, in brief, is that it is *morally* objectionable for an entire species to be punished for the sins of the first human pair; it is *logically* objectionable that perfect creatures (Adam and Eve) could sin in the first place; and it is *scientifically* objectionable that sin and suffering came about because of the first two human beings.

11.   See David Griffin's critical studies of Hick's theodicy in his *God, Power and Evil* and in his *Evil Revisited*. See also Hare and Madden's critical study of Hick's theodicy in their *Evil and the Concept of God* (Springfield, IL: C.C. Thomas, 1968).

12.   See Hick's chapter in *Encountering Evil*, "An Irenaean Theodicy," 45-48; and in his *Evil and the God of Love*, *Chapters 14 and 15* ("Pain" and "Suffering").

13.   See Hick's discussion in *Evil and the God of Love*, 309-317.

14.   See *Evil and the God of Love*, 376 and 385-386; etc. Critics, like Kane and Hare and Madden have argued that the price paid for spiritual growth is too high. There is too much gratuitous evil. Hick refers to this as the "gravest of all challenges to a Christian faith in God," and as "the greatest difficult in the way of ... [his Irenaean] theodicy."

15.   Hick argues also that the amount of evil is *relative*: if God were to eliminate the worst evils, those evils which remained would be considered the worst evils. No matter how far this elimination process extended, the situation would remain the same. Indeed, if the process were extended the point would be reached where "the world would be free of all natural evil," and this would be a world which could no longer elicit the necessary moral and spiritual growth intended by God in the soul-making process. See Hick's discussion in *Evil and the God of Love* and in "An Irenaean Theodicy."

16.   See Hick's discussion in *Evil and the God of Love*, *Chapter 16* ("The Kingdom of God and the Will of God"); and in his "An Irenaean Theodicy," 51-52; etc.

17.   Terrence Tilley, for example, argues that a universal salvation "seeks to explain the present obscurity [the problem of why God permits evil] by an appeal to a future even more obscure" ("The Use and Abuse of Theodicy," *Horizons* [1984]). Indeed, the appeal to heaven in all theodicies seems to me to succumb to this same problem. At best, it is an appeal to what *might* be a future justification for present evils, but it hardly *explains* (nor indeed do I think it could *justify*) the present evils. Hick's understanding of the afterlife, to be sure, is complex, and is not meant so much as a justification of evil or even as an explanation of evil, as much as it is a necessary tenet in his overall theodicy: if God has created an imperfect world, albeit a perfect environment for soul-making, it would be the ultimate evil if imperfect creatures were to live and die in suffering and misery, without eventually obtaining spiritual fulfilment and perfection.

18.   For the criticisms of Hick's theodicy by Griffin, Davis, Roth and Sontag (and Hick's responses), see *Encountering Evil*, edited by Stephen Davis. Griffin, of course, has published criticisms of Hick's theodicy elsewhere. Please note that publications which refer to Hick's theodicy but are not included in this chapter are indeed numerous. Those which have not been listed in this present chapter are listed elsewhere in the annotated chapters.

I   Hick's Publications on Theodicy

749.   Hick, John. *Philosophy of Religion*. Englewood Cliffs, NJ: Prentice-Hall, 1963. Fourth edition, 1990.

The section on the problem of evil acknowledges Augustinian, Irenaean and process theodicy as the three main options. The first edition did not so acknowledge the latter, which Hick regards as espousing a limited God. [See Hick's contribution to Davis's *Encountering Evil* [#763], and Griffin's response [#780]. See also Griffin's response to Hick's charge of what he regards as "elitism" in process theodicy, in Griffin's *Evil Revisited* [#873].]

750.   ———. *Evil and the God of Love*. New York: Harper and Row, 1966. Second edition, 1977. Republished, New York: Macmillan, 1985.

Hick's classic, most detailed statement of the problem of evil. The second edition deleted a chapter on Austin Farrer and added a chapter *(Chapter 17)* responding to criticisms of his position (largely by Stanley Kane [#785, #786]). The first eight chapters outline and critique the Augustinian theodicy as it is presented by Augustine, Aquinas and Journet, Calvin, Barth, and Leibniz. The final nine chapters present the Irenaean theodicy as it is portrayed in Irenaeus *(Chapter 9)*, Schleiermacher *(Chapter 10)* and by Hick's constructive, detailed theodicy *(Chapters 11-16)*. Hick proposes the justification for both moral evils and natural evils, the latter including animal suffering. A chapter is devoted to a defense, the nature and the necessity of the afterlife *(Chapter 16)*, a theme developed at great length in Hick's *Death and Eternal Life* [#760].

751.   ———. "The Problem of Evil." *Encyclopedia of Philosophy*. Paul Edwards, Editor in Chief. New York: Macmillan and Free Press, 1967: 136-141.

Outlines the problem of evil as it is presented in Augustine (the privation of good, the aesthetic theory), Aquinas, Luther, Calvin, and Leibniz. Hick criticizes this traditional "Augustinian" theodicy for its account of the origin and final disposition of moral evil. He argues that to attribute the origin of evil to the wilful crime of perfect beings is to assert that evil has created itself *ex nihilo*, a sheer contradiction. The final disposition of evil, moreover, is mired in contradiction: if God wishes to save all human creatures but is unable to do so, God would be limited in power; yet if God does not desire to save all human beings, God would be limited in goodness. Hick then outlines his "Irenaean" theodicy, noting how it overcomes these problems and others in the traditional Augustinian theodicy. He explains his solutions to moral and physical evil and, in a brief section at the end, notes that animal suffering has been addressed in various ways, including both the speculative Augustinian view that Satan's fall perverted all of creation and the eastern view that animals are part of the reincarnation cycle of rebirths and will eventually work their way to the human level and salvation. Hick concludes with a brief bibliography of historical theodicy, citing a handful of items under each the following headings: Plotinus and Augustine, Aquinas, Leibniz, Hellenistic theodicy, Jewish writings, nineteenth-century studies, twentieth-century discussions (Augustinian, Irenaean, Philosophical, and Theological).

752.   ———. "God, Evil and Mystery." *Religious Studies* 3 (1968): 539-546.

In response to Puccetti ("The Loving God—Some Observations on John Hick's *Evil and the God of Love*" [#800]), Hick argues that his critic has omitted an essential aspect of his (Hick's) theodicy, Hick's explanation of undeserved, gratuitous suffering (*Evil and the God of Love*, 369-372 [#750]). [See the revised version of this article in Hick's *God and the Universe of Faiths* [#759].]

753.   ———. "The Problem of Evil in the Last and the First Things." *Journal of Theological Studies* 19 (1968): 591-602. [Reprinted in Hick's *God and the Universe of Faiths*: 62-74 [#759].]

Response to Dom Illtyd Trethowan's "Dr. Hick and the Problem of Evil" [#809]. Hick defends his Irenaean theodicy versus Trethowan's critique and against Trethowan's defense of the traditional Augustinian theodicy.

754.   ———. "Review of E.H. Madden and P.E. Hare, *Evil and the Concept of God*" [#1210]. *Philosophy* 44 (1969): 160-161.

Hick notes that this is the first book-length study of theodicy from a sceptical point of view, and argues that while Hare and Madden rightly focus their critique of theodicy on *the problem of gratuitous evil*, they have misrepresented Hick's theodicy. They presuppose a conception of the task of theodicy which is different from Hick's approach. Hare and Madden assume that a theodicy must demonstrate that this is the best of all possible worlds. Hick's theodicy, however, argued the more modest thesis that this world is compatible with Christian belief in an all-powerful and all-loving God. It is not essential (*contra* Hare and Madden) to show how each instance of evil constitutes the most efficient way of achieving God's goal for us.

755.   ———. "Freedom and the Irenaean Theodicy Again." *Journal of Theological Studies* 21 (1970): 419-422.

Rejects Ward's contention that his (Hick's) theodicy rests on two incompatible propositions ("Freedom and the Irenaean Theodicy" [#811]). Hick denies that Irenaean theodicy contains the premises that human beings can be totally free. He denies that we do act inexplicably, incomprehensibly and unpredictably in freedom. Our nature is not neutral or alien toward God, but rather inwardly structured toward God. As such, God does not have to coerce us to respond.

756.   ———. "The Problem of Evil." *A Modern Introduction to Philosophy*. Edited by Paul Edwards and Arthur Pap. New York: Free Press, 1973. Third edition. *Chapter 39* (453-459).

[Excerpt from Hick's *Evil and the God of Love* [#750].] Presents an overview of the theodicy issue. He notes that theodicy is *negative* rather than *positive* in its conclusions: it does not claim to explain or to explain away every instance of evil, but rather points to certain considerations that prevent the fact of evil (which is largely incomprehensible) from constituting a final and insuperable bar to rational belief in God. He defends the free will defense against the criticisms of Mackie and Flew. There has been a mistaken assumption, Hick contends, that God—if such a being existed—would have created a world that was complete and perfect. The world, rather, is a place for "soul-making" in which free creatures may become the "children of God" and "heirs of eternal life." Hick's theodicy exploits insights from St. Irenaeus, the second century Church Father, who taught that God's creation is *a two-fold process*: we have been created first in the image but not yet the likeness of God, the latter revealed in Christ. Hick's version of this is that we have been created physically and now are seeking spiritual perfection through soul-making. Hick does not address the issue of animal suffering and natural evil; for discussions of this issue, Hick refers (in footnotes) to Nels Ferré's *Evil and the Christian Faith* [see #561], and Austin Farrer's *Love Almighty and Ills Unlimited: An Essay on Providence and Evil* [#555].

757.   ——. "A World Without Suffering." *The Mystery of Suffering and Death.* Edited by Michael J. Taylor. Garden City, NY: Image Books, 1973: 25-29. [Excerpt from Hick's *Evil and the God of Love* [#750].]

758.   ——. "Coherence and the God of Love Again." *Journal of Theological Studies* 24 (1973): 522-528.

Response to Rist's "Coherence and the God of Love" [#801]. Hick argues that Rist has misunderstood the Irenaean theodicy and, as such, his criticisms of it are misinformed. Hick defends his view of "universal salvation," and contends (contra Rist) that it does *not* deny freedom.

759.   ——. *God and the Universe of Faiths.* London: Macmillan, 1973.

Chapter 4 ("God, Evil, and Mystery") is a slightly different version of the article of the same title [see #752]. Hick reiterates his defense of the Irenaean theodicy with respect to the problem of undeserved suffering. If such were not the case, ethical action would be undermined; *Chapter 5* ("The Problem of Evil in the First and Last Things" [#753]) is a slightly different version of the article of the same title, in which Hick defends his Irenaean theodicy against the traditional Augustinian view. [See also Hick's *Christianity at the Centre*. London: SCM Press, 1968. New York: Herder and Herder, 1970. Revised edition, *The Centre of Christianity*. London, SCM Press, 1977; San Francisco, CA: Harper and Row, 1978.]

760.   ——. *Death and Eternal Life.* New York: Harper and Row, 1976.

An encyclopedic treatment of the experience and insights of the world's religions about death and eternal life. Hick concludes that there is a significant conceptual convergence of the Hindu teaching of liberation, the Buddhist conception of Nirvana, and the Christian mystical doctrine of the unitive state. The chapter on "Humanism and Death" *(Chapter 8)* rejects the humanist denial of an afterlife. Hick argues that any morally acceptable justification of the sufferings of humanity must postulate a life after death. He proposes his *replica theory* to which Stiver ("Hick Against Himself: Hick's Theodicy Versus His Replica Theory" [#807]) and Yates ("Survival as Replication" [#814]), among others, has responded.

761.   ——. "Remarks." *Reason and Religion.* Edited by Stuart C. Brown. Ithaca, NY: Cornell University Press, 1977: 122-128.

Response to Swinburne ("The Problem of Evil" [#596]) and Phillips ("The Problem of Evil" [#583]), both published also in *Reason and Religion*. He contends that Swinburne's theodicy is consistent with the general Irenaean approach, and that Phillips's arguments against it are unconvincing. Hick expands upon Swinburne's outline of a theodicy by utilizing aspects of his Irenaean insights.

762.   ——. "Incarnation and Atonement: Evil and Incarnation." *Incarnation and Myth: The Debate Continued*. Edited by M. Goulder. Grand Rapids, MI: Eerdmans, 1979: 77-84.

Argues that a proper understanding of the incarnation helps us meet the immense problem of evil and suffering. The Irenaean framework sees God as always involved in the world in suffering love, the cross revealing this suffering visibly as an event in history. This is in contrast to the traditional Christian view which separates creation from redemption and sees the incarnation as a specific act which undoes human sin. [See response by Charles Moule, "A Comment on Professor Hick's Critique of Atonement Doctrine" [#796], following in the text, 85-86.]

763.   ——. "An Irenaean Theodicy" and "Responses." *Encountering Evil*. Edited by Stephen T. Davis. Atlanta, GA: John Knox Press, 1981: 39-52, 63-68.

A precise, summary version of Hick's Irenaean theodicy. He summarizes his explanations for moral evil and natural evil, and responds to four critics: Sontag [#806], Davis [#775], Griffin [#780], and Roth [#802]. Hick argues that it is logically impossible for God to have created us as perfect beings and as free at the same time (at least with respect to God, if not to each other). As such, moral evil is inevitable. Physical evil is accounted for as the necessary ("perfect") environment for human soul-making. He argues that gratuitous evil is necessary; otherwise, there would be no possibility of soul-making. If all our actions were to be rewarded and punished as they merit, the basis of morality would be undermined. Hick argues also for an eschatological fulfilment, one of continued soul-making in the post mortem realm.

764.   ——. "The 'Vale of Soul-Making' Theodicy." *Exploring the Philosophy of Religion*. Edited by David Stewart. Englewood Cliffs, NJ: Prentice-Hall, 1980: 252-262. Second Edition, 1988.

[Excerpt from Hick's *Evil and the God of Love* [#750].]

765.   ——. *An Interpretation of Religion*. London: Macmillan, and New Haven, CT: Yale University Press, 1989.

Argues that all theological discourse, including the Irenaean theodicy, is mythological. The Irenaean theodicy is mythologically true in the sense that it evokes in its hearers a response appropriate to it—to seek to bring good out of evil and by cherishing an ultimate hope beyond this life. This is appropriate to the actual character of our situation in the presence of the "Real." [See response by Robert Mesle, *John Hick's Theodicy: A Process Humanist Critique* [#794]. There have been a number of other critical responses already to this latest contribution of Hick to theology, in this case, the world religions dialogue and the defining of God (the "Real") and the nature of religion.]

766.   ——. "Soul-Making and Suffering." *The Problem of Evil*. Edited by Marilyn McCord Adams and Robert Merrihew Adams. New York: Oxford University Press, 1990: 168-188.

[Excerpts from *Evil and the God of Love* [#750].]

767.   ——. "Response to Mesle." *Chapter 8* of C. Robert Mesle, *John Hick's Theodicy*. New York: St. Martin's Press, 1991: 115-134.

Hick points out several instances where Mesle [#794] has misinterpreted, indeed caricatured his theodicy. Hick reiterates his claim that a theodicy starts from an existing faith in the reality of God, a faith rooted ultimately in religious experience, and hence is capable of absorbing a considerable amount of mystery. Theodicy is not meant to convert humanists (like Mesle) but has the more modest role of demonstrating that evil is not fatally contradictory to an already existing faith. Hick rejects Mesle's two main arguments: (1) that the Irenaean conception of God as creating humanity in a religiously ambiguous world in which God hides from us to test and tease us is (according to Mesle) a cruel deception; (2) the Irenaean view of God as creating us as morally imperfect creatures who are to grow towards our ultimate perfection through our own free responses within a challenging environment is (for Mesle) a heartless device. God, Mesle argues, should have made us wholly good beings who could choose between varying goods, rather than between goods and evils. Hick counters that Mesle is incorrect in assuming that the Irenaean theodicy holds that God plans and sends *every specific evil* in order that we might learn something valuable from it. Hick rejects also Mesle's view (similar to that of Flew and Mackie) that God could have *created* us with moral values rather than having to *earn* these values through so much suffering. Hick's view is that there would be no point in God creating creatures with moral values. Hick rejects Mesle's view that there is no greater value in choosing rightly when one is free also to choose wrongly, than there is when one does not have this option. Hick repudiates also Mesle's disdain for an afterlife existence where spiritual perfection will be obtained. He rejects, finally, Mesle's rationalistic view that the only valid ground for belief in God would be a sound inference from theistically evidential aspects of the world.

768.   ——. "Reply [to Stiver]." *Problems in the Philosophy of Religion: Critical Studies of the Work of John Hick.* Edited by Harold Hewitt, Jr. New York: St. Martin's Press, 1991: 176-177.

Response to Stiver's "Hick Against Himself: Hick's Theodicy Versus His Replica Theory" [#807]. Hick grants to Stiver the logical possibility that God could create morally mature beings as though they had come to this by means of a lifetime of freely made choices; yet Hick argues (with Hewitt, "In Defense of Hick's Theodicy" [#782]) that there is no logical possibility for God to make morally mature beings whose moral maturity is the product of choices freely made. If God operates in accord with the Irenaean principle (i.e., goodness that has been developed though free choices is enormously more valuable than goodness created ready made), God would not want to create the first type of being—one which is morally perfect without having lived an earthly life. This would be pointless in the eyes of divine omniscience.

769.   ——. "Reply [to Mesle and O'Connor]." *Problems in the Philosophy of Religion: Critical Studies of the Work of John Hick.* Edited by Harold Hewitt, Jr. New York: St. Martin's Press, 1991: 82-85.

In response to Mesle's humanist critique ("Humanism and Hick's Interpretation of Religion" [#795]), Hick concedes that the word "elitist" ought not to have been used in his criticisms of humanism. Humanism may not seek to justify the sufferings and injustices of life, but Hick insists that the process theodicy which Mesle links with humanism is guilty of doing just this. Griffin has argued that the good achieved by a fortunate view justifies suffering. [See Griffin's response to Hick's charge of elitism in Griffin's *Evil Revisited* [#873]]. Hick denies that his "notorious Pascal quotation" leads to a demeaning condemnation of humanism, as Mesle argued. In response to O'Connor's "Sin and Salvation from a Feminist Perspective" [#797], Hick accepts her corrected reading of Valerie Saiving-Goldstein, "The Human Situation: A Feminine View" [#3129]. He rejects, however, O'Connor's suggestion concerning the nature of salvation/liberation, as consisting in a sense of movement and improvement, both ontologically and morally considered. O'Connor's view is too psychological.

II   Critical Discussions of Hick's Theodicy

770.   Andrus, Paul F. *Why Me? Why Thine? Clear Thinking About Suffering* Nashville, TN: Abingdon Press, 1975.

Expands upon Hick's soul-making theodicy and defends a doctrine of divine impartiality as a resolution to the problem of undeserved suffering. Undeserved suffering is needed if we are to be fully human, if we are to engage in the soul-making for which we were created.

771.   Brown, R.F. "On the Necessary Imperfection of Creation: Irenaeus' *Adversus Haereses IV, 38.*" *Scottish Journal of Theology* 28 (1975): 17-26.

Examines the arguments of Irenaeus that God created an imperfect creation, a theme used prominently by Hick in his theodicy. Brown argues that Anselm's recapitulation doctrine has two incompatible features: we are restored to our status before Adam's fall and we are elevated to a higher form of being.

772.   Cahn, Stephen M. "Cacodaemony." *Contemporary Philosophy of Religion*. Edited by Stephen M. Cahn. *Contemporary Philosophy of Religion*. New York: Oxford University Press, 1982: 20-24. [Originally published in *Analysis* 37 (1977), 69-73.]

Argues for "the problem of good" (a vindication of a malevolent demon in face of the world's goodness), and concludes that the argument is no more valid than Hick's resolution of the problem of evil. [See King-Farlow's response, "Cacodaemony and Devilish Isomorphism" [#788].]

773.   Clarke, J.J. "John Hick's Resurrection." *Sophia* 10 (1971): 18-22.

Contends that Hick's concept of resurrected bodies is obscure and unconvincing: there could be more than one version of a person resurrected, and the whole matter is too much beyond the range of human experience to make sense.

774.   Corner, Mark A. "The Umbilical Cord: A View of Man and Nature in the Light of Darwin." *Scottish Journal of Religious Studies* 4 (1983): 121-137.

Argues that Hick's view of moral progress (compared to Peter T. Forsyth's view in *The Justification of God* (London: Duckworth, 1916 [#2231]) is naïve. Darwin's theory of evolution parallels Forsyth's view of moral progress. The umbilical cord between the moral and natural worlds is not severed by Darwin's theory.

775. Davis, Stephen T. "Critique [of Hick]." *Encountering Evil*. Edited by Stephen T. Davis. Atlanta, GA: John Knox Press, 1981: 58-61.

Critique of Hick's theodicy ("An Irenaean Theodicy" [#763]). Davis agrees with Hick's insistence on keeping the traditional God of limitless power and limitless goodness (unlike the others in the text: Griffin, Roth and Sontag). Yet, he finds fault with Hick for not being entirely convincing about how to explain the amount of evil in the world. Davis argues also, against Hick, that there is a lack of convincing evidence that the world is progressing morally. He contends, furthermore, that the virtues earned by humans cost too much in pain and suffering, and that Hick's universalism contradicts Christian tradition. The latter, Davis claims, is that to which he most strongly rejects in Hick's theodicy. [See Hick's response, following in the text.]

776. Dore, Clement. "An Examination of the 'Soul-Making' Theodicy." *American Philosophical Quarterly* 7 (1970): 119-130.

Defends Hick's soul-making theodicy against various criticisms of classical theism. Dewey Hoitenga's criticism, for example ("Logic and the Problem of Evil" [#68]), that free virtuous responses to suffering commits Hick to the view that we are not obliged to prevent the suffering that evokes a virtuous response, is answered by Dore. He responds also to the common atheological claim that much suffering does *not* evoke free and virtuous responses.

777. Edwards, Paul. "Difficulties in the Idea of God." *The Idea of God: Philosophical Perspectives*. Edited by Edward H. Madden, Rollo Handy, and Marvin Farber. Springfield, IL: Charles C. Thomas, 1968.

Rejects Hick's reliance upon an afterlife as essential to his theodicy: an afterlife cannot change the facts of evil suffered in this life.

778. Fulmer, Gilbert. "John Hick's Soul-Making Theodicy." *Southwest Philosophical Studies* 7 (1982): 170-179.

Defends Hick against various critics (Paul Edwards, "Difficulties in the Idea of God" [#777]; and Ahern, *The Problem of Evil* [#1263]), both of whom argue that Hick's position necessitates that every evil should be logically necessary for the gaining of perfection. Yet, Fulmer argues that Hick's theodicy fails because he holds an inconsistent doctrine of human freedom via-à-vis God; Hick cannot explain *dysteleological* suffering; and Hick's view of God as being able to prevent evils and being able to permit evils in proportion to human deeds—and yet has *not* done so—is reprehensible.

779. Gregory, Donald R. "Would a Satanic Resurrection World Falsify Christian Theism? Reply to Gregory S. Kavka." *Religious Studies* 14 (1978): 69-72.

Rejects Kavka's argument ("Eschatological Falsification" [#787]) that a resurrection world ruled by Satan would falsify belief in God and, as such, create an insolvable problem of evil. Gregory argues that neither the evil in this world or in a resurrection world would falsify God's existence.

780. Griffin, David. "Critique [of Hick]." *Encountering Evil*. Edited by Stephen T. Davis. Atlanta, GA: John Knox Press, 1981: 53-55.

Contends that Hick has not made plausible the claim that an inherently omnipotent God is perfectly good: Hick's God could have created a better environment with less pain. There is no good reason offered by Hick as to why God wasted four billion years setting the stage for human soul-making. Griffin rejects Hick's traditional understanding of God as "limitlessly powerful," and the view that any limitation on God's power is a "self-limitation" which could be revoked at any time. Since God has the power to revoke evil and has not, Hick's God is not limitlessly good. Hick's theodicy, moreover, requires a bodily resurrection, a point which makes his theodicy implausible for many today, as his himself admits. [See also Griffin's *God, Power and Evil* [#861] and *Evil Revisited* [#873], both of which devote a chapter to refuting Hick's theodicy. The latter book rejects Hick's charge of elitism against process theodicy.]

781.   Hasker, William S. "Suffering, Soul-Making, and Salvation." *International Philosophical Quarterly* 28 (1988): 3-19.

Defends Hick's "soul-making" theodicy against the criticisms of Stump ("The Problem of Evil" [#1173]), who uses some of Kane's arguments ("The Failure of Soul-Making Theodicy" [#786]), and against the criticisms of others. He rejects Kane's argument that Hick's theodicy is pointlessly absurd, since it justifies natural evils as necessary for the development of virtues that can never be manifested in the heavenly state for which they are being cultivated. Hasker argues that virtues cultivated in this life are relevant to this life and the next. He rejects also Kane's argument that evil is not necessary for the development of virtues. Kane has not shown how the virtues he notes can be obtained in the absence of evil. Hasker defends Hick against Kane's charge that there is too much gratuitous evil: without this (Hick argued), our present ethical concepts would have no meaning. Hasker defends Hick also against the criticism that God ought to have created a different system of laws under which creatures live: the difficulty is in conceiving what this could be. Scientific knowledge argues that even minor changes might result in a universe with no intelligent life. The atheologian has not made an intelligent case for an alternative world-system. Hasker rejects, moreover, the criticism against Hick, that God could or should intervene to eliminate the worst evils: such interference by God (via miracles) would disrupt soul-making. Hasker rejects Stump's "suffering for redemption" theodicy as unsubstantiated in its central claim that evil is the best way to bring us to redemption. Stump's theodicy is both factually implausible and morally unacceptable.

782.   Hewitt, Harold. "In Defense of Hick's Theodicy." *Problems in the Philosophy of Religion: Critical Studies of the Work of John Hick.* Edited by Harold Hewitt, Jr. New York: St. Martin's Press, 1991: 173-175.

Response to Stiver's critique of Hick's theodicy ("Hick Against Himself: His Theodicy Versus His Replica Theory" [#807]). Hewitt contends that Stiver's critique is undermined by his use of concepts (for example, memory) outside their usual framework of meaning. It is logically impossible for God to create a replica of some being in this world (though not in the next), since the latter implies its "this-world" predecessor with its memories.

783.   Hollon, Ellis W., Jr. "Pain, Suffering, and Christian Theology." *Perspectives in Religious Studies* 6 (1979): 24-32.

After surveying the three main theodicies ("all is well from God's perspective," the free will solution, and "all's well that ends well"), Hollon concludes that only the latter can address adequately the question of excessive evil.

Against Kai Nielsen [see #s 1446-1448], who rejects Hick's eschatological verification, Hollon argues that it is neither merely speculation nor hypothesis that there is an ultimate justification, but rather a biblical truth.

784.   Hughes, Richard. "Bereavement and Pareschatology." *Encounter* 43 (1982): 361-375.

Examines Hick's view that theodicy requires an afterlife where suffering is redeemed (*Death and Eternal Life* [#760]). Hick rejects the "recapitulation" views of Tillich, Hartshorne and others (that the evil is not retained in the divine memory). Hughes argues from an experiential and clinical perspective, that evil *must* be remembered (*by us and by God*) if it is to be resolved.

785.   Kane, G. Stanley. "Soul-Making Theodicy and Eschatology." *Sophia* 14 (1975): 24-31.

Argues that Hick's eschatological views are fundamentally inconsistent with other aspects of his theodicy. If God's purposes will eventually be fulfilled for every human being, there cannot be freedom vis-à-vis God. To reach fulfilment, the epistemic distance that has justified free will and the world's evils must be overcome. This, Kane contends, collapses Hick's theodicy. [See response to Kane's criticisms in Hasker, "Suffering, Soul-Making, and Salvation" [#781]. See also Hick's response to Kane in *Evil and the God of Love*, second edition [#750], and in *Death and Eternal Life* [#760].]

786.   ———. "The Failure of Soul-Making Theodicy." *International Journal for Philosophy of Religion* 6 (1975): 1-22.

Rejects Hick's theodicy on several counts. He holds Hick is wrong in denying that virtues could be developed without the presence of evil. Kane argues also that Hick's scheme is inconsistent, since the virtues that are being developed by overcoming evil will not be useful in Hick's heaven. [See Hick's response to Kane in *Evil and the God of Love*, second edition [#750].]

787.   Kavka, Gregory S. "Eschatological Falsification." *Religious Studies* 12 (1976): 69-72.

Argues that Hick is mistaken in holding that the proposition "God exists" is *verifiable* but not *falsifiable*. Kavka argues that the statement is both eschatologically verifiable and falsifiable. A resurrection world controlled by Satan would falsify belief in God. [See Gregory's response to Kavka, "Would a Satanic Resurrection World Falsify Christian Theism? Reply to Gregory S. Kavka" [#779].]

788.   King-Farlow, John. "Cacodaemony and Devilish Isomorphism." *Analysis* 38 (1978): 59-61.

Refutes Cahn's argument from "the problem of good" ("Cacodaemony" [#772]), which supposedly shows atheism and theism are equally invalid. King-Farlow argues that claims about the equal consistency and probability of theism or demonism appear ludicrously irrelevant to the ordinary person committed to religious belief. It is an odd rationality to expect reasonable people to shed off a centuries' old belief for a new "ism."

789.   Madden, Edward H., and Peter H. Hare. "In Opposition to Hick's 'Vale of Soul-making' Theodicy." *Exploring the Philosophy of Religion*. Edited by David Stewart. Englewood Cliffs, NJ: Prentice-Hall, 1980: 263-273. Second Edition, 1988.

Excerpt from Hare and Madden's *Evil and the Concept of God* [#1210]. See also Hare and Madden's critical review of Hick's *Evil and the God of Love*, "A Theodicy for Today?" [#1208]. [Also relevant is John Mackie's brief review of Hick's *Evil and the God of Love*, in *Philosophical Books* 3 (1966), 17.]

790.   Mason, David R. "Some Abstract, Yet Crucial, Thoughts About Suffering." *Dialog* 16 (1977): 91-100. [Published also in *American Academy of Religion: 1974 Proceedings*. Edited by Anne Carr: 22-33.]

Considers the strengths and weaknesses of the definitions of suffering in John Hick's *Evil and the God of Love* [#750] and Daniel Day Williams's "Suffering and Being in Empirical Theology" [#2432]. Mason proposes that suffering is the experience of a partially self-directing subject being acted upon and moved from one state to another in a way that conflicts with the subject's present sense of well-being, based on its aim for that situation. There is positive value in every evil, even if this is known only to God. Not all suffering is evil. God suffers with us, experiencing and redeeming the suffering (as the process philosophy of Alfred North Whitehead held).

791.   Mathis, Terry R. *Against John Hick*. Lanham, MD: University Press of America, 1985.

The section on theodicy *(Chapter 4)* claims that Hick's system of thought can handle the problem of evil *without* the notion of eschatological verification. Hick is mistaken in thinking the awareness of evil as an instrument for God's good purposes is sufficient in some cases to remove rational doubt concerning the truth of propositions about God. There is no need (contra Hick) for an eschatological confirming experience of God to establish theistic statements as factual.

792.   Mesle, C. Robert. "The Problem of Genuine Evil: A Critique of John Hick's Theodicy." *Journal of Religion* 66 (1986): 412-450.

Maintains that Hick has misunderstood Griffin's argument—that Hick's theodicy denies *genuine* evil. Hick is mistaken to equate *genuine* evil with what Griffin means by *intrinsic* evil. Mesle contends that despite Hick's rejection of Griffin's category of merely apparent evil, he does seem to reduce all *prima facie* evils to *apparent* evil.

793.   ——. "Does God Hide From Us? John Hick and Process Theology on Faith, Freedom, and Evil." *International Journal for Philosophy of Religion* 24 (1988): 93-111.

Argues that Hick has misunderstood Griffin, who has charged that Hick's theodicy denies "genuine" evil: Hick misunderstands "genuine" evil to be synonymous with what Griffin means by "instrumental" evil. Mesle argues that Hick's claim, that every *prima facie* evil ultimately is transformed into something good, seems unnecessary for his overall position and, in fact, contradicts some of his fundamental ideas. Hick has failed to justify the basic premise of his position: his argument—that God created the world with danger in order to produce courage—is circular.

794.   ———. *John Hick's Theodicy: A Process Humanist Critique*. New York: St. Martin's, 1991.

Contains a reprinted version of Hick's chapter from *Encountering Evil* [#763]; presents a critical assessment of Hick's theodicy from "a process humanist" position; and includes a response by Hick ("Reply [to Mesle and O'Connor]" [#769]). Mesle argues that Hick's theodicy, like most theodicies (and unlike process humanism and process theism), ultimately denies the reality of evil by seeing evil and suffering as a means to a good end. Mesle contends that rather than having created a world in which there is suffering, God should have created a world free of suffering. This world is *not* the best environment in which to produce loving creatures. Mesle rejects Hick's view that God intentionally created a world of ambiguity with respect to our awareness of God. Ignorance, Mesle argues, is not the ground of freedom or faith. God should have created us with opportunities (and an environment in which) to choose between goods, rather than between goods and evils. Mesle rejects Hick's basic value judgment that it is a higher value to obtain goodness by overcoming sufferings than to have been created by God as virtuous. Mesle's argues that Hick has misunderstood David Griffin's critique [see #792], and challenges Hick's appeal to the epistemic distance [see #793]. Finally, he challenges Hick's interpretation of religion, his view of an afterlife and his critique of humanism. The final chapter argues that process theism (or process humanism) is more viable—a better "myth"—than Hick's theism. Mesle also notes where process thought and Hick's theology converge. Both theodicies, Mesle argues, dissolve into humanistic naturalism: Hick's "Real" is a myth and process theism makes God redundant.

795.   ———. "Humanism and Hick's Interpretation of Religion." *Problems in the Philosophy of Religion: Critical Studies of the Work of John Hick*. Edited by Harold Hewitt, Jr. New York: St. Martin's Press, 1991: 54-71.

Argues that Hick's *Interpretation of Religion* [#765] has made progress toward affording respect to naturalistic philosophy, but that Hick has not made that respect systematically coherent. Mesle rejects Hick's criticism of humanism as "elitist," based on the view that in denying an immortal realm after earthly death, humanism sees those who have gained success in this life as the elite. Hick's position wrongly assumes that humanism (and process theodicy) proposes to justify and approve of the suffering in the world by this elitism. A second major problem with Hick's approach is what Mesle calls "the notorious Pascal quotation," used by Hick to explain his concept of epistemic distance—which God has created to allow us room for faith and which is a central facet of his entire theological enterprise. The concept, Mesle argues, is demeaning to humanists since it implies that faith in God is an act of cognitive freedom which expresses the degree of our willingness to accept the divine reality. Humanists supposedly hide willingly from the "Real" (God). Mesle briefly suggests ways to amend Hick's position, including the sponsoring of process thought. [See O'Connor's response, "Sin and Salvation from a Feminist Perspective" [#797] and Hick's response, "Reply (to Mesle and O'Connor)" [#769].]

796.   Moule, Charles. "A Comment on Professor Hick's Critique of Atonement Doctrine." *Incarnation and Myth: The Debate Continued*. Edited by M. Goulder. Grand Rapids, MI: Eerdmans, 1979: 85-86.

Refutes Hick's views on the incarnation in "Incarnation and Atonement: Evil and Incarnation" [#762]. The incarnational christology Hick attacks amounts to a travesty of the gospels and has nothing to do with the latter. "Propitiate" should be understood as "expiate."

797.   O'Connor, June. "Sin and Salvation from a Feminist Perspective." *Problems in the Philosophy of Religion: Critical Studies of the Work of John Hick.* Edited by Harold Hewitt, Jr. New York: St. Martin's Press, 1991: 72-81.

In response to Hick's *An Interpretation of Religion* [#765], O'Connor argues that Hick has not represented feminist thought adequately. Hick's interpretation of Valerie Saiving-Goldstein's classic essay, "The Human Situation: A Feminine View" [#3129], is flawed. O'Connor proposes how Saiving's work can be integrated into Hick's enterprise. [See Hick's response, "Reply (to Mesle and O'Connor)" [#769].]

798.   Perrett, Roy. "John Hick on Faith: A Critique." *International Journal for Philosophy of Religion* 15 (1984): 15-66.

Critiques the problem of relating Hick's concept and use of "epistemic distance" to Hick's eschatology, among other issues.

799.   Pitt, Jack. "Hick on Evil: An Exercise in Critical Thinking." *Teaching Philosophy* 12 (1989): 141-144.

Points out that Hick's discussion of theodicy would have benefited from the explicit aid of logical categories. Pitt supplies these and clarifies some of Hick's "suppressed assumptions." Hick's argument, that God cannot abolish all evil, requires that it is a logical impossibility for God to create persons in a world purged of all evil. No considerations are advanced to assure us that God's inability to do the impossible does not detract from the divine perfection.

800.   Puccetti, Roland. "The Loving God—Some Observations on John Hick's *Evil and the God of Love.*" *Religious Studies* 2 (1967): 255-268.

Argues that the problem of evil is intractable, since theodicy is a subject without a proper object, and that Hick's theodicy fares no better. Puccetti maintains that Hick has not shown that an omnipotent and omniscient God would have no "morally sufficient reason" for allowing instances of innocent suffering. He rejects both Hick's appeal to *mystery* and his appeal to an *afterlife redemption*. [See Hick's response, "God, Evil and Mystery" [#752], and also the response by Yandell, "A Premature Farewell to Theism" [#1189].]

801.   Rist, John M. "Coherence and the God of Love." *Journal of Theological Studies* 23 (1972): 95-105.

Rejects Hick's theodicy on several grounds. For Hick, virtues can only be acquired by the experiences of reactions against the corresponding vices. Rist argues also that Hick's view implies a definition of human beings such that *Christ* would *not* be human. He argues also that Hick's doctrine of universal salvation is suspect, since if all of us are eventually going to be saved, this implies that there is no genuine freedom. [See Hick's reply, "Coherence and the God of Love Again" [#758].]

802. Roth, John K. "Critique [of Hick]." *Encountering Evil.* Edited by Stephen T. Davis. Atlanta, GA: John Knox Press, 1981: 61-63.

Critique of Hick's theodicy ("An Irenaean Theodicy" [#763]). Roth holds that Hick's claims of divine goodness are irreconcilable with the fact that there is so much evil and suffering. He finds fault with the inability of Hick's theodicy to account for the evil of the Holocaust: this was a waste of human life, the very antithesis of any divine providential design and soul-making purpose. Since Hick's God, moreover, *could* but *will not* intervene to disrupt the decisions and actions of human freedom, this argues against divine goodness. [Hick's response follows in the text.]

803. Rowe, William L. "Evil and Theodicy." *Philosophical Topics* 16 (1988): 119-132.

Examines Hick's theodicy for its adequacy to answer two instances of terrible evils: a fawn suffering an agonizing death in a forest and a five year old girl being brutally beaten, raped and murdered. Hick's "all-or-nothing" answer is inadequate: a world (according to Hick) that is utterly devoid of natural and moral evil would preclude the realization of the goods he postulates as justifying belief in God's permitting evils. The prevention of the two instances cited by Rowe would not leave our world devoid of natural and moral evil. For God to prevent the two evils cited, furthermore, would not imply that all evils should be prevented by God.

804. ———. "Paradox and Promise: Hick's Solution to the Problem of Evil." *Problems in the Philosophy of Religion: Critical Studies of the Work of John Hick.* Edited by Harold Hewitt, Jr. New York: St. Martin's Press, 1991: 111-124.

While Hick's theodicy provides a reasonable answer to the question as to why an omnipotent, perfectly good God would permit any evil in the world, and while his theodicy may provide an answer to the question as to why God would permit instances of different kinds of evil to occur, and finally to the question as to how an omnipotent and perfectly good God is justified in permitting instances of suffering and pain that appear to us to be excessive and unrelated to the soul-making process, Hick's theodicy has *not* explained the amount and degree of intrinsic evil and the explanation for particular evils. Rowe contends that there may be a threshold below which deity could prevent such evils only at the cost of limiting moral and spiritual development, but as Rowe argues, we are far above that threshold. The evil permitted by God is far in excess of that needed for soul-making. [See response by Linda Zagzebski, "Critical Response" [#815].]

805. Schmidt, Roger. *Exploring Religion.* Belmont CA: Wadsworth, 1980.

A chapter on suffering and death *(Chapter 14)* outlines briefly some of the main aspects of both Buddhist and Christian responses to suffering. Schmidt argues that Hick's Irenaean alternative is more viable than traditional Augustinian theodicy.

806. Sontag, Frederick. "Critique [of Hick]." *Encountering Evil.* Edited by Stephen T. Davis. Atlanta, GA: John Knox Press, 1981: 55-58.

Critique of Hick's theodicy ("An Irenaean Theodicy" [#763]). Sontag contends that Hick's God could have created us with both freedom and more desirable circumstances in which to exercise it. If God wants finite creatures to come to know and love God, why are there so many obstacles in the way? What chance have the children who die young to achieve this end? Hick's appeal to an after-life begs the theodicy issue.

807.   Stiver, Dan R. "Hick against Himself: Hick's Theodicy Versus His Replica Theory." *Problems in the Philosophy of Religion: Critical Studies of the Work of John Hick.* Edited by Harold Hewitt, Jr. New York: St. Martin's Press, 1991: 162-172.

Hick's replica theory in *Death and Eternal Life* [#760], that God can produce replicas of people after their earthly deaths, implies that Hick should admit that God is capable of producing replicas of people while sparing them the evil of this world. Since God has not done so, Stiver argues that the Irenaean theodicy fails. [See response by Harold Hewitt, "In Defense of Hick's Theodicy" [#782] and Hick's own response, "Reply (to Stiver)" [#768].]

808.   Stoeber, Michael F. *Evil and the Mystics' God: Towards a Mystical Theodicy.* Toronto, ON: University of Toronto Press, 1992.

A critical analysis of Hick's theodicy as—according to Stoeber—the best represen-tative of rational theodicy. He argues that mystical thought can answer four critical objections to Hick's theodicy. Stoeber argues (1) that Hick's theodicy does not provide the evidence needed to support the viability of his theodicy. This shortcoming is amended by the mystical theodicy of Meister Eckhart. Hick's theodicy (2) does not offer consolation for the sufferer in this present world, a problem amended in the mystical writings of Eckhart and Dostoevsky. A further problem with Hick's theodicy (3) is its failure to explain the scope and depth of evil and the origin of evil in human beings, a problem amended by the use of Boehme's "Ungrund." Finally, (4) Hick's theodicy cannot explain un-expiated, dysteleological suffering, a problem for which Stoeber finds a solution in the writings of Sri Aurobindo. [See critique of Stoeber by Barry Whitney, "Mystical and Rational Theodicy" [#1185].]

809.   Trethowan, Dom Illtyd. "Dr. Hick and the Problem of Evil." *Journal of Theo-logical Studies* 18 (1967): 407-416.

Defends traditional Augustinian theodicy versus Hick's Irenaean alternative. Hick's theodicy grants to God ultimate responsibility for all existence, includ-ing the evil within it; this is difficult to reconcile with the demonic character of evil. Hick's theodicy also affirms universal salvation and this is difficult to reconcile with a full affirmation of human responsibility and freedom. Hick's conclusions, moreover, are similar to those of the Augustinian tradition he criticizes: God is responsible for evil. Hick has not shown how humans are responsible vis-à-vis God. [See Hick's reply, "The Problem of Evil in the First and Last Things" [#753].]

810.   Tsanoff, Radoslav A. *Civilization and Progress.* Lexington, KY: University Press of Kentucky, 1971.

Contends that human beings have the capacity for greater goods and greater evils, as civilization unfolds. There is no guarantee of inevitable progress toward greater goods.

811.   Ward, Keith. "Freedom and the Irenaean Theodicy." *Journal of Theological Studies* 20 (1969): 249-254.

Argues that Hick's theodicy is built upon two incompatible postulates: human beings must be totally free in order to enter into a relationship with God and there must be an "epistemic distance" between us and God. The first requires a definition of freedom as inexplicable and unpredictable choice; the second requires a definition of freedom as choice that flows from the agent's own character. [See Hick's reply, "Freedom and the Irenaean Theodicy Again" [#755]].

812.   Weinstock, Jerome A. "What Theodicies Must But Do Not Do." *Philosophia* 4 (1974): 449-467.

A satisfactory theodicy must not only show that it is *impossible* (not logically absurd) to believe God exists, given the amount of evil in the world, but that it is *reasonable* to believe that God exists. To achieve this, theists must show, but have not, that it is reasonable to believe the "perfect balance thesis": there is a perfect balance between the amount of evil that is necessary for God's purpose in allowing for evil and the amount of evil that exists. Hick's theodicy (like other theodicies) fails to demonstrate the latter.

813.   Williams, Robert R. "Theodicy, Tragedy, and Soteriology: The Legacy of Schleiermacher." *Harvard Theological Review* 77 (1984): 395-412.

Contends that Schleiermacher's Irenaean theodicy (*The Christian Faith*, published contemporarily by Philadelphia: Fortress, 1978) is the most inclusive formulation of the Irenaean scheme to date. It avoids the problem in Hick's version (noted by Ricoeur), that Hick's theodicy is not an ethical vision of the world. If the doctrine of the fall is abandoned, the important distinction between finitude and evil cannot be maintained. Yet, the whole of traditional theodicy pivots on the free will defense, which in turn presupposes the distinction between sin and finitude. If the distinction no longer is made, theodicy—as a view of the world as ethically ordered—is no longer tenable. Williams contends, accordingly, that Hick's eschatological resolution of theodicy lapses into the very dualism he seeks to overcome: if morality should ever be actualised, it would cease to be moral. The instrumental view of evil presupposes *not* an ethical-moral vision of the world, but rather a cosmic-soteriological constitution of the world. When the instrumental view of evil is abstracted from its soteriological context, the result is a superficial Pelagian notion of progress.

814.   Yates, John C. "Survival as Replication." *Sophia* 27 (1988): 2-9.

Against Hick's "replica theory" of post mortem survival (in *Death and Eternal Life* [#760]), Yates argues that personal identity cannot be reduced to functional identity. On Hick's view, God would be the immediate origin of evil. A coherent theory of survival must be dualistic.

815.   Zagzebski, Linda. "Critical Response." *Problems in the Philosophy of Religion: Critical Studies of the Work of John Hick.* Edited by Harold Hewitt, Jr. New York: St. Martin's Press, 1991: 125-129.

Response to Rowe's critique of Hick's theodicy ("Paradox and Promise: Hick's Solution to the Problem of Evil" [#804]). Zagzebski argues that Rowe cannot hold rationally that we can know there is excessive evil in the world. She contends that the rationality of the belief that there is excessive evil neither confirms nor disconfirms soul-making theodicy. She also denies that Hick's theodicy depends on the two principles which Rowe proposes: that freely developed goodness and freely given love is better than forced love. Yet, Zagzebski suggests that the soul-making theodicy can be modified to fit the parent-child analogy more closely. The motivation of a parent in permitting a child autonomy does not depend on the superior goodness of free over forced love. Only a free person is a person. Since the existence of free souls is impossible without freedom, it is impossible also without whatever amount of evil such free will produces.

Chapter 6

Process Theodicy

A significant alternative to the traditional "Augustinian" theodicy is the comprehensive and systematic theodicy formulated by process theologians and philosophers. Process metaphysics is based on the writings of *Alfred North Whitehead* (1860-1947) and *Charles E. Hartshorne* (1897–), and while neither Whitehead nor Hartshorne worked out a systematic theodicy, others have constructed theodicies from the various strands of their writings. *David Ray Griffin's* writings, of course, were the first to formulate a systematic process theodicy, based on the writings of Whitehead and Hartshorne [see, in particular his *God, Power and Evil* (1976 and 1990), his chapter in Davis's *Encountering Evil* (1981), and *Evil Revisited* (1991)]. Griffin's published debates with various critics have advanced the process theodicy option significantly, as will be clear from the items annotated in this chapter. I would suggest that Griffin's work on theodicy (especially *God, Power and Evil*)—which elaborates and defends the writings on theodicy by Whitehead and Hartshorne—ranks with John Hick's seminal *Evil and the God of Love* and Alvin Plantinga's important work on the free will defense (*God, Freedom, and Evil*, etc.) as among the most important publications on theodicy in this century, indeed the most important since Leibniz.

The theodicy of Whitehead has been discussed in several dissertations and in various publications. One of the most comprehensive is the recently published version of *Maurice Barineau's* dissertation, *The Theodicy of Alfred North Whitehead* (1991). My 1985 book, *Evil and the Process God*, constructed a process theodicy based on (but not limited to) Hartshorne's writings, a study which was first presented in my Ph.D. dissertation (McMaster, January 1977) and preceded by my essays: "Hartshorne's New Look at Theodicy" (1979) and "Process Theism: Does a Persuasive God Coerce?" (1979), and followed by my "Hartshorne and Theodicy" (1989), "An Aesthetic Solution to the Problem of Evil" (1994), "Hartshorne on Natural Evil" (1996), and "Divine Power and the Anthropic Principle" (1998). There are also many competent and informative dissertations on aspects of Whitehead's, Hartshorne's, Griffin's, Cobb's, and other process theodicies.[1]

Process writers argue that traditional theists and atheological critics largely have had a confused and untenable conception about the meanings of the terms "God" and "creature." God was thought to be perfect in every way and it was supposed that a being who is perfect in power and goodness could eliminate or prevent much of the world's evils. Griffin's critique of the major representatives of traditional western theological thought on the theodicy issue, however, contends that they all have held an illicit understanding of God. Griffin's indictment includes such seminal figures as *Augustine, Aquinas, Luther, Calvin, Leibniz, Barth*, and other major writers in the Christian historical and contemporaneous world as well *(Hick, Plantinga,*

Maritain, Ross, etc.). His critique expands upon Whitehead's warning that traditional theology has passed over "the Galilean origin of Christianity," a vision that revealed a God who "dwells upon the tender elements of the world." Process writers support Whitehead's contention that God acts "persuasively" rather than "coercively" in the world. This understanding of God, to be sure, has elicited critical responses, contending that the process God is too "limited" and too "weak" to merit worship, since process thought denies the traditional understanding of omnipotence attributed to God. The response of Hartshorne to this common charge has been that the process conception of divine power as solely persuasive is far more viable and meaningful than the traditional conception of God as coercive: if God literally had all the power, it would be power over nothing, since creatures would have no power. This power in creatures is not a gift from God, but is inherent in the creature.[2]

It is this view of *divine persuasive power* conceived by Whitehead and defended by Hartshorne and others as "one of the greatest of all metaphysical discoveries"[3] that has led to the reformulation of a free will defense which, according to process writers, is the first viable free will defense/theodicy that has been constructed to date. The argument is that all creatures have some degree of creativity necessarily and independently of God, although God is the *sine qua non* ("without which not"), without whom nothing could exist.[4] There is, as such, a division of powers, a mutual influence between God and creatures, although God remains the greatest possible power. The "minimal solution to the problem of evil"[5] is that "risk of evil and opportunity for good are two aspects of just one thing: multiple freedom." This, according to Hartshorne, "is the sole, but sufficient reason for evil as such and in general."[6]

The problem of *physical evil* is subsumed under this logic: since all creatures— including non-human creatures—have some creativity, there is bound to be conflict. Hartshorne argues that with "a multiplicity of creative agents, some risk of conflict and suffering is inevitable," a point which Griffin has developed as the correlation between a creature's powers for good and its ability for evil.[7] God's function, according to Hartshorne, "is not to enforce a maximal ratio of good to evil, but a maximal ratio of chances of good to chances of evil."[8] God has not created the world "ex nihilo," but has existed eternally with the "other," the creation of which is in fact that aspect of God's unlimited potential, that aspect of God which has been actualised. This "other" (the entire physical universe) is not to be understood as independent of God, but as immanent in God (the process doctrine of "panentheism," all [is] in God). God is *more* than the "other" which is immanent in God: this is not "pantheism" *(all is God*, God and the world are one) but rather *all [is] in God* and God is in all. The "other" has some minimal degree of creativity over which God cannot exercise unilateral coercive power to compel it (the other) to obey the divine will. This is unlike traditional theism where God has (contentiously, to be sure) *unilateral* power to control all creatures, regardless of whether such power is used by God. God may use such power or may limit divine power to permit creaturely freedom. It amounts to the same thing: God, according to the traditional Christian theism which is challenged by process theists, has all the power.[9]

Process theodicy holds God's purpose is not to create a hedonistic, orderly utopia, but rather to provide creatures with and lure creatures toward the actualization of potentials/possibilities which, when actualized, will give us the most *aesthetic value* possible in each and every situation, at every "impasse," as Whitehead put it. It is on this point that John Hick has charged process theodicy with "elitism," arguing that while the elite have the opportunity for significant aesthetic value, most of the world's suffering and disadvantaged human creatures do not. The process view, nevertheless, is that aesthetic value is a justification for the evil that occurs, that "there is a balance of unity in diversity which is ideally satisfying"[10] for all creatures. The evil that occurs is "overcome" by God in the divine experience of all that has been actualized.

There has been a significant development among many process philosophers and theologians about *the nature of immortality* or, at least, about post mortem existence. Do we "live on" in God as merely an objective memory or do we live on in some post mortem realm as subjective, experiencing subjects? The Whiteheadian agnosticism about this matter and the endorsement of *objective immortality* by *Hartshorne, Schubert Ogden, W. Norman Pittenger, Barry Whitney*, and others, has been a major stumbling block for external critics of process theodicy. Yet *David Griffin, John Cobb, Marjorie Suchocki, Joseph Bracken, S.J.,* and others presently are arguing for the possibility of a *subjective immortality* within process metaphysics, for a more adequate eschatology than that which is presented by Whitehead and Hartshorne and the earlier generations of process thinkers.[11] This eschatology, which so many critics have claimed was lacking in process theology, has filled an immense void, although its details are still being worked out. Despite claims that Hartshorne himself has changed his mind about immortality, recognizing the need and possibility of subjective immortality, I find this to be quite problematic.

I remain convinced that theodicy does not require an eschatology of subjective immortality to be viable, although I admit that the contemporary attempts to provide such a doctrine would make process theodicy more acceptable.[12] I see this as a blending of theological beliefs with purely analytical logic. I remain unconvinced that attributing evil and suffering to a speculative being called Satan or to a "fall" of the first human pair cannot be assumed/presumed in analytical discussions. The same applies to resolving theodicy by an eschatology in which there is a continuing afterlife. The issue of combining the beliefs of Christian faith with philosophical reasoning is an unresolved issue. The time-honored Thomistic theological enterprise has held the two together, but as I noted in the introductory chapter, this has resulted in a separation of Thomistic theodicy from the mainstream discusssions in the contemporary journals. The same applies, in a certain manner, to the conservative theological stance taken by the more "fundamentalistic" of Protestant thinkers. There have been notable exceptions, as the journal *Faith and Philosophy* demonstrates clearly. Perhaps there will be more of a blending of confessional beliefs with philosophical discussions. The latter seems arid without the former, while the former lacks intellectual vigor without the latter.[13]

The annotated items which follow, listing the main writings on process theodicy, are supplemented by selected lists of publications on closely related items: *omnipotence* and the other divine attributes which process thinkers have redefined (*immutability, omniscience*, etc.). I have not attempted to offer complete annotated information on the publications by and about Whitehead and Hartshorne: there are far too many publications.[14] I have indicated only those publications that relate directly to and contribute significantly to the theodicy issue. The middle section lists some of the major publications by *Teilhard de Chardin*, whose theology resembles the Whiteheadian—Hartshornean theism in various ways. Teilhard's view is far more mystical and theological[15] and differs in significant ways from the philosophical views of Whitehead and Hartshorne. Teilhard's theodicy does not have the sophisticated Whiteheadian philosophical scheme, yet there are many strong similarities between Teilhard and Whitehead. While Teilhard is very difficult to categorize, the publications about his theodicy belong in this chapter, I think, more so than any other place. Like Whiteheadian— Hartshornean process thought, he shares some of the Irenaean "soul-making" vision that has been constructed into a theodicy by John Hick, a "character-making" theodicy. Whiteheadians refer to this as the endless creative advance in the quest for "aesthetic value." Teilhard believed, moreover, that the process ends at a specific point, the Omega Point, while the Whiteheadian—Hartshornean vision postulates an endless process, one which had no beginning *ex nihilo*, and has no end, since all reality is an aspect of God and co-eternal with God.

Process theodicy makes use of the *suffering of God* theme as much, if not more so, than any other "movement" or group of scholars. The references to this important theme are found in *Appendix C*.

Notes

1. See, for example, Dalton Baldwin, *A Whiteheadian Solution to the Problem of Evil* (Claremont Graduate School, 1975); Marvin Collins, *God and Evil in the Process Thought of A.N. Whitehead, Charles Hartshorne, and David Griffin* (Fuller Theological Seminary, 1986); Stephen Greenfield, *A Whiteheadian Perspective on the Problem of Evil* (Fordham University, 1973); Paul Eddy Wilson, *The Bearing of Process Thought on the Problem of Theodicy* (University of Tennessee, 1989); etc. There are also a number of significant dissertations on Hartshorne and process theodicy. See, for example, Philip Devenish, *Evil and Theism: An Analytic-Constructive Resolution of the So-Called Problem of Evil* (Southern Methodist University, 1977); Randall Basinger, *Divine Providence: A Comparison of Classical and Process Theism* (Northwestern University, 1978); Mary Johann Fox, *The Meaning of the Notion of Divine Power in the Neoclassical Theism of Charles Hartshorne* (Fordham University, 1977); Mark Scott, *Theodicy: Failure and Promise within the Thought of Karl Barth, David R. Griffin, and Jürgen Moltmann* (Southern Baptist Theological Seminary, 1987); Claude Storms, *The Problem of Evil for Process Thought* (Southern Baptist Theological Seminary, 1978); Barry Whitney, *The Question of Theodicy in the Neoclassical Metaphysics of Charles Hartshorne* (McMaster University, 1977); Robert Mesle, *Power and Value in Process Philosophy and Theology and Theology* (Northwestern University, 1980); Henry James Young, *Two Models of the Human Failure: A Study of the Process Theism of Teilhard and Whitehead* (Hartford Theological Seminary, 1974); and older dissertations, like Robert Cavanagh, *Toward a Contemporary Construct of Divine Providence* (Graduate Theological Union, 1968); Ronald Durham, *Process Thought and Theodicy: A Critique* (Rice University, 1974); Joseph Grange, *Tragic Vision in the Thought of A.N. Whitehead* (Fordham University, 1970); Stephen Greenfield, *A Whiteheadian Perspective on the Problem of Evil* (Fordham University, 1973); etc.
2. See Hartshorne's provocatively titled book, *Omnipotence and Other Theological Mistakes* (Albany, NY: State University of New York Press, 1984). See also Griffin's "Creation Out of Nothing and the Problem of Evil," *Encountering Evil*. Edited by Stephen Davis (Nashville, TN: John Knox Press, 1981), 101-119, 129-136.
3. Hartshorne, *The Divine Relativity* (New Haven, CT: Yale University Press, 1948), 142.
4. See Barry L. Whitney, *Evil and the Process God* (Lewiston, NY and Toronto, ON: Edwin Mellen Press, 1985), 85-87.
5. Hartshorne, *Man's Vision of God and the Logic of Theism* (Chicago, IL: Willett, Clark, 1941; reissued, Hamden CT: Archon Books, 1964), 30.
6. Hartshorne, *A Natural Theology for Our Time* (La Salle, IL: Open Court, 1967), 81.
7. Hartshorne, *Creative Synthesis and Philosophic Method* (La Salle. IL: Open Court, 1970), 237-238. See also David Griffin, *God, Power and Evil* (Philadelphia, PA: Westminster Press, 1976. Republished, Lanham, MD: University Press of America, 1991).
8. Charles Hartshorne, *Reality as Social Process* (Glencoe, IL: Free Press, and Boston, MA: Beacon Press, 1953. Republished in New York: Hafner, 1971), 107.

9. The issue is much debated, to be sure. See the debate between Nelson Pike and David Griffin in *Process Studies* (1982). See also David Basinger's *Divine Power in Process Theism* (Albany, NY: State University of New York Press, 1988), and some of his articles on this issue. See also Barry L. Whitney, *Evil and the Process God*, *Chapters 6-9*.

10. Griffin has responded to this and other criticisms in *Evil Revisited*. See also Barry L. Whitney, *Evil and the Process God* and *What Are They Saying About God and Evil?* (New York/Mahwah: Paulist Press, 1989. Updated version, 1999, from author).

11. While Whitehead left the question of immortality an open one and Hartshorne argued strongly for objective (versus subjective) immortality, contemporary process thinkers have developed strong arguments for subjective immortality. See, for example, David Griffin's "The Possibility of Subjective Immortality," *Modern Schoolman* 53 (1975); and Griffin's more recent, *Evil Revisited* (Albany, NY: State University of New York Press, 1991) and his *God and World in Post-Modern Theology* (Albany, NY: State University of New York Press, 1988); see also the arguments of Marjorie Suchocki in *God, Christ, Church* (NY: Crossroad, 1982; revised edition, 1989), and *The End of Evil* (Albany, NY: State University of New York Press, 1988); Joseph Bracken's *Society and Spirit* (Cranbury, NJ: Associated University Presses [Selinsgrove, PA: Susquehanna University Press], 1991); and others, including the eminent process thinkers, Lewis Ford and John Cobb.

12. My defense of objective immortality is found in *Evil and the Process God*. See also my "Rahner and Hartshorne on Death and Eternal Life" (co-authored with J.N. King), *Horizons, Journal of the College Theology Society* (1988).

13. This issue is obviously a complex and delicate one. I am working, at present, on the implications of immortality theory for process theodicy, and on the larger issue of the relationship of confessional beliefs and analytical philosophical/theological discussions. As a process theist, I remain firm in my belief that there is no need for a subjective immortality to justify theodicy. There may be this need for Hick's Irenaean theodicy and for the traditional theodicies, but not for process theodicy.

14. For the Whiteheadian primary and secondary bibliography to the early 1970's, see Barry Woodbridge, *Alfred North Whitehead: A Primary—Secondary Bibliography* (Bowling Green, OH: Philosophy Documentation Center, 1976). The journal, *Process Studies*, contains updated references to publications written about Whitehead, Hartshorne and other process writers and themes.

15. His Christology, for example, is central, whereas God is more central for Whitehead and Hartshorne, if not for some of their descendants. Teilhard's mystical vision which sees the Church (and the Pope) as the central nervous system of the body of Christ, etc., is far more "theological" than the Whiteheadian—Hartshornean vision, a point which I assume is obvious.

I   Process Theodicy

816.   Baldwin, Dalton D. "Evil and Persuasive Power: A Response to Hare and Madden." *Process Studies* 3 (1973): 259-272.

Defends process theodicy's use of persuasive power against five major criticisms levied by Hare and Madden, in "Evil and Persuasive Power" [#882]. He argues that there are three sets of meanings for the terms "persuasion," "coercion," and "freedom," and that a clarification of these meanings will remove some of the confusion in the arguments of Hare and Madden. [See David Griffin's response to Baldwin's arguments and also to the criticisms of Hare and Madden, in *Evil Revisited* [#873].]

817.   Barbour, Ian G. *Religion in an Age of Science*. San Francisco, CA: Harper and Row, 1990.[Revised and expanded edition, 1997.]

Volume I of The Gifford Lectures, 1989-1990. (*Volume II* is titled, *Ethics in an Age of Technology*, 1990-1991.) *Chapter 8* ("Process Thought") contains a brief presentation of process theodicy, noting some of its similarities (and main difference) from Hick's theodicy.

818.   Barciauskas, Rosemary Curran. "The Primordial and Ethical Interpretations of Evil in Paul Ricoeur and Alfred North Whitehead." *Modern Theology* 2 (1985): 64-77.

By setting the ethical interpretation of evil within the larger setting of a primordial and evolutionary understanding of evil, some of the inhibiting and destructive effects of past attempts to rationalize evil are challenged (in particular, the ethical view of evil which associates it solely with human guilt). Barciauskas holds that Ricoeur's hermeneutical, phenomenological perspective and that Whitehead's metaphysical perspective are *complementary* in their understanding of evil as primordial.

819.   Barineau, R. Maurice. "Whitehead and Genuine Evil." *Process Studies* 20 (1990): 181-188.

Refutes the contention of critics (Hare and Madden, *Evil and the Concept of God* [#1210]; Ely, *The Religious Availability of Whitehead's God* [see #844]; and Schulweis, *Evil and the Morality of God* [#1166]), that Whitehead does not allow for the actuality of genuine evils. The argument of these critics is that evils for Whitehead are *apparent* rather than *genuine*, since God utilizes every evil as a means to perfect both the world and the divine existence. Barineau employs Griffin's definitions of apparent and genuine evil, arguing that the proper definition of evil is *prima facie* evil. When judged from God's perspective, this evil is that in the place of which no other realistically possible occurrence could be better. Apparent evil is not only a means to perfection but a morally necessary and justified means. Genuine evil is not. Actual entities inevitably fail to conform to God's aims for them, and while nothing is lost in God's nature, there are elements whose contributions to higher perfection are too meager to justify their perpetuation in God's envisagement of the future. [See also Barineau's *The Theodicy of Alfred North Whitehead* [#820]].

820.   ———. *The Theodicy of Alfred North Whitehead: A Logical and Ethical Vindication*. Lanham, MD: University Press of America, 1991.

Contends that an ethical theodicy must affirm the reality of genuine evil and allow for the possibility that such evil can be overcome. An ethical theodicy, moreover, cannot deny God's omnibenevolence without qualification. An ethical theodicy, moreover, either must *deny* or *qualify* God's omnipotence. Barineau defends Whitehead's theodicy as a viable ethical theodicy, as fulfilling the cited requirements: denying divine omnipotence, affirming unqualified omnibenevolence, and affirming the reality of genuine evil.

821.   Barnhart, Joe. E. "Persuasive and Coercive Power in Process Metaphysics." *Process Studies* 3 (1973): 153-157.

Argues that Hare and Madden ("Evil and Persuasive Power" [#882]) confuse persuasive power with ineffective control and, as such, that their criticism of the process vision of God—as solely persuasive—is invalid. Yet process theists (John Cobb is cited) fail to acknowledge the argument of Hare and Madden that coercion may at times be morally justified.

822.   Basinger, David. "Divine Persuasion: Could the Process God Do More?" *Journal of Religion* 64 (1984): 332-347.

Contends that there is no good reason to assume that the model of divine omnipotence affirmed by process theism (in particular, David Griffin) is superior to that affirmed by classical theists in the free will tradition. Since human beings can at times unilaterally control the behavior of others without physical force, we ought to assume that the process God *could coerce* in this sense. But this opens process theodicy to the challenge facing the classical free will theist: if God could prevent or minimize some particularly horrible evils by the judicious use of (for example) psychological manipulation, why has God not done so? [See Griffin's response in *Evil Revisited* [#873]; see also Lewis Ford's response, "Divine Persuasion and Coercion" [#851]. See Basinger's slightly revised version of this item, "Divine Power: Do Process Theists Have a Better Idea?" *Process Theology*. Edited by Ronald Nash. Grand Rapids, MI: Baker Book House, 1987.]

823.   ———. "Griffin and Pike on Divine Power: Some Clarifications." *Philosophy Research Archives* 10 (1984): 347-352.

Maintains that Griffin has demonstrated convincingly (contra Pike) that God, given process assumptions, could not determine all the activities of any human being; that is, that God could not determine all the individual's desires, choices and actions. Yet Griffin has not answered Pike's further question: can we, given process assumptions, claim that God could determine all the bodily behaviors of any given human being? [See Pike, "Process Theodicy and the Concept of Power" [#912]; see also Griffin's response in *Evil Revisited* [#873].]

824.   ———. "Process Theology and Petitionary Prayer." *Evangelical Journal* 60 (1988): 70-81. [Reprinted in Basinger's *Divine Power in Process Theism* [#826].]

Contends that there is no basis in process theology for retaining the traditional concept of efficacious petitionary prayer. Basinger contends that Suchocki ("A Process Theology of Prayer" [#930]) has shown that petitionary prayer can justifiably be viewed as efficacious from a process perspective—as affecting the petitioner), but not that prayer initiates unilateral divine activity.

825.　　——. "Human Coercion: A Fly in the Process Ointment?" *Process Studies* 16 (1986): 161-171. [A revised version is published in Basinger's *Divine Power in Process Theism* [#826].]

Argues that if it is appropriate for human beings to coerce on occasion, and if the process God would coerce—if this were an option—it follows that process thinkers no longer can imply that divine non-coercion has a moral basis; that is, process thinkers can no longer imply that a perfect being would not coerce for moral reasons. [See David Griffin's response in *Evil Revisited* [#873]; Lewis Ford, "Divine Persuasion and Coercion" [#851]; and Barry Whitney, "Hartshorne and Theodicy" [#951].]

826.　　——. *Divine Power in Process Theism*. Albany, NY: State University of New York Press, 1988.

Much of this book has been published previously in journal articles: "Divine Persuasion: Could the Process God Do More?" [#822]; "Human Coercion: A Fly in the Process Ointment?" [#825]; "Divine Omnipotence: Plantinga Vs. Griffin" [#15]; and "Process Theology and Petitionary Prayer" [#824]. Basinger argues that process theists (mainly David Griffin) have given no good reasons why their God *could not coerce*. As such, there is no good reason to believe that their "persuasive" God is significantly different from the "coercive" God of some forms of classical theism. Nor is the process theodicy, eschatology, and vision (or lack thereof) of petitionary prayer without serious problems; process thought, as such, hardly is superior to classical theism. [Griffin has responded to many of these points in his *Evil Revisited* [#873]. For Basinger's reply to Griffin, see "Process Theism Versus Free-Will Theism: A Response to Griffin," *Process Studies* 20 (1991), 204-220.]

827.　　Belaief, Lynne. "A Whiteheadian Account of Value and Identity." *Process Studies* 5 (1975): 31-46.

Proposes a theory of moral responsibility and ethical identity in Whitehead's metaphysics. Evil is irrevocable. [See also Belaief's full-length study, *Toward a Whiteheadian Ethics* [#613].]

828.　　Bixler, Julius Seelye. "Whitehead's Philosophy of Religion." *The Philosophy of Alfred North Whitehead*. Edited by Paul Arthur Schilpp. Evanston, IL: Northwestern University Press, 489-511.

An expository discussion of evil in Whitehead's writings. Bixler argues that despite evil, the teleological intuition of religious experience provides us with a transcendental perspective. Evil arises from the incompatibility in the aims of individuals. Bixler discusses also freedom and immortality in Whitehead's philosophy of religion.

829.　　Blaisdell, Charles R. "Griffin's Theodicy." *Encounter* 50 (1989): 367-378.

Argues that Griffin's *God, Power and Evil* [#861] contains three theodicies, only the first of which is a distinctive process theodicy, although all are viable. Griffin's *metaphysical* theodicy demonstrates that the possibility of genuine evil is inescapable in any world in which there exists a multiplicity of powers; the *aesthetic* theodicy addresses the question as to whether there is too much evil; and the *axiological/existential* theodicy answers the question as to whether the good which has been achieved is worth the risk of evil. Blaisdell argues that Griffin's theodicies are powerful and credible; he suggests, however, ways to make aspects of them even stronger. For example, there was no need for Griffin to ask whether God should have created a world, since this is a metaphysical necessity.

830.   Case-Winters, Anna. *God's Power: Traditional Understandings and Contemporary Challenges*. Philadelphia, PA: Westminster, 1990.

Critically assesses the traditional concept of divine omnipotence in Calvin and Barth, supporting the alternatives in Hartshorne and feminism. Case-Winters utilizes Barry Whitney's critique of Hartshorne's conception of divine power (*Evil and the Process God* [#950]; and "Process Theism: Does a Persuasive God Coerce?" [#949]). She combines process thought and feminism into a more viable basis for theodicy, based upon the Hartshornean "relational" understanding of divine power.

831.   Clarke, Bowman L. "A Whiteheadian Theodicy." *The Defense of God*. Edited by John Roth and Frederick Sontag. New York: Paragon House, 1985: 32-47.

Defends Whiteheadian theodicy, in particular God's power and moral goodness vis-à-vis three kinds of evils: evils due to the finitude of creatures; evils due to the free moral choices of creatures (versus Mackie and Pike); and evils due to the environment of creatures.

832.   Cobb, John B., Jr. *God and the World*. Philadelphia, PA: Westminster Press, 1969.

Chapter 4 ("Evil and the Power of God," 87-102) argues that the conception of divine power is the key to the solution to the problem of evil. Divine power is persuasive, rather than coercive and all-determining. *Moral evil* is the result of the creativity of creatures; *natural evil* can be explained in the same way and it is noteworthy that there is more value in a world of creatures than in a world devoid of life. Cobb does not share the eschatological vision of Teilhard, Pannenberg, Altizer, and others, yet expresses the hope that honesty, courage, and the affirmation of life may gradually make for a better world. To affirm life and humanity is to resolve the existential question of theodicy. Cobb argues also that belief in life after death, freed from moralistic and punitive judgment, is a viable hope. [See also Cobb's "Whitehead's Philosophy and a Christian Doctrine of Man," *Journal of Bible and Religion* 32 (1964), 209-220; and his more recent defense of an afterlife, "The Resurrection of the Soul," *Harvard Theological Review* 80 (1987), 213-227.]

833.   ———. "The Problem of Evil and the Task of Ministry." *Encountering Evil*. Edited by Stephen Davis. Atlanta, GA: John Knox Press, 1981: 167-180.

A discussion of the relevance of the various theodicies discussed in this book (Griffin, Hick, Roth, Davis, and Sontag), as they relate to the practical concerns of ministry. Of these writers, Cobb notes, only Griffin [#863] holds that the goodness of the created world does not depend entirely on belief that something very different will replace it, something so good that it will counterbalance the present evils. Cobb agrees with Griffin that life is more of a blessing than a curse; otherwise, we could not continue to believe in God.

834.   ———. *Praying for Jennifer: An Exploration of Intercessory Prayer in Story Form.* Nashville, TN: The Upper Room, 1985.

A dialogue between several people who discuss the questions of intercessionary prayer, the nature of divine power, and the problem of suffering.

835.   Cole, Graham. "Towards a New Metaphysic of the Exodus." *Reformed Theological Review* 42 (1983): 75-84.

Proposes an alternative to both classical theism (as represented by H.P. Owen and E.L. Mascal) and process metaphysics (represented by Pittenger). Both have the fundamental defect of conceiving God as impersonal and are disconsonant with the ontic commitment of biblical writers. Cole's alternative is *biblical personalism* or *trinitarian*. While process metaphysics denies divine impassibility and while classical metaphysics affirms it, biblical personalism *affirms* it in the general sense (God is not acted upon from outside), yet *denies* it in the particular sense (God does feel for the creature). [See H.P. Owen's *Christian Theism.* Edinburgh: T&T Clark, 1984; *Concepts of Deity.* London: Macmillan, 1970; and *The Moral Argument for Christian Theism.* London: Allen and Unwin, 1965. Cole's references to Eric Mascal include his *He Who Is* [#1900] and *Existence and Analogy.* London and New York: Longmans, Green, 1948.]

836.   Cooper, Burton Z. *The Idea of God. A Whiteheadian Critique of St. Thomas Aquinas' Concept of God.* The Hague: Martinus Nijhoff, 1974.

The final chapter attempts to redefine redemptive faith in light of the problem of evil. Versus Ely [#844], Hare and Madden [#1210], and others, Cooper argues that the process God is sufficiently transcendent in power to permit the world to face evil with an ontologically based hope that overcomes the power of despair. Aquinas's position (the God of absolute power) is no longer relevant because of our new understanding of nature as creative.

837.   Creel, Richard. *Divine Impassibility.* Cambridge and New York: Cambridge University Press, 1986.

Argues that the enormity of evil in human history is a conclusive disproof of the existence of the *process* God, but not of the *classical* God. The difference is the kingdom of good that only the classical God can promise. Creel argues against the rejection of divine impassibility by process thinkers, concluding (for example) that there is no good reason a responsible parent or God would have a moral obligation to suffer with their suffering child. Creel argues that divine suffering is not necessary for human redemption. He discusses divine impassibility (with reference to Aquinas and Hartshorne), divine externality (versus Stump and Kretzman), evil (versus Hare and Madden), creation *ex nihilo* (versus Geach, Swinburne), and the best possible world (versus Adams, Reichenbach). God is impassible in nature, will and knowledge of abstract possibilities, but passible in knowledge of actual and concrete possibilities.

838.   Crenshaw, Robert E. "Human Suffering: Holocaust and Devastations of Worlds—A Cosmic Theology Related to Whiteheadian Thought." *The New York Times*, July 16, 1978: E7-8.

Argues that Whiteheadian thought is a viable "cosmic theology" which gives proper credit to modern scientific cosmology. Crenshaw contends that human suffering is consistent with God's power and love, since any divine intervention would constitute a destruction of the physical universe—not utter destruction, but destruction in the sense of cataclysmic explosion of the atomic universe—similar to the view of astronomy, the explosion of the primordial mass so long ago, the result of divine creative intervention.

839.   Davaney, Sheila Greeve. *Divine Power*. Harvard Dissertations in Religion. Philadelphia, PA: Fortress Press, 1986.

Argues that Hartshorne's position concerning divine power as the capacity to *influence* is far less developed and clearly articulated than is his conception of *receptive* power. The implications for theodicy is that reality is tragic, a mixture always of good and evil, with no Barthian divine triumph over evil.

840.   Davis, Stephen T. "God the Mad Scientist: Process Theology on God and Evil." *Themelios* 5 (1979): 18-23.

Review article of David Griffin's *God, Power and Evil* [#861]. Davis contends that Griffin uses the word "traditional theist" too loosely: traditional theism is not so homogeneous as process thinkers imply. He repudiates also Griffin's identification of necessity with eternity—that eternal things are necessary. He rejects Griffin's claim that traditional theism denies the reality of genuine evil. Davis also finds fault with Griffin's view that any possible world would contain self-determining entities with power over God, a claim that is not validated by Griffin. He contends that Griffin's theodicy lacks an adequate eschatology, and that this renders the theodicy much too optimistic. Davis argues the analogy that a mad scientist who created a monster that does more evil than good would be wrong to do so. The same applies for the world and God: God would be indictable if the world were to end (for humans) in the horrible suffering and death of all humans. [See Griffin's response in *Evil Revisited* [#873], and the Griffin—Davis debate in Stephen Davis, editor, *Encountering Evil* [#841].]

841.   ———. "Critique [of Griffin's theodicy]." *Encountering Evil*. Edited by Stephen Davis. Atlanta, GA: John Knox Press, 1981: 125-128.

Contends that Griffin's theodicy, presented in *Encountering Evil* [#841], fails on three counts: Davis rebuffs the necessary connection between *creatio ex nihilo* (denied by Griffin) and a denial of theistic evolution; he repudiates Griffin's denial of the traditional concept of divine omnipotence, arguing that the process God is unworthy of worship; and Davis rejects the lack of an adequate eschatology in process theodicy. [See Griffin's response in *Evil Revisited* [#873].]

842.   ———. "Why God Must Be Unlimited." *Concepts of the Ultimate*. Edited by Linda J. Tessier. New York: St. Martin's Press, 1989: 3-22.

Argues against the "limited" God of process theology. He suggests four arguments in favor of the notion of an unlimited God, and concludes that such a concept is both theologically and philosophically preferable to a limited God.

He argues (against David Griffin and process theism generally) that the view that God is all-powerful and that God voluntarily shares some of this power with the creatures is a reasonable view. [See Griffin's response, "Reply: Must God Be Unlimited? Naturalistic vs. Supernaturalistic Theism" [#871].]

843.   Durham, Ronald O. "Evil and God: Has Process Made Good Its Promise?" *Christianity Today* 22 (1978): 10-14.

Holds that by radically redefining God and the world, Whitehead's theodicy opened up radical new possibilities for theology, while classical theodicy faced more questions than credibility. Yet process theodicy has unresolved inconsistencies and other problems: God is the one exception to the metaphysical principle that all actual entities perish; process theodicy has not shown how it can avoid Kant's "limits" against moving from the phenomenal to the noumenal; the process God is incapable of functioning as Redeemer; and the central event of the Incarnation-Resurrection is debunked by Whitehead, thereby seriously denying the biblical witness and an adequate Christology.

844.   Ely, Stephen L. "The Religious Availability of Whitehead's God: A Critical Analysis." *Explorations in Whitehead's Philosophy*. Edited by Lewis Ford and George Kline. New York: Fordham University Press, 1983: 170-211.

Ely's original book, *The Religious Availability of Whitehead's God*, all of which is reprinted here, was published in 1933 (Madison, WI: University of Wisconsin Press). Ely argues that Whitehead's God is too limited to be worthy of religious worship. Whitehead's God is not responsible for evil, since his God is subsidiary to the ultimate creative forces that God did not create and cannot modify. Whitehead seeks to maintain God's goodness at the expense of divine power, yet Whitehead's God is not good in any sense in which human beings are called good. God can do little but "overcome" evils, but this does not remove the evils which we presently suffer. Whitehead's view implies that evil is an illusion of our short-sightedness. [See responses by Charles Hartshorne, "Is Whitehead's God the God of Religion?"[#886]; and Bernard Loomer, "Ely on Whitehead's God" [#901].]

845.   Ford, Lewis S. "Divine Persuasion and the Triumph of Good." *Christian Scholar* 50 (1967): 235-250.

Refutes the claim of Hare and Madden in *Evil and the Concept of God* [#1210]), that the process God is too weak to guarantee the ultimate triumph of good. Ford argues that there is final redemption from evil within God's experience.

846.   ———. "Biblical Recital and Process Philosophy: Whiteheadian Suggestions for Old Testament Hermeneutics." *Interpretation* 26 (1972): 198-209.

Contends that evil is the result of creaturely creativity, permitted by a God who acts *solely persuasively*. Divine persuasion extends to all levels of creatures (not just humans), and divine persuasive power maximizes creaturely creativity by guiding creatures toward ever greater freedom. God provides the initial aims for creatures, the process view of providence.

847.   ———. "The Power of God and the Christ." *Religious Experience and Process Theology*. Edited by Harry James Cargas and Bernard Lee. New York/Paramus: Paulist Press, 1976: 79-92.

Defends the process view of divine persuasive power as the means to resolve theodicy. He also applies this view of divine power to the question of Jesus as the Christ.

848.   ———. *The Lure of God: A Biblical Background for Process Theism.* Philadelphia, PA: Fortress Press, 1978.

This book contains, as the sub-title indicates, a detailed discussion of the biblical background of process theology. Ford maintains that while biblical theology conceives of God's power in a manner that emphasizes the coercive elements, process theology conceives of God as purely persuasive. This kind of power responds directly to the problem of evil. Classical theology conceived of divine power as efficient causation.

849.   ———. "The Whirlwind Addresses Job." *St. Luke Journal* 24 (1981): 217-221.

Ford answers Job's questions: God cannot make creatures which God can completely control, since creatures must have at least some intrinsic creative activity in order to have some sort of being vis-à-vis God. To ask how a perfectly good God could create so much evil in the world is to assume God is all-powerful and has a monopoly of power. God co-ordinates the cosmos in order that chaos—the product of the random creativity of all creatures—does not prevail.

850.   ———. "The Divine Curse Understood in Terms of Persuasion." *Semeia.* Chico, CA: Scholars Press, 1982: 81-87.

Argues that divine power ought to be conceived as *solely persuasive*: divine coercive power would be infinite, if it existed, and this would imply that it would eliminate creaturely freedom (if it were exercised) and that it would be responsible for evils that God could have prevented or taken away (if it were not exercised). Ford argues also that God can curse as well as bless. Understood in process terms, cursing is a form of divine persuasion; rather than offering to the creature the best possibility for value in the initial aim, God could offer less than the best.

851.   ———. "Divine Persuasion and Coercion." *Encounter* 47 (1986): 267-273.

Response to David Basinger's "Divine Persuasion: Could the Process God do More?" [#822] and "Human Coercion: A Fly in the Process Ointment?" [#825]; and also to Barry Whitney's *Evil and the Process God* [#950]. Ford defends divine persuasion against Basinger's claim that process theism has not shown that the process God (who cannot coerce) is more adequate in explaining evil and freedom than a version of classical theism which proposes that God *can* coerce but does not. He defends the process God (as solely persuasive) against Whitney's argument that while Hartshorne speaks of a solely persuasive God, he (Hartshorne) defines the divine activity in terms that seem to imply coercive power is, in fact, exercised by God.

852.   ———. "The Rhetoric of Divine Power." *Perspectives in Religious Studies* 14 (1987): 233-238.

Argues that God operates persuasively with "shared power," rather than coercively with such power. Ford rejects the self-sufficient power of classical Christian theism as less adequate than the process vision. Yet shared power leads to inevitable evils caused by the creativity of creatures. The problem becomes: *why is there any good?* Ford's answer is that this problem is an argument *for* God, since God must function as a cosmic orderer to prevent (solely persuasively) total chaos.

853.   Frankenberry, Nancy. "Some Problems in Process Theodicy." *Religious Studies* 17 (1981): 179-197.

Contends that process theism/theodicy has not made good on its claims to have solved the theodicy issue, based upon the distinction between divine persuasive and coercive power, the defense of the moral goodness of God, and redemptive hope. [See response by Griffin, *Evil Revisited* [#873].]

854.   Garrison, Jim. *The Darkness of God: Theology After Hiroshima.* Grand Rapids, MI: Eerdmans, 1982.

Maintains that Hiroshima confronts us as never before with taking seriously the wrath of God. Garrison contends that the greatest single question of our age is to ask why—after eons of time have evolved beauty, diversity, creativity, and freedom—we are on the brink of nuclear destruction of the species. The *darkness of God* is operating through human power and human arrogance. Garrison supports process theology as articulating affirmations about God in a way which is acceptable to our secular world. He emphasizes the process theme of dual transcendence: God and the world are integral to each other, joined in a co-operative relationship that impinges upon and changes both. God and humanity both possess light and dark elements. Garrison also employs Jungian psychology to unfold how God affects us directly within the psyche.

855.   Geisler, Norman L. "Process Theology." *Tensions in Contemporary Theology.* Edited by Stanley N. Gundry and Alan F. Johnson. Chicago, IL: Moody Press (1976): 237-286.

Contains a critique of various process themes, including theodicy. He lists eleven criticisms of process theodicy (278-279): there is no guarantee that a limited God ever can achieve a better world; the process God cannot overcome evil and, as such, its efforts to do so are wasted; the process God cannot absorb evil in its nature without becoming a dualistic combination of opposites; there is little chance for God to achieve a better world since humans seem almost totally unaware of God's purposes; etc.

856.   Grange, Joseph. "Whitehead's Tragic Vision: Process, Progress and Existentialism." *Bucknell Review* 20 (1972): 127-144.

Elaborates Donald Sherburne's argument, in "Whitehead Without God," (*Christian Scholar* 50 [1967], 251-272), that existentialism and process thought require each other. The tragic dimension of life must be affirmed if the debate over values is to be enlightened. Sartre's doctrine of freedom reinforces Whitehead's tragic vision, as does Heidegger's articulation of the interrelationship between human existence and truth (the affirmation of achievement; loss and alternatives is the "sine qua non" of authentic processive existence). Likewise, Grange affirms Nietzsche's reformulation of the tragic vision: only the affirmation of existence in the face of finitude and inexhaustible possibilities will suffice for a fulfilled life.

857. Graves, Thomas. "A Critique of Process Theodicy from an African Perspective." *Process Studies* 18 (1988): 103-111.

Notes the areas of *congruence* (reality as a society and as spiritually alive) and areas of *divergence* (the process disvalue of triviality and nature of God's persuasive power) between process theism and the third-world Shona culture of Zimbabwe. He agrees with Barry Whitney's argument (*Evil and the Process God* [#950]), that there is a need to articulate more fully the meaning of divine persuasive power in process theism.

858. Griffin, David R. "Philosophical Theology and Pastoral Ministry." *Encounter* 33 (1972): 230-244.

Rejects two views of divine action in the world: the view based on the classical conception of God as omnipotent, and the view that God does not act in the world. Griffin argues the case for the process alternative: God acts solely persuasively in the world.

859. ———. "Divine Causality, Evil and Philosophical Theology: A Critique of James Ross." *International Journal for Philosophy of Religion* 4 (1973): 168-186.

This is an earlier version of *Chapter 14* of Griffin's *God, Power and Evil* [#861]. Griffin maintains that Ross has failed to provide sound arguments for the compatibility of God's omnipotence with both human freedom and the divine goodness.

860. ———. "Relativism, Divine Causation, and Biblical Theology." *Encounter* 36 (1975): 342-369.

Contends that while the distinction between primary and secondary causation has been the most influential way theologians have understood the relationship between divine and non-divine causation, this schema not only has resulted in the problem of evil, but leads to a relativism which renders arbitrary both Christian faith and the practice of devoting special attention to the biblical texts. Whitehead's metaphysics provides a conceptuality in terms of which we can conceive of the relation between divine and non-divine causation that avoids this relativism. Since this view has important implications for biblical theology, Griffin argues that the gulf between biblical scholars and philosophical theologians can be overcome. [See Bernard Loomer's response, "Response to David Griffin," *Encounter* 36 (1975), 361-369; and George Coats, "Response to David Griffin," *Encounter* 36 (1975), 370-375. See also Griffin's reply, "Response to George W. Coats and Bernard M. Loomer," *Encounter* 36 (1975), 376-378. See *The Size of God: The Theology of Bernard Loomer in Context*. Edited by William Dean and Larry E. Axel. Macon, GA: Mercer University Press, 1987: the chapters are written by John Cobb, William Dean, Delwin Brown, Larry Exel, Bernard Lee, and Nancy Frankenberry—all discussing various aspects of Loomer's theism, in particular his final essay, "The Size of God," prepared especially for this volume. Loomer's bibliography is included, from his 1942 dissertation to his final publications in 1985, the year of his death. The aforementioned essay, "The Size of God," partially completed before his death, is included as well (20-52).]

861.   ———. *God, Power and Evil: A Process Theodicy*. Philadelphia, PA: Westminster Press, 1976. Reprinted, Lanham, MD: University Press of America, 1990.

This is the major publication on process theodicy (complemented by Barry Whitney's construction of a process theodicy based on Hartshorne's prolific publications [#950] and Maurice Barineau's construction of a process theodicy based on Whitehead's publications [#820]). The reprinted edition has the same pagination as the first edition, and includes a new preface. Griffin focuses upon the question of divine power and presents his process theodicy, after critiquing in detail the theodicies of the major classical theologians and philosophers: Plato, Aristotle, Plotinus, Augustine, Aquinas, Spinoza, Luther, Calvin, Leibniz, Barth, Hick, Ross, Fackenheim, Brunner). Griffin argues that divine power necessarily is persuasive rather than controlling, that intensity as well as harmony is required for more valuable forms of experience, and that there are necessary correlations involving value and power: the capacity for intrinsic good, for intrinsic evil, freedom (self-determination) and the capacity for instrumental goodness and for instrumental evil. The *Preface* of the second edition notes several ways the formulation of Griffin's process theodicy could be improved and he notes the ways his position has changed since the original publication. More detailed discussions of these points are contained in Griffin's *Evil Revisited* [#873]. Griffin clarifies and reformulates his definitions of "I omnipotence," "C omnipotence," etc., and inserts several major points (omitted on the recommendation of the publisher from the first edition). Efficient causation, for example, is not to be equated with coercive power, nor is final causation to be equated with persuasive power. There is also a difference between metaphysical and psychological (absolute and relative) meanings of the persuasive—coercive distinction, and an explanation why it is appropriate to use the distinction in the strictly metaphysical sense. Griffin has a much stronger view of eschatology now and accepts subjective immortality. He contends that these changes have relevance for a more fully satisfactory theodicy [See also *Chapter 6* of Griffin's *God and Religion in the Postmodern World* [#870] and his *Evil Revisited* [#873].]

862.   ———. "Values, Evil, and Liberation Theology." *Encounter* 40 (1979): 1-15.

Liberation theologies face the dilemma of rejecting the traditional doctrine of omnipotent providence and affirming that God is the supreme power in the universe. Griffin rejects as inadequate several traditional attempts to resolve this dilemma (evil is not genuine evil; divine power has been self-limited; the dilemma is beyond rational understanding; etc.), and argues that liberation theologies ought to incorporate his own solution, proposed most fully in *God, Power and Evil* [#861]: *God does not prevent all worldly evils because God cannot do so*. The advantages of holding this view outweigh the objections. There is, furthermore, a set of variables which are necessarily correlative: the capacity to enjoy values; the capacity to suffer; freedom, the power of self-determination; and causation, the power to influence others for good or evil. These variables increase proportionately to one another throughout the evolutionary process.

863.   ———. "Creation Out of Chaos and the Problem of Evil." *Encountering Evil*. Edited by Stephen Davis. Nashville, TN: John Knox Press, 1981: 101-119, 129-136.

Argues that the solution to theodicy is in denying the traditional doctrine of divine omnipotence which supposedly held God is the sole power. Griffin rejects also the traditional doctrine of *creatio ex nihilo*, in favor of the White-headian—Hartshornean view that there always has been a plurality of actualities other than God, all of which have some power of their own. As such, *divine power is necessarily persuasive*. Griffin defends his view of divine power and divine goodness vis-à-vis evil. He also defends the necessity for formulating a rational theodicy, versus merely acquiescing to the faith solution. In the final section, Griffin defends his process theodicy (presented in summary fashion here) against the critiques of Roth, Hick, Sontag and Davis (critiques which follow Griffin's presentation of his theodicy in the *Encountering Evil* text).

864.   ———. "Actuality, Possibility, and Theodicy: A Response to Nelson Pike." *Process Studies* 12 (1982): 168-179.

Response to Pike's critique in "Process Theodicy and the Concept of Power" [#912]. Griffin has revised this response to Pike in *Chapter 8* of his *Evil Revisited* [#873]. He rejects Pike's view of omnipotence as (what Pike takes to be) the standard, historical view. He rebuffs also Pike's criticisms of Griffin's arguments against "premise X": "It is possible for one actual being's condition to be completely determined by a being or beings other than itself." Griffin repudiates Pike's separation of metaphysical and logical possibility: Griffin's point is that logical possibility about actualities cannot be discussed apart from some metaphysical assertions as to the nature of actualities. He rejects also Pike's distinction between *having* and *exercising* power. For process thought, the two are necessarily correlated: an individual *is* its activity.

865.   ———. "Review of Bonnell Spencer, *God Who Dares to be Man: Theology for Prayer and Suffering*." *Process Studies* 13 (1983): 237-240.

Holds that while Spencer [#593] shares much with process theology (God is not all-controlling power and God is not impassible), he holds (contra process thought) to the doctrine of creation out of nothing, and greatly modifies Whiteheadian thought in other ways. For example, Spencer supports a divine self-limitation doctrine (as does John Hick), contradicting his (Spencer's) own position. He also develops a Christology that supposedly is based on White-headian thought, but is problematic at several points.

866.   ———. "Power Divine and Demonic: A Review Article." *Encounter* 45 (1984): 67-75.

Review of the 1982 reprinting of Arthur McGill's *Suffering: A Test of Theological Method*, first published in 1968 [#1139]. McGill argues that God's power is revealed in Christ as non-dominating power, in contrast to demonic power that is coercive and dominating. Griffin argues that process theists would agree that divine power is persuasive, yet would disagree that all power which differs from divine power is demonic: creatures exercise both kinds of power—creative/persuasive and coercive/domineering.

867.   ———. "The Rationality of Belief in God: A Response to Hans Küng." *Faith and Philosophy* 1 (1984): 16-26.

Response to Küng's *Does God Exist?* [#1893]. He holds that while some of Küng's statements suggest that he wishes to modify the traditional conception of divine omnipotence, there are contradictory statements in Küng's text, as well as an ultimate appeal to mystery and the insolvability of theodicy. Griffin argues that this appeal to incomprehensibility is in serious tension with other elements of Küng's theological enterprise.

868.   ———. "Creativity in Post-Modern Religion." *Creativity in Art, Religion and Culture.* Edited by Michael Mitias. Amsterdam: Rodopi, 1985: 64-85.

Maintains that the Whiteheadian view of creativity provides new perspectives on various issues, including evil. Given the ultimacy of creativity, there must always be a multiplicity of creative individuals. All exemplify creativity, while God is the ultimate instance of this exemplification. The creativity of creatures is not a contingent matter.

869.   ———. "*Creation Ex Nihilo*, The Divine *Modus Operandi*, and The *Imitatio Dei.*" *Faith and Creativity: Essays in Honor of Eugene H. Peters.* Edited by George Norgulen and George Shields. St. Louis, MO: CBP Press, 1987: 95-123.

Griffin contends that divine persuasive power alone explains the creation of the world, and yet there were good reasons for early Christianity to retain the idea of God's power as coercive, thereby missing the central revelatory significance of Jesus and creating an insoluble problem of evil.

870.   ———. *God and Religion in the Postmodern World.* Albany, NY: State University of New York Press, 1988.

Discusses various aspects of theodicy, among other themes, throughout this book. He denies creation out of nothing as self-contradictory and holds that because each occasion is affected by the creative influences of all previous creatures, God cannot be the total cause of every event. Evil is the result. The theodicy problem has developed in modern times, Griffin argues, largely because the founders of modernism (Descartes, Boyle, Newton, Luther, Calvin, and others) subscribed to the Augustinian voluntaristic tradition that stressed the absolute omnipotence of God far more than had the medieval thinkers (Aquinas, etc.). The chapter on post mortem life (*Chapter 6*, "Postmodern Animism and Life After Death") presents Griffin's arguments for an afterlife and its application for theodicy: process theodicy often has been attacked for its lack of an eschatology, a situation Griffin seeks to amend in this and other recent publications. [For Griffin's earliest publication on the question of Whiteheadian "subjective immortality," see his "The Possibility of Subjective Immortality," *Modern Schoolman* 53 (1975), 35-57. Originally published in *University of Dayton Review* 8 (1971), 43-56.]

871.   ———. "Reply: Must God Be Unlimited? Naturalistic Vs. Supernaturalistic Theism." *Concepts of the Ultimate.* Edited by Linda J. Tessier. New York: St. Martin's Press, 1989: 23-31.

Response to Davis's "Why God Must Be Unlimited" [#842]. Griffin defends process theism as a *naturalism* which holds that the existence of a realm of finite beings with power is not a contingent, arbitrary fact, based upon a divine decision. This is opposed to Davis's supernaturalistic theism with its view that God has all the power and will one day overcome all the evil with it. [See the Griffin—Davis debate in *Encountering Evil* [#863].]

872.   ———. "Review of Marjorie Suchocki, *The End of Evil: Process Eschatology in Historical Context.*" *Process Studies* 19 (1989): 57-63.

Griffin concedes that he agrees with Suchocki's view [#932] that an adequate theodicy requires an eschatology and a portrayal of God's power as sufficient to guarantee the victory of good over evil. He agrees that the Whiteheadian doctrine of "objective immortality" is not the basis for a sufficient eschatology. Yet, Suchocki's modification of Whitehead's texts to formulate a process eschatology fails in three ways: it is incompatible with fundamental Whiteheadian categories; it is not intelligible; and it does not make contact with ordinary intuitions and yearnings for salvation. [See Suchocki's reply, "Evil, Eschatology, and God: Response to David Griffin" [#933].]

873.   ———. *Evil Revisited: Responses and Reconsiderations*. Albany, NY: State University of New York Press, 1991.

Response to criticisms of his theodicy by Plantinga, David and Randall Basinger, Frankenberry, Pike, Hefner, Knasas, Hare and Madden, and others. He offers various clarifications and reformulations of his views (the latter also noted briefly in the *Preface* of the second edition of his *God, Power and Evil* [#861]). The major changes are a stronger doctrine of evil (a dimension of evil Griffin calls "the demonic") and a more robust doctrine of divine power which gives a stronger basis for the hope evil will be overcome in the long run. A fully adequate theodicy, he now asserts, requires a more adequate eschatology than he presented previously. Griffin holds fast to the view that the only possible way to solve the problem of evil is to modify the traditional doctrine of divine power. He presents a detailed clarification of persuasive and coercive power, and distinguishes them from efficient and final causation. He distinguishes also between metaphysical and psychological persuasion and coercion.

874.   Griffin, David R., and John Cobb. *Process Theology: An Introductory Exposition*. Philadelphia, PA: Westminster, 1976.

Griffin's brief discussion of theodicy (69-75) distinguishes divine ultimate *responsibility* for evil without being *indictable* for it. He clarifies why evil is necessary in the world.

875.   Griffin, David R., and Joseph A. Deegan and Daniel E.H. Bryant. *How Are God and Evil Related?* Claremont, CA: Center for Process Studies, 1988.

A simplified version of some of the major aspects of Griffin's process theodicy. He contrasts process theism with supernaturalism, pragmatism and atheism.

876.   Griffin, David R., and Huston Smith. *Primordial Truth and Postmodern Theology*. Albany, NY: State University of New York Press, 1989.

The book is a dialogue between the two authors: two rounds of Griffin's critique of Smith's views *(Chapters 2 and 4)*, with Smith's responses *(Chapters 3 and 5)*. Griffin takes issue with Smith's denial of genuine evil (Smith supports the Augustinian privation of good and the principle of plenitude theory in the context of the great chain of being) and his defense of a traditional notion of divine omnipotence. Against Smith's gnostic dualism, Griffin argues for a post mortem realm of continued conscious existence (unlike his earlier view and the more general Whiteheadian agnosticism on this issue, and the Hartshornean view that there is merely objective immortality "in God" after a creature's earthly death). Smith insists that the classical God is much more powerful than the process God and much more benevolent, since everything is as it should be, the result of divine causation—nothing that occurs would have been better, had it been otherwise. God transmutes everything into perfect goodness.

877.   Gruenler, Royce G. *The Inexhaustible God*. Grand Rapids, MI: Baker Book House, 1983.

In this major critique of process theology from an evangelical point of view, Gruenler contends that biblical faith is superior to the improvements suggested by process theologians. *Chapter 1* ("Theodicy, Anthropodicy, and Power in Process Theism: A Critique") refutes process theodicy, rejecting the fact that it ignores God's self-revelation, as witnessed in Scripture. He refutes also "the finite God" of process theology, the difficulties process theology has in setting out the ratio of power between God and creatures, the lack of an eschatology, etc. He also criticises evangelicals (like Richard Rice, *The Openness of God* [#127]), who are sympathetic to process theology.

878.   Hamilton, Peter. *The Living God and the Modern World*. London: Hodder and Stoughton, 1967.

Chapter 4 ("Suffering, Death and Heaven in the Light of Process Thinking") offers a sympathetic interpretation of process thinking (Whitehead and more so, Hartshorne) on the problem of evil and immortality.

879.   Hare, Peter H., and Edward H. Madden. "Evil and Unlimited Power." *Review of Metaphysics* 20 (1966): 278-289.

Argues that the problem of evil should focus on *the problem of gratuitous evil*. The "quasi-theism" of Whitehead and Hartshorne fails on three counts: (1) it cannot make meaningful the distinction between a "limited" and a "relative" God; (2) its God cannot guarantee the triumph of good over evil; and (3) its characterization of evil and value is incompatible with theism. [See Hare and Madden, *Evil and the Concept of God* [#1210].]

880.   Hare, Peter H. "Evil and the Concept of a Limited God." *Philosophical Studies* 18 (1967): 65-70.

Contends that the problem of evil should not seek to answer the question as to why God did not create a world in which there is no evil, but answer why there is *gratuitous* evil. Hare contends that the concept of a limited God (of process theology) is an inadequate response to gratuitous evil. [See Hare and Madden, *Evil and the Concept of God* [#1210].]

881.   ——. "Review of David Griffin, *God, Power and Evil*." *Process Studies* 7 (1977): 44-51.

Hare suggests that Griffin's process theodicy [#861] is weakened by the fact that neither Griffin nor other process theists have described what imaginable state of affairs would *falsify* the deity of process theism, what imaginable evil events would have to take place in the world to constitute a preponderance of evidence against process theism. [See Griffin's response in *Evil Revisited* [#873].]

882.   Hare, Peter H., and Edward H. Madden. "Evil and Persuasive Power." *Process Studies* 2 (1972): 44-48.

Asserts that process theodicy has not defended its thesis that God acts solely persuasively. Process theodicy has not shown how the high proportion of persuaded actuality is compatible with divine persuasive power. A *mixture* of persuasive and coercive power in God seems more appropriate than solely persuasive power. [See Baldwin's response, "Evil and Persuasive Power: A Response to Hare and Madden" [#816]. See also Griffin's response to Baldwin and to Hare and Madden, in *Evil Revisited* [#873].]

883.   Hartshorne, Charles E. "Whitehead and Berdyaev: Is There Tragedy in God?" *Journal of Religion* 37 (1957): 71-84.

Argues that Berdyaev and Whitehead share many similarities, including the view that there is tragedy in God. Alternative possible values and multiple freedom render the total avoidance of conflict unachievable. God is not sheer cause, mere being, independent of all becoming and creating, but is relative to the world, the "fellow sufferer."

884.   ——. "A New Look at the Problem of Evil." *Current Philosophical Issues: Essays in Honor of Curt John Ducassé*. Edited by Frederick C. Dommeyer. Springfield, IL: Charles C. Thomas, 1966: 201-212.

This is Hartshorne's most systematic treatment of the theodicy issue. He argues that God's power is persuasive, not coercive and, as such, the mutual conflict arising from creaturely freedom is the cause of evil. There is a multiplicity of powers, not just divine power, operating in the world. God provides laws of nature within which creaturely freedom is possible and "lures" us to actualise the greatest possible values at each moment. God also preserves eternally the goods and evils, both in their full and complete value.

885.   ——. *A Natural Theology for our Time*. La Salle, IL: Open Court, 1967.

Contains references (as do many of Hartshorne's numerous publications) to the theodicy issue, although Hartshorne has not presented a systematic theodicy. [For such a systematic construction of a theodicy from these many and varied references, see Barry Whitney, *Evil and the Process God* [#950].] Hartshorne holds that there is no utterly senseless or unredeemed evil: all evil has value from some perspective. The source of evil lies in creaturely creativity (which is conscious freedom in human beings). The risk of evil and opportunity for good arise from the same source: the multiple creativity/freedom of creatures. Hartshorne argues also that evils are not an empirical disproof of God's necessary existence. [On this latter point, see Hartshorne's *Anselm's Discovery: A Re-Examination of the Ontological Argument for God's Existence*. La Salle, IL: Open Court, 1965; and *The Logic of Perfection*. La Salle, IL: Open Court, 1962. For the implications of Hartshorne's ontological argument for theodicy, see Barry Whitney, *Evil and the Process God, Chapter 5*.]

886.   ——. "Is Whitehead's God the God of Religion?" *Whitehead's Philosophy: Selected Essays, 1935-1970*: 99-110. Lincoln, NE: University of Nebraska Press, 1972.

Defends Whitehead's God against the criticisms of Stephen Ely (*The Religious Availability of Whitehead's God* [see #844]). Whitehead's God is benevolent: in

God, altruism and self-interest are one; creaturely values are enjoyed by God, without this being selfishness on God's behalf. Ely misunderstands Whitehead's theory of the overcoming of evils and mistakenly holds that Whitehead's God deindividualizes us.

887.   ———. "Theism in Asia and Western Thought." *Philosophy East and West* 28 (1978): 401-409.

Rejects the traditional doctrine of divine omnipotence. Evil is the result of multiple decision-making by creatures. God sets limits to the tendency toward chaos inherent in this multiple freedom.

888.   ———. *Omnipotence and Other Theological Mistakes*. Albany, NY: State University of New York Press, 1984.

Presents a simplified version of his theodicy, dispersed throughout the book with other themes. The only solution is that which uses the idea of freedom and generalizes it to all of creaturely life. Hartshorne rejects absolute divine determinism, the view implicit in the traditional use of "omnipotence."

889.   ———. "[Response to] Barry Whitney." *Hartshorne, Process Philosophy and Theodicy*. Edited by Robert Kane and Stephen Phillips. Albany, NY: State University of New York Press, 1989: 184-185.

Response to Whitney's critique of his [Hartshorne's] theodicy ("Hartshorne and Theodicy" [#951]). Hartshorne concedes that Whitney is justified in arguing that he (Hartshorne) has been less clear about God as cosmic *cause* than as cosmic *effect*. He reaffirms that divine power is solely persuasive and that this Whiteheadian insight is adequate to guarantee there will always be a cosmic order sufficient to make the world a possible set of data for the divine psyche. Hartshorne maintains that the world cannot degenerate into either hopeless chaos or hopeless monotony. He holds that the divine irresistible power which guarantees this is not coercive.

890.   Hefner, Philip J. "Is Theodicy a Question of Power?" *Journal of Religion* 59 (1979): 87-93.

Review article of Griffin's *God, Power, and Evil* [#861]. Hefner argues that Griffin's formulation of the problem of evil is inadequate on several counts: his rejection of *creatio ex nihilo* diminishes the essential Christian belief that God is the origin of all things; his concept of "genuine" evil is ambiguous; and his explanations of freedom, value and triviality lead to the same conclusion as the traditional theodicies Griffin rejects: freedom is worth the risk of the evils it produces. [See Griffin's response to Hefner in *Evil Revisited* [#873].]

891.   ———. "The Problem of Evil: Picking Up the Pieces." *Dialog* 25 (1986): 87-92.

Maintains that there is no rational solution to the problem of evil: we must live with the faith that evil will be overcome by God eventually. Hefner questions whether Griffin's process theodicy and Rabbi Harold Kushner's version of it (*When Bad Things Happen to Good People* [#1132]) compromise too much the traditional Christian understanding of divine power and creation *ex nihilo*. John Hick's version of theodicy is seen as more adequate, since divine power is not so comprised.

892. Henry, Carl F.H. "The Stunted God of Process Theology." *Process Theology*. Edited by Ronald H. Nash. Grand Rapids, MI: Baker Book House, 1987: 357-376.

Citing Whitehead, Hartshorne, Ogden, Griffin, Pittenger and D.D. Williams, Henry argues that process theology repudiates the Word of God mediated solely through Christ. Process theologians misidentify the God of biblical theism and of evangelical orthodoxy with the immovable divinity postulated by certain Greek philosophers and present secular thinkers. The denial of divine omnipotence invalidates process theodicy, since a non-omnipotent God cannot transform a non-ideal world into an ideal one.

893. Hick, John. "Critique." *Encountering Evil*. Edited by Stephen Davis. Atlanta, GA: John Knox Press, 1981: 122-123.

Rejects Griffin's theodicy for its limited God. Hick rejects also Griffin's invalid distinction between genuine and apparent evils. [See also Hick's brief critique of Griffin's theodicy, in Mesle, *John Hick's Theodicy* [#794]; Griffin's responses are found in Davis, editor, *Encountering Evil* [#780] and Griffin's *Evil Revisited* [#873].]

894. Holmes, Arthur F. "Why God Cannot Act." *Process Theology*. Edited by Ronald H. Nash. Grand Rapids, MI: Baker Book House, 1987: 177-195.

Maintains that since Whitehead's God is unable to act other than persuasively, there is no assurance that good will prevail. Without unilateral divine action, the process metaphysics is an overly romanticised idealism caught up in the evolutionary optimism that preceded the holocausts of this century.

895. Inbody, Tyron. "Religious Empiricism and the Problem of Evil." *American Journal of Theology and Philosophy* 12 (1991): 35-48.

Evaluates the empirical theologies and theodicies of Henry Nelson Wieman, Bernard Meland and Bernard Loomer. [For Meland's bibliography, see Barry Woodbridge, compiler, "Bernard Eugene Meland: A Primary and Secondary Bibliography," *Process Studies* 5 (1975), 285-302. See also the listings for Meland and Wieman in Barry Woodbridge, editor, *Alfred North Whitehead: A Primary—Secondary Bibliography* (Bowling Green, OH: Bowling Green State University: Philosophy Documentation Center, 1976)]. Inbody argues that by concentrating more on the depth of experience than on a rational analysis of necessary ideas and on a speculative vision of the whole grounded in experience, the empirical theologians construct a more ambitious view of divine goodness than have the majority of process theologians. The strength of such an approach is that it reframes the theodicy question. The danger is the threat of moving too far toward a pantheism in which one might lose the object of religious devotion in a sea of natural piety.

896. Jackson, Gordon E. *Pastoral Care and Process Theology*. Lanham, MD: University Press of America, 1981.

The section on theodicy contends that the Whiteheadian notion of evil contributes in two significant ways (differently than does traditional theodicy) to pastoral care: in the location of moral evil or sin within the self-causing subject, and in seeing how God is required as Savior.

897.   Janzen, J. Gerald. "Modes of Power and the Divine Relativity." *Encounter* 36 (1975): 379-406.

Critically assesses Lewis Ford's major writings on divine power ("Divine Persuasion and the Triumph of Good" [#845]; "Biblical Recital and Process Philosophy" [#846]; and "God as King: Benevolent Despot or Constitutional Monarch?" [#993]). Janzen contends that Ford's effort to conceive of God as wholly persuasive is misconceived, but with appropriate modifications, two models of divine power can be fused into one model that articulates power in terms both of efficacy and of finality (coercion and persuasion).

898.   Jones, William R. "Process Theodicy: Guardian of the Oppressor or Goad to the Oppressed? An Interim Assessment." *Process Studies* 19 (1989): 268-281.

Claims that process theodicy fails to deal with the ethnic factor in suffering. This renders suspect the benevolence of God in process theodicy, question-begging assumption.

899.   Knasas, John. "Super God: Divine Infinity and Human Self-Determination." *American Catholic Philosophical Association Proceedings* 55 (1981): 197-209.

Defense of Aquinas versus Griffin's theodicy and his (Griffin's) challenging of the all-powerful God. For Aquinas, God works in the human will without detriment to the real ability of the will to act otherwise. When omnipotence is seen as the infinity of "subsistens esse," creatures can be the loci of self-determination. Knasas concludes that the traditional notion of God in Aquinas remains an intelligible standard by which to judge Griffin's process God as finite and imperfect. [See Griffin's response in *Evil Revisited* [#873].]

900.   Kraus, Elizabeth M. "God the Savior." *New Essays in Metaphysics*. Edited by Robert C. Neville. Albany, NY: State University of New York Press, 1987: 199-215.

Argues for the Whiteheadian view that evil (as the loss of aesthetic intensity) is an essential component in the finite process, and that a complex divine activity that overcomes evil is equally essential.

901.   Loomer, Bernard M. "Ely on Whitehead's God." *Process Philosophy and Christian Thought*. Edited by Delwin Brown, Ralph James, and Gene Reeves. Indianapolis, IN: Bobbs-Merrill, 1971: 264-286.

Defense of Whitehead against Ely's criticisms (*The Religious Availability of Whitehead's God* [#844]): the preservation of values, the transmutation of evil into good (which includes the problem of evil and God's goodness), and the problem of the relation of God's goodness and the preservation of individuals as such. Ely misinterprets Whitehead at several points, including the concept of objective immortality: Whitehead does not (contra Ely) hold that evils disappear for God. The immortality of the past retains *all* goods and evils in God's experience. Loomer argues also that Ely's misinterpretation of Whitehead's concept of transmutation reduces Whitehead's theology to an absurdity: all evil is not to be seen as good in God's eyes. Evil is real, yet transformed by God. Ely mistakenly interprets Whitehead's view of aesthetic value as implying God is not good. Ely also mistakenly holds that divine goodness is contingent upon human immortality.

902. ——. "Two Conceptions of Power." *Process Studies* 6 (1976): 5-32.

Contrasts *unilateral* (or linear) power with *relational* power. The former is the traditional view, the power of influencing others; the latter is the process view, the power of being influenced and influencing. [For a discussion of various views of divine power in process theology, see Barry Whitney, *Evil and the Process God* [#950], etc.; David Basinger, *Divine Power in Process Theism* [#826]; David Griffin, *God, Power and Evil* [#861], and *Evil Revisited* [#873]; Gerald Janzen, "Modes of Power and the Divine Relativity" [#897]; Lewis Ford, "Divine Persuasion and Coercion," [#851], "Divine Persuasion and the Triumph of Good" [#845]; etc. See also the recent publication of Nicholas Gier, "Three Types of Divine Power," *Process Studies* 20 (1991), 221-232: he argues for the relational "power-sharing" model of power in process theology and feminism, versus the unilateral divine power in traditional theism and the free will defense of Nelson Pike and David Basinger.]

903. Mazzuca, John Louis. "Reflections on the Divine Tragedy in the Universe of A.N. Whitehead." *Encounter* 33 (1972): 185-202.

Asserts that the God of Whitehead is the crystallization of a tragic symbol. Whitehead's God is not and cannot be the *sole* determiner of actualities; God is only one fact amid a welter of facts. God influences the world only by persuasion and, as such, lacks "power" and is unworthy of "praise." God cannot make all things well in the end, since evil is irrevocable. Mazzuca concedes that some may find relevant Whitehead's reference to the intuition of a "rightness" in things, yet he argues that tragedy reigns: the actualization of our ideals is rare and our sorrow is profound.

904. Mesle, C. Robert. "Review of Stephen Davis, editor, *Encountering Evil*." *Process Studies* 15 (1986): 137-139.

Argues that Davis, Roth, Sontag, and Hick offer no rational basis for determining the nature of divine power or love. Griffin and other process theologians succeed in offering arguments against the coherence of some of the concepts of omnipotence; but they do so at the expense of divine love.

905. ——. "Review of Barry Whitney, *Evil and the Process God*." *Process Studies* 17 (1987): 57-61.

Concurs that Whitney's process theodicy [#950] uncovers a major problem in process theodicy: God's activity is said to be solely persuasive, yet Hartshorne describes this action in terms indistinguishable from coercion. Mesle argues that Whitney's proposal—that the process God be seen as operating persuasively within natural laws and yet coercively in having established those laws—put him (Whitney) in close proximity with John Hick who has argued that God has created the best kind of world possible for soul-making. Unlike Whitney, other process theists have insisted that God does not set the limits within which freedom is to operate and, as such, they do not have to address issues that face Whitney. [See Whitney's response to Mesle and others in "Hartshorne and Theodicy" [#951].]

906. Miller, Randolph Crump. "Process, Evil and God." *American Journal of Theology and Philosophy* 1 (1980): 60-70.

An exposition of some central features of process theodicy, drawing upon Whitehead, Hartshorne and Griffin. Miller concludes that process theodicy is a viable solution to the problem of evil. God is not responsible for evil but suffers along with us.

907.   Nobuhara, Tokiyuki. "Whitehead and Nishida on Time." *Japanese Religions* 12 (1982): 41-50 and 47-64.

Argues that Whitehead's concept of God solves the problem of time and evil differently and more effectively than does Nishida. Whitehead's concept of God as *Primordial* is not in danger of being identified with the demonic; God as *Consequent* experiences evil in a redemptively creative way.

908.   Nordgulen, George. "New Spokesman in an Old Dialogue." *New Scholasticism* 47 (1973): 324-338.

Holds that Hume's cosmological and metaphysical context was inadequate to elucidate and clarify the theistic issue (see Hume's *Dialogues Concerning Natural Religion*). Process theism offers a new cosmology, a new theism, and a new understanding of the problem of evil: God does *not* have all the power.

909.   Ogden, Schubert M. "Evil and Belief in God: The Distinctive Relevance of a 'Process Theology'." *Perkins Journal of Theology* 31 (1978): 29-34.

Following Hartshorne's lead, Ogden argues that process theology has relevance in resolving the traditional problem of evil by demonstrating that the understanding of omnipotence is a meaningless concept and theodicy, as such, is a pseudo-problem.

910.   Peel, David R. "Is Schubert Ogden's 'God' Christian?" *Journal of Religion* 70 (1990): 147-166.

Defense of process theology and theodicy against attacks by some British thinkers. Peel defends Ogden's claim that neoclassical metaphysics proposes a way of conceiving God without succumbing to the supernaturalism of classical theism.

911.   Peterson, Michael L. "God and Evil in Process Theology." *Process Theology.* Edited by Ronald H. Nash. Grand Rapids, MI: Baker Book House, 1987: 117-139.

Contends that process theodicy fails to do justice to the historic Christian understanding of God and evil, and that it fails to present an adequate philosophical answer to the problem of evil. Process theodicy distorts divine power, divine goodness, the nature of evil, and fails to provide a satisfactory eschatology. [See Lewis S. Ford's response to Peterson and others in Nash, *Process Theology*, "Evangelical Appraisals of Process Theism" [#999].]

912.   Pike, Nelson. "Process Theodicy and the Concept of Power." *Process Studies* 12 (1982): 148-167.

Argues against Griffin's claim that God, defined as all-powerful, would have all the power there is. The standard view of omnipotence has held that God could completely determine all of the activities of all other beings; yet this does not make creatures other than God devoid of power, since God willingly refrains from exercising some of the divine power. Pike rejects Griffin's arguments versus the premise that it is possible for one actual being to be completely determined by a being or beings other than itself: Pike rejects Griffin's distinct and incompatible claims that this premise is meaningless and both logically and metaphysically false. [Griffin responds in "Actuality, Possibility, and Theodicy: A Response to Nelson Pike" [#864] and in *Evil Revisited* [#873].]

913.   Pittenger, W. Norman. "Process Theology Revisited." *Theology Today* 27 (1970): 212-220.

Defends process theism against the charge that it does not take evil seriously. The God of Whitehead and Hartshorne experiences all creaturely goods and evils: God positively prehends whatever is useable, and negatively prehends "surd" evils.

914.   ———. *Goodness Distorted*. Bath, England: A.R. Mowbracy and Co., 1970.

Exposition of the process understanding of evil and the nature of God as love. Love is central to the nature of God and to the universe; love makes it possible for us to face evil and overcome it. God takes into the divine reality all the good; evil is prehended negatively, after all possible good has been extracted from it. God suffers with us, as shown in the redemptive suffering of Christ. Pittenger then shows how the doctrine of God as love illuminates various theological concerns: sin, human beings, the church, human destiny and the ultimate meaning of life.

915.   ———. "Process Theology and the Fact of Evil." *Expository Times* 82 (1971): 73-77.

Defends process theology against the charge that it minimalizes evil. Evils hold back, diminish and distort the creative advance of the cosmos toward the shared increase of good sought by God's lure. Pittenger summarizes the discussion of the types of evils noted in his *Goodness Distorted* [#914], and rejects the separation of creation and redemption. Creation is good. Sin is the violation of proper divine and human relationships, and original sin is an accumulation of wrong choices which make good acts impossible. Divine omnipotence is best understood as the power of God to accomplish the divine will through, rather than in spite of, the decisions of creatures.

916.   ———. "Suffering and Love." *Expository Times* 84 (1973): 19-22.

Holds that suffering has positive value in deepening our understanding of life, purifying our feelings, enriching our relationships with others, and in grasping the nature of divine love.

917.   ———. "An Interpretation of Sin." *Religion in Life* 44 (1975): 428-431.

Maintains that sin is our failure to live in proper relationships with each other and with God.

918.   ———. "Is God Responsible for Evil?" *Modern Churchman* 19 (1976): 86-89.

Rejects the classical Christian understanding of God's power as responsible for all goods and evils. Divine omnipotence means *sovereign rule*, not *all-mightiness*. God uses force or coercion only to prevent contrasts from becoming totally destructive conflicts, such that would reduce creation to a state of anarchy and chaos. Creaturely creativity is responsible for the world's evil, not God. God suffers with creation.

919. ———. *Cosmic Love and Human Wrong: The Reconstruction of the Meaning of Sin in the Light of Process Thinking*. New York: Paulist Press, 1978.

Redefines sin and human wrongness in terms of process theology; God is not responsible for the world's evil, but is rather a participant in our struggle to overcome evil. The world is a process and not a completed product. God lures us to actualize the best value available at each moment, but creatures are free to accept or reject this lure to aesthetic value. Since God is love, God cannot use coercion except in those very restricted areas of subhuman and human life where only by coercion can chaos be prevented. This is the wrath of God, but whatever force God uses is minimal.

920. ———. *After Death, Life in God*. New York: Seabury Press, 1980.

Defends the Whiteheadian view that we live on as "objectively immortal" *in God*. Pittenger argues that we rise *in the risen Christ*. God is the recipient of all creaturely experiences.

921. ———. *Catholic Faith in a Process Perspective*. New York: Orbis Books, 1981.

Chapter 5 ("Process Theology and the Fact of Evil") and *Chapter 6* ("Suffering and Love") present Pittenger's process view of the nature of sin and its overcoming by God's love. While not wishing to minimalize the reality of evil, Pittenger argues that suffering can contribute to a deeper understanding of life, purify our motives and desires, enrich our relationships with one another, and to grasp more profoundly the nature of God as cosmic love who shares in our suffering.

922. Platt, David. "Does Whitehead's God Possess a Moral Will?" *Process Studies* 5 (1975): 114-122.

Response to critics (Ely's *The Religious Availability of Whitehead's God* [see #844], and others) who have argued that Whitehead's moral philosophy is deficient. From a Kantian perspective, there is a difficulty with Whitehead's aesthetic model of value. The crucial issue is the apparent amorality of Whitehead's God. If God seeks maximum value within the realm of finite occasions, God does not seem to favor some value-realizations over others. Platt defends Whitehead against this criticism, contending that Whitehead's primary focus on aesthetic value must be supplemented by moral concerns. Otherwise, a new problem of evil would arise: God lures and experiences all human value, including hideous acts.

923. Reynolds, A. "God and Evil: A Rejoinder." *Modern Churchman* 24 (1981): 183-186.

Argues against Norman Pittenger's process theodicy [see the several Pittenger items listed in this chapter] and claims that the "orthodox" position can be exonerated quite simply, if the concept of omnipotence is understood correctly. Pittenger's process theism is a return to the finite God invoked by John Stuart Mill. It overlooks the fact that it is impossible for God to prevent evil without interfering with the very purpose of creation. God cannot eliminate imperfection from a finite world: this is not a limitation on God, however, but an empirical fact.

924. Roth, John K. "Critique." *Encountering Evil.* Edited by Stephen T. Davis. Atlanta, GA: John Knox Press, 1981: 119-121.

Rejects Griffin's theodicy on various grounds. Griffin's claim for the necessity of metaphysical correlates (that every increase in the capacity to enjoy intrinsic goodness is an increase in the capacity to suffer, etc.) is unsubstantiated by experience. Griffin's God, moreover, is too weak, and the lack of an adequate eschatology is a crucial gap in his theodicy. [See Griffin's response in *Encountering Evil* [#863], and *Evil Revisited* [#873].]

925. Sia, Santiago. *God in Process Thought.* Boston, MA: Martinus Nijhoff Publishers, 1985.

This book contains a brief and uncritical exposition of Hartshorne's theodicy and the question of immortality (96-109). [Sia has argued since, in an unpublished paper, that the process God coerces. See also his edited volume, *Charles Hartshorne's Concept of God.* Dordrecht: Kluwer Academic Publishers, 1990.]

926. ———. "Suffering and Creativity: A Contribution to Hartshorne's Concept of Sole Reality." *Ultimate Reality and Meaning: Interdisciplinary Studies in the Philosophy of Understanding* 12 (1989): 210-220.

Exposition of Hartshorne's theodicy: God governs the world by establishing a general order within which creatures have freedom. This causes the evil and suffering we endure. Sia rejects the criticisms of Luther Evans and Colin Gunton, that Hartshorne's theism has denied divine activity by focusing solely on passivity. He argues that divine power is persuasive, yet holds that the idea of controlling power in the sense of overriding others is not in itself objectionable, if this power is exercised by God. God would override our freedom only when circumstances demand it and when it would benefit us all.

927. Siebert, Steve. "Why Is There Evil?" *Christianity Today* 22 (1978): 28-31.

Review article of David Griffin's *God, Power and Evil* [#861]; Brian Hebblethwaite's *Evil, Suffering and Religion* [#2254]; Michael Galligan's *God and Evil* [#1092]; and Sibley Towner's *How God Deals with Evil* [#1788]. Siebert argues that all four books share a conviction that the traditional Augustinian theodicy is no longer credible; yet all four fail to deal adequately with important aspects of scripture: original sin, angels, the devil, hell, etc. He argues also that Griffin's central thesis (the self-contradictory nature of traditional theism) is suspect, since Griffin mistakenly based this claim on the premise that God's knowledge, will, and causation are identical for Aquinas.

928. Sontag, Frederick. "Critique [of Griffin] by Frederick Sontag." *Encountering Evil.* Edited by Stephen Davis. Atlanta, GA: John Knox Press, 1981: 119-122.

Argues that Griffin's God is limited and that an eschatology is lacking. [See Griffin's response, following in the text.]

929. Straton, George Douglas. *Theistic Faith for our Time: An Introduction to the Process Philosophies of Royce and Whitehead.* Washington, DC: University Press of America, 1979.

Critical comparison of Royce and Whitehead on various issues, including theodicy. Straton differs with Griffin on the issue of *divine self-limitation*, arguing that God is not limited by metaphysical principles. For Straton, God's self-limitation is a moral act, a viable option, he suggests, for process thought. This interpretation of Whitehead avoids the difficulties of Brightman and dissipates difficulties in the theodicies of Royce and Whitehead. Freedom is a moral necessity, if ours is to be a moral universe. [See also Straton's much earlier "God, Freedom and Pain," *Harvard Theological Review* 55 (1962), 143-159.]

930.   Suchocki, Marjorie. "A Process Theology of Prayer." *American Journal of Theo- logy and Philosophy* 2 (1981): 33-45.

Contends that process theology enhances the understanding and practice of prayer. Prayer (confessional, intercessory, prayers of praise, and liturgical) is a way in which we optimize our ability to transform the world, deepen the congruity of our own will with the divine will and, as such, cooperate in the divine acting in history. We aid in the redemptive process. [See Basinger's critique in *Divine Power and Process Theology* [#826].]

931.   ———. *God, Christ, Church*. New York: Crossroad, 1982. Second (revised and expanded) edition, 1989.

A systematic process theology that expresses the process perspective of God, Christ and the Church. *Chapter 2* ("Sin in a Relational World") interprets original sin and the demonic from a process perspective, and *Chapters 15-17 (Part V)* present a process eschatology, developed more fully by Suchocki in her *The End of Evil: A Process Eschatology* [#932]. God prehends all actual occasions (humans and all other beings) in their full subjectivity. Redemption from evil is not obtained merely by immortality in God, but in subjectively experiencing God's prehension of the subject. [See the following item and Griffin's critique noted therein.]

932.   ———. *The End of Evil: Process Eschatology in Historical Context*. Albany, NY: State University of New York Press, 1988.

Argues for the possibility of an adequate process eschatology from a Whiteheadian perspective, claiming that this is necessary for a viable process theodicy. Since finitude is inherently the source of evil as well as good, a post-historical redemption is needed. Whitehead's "objective immortality" is not adequate for theodicy. Suchocki argues that actual occasions can be *subjectively immortal* in God. [See Griffin's critical review [#872] and Suchocki's response, "Evil, Eschatology and God: Response to David Griffin" [#933]. See also Suchocki's recent "Original Sin Revisited." *Process Studies* 20 (1991), 233-243.]

933.   ———. "Evil, Eschatology, and God: Response to David Griffin." *Process Studies* 19 (1989): 63-69.

Defends her arguments against Griffin's disagreement ("Review of Suchocki, *The End of Evil: Process Eschatology in Historical Context*" [#872]), that Whitehead's notion of God as an actual entity is adequate as a basis upon which to build a metaphysical eschatology of the kind attempted by Suchocki. Suchocki insists that her positing of a third form of creativity, intermediate between concrescent and transitional creativity, becomes the ground for a prehension which retains the immediacy of the occasion. Without this third form, there is no real distinction between the other two forms of creativity.

934.   Thelakat, Paul. "God Suffers Evil." *Louvain Studies* 14 (1989): 16-25.

Summary of some of the main conclusions of his doctoral thesis (*God Suffers Evil: An Attempted Rapprochement of Classical and Neo-Classical Theism*). He responds to Griffin's *God, Power and Evil* [#861]. Thelakat accepts Griffin's view that God suffers, yet rejects Griffin's view that the classical definition of evil as privation of good is inadequate and unacceptable. He qualifies Griffin's position that there is no intelligibility in the belief that the classical God permits evil. With respect to the latter, he argues that the possibility of permitting evil is the same as the possibility for permitting good.

935.   ———. "Process and Privation: Aquinas and Whitehead on Evil." *International Philosophical Quarterly* 26 (1986): 287-296.

Argues that there are areas of fundamental agreement between Aquinas and Whitehead with respect to the philosophic description of evil as the privation of good. There is agreement that (1) things or actualities in themselves are good; (2) evil arises out of the conflict or opposition of goods; (3) there are two kinds of evil: *privari* in Aquinas is equivalent to destruction in Whitehead, and *privatum esse* in Aquinas is equivalent to degradation or unnecessary triviality in Whitehead. The major difference between Aquinas and Whitehead, however, is that for Aquinas evil pertains to the categories of accidents, while for Whitehead evil is essential/relational.

936.   Thompson, Kenneth F., Jr. *Whitehead's Philosophy of Religion*. The Hague: Mouton and Company, 1971.

Expository analysis of various themes in Whitehead's philosophy of religion. He notes that unqualified omnipotence is problematic for the problem of evil, and responds to Ely's critiques (*The Religious Availability of Whitehead's God* [#844]). Thompson defends the process view of divine goodness and the overcoming of evil by God. He rejects the suggestion of Daniel Day Williams's ("Deity, Monarchy and Metaphysics" [#2428]), that there are coercive as well as persuasive aspects in Whitehead's God. Coercive action would be unworthy of divine perfection.

937.   Tilley, Terrence W. "Life After Theology and Other Thoughts About Eternity." *Books in Religion* 5 (1986): 5, 14-15.

Contains a critical review of Barry Whitney's *Evil and the Process God* [#950]: Tilley claims that process theodicy lacks the imagination to develop an eschatology. Tilley reviews also Richard Kropf's *Evil and Evolution* [#966]) Brian Hebblethwaite's *The Christian Hope*. Grand Rapids, MI: Eerdmans, 1984; Richard Viladesau's *The Reason for our Hope*. New York: Paulist Press, 1984); Pheme Perkins's *Resurrection*. New York: Doubleday, 1984; Morton Kelsey's *Resurrection*. New York: Paulist Press, 1985; and Rowan Williams's *Resurrection*. Philadelphia, PA: Pilgrim Press, 1985.

938.   Vitali, T.R. "The Importance of the *A Priori* in Whiteheadian Theodicy." *Modern Schoolman* 62 (1985): 277-291.

Argues that Nancy Frankenberry has developed the basis for Whiteheadian theodicy, founded upon some critical emanations of the Whiteheadian theory of actual occasions and the role of divine efficient causality in every concrescent event.

[See Frankenberry entries: [#1000-1004].] Frankenberry's revised Whiteheadian theism/theodicy meets Norris Clarke's objections (*The Philosophical Approach to God* [#1838]]), but not those of Robert Neville (*Creativity and God* [#1024]). Hartshorne's *a priori* theism, however, answers the problem as to the intrinsically normative status of creativity. Frankenberry sees creativity as everlasting on the basis of intuition and her reformed theory of efficient causality; the *a priori* reason is that God exists necessarily.

939.   Watt, Trevor. "Death and Evil: A Process Perspective." *Philosophy of Religion and Theology*. Compiled by David R. Griffin. American Academy of Religion, Wilson College: Chambersburg, PA, 1972: 160-173.

Contends that Whitehead's view of redemption through suffering, which accepts suffering as real and evil but not ultimate, is in opposition to Berger's view of the Judaeo-Christian tradition as embracing only a pathological view of suffering.

940.   Whitehead, Alfred North. *Science and the Modern World*. New York: Macmillan, 1925. Cambridge: Cambridge University Press, 1926. New York: Free Press, 1967.

See, in particular, the sections entitled "God" and "Religion and Science." In place of Aristotle's *God as Prime Mover*, Whitehead's God is the *Principle of Concretion*. Medieval thinkers, anxious to establish the religious significance of God, paid God "metaphysical compliments" by conceiving God as the foundation of the metaphysical situation with its ultimate activity. This conception rendered God the origin of all evil as well as all good. Yet, as the supreme ground for limitation, God divides the good from the evil. Whitehead argues also that while religious truths are eternal, the expression of those truths requires continual development. The presentation of God under the aspect of power awakens every modern instinct of critical reaction. Modern science has weakened the old hold of religious forms of expression. The religious vision is our one ground for optimism: "Apart from it, human life is a flash of occasional enjoyments lighting up a mass of pain and misery, a bagatelle of transient experience" (192).

941.   ——. *Religion in the Making*. New York: Macmillan, 1926. Cambridge: Cambridge University Press, 1926, 1936.

See, in particular, the sections entitled "Body and Spirit" and "Truth and Criticism." Evil, Whitehead argues, is exhibited in the loss of the higher experience in favor of the lower. Evil is a good in itself, but a destructive agent among things greater than itself. While evil is positive and destructive, what is good is positive and creative. Evil, by its nature, is unstable and promotes its own destructiveness. God's experience includes a synthesis of the entire universe. The purpose of God is to seek value in the temporal world, in each self-creating entity.

942.   ——. *Process and Reality: An Essay in Cosmology*. New York: Macmillan, 1929. Cambridge: Cambridge University Press, 1929. New York: Social Science Bookstore, 1941. New York: Harper and Brothers, 1960. Corrected Edition edited by David R. Griffin and Donald Sherburne. New York: Free Press, 1977.

This is Whitehead's acknowledged greatest work. It is, as are most of his publications, written in highly technical and complex language. He has not formulated a systematic theodicy here or elsewhere, yet see, in particular, the sections entitled "The Opposite Ideals," "God and the World," and "The Theory of Truth." Whitehead argues, for example, that the ultimate evil in the world is that time is a "perpetual perishing," "the past fades." He articulates also his doctrine of "objective immortality" and the doctrine of aesthetic value, etc.

943.   ——. *Adventures of Ideas*. New York: Macmillan, 1933. Cambridge: Cambridge University Press, 1933, 1938.

See, in particular, the sections entitled "Beauty," "Truth and Beauty," and "Adventure." Whitehead argues that progress is founded on the experience of discordant feelings. An individual experience can deal with evil in various ways: evil can be negatively prehended; there can be positive realization in the positive feeling of discordance; the discordance can be eliminated by reducing it to the background; etc. He argues that Beauty is more fundamental than Truth, and various other seminal Whiteheadian themes.

944.   ——. *Modes of Thought*. New York: Macmillan, 1938. Cambridge: Cambridge University Press, 1938.

See, in particular, the section entitled "Activity." He discusses the relation of order to the good. Life needs more than mere conformity and order; vague and disorderly elements of experience are essential for the advance of novelty.

945.   ——. "Mathematics and the Good." *Harvard Divinity School Bulletin* 39 (1941): 5-21. [Also published in *The Philosophy of Alfred North Whitehead*. Library of Living Philosophers. Edited by Paul Arthur Schilpp. Evanston and Chicago, IL: Northwestern University Press, 1941, 666-681.]

Holds that Good and Evil cannot be discussed without reference to the interweaving of diverse patterns of experience. There is the evil of triviality and the intense evil of active deprivation, among other types of evil.

946.   ——. "Immortality." *The Philosophy of Alfred North Whitehead*. Library of Living Philosophers. Edited by Paul Arthur Schilpp. Evanston and Chicago, IL: Northwestern University Press, 1941: 682-700. [Also published by Cambridge: Cambridge University Press, 1951, and New York: Tudor Publishing Company, 1951.]

Presents his theory of *objective immortality*. Personal identity survives within the immediacy of a present occasion, and survives fully within God's experience of that entity's actuality. Apart from God, the world would dissolve into the nothingness of confusion. Whitehead discusses the World of Value and World of Activity: the immortality of Value enters into the changefulness that is the essential character of Activity.

947.   Whitla, William. "Sin and Redemption in Whitehead and Teilhard de Chardin." *Anglican Theological Review* 47 (1965): 81-95.

Argues that Teilhard de Chardin's view of redemption goes beyond Whitehead's view of evil as overcome by God. Whitehead's weakness is his inadequate theological perspective, a gap filled by Teilhard's redemptive soteriology.

948.   Whitney, Barry L. "Hartshorne's New Look at Theodicy." *Studies in Religion* 8 (1979): 281-291.

Hartshorne has presented two distinct, though interrelated theodicies. The first is based upon the necessary existence of God (Hartshorne's revised version of the *a priori* ontological argument); the second is in the more traditional seeking of a reconciliation of divine power and creaturely freedom. Hartshorne defines God as solely persuasive and holds that evil results from the conflicting creativity of creatures.

949.   ———. "Process Theism: Does a Persuasive God Coerce?" *Southern Journal of Philosophy* 17 (1979): 133-143.

Contends that Hartshorne's understanding of God as solely persuasive is unjustified in his writings. Hartshorne defends his view of God as persuasive in terms which are indistinguishable from coercion. Later versions of this argument are contained in Whitney's *Evil and the Process God, Chapter 6* [#950] and "Hartshorne and Theodicy" [#951]].

950.   ———. *Evil and the Process God: Hartshorne Process Theodicy*. Toronto Studies in Theology, *Volume 19*. Lewiston, NY, London, and Toronto, ON: Edwin Mellen Press, 1985.

A detailed critical analysis of Hartshorne's theism and its implications for theodicy. Whitney surveys biblical theodicy and classical theism in light of process theism, and critiques Hartshorne's theodicy. Hartshorne has not been clear as to how God acts solely persuasively: he writes in a manner that *coercion* can be inferred when Hartshorne uses the term and wants to argue for *persuasion*. Whitney argues that Hartshorne's God is coercive in imposing natural laws and acting as an irresistible, unconscious lure to creaturely creativity within those laws. Whitney defends Hartshorne's doctrine of divine immutability against classical theism and defends Hartshorne's doctrine of objective immortality as adequate to resolve the theodicy issue. [See responses by Lewis Ford, "Divine Persuasion and Coercion" [#851]; Robert Mesle, "Review of Barry Whitney, *Evil and the Process God* [#905]; David Basinger, *Divine Power and Process Theism* [#826]; Anna Case-Winters, *God's Power* [#830]; David Griffin, "Hartshorne's Postmodern Theology," *Hartshorne, Process Philosophy and Theology*. Edited by Robert Kane and Stephen Phillips. Albany, NY: State University of New York Press, 1989, 1-32; etc.]

951.   ———. "Hartshorne and Theodicy." *Hartshorne, Process Philosophy and Theology*. Edited by Robert Kane and Steven Phillips. Albany, NY: State University of New York Press, 1989: 55-71.

Holds that Hartshorne's theodicy rests on a revised conception of divine omnipotence. Whitney expands and clarifies his argument in *Evil and the Process God* [#950]: Hartshorne argues that God acts solely persuasively, yet the language he uses to justify this view is far from clear, suggesting (against Charles Hartshorne's intentions) that there are coercive aspects in the divine activity in the world, not only with respect to the imposition of natural laws as the limits to freedom but in the divine luring of creatures within the confines of those natural laws. Whitney responds to Ford's comments in "Divine Persuasion and Coercion" [#851]; Basinger's *Divine Power and Process Theism* [#826]; and Mesle's review article [#905]. He argues that the Hartshornean principle of the law of polarity (Morris Cohen's) implies that divine power is best conceived as a *mixture* of persuasion and coercion: solely persuasive power is as meaningless as solely coercive power. [See Hartshorne's response, "Barry Whitney," in *Hartshorne, Process Philosophy and Theology* [#889]. More recently, see Barry Whitney, "An Aesthetic Solution to the Problem of Evil," *International Journal for Philosophy of Religion* 35 (1994), 21-37, "Hartshorne and Natural Evil," *Sophia* 35 (1996), 39-46, and "Divine Power and the Anthropic Principle," *The Personalist Forum* (forthcoming, 1998).]

952.   Whitney, Barry L., and J. Norman King. "Rahner and Hartshorne on Death and Eternal Life." *Horizons, Journal of the College Theology Society* 15 (1988): 239-261.

Defends Hartshorne's doctrine of objective immortality in comparison with Rahner's more traditional view. There is no justification in seeking to resolve theodicy by means of subjective immortality. [See also Whitney, "Divine Immutability in Process Philosophy and Contemporary Thomism" [#1048]].

953.   Williams, Daniel Day. "Moral Obligation in Process Philosophy." *Journal of Philosophy* 56 (1959): 263-267. [Published also in *Alfred North Whitehead: Essays on his Philosophy*. Edited by George L. Kline. Englewood Cliffs, NJ: Prentice-Hall, 1963, 189-195. For further relevant publications by Williams, see [#2425-2432].]

Contends that process metaphysics provides both a theory of the absoluteness of moral obligation and an acknowledgment of tragic forces which pervade a world in process.

954.   Wood, Forrest Jr. "Some Whiteheadian Insights into the Problem of Evil." *Southwestern Journal of Philosophy* 10 (1979): 147-155.

Argues that the demand that the goodness of God entails the absence of evil and destructiveness is based upon an inadequate metaphysics. Claims that evil is part of Whitehead's God and that evil, for Whitehead, has aesthetic value. Wood maintains that the advancement of theological thought has been held back by the denial of these doctrines.

II   Publications on Teilhard's Theodicy [Selected]

955.   Barthélemy-Madaule Madeleine. "Teilhard de Chardin, Marxism, Existentialism: A Confrontation." *International Philosophical Quarterly* 1 (1961): 648-667.

956.   Braybrooke, Neville, editor. *Teilhard de Chardin: Pilgrim of the Future.* New York: Seabury Press, 1964.

957.   Chauchard, Paul. *Teilhard de Chardin on Love and Suffering.* Glen Rock: Paulist Press, 1966.

958.   Crespy, Georges. "Teilhard de Chardin—Evil and the Cross." *Philosophy Today* 8 (1964): 84-100. [See also his book, *La pensée théologique de Teilhard de Chardin*. Paris: Editions universitaires, 1961, 109-133.]

959.   ———. "The Problem of Evil in Teilhard's Thought." *Process Theology*. Edited by E. Cousins. New York: Newman Press, 1971: 283-298.

960.   Faricy, Robert. "Teilhard de Chardin's Spirituality of the Cross." *Horizons, Journal of the College Theology Society* 3 (1976): 1-15.

961.   Francoeur, Robert. *Perspectives in Evolution*. Baltimore, MD: Helicon, 1965: 185-229.

962.   ——. *Evolving World, Converging Man*. New York: Rinehart and Winston, 1970: 124-174.

963.   Gray, Donald P. "Involution and the Problem of Evil." *The One and the Many: Teilhard de Chardin's Vision of Unity*. New York: Herder and Herder, 1969: 52-74.

964.   Kim, Dai Sil. "Irenaeus of Lyons and Teilhard de Chardin: A Comparative Study of 'Recapitulation' and 'Omega'." *Journal of Ecumenical Studies* 13 (1976): 69-93.

965.   King, Thomas M. *Teilhard, Evil and Providence*. Chambersburg, PA: Anima Books, 1989.

966.   Kropf, Richard W. *Evil and Evolution*. London and Toronto, ON: Associated University Presses, 1984. *Chapter 8* ("The God who Suffers").

967.   Mooney, Christopher F. *Teilhard and the Mystery of Christ*. New York: Harper and Row, 1966.

968.   ——. "Teilhard de Chardin on the Problem of Suffering." *The Mystery of Suffering and Death*. Edited by Michael J. Taylor. Garden City, NY: Image Books, 1973: 57-70. [Originally published in *Journal of Religion and Health* 11 (1965), 429-440.]

969.   Murray, Michael H. *The Thought of Teilhard de Chardin*. New York: Seabury Press, 1966.

970.   Nogar, Raymond J. "The Lord of the Absurd: A Non-Teilhardian View." *The Mystery of Suffering and Death*. Edited by Michael J. Taylor. Garden City, NY: Image Books, 1973: 101-107.

971.   Robbins, Lee. "Being in Darkness: A Jungian Commentary on Teilhard's 'Passivities of Diminishment'." *Anima* 11 (1984): 17-23.

972.   Singleton, Michael. "Teilhard on Camus." *International Philosophical Quarterly* 9 (1969): 236-247.

973.   Smith, R.B. "The Place of Evil in a World of Evolution." *Teilhard Reassessed*. Edited by Anthony Hanson. London: Darton, Longman and Todd, 1970: 59-77.

974.   Smulders, Piet. *The Design of Teilhard de Chardin: An Essay in Theological Reflection*. Westminster, MD: Newman Press, 1967: 140-195.

975.   Teilhard de Chardin, Pierre. *Oeuvres de Pierre Teilhard de Chardin, 10 Volumes*. Paris: Seuil, 1955-1969.

976.   ——. *The Future of Man*. New York: Harper and Row, 1964.

977.   ——. *The Phenomenon of Man*. Revised English edition. New York: Harper and Row, 1965.

978.   ——. *The Divine Milieu*. New York: Harper and Row, 1965.

979.   ——. *Hymn to the Universe*. New York: Harper and Row, 1965.

980. ——. *Science and Christ*. New York: Harper and Row, 1968.

981. ——. *Writings in Time of War*. New York: Harper and Row, 1968.

982. ——. *On Suffering*. New York: Harper and Row, 1974. [Extracts from various of Teilhard's writings: *Writings in Time of War* (1968); *The Making of a Mind* (1965); *Letters to Léontine Zanta* (1969); *Science and Christ* (1968); *Letters to Two Friends, 1926-1952* (1968); *The Divine Milieu* (1960); *Human Energy* (1971); and new translations from *Ecrits du temps de la guerre* (1965); *Preface* from *L'Energie spirituelle de la souffrance* (1951); and unpublished letters of Teilhard to Edouard Le Roy and Madame Henry Cosme.]

983. Wilburn, Ralph G. "Reflections on the Problem of Evil." *Lexington Theological Quarterly* (1981): 126-141. [Discusses various theodicies and rejects them all as inadequate. Teilhard's theodicy, which explains evil as part of an evolving world, cannot explain moral evil adequately.]

III Related Publications on Process Thought
[Selected]

984. Axel, Larry E. "Reshaping the Task of Theology." *American Journal of Theology and Philosophy* 8 (1987): 59-63.

985. Clarke, W. Norris. "Christian Theism and Whiteheadian Process Philosophy." *Logos* 18 (1980): 9-41. [Reprinted in *Process Theology*. Edited by Ronald H. Nash. Grand Rapids, MI: Baker Book House, 1987, 217-251].

986. Cobb, John B., Jr. *Hope and the Future of Man*. Philadelphia, PA: Fortress Press, 1972.

987. ——. "Natural Causality and Divine Action." *Idealistic Studies* 3 (1973): 207-222.

988. ——. "Befriending an Amoral Nature." *Zygon, Journal of Religion and Science* 23 (1988): 431-436.

989. Craig, William L. "Process Theology's Denial of Divine Foreknowledge." *Process Studies* 16 (1987): 198-202.

990. ——. "Divine Foreknowledge and Future Contingency," in *Process Theology*. Edited by Ronald Nash. Grand Rapids, MI: Baker Book House, 1987: 93-115. [See Donald Wayne Viney's response to Craig, "Does Omniscience Imply Foreknowledge? Craig on Hartshorne" [#1045].]

991. Donnelley, Strachan. "Whitehead and Nietzsche: Overcoming the Evil of Time." *Process Studies* 12 (1982): 1-14. [Both Whitehead and Nietzsche saw time as a threat to the ultimate significance of human life. Both found ultimate significance in this temporal life.]

992. Ford, Lewis S. "The Viability of Whitehead's God for Christian Theism." *Proceedings of the American Catholic Philosophical Association* 44 (1970): 141-151.

993. ——. "God as King: Benevolent Despot or Constitutional Monarch?" *Christian Scholar's Review* 1 (1971): 318-322.

994. ——. "The Non-Temporality of Whitehead's God." *International Philosophical Quarterly* 13 (1973): 347-376.

995. ——. "The Immutable God and Father Clarke." *New Scholasticism* 49 (1975): 189-199.

996. ——. "The Eternity of God and the Temporality of the World." *Encounter* 36 (1975): 115-122.

997. ——. "A Response to Neville's Creativity and God." *Process Studies* 10 (1980): 105-109.

998. ——. "Divine Activity of the Future." *Process Studies* 11 (1981): 169-179.

999. ——. "Evangelical Appraisals of Process Theism." *Christian Scholar's Review* 20 (1990): 149-163.

1000. Frankenberry, Nancy. *Religion and Radical Empiricism.* Albany, NY: State University of New York Press, 1982.

1001. ——. "The Emergent Paradigm and Divine Causation." *Process Studies* 13 (1983): 202-217.

1002. ——. "The Power of the Past." *Process Studies* 13 (1983): 132-144.

1003. ——. "The Logic of Whitehead's Intuition of Everlastingness." *Southern Journal of Philosophy* 21 (1983): 31-46.

1004. ——. "Meland's Empirical Realism and the Appeal to Lived Existence." *American Journal of Theology and Philosophy* 5 (1984): 117-129.

1005. Goetz, Ronald. "Process Theology Debate Continues (Rejoinder to John Cobb)." *Christian Century* 104 (1987): 22-24.

1006. Goss, James. "Camus, God, and Process Thought." *Process Studies* 14 (1974): 114-128.

1007. Grant, Colin. "Possibilities for Divine Passibility." *Toronto Journal of Theology* 4 (1988): 3-18.

1008. Griffin, David R. "Is Revelation Coherent?" *Theology Today* 28 (1971): 278-293.

1009. ——. "A New Vision of Nature." *Encounter* 35 (1974): 95-107. [Originally published in *The Proceedings for Earth Ethics Today and Tomorrow.* Edited by Donald Scherer. Bowling Green, OH: Bowling Green State University, 1973), 95-107.]

1010. Hancock, Lee. "Incarnate Suffering and Faith: AIDS and the Power of God." *Christianity and Crisis* 47 (1988): 240-242.

1011. Hartshorne, Charles. *Aquinas to Whitehead: Seven Centuries of Metaphysics of Religion.* Milwaukee, WI: Marquette University Publications, 1976.

1012. Hartshorne, Charles, and John Kennedy and Piotr Gutowski. "Charles Hartshorne on Metaphilosophy, Person and Immortality, and Other Issues." *Process Studies* 19 (1990): 256-277. [Interview with Hartshorne.]

1013. Hershinow, Sheldon. "Bernard Meland and Jewish Humanism." *Religious Humanism* 13 (1979): 56-63.

1014.   Jacobson, Nolan P. "Whitehead and Buddhism on the Art of Living." *Eastern Buddhist* 9 (1975): 8-36.

1015.   Jesse, Jennifer G. "A Process Perspective of Revelation." *Encounter* 48 (1987): 367-384.

1016.   Keller, J.A. "Niebuhr, Tillich, and Whitehead on the Ethics of Power." *American Journal of Theology and Philosophy* 7 (1986): 132-148.

1017.   Lawrence, Nathaniel. "The Vision of Beauty and the Temporality of Deity in Whitehead's Philosophy." *Journal of Philosophy* 58 (1961): 534-553.

1018.   Mason, David R. "Reflections on Prayer from a Process Perspective." *Encounter* 45 (1984): 347-356.

1019.   McDaniel, Jay. "The God of the Oppressed and the God Who is Empty." *God and Global Justice: Religion and Poverty in an Unequal World*. Edited by Frederick Ferré and Rita Matarangnon. New York: Paragon House, 1985: 185-204. [Slightly revised version published in *Journal of Ecumenical Studies* 22 (1985), 687-702.]

1020.   ———. "Where is the Holy Spirit Anyway? Response to a Sceptic Environmentalist." *Ecumenical Review* 42 (1990): 162-174.

1021.   Moskop, John. *Divine Omniscience and Human Freedom: Thomas Aquinas and Charles Hartshorne*. Macon, GA: Mercer University Press, 1984.

1022.   Muray, Leslie A. "The Doctrine of Grace in Whiteheadian Categories." *Encounter* 45 (1984): 359-371. [See also Muray's *An Introduction to the Process Understanding of Science, Society and the Self*. New York and Toronto, ON: Edwin Mellen Press, 1988.]

1023.   Neville, Robert C. "The Impossibility of Whitehead's God for Christian Theology." *Proceedings of the Catholic Philosophical Association* 44 (1970): 130-140.

1024.   ———. *Creativity and God: A Challenge to Process Theology*. New York: Seabury Press, 1980.

1025.   ———. "Concerning 'Creativity and God': A Response." *Process Studies* 11 (1981): 1-10. [A response to criticisms of Neville's *Creativity and God* [#1024] by various process thinkers (Hartshorne, Ford, Cobb).]

1026.   O'Hanlon, Gerald F. "Does God Change?" *Irish Theological Quarterly* 55 (1987): 161-183. [See also O'Hanlon's *The Immutability of God in the Theology of Hans Urs von Balthasar* [#2359].]

1027.   Pittenger, W. Norman. "Process Theology." *Expository Times* 79 (1968): 56-57.

1028.   ———. *Unbounded Love*. New York: Seabury, 1970.

1029.   ———. "'Personal Survival' in Biblical Thought and Process Thought." *Encounter* 36 (1975): 91-100.

1030.   ———. "Beauty in a World of Process." *Andover Newton Quarterly* 17 (1977): 243-249.

1031.   ———. *The Lure of Divine Love*. New York: Pilgrim Press, 1979.

1032.   ———. "The Divine Activity." *Encounter* 47 (1986): 257-266.

1033.   ———. *Freed to Love: A Process Interpretation of Redemption*. Wilton, CT: Morehouse-Barlow, 1987.

1034.   ———. *Becoming and Belonging: The Meaning of Human Existence and Community*. Harrisburg, PA: BSC Litho, 1989. [The relevant chapter is *Chapter 2*, "The Loving God and the Fact of Evil".]

1035.   Rodier, David F.T. "The Problem of Ordered Chaos in Whitehead and Plotinus." *The Significance of Neoplatonism*. Edited by R. Baine Harris. Norfolk, VA: Old Dominion University Research Foundation, 1976: 301-317.

1036.   Ross, James F. "God and the World: A Review Article of *God and the World*, by John Cobb" [#832]. *Journal of the American Academy of Religion* 38 (1970): 310-315.

1037.   Shaw, Marvin C. "The Romantic Love of Evil: Loomer's Proposal of a Reorientation in Religious Naturalism." *American Journal of Theology and Philosophy* 10 (1989): 33-42.

1038.   Simmons, James R. "Whitehead's Metaphysic of Persuasion." *Philosophy and Rhetoric* 2 (1969): 72-80.

1039.   Stokes, Walter E. "God for Today and Tomorrow." *New Scholasticism* 43 (1969): 351-378.

1040.   Suchocki, Marjorie. "The Question of Immortality." *Journal of Religion* 57 (1977): 288-306.

1041.   ———. "The Appeal to Ultimacy in Meland's Thought." *American Journal of Theology and Philosophy* 5 (1984): 80-88.

1042.   Terry, R. Franklin. "The Problem of Evil and the Promise of Hope in the Theology of Henry Nelson Wieman." *Religion in Life* 39 (1970): 582-594.

1043.   Towne, Edgar A. "Henry Nelson Wieman: Theologian of Hope." *Iliff Review* 27 (1970): 13-24.

1044.   Viney, Donald Wayne. *Charles Hartshorne and the Existence of God*. Albany, NY: State University of New York Press, 1985.

1045.   ———. "Does Omniscience Imply Foreknowledge? Craig on Hartshorne." *Process Studies* 18 (1989): 30-37. [Response to William Craig's "Divine Foreknowledge and Future Contingency" [#990].]

1046.   Westphal, M. "On Thinking of God as King." *Christian Scholar's Review* 1 (1970): 29-34.

1047.   ———. "God as King: A Reply to Lewis Ford." *Christian Scholar's Review* 2 (1971): 323-324.

1048.   Whitney, Barry L. "Divine Immutability in Process Philosophy and Contemporary Thomism." *Horizons, Journal of the College Theology Society* 7 (1980): 49-68.

1049.   ———. "Does God Influence the World's Creativity? Hartshorne's Doctrine of Possibility." *Philosophy Research Archives* 6 (1981): 613-622.

1050.   ———. "Charles Hartshorne." *Non-Violence—Central to Christianity*. Edited by Joseph T. Culliton. Lewiston, NY, London, and Toronto, ON: Edwin Mellen

Press, 1982: 217-237. [Divine persuasive power is the model for human interaction, although there are times when pacifism, non-violence, is inappropriate for human action.]

1051. ———. "Religion, Science and Process: A Contemporary Understanding of God." *The Reality of God in the Contemporary World*. Edited by F. Temple Kingston. Windsor, ON: University of Windsor, Canterbury College Monograph Series, 1982: 35-57. [An overview of divine persuasive power in process thought, in contradistinction to the coercive power in traditional, classical western theism.]

Chapter 7

Other Philosophical Theodicies

This chapter covers a great mass of published literature on the theodicy issue, publications largely from analytic theologians and philosophers.[1] These publications are more "philosophical" than "theological" (i.e., more analytic than confessional). The latter have been assigned primarily to *Appendix D*, as less central to the important on-going debates and discussions of theodicy in the academic philosophical and theological journals.[2]

The mass of published material included in this chapter has been sub-divided into five sections: "*Some Constructive Theodicies*"; "*Some Challenges to Theism*"; "*Other Critical Discussions*"; "*God and the Good*"; and "*Related Publications.*" It was a difficult task to determine how best to organize the material, a task rendered even more challenging by the decision not to cross-list the several hundreds of items that could have been listed two or more times throughout this book.[3] Other "constructive theodicies," for example, have been presented by theologians like *John Hick (Chapter 5)*, by process theists *(Chapter 6)*, by *Alvin Plantinga (Chapters 2 and 3)*, and by a host of others who are listed elsewhere. The reason for this organization of the material was (ideally) to distinguish more clearly the various facets and approaches which make up the theodicy issue.

Over the past thirty years, the theodicy issue has become an ever-increasing focus of interest for philosophers and theologians. During the past few years, however, there has been a shift in emphasis. This shift may be more subtle than discernible, and it is clearer in some publications than in others. Not all who address the issue have accepted the change in focus, as would be expected in any "paradigm" change, albeit one of less than earth-shattering proportions. Some are still writing from the former perspective, but the dominant trend seems to be turning to the new set of issues. In short, the *logical problem of evil* has given way to the *inductive problem of evil*.

The initial challenge led by *John Mackie* and *Antony Flew* in the late 1950s and 1960s has been characterized variously as *the logical problem of evil, the deductive problem of evil*, or as *the a priori argument*.[4] The argument alleges that there is a logical inconsistency between the propositions regarding God's attributes (omnipotence and omnibenevolence) and the proposition that evil exists. One of the main issues centers about the questions as to whether or not God has a morally sufficient reason for permitting evil; another is whether or not evil is connected logically to greater goods. Theists like *M.B. Ahern, Alvin Plantinga, Keith Yandell, Nelson Pike, George Mavrodes, Philip Yancey, John King-Farlow*, and others *(Robert and Marilyn Adams, David and Randall Basinger, Clement Dore, Norman Geisler, Douglas Hall, Errol Harris, William Hasker, Yeager Hudson, Michael Peterson, James Ross, Harold Schulweis, Eleonore Stump*, etc.) have attempted in various ways to reconcile God's attributes with the stark reality of suffering and evil.

These efforts, particularly the free will defense of Alvin Plantinga, have succeeded in advancing the issue to another focus: *the evidential problem of evil*, also referred to as *the inductive argument from evil, the a posteriori argument from evil*, and *the probabilistic argument of evil*. This has led to an increasing awareness of *the problem of gratuitous evil*. The work of *Michael Peterson*, following in the steps of his teacher, *Edward Madden*, is relevant here, as is the writing of *Keith Yandell, Keith Chrzan*, and others.[5] Theists argue for the probability of theism despite the reality of evil, while atheists argue for the improbability of theism in face of the preponderance of evil, and demand not merely theological appeals to *probability* (as is the case with Plantinga's free will defense) but *theodicies* that explain evil, particularly its relationship to God as powerful, loving, and just. Hick's Irenaean theodicy, process theodicy, natural evil theodicies, and so on (listed in separate chapters) have responded to this challenge.

The five sections of this present chapter cover major apologists for theism, major critics, and discussions which deal with a variety of relevant issues: God's relationship with "the good," *Frederick Sontag's* call for a revised theism, *John Roth's* theodicy of protest, *Stanley Hauerwas's* appeal to more existential awareness (a theme which occupies much of *Appendix D*), and various other philosophical aspects of the problem of evil. Among the major critics (those who argue from the evidence of evil against God's existence, whether from the logical or the evidential perspective) are *John Mackie, H.J. McCloskey, Peter Hare, Edward Madden, William Rowe, Michael Martin*, and others. *Terrence Tilley* and *Kenneth Surin* are objecting that the very enterprise of philosophical theodicy is misguided, while some feminists are arguing that feminism will not support the continuation of philosophical theodicy.[6]

I trust that it does not seem arbitrary to have designated various authors as *theists*, and/or *proponents of theism* and others as *atheists, sceptics,* and/or *opponents of theism*. In many cases, the author's position is clearly such, but there are many instances where it is the *argumentation*, not the author's *personal orientation* (as a theist or atheist or whatever) that is important.

Section I lists publications which argue the case for theism despite the evil and suffering in the world. Besides the construction of theodicies and arguments against anti-theists, this section includes also reference to the claims of philosophers like Alvin Plantinga that religious beliefs are "basic" and, as such, require no theoretical defense. Many are convinced by this; yet there are many others who demand *theodicies* rather than merely *defenses* and theological assumptions. *Section II* lists publications that argue variously the case against theism from the evidence of the world's evil and suffering. *Sections III-V* list publications that discuss many of the diverse issues which make up the philosophical problem of evil.[7] These items could not be characterized under the rubric of the first two sections, nor was it appropriate to list them in any of the other annotated chapters, despite the frequent references in these publications to issues discussed in the other annotated chapters. The items in the final three sections (and elsewhere—indeed, throughout the bibliography), moreover, could have been expanded considerably, since the number of publications which could be deemed peripheral is staggering, to say the least. Indeed, as noted below, if all of the (more or less relevant) references in books on the general topic of "philosophy of religion" were included, with the incredible variety and complexity of issues this field considers—*miracles, faith healing, divine attributes, the rationality of religious belief* and *mystical intuitions, revelation*, and more theological/confessional themes, like the questions of *immortality, Christology, heaven and hell, Satan*, etc.—the list would be all but endless. Publications on some of the most relevant (in my opinion) of these themes have been listed in the appendices.

Notes

1. See *Appendix E* for some relevant dissertations. Among the most significant are the following: Michael Beaty, *The Univocity Thesis and the Moral Goodness of God* (University of Notre Dame, 1986); Richard Bavier, *The Justification of Evil in Teleological Theodicy* (Brown University, 1974); Paul Draper, *The Evidential Problem of Evil* (University of California, 1985); Frederick Bolton, *Theodicy: A Study of the Thought of Some British Theologians of the Twentieth Century with Reference to the Problem of Evil* (Princeton Theological Seminary, 1964); Rowan Crews, *The Praise of God and the Problem of Evil: A Doxiology Approach to the Problem of Evil and Suffering* (Duke University, 1989); David Faber, *The Problem of Omnipotence and God's Ability to Sin* (University of Massachusetts, 1989); William Frierson, *The Problem of Evil: A Metaphysical and Theological Inquiry* (Emory University, 1977); Loren Meierding, *The Argument from Evil* (University of Texas, 1978); Stephanie Gindes, *The Psychology of Evil* (United States International University, 1976); Sandra Menssen, *Foundations of Theodicy: Is There a Criterion of Goodness for Worlds?* (University of Minnesota, 1984); Tom Milazzo, *The Protest and the Silence: Suffering and Death as a Theological Problem* (Emory University, 1988); Alan Nasser, *The Ontological Argument and the Problem of Evil* (Indiana University, 1972); Louis Ruprecht, *The Tragic Posture in the Modern Age: An Essay on Tragedy—Classical, Christian and Modern* (Emory University, 1990); Ben Nowlin, *The Reasonableness of Faith as a Response to the Problem of Evil* (University of Oklahoma, 1981); Chandler Pauling, *The Problem of Evil in Contemporary Theology* (Aquinas Institute, 1971); Osmond Ramberan, *Faith, Language, and the Problem of Evil in Recent Analytic Philosophy* (McMaster University, 1974); Thomas Warren, *God and Evil: Does Judaeo-Christian Theism Involve a Logical Contradiction?* (Vanderbilt University, 1969); Adrian McFarlane, *Toward a Grammar of Fear: A Phenomenological Analysis of the Experience and the Interpretation of Fear as a Propaedeutic to the Study of the Problem of Evil* (Drew University, 1985); Andrea Weisberger, *A Defense of the Argument from Evil: A Critique of Pure Theism* (Vanderbilt University, 1990); Terrence White, *God and Evil: A Study of the Problem of Evil* (New York University, 1979); Ira Adler, *Theism and Evil: An Analytic Approach* (New York University, 1975); Terry Christlieb, *Theism and Evil: Consistency, Evidence, and Completeness* (Syracuse University, 1988); Douglas Davis, *Is Evil a Relation? A Study in the Metaphysics of Value* (State University of New York, 1986); Douglas Geivett, *The Logic of the Problem of Evil* (University of Southern California, 1985); Samuel Hughes, *The Problem of Evil as Discussed in the Gifford Lectures from 1889-1986* (Baylor University, 1989); Robert Jooharigian, *Evil and the Existence of God* (University of Wisconsin, 1977); etc.

2. The distinction between philosophical and theological may not be clear in the minds of some readers. It is not an easy issue to define. I regard the confessional perspective, which takes in much of classical or traditional Christianity, as "theological," rather than analytical or philosophical. Much of the traditional and contemporary Thomistic writings are theological in this sense: the listings on Thomism in *Appendix B* certainly contain sophisticated philosophical themes, but many of them also assume traditional beliefs in heaven and hell, miracles, divine unilateral power, Christology, etc. Again, I note that it may be a contentious issue to define these themes and perspectives as theological, rather than philosophical, but there is a clear difference between the majority of publications assigned to *Appendix B* (and also *Appendix D)* and the majority of publications listed in the annotated chapters. Had this bibliography been written by a Roman Catholic committed to the Thomistic perspective, I assume that there might be a difference of opinion on this point and that the publications listed in the Thomistic section of *Appendix B* would be given a much higher profile. Perhaps the attempt might be made to interrelate the items in the annotated sections and the Thomistic publications. I would welcome such a dialogue, and while there are publications in the Thomist section which

address the issues in the annotated chapters, there is also a distinct difference of perspective and presuppositions which militates against more fruitful dialogue. The same may apply to an evangelical, conservative Protestant writer. I am neither a conservative Protestant nor a Thomist. My religious background is Anglican, but while I am a theist, I do not assume denominational dogmas as aspects of my philosophical theology. I seek only reasoned arguments and rationality of thought.

3.   There are hundreds of books on "philosophy of religion," and many of them have sections on the theodicy issue. Many of these are expository rather than original, critical contributions to the issue. I have included the most relevant (critical) publications. [See also William Wainwright's annotated bibliography, *Philosophy of Religion* (New York: Garland Publishing Company, 1976).]

4.   Among the most informative publications on the classification of the various types of theodicies are those of Michael Peterson. See, in particular, his *Evil and the Christian God* (Grand Rapids, MI: Baker Book House, 1982). See also Bruce Reich enbach's *Evil and a Good God* (New York: Fordham University Press, 1982). Peterson's most recent book, *The Problem of Evil: Selected Readings* (Notre Dame, IN: University of Notre Dame Press, 1992), which was published as this present annotated bibliography was in the final stages of printing, includes a helpful introduction to the distinct facets of the theodicy question. Peterson's 25-page bibliographical list contains a selected number of items, all of which, of course, are entered in this present annotated bibliography. Peterson's list is not broken down into various sub-divisions, as is the shorter bibliography of Robert and Marilyn Adams in their recent source book, *The Problem of Evil* (New York: Oxford University Press, 1990). Peterson's introductory analysis of the various issues involved in the theodicy issue, however, is consistent with his previous publications, though expanded somewhat, and is very helpful. Also of particular help are several other general works of this kind: Paul Schilling's *God and Human Anguish* (Nashville, TN: Abingdon, 1977); Hare and Madden's classic critique, *Evil and the Concept of God* (Springfield, IL: C.C. Thomas, 1968); Michael Martin's caustic analysis, *Atheism: A Philosophical Analysis* (Philadelphia, PA: Temple University Press, 1990); Stephen Davis, "The Problem of Evil in Recent Philosophy" (*Review and Expositor* [1988]); my own *What Are They Saying About God and Evil?* (New York and Mahwah, NJ: Paulist, 1989); among many others, including David Griffin's *God, Power and Evil* (Philadelphia, PA: Westminster, 1976 and Lanham, MD: University Press of America, 1990) and John Hick's *Evil and the God of Love* (New York: Harper and Row, 1966 and 1977 and New York: Macmillan, 1985); etc.

Peterson, in the aforementioned 1992 source book makes reference to Daniel Clendenin's forthcoming, *Evil: A Bibliography*. This is a project which, until now, had been unknown to me. I infer from Peterson's reference that the book is not annotated and that it focuses upon the problem of evil in literature. I look forward to its publication, since the theodicy issue is a very complex one and scholars need as many resources as possible to deal with the theodicy issues in an informed manner. There is far too much writing on the issue "in the dark," as it were, in apparent ignorance of major publications on the very aspect(s) of the problem(s) under discussion. [Note: this book has not been published to my knowledge, as I write this in early 1998.]

There is much more work to be done to organize the material and make what has been published far more generally available to those researching and writing on the issue. The task of organizing and annotating the biblical and historical references remains incomplete *(Appendices A and B)*. The "suffering of God" theodicy *(Appendix C)* is also one which needs to be pursued, and of course, the publications listed in the miscellaneous appendix—with its numerous sub-divisions—beg for completion *(Appendix D)*. The areas of (what I have referred to often as) peripheral relevance, like the question of *immortality* and the question of *miracles, faith healing, animal suffering,* the *rational status of religious belief, religion in literature, women and theodicy, non-Judaeo-Christian theodicy,* the understanding and nature of *pain,* the question of defining *sin* and the issue of *original sin,* etc.—all have relevance to the theodicy issue, as does the immense issue of redefining the *divine attributes,* omnipotence, impassibility, omniscience, and the like. There is much work to be done, and while I hope to update this present bibliography's annotated chapters periodically and contribute companion volumes of critical essays, the task of organizing the vast and accumulating material on the topic and related areas is of urgent importance. We are in the electronic, computer age, but not yet at the point where computer data bases can provide the material we seek. Too much material, not all of which is directly relevant, is dispersed among the four or five available data bases, and there is much which is left out of these bases, since it takes a professional in the field to recognize relevant peripheral areas. The question of relevance, of course, may vary widely also according to the viewpoint and background of the individual scholars who address the theodicy issue. The more organized the material we have, the better. The more available the material, the better. Uninformed scholarship leads to needless repetition and improvident efforts.

5. See Michael Peterson, *Evil and the Christian God* (Grand Rapids, MI: Baker Book House, 1982), and Peter Hare and Edward Madden, *Evil and the Concept of God* (Springfield, IL: C.C. Thomas, 1968). The many others who have contributed to the issue, in defense of theism or in opposition, are noted in the annotated chapters. The issue is becoming one of increasing significance. Keith Yandell's arguments are listed in this chapter, as are the relevant writings of Trau, King-Farlow, Hasker, Wainwright, and others. The critiques not only of Peter Hare and Edward Madden, but also Keith Chrzan, among others, are included. Chrzan, for example, has criticised the efforts of Peterson, Yandell and Yeager Hudson, all of whom seek to resolve the issue of gratuitous evil.

6. References are entered in this chapter.

7. Some items of a more "theological" or "confessional" nature have been entered in this and in the other annotated chapters, where relevant. The vast majority of publications of this kind, however, have been relegated to the appendices.

I   Some Constructive Theodicies

1052.   Adams, Marilyn McCord. "Hell and the God of Justice." *Religious Studies* 11 (1975): 433-447.

Rejects the doctrine of hell as inconsistent with divine love. There are no valid principles of justice that require God to condemn people to hell.

1053.   ———. "Divine Justice, Divine Love and the Life to Come." *Crux* 13 (1976/ 1977): 13-28.

Argues against retributive justice by God; both its ethical premise and its assessment of God's character and purpose are problematic. Since God is love, God will not deny anyone the possibility of heaven. [See also her "Hell and the God of Justice" [#1052].]

1054.   ———. "Redemptive Suffering: A Christian Solution to the Problem of Evil." *Rationality, Religious Belief, and Moral Commitment.* Edited by Robert Audi and William J. Wainwright. Ithaca, NY: Cornell University Press, 1986: 248-287.

Argues that redemptive suffering affords a solution to theodicy for the believer and unbeliever alike. The cross of Christ is a revelation of God's righteous love and a paradigm of redemptive suffering. Martyrdom is also a paradigm of redemptive suffering, redeeming the onlooker, the persecutor and the martyr. Mystics reveal that suffering is a revelation of the inner life of God.

1055.   ———. "Duns Scotus on the Goodness of God." *Faith and Philosophy* 4 (1987): 486-505.

Contends that rather than formulating defenses against the attacks on the problem of evil by analytical philosophers, Christian philosophers should be formulating what they believe about God's goodness and how God is solving the problem of evil. Adams utilizes Duns Scotus's conception of divine goodness and his understanding of God's creative and redemptive purpose: Scotus's theology is not immune to the problem of evil, but he has re-identified its location in the light of Christian soteriology.

1056.   ———. "Theodicy Without Blame." *Philosophical Topics* 16 (1988): 215-245.

Rejects the theodicy of moral blame (the "moralistic approach"), the paradigm case being that of St. Augustine. Adams argues for an alternative non-moralistic theodicy "without blame": the argument is that horrendous evils can be defeated both globally and within the context of the created participant's life, by integrating them into a relationship with God. Adams argues that Augustinian moralistic theodicy cannot account for horrendous evils.

1057.   ———. "Problems of Evil: More Advice to Christian Philosophers." *Faith and Philosophy* 5 (1988): 121-143.

Citing Alvin Plantinga's "Advice to Christian Philosophers" (*Faith and Philosophy* 4 [1984]: 253-271), Adams notes that the theodicy issue can be formulated either *aporetically* (a constructive challenge) or *atheologically* (as a proof versus God). Pike's *epistemic* defense ("Hume on Evil" [#1157]) and Plantinga's *demonstrative* defense (*The Nature of Necessity*) [#110], as well as paradigm defenses of theodicy, all respond to atheological challenges within a religion-neutral (shared) value theory. Adams notes, however, that there are serious problems with this reliance and its neutral value assumption: it diverts attention from God's agent-centered goodness. We must systematize, deepen, and clarify Christian thought about evil.

1058.   ———. "Horrendous Evils and the Goodness of God." *Proceedings of the Aristotelian Society: Supplement* 63 (1989): 297-310. [Revised version published in *The Problem of Evil.* Edited by Marilyn McCord Adams and Robert Merrihew Adams. New York: Oxford University Press, 1990, 209-221.]

Focuses on the issue of horrendous evils (evils which threaten the positive meaning of a person's life), largely ignored in theodicy discussions. Adams contends that global and generic solutions are incomplete, and agrees with Plantinga ("Self-Profile" [#114]) that we cannot know why God permits horrendous evils. Yet this inability does not make belief in God irrational: it is enough to show how God can be good by defeating horrendous evils within the context of an individual's life. God is understood by Christians as the greatest conceivable being and as good, to the extent that even horrendous evils cannot dispute. God can overcome such evils in three ways: our suffering identifies us with the suffering of Christ; our suffering will elicit divine gratitude (as in Julian of Norwich); and our suffering leads to an inner mystical vision of God, containing both the deepest sufferings and the highest joys. [See response by Sutherland, "Horrendous Evils and the Goodness of God–II" [#1368]. See also Adams, "Sin as Uncleanness." *Philosophical Perspectives* 5 (1991), 1-27.]

1059.   Appleby, Peter C. "Reformed Epistemology, Rationality and Belief in God." *International Journal for Philosophy of Religion* 24 (1988): 129-141.

Defends Plantinga's thesis of proper basicality: see Plantinga's various publications on this theme: *God and Other Minds* [#107]; "Is Belief in God Rational?" (*Rationality and Religious Belief.* Edited by C.F. Delaney (Notre Dame, IN: University of Notre Dame Press, 1979), 7-27; "Is Belief in God Properly Basic?" (*Noûs* 15 [1981], 41-51); "Reason and Belief in God" (*Faith and Philosophy.* Edited by Alvin Plantinga and N. Wolterstorff. Notre Dame, IN: University of Notre Dame Press, 1979). Appleby defends Plantinga against Alston ("Plantinga's Epistemology of Religious Belief," *Alvin Plantinga, Profiles, Volume 5.* Edited by James Tomberlin and Peter van Inwagen. Boston, MA: Reidel, 1985); and Jay Van Hook ("Knowledge, Belief and Reformed Epistemology," *Reformed Journal* 31 [1981], 12-17). The rationality of truths and beliefs is culturally variant. There are rational grounds, as Plantinga argued, for belief in God as properly basic and, as such, the problem of evil is not insurmountable. [For some of the most recent publications on this issue, see Terry Christlieb, "Which Theisms Face an Evidential Problem of Evil?" *Faith and Philosophy* 9 (1992), 45-64; Paul Draper, "Evil and Proper Basicality of Belief in God," *Faith and Philosophy* 8 (1991), 135-147; Richard Grigg, "Theism and Proper Basicality: A Response to Plantinga," *International Journal for Philosophy of Religion* 14 (1983), 123-127; Garth L. Hallett, "Evil and Human Understanding," *Heythrop Journal* 32 (1991), 467-476; etc.]

1060.   Basinger, David. "Evil as Evidence Against the Existence of God: A Response." *Philosophy Research Archives* 4 (1978): 55-67.

Response to Pargetter's argument ("Evil as Evidence Against the Existence of God" [#1146]), that the atheist is not justified in arguing against God's existence on the basis of evil. Basinger argues that Pargetter's argument is unconvincing because of unclarity in his understanding of "plausibility" and "possibility," as these terms are applicable to explanatory hypotheses. Pargetter also fails to understand clearly the conditions under which a *prima facie* moral conflict exists.

1061.   ——. "Evil as Evidence Against God's Existence: Some Clarifications." *Modern Schoolman* 58 (1981): 175-184.

Response to Michael Martin ("Is Evil Evidence Against the Existence of God?" [#1227]). Basinger refutes Martin's atheological argument from evil, that the existence of evil in great abundance counts as evidence against God's existence (as omnipotent, omniscient, and all-good) and the ability of the theist to respond is so limited that it is more rational to believe that God does not exist. Basinger counters that the atheologian has not yet demonstrated that God could have created a better world, one with less evil. *Contra* James Cornman and Keith Lehrer (*Philosophical Problems and Arguments* [#1205]), it cannot be assumed that God can create any logically possible world or that God would intervene to reduce certain evils.

1062.   ——. "Why Petition An Omnipotent, Omniscient, Wholly Good God?" *Religious Studies* 19 (1983): 25-41.

Discusses Stump's "Petitionary Prayer" [#1172]. Basinger argues that it is debatable whether the proponents of petitionary prayer can affirm *both* that certain states of affairs occur because God's assistance is requested *and* the claim that God desires to maximize the quality of life for each individual.

1063.   ——. "Evil and a Finite God: A Response to McGrath." *Philosophy Research Archives* 13 (1987/1988): 285-287.

Rejects McGrath's claim ("Evil and the Existence of a Finite God" [#1320]), that to escape the problem of evil one needs only to alter the conception of God, as limited in either power or goodness. McGrath fails to distinguish between the *deductive* and *inductive* problems of evil and between the limitations in God's *strength* and God's *ability* to act.

1064.   ——. "Hauerwas on the Problem of Evil: A Response." *Christian Scholar's Review* 19 (1989): 289-295.

In response to Hauerwas ("God, Medicine, and the Problem of Evil" [#1295]), Basinger concurs that evil is a problem for theists, but not the "mistake" Hauerwas claims. Hauerwas's critique of the manner in which most theologians have presented the theoretical problem of evil is invalid: not all Christians seek to resolve the issue at this level. Likewise, Hauerwas is wrong in his arguments that theodicy has been based on other assumptions: that the problem of innocent sufferers is a *theoretical* (rather than an *existential*) question, and that the theoretical problem is a challenge to faith.

1065.   Basinger, David, and William S. Hasker, Michael L. Peterson, and Bruce R. Reichenbach. *Reason and Religious Belief*. Oxford: Oxford University Press, 1990.

Chapter 6 ("The Problem of Evil: The Case Against God's Existence," 92-116), written by Michael Peterson, surveys the logical problem of evil, the evidential problem of evil, the issue of a defense versus a theodicy, the range of responses, and some criticisms (including the best possible world theodicy, the higher-divine-morality approach, natural law theodicy, free will theodicy, Hick's theodicy, Augustinian, and process theodicy), and concludes that there is one common thread that runs through all theistic theodicies: evil is necessary to a greater good. The common thread that runs through the atheistic rebuttals, moreover, is the argument that at least some evil or some kinds of evil do not seem necessary for a greater good. Peterson recommends developing the distinction between two sorts of "greater-good" theodicies, distinguishing the actuality of evil as necessary for the greater good from the possibility of evil as such. The former seems less viable.

1066. Beaty, Michael. "The Problem of Evil: The Unanswered Questions Argument." *Southwestern Philosophical Review* 30 (1988): 57-64.

Outlines three formulations of the problem of evil: the logical version (Mackie), the probabilistic version (Plantinga), and the "unanswered questions" version (Hume's Philo and Dostoevsky's Ivan). Beaty contends that theism does not need to answer the unanswered questions for religious belief in God to be rational: What is the source of evil?; What are God's reasons for permitting certain kinds of evils?; and What are God's reasons for permitting particular instances of certain kinds of evils? Human beings grasp only opaquely God's providential governance of the world.

1067. Birnbaum, David. *God and Evil*. Hoboken, NJ: KTAV Publishing, 1989.

Purports to provide a solution to the theodicy issue from a Jewish perspective. He argues that God's power "contracts" as human freedom grows, thereby leaving us more and more susceptible to evil.

1068. Blocher, Henri. "Christian Thought and the Problem of Evil." Translated by Dustin E. Anderson. [Four Parts]. *Churchman* 99 (1985): 6-24; 101-130; 197-215; 293-316.

Rejects three main rational theodicies: understanding evil as necessarily attached to finitude, as the privation of good, and as the result of free will. Blocher proposes a biblically based theodicy, grounded on three truths: the hateful reality of evil, the complete sovereignty of God who determines every event including free acts and evil acts, and the goodness of God. These truths remain opaque, yet what we must understand is that we cannot understand. The cross of Christ is at the center of God's plan and the foundation of hope.

1069. Bowker, John W. "Suffering as a Problem in Religions." *The Meaning of Suffering*. Edited by Flavian Dougherty. New York: Human Sciences Press, 1982: 15-54.

Maintains that while Freud and Marx regarded suffering as the basic problem of religion, religion is, in fact, profoundly realistic in dealing with suffering—rather than being illusory and compensatory.

1070. Breton, Stanislas. "Human Suffering and Transcendence." *The Meaning of Suffering*. Edited by Flavian Dougherty. New York: Human Sciences Press, 1982: 55-94.

Holds that the problem of suffering arises from the mere fact that we never resign ourselves to its inevitability. We seek unsatisfying scientific/naturalistic and philosophical/religious explanations.

1071.   Cain, David. "Arthur McGill: A Memoir." *Harvard Theological Review* 77 (1984): 95-111.

An overview of major points in McGill's theology [#see 1139], including comments about his theodicy. Cain notes that we must remain open to receiving and giving in the presence of death and suffering. This implies the acceptance of suffering, since this is not yet God's world. The cross (not the resurrection) is the decisive, overwhelming and unimpeachable triumph of God's power over evil and sin: it is an openness despite the suffering. The chapter includes a selected bibliography of McGill's writings (1954-1982).

1072.   Calvert, Brian. "Dualism and the Problem of Evil." *Sophia* 22 (1983): 14-28.

Proposes a dualistic solution to the problem of evil, one that retains the conception of God in orthodox Christian belief and does not limit God's power, as do other forms of dualism. Calvert argues that there are two necessary beings: God and an ultimate evil being. It is not a limitation on God's power, he contends, not to be able to destroy this evil being, since its existence is necessary and God cannot do what is logically impossible (destroy a necessary being). The evil being is responsible for evil, and this constitutes a solution to the problem of evil. [See Novak's response, "Comments on Calvert's 'Dualism and the Problem of Evil'" [#1328].]

1073.   Chiari, Joseph. *The Necessity of Being*. New York: Gordian Press, 1973.

Chapter 5 ("Evil and Suffering," 70-84) argues that evil has its source in the naturally destructive character of things, each struggling to realize its own essence. Evil is part of the conflict of opposites, unavoidable and contingent to the final aim of the everlastingness and permanence of good. Evil is negative and will be eliminated, but the negativity is part of the necessary growth of good. Suffering (as shown by the biblical Book of Job) can be a means to open up and raise the individual to the knowledge and apprehension of God.

1074.   Chisholm, Roderick M. "The Defeat of Good and Evil." *Proceedings and Addresses of the American Philosophical Association* 42 (1968-1969): 21-38. [Also published in *Contemporary American Philosophy*. Edited by John E. Smith. New York: Humanities Press, 1970, 152-169; and in *The Problem of Evil*. Edited by Marilyn McCord Adams and Robert Merrihew Adams. New York: Oxford University Press, 1990, 53-68.]

Distinguishes between the intrinsic goodness or intrinsic badness (evil) of a certain situation being "balanced off" and "defeated" by some other situation. Against those (Mackie, McCloskey, Aiken, Flew, etc.) who argue that it is not possible for a world that is at least as good as any other possible world to include intrinsically bad states of affairs, Chisholm argues that this is not so, provided that the badness of each of these states of affairs is defeated. The world's evil is defeated and contained in a larger whole, a whole which is absolutely good. [See Penelhum's comments, "Divine Goodness and the Problem of Evil" [#1408]; and Flemming's response, "Omnibenevolence and Evil"

[#1089]. See also Chisholm and Ernest Sosa, "On the Logic of 'Intrinsically Better'," *American Philosophical Quarterly* 3 (1966), 244-249. See Chisholm's *The Foundations of Knowing*. Brighton: Harvester Press, 1982; and his earlier *Theory of Knowing*. Englewood Cliffs, NJ: Prentice-Hall, 1966.]

1075. Chryssides, George D. "Evil and the Problem of God." *Religious Studies* 23 (1987): 467-475.

Proposes a solution to the problem of evil, based on a revisionist concept of God. Christians must abandon the concept of God as a person or as a disembodied agent; they must conceive of God in a less overtly personalistic manner. If God is not a person, there is no divine being to be morally censured or morally defended. [See also Chryssides's "God and the Tao," *Religious Studies* 19 (1983), 1-12.]

1076. Dore, Clement. "Do Theodicists Mean What They Say?" *Philosophy* 49 (1974): 357-374.

Discusses the claims of McCloskey and Penelhum, that the so-called values made possible by evils (courage, endurance, charity, sympathy, etc.) are not worth the evil that gave rise to them (McCloskey, "God and Evil" [#1231]; and Penelhum, *Religion and Rationality* [#95]). Either the theodicist really *does believe* that heroic responses to suffering are sufficiently valuable to outweigh the suffering, or the theodicist really *does not believe* a person can be justified in permitting suffering on the ground that it gives rise to such responses. Dore seeks to show how a rational theodicist could hold *both* that God can be justified in causing suffering on the ground that it serves good ends *and* that human beings cannot be justified in causing suffering on the same ground. He points out the difference between God and human beings, explaining that, while God is cleared of blame for causing suffering, humans beings are not. [See response by Brecher, "Notes and Comments: Knowledge, Belief and the Sophisticated Theodicist" [#360].]

1077. ———. "Do Theists Need to Solve the Problem of Evil?" *Religious Studies* 12 (1976): 383-390.

Discusses the atheist's challenge that theists have failed to show that neither God nor human beings are morally justified in not preventing instances of intense innocent suffering. Dore argues that God may have a property (indiscernible to us) which accounts for God's refusal to eliminate morally reprehensible evils. Perhaps the elimination of such evil would bring about an undesirable state of affairs.

1078. ———. "Agnosticism." *Religious Studies* 18 (1982): 503-507.

Rejects the claim that agnosticism (the suspension of judgment) is more rational than theism or atheism. He contends that theism, atheism and agnosticism are equally rational positions.

1079. ———. *Theism*. Dordrecht and Boston, MA: Reidel, 1984.

Chapter 1 ("Does Suffering Serve Valuable Ends?") claims to refute the atheistic argument from suffering by arguing that suffering is a logically necessary condition of the existence of some valuable ends. Dore defends this thesis against various critical arguments.

1080.   ———. "A Reply to Professor Rowe." *Faith and Philosophy* 3 (1986): 314-318.

Response to Rowe's critical review *(Faith and Philosophy* 3 [1986], 202-206) of Dore's *Theism* [#1079]. Dore reaffirms his argument that God is not a non-existing object, and that Rowe's criticism of this is incoherent. Against Rowe's concept of metaphysical impossibility, Dore contends that God's non-existence, non-omnipotence and non-omniscience are logically (not just metaphysically) impossible. Dore defends his claim also that since "God" means supremely perfect being, it is unlikely that anyone who has experienced God has failed to experience God *qua* supremely perfect being. As such, he holds that it is logically possible that a supremely perfect being exists.

1081.   ———. *God, Suffering, and Solipsism.* New York: St. Martin's Press, 1989.

Expanded and revised version of some of the issues covered in Dore's *Theism* [#1079]. The discussion of the theodicy issue *(Chapters 5-7)* is expanded in this later book: the solution is extensively revised and the free will defense is taken more seriously *(Chapters 5 and 6). Chapter 7* is a reprinted version of "Does Suffering Serve Discernible Ends?" which is similar to *Chapter 1* in Dore's *Theism,* "Does Suffering Serve Valuable Ends?" Dore expands upon the free will defense of Alvin Plantinga and John Hick's "soul-making" version of the free will defense. He contends that these are promising responses to the challenge of solipsism.

1082.   Downing, F. Gerald. "God and the Problems of Evils." *Sophia* 7 (1968): 12-18.

Maintains that evil is not incompatible with theism, when theism is understood as being concerned not with questions of *logical inconsistency* but with *practical responses*; namely, how to maintain and enjoy the good and how to avoid the evil.

1083.   Dupré, Louis. "Evil—A Religious Mystery: A Plea for a More Inclusive Model of Theodicy." *Faith and Philosophy* 7 (1990): 261-280.

Contends that theodicies employ a rationalistic conception of God (which is alien to living faith) and an abstract, theologically neutral definition of good and evil. He proposes an alternative model that rests upon a more intimate union of finite and infinite Being, allowing creatures greater autonomy and responsibility, and enabling the creator to share in our suffering. God redeems us in this way.

1084.   Ehman, Robert R. "On Evil and God." *Monist* 46 (1963): 478-487.

The argument is that since God is self-sufficient and creation is contingent, there is no necessity for the creation of more good than we find in the world. Since God freely creates, we have no claim on God. To reject God because of the world's evil is to measure God in terms of the standards of human beings and, as such, to regard the world (falsely) as divine. Since the world is other than God, there is no contradiction between evil and the goodness of God.

1085.   Ewing, Alfred Cyril. "The Problem of Evil." *Value and Reality: The Philosophical Case for Theism.* New York: Humanities Press, 1973: 209-237.

After rejecting various theodicies, including Hartshorne's *a priori* argument, the free will defense, and the limiting of divine power, Ewing argues that the most promising solution is to see evil as a condition without which certain goods could not be attained. He argues also for indeterminism and universal salvation: the theistic hypothesis demands that all human beings reach salvation, even if it takes place through a succession of lives. [See critical comments of John Knox, "A.C. Ewing: A Critical Survey of Ewing's Recent Work" [#73].]

1086. Faricy, Robert. "The Problem of Evil in Perspective." *Communico: International Catholic Review* 6 (1979): 173-191.

Contends that traditional Augustinian theodicies fail and that the new theologies of Teilhard, liberationists and Pannenberg are more promising. The problem of evil cannot be considered properly apart from the principle elements of the Christian apocalyptic tradition. The *apocalyptic—*versus *metaphysical—*framework sees evil under three aspects: teleological (Teilhard), prophetic (liberationists), and apocalyptic (Pannenberg). Faricy claims that Catholic theological reflection on theodicy since the late 1950s has moved from the teleological to the prophetic, and now into the apocalyptic.

1087. Farrell, P.M. "Evil and Omnipotence." *Mind* 67 (1958): 399-403.

Challenges Mackie's suggestion ("Evil and Omnipotence" [#1217]) that no proposed solution to the problem of evil can withstand criticism. He argues for a more complete understanding of the nature of evil, as the privation of good. [See Zimmerman's response, "A Note on the Problem of Evil" [#1376].]

1088. Feinberg, John S. *Theologies and Evil*. Washington, DC: University Press of America, 1979.

Discusses several theodicies: theonomy, Liebnizian rationalism, and the modified rationalism of Schlesinger, Hick, Plantinga, Yandell, and Ross. Feinberg argues that these theodicies are internally consistent (except for Schlesinger's and Ross's)—versus Mackie's claim that this is not possible—and yet that there are external criticisms which render them inadequate. The free will defense of modified rationalists, for example, is rejected because Feinberg is not convinced that incompatibility is correct. Nor is such a view of freedom as valuable as claimed, when it is possible to have compatibilistic freedom and no evil. Feinberg's own theodicy proposes that moral evil is consistent with God and that natural evil reduces to a problem of moral evil or, in fact, to a religious problem. Feinberg's theodicy is a version of modified rationalism that incorporates a nonconsequentialist account of ethics. It does not rest on incompatibilistic free will.

1089. Flemming, Arthur. "Omnibenevolence and Evil." *Ethics* 96 (1986): 261-281.

Regards the problem of evil not simply as an epistemic or logical difficulty, but as a *casuistical question for ethics*: is there a moral justification for allowing evil which could have been prevented? Flemming argues that traditional theistic efforts fail to answer this question adequately. There is a more promising solution: divine benevolence is the same virtue as it is in human beings, but with the one exception, that divine omnipotence puts greater demands on divine benevolence. Divine benevolence must admit some evil in the world. [See Chisholm's "The Defeat of Good and Evil" [#1074].]

1090.   Foster, Andrew Durwood. "The Problem of Understanding Evil." *Religion in Life* 37 (1969): 555-569.

While Christianity has affirmed that God is all-powerful and all-loving, the question to be addressed is to define the third proposition, that evil exists. Christianity must maintain the reality of evil despite those who have tried to deny its reality: evil is *real* but not *ultimate*. Foster argues that all evil either is sin or is rooted immediately or ultimately in sin.

1091.   Frank, Simon Lyudvigovich. *The Unknowable: An Ontological Introduction to the Philosophy of Religion*. Athens, OH: Ohio University Press, 1983. Translated by Boris Jakim. Originally published in 1939.

Chapter 10 ("God and the World," 261-296) argues that the problem of evil is unsolvable rationally: to explain evil would be to ground and justify it; but this would contradict its very essence as illegitimate, as that which should not be. The overcoming of evil in the awareness of guilt and in the endurance of suffering is based in our being in God, in our return to God. He rejects the free will defense: evil is never freely chosen. Evil is generated in the ineffable abyss which lies on the threshold between God and "not-God." Yet the question of the *origin* of evil is really the question of *responsibility* for evil (human responsibility).

1092.   Galligan, Michael. *God and Evil*. New York: Paulist Press, 1976.

Critiques both the Augustinian (Augustine, Aquinas, Calvin) and Irenaean theodicies (Schleiermacher, Hick, Teilhard). Karl Rahner shares with Augustinian theodicy the abandonment of the theodicy of free will (as internally incoherent). Augustinian and Irenaean theodicy both fail to define divine power adequately, while the Irenaean theodicy's instrumentallist view of evil is prejudicially selective. Process thinkers (Hartshorne, Cobb) define divine power more adequately, but without divine coercion they have an inadequate account of immortality and salvation by God.

1093.   Geisler, Norman L., and Winfried Corduan. *Philosophy of Religion*. Grand Rapids, MI: Zondervan, 1974. Grand Rapids, MI: Baker Book House. Second edition, 1988.

Part Four ("God and Evil," *Chapters 14-17)* addresses theodicy. Geisler rejects various solutions to theodicy (evil as illusion, the finite God, cosmic sadism, determinism, etc.) and argues that while this is not the best of all possible worlds, it is the best of all possible ways to achieve the best of all possible worlds *(Chapter 14)*. The following three chapters address the questions: why did God create anything imperfect?—*the metaphysical problem of evil (Chapter 15)*: Geisler argues for the Augustinian—Thomist principle of evil as privation; why does God permit the imperfect to exist?—*the moral problem of evil (Chapter 16)*: Geisler argues that permitting evil is the best way to the best possible world, and he defends a version of eschatological verification (versus Hick's version); and why does unnecessary human suffering and pain exist if there is an absolutely perfect God?—*the physical problem of evil (Chapter 17)*: Geisler argues that physical evils are a necessary condition and concomitant of the best kind of world for achieving the best of all possible moral worlds.

1094.   ———. *The Roots of Evil*. Grand Rapids, MI: Zondervan Publishing House, 1979. Second Edition, 1989.

Proposes various philosophical options to answer the apparent contradictions between the existence of (moral and physical) evil and God. He evaluates and supports biblical theism for its ability to answer some of the major questions about metaphysical, moral and physical evil.

1095.   Gellman, Jerome I. "The Meta-Philosophy of Religious Language." *Noûs* 11 (1977): 151-161.

Argues that no theological understanding of God and evil can conclude that the problem of evil could not arise. Contends also that the problem is an authentic articulation of the Judaeo-Christian tradition: the theodicy problem is internal to that tradition. He argues for an analogical theory of God over the *via negativa*: the former, but not the latter, makes the problem of evil possible.

1096.   ———."Omnipotence and Impeccability." *New Scholasticism* 51 (1977): 21-37.

Response to Pike's "Omnipotence and God's Ability to Sin" [#98]. Pike has not provided an adequate characterization of divine omnipotence: if God is omnipotent, is God incapable of sinning? Gellman holds that there are morally unjustified states of affairs which is logically impossible for an essentially perfect being to create.

1097.   ———. "Religion as Language." *Religious Studies* 21 (1985): 159-168.

Reformulates the argument presented in his "The Meta-Philosophy of Religious Language" [#1095]. Gellman distinguishes *religious* and *metaphysical* beliefs, with respect to the problem of evil, arguing for the relative-identity of belief. Religious belief in the seriousness of the theodicy problem engages in the use of a shared institutional language (internal); metaphysical belief in the problem arises in one's theological system (external). [See also Gellman's more recent, "A New Look at the Problem of Evil," *Faith and Philosophy* 9 (1992), 209-215.]

1098.   Gilkey, Langdon. "The Christian Understanding of Suffering." *Buddhist Christian Studies* 4 (1985): 49-65.

Outlines (what he understands to be) the Christian understanding of suffering: the affirmation of our finitude, the surrender of this finitude in repentance and faith, and the gifts through grace of a new self, united with the divine. [See responses by Masao Abe and Francis H. Cook, "Responses to Langdon Gilkey" [#3009]. See also Gilkey's "Theodicy and Plurality" [#2495]; and Gilkey's *Maker of Heaven and Earth* ("Creation and Evil," *Chapter 7*). Garden City, NY: Anchor Books, 1965. Originally published in 1959. See also Gilkey's *Renaming the Whirlwind*. Indianapolis, IN and New York: Bobbs-Merrill, 1969.]

1099.   Gordon, David. "Is the Argument from Evil Decisive?" *Religious Studies* 19 (1983): 407-410.

Refutes Lugenbehl's defense of the argument from evil against several theistic objections to it ("Can the Argument from Evil Be Decisive After All?" [#1216]). Gordon argues that Lugenbehl is incorrect in claiming that since God could not achieve a certain end without the use of a painful means, there are sufficient grounds to show that God is not all-powerful. It is incorrect to assume the principle that an all-good God would achieve ends with the least amount of pain. Gordon holds that Lugenbehl too readily assumes that God ought to act as human beings act in moral situations.

1100.   Grisez, Germain. *Beyond the New Theism: A Philosophy of Religion*. Notre Dame, IN: University of Notre Dame Press, 1975.

The section on theodicy argues against consequentialist theories of morality and addresses various aspects of the problem of evil. Grisez argues that evil is real but not created; and that evil is a privation of good.

1101.   Gruner, Rolf. "The Elimination of the Argument from Evil." *Theology* 83 (1980): 416-424.

Claims that it makes no sense to think that there could be a world in which there is no evil. Those who argue from evil against God's existence make, by implication, this mistaken assumption. A perfect state of this world cannot be imagined, since it would no longer be *this* world. The more fundamental question is why God created this world, rather than none at all. We must choose to accept this world and its inevitable evil or to reject the world; we must choose between no world and an imperfect one.

1102.   Hagner, Donald A. "A New Look at the Problem of Evil." *Christianity Today* 13 (1969): 1122-1124.

Contends that *revelation* is the solution to theodicy: the three propositions (God is omnipotent, omnibenevolvent, and yet evil exists) are inconsistent and not resolvable by rational means. Revelation also reveals this is not the best possible world and not the world originally created by God. Revelation reveals also that there must be a good reason for evil.

1103.   Hall, Douglas. *God and Human Suffering*. Minneapolis, MN: Augsburg, 1986.

Argues that various aspects of what we refer to as suffering (loneliness, the experience of limits, temptation, anxiety) are necessary parts of God's good creation. These are distinguished from suffering in a post-fallen state. God's response to and preoccupation with our suffering is nothing less than the suffering of God. Hall structures his theodicy with explicit reference to the *creation* (suffering as becoming; some suffering is the result of finitude); to the *fall* (suffering as burden: some suffering is the result of human freedom used distortedy); and to *redemption* (the conquest from within). Christian faith affirms the conquest of suffering and Hall argues that the Church is a vital part in God's response to suffering. An appendix critiques several theodicies: Kushner, *When Bad Things Happen to Good People* [#1132]; C.S. Lewis, *The Problem of Pain* [#3435]; Allen, *Traces of God in a Frequently Hostile World* [#544]; Buttrick, *God, Pain and Evil* [#1511]; and Weatherhead, *Salute to a Sufferer* [#3703].

1104.   Hall, Thor. "Theodicy as a Test of the Reasonableness of Theology." *Religion in Life* 43 (1974): 204-217.

Surveys and critically assesses various methodical approaches to theodicy. He argues that the critical method of the Lundensian school, particularly Anders Nygren and Ragnar Bring, is the most reasonable option for theodicy. Hall rejects various alternative options: revelational, secular, metaphysical, historical, existential, correlative, and dialectical. [See also Thor Hall's *A Framework for Faith*. Leiden: E.J. Brill, 1970.]

1105.　——. "Creation as Historic-Dramatic Category in Gustaf Aulén's Theology." *Creation and Method: Critical Essays on Christocentric Theology.* Edited by Henry Vander Goot. Washington, DC: University Press of America, 1981.

Discussion of Aulén's theology, including his theodicy (see *The Faith of the Christian Church.* Philadelphia, PA: Muhlenberg, 1960; and *The Drama and the Symbols* [#1268]). Aulén holds that there is no rational solution to theodicy; the task is to *overcome* evil. He removes theodicy from the context of theoretical speculation concerning the origin of evil, placing it rather in the context of existential interpretation of meaning. Hall contends that Aulén has resolved the problem of God's relation to the world (God as cause, etc.), a problem that has "haunted Christian theologians as long as theology has existed." There is no need to explain God's providence as the cause of what happens.

1106.　Harris, Errol E. "Selfhood and Godhood." *Philosophical Review* 67 (1958): 538-545.

Argues that Campbell (*On Selfhood and Godhood* [#1386]) did not need to propose the dubious doctrine of an afterlife with its compensating joys as a solution to theodicy. Harris contends that suffering is the means by which the highest values can be achieved.

1107.　——. *Revelation Through Reason: Religion in the Light of Science and Philosophy.* New Haven, CT: Yale University Press, 1959.

Chapter 6 ("Evil and Divine Power, 126-155) extends Flew's arguments ("Divine Omnipotence and Human Freedom" [#45]) which seek to dismiss the Augustinian God of absolute power as implying a negation of human freedom. Harris argues that pain and evil are not identical; pain is an integral aspect of some things which are deemed good. He supports the view that evil is inherent in the world's process; creation is the process of generation of value through the progressive elimination of evil.

1108.　——. *The Problem of Evil.* Milwaukee, WI: Marquette University, 1977.

This brief book is very similar to the author's *Atheism and Theism, Chapter 6* ("Evil and Transfiguration" [#1109]).

1109.　——. *Atheism and Theism.* New Orleans, LA: Tulane University Press, 1977.

The chapter on theodicy (*Chapter 6*, "Evil and Transfiguration," 105-132) responds to Brand Blanshard's *Reason and Belief* [#1197]. Blanshard argued that theists must take refuge in blind faith or revolt against reason altogether with respect to the failure of their attempts to resolve the problem of evil. Harris answers Blanshard's critique by contending that evil is transfigured in the progressive sublation of the finite toward the ultimate realization of an absolute redemption. Perfection requires imperfection in the stages of its generation. As such, the idea of an absolutely benevolent and omnipotent God who might create a world devoid of evil is an impossible abstraction.

1110.　——. "Reply to Hepburn's 'The Problem of Evil'." *Dialectic and Contemporary Science: Essays in Honor of Errol E. Harris.* Edited by Philip T. Grier. Lanham, MD: University Press of America, 1989: 125-135.

Reaffirms basic features of his theodicy against Hepburn's critique ("The Problem of Evil" [#1299]) regarding the privation of good and the necessity and unavoidable nature of natural evil as a result of human finitude. He contends that a world without finites is inconceivable, and a world without pain in finite creatures would be a world without life and consciousness. This may be the best of all possible worlds, the only world ontologically possible. Harris argues also against Hepburn's critique that God does not need nature and its sufferings for the divine self-articulation.

1111.   Hasker, William S. "On Regretting the Evils of this World." *Southern Journal of Philosophy* 19 (1981): 425-438.

Holds that we should not blame God for creating a world with so much evil and suffering if we are glad *on the whole* that we exist and that the evils likely are necessary for our existence. Had the world's past events been different, it would be likely that we who now exist would not exist. [See Morriston's reply, "Gladness, Regret, God, and Evil" [#1325]. See also Hasker's more recent "The Necessity of Gratuitous Evil," *Faith and Philosophy* 9 (1992), 23-44].

1112.   Hatcher, William S. "A Logical Solution to the Problem of Evil." *Zygon, Journal of Religion and Science* 9 (1974): 245-255.

Demonstrates that the problem of evil is a real, logical contradiction (rather than merely a paradox), and argues that the problem can be resolved by denying that evil is an *absolute* term: the contradiction in propositions no longer exists in the *relativist* framework. The problem of evil can be formulated in relative terms. Hatcher replaces the absolute term Ev(X) ["X is evil"] with the relative term Ev(X,Y) ["X is more evil than Y"]. [See Quinn's response, "A Pseudosolution to the Problem of Evil" [#1335]; and Hatcher's reply, "The Relative Conception of Good and Evil" [#1113].]

1113.   ———. "The Relative Conception of Good and Evil." *Zygon, Journal of Religion and Science* 10 (1975): 446-448.

Refutes Quinn's criticisms ("A Pseudosolution to the Problem of Evil" [#1335]) of Hatcher's contention that the problem of evil can be disposed of ("A Logical Solution to the Problem of Evil" [#1112]). Quinn's critique is irrelevant to Hatcher's solution, since Quinn continues to use an absolute framework involving the use of good and evil as absolute (monadic) predicates. Hatcher rejects Quinn's criticism that the relativist account of good and evil does not take evil seriously. The relativist account is closer to experience and enables us to see God's purpose much more clearly.

1114.   Hebblethwaite, Brian L. "MacKinnon and the Problem of Evil." *Christ, Ethics and Tragedy: Essays in Honour of Donald MacKinnon.* Edited by Kenneth Surin. Cambridge: Cambridge University Press, 1989: 131-145.

Critical analysis of MacKinnon's theodicy [see #1315]: his rejection of evil as the privation of good; his insistence that there is no theoretical solution to theodicy; and his insistence on the ineradicability of the tragic from Christianity. Hebblethwaite refutes all three of these aspects of MacKinnon's theodicy. He also rejects Stewart Sutherland's view (*God, Jesus and Belief* [#3653]), that the insolubility of the problem of evil is axiomatic: this (according to Hebblethwaite) leads to an impersonal God. He rejects also Karl Rahner's solution of theodicy ("Why Does God Allow us to Suffer?" [#1927]): Rahner wrongly grounds suffering in the incomprehensibility of God as his ultimate solution.

1115. Hicks, David C. "Moral Evil as Apparent Disvalue." *Religious Studies* 13 (1977): 1-16.

Argues that moral evil, in additional to the free will defense, can be explained as apparent disvalues (rather than a kind of positive entity), attitudes, and behaviors which are not consistent with the norm of a given society. He argues also for the relativity of moral norms, such as are ultimately derived from and subject to the certain things of objective value: human persons, living things in general, and the holy or divine being.

1116. Hudson, Yeager. "Is There Too Much Evil in the World?" *International Philosophical Quarterly* 25 (1985): 343-348.

Formulates a theodicy against the deduction from the existence of *any* evil in the world. He argues that the deduction from the quantity of evil necessarily degenerates into the more standard deduction from any evil. Defenses against the former abound, and since deduction from the quantity of evil collapses into deductions from any evil, it fails as well. The argument that there is too much evil in the world is a subjective and psychological argument, not a logical one. God's morally sufficient reason for allowing evil is that it is a necessary condition of conscious and moral human beings. [See response by Chrzan, "Hudson on 'Too Much Evil'" [#1201]; and Hudson's reply [#1117].]

1117. ———. "Response to Chrzan's 'Hudson on "Too Much" Evil'." *International Philosophical Quarterly* 27 (1987): 207-210.

Refutes Chrzan's claim that some "too much evil" arguments are more valid or more plausible and convincing than others. He maintains his former point, that there is a collapse of the argument from the deduction from the *quantity* of evil into the deduction from *any* evil.

1118. ———. *The Philosophy of Religion*. Mountain View, CA: Mayfield Publishing Company, 1991.

Chapter 4 ("Objections to Theism,") critically assesses the challenge of theodicy. Hudson holds that the problem remains a major concern for theists, since atheological objections have not been answered sufficiently. Theistic attempts to justify both moral evil (through the free will defense) and natural evil are based on a modified understanding of omnipotence. An adequate theodicy, he holds, must preserve both human freedom and God's "great-making attributes." He argues that the possibility of evil is a necessary condition for the existence of any and all good.

1119. Hughes, Philip Edgecumbe. "Has God Lost Control?" *Christianity Today* 18 (1974): 1390-1394.

The argument is that God controls all things and will intervene in judgment (as in creation and redemption) at the end of the age.

1120. Keene, G.B. "A Simpler Solution to the Paradox of Omnipotence." *Mind* 69 (1960): 74-75.

Refutes Mackie's paradox of omnipotence ("God and Evil" [#1217]). Keene denies the suggestion that God is limited if God cannot make things which God cannot control. He restructures this proposition to avoid Mackie's paradox:

there is nothing of which it is true that both God can make it and that God cannot control it. Thus, if God can make something, God can control it. It is impossible that an omnipotent being can make things it cannot control, and it is false that an omnipotent being cannot make things it cannot control.

1121.   ———. "Capacity-Limiting Statements." *Mind* 70 (1961): 251-252.

Response to Mayo's critique ("Mr. Keene on Omnipotence" [#1318]) of Keene's argument ("A Simpler Solution to the Paradox of Omnipotence" [#1120]). The latter sought to resolve the paradox of omnipotence. Keene reaffirms that if the statement—God cannot make things which God cannot control—is not a capacity-limiting statement, there is no paradox of omnipotence obtainable from it.

1122.   Kekes, John. "Understanding Evil." *American Philosophical Quarterly* 25 (1988): 13-24.

Maintains that the way we understand evil directly affects our concept of morality. Of the three traditional views of *gratuitous evil* (corruption of an essentially good nature, the uncontrolled expression of our brutish nature, and the mixture of good and evil potentialities in human nature), only the third is valid. It is only from this latter view that a valid conception of morality can be formulated, one which is incompatible with several meta-ethical theories. [See also Kekes, "The Problem of God," *Journal of Value Inquiry* 18 (1984), 99-112.]

1123.   Kielkopf, Charles F. "Emotivism as the Solution to the Problem of Evil." *Sophia* 9 (1970): 34-38.

Resolves the problem of evil by denying the existence of evil (and good). Adopting an emotivist (non-cognitivist) analysis of value judgments, he shows that the problem of evil cannot be a *logical* problem which tests the consistency of propositions. Nor is there a *moral* problem of finding excuses for God's toleration of evil. The problem of evil is best understood as a *religious* problem. To state that "God is omnibenevolent" has no truth value, yet we can convince ourselves through conditioning that the statement is true.

1124.   King-Farlow, John. "Through a Glass Darkly: God and Evil." *Chapter 5* of his *Reason and Religion: Philosophy and Religion in a Scientific Age*. London: Darton Longman Todd, 1969: 73-85.

Denies the argument that there is a logical inconsistency in the propositions about God's attributes and the existence of evil. He discusses also the atheistic argument that the forms and amounts of evil render it improbable God exists. King-Farlow holds that this does not take into account other facts, an afterlife, for example.

1125.   ———. "The Liabilities of Limited Gods." *Philosophical Studies* 20 (1969): 46-48.

Response to Madden's "Evil and the Concept of a Limited God" [#1223]. King-Farlow argues that Madden confuses *ethical* and *existential* matters in arguing for his metaphysical thesis, that evil in the world is incompatible with any limited God's existence.

1126.   ———. "Must Gods Madden Madden?" *Philosophy and Phenomenological Research* 30 (1969): 451-455.

Critique of Madden ("The Many Faces of Evil" [#1221] and Hare and Madden, "On the Difficulty of Evading the Problem of Evil" [#1209]). He argues that Madden has not acknowledged the counter-argument of Nelson Pike ("Hume on Evil" [#1157]), and has not proven that there is a formal inconsistency between theistic beliefs and the existence of evil in the world. King-Farlow rejects Madden's argument that gratuitous evil is unanswerable by the theist. Perhaps such evil is explainable by reference to a doctrine of *the transmigration of souls* and/or free will. [See King-Farlow's "Evil and Other Worlds" [#383]]. Also, despite the sufferings and defects in the world, he contends that the very existence of rational persons offers strong evidence that there is at least one benevolent cosmic person at work. [See response by Hare and Madden, "Why Hare Must Hound the Gods" [#1211].]

1127.   ———. "Scepticism, Evil and Original Sin." *The Challenge of Religion Today: Essays on the Philosophy of Religion*. Edited by John King-Farlow. New York: Science History Publications, 1976: 26-42.

Argues that there may well be a rational basis for belief in God, despite evil. He considers traditional Christian belief, reincarnation, and Pascal's wager, and argues—against the sceptic—that there are many possible cosic models which can integrate biblical teachings, human experience of good and evil, and moral intuitions.

1128.   King-Farlow, John, and K.G. Gotkürdel. "Über Formal Entscheidbare Sätzenkonjunktionen Der Principia Theologica Und Verwandter Systeme." *Analysis* 30 (1970): 140-144.

Argues that Hare and Madden (*Evil and the Concept of God* [#1210]) are confused about the appropriate "rationality criteria" for judging reasonable beliefs and decisions. Pike ("God and Evil: A Reconsideration" [#1156]) has inadvertently encouraged this sort of confusion. The formally decidable consistency of various important theological propositions sheds far more light on the theodicy issue than is appreciated by Pike and by Hare and Madden.

1129.   Kolakowski, Leszek. *Religion: If There is No God: On God, the Devil, Sin, and Other Worries of the So-Called Philosophy of Religion*. Oxford: Oxford University Press, 1982.

Argues a utilitarian view of evil. Since God is a utilitarian, we live in the best of all possible worlds, a world in which the global amount of good outweighs the mass of evil to the maximum degree possible. All things are building blocks for a future perfection, and nothing will be wasted in the process. [See response by Moulder, "In Search of a Theodicy" [#1327].]

1130.   Kropf, Richard W. *Evil and Evolution: A Theodicy*. Rutherford, NJ: Fairleigh Dickinson University, 1984.

Influenced by process theodicy (David Griffin), and the writings of many others (Dostoevsky, Ricoeur, Ahern, Weil, Kitamori, and most notably, Teilhard), Kropf discusses the attributes of divine power and goodness, the nature of evil, original sin ("ultimate sin"), moral and physical evil, and the suffering of God. He argues that suffering is the result of chance; true freedom is won only through suffering amid the evolutionary struggle toward consciousness and freedom. God "has taken a chance on chance."

1131. Kushner, Harold S. "Why Do the Righteous Suffer? Notes Toward a Theology of Tragedy." *Judaism* 28 (1979): 316-323.

Written before his popular book, *When Bad Things Happen to Good People* [#1132], Kushner maintains that suffering is the result of human freedom, human insensitivity, and the chance occurrences of impersonal laws of nature. His point is that evil and suffering are not to be attributed to God's cruelty, as has been traditionally believed and taught.

1132. ———. *When Bad Things Happen to Good People*. New York: Schocken, 1981.

This book has been a phenomenon, selling over three million copies in several languages. Kushner argues for the rejection of the traditional view which attributes evil to God. Kushner argues that God does not will the tragedies of human life. Evils are the result of randomness; God's role is to give us the ability to cope with our suffering and also to suffer with us. [See also Kushner's *Who Needs God?* New York: Pocket Books, 1989; and *When Children Ask About God*. New York: Schocken, 1989. First published in New York: Reconstructionist Press, 1971.]

1133. Langton, Douglas C. "The Argument from Evil: Reply to Professor Richman." *Religious Studies* 16 (1980): 103-113.

Rejects Richman's argument ("The Argument from Evil" [#1243]), that the theist must specify the morally sufficient reasons why God permits suffering in order to be justified rationally in maintaining belief in God in face of the suffering in the world. Langton argues that Richman wrongly believes that the same standards about morally sufficient reasons apply both to cases of *omission* and cases of *commission*.

1134. Luhman, Reginald S. "Belief in God and the Problem of Suffering." *Evangelical Quarterly* 57 (1985): 327-348.

Argues that no complete solution to the problem of evil can be forthcoming, since such a solution must account for all actual suffering which has existed or will exist. The onus of proof is on the atheist to show that the theist is wrong in the assessment of the limitation of human knowledge of God. Luhman argues that the free will defense, allied to belief in an afterlife, is the most promising of solutions, despite certain difficulties. The afterlife, for example, may be filled with dangers and pain (Hick). He rejects various theodicies: suffering is illusion; pain is beneficial; suffering is the result of sin; suffering is God's will; suffering is a result of natural laws; and the belief that God suffers.

1135. Mauldin, Frank L. "Misplaced Concreteness in the Problem of Evil." *Perspectives in Religious Studies* 11 (1984): 243-255.

Contends that the theoretical formulation of the problem of evil substitutes the part for the whole (the Whiteheadian *fallacy of misplaced concreteness*). It focuses on the logical paradox rather than on the important biblical and concrete historical basis of Christian faith: the trinity, the cross, and so on.

1136. Mavrodes, George I. "The Problem of Evil as a Rhetorical Problem." *Philosophy and Rhetoric* 1 (1968): 91-102.

Theodicy should not be treated solely as a *logical* problem but as a *rhetorical* problem of seemingly incomparable beliefs. Rhetorical parameters include the requirements of psychological effectiveness (persuasiveness), as well as those of truth and logic.

1137.   ———. *Belief in God: A Study in the Epistemology of Religion.* New York: Random House, 1970.

Chapter 4 (90-111) addresses the problem of evil. Mavrodes contends that the formulations of the problem of evil by David Hume and John Mackie are irrelevant to the beliefs of a theist. He argues that answering the theodicy questions (the set of supposed incoherent propositions or beliefs) will not alter the believer's beliefs).

1138.   ———. "Keith Yandell and the Problem of Evil." *International Journal for Philosophy of Religion* 20 (1986): 45-48.

Refutes Yandell's claim ("The Problem of Evil and the Content of Morality" [#1193]), that since God allows evil, God must have a morally sufficient reason for doing so. Mavrodes argues that this claim is unsubstantiated, since it is hypothetical and conditional on God's existence. Yandell's argument can be used to argue the absurd conclusion that no fact whatsoever provides any evidence against anything at all: everything is critically cancelled.

1139.   McGill, Arthur C. *Suffering: A Test of Theological Method.* Philadelphia, PA: Westminster Press, 1982. First published in 1968.

Distinguishes divine power from demonic power and discusses the implications for the trinity, the nature of evil, and for christology. True power belongs only to God, a power revealed in Christ. Dominating power, demonic power, is essentially and ultimately impotent. This realization frees us from fear, as we identify with the divine giving and receiving power. [See Griffin's response, "Power Divine and Demonic" [#866].]

1140.   Miller, Ed. L. *God and Reason: A Historical Approach to Philosophical Theology.* New York: Macmillan, 1972: 137-158.

Chapter 9 ("The Problem of Evil") dismisses Leibniz's theodicy. Miller argues in support of the Stoics' aesthetic view and the privation view of evil in Augustine and Aquinas. He defends traditional Augustinian theodicy versus Hick's charge that it is internally incoherent. He acknowledges that atheistic existentialists like Sartre and Camus view the world differently than theists and, as such, cannot resolve the theodicy issue.

1141.   Mora, Freya. "Thank God for Evil?" *Philosophy* 58 (1983): 399-401.

Argues that love is necessary for happiness and that evil is a necessary condition for love. As such, God is not indictable for creating a world with evil.

1142.   Nash, Ronald H. *Faith and Reason: Searching for a Rational Faith.* Grand Rapids, MI: Academic Books, 1988.

Three chapters focus on the problem of evil: "The Deductive Problem of Evil"; "The Inductive Problem of Evil"; and "The Problem of Gratuitous Evil." Nash gives particular emphasis to the work of Plantinga and to the thesis that religious faith does not need rational support. Nash supports Plantinga's response to the deductive problem of evil and supports also his free will defense. He agrees with the theistic responses to the inductive problem of evil: free will theodicy, natural law theodicy, and soul-making theodicy. The problem of gratuitous evil, he argues, can be answered by the doctrine of *meticulous providence*.

1143. Oakes, Robert A. "The Problem with the 'Problem of Evil'." *Personalist* 55 (1974): 106-114.

Asserts that evil, a contingent fact, does not refute God's existence, since it has not been shown that God's existence is *contingent* rather than *conceptual*. Hartshorne, Malcolm and Findlay have made a strong case for the conceptual/necessary status of God's existence. Yet, even if the theistic question were to be shown to be contingent, evil still would not count against the existence of God. The probability criteria and unique cases present serious difficulties for the atheistic claim that evil constitutes negative import for the truth of theism.

1144. ———. "God, Suffering, and Conclusive Evidence." *Sophia* 14 (1975): 16-20.

Rejects Pike's widely held claim ("Hume on Evil" [#1157]) that the existence of suffering or evil constitutes conclusive evidence for the falsity of classical theism *only* if it is a necessary truth that a perfectly good God would have no "morally sufficient reason" for permitting the existence of evil or suffering. Oakes argues that proponents of this belief have invalidly conflated *epistemic* and *logical* possibility.

1145. Palma, A.B. "Notes Towards a God." *Sophia* 25 (1986): 4-17.

Refutes Mackie's view (*The Miracle of Theism* [#1220]) that reasonable belief can rest only upon logically sufficient conditions. Palma argues that love can be the basis for reasonable belief in God. The world must be "ontologically independent" of God, if God is to love the world. As such, suffering is inevitable in the world.

1146. Pargetter, Robert. "Evil as Evidence Against the Existence of God." *Mind* 85 (1976): 242-245.

Argues that there is no justification for the claim that evil is strong evidence against the existence of God. He contends that atheists wrongly assume that God and evil are in conflict and that atheism is more plausible than theism. [See Basinger's response, "Evil as Evidence Against the Existence of God: A Response" [#1060].]

1147. ———. "Evil as Evidence." *Sophia* 21 (1982): 11-15.

Response to Martin's "Is Evil Evidence Against the Existence of God?" [#1227]. Martin has failed to show that evil is *prima facie* evidence against God's existence: his definition is too problematic to be taken seriously. Martin's assumption that evil constitutes *prima facie* evidence against God's existence is relative to the assumption that the existence of evil in great abundance is not logically necessary, and that there is no sufficient reason for God to allow evil in great abundance. Pargetter rejects this assumption as well as other aspects of Martin's presentation of a reformulated problem from evil. Martin's argument, for example, violates the "principle of total evidence."

1148. ———. "Experience, Proper Basicality and Belief in God." *International Journal for Philosophy of Religion* 27 (1990): 141-160.

Following upon Plantinga's arguments ("Is Belief in God Properly Basic?" [see #1059], and *Rationality and Religious Belief* [see #1059]), Pargetter proposes what he takes to be an adequate account of the concept of "properly basic belief," in support of the contention that theism is indeed a properly basic belief. Reliable persons must have experiences in circumstances which do not undermine their reliability. The resulting belief systems depend on the holistic rationality of the overall belief system.

1149. Peterson, Michael L. "Christian Theism and the Problem of Evil." *Journal of the Evangelical Theological Society* 21 (1978): 35-46.

Surveys various formulations of the problem of evil and focuses upon two of them: the problem of *logical consistency* and the problem of *gratuitous evil*, views which hold that theism is irrational and improbable, respectively. He recommends various responses to these formulations for Christian theologians and philosophers. Many theists, he notes, have not understood the logic of the problem of gratuitous evil.

1150. ———. "Evil and Inconsistency: A Reply." *Sophia* 18 (1979): 20-27.

Response to La Croix ("Unjustified Evil and God's Choice" [#78]). Peterson contends that La Croix has not succeeded in showing any inconsistency in traditional theism's beliefs about God and evil. All such attempts to define the problem of evil as a logical inconsistency fail. Theodicy is a problem not of *a priori* logical inconsistency but of *a posteriori* acceptance or probability of theism in light of relevant external evidence.

1151. ———. "God and Evil: Problems of Consistency and Gratuity." *Journal of Value Inquiry* 13 (1979): 305-313.

Delineates two main aspects of the problem of evil: the problem of *prima facie* gratuitous evil and the problem of logical consistency. The former is the more important problem: the theodicy problem involves a mixture of moral values, ontological commitments, logical principles and existential feelings. Peterson argues that analyses like those of Plantinga and Ahern miss several crucial points — analyses which point out the inherent inconclusiveness and psychological nature of the opponents' case, while being unable to explain all the apparently gratuitous evil in the world.

1152. ———. "The Inductive Argument of Evil." *Journal of the American Scientific Affiliation* 33 (1981): 82-87.

Notes that while twentieth century philosophers have been preoccupied largely with the *deductive* argument from evil (the logical problem), there has been a shift in interest lately in the *inductive* argument. He distinguishes various formulations of the argument and focuses upon the most formidable version: the inductive argument from gratuitous evil. Peterson rejects atheistic attempts which use such inductive arguments to view evil as evidence against God's existence. He contests the basis and accuracy of the factual premise about the actual gratuity of evil. There is evidence which tends to confirm (rather than disconfirm) theism. He questions, finally, the legitimacy of the assumption that stipulates how God should dispose of evil.

1153.   ———. *Evil and the Christian God*. Grand Rapids, MI: Baker Book House, 1982.

Critically discusses the logical version of the problem of evil *(Chapter 2)*, the evidential version *(Chapter 3)*, and then focuses on the problem of gratuitous evil *(Chapters 4-6)*, the latter constituting the most formidable of all versions of the problem of evil. He notes that the logical argument has been in decline thanks to the efforts of Hick, Plantinga, Ahern, Yandell, and others. Peterson expands upon Plantinga's theodicy in order to address the issue of gratuitous evil. God cannot preclude gratuitous evil and at the same time permit human freedom. God cannot preclude gratuitous evil, he holds, and at the same time permit natural evils (versus McCloskey, etc.). Peterson rejects the idea of divine meticulous providence as untenable. He supports Hick's soul-making premise.

1154.   ———. "Recent Work on the Problem of Evil." *American Philosophical Quarterly* 20 (1983): 321-339.

Surveys recent work in theodicy: the logical problem, the evidential problem, Hick's theodicy, process theodicy, natural law theodicy, and free will theodicy. Contains a brief bibliographical list (335-339). [See also the recent source book edited by Michael Peterson, *The Problem of Evil: Selected Readings*. Notre Dame: University of Notre Dame Press, 1992. This book contains sections on classical statements of theodicy, the various versions of the problem of evil (logical, evidential, existential), perspectives (Augustinian, Irenaean, process theodicies), and the various issues involved (omnipotence and free will, natural evil, best possible world). The book contains also a bibliographical listing of selected publications on theodicy (367-391).]

1155.   ———. "Evil as Evidence for the Existence of God." *Kerygma and Praxis*. Edited by W. Vanderhoof and David Basinger. Winoma Lake, IN: Robert Wesleyan College Press; Light and Life Press, 1984: 115-131.

Argues that evil confirms theism rather than being evidence against God. A sophisticated view of the relation of God and evil grounds this assumption. God allows some evil, that which is morally justifiable.

1156.   Pike, Nelson. "God and Evil: A Reconsideration." *Ethics* 68 (1958): 116-124.

Response to Aiken's "Evil and God: A Study of Some Relations Between Faith and Morals" [#1195]. Pike argues that the *theological thesis* (an all-powerful, all-good, all-knowing God exists) is not incompatible with the *ethical thesis* (evil exists). The two theses are axiomatic. It follows that there is a good reason for evil despite the fact that we cannot know it. The fact that we are unable to explain many evils should not lead to the rejection of God's existence. The arguments for God's existence are relevant here. There should be no conflict of attitudes in holding both theses.

1157.   ———. "Hume on Evil." *Philosophical Review* 72 (1963): 180-197. [Reprinted in Pike's *God and Evil*. Englewood Cliffs, NJ: Prentice-Hall, 1964, 85-102.]

Argues that God may have "a morally sufficient reason" for permitting evil. The critic must show that the opposite is necessarily true. Also, since there are independent reasons for the theist's belief in God, there is no need to produce God's morally sufficient reason for permitting evils. [Among the many responses to this seminal essay, see Pentz's defense of Pike ("Rules and Values and the Problem of Evil" [#1409]) contra Penelhum's "Divine Goodness and the Problem of Evil" [#1408].]

1158. Plantinga, Theodore. *Learning to Live with Evil*. Grand Rapids, MI: Eerdmans, 1982.

Examines four major conceptions of evil: evil as *ultimate* (Manichean); evil as *necessary* (Hegel, Schleiermacher); evil as *non-being* (Platonism); and evil as *alienation* from God (Augustine and Calvin). From within the Augustinian-Calvinist perspective, Plantinga examines the various issues involved, concluding that the only response to the problem of evil is eschatological: God will overthrow the forces of evil.

1159. Prasad, Rajendra. "Suffering, Morality and Society." *Indian Philosophical Quarterly* 4 (1983): 161-171.

Argues that in a societal context, all suffering is not evil—as is too often assumed. There are, for examples, reasons which morally justify suffering. Suffering the consequences for morally wrong actions is one case in point.

1160. Ramberan, Osmond G. "Religious Belief and the Problem of Evil." *Studies in Religion* 5 (1975/1976): 177-185.

Maintains that belief in God is unfalsifiable by evil since the believer holds a particular set of beliefs, a "form of life" to which the believer is committed.

1161. ——. "Evil and Theism." *Sophia* 17 (1978): 28-36.

Contends that the five propositions generally held to formulate the problem of evil (God exists; God is omnipotent; God is omniscient; God is all-good; and evil exists) must be extended by an additional premise, that a good thing would always, as far as it could, eliminate or prevent evil. But several candidates for this additional premise are rejected on the grounds that they are not necessarily true, or essential to theism, or a logical consequence of such propositions. Ramberan concludes that the logical formulation of the problem of evil is not a threat to the theist.

1162. ——. "Evil, Falsification and Religious Language." *Indian Philosophical Quarterly* 2 (1981): 227-246.

Asserts that when the theist offers a solution to the problem of evil by claiming that the proposition "There is evil in the world" does not count against the proposition "God exists and is all-powerful and all-good," this is not a selling out in the sense of Flew's falsification challenge. Religious statements are neither verifiable nor falsifiable, yet they have meaning in their *use* (as in Ludwig Wittgenstein); religious beliefs make a difference to the believer. [For relevant publications on the falsification debate, see Antony Flew and Alasdair MacIntyre, *New Essays in Philosophical Theology* [#45]. This seminal book contains essays by Flew, R.M. Hare, Basil Mitchell, Ian M. Crombie (on falsification), Flew's "Divine Omnipotence and Human Freedom" [#45], and other important essays, many of which were published previously.]

1163. Ross, James F. *Philosophical Theology*. Indianapolis, IN: Bobbs-Merrill, 1969.
Chapter 6, "'God is Good' and 'The Problem of Evil'" (222-278), claims to dissolve the problem of evil. God is not accountable for the world's evil,

despite the fact that God could have created a better world and prevented present evils from occurring. God is on a higher level of reality than the world, and is not responsible for the evil produced by the lower levels. [See responses by Griffin, *God, Power and Evil* [#861]; Mavrodes, "Some Recent Philosophical Theology" [#85]; and Oakes, "God, Evil and Professor Ross" [#93]. See also James Ross, "Evil," in his *Introduction to the Philosophy of Religion*. New York: Macmillan, 1969.]

1164.   Schilling, S. Paul. *God and Human Anguish*. Nashville, TN: Abingdon, 1977.

Critiques the faith solution to the problem of evil, the denial of the positive reality of evil, the dualism of good and evil, and suffering as judgment. He supports (yet criticizes aspects of) Hick's soul-making theodicy, and locates evil in the evolutionary natural order. Passing references to process theodicy are sympathetically appropriated by Schilling in his formulation of an adequate theodicy. He argues, for example, that there are some misleading views of divine power and providence. Schilling holds that human beings are genuinely free and that there are ultimate principles within the eternal nature of God, principles which limit God's control over creatures. He argues for divine suffering-love and for Christian hope as essential aspects of theodicy.

1165.   Schmitz, Kenneth L. "Entitative and Systemic Aspects of Evil." *Dialectics and Humanitas* 9 (1978): 149-161.

The *entitative* interpretation of evil (Aristotle, Aquinas) resolves the problem of evil by recovering an originally intended good, while the *systemic* interpretation (Hegel, Berdyaev, Simone Weil) resolves the problem of evil by means of a radical and comprehensive modulation of the system.

1166.   Schulweis, Harold M. *Evil and the Morality of God*. Cincinnati, OH: Hebrew Union College Press, 1984.

After presenting critiques of several "subject" theodicies (Maimonides, Aquinas, Leibniz, Hartshorne, Weiman, Tillich, Barth, Hick), Schulweis proposes an alternative form of theology and theodicy, based on Feuerbach; his so-called "predicate theodicy." Godly qualities are assigned to humans and the traditional questions as to why God does/causes/permits evil no longer are relevant. God cannot be understood as an entity (subject) apart from humans (predicates).

1167.   ———. "Predicate Theodicy: 'Why Did it Happen?'" *Religious Education* 84 (1989): 16-25.

Rejects "subject theodicy" which, he claims, is based on unarticulated presumptions. Asking "why" some evil occurs assumes there is a subject (God) who caused or permitted it for a reason. Predicate theodicy traces the roots of evil, not vertically, but horizontally. Evils are not attributed to God but to natural processes and human beings. Our response to the evils in history and nature can exhibit godly characteristics.

1168.   Schütze, Alfred. *The Enigma of Evil*. Edinburgh: Floris Books, 1978. [Originally published in German by Verlag Urachhaus: Stuttgart, 1969.]

Discusses the evolution of evil and argues that God permits evil for the sake of the growth of human freedom. He discusses also the nature of evil, with particular emphasis on Christian theological themes: the fall, Lucifer and the inevitable coming of the anti-Christ.

1169.   Shuster, Marguerite. "The Good, the Bad and the Troubled: Studies in Theodicy." *TSF Bulletin* 7 (1983): 6-7.

Argues that Michael Peterson's *Evil and the Christian God* [#1153] is logically unimpressive, humanly callous and theologically disastrous. Yet she finds Theodore Plantinga's *Learning to Live with Evil* [#1158] worthwhile; Kushner's *When Bad Things Happen to Good People* [#1132] is rejected (as is process theodicy) for its denial of God's all-controlling power, yet the verdict on Lewis Smedes's *How Can It Be All Right When Everything Is All Wrong?* [#3630] is that this book is useful for its emphasis on divine grace as the source of hope and faith.

1170.   Snyder, Daniel T. "Surplus Evil." *Philosophical Quarterly* 40 (1990): 82-86.

Rejects Rowe's claim ("The Problem of Evil and Some Varieties of Atheism" [#1246]), that the intense suffering which an omnipotent being could have prevented without losing some greater good, is an argument against theism. Snyder distinguishes Rowe's "pointless" evil from "surplus" evil. Not every pointless evil is surplus. The disvalue of surplus evil exceeds whatever value there is in the relevant range of possibilities of freedom. As such, free will theodicists cannot admit surplus evil. Rowe's argument requires surplus evil to render it a viable objection to theism.

1171.   Stearns, J. Brenton. "Divine Punishment and Reconciliation." *Journal of Religious Ethics* 9 (1981): 118-130.

Argues that divine punishment is suffering understood as a divine moral concept. Suffering can be retributive, but after reconciliation with God, it loses its status as punishment.

1172.   Stump, Eleonore. "Petitionary Prayer." *American Philosophical Quarterly* 16 (1979): 83-85.

The argument is that God works through prayer as an intermediary, rather than God taking the initiative for our sake. Prayer acts as a buffer between God and humankind. Not every prayer is answered. [See Basinger's response, "Why Petition an Omnipotent, Omniscient, Wholly Good God?" [#1062]].

1173.   ——. "The Problem of Evil." *Faith and Philosophy* 2 (1985): 392-423.

Proposes a solution to the Christian problem of evil which, she contends, is consistent and coherent, and which escapes some of the problems incurred in the solutions of Hick, Swinburne, and Plantinga. Stump argues that the solution rests on the fixing of our defective wills by freely willing that God fix our wills; our freedom remains intact. Moral and physical evil contribute toward this free willing on the creatures' part and lead to a good end, culminating in heaven. [See responses by Schuurman, "The Concept of a Strong Theodicy" [#426]; Fales, "Antediluvian Theodicy: Stump on the Fall" [#1287]; and Smith, "What's So Good About Feeling Bad?" [#1347].]

1174.   ——. "Suffering for Redemption: A Reply to Smith." *Faith and Philosophy* 2 (1985): 430-435.

Responds to Michael Smith's various criticisms ("What's So Good about Feeling Bad?" [#1347]), including the moral concern that there is too much evil in the world to believe that evil is to be understood as an instrumental means to the good end. Stump contends that all evil leads to some good, even if it is unknown to us as finite human beings.

1175.   Trau, Jane Mary. "Fallacies in the Argument from Gratuitous Evil." *New Scholasticism* 60 (1986): 485-489.

Claims that the argument for *gratuitous* (unmerited) suffering is circular and should be eliminated from discussions about the existence of God. If God exists, it is reasonable to assume there is some purpose in all suffering, even if the purpose is unknown to us. The atheist cannot argue that there is gratuitous evil since there appears to be no purpose in some suffering. One cannot be certain there is gratuitous suffering unless one is certain there is no God, but this is a circular argument since it is the existence of God that is in question.

1176.   ———. "The Positive Value of Evil." *International Journal for Philosophy of Religion* 24 (1988): 21-33.

Suggests a third proposition can illuminate the claim that the two propositions—God exists and evil exists—are incompatible. Trau establishes this proposition with a metaethical theory. Evil is a necessary double effect of the existence of goodness. Moral evil, for example, is a double effect of the possibility of moral evil (that is, free will). Natural evil is a double effect of natural goods. Evil possesses instrumental goodness sufficient to outweigh its intrinsic badness. She concludes that the argument of gratuitous evil against the positive value of evil cannot be proven.

1177.   ———. *The Co-Existence of God and Evil.* New York: Peter Lang, 1991.

Expands upon the arguments in her "Fallacies in the Argument from Gratuitous Evil" [#1175], and "The Positive Value of Evil" [#1176]. Trau contends that there is positive value in all evil and that this proposition establishes the compatibility of the propositions, "God exists" and "evil exists," (the logical argument from evil). She suggests a modified version of the principle of double effect. The traditional version (as in Charles Journet) implies agency; Trau's version does not. The double effect doctrine refers to the necessary relation between moral evil, free will and the existence of moral evil. God's primary intention is to make moral goodness possible and this cannot be accomplished without the double effect possibility of evil. [See the critical review by Barry Whitney, "Mystical and Rational Theodicy" [#1185].]

1178.   Tripathi, R.K. "Two Approaches to the Problems of Evil." *Journal of Dharma* 2 (1977): 312-317.

Discusses the two approaches to theism, the religious and the reflective. He then argues that there are two kinds of reflective or philosophical approaches to the problem of evil: naturalism and idealism. For both, the problem of evil is not a problem if it is appreciated that evil is *not real* but only an *illusion*.

1179.   Van Inwagen, Peter. "The Magnitude, Duration, and Distribution of Evil: A Theodicy." *Philosophical Topics* 16 (1988): 161-187.

Acknowledges Plantinga's comment that a theodicy is presumptuous, and offers a theodicy of moral evil based on the free will defense and on a philosophical reflection of the data of Christian revelation. He expounds and defends his theodicy by addressing four questions about the magnitude, duration and distribution of evil: (1) God could not redeem creatures without grave deception (memories would be lost, etc.); (2) God cannot protect us from pain and suffering without reducing our existence to something meaningless and denying our awareness of the need for atonement; (3) the existence of evil has persisted because it takes us a long time to respond to God's guidance and God can enter a people's history only when the ground has been prepared; and, finally, (4) there is so much horrific suffering among the innocent for reasons unknown to us, except to acknowledge that we live in a fallen world, separated from God. [The final point is developed in van Inwagen's "The Place of Chance in a World Sustained by God" [#1180].]

1180. ———. "The Place of Chance in a World Sustained by God." *Divine and Human Action: Essays on the Metaphysics of Theism.* Edited by Thomas V. Morris. Ithaca, NY: Cornell University Press, 1988: 211-234.

The question of innocent and apparently undeserved suffering cannot be answered fully. There is no reason known to human beings for such evils, except that we are in a fallen state. Otherwise, we would not have been susceptible to these evils. Our destructive potential has become actual by our rebellion and folly. God may intervene (miraculously) to prevent certain evils, yet to do so perpetually would be to deceive us into thinking we could live apart from God and are not subjected to chance. [See also Peter van Inwagen's more recent, "The Problem of Evil, the Problem of Air, and the Problem of Science," *Philosophical Perspectives* 5 (1991), 135-165.]

1181. Wall, George B. *Is God Really Good? Conversations with a Theodicist.* Lanham, MD: University Press of America, 1983.

A book in the form of a dialogue between a theist, a humanist, and others, during which Walls constructs a theodicy, a version of the free will defense. [See also his "A New Solution to an Old Problem" [#155], and "Heaven and a Wholly Good God" [#437]]. Walls holds a view of divine omniscience that is compatible with freedom in human beings. God's role is to induce us to be responsible moral agents. God does not intervene to prevent evils caused by the misuse of human freedom. Natural evil, furthermore, provides additional occasions and stimuli to which in freedom we can respond. Animal suffering is explained on the basis of animals lacking foresight and self-consciousness, and as the necessary function of pain in animals.

1182. Ward, Keith. *Rational Theology and the Creativity of God.* Oxford: Blackwell, 1982.

Seeks to show that the idea of God is internally consistent and coherent with other knowledge of the universe and compatible with the beliefs of major theistic religion. Ward argues also that belief in God is the highest expression of human rationality. In *Chapter 9* ("The Existence of Evil," 189-210), he suggests that it is a morally unexceptionable axiom that the existence of evil can be justified on the grounds that it is the necessary implication of some otherwise unobtainable good. Immortality for animals, as well as humans, is a necessary condition of any theodicy. Ward rejects the impassible God of traditional theology, and argues that suffering with the creature is a necessary aspect of divine perfection—although God overcomes the suffering and sorrow. He argues that traditional theodicy, in retrospect, lacks an evolutionary theory; it holds to the Adamic myth that God created a perfect world. [See response by Moulder, "In Search of a Theodicy" [#1327]. See also Ward's *Holding Fast to God: A Reply to Don Cupitt*. London: SPCK Press, 1982. See Don Cupitt's *Taking Leave of God*. London: SCM Press, 1980.]

1183.   White, David. "The Problem of Evil." *Second Order* (Nigeria) 4 (1975): 14-24.

Contends that the argument against an omnipotent and wholly good God—on the basis of the existence of evil—is not conclusive. No suggestion offered for the elimination of the existence of some particular evil would make the world better. Indeed, the elimination of any known evil likely would make the world worse. There is no evidence for the actual existence of unnecessary evil in light of the premise of free will.

1184.   Whitney, Barry L. *What Are They Saying About God and Evil?* New York and Mahwah, NJ: Paulist Press, 1989 [Revised and updated version, 1999, from the author.]

Presents an overview (exposition and critique) of contemporary theodicies: Biblical, Augustinian-Thomistic, Hick's Irenaean theodicy, Process theodicy, various philosophical theodicies, conservative and popular theodicies, suffering of God theodicy, and Jewish reactions to the holocaust. Whitney concludes with a proposal for an explanation of moral evil (a free will defense, as found in process theodicy) and for physical evils (based on the necessity of natural laws, as proposed by various writers). He contends that a more critical understanding of theodicy is an effective means by which to cope (existentially) with evil.

1185.   ———. "Mystical and Rational Theodicy" [Review Article of Trau and Stoeber]. *Method and Theory in the Study of Religion* 3 (1992).

A critical discussion of Jane Mary Trau's *The Co-Existence of God and Evil* [#1177] and Michael Stoeber's *Evil and the Mystics' God: Towards a Mystical Theodicy* [#808]. Trau's book is an expansion of two previous articles ("The Positive Value of Evil" [#1176] and "Fallacies in the Argument from Gratuitous Evil" [#1175]). She claims that the logical problem of evil can be resolved by establishing the compatibility of the proposition "All Evil has positive value" with the propositions "God exists" and "Evil exists." While this solution to the logical problem is valid, Whitney argues that Plantinga's prior version of the same strategy generally has been conceded to have resolved the logical version. Trau offers a modified version of the Thomistic principle of double effect and, in arguing that all evil has some positive value, she can insist that there is no gratuitous evil. Stoeber's book rightly objects to this kind of arid theological discourse, far removed as it is from suffering itself. He cites John Hick's theodicy as the paradigm case of what is best in traditional theodicy, particularly for its teleological focus, and then proceeds to show that the four main weaknesses in Hick's theodicy can be answered by various mystical writings: Underhill, Eckhart, Dostoevsky, Boehme, and Aurobindo. Whitney's main argument against Stoeber is his (all-too-common) lack of awareness and critical appropriation of directly relevant publications on the topic at hand.

1186.   Wierenga, Edward R. "Reply to Harold Moore's 'Evidence, Evil and Religious Belief.'" *International Journal for Philosophy of Religion* 9 (1978): 246-251.

Defends Plantinga's rejoinder to the probabilistic argument from evil (*God, Freedom, and Evil* [#109]). Wierenga argues against Moore ("Evidence, Evil and Religious Belief" [#1238]), that Plantinga's account of confirmation is not "internally inconsistent," nor "impoverished and unacceptable." Wierenga argues also that there is a difficulty with Plantinga's concept of evidence as not being applicable to questions about the existence of God: Plantinga presupposes that the conditional probability of every proposition is defined without reference to any background knowledge. [See Moore's response, "Evidence—Once More" [#1239].]

1187.   Williamson, Clark M. "Things Do Go Wrong (And Right)." *Journal of Religion* 63 (1983): 44-56.

Maintains that theodicy is a problem that arises from the conflict between experience and formal propositions that are inadequate to experience (as Alfred North Whitehead has determined such adequacy). Williamson argues that the *problem of goodness* is as problematic as the problem of evil.

1188.   Wykstra, Stephen J. "The Humean Obstacle to Evidential Arguments from Suffering: On Avoiding the Evils of 'Appearance'." *International Journal for Philosophy of Religion* 16 (1984): 73-93. [Also published in *The Problem of Evil*. Edited by Marilyn McCord Adams and Robert Merrihew Adams (New York: Oxford University Press, 1990), 138-160.]

Critically assesses Rowe's argument ("The Problem of Evil and Some Varieties of Atheism" [#1246]), that much suffering does not appear to serve any outweighing good. Wykstra rejects two criticisms of Rowe's argument (Reichenbach, "The Inductive Argument from Evil" [#584], and Swinburne, *The Existence of God* [#600]). He does not accept Rowe's assumption that the reasons why God permits suffering would be clear to finite minds. Despite the fact that many evils seem pointless, this should not lead us to reject belief in God. If theism is true, what we would expect is that the goods by virtue of which God permits suffering are beyond our comprehension. As such, this is not evidence against theism. [See Rowe's response: "Evil and the Theistic Hypothesis: A Response to Wykstra" [#1247]. See also the response by Chrzan, "Debunking Cornea" [#1200].]

1189.   Yandell, Keith E. "A Premature Farewell to Theism (A Reply to Roland Puccetti)." *Religious Studies* 5 (1969): 251-256.

Rejects Puccetti's claim ("The Loving God—Some Observations on John Hick's *Evil and the God of Love*" [#800]), that theodicy is an intractable problem since an all-knowing, all-powerful, and all-good being can reasonably be said to have morally sufficient reasons for allowing persons to endure suffering. He argues that this is not a punishment for any of our wrong-doing only if some instance can be provided to explains the fact of such suffering in a way compatible with the truth of God's existence as all-knowing, all-powerful, and all-good. [See Hick's response, "God, Evil and Mystery" [#752]].

1190.   ———. "The Problem of Evil." *Basic Issues in the Philosophy of Religion.* Boston, MA: Allyn and Bacon, 1973: 43-66.

Defends theism against both strong and weak formulations of the problem of evil (the alleged logical contradiction and the probability scenario, respectively). He suggests cases where evils should not be prevented by an omnipotent and omnibenevolent God, and questions the coherence of the concept of a best possible world. Yandell offers a free will defense similar to Plantinga's [see Chapter 2].

1191. ——. "A Proposed Solution to the Problem of Evil." *TSF Bulletin* 5 (1982): 7-8.

Defends various claims which contribute to a resolution of the problem of evil. God, for example, must have a morally sufficient reason for allowing evil. Yandell argues also that ethical considerations take precedence over issues of logical consistency. Evil cannot disprove God's existence unless God's existence could be disproved on other grounds.

1192. ——. *Christianity and Philosophy*. Grand Rapids, MI: Eerdmans, 1984: 214-245.

Chapter 6 ("Is the Existence of Evil Evidence Against the Existence of God?") argues that the fact there are evils which have no explanation conceivable to human knowledge is *not* evidence that there is, in fact, *no* reason for such evils. Ethical theories which contend that worlds containing evil are not worth creating are unpersuasive. There are worlds an omnipotent deity cannot create. Yandell concludes that evil is decisive evidence against God's existence only if we know that there is not a morally sufficient reason for God's permitting them. We could know this only if we know that God does not exist. Yandell concedes, however, that theists have a responsibility to provide an ethical theory that suggests how evil is not merely gratuitous.

1193. ——. "The Problem of Evil and the Content of Morality." *International Journal for Philosophy of Religion* 17 (1985): 139-165.

Contends that if God exists, God has a morally sufficient reason for allowing evil and, as such, every and all evil is "critically cancelled." Yet, if there were no morally sufficient reason, it would not refute theism, since God does not have to have such a reason. There is no best possible state of affairs God could have created; for any state of affairs there is a creatable morally superior state. Creation is better than no creation and, hence, God needs no reason for creating the world as it is. Yandell defends the Kantian moral agent, Kantian freedom versus Spinozean persons. A Kantian world is indeterminate in a way in which the creation of a Spinozean world is not. [See response by Mavrodes, "Keith Yandell and the Problem of Evil" [#1138].]

1194. ——. "Gratuitous Evil and Divine Existence." *Religious Studies* 25 (1989): 15-30.

Considers the "root argument" for gratuitous evils, that since there are gratuitous evils, there is no God. Yandell examines the meaning of gratuitous evils and expands the argument for gratuitous evils into several more sophisticated versions. His conclusion is that it is not obvious what sort of evil God could not allow without tainting the divine goodness. [See the response by Chrzan, "God and Gratuitous Evil: A Reply to Yandell" [#1204]].

II   Some Challenges to Theism

1195.   Aiken, Henry David, "Evil and God: A Study of Some Relations Between Faith and Morals." *Ethics* 68 (1958): 77-79.

Attempts to reinterpret the *logical* problem of evil as a *practical* or *existential* problem. He distinguishes between the *theological* thesis (belief in God) and the *ethical* thesis (evil exists). [See response by Pike, "God and Evil: A Reconsideration" [#1156]; and Novak, *Belief and Unbelief* [#1329].]

1196.   Angeles, Peter A. *The Problem of God*. Buffalo, NY: Prometheus Press, 1980.

Chapter 8 ("God as All-Good and Omnipotent: The Problem of Evil," 131-148) contends that the instances of evil in the evolutionary advance count against God's existence, and that this does not appear to be the best possible world. He rejects the arguments that evil is illusion; the privation of good; that divine goodness is different from human understandings of goodness; that evil is a test; that good comes from evil; that evil exists to build character; that the whole is good from God's perspective; that good would not be known without evil; that there is a good explanation for natural evil; and that the free will defense is consistent with divine omnipotence and omniscience.

1197.   Blanshard, Brand. *Reason and Belief*. New Haven, CT: Yale University Press, 1975.

Argues that the problem of evil is an insurmountable obstacle to rational belief in God. He asserts that the treatment of the problem in theology has been an "intellectual disgrace." Theistic arguments break down so easily that theologians must take refuge in blind faith or revolt against reason altogether. [See response by Harris in his *Atheism and Theism* [#1109].]

1198.   Bradley, R.D. "A Proof of Atheism." *Sophia* 6 (1967): 35-49.

Claims that the problem of evil constitutes a *reductio ad absurdum* proof of the non-existence of God, *a reductio ad absurdum* proof for atheism. Bradley contends that the premises of the logical version of the argument from evil are valid and the conclusion (that God does not exist as omnipotent and omnibenevolent) likewise holds. The *reductio ad absurdum* is persuasive since the fact that evil exists must be false if God, as defined by theists, exists. The *reductio ad absurdum* is shown also in the presupposition that God, as defined by theists, entails that evil exists, since God is defined as just, righteous, and merciful, all of which entail the existence of evil. Theistic belief entails, in short, both that *evil exists* and that *evil does not exist*. [See response by Ahern, "God and Evil—A Note" [#1262].]

1199.   Burns, J. Patout. "Review Symposium." *Horizons, Journal of the College Theology Society* 18 (1991): 300-303.

Review of Tilley's *The Evils of Theodicy* [#1254]. Burns agrees with Tilley that Augustine offered a *defense* rather than a *theodicy*, in contrast to those who (like John Hick) have amalgamated elements from Augustine's writings into an "Augustinian theodicy." Burns advances Tilley's argument by suggesting that Augustine in fact *argued against* the very possibility of a theodicy. [Tilley's response follows in the text.]

1200. Chrzan, Keith. "Debunking Cornea." *International Journal for Philosophy of Religion* 21 (1987): 171-177.

Response to Stephen Wykstra's attempt ("The Humean Obstacle to Evidential Arguments from Suffering: On Avoiding the Evils of 'Appearance'" [#1188]) to refute Williams Rowe's probabilistic argument for atheism ("The Problem of Evil and Some Varieties of Atheism" [#1246]). Chrzan argues that Wykstra's epistemological principle—the "condition of reasonable access" (cited as COR-NEA, the Condition of Reasonable Epistemic Access)—is faulty. [See Wykstra and Russell, "The 'Inductive Argument from Evil': A Dialogue" [#1344].]

1201. ———. "Hudson on 'Too Much' Evil." *International Philosophical Quarterly* 27 (1987): 203-210.

Refutes Yeager Hudson's value judgment ("Is There Too Much Evil in the World?" [#1116]), that too much evil is meaningless. Chrzan contends that Hudson's arguments are either *trivial*—if he intends them against the deductive from the quantity of evil or *false*—if he intends them against the induction from the quantity of evil. [See Hudson's reply, "Response to Chrzan's Hudson on 'Too Much' Evil" [#1117].]

1202. ———. "Plantinga on Atheistic Induction." *Sophia* 27 (1988): 10-14.

Refutes Plantinga's argument (*The Nature of Necessity* [#110]) against the inductive or probabilistic argument from evil, which holds the actual quantity, diverssity and dispersion of evil is evidence that renders unlikely the existence of God. Chrzan argues that Plantinga's argument succumbs to various logical errors. [See Langtry's response, "God, Evil, and Probability" [#1310].]

1203. ———. "When is Gratuitous Evil Really Gratuitous?" *International Journal for Philosophy of Religion* 24 (1988): 87-91.

Argues against Peterson's attempt to defend theism despite gratuitous evil (*Evil and the Christian God* [#1153]). Peterson's argument fails because of an equivocation regarding the term "gratuitous," and he resorts to denying that gratuitous evil exists.

1204. ———. "God and Gratuitous Evil: A Reply to Yandell." *Religious Studies* 27 (1991): 99-103.

Response to Yandell's "Gratuitous Evil and Divine Existence" [#1194]. He contends that Yandell's arguments to refute the premises of the probabilistic argument from evil fail—"if there is gratuitous evil then there is no God," and "there is gratuitous evil." Chrzan argues that Yandell's argument against the latter premise is analytically false and his argument against the former demonstrates only that it is possibly false.

1205. Cornman, James W., and Keith Lehrer. *Philosophical Problems and Arguments*. New York: Macmillan, 1974.

The section on theodicy (340-352) argues that evil is the evidence available to us as an argument against God's existence. They reject various traditional theodicies.

1206. Fulmer, Gilbert. "Evil and Analogy." *Personalist* 58 (1977): 333-343.

Refutation of Ross's theodicy (*Philosophical Theology* [#1163]) as internally inconsistent and question-begging, and as incompatible with the doctrine of analogical predication which (Ross holds) is the only form of speech by which we can speak about God meaningfully. Fulmer refutes Ross's argument that God should be called "good." David Griffin ("Divine Causality, Evil and Philosophical Theology" [#859]) has shown that Ross's theodicy is *morally* odious; Fulmer seeks to show it is also *logically* untenable.

1207.   Gupta, Santosh Sen. "God and Evil." *Visvabharati Quarterly* 21 (1955): 340-351.

The problem of evil is solely a logical problem, the problem of reconciling the triad of propositions. Gupta argues that there are two types of solutions: those which deny one of the propositions and those which affirm them all. He rejects various proposed solutions: that evil is a means to a good end; that suffering has a disciplinary effect; and the free will solution. The latter is invalid, he argues, since God could have designed human beings such that we always freely choose the good. He concludes that the problem of evil is a problem only on the assumption that God exists. The problem cannot be resolved, since the attempt to reconcile God with evil is a virtual denial of the evil character of evil.

1208.   Hare, Peter H., and Edward H. Madden. "A Theodicy for Today?" *Southern Journal of Philosophy* 4 (1966): 287-292.

Critical review of John Hick's *Evil and the God of Love, Part Four* of which is titled "A Theology for Today" [#750]. Hare and Madden regard Hick's theodicy as a version of the "third" type of tactic they have defined; that is, an attempt to resolve the problem within a traditional theistic framework (rather than evade the problem, an attempt to show the problem is meaningless, or to modify traditional theistic concepts: see Hare and Madden's *Evil and the Concept of God* [#1210]]. They argue that Hick's free will solution is an example of the "all or nothing" fallacy; that Hick cannot show how the world's suffering is the most efficient way to achieve the soul-making goal; and that Hick's alternative move is an equally invalid "slippery slope" argument: if God were to eliminate some of the worst evils, there would be no place to stop. Hare and Madden claim that God would know where to stop. They reject Hick's appeal also to his argument that a world with no gratuitous evil would be worse than the present world. Only a minute amount of the present evil would be sufficient, Hare and Madden insist, to answer Hick's point that the lack of gratuitous evil would undermine the soul-making process. God, moreover, would know enough to assign good or evil consequences of actions as a result of *motives* and not simply as a result of what an agent *does*. [See Hick's response in his review of Hare and Madden's *Evil and the Concept of God* [#754].]

1209.   ——. "On the Difficulty of Evading the Problem of Evil." *Philosophy and Phenomenological Research* 27 (1967): 58-69.

Repudiation of the attempts of Karl Barth, Paul Tillich and the linguistic philosophers (following the later Wittgenstein and Austin) to evade the problem of evil by the "theological circle" and the "linguistic circle." [See King-Farlow's response, "Must Gods Madden Madden?" [#1126] and their response (Hare and Madden), "Why Hare Must Hound the Gods" [#1211].]

1210.   ——. *Evil and the Concept of God.* Springfield, IL: Charles C. Thomas, 1968.

Contains critical discussions of several types of theodicies, and rejects them all. The first type of theistic solution is to *evade* the problem (Tillich, Barth, mysticism); the second attempts to *deny* the problem (Schlesinger, Hartshorne, Patterson Brown); the third seeks to resolve theodicy within the confines of *traditional theism* (the character-building theory of Tennant, William Temple, Schleiermacher and John Hick, Leibniz's "best possible world theodicy," Augustine's "privation of good," Farrer's use of the "principle of plenitude," the free will defense, and other traditional aspects of theodicy); the fourth, characterized as *"quasi theism,"* seeks to resolve the problem by modifying the traditional attributes of God (the Whiteheadian-Hartshornean process theism, Brightman's finite God, and Royce's metaphysics of absolute idealism). In their discussion of process theodicy, defined as "hybrid theism-temporalism" (115-125), Hare and Madden reject its distinction between limited and relative as spurious; they find difficulties in both the Primordial Nature and Consequent Nature of God as the guarantor of the growth of value; and they argue that the definition of evil and the sacrificing of aesthetic value for human good is a challenge to divine goodnness. [Among the many responses to this seminal book, see David Griffin, *Evil Revisited* [#873].]

1211.   ———. "Why Hare Must Hound the Gods." *Philosophy and Phenomenal Research* 29 (1969): 456-459.

Response to King-Farlow's "Must Gods Madden Madden?" [#1126]. Hare and Madden reject the claim of King-Farlow and Nelson Pike ("Hume on Evil" [#1157]), that they (Hare and Madden) consider the problem of evil a logical problem. It is rather the problem of gratuitous evil. They note that their *Evil and the Concept of God* [#1210] makes this clear.

1212.   ———. "Evil and Inconclusiveness." *Sophia* 11 (1972): 8-12.

Elaboration of the argument (*Evil and the Concept of God* [#1210]) against the theistic inconclusivist argument. This argument holds that it is logically possible there are reasons for evil of which we are ignorant (Yandell, "Ethics, Evil, and Theism" [#441]; and "A Premature Farewell to Theism" [#1189]; Ahern, *The Problem of Evil* [#1263], Mavrodes, *Belief in God* [#1137], and "Some Recent Philosophical Theology" [#85]). Hare and Madden insist that this argument is irrelevant and an abdication of a genuine responsibility to produce an adequate theodicy. The note that even Hick's elaborate theodicy is inadequate on this point (as well as on other points).

1213.   ———. "The Problem of Evil." *Encyclopedia of Unbelief*. Edited by Gordon Stein. Buffalo, NY: Prometheus Press, 1985: 187-195.

As in *Evil and the Concept of God* [#1210] and various articles, Hare and Madden offer brief critiques of assorted theodicies: the traditional Christian view of inherent depravity; the free will defense; natural evil theodicies; Hick's Irenaean solution; process theodicy; and others.

1214.   Joy, Morny. "Review Symposium." *Horizons, Journal of the College Theology Society* 18 (1991): 303-306.

Review of Tilley's *The Evils of Theodicy* [#1254], focusing on his chapter on Boethius's *The Consolation of Philosophy*. Joy holds that Tilley's combination of narrative theory, speech-act theory and communicative praxis overcomes the sterility that has plagued discussions on theodicy. He argues that philosophy needs more emotional indulgence, that philosophy is too ascetic. [See Tilley's response, following in the text (307-312) after the critical reviews of Joy and three others [see #1254].]

1215.   Laffey, Alice L. "Review Symposium." *Horizons, Journal of the College Theology Society* 18 (1991): 296-300.

Review of Tilley's *The Evils of Theodicy* [#1254]. She concurs with Tilley's conclusion that the Book of Job should not be used to defend theodicy, but arrives at this conclusion by means of a more extensive canonical criticism and historical criticism than Tilley's speech-act theory of literary criticism. As a feminist, Laffey notes, she agrees with Tilley's rejection of theodicy, claiming that women would not have produced theodicy and that women will not support the survival of academic theodicy. [Tilley's response follows in text, 307-312.]

1216.   Lugenbehl, Dale. "Can the Argument from Evil Be Decisive After All?" *Religious Studies* 18 (1982): 29-35.

Refutes the contention that even if there is a morally sufficient reason why God allows evil and this reason cannot be conceived, it still could be the case that God might not be held morally blameless. Lugenbehl argues that if God could prevent suffering and does not, it is reasonable to hold God blameworthy for not making the reasons known to us. Also, to hold God blameless for suffering, by believing that all will turn out for the best in the long run, implies that God is not all-powerful. [See response by Gordon, "Is the Argument from Evil Decisive?" [#1099].]

1217.   Mackie, John L. "Evil and Omnipotence." *Mind* 64 (1955): 200-212. Reprinted in *God and Evil*. Edited by Nelson Pike. Englewood Cliffs, NJ: Prentice-Hall, 1964: 46-60.

Argues against various solutions to the theodicy issue, including the argument that God could have made us free, yet such that we always act for good. In this seminal article, Mackie argues also that "first order evils" (pain) does not justify "second order goods" (endurance, compassion). "Second order evils" (moral evils) are also the result. He proposes also his infamous "paradox of omnipotence," to which there have been numerous responses.

1218.   ———. "Omnipotence." *Sophia* 1 (1962): 13-25.

While Mackie had argued, in "Evil and Omnipotence" [#1217], that the paradox of omnipotence could be resolved by modifying the traditional notion of omnipotence, he grants that the paradox can be resolved also by denying the possibility of the sort of freedom of the will that a successful free will defense would require.

1219.   ———. "Theism and Utopia." *Philosophy* 37 (1962): 153-158.

Response to various critics: Ninian Smart ("Omnipotence, Evil and Supermen" [#429]); S.A. Grave ("On Evil and Omnipotence" [#241]); and P.M. Farrell ("Evil and Omnipotence" [#1087]). Mackie restates his argument that since free choices are determined by our characters (rather than being random), a powerful God could have made us such that we always freely choose the good.

1220.   ———. *The Miracle of Theism: Arguments For and Against the Existence of God*. New York: Oxford University Press, 1982.

In *Chapter 9* ("The Problem of Evil," 150-176), Mackie refutes the theological proofs and concludes that the central doctrines of theism cannot be defended rationally. He dismisses various attempts to resolve the problem of evil, arguing that an omnipotent God could create beings who were free and who used that freedom only for good. [See also Mackie's *Ethics: Inventing Right and Wrong*. Middlesex, England: Harmondsworth, and New York: Penguin, 1977.]

1221.   Madden, Edward H. "The Many Faces of Evil." *Philosophy and Phenomeno-logical Research* 24 (1964): 481-92.

Rejects several of the main traditional solutions to the problem of evil, focusing in most detail upon the free will defense and the ultimate harmony solution. Madden contends that "the problem of good" is isomorphic to the problem of evil and that theodicy is insoluble.

1222.   ———. The Riddle of God and Evil". *Current Philosophical Issues: Essays for C.J. Ducassé*. Edited by Frederick Dommeyer. Springfield, IL: Charles C. Thomas, 1966: 185-200.

Rebuffs several of the main traditional solutions to the problem of evil. He rejects the ultimate harmony solution and, in particular, the argument known as the best possible world thesis and its version in Schlesinger's theodicy ("The Problem of Evil and the Problem of Suffering" [#415]), as well as in Robert E. Larson's (unpublished) manuscript, "The Problem of Evil and the Language of Religion."

1223.   ———. "Evil and the Concept of a Limited God." *Philosophical Studies* 18 (1967): 65-70.

Argues that advocates of a limited theism are not successful in solving the problem of gratuitous evil. He holds that the ultimate triumph of good cannot be guaranteed by a limited God: a limited God who cannot control evil would have no good reason for creating the world; a limited God is limited in the very ways which are useless to solve the theodicy problem; and a limited God cannot guarantee that evils lead to good ends.

1224.   Martin, Michael. "Religious Commitment and Rational Criticism." *Philosophi-cal Forum* 2 (1970): 107-122.

Argues against William W. Bartley's appeal to commitment in contemporary Protestant theology (*The Retreat to Commitment*. Toronto, ON: Random House, and New York: A.A. Knopf, 1962). Martin rejects Bartley's definition of ration-ality, contending that Bartley's own standards for criticism are themselves not criticizable. Religious beliefs are criticizable, despite Bartley's arguments.

1225.   ———. "The Formalities of Evil and a Finite God." *Critica* 9 (1977): 89-92.

Argues that since a perfectly good being may have sufficient reason for allow-ing evils, Walton's argument ("The Formalities of Evil" [#1257]) is invalid. [See following item.]

1226.   ———. "The Formalities of Evil and a Finite God: Correngenda." *Critica* 10 (1978): 133-135.

Corrects several errors in the original argument ("The Formalities of Evil and a Finite God" [#1225]). He mistakenly attributed to Walton, for example, a premise different from the one Walton actually holds. He also assumed a very finite God, a God that is merely more powerful than any human being, and this (he corrects) with the view that it is too weak an assumption to be plausible. He reformulates his argument to eliminate these and other problems in the first formulation.

1227.   ———. "Is Evil Evidence Against the Existence of God?" *Mind* 87 (1978): 429-432.

Objects to Pargetter's contention that the existence of evil has yet to be shown as strong evidence for the non-existence of God (Pargetter, "Evil as Evidence against the Existence of God" [#1146]). Martin outlines an argument and defends it against various objections, an argument that meets Pargetter's challenge and shows that the existence of evil is evidence against God in a way that is free from the problems Pargetter raised. The argument centers on the proposition that the existence of evil in great abundance is not logically necessary and there is no sufficient reason for God to allow evil in great abundance. This proposition contradicts belief in God, and while there is no *a priori* way to demonstrate its truth, attempts to show that it is false have failed. [See Basinger's response, "Evil as Evidence Against God's Existence: Some Clarifications" [#1061]; see also Fitzpatrick's comments, "The Onus of Proof in Arguments about the Problem of Evil" [#370].]

1228.   ———. "Does the Evidence Confirm Theism More than Naturalism?" *International Journal for Philosophy of Religion* 16 (1984): 257-262.

Critiques Schlesinger's arguments in *Religion and the Scientific Method* [#418], that theism is more *probable* than atheism. The principle on which Schlesinger's argument is based ("When a given piece of evidence E is more probable on H than on H' then E confirms H more than H'") is unacceptable. Even if this principle were granted, Schlesinger's argument would fail, since there is evidence that cancels out the confirmatory effect of the evidence cited by Schlesinger. He has not taken into account the total available evidence for theism and naturalism.

1229.   ———. "A Theistic Inductive Argument from Evil." *International Journal for Philosophy of Religion* 22 (1987): 81-87.

Rejects Peterson's argument (*Evil and the Christian God* [#1153]), that evil produces inductive evidence for God's existence. Peterson's use of inductive argumentation is at odds with more standard inductive reasoning. This leads to the possibility of inductive support for various creatures—fairies and the like.

1230.   ———. *Atheism: A Philosophical Analysis*. Philadelphia, PA: Temple University Press, 1990.

Contains detailed critiques of arguments for the existence of God and defends arguments that reject the existence of God. The final third of the book contains an overview of recent theodicies (*Chapters 14-18*): the free will defense of Plantinga fails; counterfactuals of freedom are rejected; natural evil theodicies (Plantinga, Reichenbach, Swinburne) fail; Hick's soul-making theodicy fails; and a host of "minor theodicies" fail.

1231.   McCloskey, H.J. "God and Evil." *Philosophical Quarterly* 10 (1960): 97-114. [Reprinted in Nelson Pike, editor. *God and Evil*. Englewood Cliffs, NJ: Prentice-Hall, 1964: 61-84.]

Refutes various proposed solutions to the problems of moral and physical evil. McCloskey concludes that if God is all-powerful and perfectly good, such a God ought to have created a world without unnecessary evils. Since the most popular philosophical and theological attempts to explain this unnecessary evil are unconvincing, God cannot exist as an omnipotent, omnibenevolent Being.

1232.   ——. "The Problem of Evil." *Journal of Bible and Religion* 30 (1962): 187-197.

Rejects the theistic argument that evils are parts of a good whole and that evils may be means to good ends. McCloskey argues also that freedom does not have the great value ascribed to it in the free will defense.

1233.   ——. "Would Any Being Merit Worship?" *Southern Journal of Philosophy* 2 (1964): 157-164.

Contends that no being, finite or infinite, merits worship. It is possible to conceive of a being which, if it existed, might merit respect and reverence, but not adoration and submission. McCloskey rejects various versions of defining a being (God) that might merit worship, including a perfect, all-powerful being. Such a being is incomprehensible, possibly not personal, and there are problems with the concept of omnipotence, etc.

1234.   ——. "Evil and the Problem of Evil." *Sophia* 5 (1966): 14-19.

Refutes Ahern's claim ("A Note on the Nature of Evil" [#1260]), that McCloskey ("The Problem of Evil" [#1232]) construes the privation theory as a solution to the problem of evil when in fact the theory is about the *nature* of evil. Ahern's defense of the privation theory of evil fails: Ahern has not shown that all pain is useful and (in this sense) good (the privation of good).

1235.   ——. *God and Evil*. The Hague: Nijhoff, 1974.

Draws on material from three of his previously published articles ("God and Evil" [#1231]; "The Problem of Evil" [#1232]; and "Would Any Being Merit Worship?" [#1233]). McCloskey critiques the conception of a finite God (J.S. Mill), the free will defense (Maritain), the best possible worlds defense (Leibniz), and various Christian solutions to moral and physical evil.

1236.   McPherson, Thomas. *Philosophy and Religious Belief*. London: Hutchinson University Library, 1974.

Discusses various issues in philosophy of religion, including theodicy (*Chapter 4, Part 4*: "The Problem of Evil," 71-77). He critiques the limiting of God; the free will defense; and the redefining of the notion of evil.

1237.   Meynell, Hugo. "Evil." *God and the World: The Coherence of Christian Theism*. London: SPCK Press, 1971: 64-83.

Argues that the problem of evil leads the theist either to resort to an analysis of God's goodness in terms of metaphysical excellence or to give up the doctrine of divine omnipotence (process theism), or both, or indeed, to argue that divine omnipotence uses evil as a means to a good end (Hick). The first seems an evasion, the second a capitulation, and the third is questionable. He makes critical reference also to Barth, Aquinas, Augustine, and the free will defense.

1238.   Moore, Harold F. "Evidence, Evil and Religious Belief." *International Journal for Philosophy of Religion* 9 (1978): 241-245.

Refutes Plantinga's argument (*God, Freedom, and Evil* [#109]) against the contention of Cornman and Lehrer (*Philosophical Problems and Arguments* [#1205]), that even if the existence of God can be logically reconciled with the existence of evil, the existence of God is rendered improbable by the reality of evil. Moore argues that the conditions for using evidence to assess fundamental religious issues (like the existence of God and the problem of evil) do not exist. [See Wierenga's response, "Reply to Harold Moore's 'Evidence, Evil and Religious Belief'" [#1186].]

1239.   ——. "Evidence—Once More: Reply to E. Wierenga's 'Reply to H. Moore's "Evidence, Evil and Religious Belief".'" *International Journal for Philosophy of Religion* 9 (1978): 252-253.

Reaffirms his claim that theistic belief cannot be assessed in terms of evidence. Moore argues that Plantinga's account of the confirmation of theism is impoverished and unacceptable. Other ways must be found to deal with the inductive problem of evil. Evil does not count against the existence of God, but this is not because evidence has been applied to the issue and found to be decisive; rather, it is because we do not know *how* to assess such beliefs in terms of evidence.

1240.   Parsons, Keith M. *God and the Burden of Proof: Plantinga, Swinburne, and the Analytic Defense of Theism.* Buffalo, NY: Prometheus Press, 1990.

Book-length critique of the theologies of Alvin Plantinga [see Chapters 2 and 3] and Richard Swinburne [see Chapter 4]. Plantinga's arguments are presented in *Chapter One* ("Plantinga and the Rationality of Theism"), the argument in particular that theism is not irrational even though it cannot meet the evidentialist challenge. Parsons concludes that this is valid, yet that it has consequences other theists might reject. Plantinga's free will defense (*Chapter Three*, "Evil and the Burden of Proof") is valid if its premises and assumptions are granted. Yet, it seems to imply a dualism which cannot be of any use, even as a hypothesis; Plantinga's assumption that free will has the absolute value he deems it to have is questionable; etc. Swinburne's cosmological argument for theism, presented by Parsons in *Chapter Two* ("Swinburne and the Cosmological Argument") fails. Swinburne has not given good reasons for thinking that God could not have given us noninductive knowledge of the consequences of our actions. Parsons argues that the atheist argument from evil succeeds in meeting the burden of proof against God's existence (*Chapter Three*).

1241.   Perkins, R.K., Jr. "An Atheistic Argument from the Improvability of the Universe." *Noûs* 17 (1983): 239-250.

Formulates a new argument from evil against the existence of God. He argues not that evil is logically incompatible with God's existence but that evil is incompatible with the fact that this world could have been *improved* by God. He attempts to escape some of Plantinga's objections to his argument and to show the *reductio ad absurdum* of theism by contending *both* that "God exists entails that this universe is as good as any which God can bring about" *and* that "God exists entails that this universe could be improved by God."

1242.   Puccetti, Roland. "The Concept of God." *Philosophical Quarterly* 15 (1965): 237-245.

Contends that the concept of God is self-contradictory. He proposes an *onto-logical disproof* of God (as had Findlay, "Can God's Existence Be Disproved?" *New Essays in Philosophical Theology*. Edited by Antony Flew and Alasdair MacIntyre. London: SCM Press, 1955: 47-56). Puccetti argues that there are no known reasons why God should not eliminate innocent pain and suffering.

1243.   Richman, Robert J. "The Argument from Evil." *Religious Studies* 5 (1969): 203-212.

Argues that the theist must specify the morally sufficient reason why God permits suffering if theism is to be rationally justified in maintaining that God exists in face of the suffering in the world. He reformulates the problem of evil in terms of "the logic of our moral judgements" and claims that it is successful in refuting theism. [See response by Langton, "The Argument from Evil: Reply to Professor Richman" [#1133].]

1244.   Rowe, William L. "C.B. Martin's Contradiction in Theology." *Australasian Journal of Philosophy* 40 (1962): 75-79.

Response to aspects of C.B. Martin's *Religious Beliefs* (Ithaca, NY: Cornell University Press, 1959). Rowe rejects Martin's argument that the propositions— "It is not logically possible that God did evil," "Christ is God," and "It is logi-cally possible that Christ did evil"—are incompatible logically if the second proposition is necessarily true. Rowe notes that Christ is an historical figure, not a necessary truth.

1245.   ——. *Philosophy of Religion: An Introduction*. Belmont, CA: Dickinson, 1978.

Chapter 6 ("The Problem of Evil," 79-95) concludes that the *logical* problem of evil has been shown to be unsuccessful, while the *evidential* problem of evil remains a problem for theists: the latter shows that the variety and profusion of evil provides rational support for atheism.

1246.   ——. "The Problem of Evil and Some Varieties of Atheism." *American Philo-sophical Quarterly* 16 (1979): 335-341. [Also in *The Problem of Evil*. Edited by Marilyn McCord Adams and Robert Merrihew Adams. New York: Oxford University Press, 1990.]

Argues that there is an argument for atheism based on the existence of evil. It is rational and reasonable that there exist instances of intense suffering which an omnipotent, omniscient being could have prevented, without thereby losing some greater good or permitting some evil equally bad or worse. As such, God cannot exist. The informed atheist has three options concerning the rationality of theism: *unfriendly atheism* (rejects the rational basis of theism); *indifferent atheism*; and *friendly atheism*, the latter defended by Rowe. Friendly atheism holds that some theists are rationally justified in believing that God exists, but the atheist is not committed to thinking this is a true claim. [See responses by Delmas Lewis, "The Problem with the Problem of Evil" [#1311]; and Snyder, "Surplus Evil" [#1170].]

1247.   ———. "Evil and the Theistic Hypothesis: A Response to S.J. Wykstra." *International Journal for Philosophy of Religion* 16 (1984): 95-100.

Response to Wykstra's critique ("The Humean Obstacle to Evidential Arguments from Suffering" [#1188]) of Rowe's "The Problem of Evil and Some Varieties of Atheism" [#1246]. Rowe rejects Wykstra's claim that seemingly pointless evil is not evidence against God's existence, that things would seem more or less the same to us whether or not there were a reason for the suffering. The good in the suffering is beyond our knowledge. Rowe argues, to the contrary, that some evils do seem pointless; for example, a fawn's meaningless suffering alone and unknown in the forest.

1256.   Varman, Ved Prakash. "Monotheism and the Problem of Evil." *Indian Philosophical Quarterly* 2 (1975): 341-352.

Considers various attempts (including the free will defense) to resolve the problem of evil within a monotheistic religion and finds them all unimpressive. The only solution is to reject monotheism. The limiting of divine God such that God cannot do everything is unsatisfactory, since this would be an abandonment of monotheism.

1257.   Walton, Douglas. "The Formalities of Evil." *Critica* 8 (1976): 3-9.

Argues that a consistent theism must reject at least one of the formal premises it holds. [See responses by Martin, "The Formalities of Evil and a Finite God" [#1225] and "The Formalities of Evil and a Finite God: Correngenda" [#1226].]

III   Other Critical Discussions

1258.   Abraham, William J. "The Problem of Evil." *An Introduction to the Philosophy of Religion*. Englewood Cliffs, NJ: Prentice-Hall, 1985: 62-74.

Rejects the "limited God solution" to theodicy (see Kushner, *When Bad Things Happen to Good People* [#1132]). Rejects also the free will defense (as incompatible with the Christian view that God is causally operative in all things); and rejects Plantinga's explanation for physical evil. He concludes that theodicies assume a commitment to a utilitarian moral theory, and that natural evil is justified on the grounds that it leads eventually to a good end.

1259.   Ahern, M.B. "An Approach to the Problem of Evil." *Sophia* 2 (1963): 18-26.

Challenges Mackie's "basic principle," that "good is opposed to evil, in such a way that a good thing always eliminates evil as far as it can." Ahern argues that while God cannot will or approve of evil, God can (negatively) permit evil to exist. Ahern also challenges various other aspects of Mackie's argument ("Evil and Omnipotence" [#1217]).

1260.   ———. "A Note on the Nature of Evil." *Sophia* 4 (1965): 17-25.

In response to McCloskey's "The Problem of Evil" [#1232], Ahern defends the *privation theory of evil*. Evil is not something wholly positive, wholly negative, or positive but harmful. Evil is something negative but not *wholly* negative. All evils are useful and, in this sense, a good—the privation of good. McCloskey has argued (against this theory of the nature of evil) that theists must look elsewhere to explain why God permits it. Ahern's point is that the privation theory is concerned only with the former—the nature of evil. [See McCloskey's reply, "Evil and the Problem of Evil" [#1234]. See also *Appendix B* for many other publications about the *privation of good* theory. Other references are dispersed throughout the annotated chapters.]

1261.   ——. "The Nature of Evil." *Sophia* 5 (1966): 35-44.

A further response to McCloskey's "Evil and the Problem of Evil" [#1234]. Ahern defends his former critique of McCloskey's criticism of the *privation* theory of evil. McCloskey is wrong in his supposition that theists employ (or should employ) the privation theory as a solution to the problem of evil. [For a recent response to Ahern, see Peter Drum, "The Intrinsic Value of Pain," *Sophia* 31 (1992), 97-99.]

1262.   ——. "God and Evil—A Note." *Sophia* 6 (1967): 23-26.

Rejoinder to R.D. Bradley's "A Proof of Atheism" [#1198]. Ahern refutes Bradley's claim that it is analytically true that God is not good since God *could* prevent evil and does not, and thus is responsible for evil. Ahern argues that proper linguistic usage does not entail that anyone who does not prevent evil is responsible for the evil. Bradley has not shown that God is obliged to prevent some specific evils or that there can be no justifiable reasons for not preventing them.

1263.   ——. *The Problem of Evil*. New York: Schocken Books, 1971.

Discusses three sets of theodicy questions: the general problem, the specific abstract problem, and the specific concrete question. He concludes that conditions for the compatibility or incompatibility of God and evil cannot be met.

1264.   Allen, Diogenes. "Theodicies: Rebuttals to a Challenge." *The Reasonableness of Faith: A Philosophical Essay on the Grounds for Religious Beliefs*. Washington, DC: Corpus Books, 1968: 96-114.

Contends that theodicies must meet three standards: they must show that the *a priori* incompatibility of God and evil is not a fatal threat; they must not lead to apathy or despair; and their account of evils in this world must be in keeping with Christian beliefs.

1265.   Amend, Edward A. "The Problem of Evil." *Dialog* 22 (1983): 65-66.

Maintains that as a universal power, evil is in opposition to the equally universal and even more powerful good. From the human point of view, the problem of evil has no apparent solution; yet from God's perspective, evil is overcome by the positive good that made evil known in the first place. Ultimately, evil disappears in the power and reality of God. Existentially, evil is to be engaged and resisted.

1266.   Anderson, Susan Leigh. "Evil." *Journal of Value Inquiry* 24 (1990): 43-53.

Argues that evil is not an *entity* but an *activity*. Anderson defines "evil action" as (among other things) action done consciously, voluntarily and wilfully. The agent must cause harm or allow harm to be done when the agent could have prevented it. A minimum of harm must occur, and the more harm, the more evil the action is.

1267.   Andre, Shane. "The Problem of Evil and the Paradox of Friendly Atheism." *International Journal for Philosophy of Religion* 17 (1985): 209-216.

Critique of William Rowe's "The Problem of Evil and Some Varieties of Atheism" [#1246]. Andre distinguishes Rowe's "special grounds atheism" (that concedes the rationality of theism but holds that the atheist's position has more evidential merit) from Rowe's "paradoxical atheism" (that concedes the rationality of theism without claiming the superiority of the atheist's evidential worth). Andre argues that the former is inconsistent in arguing that evil and suffering render atheism reasonable while it does not render theism unreasonable; the latter is incoherent and paradoxical.

1268.   Aulén, Gustof. *The Drama and the Symbols: A Book of the Images of God and the Problems They Raise.* Philadelphia, PA: Fortress Press, 1970.

Argues that all forms of theodicy must compromise the Christian promise of divine love as long as God's power is conceived as "all-causality." [See also Aulén's *The Faith of the Christian Church* [see #1105].]

1269.   Baker, Tom. "And the Life Everlasting: Some Personal Reflections." *Thought* 61 (1986): 425-433.

Based on John Baillie's *And the Life Everlasting* (New York: Scribner's Sons, 1933, and New York: Oxford University Press, 1934; reprinted in 1950), in which Baillie inextricably links belief in heaven and the theodicy question. Baker argues that it is difficult for modern sensibilities to accept belief in an afterlife. He argues that belief in heaven is based neither on self-interest nor on the need for consolation, but on the need to justify God. Belief in heaven is aligned intricately with belief in God.

1270.   Bash, J.A. "Religion and Evil." *Academic Study of Religion: 1974 Proceedings.* Edited by Anne Carr. University of Montana, Missoula, MT: Scholars Press, 1974: 15-21.

Discusses three significantly different ways of interpreting the *nature* of evil: evil is the incongruity in human events and experiences; evil is the privation of good; and evil is a concrete and independent reality. Bash discusses also the alternative resolutions offered for *coping* with evil as it is interpreted in each of these formulations.

1271.   Black, Hubert P. "The Problem of Evil." *Christianity Today* 15 (1971): 689-694.

Rejects the atheistic contention regarding the alleged inconsistency of the propositions—God is omnipotent, God is omnibenevolent, and evil exists. There is no inconsistency in as much as God permits creatures to commit moral evils (due to a defection from being).

1272.   Burke, Michael B. "Theodicy with a God of Limited Power: A Reply to McGrath." *Analysis* 47 (1987): 57-58.

Rejects McGrath's assumption ("Evil and the Existence of a Finite God" [#1320]) that the problem of evil can be solved if God is conceived as limited in power. Burke suggests that, rather than God's power being limited, perhaps God has not eliminated various evils because God can attend to only a dozen galaxies at a time and ours may not be among the most urgently in need of attention. [See McGrath's response, "Children of a Lesser God? A Reply to Burke and Crisp" [#1321].]

1273. Burkle, Howard R. *God, Suffering and Belief*. Nashville, TN: Abingdon Press, 1977.

Holds that evil is the result of *human* inactivity, not *divine* activity or inactivity. God suffers with us and is actively involved in every human situation. The question is not whether there is divine participation, but whether we will take responsibility to join with God to eliminate the evils in the world. [See the numerous other entries in the "Suffering of God Theodicy" appendix and other entries dispersed throughout this various chapters.]

1274. Cartwright, Nancy. "Comments on Wesley Salmon's 'Science and Religion'." *Philosophical Studies* 33 (1978): 177-183.

Response to Salmon's "Religion and Science: A New Look at Hume's *Dialogues*" [#1250]. Cartwright holds that the inductive approach to theodicy is embedded in question-begging. Statistical data, moreover, are inappropriate to discussions of God's existence and other metaphysical issues.

1275. Casserley, Julian. *Evil and Evolutionary Eschatology: Two Essays*. Edited and Introduced by C. Don Keyes. New York and Toronto, ON: Edwin Mellen Press, 1990.

Contains a revised version of Keyes's "Casserley's Theodicy in Relation to his Critique of Power" [#1306] and also a reprint of Julian Casserley's *Why Pain and Evil?* (1950), as well as Casserley's *Theology of Man*, previously unpublished. Casserley defends humanism from the perspective of eschatology, and subsumes history into biological evolution. God is not to be defined primarily in terms of sovereignty and power. God achieves the eschatological future by inspiring a desire for progress, rather than using coercive force.

1276. Chaves, Eduardo O.C. "Logical and Semantical Aspects of the Problem of Evil." *Critica* 10 (1978): 3-42.

Contends that *semantical equivocation* prevents the settlement of the problem of evil in its logical aspects. He seeks to clarify the presuppositions and assumptions of various theodicists, Nelson Pike in particular.

1277. Clark, Kelly James. "Evil and Christian Belief." *International Philosophical Quarterly* 29 (1989): 175-189.

The argument is that God's redemptive work brings good out of evil. [See also his *Return to Reason* [#1278].]

1278. ———. "God and Evil." *Return to Reason*. Grand Rapids, MI: Eerdmans, 1990: 55-91.

Sympathetic expository discussion of the theodicy issue: moral and physical evil; the free will defense versus free will theodicy; the best possible world; Plantinga's version of the free will defense; and Plantinga's transworld depravity (versus John Mackie, *The Miracle of Theism* [#1220]; and William Abraham, *An Introduction to the Philosophy of Religion* [#1258]). He contends that the problem of gratuitous evil is resolved by the Christian's commitment to a redeeming God. Clark rejects attempts at constructing a theodicy; such are of little help with respect to the existential problem of evil (as C.S. Lewis noted in *A Grief Observed* [#3438]).

1279.   Clark, Stephen R.L. *The Mysteries of Religion.* Oxford: Blackwell, 1986.

Chapter 8 ("War and the Problem of Evil," 144-161) argues that the problem of evil centers on the question—how can an "Abrahamic theism" serve God from any motive other than fear? Clark rejects the free will defense as anti-deterministic. He focuses upon God's omnipotence in terms of the promise of eventual success in overcoming evil. He rejects both the doctrine of original sin and reincarnation/karma as explanations for evil. He rejects also, with some qualifications, the dualistic vision of God warring with evil spirits.

1280.   Collins, John. "C.A. Campbell and the Problem of Suffering." *Religious Studies* 16 (1980): 307-316.

Assesses Campbell's theodicy, in *On Selfhood and Godhood* [#1386] and "Reason and the Problem of Suffering," *Philosophy* 10 (1935), 154-167. Collins finds problems with Campbell's understanding of deserved and undeserved suffering, and problems with Campbell's principle of compensation, as well as with his use of the best possible world theodicy.

1281.   Conway, David A. "The Philosophical Problem of Evil." *International Journal for Philosophy of Religion* 24 (1988): 35-66.

Rejects theistic attempts (Plantinga's in particular) to resolve the problem of evil in its logical and evidential forms. Conway argues that the supposed differences between the two types of arguments are not really differences. He concludes that theists should abandon the meta-discussion about what the problem of evil is. Evil is a problem for theism in so far as there exists evil that appears to be omni-preventable. We must abandon strategies which claim that the problem of evil can be disposed of by referring to the inapplicability of probability theories or by the lack of an apparent inconsistency between the existence of God and evil. The real issue is whether evil is *omni-preventable*, and this involves such philosophical issues as modalities, values, and metaphysical ontologies—issues that are not matters of simple or obvious consistency or inconsistency, or of probability.

1282.   Crisp, Roger. "The Avoidance of the Problem of Evil: A Reply to McGrath." *Analysis* 46 (1986): 160.

Refutes McGrath's contention ("Evil and the Existence of a Finite God" [#1320]), that theism cannot avoid the problem of evil by denying divine omnipotence or divine goodness. Crisp proposes that we consider the possibility of an infinitely evil power at work in the universe. He recommends also the traditional doctrine of *acts of omission*.

1283.   Davis, Stephen T. "The Problem of Evil in Recent Philosophy." *Review and Expositor* 82 (1985): 535-548.

Davis presents an overview of recent theodicies, noting various strengths and weaknesses in all of them. He considers the theodicies of John Roth (theodicy of protest), David Griffin (process theodicy), John Hick (Irenaean theodicy), and Alvin Plantinga (free will defense). [See also Davis's edited book, *Encountering Evil* [see #1284] in which his theodicy is presented and criticized along with the theodicies of Griffin, Roth, Sontag and Hick.]

1284.   ——. "Critique [of Sontag]." *Encountering Evil*. Edited by Stephen T. Davis. Atlanta, GA: John Knox Press, 1981: 154-157.

Critique of Sontag's "Anthropodicy and the Return of God" [#1352]. Davis rejects Sontag's denial of divine goodness and eschatological hope. He rejects also Sontag's claim that evil is not cost-effective. [Sontag's response follows in the text.]

1285.   Davis, Thomas D. *Philosophy: An Introduction Through Original Fiction and Discussion*. New York: Random House, 1979.

In a brief discussion (*Chapter 3*, "God and the Problem of Suffering"), Davis rejects the free will defense: God could have created people without free will who were lively, emotional, thoughtful, etc. He rejects also "the virtue defense" (there can be no virtues without suffering). He contends that suffering contradicts the very nature of virtue as the relief of suffering.

1286.   Eby, Lloyd. "Is God Good and Can God Be Defended?" *The Defense of God*. Edited by John K. Roth and Frederick E. Sontag. New York: Paragon House, 1985: 48-67.

Constructs a theodicy based on Unification texts and doctrine. God did not prevent the fall of Adam for various reasons; God had established the principle which limited the divine dominion over imperfect people, and God cannot violate that principle; Adam and Eve were to reach perfection by responsible exercise of free will, and if God had intervened it would have acknowledged Satan as a co-creator. Eby denies that natural evils are evils as such, and contends that in an ideal world, humans would have mastery over nature. He denies also the doctrine of eternal damnation, arguing that eventually all will be saved. He contends that this (Unification) theodicy has features in common with process theodicy: God is bound by the choices made by humans. Eby's conclusion is that Unification theodicy is the best answer that exists for this issue.

1287.   Fales, Evan. "Antediluvian Theodicy: Stump on the Fall." *Faith and Philosophy* 6 (1989): 320-329.

Response to Stump's "The Problem of Evil" [#1173]. Despite some desirable features (her utilization, for example, of major doctrines of the Judaeo-Christian faiths), Stump's theodicy, with its conceptions of hell and original sin, raises more problems than it solves. [See other relevant publications by Fales: "Should God Not Have Created Adam?" *Faith and Philosophy* 9 (1992), 192-208; and his much earlier, "Evil and Omnipotence," *Australasian Journal of Philosophy* 36 (1958), 216-221.]

1288.   Ford, David F. "Tragedy and Atonement." *Christ, Ethics and Tragedy*. Edited By Kenneth Surin. Cambridge: Cambridge University Press, 1988: 117-130.

A critical discussion of the themes of tragedy and atonement in MacKinnon's theology [see #1315].

1289. Friedman, R.Z. "Evil and Moral Agency." *International Journal for Philosophy of Religion* 24 (1988): 3-20.

Contends that the conceptual framework for theodicy is the idea of human beings as moral agents. For this idea to be meaningful, religion requires *both* God and evil. Both are required to render intelligible the concept of moral agency. Friedman contends that theodicies fail—in seeking to defend the goodness of God, theodicies undermine moral agency. Paradoxically, anti-theologies encounter the same difficulty, establishing conclusions that have negative implications for our understanding of moral agency. They undermine the contention, central to the moral view, that we can discern the difference between good and evil. The Book of Job addresses evil in a way that is far more sophisticated than either theodicy or anti-theodicy: it accepts the reality of the theodicy problem and the impossibility of a resolution.

1290. Gordon, Jeffrey. "The Dilemma of Theodicy." *Sophia* 23 (1984): 22-34.

Argues that a resolution to the problem of evil would be as destructive to theism as the failure to resolve the issue. The *dilemma* for theodicy is that it either fails to answer the argument from evil or that it adduces a compensation for misfortune that requires no necessary recourse to God.

1291. Görman, Ulf. *A Good God? A Logical and Semantical Analysis of the Problem of Evil*. Stockholm: H. Ohlsson, 1977.

Maintains that the problem of evil is mainly an *evaluative* problem and that the disagreement between the apologist and the sceptic depends on their having different value hierarchies. The problem of evil considers the acceptability of the goodness of God in view of the evaluations ascribed to God. The most intricate problem is for the theist who wants to give the avoidance of suffering priority over other values. Görman considers also the debate between Flew and Plantinga: he rejects the positions of both.

1292. Griffin, David R. "Critique [of Sontag]." *Encountering Evil*. Edited by Stephen T. Davis. Atlanta, GA: John Knox Press, 1981: 152-154.

Refutes Sontag's "Anthropodicy and the Return to God" [#1352]. Griffin rejects Sontag's view that every aspect of the structure of the world must be thought of as the result of God's decisions. Griffin argues that Sontag does not distinguish between necessary actuality and necessary possibility because he does not believe God could create a world in which free creatures reside. Sontag does not refute Griffin's alternative view that there are necessary elements of the world beyond God's control. [Sontag's response follows in the text.]

1293. Harper, Albert W.J. *The Theodicy of Suffering*. San Francisco: Mellen Research University Press and New York: Edwin Mellen Press, 1990.

Holds that God (as pure Godhead) is eternal, without form and property. Harper argues that human beings, not God, are in need of vindication in view of the ills we are called upon to bear.

1294. Hauerwas, Stanley. *Suffering Presence: Theological Reflections on Medicine, the Mentally Handicapped, and the Church*. Notre Dame, IN: University of Notre Dame Press, 1986.

A collection of essays which argues that the "sufferer-healer interaction" is a spiritual and moral exchange. He rejects the modern medical ethics which ignores the human story and the religious dimensions of medicine.

1295.   ———. "God, Medicine, and the Problems of Evil." *Reformed Journal* 38 (1988): 16-22.

Contends that the attempt to answer the problem of evil is a mistake. Suffering cannot challenge belief in the existence of God. He argues also that it is a philosophical and theological mistake to assume there is a single problem of evil. Hauerwas agrees with Surin (*Theology and the Problem of Evil* [#1364]), that the theodicy question has been abstracted from the concrete situation. [See Basinger's response, "Hauerwas on the Problem of Evil" [#1064].]

1296.   ———. *Naming the Silences: God, Medicine and the Problem of Suffering*. Grand Rapids, MI: Eerdmans, 1990.

Focusing upon the illness of children, Hauerwas argues that attempts to explain evil vis-à-vis God is a mistake. The context of suffering is important, as is the manner in which the sufferer continues to cope. As Surin argued (*Theology and the Problem of Evil* [#1364]), the philosophical theism of the Enlightenment has generated the problem of evil and is far removed from those who see suffering as a practical challenge for Christian living.

1297.   Helm, Paul. "Problems of Evil." *Sophia* 5 (1966): 20-23.

There are at least two different aspects of the problem of evil, both of which must be addressed: there is the problem of the *epistemological* barrier to belief in the existence of God, and there is the *moral* problem, the problem of reconciling belief in God despite the world having certain features which seem incompatible with an infinite, loving God.

1298.   Henze, Donald. "On Some Alleged Humean Insights and Oversights." *Religious Studies* 6 (1970): 369-377.

Refutes Pike's argument ("Hume on Evil" [#1157]), that Hume's argument from evil overlooked the possibility that God might have a morally sufficient reason for permitting evil. Pike has not shown that this reason can be applied to an omni-being (God). It is only to persons and their actions (under specified conditions) that the concept of a "morally sufficient reason" applies. There is no clear sense in which omni-beings can be thought of as moral agents. Pike, moreover, has not shown that suffering must be a necessary component in the best of all possible worlds. Henze rejects also Pike's attempt to avoid the problem of evil on *a priori* grounds.

1299.   Hepburn, Ronald. "The Problem of Evil." *Dialectic and Contemporary Science: Essays in Honor of Errol E. Harris*. Edited by Philip T. Grier. Lanham, MD: University Press of America, 1989: 111-124.

Refutes various aspects of the theodicy of Errol Harris [see #1106-1110]. The problem of natural evil (in individual animals) has not been adequately addressed by Harris by his appeal to the ultimate perfection of the whole. Hepburn contends that Harris's God is finite, since evils are the inevitable consequences of finitude, essential to the procession of phases, and without which there can be no self-realization and self-differentiation of deity. Harris's God lacks moral perfection.

1300. Hick, John. "Critique [of Sontag]." *Encountering Evil*. Edited by Stephen T. Davis. Atlanta, GA: John Knox Press, 1981: 151-152.

Refutes Sontag's "Anthropodicy and the Return of God" [#1352]. Hick argues that Sontag caricatures an eschatological theodicy and thereby avoids taking this option seriously. Hick defends his (Hick's) eschatological theodicy against Sontag's refutation of it. The issue is not *compensation*, but eschatological perfection of human animals into children of God. [Sontag's response follows in the text.]

1301. Hitterdale, Larry. "The Problem of Evil and the Subjectivity of Values Are Incompatible." *International Philosophical Quarterly* 18 (1978): 467-469.

Argues that many philosophers hold two incompatible doctrines: that the problem of evil furnishes weighty and perhaps decisive evidence against belief in God, and that judgments of value are only subjective. David Hume and Bertrand Russell held these incompatible theories, as (more recently) does Antony Flew (*God and Philosophy* [#223]). The atheistic argument from evil does not work unless values are non-subjective. Agnosticism is the most that the sceptic can affirm.

1302. Hoffman, Joshua. "Can God Do Evil?" *Southern Journal of Philosophy* 17 (1979): 213-220.

Holds that Pike's solution to the theodicy dilemma ("Omnipotence and God's Ability to Sin" [#98]) fails because it commits him to the view that God is *contingently* omnibenevolent. Hoffman argues that to defend the traditional Christian doctrine of God, God must be viewed as *necessarily* omnibenevolent. Contingent omnibenevolence is incompatible with the divine command theory. *God cannot do evil*, and this does not deny the divine omnipotence, since doing evil is logically impossible for God.

1303. Huber, C.E. "A Philosophical View of Providence." *The Caring God: Perspectives on Providence*. Edited by Carl S. Meyer and Herbert T. Mayer. St. Louis, MO: Concordia Publishing House, 1973: 67-92.

Hume, Russell, Flew and others hold two incompatible doctrines—that judgments of values are subjective, and that the problem of evil furnishes decisive evidence against belief in God. The atheistic conclusion from the problem of evil (that there is no God) alleges something about how the world is *objectively*, yet the premises (assertions about good and evil) are *subjective*. Hence, Huber concludes that the atheistic argument from evil fails. Subjectivism diminishes severely the case for atheism. Yet, for a religious believer who is a subjectivist about values, agnosticism is the only conclusion.

1304. Johnson, Jeff. "Inference to the Best Explanation and the Problem of Evil." *Journal of Religion* 64 (1984): 54-72.

Argues that if the deductive argument from evil is sound, any proposed theodicy must be rejected as contradictory (as Mackie noted [#1217]). Yet, the theist need only produce a logically possible explanation of evil to defeat the argument. Inductive arguments are more sound. Given the facts of evil, however, atheism is more likely the inference to the best explanation than are theistic accounts of Satan, Hick's soul-making, and the appeal to mystery.

1305.   Keller, James A. "The Problem of Evil and the Attributes of God." *International Journal for Philosophy of Religion* 26 (1989): 155-171.

Theists should respond to the probabilistic argument from evil by reexamining God's attributes, rather than holding that evil has no evidential force against theism. It is not enough to posit that God is beyond human comprehension.

1306.   Keyes, C. Don. "Casserley's Theodicy in Relation to his Critique of Power." *St. Luke Journal of Theology* 32 (1989): 37-48.

This is an earlier version of Keyes's essay in Casserley's *Evil and Evolutionary Eschatology* [#1275].

1307.   King-Farlow, John, and Naill Shanks. "Theodicy: Two Grand Extremes." *Scottish Journal of Theology* 41 (1987): 153-176.

Dismisses the two contrasting theodicies of Fedor Dostoevsky's Ivan Karamazov in *The Brothers Karamazov* (New York: Bantom Classic, 1970) and Peter Geach's *Providence and Evil* [#1426]: both, he argues, are extremist and flawed.

1308.   Kohl, Marvin. "On Suffering" and "Reply" [to Paul Kurtz]. *Humanist Ethics*. Edited by Morris B. Storer. Buffalo, NY: Prometheus Press, 1980: 173-178.

Argues that the problem of pain poses a problem for the humanist, as well as for the theist, a problem the humanist cannot resolve merely by rejecting theism or by embracing egoism. [See Kurtz's response, "Comment by Kurtz" [#1309].]

1309.   Kurtz, Paul. "Comments by Paul Kurtz." *Humanist Ethics*. Edited by Morris B. Storer. Buffalo, NY: Prometheus Press, 1980: 177-178.

Rejects Kohl's argument ("On Suffering" [#1308]), that Promethean humanism must be universalistic and altruistic. He points out (contra Kohl) that there is a form of humanism that has avoided the pitfall of egoism.

1310.   Langtry, Bruce. "God, Evil and Probability." *Sophia* 28 (1989): 32-40.

Response to Chrzan's criticisms of Plantinga, in "Plantinga on Atheistic Induction" [#1202]. Langtry argues that Chrzan's appraisals are confused, and yet that aspects of Plantinga's argument of epistemic probability for God is also somewhat confused. Langtry concludes that while the atheological claim (that the existence of the amount of evil in the world makes God's existence improbable) is far from certain, Plantinga's claim (that there is no reason to think that the atheological claim is true) is short-sighted.

1311.   Lewis, Delmas. "The Problem with the Problem of Evil." *Sophia* 22 (1983): 26-36.

Refutes Rowe's claim ("The Problem of Evil and Some Varieties of Atheism" [#1246]), that pointless suffering can be used as a formidable argument against belief in God's existence. Rowe has not succeeded in showing that apparently pointless evils lead to the conclusion that there *are* in fact cases of genuinely pointless (gratuitous) evils.

1312. ——. "Eternity Again: A Reply to Stump and Kretzmann." *International Journal for Philosophy of Religion* 15 (1984): 73-79.

Refutes the argument of Stump and Kretzmann ("Eternity" [#262]), that God is unchanging and atemporal. Lewis argues that such a God would be unaffected by the experiences of temporal beings.

1313. Lewis, Hywel David. *Philosophy of Religion*. London: English University Press, 1965.

The chapter on theodicy, miracles and immortality critiques various theodicies (dualistic, monistic, free will, etc.). Lewis concludes that the religious apologist should not put further effort into such arguments. Rather, trust should be placed on faith in God.

1314. Lowe, Susan. "No Love for God?" *Philosophy* 60 (1985): 263-264.

Response to Mora's "Thank God for Evil?" [#1141]. Lowe's argument is that Mora's God is unlovable since the beloved must be perishable and susceptible to misfortunes. [MacKinnon has responded in "Evil and the Vulnerability of God" [#1316].]

1315. MacKinnon, Donald M. "Theology and Tragedy." *Religious Studies* 2 (1966): 163-169.

Argues that a renewed sense of awareness regarding the term "tragic" can be predicated to the Gospel records. [See also MacKinnon's "Atonement and Tragedy" and his "Order and Evil in the Gospel," both of which are published in MacKinnon's *Borderlands of Theology*. London: Lutterworth Publishing, 1968.]

1316. ——. "Evil and the Vulnerability of God." *Philosophy* 62 (1987): 102.

Defends Mora's argument ("Thank God for Evil?" [#1141]), that the object of love must be perishable, against Lowe's critique ("No Love for God?" [#1314]). Lowe claims that Mora's God cannot be loved, yet Mora's argument can be amended by substituting "vulnerable" for "perishable."

1317. Matson, Wallace I. *The Existence of God*. Ithaca, NY: Cornell University Press, 1965.

The chapter on evil (135-170) denies there is a logical contradiction in the Epicurean paradox (the triad of propositions). Matson rejects various solutions: that evil is illusion; the privation of good; the aesthetic view of evil as part of a good whole; the argument that evil exists as a means to a greater good; the free will defense; and an afterlife compensation. He concludes that there cannot exist a being who is at once omnipotent, omnibenevolent and omniscient. [See response by Oakes, "Actualities, Possibilities, and Free Will Theodicy" [#91].]

1318. Mayo, Bernard. "Mr. Keene on Omnipotence." *Mind* 70 (1961): 249-250.

Refutes Keene's solution to the paradox of evil, in "A Simpler Solution to the Paradox of Omnipotence" [#1120]. Keene's statement that "X cannot make things which X cannot control" resolves Mackie's paradox of omnipotence, but only at the price of another dilemma: either all "cannot" statements are rewordable in the same form, or only some such statements are. If only some are, Keene has given no reason for deciding that his rewording of Mackie's second horn is one of them. If all such statements are rewordable, then it follows that the statement entails that anyone's capacity is limited—and this is absurd.

1319. McCullough, H.B. "Theodicy and Mary Baker Eddy." *Sophia* 14 (1975): 12-18.

Contends that virtues like compassion and mercy entail the reality of evil, contra the views of Mary Baker Eddy. The mere appearance of evil as evil is not a sufficient argument, and if there were a world without evil, it is not necessarily better than this world.

1320. McGrath, P.J. "Evil and the Existence of a Finite God." *Analysis* 46 (1986): 63-64.

Rejects Mackie's proposal that theodicy can be resolved only if divine omnipotence or goodness is rejected. A finite God would result from the rejection of divine omnipotence and an indifferent God would result from rejecting divine goodness. Neither is acceptable. [See responses by Suttle, "On God Tolerating Evil" [#143]; Basinger, "Evil and a Finite God: A Response to McGrath" [#1063]; Burke, "Theodicy with a God of Limited Power: A Reply to McGrath" [#1272]; and Crisp, "The Avoidance of the Problem of Evil: A Reply to McGrath" [#1282].]

1321. ———. "Children of a Lesser God? A Reply to Burke and Crisp." *Analysis* 47 (1987): 236-238.

Rejects arguments against his thesis, in "Evil and the Existence of a Finite God" [#1320], by Burke ("Theodicy with a God of Limited Power: A Reply to McGrath" [#1272]); and by Crisp ("The Avoidance of the Problem of Evil" [#1282]). McGrath's point is *not* that the problem of evil remains insoluble when God is conceived as limited in goodness or in power, but the more modest claim that the problem is not eliminated. The argument of critics, that a powerful but finite God cannot eliminate all the world's evils, does not explain why God does not assist us in eliminating evil. [For a response to the McGrath–Burke–Crisp debate, see Peter Hutcheson, "Omniscience and the Problem of Evil," *Sophia* 31 (1992), 53-58. He argues that the option overlooked in the debate is that one option open to the theist is to conceive of God as having limited knowledge. Hutcheson contends that conceiving of God as such, as less than omniscient, does not resolve the theodicy problem.]

1322. Midgley, Mary. *Wickedness: A Philosophical Essay.* London: Routledge and Kegan Paul, 1984.

Argues that moral evil is negative in character and that moral evil is understood best as what is lacking in wickedness, in the lack of concern for others, negligence, aggressiveness, and pride.

1323. Miller, Jerome A. *The Way of Suffering: A Geography of Crisis.* Washington, DC: Georgetown University Press, 1990.

Not a philosophical study of theodicy, but a phenomenological reflection on suffering and crisis, informed by Nietzsche, Heidegger and Sophocles, among others. Suffering is the greatest spiritual teacher, and while the experience of crisis is that which threatens the control we seek over our lives, the lesson we must learn is that we are not ultimately in control of our lives, that suffering is both inevitable and yet the only way to access the deepest realities which admittedly are terrifying and over which we have no control. Miller describes and evaluates a series of different attitudes and modes of being, different existential approaches to life, each progressively harsher than the previous, until he reaches the ultimate crisis of facing death in a heroic manner. He documents the journey that must be undertaken by the individual who allows crisis to uproot his or her life. This is the only means to the spiritual world. [See Miller's "The Way of Suffering: A Reasoning of the Heart" [#1324] for a refinement of the more optimistic aspects of his argument.]

1324.   ———. "The Way of Suffering: A Reasoning of the Heart." *The Existence of God.* Edited by John R. Jacobson and Robert Lloyd Mitchell. London, Lewiston, NY, and Toronto, ON: Edwin Mellen Press, 1988: 281-301.

Maintains it is through suffering that we learn whether God exists. The image of God in classical Christianity betrays us when we suffer the inevitable pains and losses. Our deepest intuition is of despair and the intuition of nothingness. Yet God is found in this nothingness; indeed, God is found *only* in and through nothingness [see #1323].

1325.   Morriston, Wesley. "Gladness, Regret, God, and Evil: A Reply to Hasker." *Southern Journal of Philosophy* 20 (1982): 401-407.

Response to Hasker's "On Regretting the Evils of this World" [#1111]. Morriston rejects Hasker's argument that the suffering and evils in the world cannot be held against God since they were necessary for our existence, and that we are (and should be) glad that we exist. Morriston argues that even if it is correct that all major events of history are necessary for our existence, they are necessary *only* given the natural order that God has established. If God is omnipotent, could there not have been established an order without evils? Hasker's argument is unclear about the conditions under which it is reasonable to lodge a moral complaint against someone.

1326.   Moulder, James. "Philosophy, Religion, and Theodicy." *South African Journal of Philosophy* 3 (1984): 147-150.

This is a review of the theodicies in John Hick's *Philosophy of Religion*, third edition [#749]; Richard Taylor's *Metaphysics*, third edition. Englewood Cliffs, NJ: Prentice-Hall, 1983; George Schlesinger's *Metaphysics* [#420]; and James Crenshaw's edited book, *Theodicy in the Old Testament* [see #1649].

1327.   ———. "In Search of a Theodicy." *Religion in South Africa* (1984): 75-80.

This is a review of *Contemporary Philosophy of Religion*, edited by Cahn and Shatz [#772]; Davies's *An Introduction to the Philosophy of Religion* [#1852]; Kolakowski's *Religion* [#1129]; Mackie's *The Miracle of Theism* [#1220]; and Ward's *Rational Theology and the Creativity of God* [#1182]. Moulder argues that liberation theology needs a theodicy: if God can liberate the oppressed, why does God not do so? Utilitarian responses are unhelpful to the oppressed (Kolakowski and Ward) in arguing that God strives to eliminate not *all* evil, but *unnecessary* evil. Likewise, Libertari an responses that utilize the free will defense are unhelpful: Mackie is correct that there is lack of clarity in what constitutes a free choice. Davies's support of the Thomistic view, that God is the author of all good and evil, likewise is unhelpful to the oppressed.

1328.   Novak, Joseph A. "Comments on Calvert's 'Dualism and the Problem of Evil'."
         Sophia 26 (1987): 42-50.

         Refutes Calvert's arguments ("Dualism and the Problem of Evil" [#1072]) for *a
         necessary evil being*. Novak argues that Calvert assumes some unacceptable
         propositions, and that his arguments are historically inaccurate.

1329.   Novak, Michael. *Belief and Unbelief: A Philosophy of Self-Knowledge*. New
         York: Macmillan, 1965.

         The chapter on theodicy (*Chapter 4*, "God and Evil," 159-174) critiques Aiken's
         theodicy ("Evil and God" [#1195]). Aiken mistakenly understands key terms (omni-
         potence, omniscience, person, moral agent, etc.) as having the same meaning for
         both God and human beings. Novak considers also the nature of the good, making
         use of the definition of good outlined by Gertrude Anscombe (in *Three Philo-
         sophers*. Oxford: Blackwell, 1961, 1963).

1330.   O'Connor, David. "On Failing to Resolve Theism–Versus–Atheism Empirically."
         Religious Studies 26 (1990): 91-103.

         Argues that we cannot make comparisons between how the world would be if God
         did or did not exist. Atheists and theists falsely believe such comparisons can be
         made, and they erroneously draw conclusions about God's existence or non-exis-
         tence, based on the state of the world.

1331.   O'Hear, Anthony. "Suffering and Evil." *Chapter 6* of *Experience, Explanation
         and Faith: An Introduction to the Philosophy of Religion*. London: Routledge and
         Kegen Paul, 1984: 202-234.

         A discussion of theodicies in modern western literature as well as in eastern reli-
         gions. He holds that critics of theism are mistaken in thinking that a life without
         suffering would be better than this present life. Suffering is the catalyst of moral
         qualities. O'Hear contends that hedonistic attacks on religion (e.g., John Mackie)
         fail to the extent that they imply a better world without suffering is possible. He
         rejects Hick's explanation of gratuitous evil, yet defends (with some qualifica-
         tions) Plantinga's free will defense versus Mackie. He defends also Aquinas's
         privation account, process theodicy, and eastern theodicies (Hinduism, Bud-
         dhism). O'Hear concludes that western theodicies see this life merely as a prelude
         to another and that suffering is a mere pitfall along the way. He argues that eastern
         and process theodicies disvalue the process by postulating an Absolute that under-
         lies and completes the process.

1332.   Oates, David. "Social Darwinism and Natural Theodicy." *Zygon, Journal of
         Religion and Science* 23 (1988): 439-454.

         Notes that social Darwinists (Darwin, Wallace, Spenser) utilized various re-
         sponses to the theodicy question: sentimental denial of the problem; optimistic
         belief in progress; and belief in perfection.

1333.   Prazic, Alexander. "An Argument Against Theism." Translated by Bojana Mlade-
         novic. *Contemporary Yugoslav Philosophy: The Analytic Approach*. Edited by
         Alexander Pavković. Boston, MA: Kluwer Academic Publishers, 1988: 251-262.

Rejects the "paradox of omnipotence" (used by John Mackie and others), that if God created a stone that God could not lift, then God would not be omnipotent, and if God could not create such a stone, then God likewise would not be omnipotent. Prazic argues that God is omnipotent *by definition* and, as such, this excludes the very possibility of the creation of such a stone. The argument against divine omnipotence, then, is a sophism which confuses divine power and logical possibility. Prazic argues also that some consequences of omnipotence contradict omniscience: God cannot be conceived as having both attributes without contradiction.

1334.   Prevost, Robert. *Probability and Theistic Explanation.* Oxford: Clarendon Press, 1990.

This is a book-length study of the theologies of Richard Swinburne and Basil Mitchell. The relevant readings discussed include the following: Basil Mitchell, *Justification and Religious Belief.* London: Macmillan, 1973; and *Morality: Religious and Secular.* Oxford: Oxford University Press, 1980; Richard Swinburne, *An Introduction to Confirmation Theory.* London: Methuen, 1973; *Faith and Reason.* Oxford: Oxford University Press, 1980; "Mackie, Induction and God," *Religious Studies* 19 (1983), 385-391; *The Coherence of Theism* [#598]; and *The Existence of God* [#600].

1335.   Quinn, Philip L. "A Pseudosolution to the Problem of Evil." *Zygon, Journal of Religion and Science* 10 (1975): 444-446.

Argues that Hatcher's reformulation of the problem of evil in relative terms ("A Logical Solution to the Problem of Evil" [#1112]) does not take evil seriously. Quinn contends that it is unreasonable to restrict the use of good and evil in a purely relative way: the holocaust is an instance of an absolute evil. [See Hatcher's response, "The Relative Conception of Good and Evil" [#1113].]

1336.   Ray, Bendy Gopal. "Reformulation of the Problem of Evil." *Darshana Institute* 7 (1967): 48-51.

Contends that the problem of evil is a problem of tension that has its source within our being. We seek "the more" (there must be "more" than this life of suffering) and regard it as good, while the fall from "the more" is regarded as evil. Evil is not a problem, then, as far as existence is concerned. The problem arises from reason's attempt to classify things (for example, that God is all-powerful and all-good).

1337.   Resnick, Lawrence. "Evidence, Utility, and God." *Analysis* 31 (1971): 87-90.

Refutes the argument of King-Farlow and Gotkürdel ("Über Formal Entscheidbare Sätzenkonjunktionen der Principia Theologica und Verwandter Systeme" [#1128]), that defends the legitimacy of theism: evil is evidence against God's existence but good is evidence to the contrary. Resnick argues that their appeal to utility of belief, evidence and hypothesis is invalid.

1338.   Rintelen, Fritz J. Von. "Ideas of Good and Evil in Theories of Creation." *Anima* 4 (1978): 52-55. [Translated, revised and abridged from the original German by the editors of *Anima*.]

Sketches the evolution of human deconceptions of creation in order to clarify our present dilemmas in understanding and coping with evil. Irenaeus, Augustine and

Aquinas spoke of a continuous creation, reaffirmed in more modern times by Schleiermacher and Hegel. Despite the inevitable evils of the evolutionary processes, we can exceed to good and to personal dignity.

1339.   Root, Michael. "Creation, Redemption and the Limits of System: A Study of Regin Prenter." *Creation and Method*. Edited by Henry Vander Goot. Washington, DC: University Press of America, 1981: 13-28.

Argues that Regin Prenter's christological focus (*Creation and Redemption*, translated by Theodor I. Jensen. Philadelphia, PA: Fortress Press, 1967) makes his explanation of moral evil unsatisfactory: the "divine victory" theme leads to an understanding of evil as in some sense independent of God, while the "human sacrifice" theme leads to an understanding of evil as grounded in some structure of creation.

1340.   Roth, John K. "The Defense of God: A Reprise." *The Defense of God*. Edited by John Roth and Frederick E. Sontag. New York: Paragon, 1985.

Refers to Reeve Robert Brenner's *The Faith and Doubt of Holocaust Survivors* [#2707], and critiques the responses to the Holocaust of Paul van Buren (*Discerning the Way: A Theology of Jewish Christian Reality* [#2904]) and Arthur Cohen (*The Tremendum: A Theological Interpretation of the Holocaust* [#2730]). Roth finds van Buren's suffering God too weak and contends that Cohen's God of "plenteous unfolding" cannot answer the disaster of the holocaust. Neither can make a strong enough case for redemption by a God who permitted the holocaust. God did not stop the holocaust, Roth argues, and to hope in this God is also to protest against this God. God's involvement with evil is, at times, more than human beings can bear. God alone can end the suffering of the world, but hope that such will take place is not firm in light of the holocaust.

1341.   ———. "Against Despair." *God: The Contemporary Discussion*. Edited by Frederick E. Sontag and M. Darrol Bryant. Barrytown, NY: Rose of Sharon Press, 1982: 345-361.

Contends that the free will defense is no longer credible after Auschwitz. God has given us too much freedom, too soon. The destructive power of human freedom discredits this very freedom. Roth's "theodicy of protest" despairs over the hope that history is evolving toward a final victory, toward a Kingdom of God on earth. His theodicy of protest despairs that there will be any future good to render acceptable the wickedness and suffering in the whole of human experience.

1342.   ———. "A Theodicy of Protest" and "Response." *Encountering Evil*. Edited by Stephen Davis. Atlanta, GA: John Knox Press, 1981: 7-22, 30-37.

Affirms the omnipotence of God and argues that God could intervene but does not do so, in order to permit full reign to freedom in creatures. There is, as such, no divine plan for history. History refutes more than it affirms the providential care of God. Roth rejects the "suffering of God" theme as an inadequate vision of divine power. He rejects theodicies that legitimate evil, and posits a demonic or dark side of God as an explanation for permitting so much devastating evil in the world. [See also Roth's *Problems in the Philosophy of Religion*. Scranton, NY: Chandler, 1971; Relevant also is Roth's "Williams James and Contemporary Religious Thought: The Problem of Evil," *The Philosophy of William James*. Edited by Walter R. Corti. Hamberg: Felix Meiner, 1976.]

1343. ———. "Critique [of Sontag]." *Encountering Evil*. Edited by Stephen T. Davis. Atlanta, GA: John Knox Press, 1981: 157-159.

Refutes Sontag's "Anthropodicy and the Return to God" [#1352]. Roth argues that a clear epistemological basis for Sontag's theodicy is lacking, as is an ethical component: Sontag does not tell us how we are to relate to a God who has forced a game of Russian roulette on us. [Sontag's response follows in the text.]

1344. Russell, Bruce, and Stephen Wykstra. "The 'Inductive Argument from Evil': A Dialogue." *Philosophical Topics* 14 (1988): 133-160.

Written in the form of a dialogue between three professional women in their 30s. The women discuss the recent death of the six-year-old daughter of one of the women. The authors make reference to Swinburne and to the Rowe—Wykstra debate (see Wykstra's "The Humean Obstacle to Evidential Arguments from Suffering: On Avoiding the Evils of 'Appearance'" [#1188] which refutes Rowe's "The Problem of Evil and Some Varieties of Atheism" [#1246]; and Rowe's response, "Evil and the Theistic Hypothesis: A Response to Wykstra" [#1247]). The authors defend Wykstra's argument that God sees goods we cannot see and that, since the universe is the creation of God, it is eminently likely that it is morally good rather than morally shallow. Russell rejects the latter, arguing that it begs the question of God's existence. Wykstra's response is that he needs to show only that it is *possible* that God exists for there to be goods in the evils we experience, goods experienced only by God. [See Russell's "The Persistent Problem of Evil" [#1249].]

1345. Scherer, Donald. "Axiology and the Problem of Evil." *Canadian Journal of Theology* 14 (1968): 222-227.

Contends that there is a problem of evil only if evil is conceived, not as alienation from God, but as moral wrongdoing or as suffering.

1346. Smith, George H. *Atheism: The Case Against God*. Buffalo, NY: Prometheus Press, 1979.

A detailed defense of atheism. Smith presents both philosophical and psychological critiques against the concept of God. *Part Four* discusses the harmful effects of religious teachings: the concepts of hell and sin, and the cultivation of guilt and obedience, in particular.

1347. Smith, Michael. "What's So Good about Feeling Bad?" *Faith and Philosophy* 2 (1985): 424-429.

Presents several criticisms of Stump's theodicy ("The Problem of Evil" [#1173]). Versus the Anselmian-Stump characterization of free will, Smith argues that the nature of the will determines whether or not a will is free, but not how this nature has come about. Versus Stump's strong reliance on heavenly compensation, Smith argues against the view that all evils are instrumental goods. [See Stump's reply, "Suffering for Redemption: A Reply to Smith" [#1174].]

1348. Sontag, Frederick E. *The God of Evil: An Argument from the Existence of the Devil*. New York: Harper and Row, 1970.

Constructs a concept of God from the existence of evil (symbolized in the Devil), rather than from abstract theological concepts. He argues that the only possible answer to atheism is to take all the forces that lead to it and accept these into the nature of God. He argues that God permitted more evil and destructiveness in the world than was necessary. The God of evil may be the only God strong enough to withstand the natural tendency toward atheism. Sontag argues that we must begin the discussion of theodicy with the reality of evil. This defines a conception of a God who tolerates the existence of suffering and misery without being overcome by them. Non-being is the foundation of being. The non-being is God and is responsible for the non-being in the world. [See also Sontag's earlier, "God and Evil," *Religion in Life* 34 (1965), 215-223.]

1349.   ———. *God, Why Did You do That?* Philadelphia, PA: Westminster Press: 1970.

Constructs a concept of God consistent with the reality of the world as it is experienced. In creating the world as it is, God created more evil than was necessary for good ends. God failed to create a world in which more than a few succeed. Sontag argues that God is beyond good and evil, and that the creation and actions by God seem voluntaristic.

1350.   ———. *What Can God Do?* Nashville, TN: Abingdon Press, 1979.

Outlines various options that can be exercised by God and options which cannot be exercised by God in face of the world's evil. God *can* suffer, love, act freely, use force, heal, etc.; God *cannot* control those who represent God, avoid evil, predict the future, speak to us directly, etc. [See also Sontag's *Love Beyond Pain: Mysticism Within Christianity*. New York: Paulist Press, 1977.]

1351.   ———. "Technology and Theodicy: Is God Present in the History of Technology?" *Nature and System* 1 (1979): 265-275. [Reprinted in his *Theology and Technology: Essays in Christian Analysis and Exegesis*. Edited by Carl Mitcham and Jim Grote. Lanham, MD: University Press of America, 1984, 291-301.]

Maintains that with the disillusionment over science and technology as "progress," and the rise of violence in the twentieth century, it is hard to make the case that divine justice is being worked out in the world, despite Teilhard de Chardin's claims to the contrary.

1352.   ———. "Anthropodicy and the Return of God" and "Response." *Encountering Evil*. Edited by Stephen T. Davis. Atlanta, GA: John Knox Press, 1981: 137-151, 160-166.

A summary version of his theodicy. Sontag argues for a new understanding of God. Until this is accomplished, theodicy will continue to be *anthropodicy*, without reference to God. Sontag questions whether we should be arguing that God is free of all responsibility for evil. Since God has remained silent, we have the task of constructing answers to the reasons why God has created a world with so much evil. There may well be *a demonic side to God*, a God who may cause evil for no morally good reason. Intellect and goodness alone do not determine the divine goodness. God's goodness is not evident, simple, beyond debate, nor does it exclude evil. God is responsible for all the structural features of the world and has created a harsher world than was necessary. There is no guarantee that such a God will balance things in the end. Sontag concludes that God must take chances and that the divine control over the world must be loose; this is the reality of a world of the holocaust. [In the "Response," Sontag defends his theodicy against the criticisms of Griffin, Davis, Roth, and Hick, all of which are included in the *Encountering Evil* book.]

1353. ——. "Evil, Being Black and Love." *Journal of the Interdemoninational Theological Center* 10 (1982/1983): 15-19.

Argues that the plight of blacks in America is akin to a continued, slow slavery. He contends, however, that the black church holds the key to a renewed Christian love—if it is able to turn its love and forgiveness outward. The black church has found God in the midst of evil.

1354. ——. "The Discriminatory God: A Theodicy of Inequality." *Encounter* 44 (1983): 391-393.

Holds God responsible for the inequality in the world, women's inequality in particular. As such, God is a discriminatory God. Women were created in a way which disadvantaged them from men, both physically and as those who bear the burden of reproduction.

1355. ——. "Evil, Freedom and the Future." *Encounter* 45 (1984): 139-157.

Contends that America faces the problem of evil anew, due to a number of factors, including the Viet Nam war. The concept of God must be a democratic sharing of power, yet divine love (with reference to Aristotle and Aquinas) provides a way to interpret freedom that stops short of personal and social disintegration. God's omnipotence, as such, is maintained without a wholesale determination of every event.

1356. ——. "The Defense of God." *The Defense of God.* Edited by John K. Roth and Frederick E. Sontag. New York: Paragon Books, 1985: 1-14.

Questions why God has not offered a defense against the attacks made on God via the theodicy issue. From the abuse of Jesus on the cross, down through the centuries, God has not explained the lapses of power and has not made the divine purpose clear. As such, Sontag holds that it is left to theologians to defend God. This is the meaning of faith: to do what God *could* do but *refuses* to do.

1357. ——. "Master of the Universe: Why?" *Encounter* 50 (1989): 141-149.

Recognizing that God is Master of the Universe explains evil in the sense that we now know a God of might, a God who is free to choose a world of destruction and beauty, rather than a God who could have created a less harsh world. Sontag suggests that perhaps the imbalance between good/evil, terror/peace, love/hate, etc., is meant by God to teach us patience until God restructures the world anew.

1358. ——. "The Birth of God." *Encounter* 51 (1990): 285-292.

Argues that theism must become more pluralistic, that we need several doctrines of God.

1359. Sontag, Frederick E., and John K. Roth. "Toward a New American Theodicy." *Drew Gateway* 46 (1975/1976): 56-64.

Maintains that we can no longer hold, as did the colonials, that evil and suffering are the result of divine retribution. Nor can we hold that America will achieve an earthly paradise. God's power has been democratically distributed so that evil and destruction inevitably ensue. The notion of America as the New Israel, as such, implies suffering, as was the case with ancient Israel. [See also other relevant collaborations by Sontag and Roth: *God and America's Future*. Wilmington, NC: Consortium Books, 1977, and *The American Religious Experience*. New York: Harper and Row, 1972.]

1360.   Springsted, Eric O. "Is There a Problem with the Problem of Evil?" *International Philosophical Quarterly* 24 (1984): 303-312.

Holds that in order to discuss the problem of evil, it is necessary to understand how the believer regards evil. Failure to do so results in an argument against belief that is not convincing to the believer, and to a distorted picture of the religion that is being discussed philosophically. The *logical* problem of evil interpenetrates with the *existential* problem of evil, and it is mistaken to reduce one of the problems to the other. Theists often believe in a sovereign good that is not incommensurable with evil of any kind and, as such, philosophical discussion of the problem of evil often fails to convince anyone who already believes in God. Flew's argument, that theism dies the death of a thousand qualifications ("Divine Omniscience and Human Freedom" [#45]), is an example of mistaking what the believer really is doing.

1361.   Stace, Walter. "The Problem of Evil." *Philosophy, Religion, and the Coming World Civilization*. Edited by L.S. Rouner. The Hague: Martinus Nijhoff, 1966: 123-134.

Contends that neither absolute idealism nor mysticism can solve the problem of evil. The solution lies, rather, in comprehending that it is logically impossible for there to be a world without evil, just as a concave entails a convex.

1362.   Surin, Kenneth. "Atonement and Christology." *Neue Zeitschrift für Systematische Theologie und Religionsphilosophie* 24 (1982): 131-149.

Argues that "functional" christologies are lacking inasmuch as they cannot derive a salvation-scheme which accords fully with the central Christian affirmation that in Jesus, God acted decisively in history to bring salvation to humankind. Surin argues for a view of christology and atonement that conceives the incarnation in ontological terms, following Irenaeus, and as defined by Stephen Sykes. [See Sykes, "The Theology of the Humanity of Christ," in *Christ, Faith and History: Cambridge Studies in Christology*. New York and Cambridge: Cambridge University Press, 1972.]

1363.   ———. "Revelation, Salvation, the Uniqueness of Christ and Other Religions." *Religious Studies* 19 (1983): 323-343.

Notes that one of the methodological difficulties which encompasses attempts to formulate a plausible syncretism (Hinduism and Christianity) is enlightened by the construction of a phenomenology of moral evil and a religious anthropology. Surin argues for an incarnational view of salvation.

1364.   ———. *Theology and the Problem of Evil*. Oxford: Blackwell, 1986.

Argues that theodicy cannot be a responsible theological discourse as long as it remains historical and of merely theoretical interest. Surin seeks a new kind of discourse about the problem of evil (following Dorothee Soelle, Moltmann, and P.T. Forsyth), a *practical*, versus *theoretical*, theodicy. The focus should be on historically situated evils, and practical concerns about the elimination of evil, rather than on explanations for evil. There should be concern also with the political and societal consequences of such. [See also Surin's "Theistic Arguments and Rational Theism," *International Journal for Philosophy of Religion* 16 (1984), 123-125.]

1365.   ——. "Theodicy?" *Harvard Theological Review* 76 (1983): 225-247.

Asserts that there are three main reasons why theodicy fails: (1) the Enlightenment (as Becker notes) turned *theodicy* into *anthropodicy*; (2) the abstract conception of evil used by theodicists; and (3) theodicy involves the application of principles of reason to a problem which defies reason. Surin argues that theodicy must be addressed from its practical and soteriological aspects, rather than theoretically. This supports Whitehead's and Moltmann's theology of the "suffering God," rather than a theoretical theodicy, like John Hick's.

1366.   ——. "Tragedy and the Soul's Conquest of Evil." *New Blackfriars* 62 (1981): 521-532.

Response to W.W. Bartley's arguments in "The Soul's Conquest of Evil" (in *Talk of God*. Edited by G.N.A. Versey. London: Macmillan, 1969, 86-99). Surin challenges Bartley's contention that only a few gifted individuals are capable of acting in a truly moral manner, and that it is impossible for a person to subdue his or her own evil will. He agrees with Bartley that self-knowledge is a necessary condition of the soul's conquest of evil, but not the sufficient condition. While Bartley is right to be pessimistic about our ability to overcome tragic evil, he is right for the wrong reasons. Such evil can only be overcome by the creator.

1367.   ——. "Review Symposium." *Horizons, Journal of the College Theology Society* 18 (1991): 290-295.

Review of Tilley's *The Evils of Theodicy* [#1254], which incorporates and extends Surin's own work, as well as the writings of others like Michael Buckley and Jeffrey Stout. Surin agrees that theodicy is possible only in the historical, cultural and intellectual context of the European Enlightenment. He contends that Tilley's failure to take into account the exchange between John R. Searle (Limited, Inc. Evanston, IL: Northwestern University Press, 1988, containing collected essays of Searle's) and Jacques Derrida ("Reiterating the Differences," *Glyph* 1 [1977], 198-208) is problematic. [Other references to Searle and Derrida are listed in the bibliography in Tilley's book. See also Tilley's response, following in the text, 306-312.]

1368.   Sutherland, Stewart. "Horrendous Evils and the Goodness of God—II." *Aristotelian Society: Supplementary Volume* 63 (1989): 311-323.

Response to Marilyn McCord Adams ("Horrendous Evils and the Goodness of God" [#1058]). Sutherland contrasts Adams's response to horrendous evil with that of Tolstoy (*Confessions*). Adams appeals to transcendent goods that defeat horrendous evils. Such a solution was not available to the secular Tolstoy. Adams substitutes "how" questions for "why" questions. [See the response by

Adams in her slightly revised version of the original article, in *The Problem of Evil*, edited by Marilyn McCord Adams and Robert Merrihew Adams [see #1058].]

1369.   Sutton, Robert C. "The Human Question: Reflections on the Problem of Evil." *Drew Gateway* 53 (1983): 47-54.

Following a distinction made by Alan Watts (*The Two Hands of God: The Myth of Polarity*. New York: Collier Books, 1963), Sutton argues that discussions of the problem of evil often confuse spheres (existential/narrative, logical/propositional, psychological/scientific, religious/mythological, and theological/propositional). He argues also that it is a categorial mistake to deny or criticize the reasoning and expression of one sphere, based on modes appropriate to another. [See also Alan Watts's chapter, "The Problem of Evil," in his *The Supreme Identity: An Essay on Oriental Metaphysics and the Christian Religion*. New York: Vintage Books, 1972.]

1370.   Wainwright, William J. "The Presence of Evil and the Falsification of Theistic Assertions." *Religious Studies* 4 (1969): 213-216.

Argues that several arguments which have been offered to show that theistic assertions are not falsifiable are, in fact, inconclusive. The presence of a certain amount of evil does count against belief, and people indeed have abandoned faith because of the presence of evil. Evil, as such, can falsify belief (*contra* the falsification challenge of Flew).

1371.   ———. *Philosophy of Religion*. Belmont, CA: Wadsworth, 1988.

Chapter 3 ("The Problem of Evil," 66-98) rejects the greater goods defense and the free will defense. The former does not account for the quantity of evils, while the latter cannot account for natural evils. Wainwright argues that theists do not explain evil, gratuitous evil in particular.

1372.   West, Philip. "Christology as 'Ideology'." *Theology* 88 (1985): 428-436.

Critique of MacKinnon's theology (*Borderlands of Theology* [see #1315]). West rejects MacKinnon's characterization of the work of Christ as "tragedy." [See response by Surin, "Christology, Tragedy and 'Ideology'" [#2403].]

1373.   Wetzel, James. "Can Theodicy be Avoided?: The Claim of Unredeemed Evil." *Religious Studies* 25 (1989): 1-13.

Examines Surin's argument for practical theodicy, comparing it with the minimalist theodicy of Plantinga and the speculative theodicies of Hick and Swinburne. Wetzel concludes that practical theodicies (Surin's and Soelle's) will be hard pressed to eliminate traditional theoretical theodicy. The latter is necessary as long as we have not explained unredeemed evil.

1374.   Williams, Robert R. "Sin and Evil." *Christian Theology*. Edited by Peter C. Hodgson and Robert H. King. Philadelphia, PA: Fortress Press, 1982: 168-195.

Critically assesses the Augustinian formulation of the doctrine of original sin that has dominated Christian theodicy until the modern period. Williams concludes that there are several problems with the Augustinian doctrine. The doctrine of the elect, for example, casts doubt upon the benevolence of God, and in deriving all evil from the fall, the doctrine fails to acknowledge the tragic depth and flaw in human freedom. Williams concludes that Hick's Irenaean theodicy offers more promise and rightly has become dominant among contemporary theodicies.

1375. Wisdom, John. "God and Evil." *Mind* 44 (1935): 1-20.

Contends that God and evil are not incompatible, if evils are logically necessary parts of good wholes and if less evil would imply less value could be realized. Also, the goodness of the wholes is not derived entirely from the goodness of the parts. It cannot be proved that no world containing evil could be the best logically possible world; yet only if this could be proved could evil be used as proof for the non-existence of God, defined as an all-powerful perfection.

1376. Zimmerman, Marvin. "A Note on the Problem of Evil." *Mind* 70 (1961): 253-254.

Response to Farrell's challenge ("Evil and Omnipotence" [#1087]) to Mackie's contention ("Evil and Omnipotence" [#1217]) that no proposed solution to the problem of evil can withstand criticism. Zimmerman contends that Farrell's solution has inconsistencies and contradictions, thereby adding weight to Mackie's original contention.

IV God and the Good [Ethics and Theodicy]

1377. Adams, Robert Merrihew. "A Modified Divine Command Theory of Ethical Wrongness." *Religion and Morality*. Edited by Gene Outka and John P. Reeder, Jr. New York: Doubleday, 1973: 318-347.

Defends the metaethical interpretation of "wrong" as meaning "contrary to God's commands."

1378. ———. "Autonomy and Theological Ethics." *Religious Studies* 15 (1979): 191-194.

Defends the belief that right action is commanded by God, and responds to the common objection to this view—that it is incompatible with autonomy. He discusses the concepts of "responsibility" and "motives," in order to argue against reasons to believe that we ought to be autonomous, automonous in a sense that is incompatible with seeing moral action as obedience to God.

1379. ———. "Divine Command Meta-ethics Modified Again." *Journal of Religious Ethics* 7 (1979): 66-79. [Reprinted in Adams's *The Virtue of Faith*. New York and Oxford: Oxford University Press, 1987, 128-143.]

Maintains that the property of ethical wrongness is identical with the property of acting contrary to the commands of a loving God.

1380. Basinger, David. "Kai Nielsen and the Nature of Theistic Ethics." *Journal of the Evangelical Theological Society* 24 (1981): 233-238.

Argues against Kai Nielsen's view [see #1407, one of Nielsen's numerous books and articles on this topic]. Basinger refers specifically to Nielsen's "History of Ethics," *Encyclopedia of Philosophy* III (New York: Macmillan, 1967): 108; and Nielsen's *Ethics Without God* [#1447], etc. Nielsen holds that the nonexistence of God does not preclude the possibility of there being an objective standard on which to base moral judgments. Basinger contends that theists must admit Nielsen's point, that they affirm "God is good" because the actions and attitudes in question are consistent with their moral sensibilities. To affirm "God is a being worthy of worship" has been tested by its consistency with moral expectations. But, contra Nielsen, the theist need not grant the point that the moral criteria used by theists to evaluate God's goodness constitute a moral standard that is separate from and more fundamental than is the divine moral code being judged. The theist can hold that we are created by God with an innate moral sense that is divine in principle.

1381. Brown, Patterson. "Religious Morality." *Mind* 72 (1963): 235-244.

Argues that there would be no necessity for salvation without evil. Since God causes or allows evil to exist as evil, it is a good; otherwise, God would not be God. [Reprinted in Keith Yandell, *God, Man and Religion* [#170], with a response by Campbell, "Patterson Brown on God and Evil" [#1387].]

1382. ———. "God and the Good." *Religious Studies* 3 (1967): 269-276.

Contains a unified version of his arguments in "Religious Morality" [#1381] and "Religious Morality: A Reply to Flew and Campbell" [#1383]. If moral judgments are made on religious grounds (as God's will), then God's existence has been presupposed. As such, the judgments about evils as judged by God's will cannot count against God's existence. [Reprinted in Yandell's *God, Man and Religion* [#170]. See Dore's critique, "Ethical Supernaturalism and the Problem of Evil" [#1390].]

1383. ———. "Religious Morality: A Reply to Flew and Campbell." *Mind* 77 (1968): 577-580.

Response to Flew ("The Religious Morality of Mr. Patterson Brown" [#1394]), and Campbell ("Patterson Brown on God and the Good" [#1387]). Brown defends his arguments in "Religious Morality" [#1381]. He contends that Campbell's position leads to an infinite regress regarding the criterion of goodness. [Reprinted in Yandell, *God, Man and Religion* [#170].]

1384. Brown, Robert F. "God's Ability to Will Moral Evil." *Faith and Philosophy* 8 (1991): 3-20.

Elaborates upon and extends the arguments of Pike ("Omnipotence and God's Ability to Sin" [#98]); Reichenbach ("Why is God Good?" [#1412]); and others (e.g., Harrison, "Geach on God's Ability to Do Evil" [#246]), all of which hold that classical Christianity has an inadequate view of God's goodness in relation to God's freedom and the power to do what is morally evil. Pike's position has not shown how to conceive God as having the freedom to will (and the power to carry out) moral evil. The traditional doctrine of God needs more extensive modification than Pike and others realize. Brown proposes a *voluntaristic* (libertarian) conception of God's will as the means to carry through consistently the program of Pike and Reichenbach. God's free will must be coequal with God's ontologically good nature.

1385. Brümmer, Vincent. "Divine Impeccability." *Religious Studies* 20 (1984): 203-214.

Holds that it is logically impossible that God could be the author of any state of affairs which God has not approved, and that God could approve any state of affairs which is evil. God does not approve evil and is not the cause of states not approved by God; God cannot sin. [See Helm's response, "God and the Approval of Sin" [#1397].]

1386. Campbell, C.A. "Theism and the Problem of Evil: (1) Sin"; and "Theism and the Problem of Evil: (2) Suffering." *On Selfhood and Godhood.* London: Allen and Unwin. New York: Macmillan, 1957: 269-306.

Contends that moral evil presents no problem for theism. Undeserved suffering that is intense and of long duration is a serious problem, and it makes no sense to speak of discipline and spiritual enrichment with respect to such evils. Campbell rejects the solutions that deny God is all-powerful, and that hold the devil responsible for evil and suffering. He rejects also the solution that there is no undeserved suffering, since humans are innately bad. Undeserved suffering may be explained as logically bound up with the conditions of a world that is the best possible (conceivable); yet this theory is ultimately inadequate: God could have made creatures such that we cannot experience intense and prolonged agony. Campbell supports the theory of immortality as the most promising solution to theodicy. [See two relevant responses by Errol Harris, "Selfhood and Godhood" [#1106]; and John Collins, "C.A. Campbell and the Problem of Suffering" [#1280].]

1387. Campbell, Keith. "Patterson Brown on God and Evil." *Mind* 74 (1965): 582-584. [Reprinted in Yandell, *God, Man and Religion* [#170].]

Response to Brown's "Religious Morality" [#1381]. Campbell argues that there is no prior system of evaluation by which to judge God's word as the standard of morality. He contends that Brown's appeal to God as such as standard is irrational. [See Brown's response, "Religious Morality: A Reply to Flew and Campbell" [#1383].]

1388. Clark, Stephen R.L. "God, Good and Evil." *Proceedings of the Aristotelian Society* 77 (1976/1977): 247-264.

Maintains that the problem of evil is not a refutation of theism since, in a world created by God, there can be no independent standard of right. Whether things were good or bad, there can be no charge against God.

1389. Donnelly, John. "Some Remarks on Geach's Predicative and Attributive Adjectives." *Notre Dame Journal of Formal Logic* 13 (1971): 125-128.

Argues that Geach's distinction ("God and Evil" [#1424]) between logically *predicative* adjectives and logically *attributive* adjectives is invalid. [See response by Stevenson, "Donnelly on Geach" [#1456].]

1390. Dore, Clement. "Ethical Supernaturalism and the Problem of Evil." *Religious Studies* 8 (1972): 97-113.

Rejects Patterson Brown's claim ("God and the Good" [#1382]), that the theist as an ethical supernaturalist—as one who identifies the good as having its source in God's will—need not be concerned with theodicy. Dore argues that

Brown's arguments—that the theist is an ethical supernaturalist and that theists are ethical supernaturalists with respect to all their moral judgements—are questionable contentions.

1391. Ehman, Robert R. "On the Reality of the Moral Good." *Review of Metaphysics* 16 (1962): 45-54.

Holds that moral failure is inseparable from the very conception of the good. The proper conception of the realization of good includes moral failure.

1392. Faber, Paul. "The Euthyphro Objection to Divine Normative Theories: A Response." *Religious Studies* 21 (1985): 559-572.

A defense of divine normative theories, versus MacIntyre's contemporary version of the Euthyphro objection (Alasdair MacIntrye, "Atheism and Morals" [see #1405]). Faber argues that the Euthyphro objection is not troublesome for the divine normative theorist. If one has grounds for holding a divine normative theory, the theory is not threatened by the Euthyphro objection.

1393. Fletcher, Joseph. "An Odyssey: From Theology to Humanism." *Religious Humanism* 18 (1979): 146-157.

Contends that God is dead, as far as ethics is concerned. There is an autonomy of ethics from theism. Morality is not based on God: God is based on morality and on human images.

1394. Flew, Antony G. "The Religious Morality of Mr. Patterson Brown." *Mind* 74 (1965): 578-581.

Rejects Brown's view of morality ("Religious Morality" [#1381]) as dependent upon God and, as such, supposedly (according to Brown) a solution to the theodicy issue. Flew holds that Brown's position assumes an understanding of God as naked power, and that even if Brown were correct, there would be a new version of the problem of evil: how is the suffering we experience compatible with other divine attributes (love and knowledge)? [Reprinted in Yandell, *God, Man and Religion* [#170].]

1395. Fulmer, Gilbert. "Review of Peter Geach, *Providence and Evil*." *Southwestern Journal of Philosophy* 10 (1979): 203-209.

Argues that Geach [#1426] has not defined divine almightiness fully, despite its central importance for his enterprise. Fulmer rejects also Geach's view that God knows the future because God has caused it. Geach's chapter on theodicy *(Chapter 4)* does not acknowledge recent arguments about the issue, and Geach falsely *assumes* God's existence and nature by an appeal to revelation. Fulmer rejects also Geach's explanation of animal pain. God, according to Geach, cannot be reproached for permitting such suffering, since God cannot feel sympathy for physical pain. Fulmer objects, moreover, to Geach's view that God cannot be judged by the same standards by which we judge human actions. As such, the battle to justify divine goodness is not won but, rather, abandoned by Geach. Other criticisms are centered about Geach's naïve rejection of evolutionary theory and his attribution of acts of God that would be evil if performed by human beings. [See Geach's response in "An Exchange (between Peter Geach and Gilbert Fulmer)" [#1428].]

1396.   Goldstick, D. "Monotheism's Euthyphro Problem." *Canadian Journal of Philosophy* 4 (1974): 585-589.

Proposes a moral argument against theism. Goldstick argues that the view that whatever God wills is morally right commits the theist to the ethical position that "might is right." This is a good moral reason for the rejection of theism.

1397.   Helm, Paul. "God and the Approval of Sin." *Religious Studies* 20 (1984): 215-222.

Refutation of Brümmer's argument ("Divine Impeccability" [#1385]), that God (logically) cannot sin. Helm contends that Brümmer's account is cogent only if Swinburne's account (with which he disagrees) is, and hence that Brümmer's account is either not cogent or collapses into Swinburne's. Brümmer is wrong in assuming that only a God who could (logically) sin would be omnipotent. Helm rejects also Brümmer's claim that since it is logically impossible for God to sin, God's agency cannot be rational. He argues also that if the free will defense succeeds, Brümmer's thesis fails, and vice versa. The free will defense succeeds by showing that the proposition "God creates free individuals such that it is impossible for them to do moral evil" is inconsistent; yet if this were so, the proposition that "God is such that he can perform morally evil actions" is inconsistent. [See Brümmer's response, "Paul Helm on God and the Approval of Sin" [#22]. See also Paul Helm's *Divine Commands and Morality*. Oxford: Oxford University Press, 1981.]

1398.   Howsepian, A.A. "Is God Necessarily Good?" *Religious Studies* 27 (1991): 473-484.

Contends that God's goodness is accidental to the divine nature. He argues that God is *contingently* good, and that this is a faithful articulation of one facet of Anselm's core intuition of God's "greatest conceivable being." Maximal benevolence means to be wholly good and to have the ability to perform a maximal set of good actions. Also, if refraining from an evil action can be a good action or part of a good action, Howsepian concludes that a *necessarily* omnipotent and omniscient being could not be both necessarily good and maximally good, since a necessarily good, omniscient and omnipotent being could not possibly refrain from evil.

1399.   Kane, G. Stanley. "The Concept of Divine Goodness and the Problem of Evil." *Religious Studies* 20 (1984): 49-72.

Argues that we must accept "goodness" as applying both to humans and to God. One cannot defend traditional theism by maintaining that God's goodness differs from ours. Kane rejects the view that divine goodness is unintelligible to human beings. He refutes the theodicies of Barth and Brunner, in particular the "Ash'arite views" expressed in them. [See G. Legenhausen, "Notes Towards an Ash'arite Theodicy" [#1402].]

1400.   King, James T. "The Problem of Evil and the Meaning of Good." *Proceedings of the American Catholic Philosophical Association* 44 (1970): 185-194.

Response to William McMahon's claim ("The Problem of Evil and the Possibility of a Better World" [#389]), that a satisfactory solution to the problem of evil has not been elaborated sufficiently by either theists or anti-theists. King argues that the problem of evil, given an emotive or intuitionist or theonomous reading, disappears. So likewise do its solutions. Theodicy is a genuine problem only if it is given a utilitarian reading.

1401. ———. "The Meta-Ethical Dimension of the Problem of Evil." *Journal of Value Inquiry* 5 (1971): 174-184.

Argues that if the moral language employed in the problem of evil is accepted according to some forms of emotive, intuitive or theonomous interpretations, the problem will vanish and the question of the existence or nonexistence of God will be settled on the grounds of the usages involved. Accordingly, King argues that the problem of evil ought to be stated in utilitarian language; as such, the problem has the logical status of a genuine problem.

1402. Legenhausen, G. "Notes Towards an Ash'arite Theodicy." *Religious Studies* 24 (1988): 257-266.

Examines the implications for theodicy of the writings of tenth century Muslim theologian, al-Ash'ari, who advocated the divine command theory of morality (that God, as author of moral law, is not subject to it). Legenhausen argues that this theory need not been accepted in order to endorse the al-Ash'arite's contention that it is not wrong for God to permit avoidable evil. All that is required is a moral relativism, according to which the moral quality of an act is relative to whether it is performed by God or by creatures. Avoidable evil is *existentially*, but not *morally* permitted by God. Legenhausen defends Ash'arite theodicy against the criticisms by Stanley Kane ("The Concept of Divine Goodness and the Problem of Evil" [#1399]), who rejected its versions in Barth and Brunner. Legenhausen concludes that the problem of evil is resolved, not by compromising divine power, but by exalting God above human morality.

1403. Lewis, Charles. "Divine Goodness and Worship Worthiness." *International Journal for Philosophy of Religion* 14 (1983): 143-158.

Seeks a concept of divine goodness as a "religious" concept with respect to its origin within the biblical attitude of worship. The problem of evil has become more of a problem because philosophers and theologians have sought a God, based on the Greek influence, who is worthy of worship. This is contrary to the biblical God who was worshipped as a power which sent both good and evil. According to the biblical accounts, God's goodness is based in the divine salvific power.

1404. Linville, Mark D. "On Goodness: Human and Divine." *American Philosophical Quarterly* 27 (1990): 143-52.

Proposes a solution to the Euthyphro dilemma. The key is to identify the ultimate moral criterion as God's necessarily good nature and then understand this goodness *analogically* rather than *literally*. This provides moral grounds for obeying God without thereby presupposing some moral principle independent of God.

1405. MacIntyre, Alasdair C. *The Religious Significance of Atheism*. New York: Columbia University Press, 1963.

A chapter entitled "Atheism and Morals" presents a contemporary version of the Euthyphro objection: if a divine normative theory is true, then God's power, not

God's goodness, justifies worship of God. [See response by Faber, "The Euthyphro Objection to Divine Normative Theories: A Response" [#1392].]

1406.   McDonnell, Devin. "The Consequentialist Controversy." *Modern Schoolman* 56 (1979): 201-215.

Argues against Richard McCormick's consequentialist theory of morality (*Ambiguity in Moral Choice* [#3476]), and supports the arguments of Germain Grisez and Russell Shaw against consequentialism (*Beyond the New Morality: The Responsibilities of Freedom*, Notre Dame, IN: University of Notre Dame Press, 1974). McDonnell argues that the latter is compatible with moral freedom and evil.

1407.   Nielsen, Kai. "God and the Basis of Morality." *Journal of Religious Ethics* 10 (1982): 335-350.

Contends that belief in God is not necessary to give morality an appropriate ground and rationale, an argument that has been repeated in various forms. [See Kai Nielsen's "Some Remarks on the Independence of Morality from Religion," *Mind* 70 (1961), 175-186; "God and the Good: Does Morality Need Religion?" [#1446]; *Ethics Without God* [#1447]; and "On Religion and the Grounds of Moral Belief," *Religious Humanism* 11 (1977), 33-34; and numerous other publications by Nielsen.]

1408.   Penelhum, Terence. "Divine Goodness and the Problem of Evil." *Religious Studies* 3 (1967): 95-108. [Also published in *The Problem of Evil*. Edited by Marilyn McCord Adams and Robert Merrihew Adams. New York: Oxford University Press, 1990, 69-82.]

Refutes the claim of Pike ("Hume on Evil" [#1157]) and Chisholm (in a seminar discussion: see Chisholm's published version, "The Defeat of Good and Evil" [#1074]), that an agnostic stance is sufficient to refute the logical problem of evil. Penelhum argues that agnosticism challenges belief in the goodness of God. The theist is committed to some theodicy, since one cannot remain agnostic about the range of purposes for which God would allow evil. The more specific the moral code, the more precise must be the suggestions about the possible divine reasons for allowing particular evils. The theist cannot be totally agnostic about the reasons God would permit evil since the theist's moral principles exclude many possible reasons. Thus, the theist's moral principles must implicitly or explicitly include every possible justification for evil. Penelhum rejects the claim of theists that the atheist must show it is a necessary truth that God has no morally sufficient reason for allowing evil. The Protestant ethic has two prominent features that delimit the reasons for evil, reasons that count as morally sufficient: (1) principles that assign priorities and guidelines in moral situations, and (2) the personal qualities and relationships founded upon love. [See Pentz's response, "Rules and Values and the Problem of Evil" [#1409]; and Delmas Lewis's comment in "The Problem with the Problem of Evil" [#1311].]

1409.   Pentz, Rebecca D. "Rules and Values and the Problem of Evil." *Sophia* 21 (1982): 23-29.

Defends Pike's claim ("Hume on Evil" [#1157]) against Penelhum ("Divine Goodness and the Problem of Evil" [#1408]). Pike (see also Chisholm, "The

Defeat of Good and Evil" [#1074]) has argued that it is possible for an omnipotent and omniscient being to allow suffering without being morally culpable. Pentz refutes Penelhum's claim that the moral principles endorsed by the theist are restrictive enough to ensure God's culpability. Penelhum fails to identify the difference between moral rules and moral values.

1410.   Post, H.R. "On a Good-Evil Asymmetry." *Mind* 71 (1962): 96-97.

Argues that there are some cases where an objective assignment of the terms "good" and "evil," respectively, to two alternative courses of action or motives is possible.

1411.   Reichenbach, Bruce. "The Divine Command Theory of Objective Good." *The Georgetown Symposium on Ethics.* Edited by Rocco Porreco. Lanham, MD: University Press of America, 1984: 219-233.

Defends the divine command theory of ethics against various criticisms: [1] that it entails arbitrariness on behalf of the divine will (Patrick Nowell-Smith, "Religion and Morality" [#1449]; Thomas Mayberry, "Morality and the Deity" [#1444]; [2] that there is a vicious circularity in defining God in terms of goodness and goodness in terms of God (A.C. Ewing, *Prospects for Metaphysics* [#1420]; and A.C. Ewing, "Ethics and Belief in God," *Hibbert Journal* 39 [1941], 375-388; [3] that it violates moral authority (K. Campbell, "Patterson Brown on God and Evil" [#1387]); and [4] that it is a relic of an infantile stage of moral theory (Patrick Nowell-Smith, "Morality: Religious and Secular" [#1449]. Reichenbach argues that utilizing the kind of approach of Henry Veatch (*The Ontology of Morals* [#1458], and "Language and Ethics: What's Hecuba to Him or He to Hecuba?" [see #1458]) provides the kind of metaphysical framework within which can be constructed the kind of justification demanded by the ethical theorist, without appealing to an autonomous ethic. There is objective good in the telos of created beings; divine commands are justified and reasonable insofar as they are grounded in that telos; they are commands whose character aids in human self-actualization or self-fulfilment.

1412.   ———. "Why is God Good?" *Journal of Religion* 60 (1980): 51-66.

Contends that God is good because of the divine nature and divine actions, perfection and moral quality, respectively. Reichenbach rejects Aquinas's account of divine goodness: Aquinas's God cannot be significantly free, since his God is not free with respect to the rightness of the divine acts. Aquinas's God is not good in the *moral* sense, but is good only *ontologically*.

1413.   Rigali, Norbert J. "Evil and Models of Christian Ethics." *Horizons, Journal of the College Theology Society* 8 (1981): 7-22.

Asserts that relational moral theology should replace the moderate consequentialism of much moral theology. The latter developed out of an insufficient reconsideration of the traditional ethical categories (moral and physical evils), and resulted in only a slight modification of them. What is needed is a radical reconsideration of evil that introduces a theological understanding of evil into moral theology. Rigali proposes that evil must be understood in terms of a *relational* model of moral norms and decision-making. This view sees the moral subject as a person in relation to all of reality, rather than as a person with ends and means (as in consequentialism).

1414. Swinburne, Richard G. "Duty and the Will of God." *Canadian Journal of Philosophy* 4 (1974): 213-227.

Proposes a resolution to the problem first stated in Plato's *Euthyphro*. Are actions that are obligatory, obligatory since God makes them so (by commanding them), or does God urge us to do them because they are obligatory anyway? The theist can hold the first view for actions that are contingently obligatory and the second for actions that are necessarily obligatory, actions for which the obligation is a *necessary*, rather than a *contingent* moral truth.

1415. Tan, Tai Wei. "Morality and the God of Love." *Sophia* 26 (1987): 20-26.

Resolves the dilemma of ethical monotheism posed by Plato in *Euthyphro*. Can a thing be good because God wills it? Is God subject to the moral law? Would this not deny God's supremacy as creator of all? The dilemma can be resolved through an understanding of the nature of morality in relation to love. Divine love fulfils the moral law. Tan argues that love transcends itself into moral behavior, without being tied up with the notion of obedience to the moral law.

V   Related Publications on God and the Good
[Selected]

1416. Adams, Robert Merrihew. "Christian Liberty." *Philosophy and the Christian Faith*. Edited by Thomas V. Morris. Notre Dame, IN: University of Notre Dame Press, 1988: 151-171.

1417. Alston, William P. "Some Suggestions for Divine Command Theorists." *Philosophy and the Christian Faith*. Edited by Thomas V. Morris. Notre Dame, IN: University of Notre Dame Press, 1988: 303-326.

1418. Bennett, James O. "Beyond 'Good and Evil': A Critique of Richard Taylor's 'Moral Voluntarism'" [A section of Taylor's *Good and Evil* [#3658]], *Journal of Value Inquiry* 12 (1978): 313-319.

1419. Carney, Frederick S. "On McCormick and Teleological Morality." *Journal of Religious Ethics* 16 (1978): 81-107. [Discussion about Aquinas.]

1420. Ewing, A.C. *Prospects for Metaphysics*. London: Allen and Unwin, 1961. [See also Ewing's "Ethics and Belief in God," *Hibbert Journal* 39 (1941), 375-388.]

1421. Fisher, Carlton D. "Because God Says So." *Philosophy and the Christian Faith*. Edited by Thomas V. Morris. Notre Dame, IN: University of Notre Dame Press, 1988: 355-377.

1422. Frank, Richard. "Can God Do What is Wrong?" *Divine Omniscience and Omnipotence in Medieval Philosophers*. Edited by Tamar Rudavsky. Dordrecht and Boston, MA: Reidel, 1985: 69-79.

1423. Garcia, Jorge J.E. "Evil and the Transcendentality of Goodness: Suaréz's Solution to the Problem of Positive Evils." *Being and Goodness*. Edited by Scott MacDonald. Ithaca, NY: Cornell University Press, 1991: 151-176. [Defends a Thomist doctrine of transcendence of goodness. See also J. Garcia's "Goods and Evils" *Philosophy and Phenomenological Research* 47 (1987), 385-412; J. Garcia's

"Good and Evil," *Handbook of Metaphysics/Ontology*. Edited by H. Berkhardt and B. Smith. München, Hamden, and Wien: Philosophia Verlag, 1991; and J. Garcia and Douglas Davis, *The Metaphysics of Good and Evil According to Suaréz: Metaphysical Disputations X and XI and Selected Pages from Disputations XXIII and Other Works*. Translated and with an introduction and notes. München, Hamden, and Wien: Philosophia Verlag, 1989.]

1424.   Geach, Peter T. "Good and Evil." *Analysis* 17 (1956): 33-42. [See response by MacIver, "Good and Evil and Mr. Geach" [#1442].]

1425.   ———. *God and the Soul*. New York: Schocken Books, 1969, and London: Kegan Paul, 1969. [Discusses reincarnation *(Chapter 1)*; immortality *(Chapter 2)*; and various issues, including "The Moral Law and the Law of God" *(Chapter 9)*. He argues that knowledge of God's moral law is not the prerequisite of all moral knowledge; we must know God's law to know that we must not do evil in order that good may come about.]

1426.   ———. *Providence and Evil*. New York: Cambridge University Press, 1977. [Discusses four possible views of divine omnipotence *(Chapters 1-3)*, animal pain and a rejection of evolutionary theory *(Chapter 4)*, original sin *(Chapter 5)*, freedom: chance is compatible with divine providence *(Chapter 6)*, and hell *(Chapter 7)*. Argues that what is good for God is not necessarily what humans regard as good. See Fulmer's critical response, "Review of Peter Geach, *Providence and Evil*" [#1395].]

1427.   ———. "Can God Fail to Keep Promises?" *Philosophy* 52 (1977): 93-95. [Response to Harrison, "Geach on God's Alleged Inability to Do Evil" [#246], which refutes Geach's arguments in "Omnipotence" [#233].]

1428.   Geach, Peter T., and Gilbert Fulmer. "An Exchange." *Southwestern Journal of Philosophy* 11 (1980): 165-170. [An exchange occasioned by Fulmer's "Review of Peter Geach, *Providence and Evil*" [#1395]. Each accuses the other of mispresenting his position. Fulmer concludes that there is nothing enlightening about Geach's understanding of the problem of evil.]

1429.   Gibbs, Benjamin. "Can God Do Evil?" *Philosophy* 50 (1975): 466-469. [Reply to Geach's "Omnipotence [#233].]

1430.   Graesser, Carl. "Righteousness, Human and Divine." *Currents in Theology and Mission* 10 (1983): 134-141.

1431.   Green, Ronald M. *Religious Reasons: The Rational and Moral Basis of Religious Belief*. Oxford: Oxford University Press, 1978.

1432.   Hare, R.M. "Geach, Good and Evil." *Analysis* 17 (1956): 103-111.

1433.   Harrison, Jonathan. "Geach on Harrison on Geach and God." *Philosophy* 52 (1977): 223-226. [Refutes Geach's response, "Can God Fail to Keep Promises?" [#1427], which responds to Harrison's "Geach on God's Alleged Ability to do Evil" [#246], which, in turn, is a response to Geach's "Omnipotence" [#233]. Harrison argues that Geach has not made the distinction between "God cannot break his promises" and "It cannot be that God will break his promises."]

1434.   ———. "Malt Does More than Peter Can or On Behalf of the Damned." *Religious Studies* 14 (1978): 525-537. [Review article of Geach's *Providence and Evil* [#1426]. Harrison argues that Geach's attempt to resolve the theodicy issue is yet another in a long line of failures. See Harrison's "Geach on God's Alleged Ability to do Evil" [#246]. He rejects, for example, Geach's distinction between God being *almighty* and *omnipotent*. He rebuffs also Geach's view of freedom and divine omniscience, his answer to animal suffering, etc. He rejects Geach's view that a universe in which there is chance is incompatible with a universe in which everything is determined, and disputes also Geach's view of hell.]

1435. Jordon, Mark D. "The Transcendentality of Goodness and the Human Will." *Being and Goodness.* Edited by Scott MacDonald. Ithaca, NY: Cornell University Press, 1991: 129-150.

1436. Keane, Philip S. "The Objective Moral Order: Reflections on Recent Research." *Theological Studies* 43 (1982): 260-278. [Discusses Roman Catholic principles regarding moral objectivity and contemporary Roman Catholic thinking of moral objectivity.]

1437. Khatchadourian, Haig. "Is the Principle of Double Effect Morally Acceptable?" *International Philosophical Quarterly* 28 (1988): 21-30. [Argues against various formulations of the principle of double effect used in ethical theories. He constructs a more plausible formulation.]

1438. Kretzmann, Norman. "God Among the Causes of Moral Evil: Hardening of Hearts and Spiritual Blinding." *Philosophical Topics* 16 (1988): 189-213. [Argues that Aquinas's God is the cause of sin.]

1439. Kretzmann, Norman, and Eleonore Stump. "Being and Goodness." *Divine and Human Action: Essays in the Metaphysics of Theism.* Edited by Thomas V. Morris. Ithaca, NY: Cornell University Press, 1988: 281-312. [Reprinted in *Being and Goodness.* Edited by Scott MacDonald [#1892].]

1440. Lee, Patrick. "Permanence of the Ten Commandments: St. Thomas and His Modern Commentators." *Theological Studies* 42 (1981): 422-443.

1441. MacDonald, Scott. "Egoistic Rationalism: Aquinas's Basis for Christian Morality." *Philosophy and the Christian Faith.* Edited by Thomas V. Morris. Notre Dame, IN: University of Notre Dame Press, 1988: 327-354.

1442. MacIver, A.M. "Good and Evil and Mr. Geach." *Analysis* 18 (1957): 7-13.

1443. MacKay, Alfred F. "Attributive-Predicative." *Analysis* 30 (1970): 113-120. [Argues that Peter Geach ("Good and Evil" [#1424]) and R.M. Hare ("Geach, Good and Evil" [#1432]) have not shown that "good" is always attributive, never predicative.]

1444. Mayberry, Thomas. "Morality and the Deity." *Southwestern Journal of Philosophy* 1 (1970).

1445. Nelson, Mark. "Naturalistic Ethics and the Argument from Evil." *Faith and Philosophy* 8 (1991): 368-379.

1446. Nielsen, Kai. "God and the Good: Does Morality Need Religion?" *Theology Today* 21 (1964): 47-58.

1447. ———. *Ethics Without God.* London: Pemberton Books, 1973.

1448. ———. "On Religion and the Grounds of Moral Belief." *Religious Humanism* 11 (1977): 33-34.

1449.   Nowell-Smith, Patrick. "Religion and Morality." *The Encyclopedia of Philosophy*. New York: Macmillan, 1970. [See also his "Morality: Religious and Secular," *Readings in the Philosophy of Religion*. Edited by Baruch A. Brody. Englewood Cliffs, NJ: Prentice-Hall, 1974. Originally published in *The Rationalist Annual*. London: Pemberton Publishing Company, 1961. This chapter was not included in the second revised edition of Brody's *Readings in the Philosophy of Religion*, 1992.]

1450.   Peter, Carl J. "Divine Necessity and Contingency: A Note on R.W. Hepburn." *Thomist* 53 (1969): 150-161. [Response to Hepburn's *Christianity and Paradox*. New York: Pegasus, 1968].

1451.   Pigden, Charles R. "Geach on Good." *Philosophical Quarterly* 40 (1990): 129-154.

1452.   Prior, Arthur N. "The Autonomy of Ethics." *Australasian Journal of Philosophy* 38 (1960): 199-206.

1453.   Quinn, Phillip L. "Religious Obedience and Moral Autonomy." *Religious Studies* 11 (1975): 265-281.

1454.   ———. "An Argument for Divine Command Theory." *Philosophy and the Christian Faith*. Edited by Thomas V. Morris. Notre Dame, IN: University of Notre Dame Press, 1988: 289-302.

1455.   Rachels, James. "God and Human Attitudes." *Religious Studies* 7 (1971): 325-327.

1456.   Stevenson, J.G. "Donnelly on Geach." *Notre Dame Journal of Formal Logic* 13 (1972): 429-430. [Refutes Donnelly's claims ("Some Remarks on Geach's Predicative and Attributive Adjectives" [#1389]) regarding Peter Geach's distinction ("Good and Evil" [#1424]) between "logically predicative" and "logically attributive."]

1457.   Taliaferro, Charles. "The Divine Command Theory of Ethics and the Ideal Observer." *Sophia* 22 (1983): 3-8.

1458.   Veatch, Henry. *The Ontology of Morals*. Evanston, IL: Northwestern University Press, 1971. [See also Veatch, "Language and Ethics: What's Hecuba to Him or He to Hecuba?" *Proceedings of the American Philosophical Association* 44 (1972): 45-62.]

1459.   Yandell, Keith E. "Divine Necessity and Divine Goodness." *Divine and Human Action*. Edited by Thomas V. Morris. Ithaca, NY: Cornell University Press, 1988: 313-344.

Appendix A

Biblical Theodicy

It is accepted generally that there is no single, systematic theodicy within the biblical writings. Constructing a rational, coherent theodicy obviously was not the intent of the authors. Indeed, with reference to the Hebrew Scriptures, there was a distinct "indiffernce toward problems of theory and structure," as noted by Erhard Gerstenberger, co-author (with Wolfgang Schrage) of *Suffering*, one of the most significant publications on biblical understandings of God and evil).[1] Schrage confirms the same with respect to the New Testament. He points out, furthermore, that the very fact there are numerous solutions offered is in itself a "warning against absolutizing one of them or trying to bring them all together into a harmonized system."[2]

There is a way, nevertheless, to explain—from an overall, generalized perspective— the complex assortment of biblical assumptions and speculations about the problem of understanding evil and its relationship to God. Hopefully, such an overview does not oversimplify a very enigmatic set of views espoused by many biblical authors over several centuries. There are many publications which address this theme. David Griffin, for example, has argued convincingly that there are two dominant understandings of God's relationship with creatures within the biblical writings. The primary view holds that all goods and evils are the product of divine sovereignty. The secondary view holds, paradoxically, that human free will is the cause of moral evils.[3]

The issue also has been addressed competently by D.A. Carson under the rubric of divine sovereignty and human responsibility.[4] Focusing mainly on the Gospel of John, but also on relevant Hebrew Bible and intertestamental sources (the Apocrypha and pseudepigrapha, Dead Sea Scrolls, targums and rabbinic literature), Carson's conclusion is that such texts often juxtapose divine sovereignty and human responsibility without manifesting an awareness or concern with the theoretical difficulties which have become so important in the theological tradition and contemporary debates. In those passages where the ancient writers *do* seek to address the issue, "their interests focused on a practical area, viz, how to reconcile God's goodness and power and elective purposes with the vicissitudes they actually experience."[5]

By the time of the apocalyptic writings and the New Testament, there had been a historical progression in understanding the relationship between divine causation and human freedom. The question of God and evil had to be faced with new urgency because of the crisis of 587 BC and the emergence of the exilic and post-exilic communities.[6] Serious questions about the divine distribution of justice are raised in Habakkuk, Jeremiah and Job. As James Crenshaw has argued, the wisdom, apocalyptic and creation faith were responses to this issue, at a time when the historic tradition seemed to be inadequate.[7] D.A. Carson suggests, moreover, that the tension was such that it could *not* be resolved. His recommendation is that both divine sovereignty and human responsibility must be acknowledged. Most biblical writers "presuppose human responsibility," but "they not only presuppose divine sovereignty but insistently underscore it, even when the devastation of observable phenomena appear to fly in the face of such belief."[8]

Besides the predominant feature of biblical writings, which attributes all goods and evils to the causal will of God, another basic feature of the biblical writings on God's relationship to evil is the assumption of *the Adamic myth* as the explanation of the source of evil in God's otherwise good creation. The various biblical explanations for evil, which attempt to clarify why God allows evil and suffering in the world, assume that God has a morally justifiable reason *because* of the fall and its ramifications. The biblical references suggest that perhaps we are being punished, or tested, or disciplined; or perhaps our suffering will bring about a better end, as did the redemptive suffering of Christ, etc. All such theories assume that humans have fallen from the original Adamic state of goodness (or from a state of perfection, as Augustine interpreted Genesis).[9]

Theological scholarship and the rise of modern science over the past three centuries, of course, have discredited a literal, historical interpretation of the Adamic story as the primary explanation for the world's evils. Bultmann's celebrated "demythologizing" and the more recent work of scholars like James Barr have denied a strict fundamentalist or literalistic interpretation of biblical texts, inspired though these texts may be. F.D. Fohr's recent book, *Adam and Evil: The Spiritual Symbolism of Genesis and Exodus*,[10] aptly substantiates this point, as have many others.

As such, traditional biblical speculations about evil are being seriously questioned by modern scholarship, despite their long and privileged history. The fact that the word "pain," for example, has its roots in the same word as "punishment" indicates just how influential the biblical understanding of *evil as divine punishment* has been from biblical times to the present. Klaus Koch, among growing numbers of others—theists and sceptics alike—disputes this explanation for evil. Koch's examination of the biblical passages which seem to make the case for divine retribution most strongly leads him to conclude that they do *not*, in fact, support the traditional interpretations.[11] Walter Brueggemann has extended Koch's analysis to consider theodicy in its social dimensions, while others like James Crenshaw are arguing that the doctrine of divine retribution places inappropriately severe limitations on divine power. Still others argue that the divine punishment theory is a primitive view of God, depicting God as continually intervening in the world to reward the good and punish the wicked. The arbitrary and disproportionate distributions of evils in the world argues against this view.[12] The same applies to attributing evil to *divine warnings or as tests of faith*, again seen as a result of our "fallen" state. This was the case with Paul, who saw his suffering as a test, as a call to remain steadfast in faith and patient amid adversity (2 Cor 2:8). It was also the lesson of the Book of Job, the classic example of the "faith solution." While there is an unmanageable mass of literature centered on the analysis and interpretation of the Book of Job, there have been an increasing number of eminent scholars who challenge its understanding of evil as the result of divine causation, no matter what justifiable reason there might be. Crenshaw, for example, cautions that divine testing should not be seen in isolation from divine pathos,[13]—see *Appendix C* for more on this "suffering of God" theology—while others stress even more strongly that the understanding of suffering as a test of faith (or as a warning) rests upon an inadequate representation of divine power vis-à-vis human freedom.[14] This, of course, has been one of the central themes of Whiteheadian-Hartshornean process theism.

Daniel Simundson, in his popularized interpretation of biblical views on God and evil, *Faith Under Fire*,[15] argues that the New Testament contributed to the Hebrew scriptures three new explanations for suffering: that it has *redemptive value*; that it is the result of *evil powers* (Satan and the evil cohorts); and that suffering can be softened by the belief in *an afterlife redemption*. Against the first of these, he points out that most human suffering seems not to have redemptive value for others, although such may well have been the case for persecuted Christians in the first centuries.[16] The argument, moreover, that Satan is the cause of evil, leads to a dualism and metaphysical speculation which does not answer the theodicy issue rationally, nor the prior question as to why God would create such an evil being to torment us.[17]

The speculation and belief in an afterlife redemption as bringing to an end the anguish and suffering (or as justification for earthly suffering), as is the case with the speculation that evil powers are the source of human suffering, have been mainline Christian views since the New Testament era. Such views, however, as is the case for the aforementioned views, are being questioned by growing numbers of scholars. Biblical writers, of course, were not seeking to formulate systematic theodicies, yet historical theologians from at least the time of Augustine did so, and used the biblical theories as the bases of their speculations. The theories of redemptive suffering and the afterlife redemption have dominated the western Judaeo–Christian tradition for centuries, until the seminal work of Schleiermacher in the nineteenth century and John Hick[18] and process philosophers in this century.[19] While Hick's contemporary theodicy requires an afterlife for its viability, the assumption of an afterlife is a faith statement, a belief, rather than a rational premise that would be used by most analytic philosophers and theologians—although, as always, there are major exceptions to this position.

The *faith solution*, represented in the Book of Job and other biblical texts (Paul's exhortation, for example, about the unsearchableness of God's ways, reflecting passages in the Hebrew scriptures) encourages a trusting faith that all goods and evils which occur in human life are part of God's incomprehensible plan and, as such, have a meaning and purpose, albeit known only to God. This solution has remained dominant for centuries because of its incredibly simple solution to theodicy and its apparent resolution of the problem of evil. It brings also a curious and sombre reassurance that since all goods and all evils are the result of divine action, they are justified. The problem with this view is that it may encourage social and personal apathy and despair, among other negative effects, as noted in *Chapter 1*.

For detailed discussions about the various biblical solutions to the problem of evil, even though these are not meant to be formal theodicies, there are a number of books available.[20] In the lists which follow, I have included those writings I judge to be among the most important discussions, at least in the English language.[21] The biblical writings and the writings of biblical scholars on the relationship between God and evil involve many peripheral themes, peripheral at least to this bibliography's focus on explicit, analytic contributions to the theodicy issue. Biblical discussions of divine justice, righteousness, sin, and technical analyses of texts and words are far more common than are concerted attempts of biblical theologians to enter the debates with analytic philosophers and theologians in the attempt to construct or discuss theodicies. Yet there are exceptions. The writings of James Crenshaw, Walter Brueggemann, Klaus Koch, D.A. Carson, Sibley Towner, Daniel Simundson, among others noted in this appendix, have approached the subject in ways which should be of serious interest to those who engage in the ongoing debates represented in the annotated chapters of this bibliography.

As is the case with respect to the numerous books on the general topic of "philosophy of religion" (many of which contain summary statements of the philosophical analyses of the theodicy issue), there are innumerable books, too abundant to list, which offer introductions to biblical thought and critical methods, even though these books mercy, divine sovereignty, and the like, and an incredibly massive literature on Job. Most of these are not *directly relevant* to theodicy, as defined by analytic theological and philosophical writings, yet these themes are of utmost importance in their own context, obviously.

In what follows, I have listed what I consider to be the most important of the publications on biblical theodicy, or rather, on biblical thinking about God and evil. My intent was to list as many of these publications as possible, those which have the most direct relevance to the issues discussed in the annotated sections of this bibliography. I have not separated the publications on Job from the others, although a good portion are about this seminal text.[22]

Notes

1.   Erhard Gerstenberger and Wolfgang Schrage, *Suffering* (Nashville, TN: Abingdon Press, 1977).

2.   Gerstenberger and Schrage, *Suffering*, 132, 206.

3.   See David R. Griffin, *God, Power and Evil* (Lanham, MD: University Press of America, 1990): 31-37; see also Barry L. Whitney, *Evil and the Process God* (New York and Toronto, ON: Edwin Mellen Press, 1985): *Chapters 2 and 3*; and Barry L. Whitney, *What Are They Saying About God and Evil?* (New York/Mahwah, Paulist Press, 1989): *Chapters 2 and 3*. As process theists, Griffin and Whitney hold these two views to be paradoxical to the point of contradiction. Many others who are not process theists would agree. The Gerstenberger–Schrage volume, *Suffering*, is also a very useful reference, as is Daniel Simundson's *Faith Under Fire* (Minneapolis, MN: Augsburg, 1980).

4.   D.A. Carson, *Divine Sovereignty and Human Responsibility* (Atlanta, GA: John Knox Press, 1981).

5.   Carson, *Divine Sovereignty*, 38.

6.   See Walter Brueggemann, "Theodicy in a Social Dimension," *Journal for the Study of the Old Testament* 33 (1985): 3.

7.   James Crenshaw. *A Whirlpool of Torment* (Philadelphia, PA: Fortress Press, 1984); etc.

8.   Carson, *Divine Sovereignty*, 24.

9.   See John Hick's cogent argument about the manner in which Augustine misinterpreted the Genesis story of the Garden of Eden and the Fall. The garden becomes a state of perfection; the innocent children, Adam and Eve, become creatures with full knowledge of God, etc. It is this misinterpretation of Genesis which led to the unresolvable paradoxes in the Augustinian account. A perfect world *in the beginning*, contradicts our contemporary scientific knowledge, and it was all but impossible for Augustine to explain how perfect creatures could sin. See Hick, *Evil and the God of Love* (New York: Harper and Row, 1977), 245-253.

10.   F.D. Fohr. *Adam and Eve: The Spiritual Symbolism of Genesis and Exodus* (Lanham, MD: University Press of America, 1986).

11.   Klaus Koch, "Is There a Doctrine of Retribution in the Old Testament?" in *Theodicy in the Old Testament*. Edited by James Crenshaw (Philadelphia, PA: Fortress Press, 1983): 57-87.

12.   Brueggemann's "Theodicy in a Social Dimension" (see note 6).

13.   James Crenshaw, *A Whirlpool of Torment*.

14.   See Whitney, *Evil and the Process God (Chapters 2* and *3)*.

15.   Daniel Simundson, *Faith Under Fire*.

16.   Simundson, *Faith Under Fire*, 131-132.

17.   For more detailed discussions of this point, see Barry L. Whitney, *Evil and the Process God* and *What Are They Saying About God and Evil?*

16. Simundson, *Faith Under Fire*, 131-132.
17. For more detailed discussions of this point, see Barry L. Whitney, *Evil and the Process God* and *What Are They Saying About God and Evil?*
18. See the introductory notes to *Chapter 5*.
19. See the introductory notes to *Chapter 6*.
20. See Barry L. Whitney, *What Are They Saying About God and Evil?* (Paulist, 1989 and new edition available from author, 1999) and *Evil and the Process God* (Mellen, 1985); David Griffin, *God, Power and Evil* (Westminster, 1976 and University Press of America, 1990) and *Evil Revisited* (Albany, NY: State University of New York Press, 1991); and the Gerstenberger/Schrage study, *Suffering* (Abingdon, 1977).
21. The fact that the text of this present bibliography consumes 650 pages (first edition) precluded a full listing of foreign-language publications. There are many relevant publications in German, of course, but this bibliography has set limits which make it manageable. It is encouraging that many of the most important publications have been translated into English.
22. One of the most recent collections of 34 essays and a select bibliography on Job ought to be mentioned: *Sitting with Job: Selected Studies on the Book of Job*. Edited by Roy B. Zuck (Grand Rapids, MI: Baker Book House, 1992). Authors cited include the following: Gregory Parsons, Claus Westermann, John Hartley, Robert Dhorme, Norman Habel, David Clines, Phiip Yancey, Laird Harris, Francis Andersen, Matitiahu Tsevat, Elmer, David Clines, Mark Littleton, Roy Zuck, Albert Barnes, Michael Cisk, Édouard Dhorme, Sylvia Scholnick, James Williams, David McKenna, and Lynne Newell.

Biblical Theodicy [Selected Publications]

1460.   Abba, Raymond. "Perfect Through Suffering." *Expository Times* 98 (1987): 145-146. [Sermon, 3rd. Sunday in Lent: Hebrews 2:10.]

1461.   Ackroyd, Peter. *Exile and Restoration*. Philadelphia, PA: Westminster Press, 1968.

1462.   Addinall, Peter. "What is Meant by a Theology of the Old Testament?" *Expository Times* 97 (1986): 332-336. [Theodicy section discusses Job.]

1463.   Ahern, Barnabas M. "The Fellowship of His Sufferings (Phil 3:10): A Study of St. Paul's Doctrine of Christian Suffering." *Catholic Biblical Quarterly* 22 (1960): 1-32.

1464.   Akin, Daniel L. "Triumphalism, Suffering, and Spiritual Maturity: An Exposition of 2 Corinthians 12: 1-10 in its Literary, Theological, and Historical Context." *Criswell Theological Review* 4 (1989): 119-144.

1465.   Allison, Dale C., Jr. "Matthew 10:26-31 and the Problem of Evil." *St. Vladimir's Theological Quarterly* 32 (1988): 293-308.

1466.   Andersen, Francis I. *Job: An Introduction and Commentary*. London: Inter-Varsity Press, 1976. [See also Andersen's "The Problem of Suffering in the Book of Job," in Roy B. Zuck, editor. *Sitting With Job* [see #1826]: 181-188.]

1467.   Anderson, Megory, and Philip Culbertson. "The Inadequacy of the Christian Doctrine of Atonement in Light of Levitical Sin Offering." *Anglican Theological Review* 68 (1986): 303-328.

1468.   Archer, Gleason L. *The Book of Job*. Grand Rapids, MI: Baker, 1982.

1469.   Armstrong, David R. "When God Isn't Good." *Church Divinity*. Edited by John H. Morgan. Notre Dame, IN: Foundations Press, 1984: 13-33. [Jeremiah on suffering.]

1470.   Balentine, Samuel E. "Prayers for Justice in the Old Testament: Theodicy and Theology." *Catholic Biblical Quarterly* 51 (1989): 597-616.

1471.   Barr, James. "The Book of Job and its Modern Interpreters." *Bulletin of the John Rylands University Library of Manchester* 54 (1971/1972): 28-46.

1472.   ———. *The Bible in the Modern World*. New York: Harper and Row, 1973.

1473.   ———. *Fundamentalism*. Philadelphia, PA: Westminster Press, 1977.

1474.   ———. *Escaping From Fundamentalism*. London: SCM Press, 1984.

1475.   Barraclough, Ray. "A Re-Assessment of Luke's Political Perspective." *Reformed Theological Review* 38 (1979): 10-18.

1476.   Barton, John, and Robert P. Carroll, Jan P. Fokkleman, et al. *Prophets, Worship and Theodicy*. Leiden: E.J. Brill, 1984.

1477.   Barton, Stephen. "Paul and the Cross: A Sociological Approach." *Theology* 85 (1982): 13-19. [See also his "Paul and the Resurrection: A Sociological Approach." *Religion* 14 (1984), 67-75.]

1478.   Beasley-Murray, George R. "The Righteousness of God in the History of Israel: Romans 9-11." *Review and Expositor* 73 (1976): 437-450.

1479. Beker, Johan Christiaan. *Paul the Apostle: The Triumph of God in Life and Thought*. Philadelphia, PA: Fortress Press, 1980.

1480. ———. *Paul's Apocalyptic Gospel: The Coming Triumph of God*. Philadelphia, PA: Fortress Press, 1982.

1481. ———. "Suffering and Triumph in Paul's Letter to the Romans." *Horizons in Biblical Theology* 7 (1985): 105-119.

1482. ———. *Suffering and Hope: A Biblical Vision of the Human Predicament*. Philadelphia, PA: Fortress Press, 1987. [Chapters on the Old Testament response to evil, the early Christian response to evil, Paul's response to evil, and recent responses: Kushner's *When Bad Things Happen to Good People* [#1132], and Soelle's *Suffering* [#2397].]

1483. Bennett, Georgann. *What the Bible Says About Goodness*. Joplin, MO: College Press Publishing Co., 1981.

1484. Bennett, Robert Avon. "Joseph: Can Good Come Out of Evil?" *Preaching on Suffering and a God of Love*. Edited by Henry J. Young and Nathan A. Scott. Philadelphia, PA: Fortress Press, 1978: 22-28.

1485. Bennett, W.J. "The Son of Man Must ..." *Novum Testamentum* 17 (1975): 113-129. ["The Son of Man must *suffer*": Mark 8:31.]

1486. Bertrangs, A. *The Bible on Suffering*. Translated by F. Vander Heijden. De Pere, WI: St. Norbert Abbey Press, 1986. [Concludes that suffering is the result of the inscrutable wisdom of God, not a catastrophe brought about by blind fate.]

1487. Bigger, Charles. "Kant and Job's Comforters: A Review Article." *King's Theological Review* 1 (1987): 62-63.

1488. Blazen, Ivan T. "Suffering and Cessation from Sin According to 1 Peter 4:1." *Andrews University Seminary Studies* 21 (1983): 27-50.

1489. Blenkinsopp, Joseph. "We Rejoice in Our Sufferings." *The Mystery of Suffering and Death*. Edited by Michael J. Taylor. Garden City, NY: Image Books, 1973: 45-55. [Reprinted from *The Way* 7 (1967), 36-44.]

1490. Bochet, Marc. "Job in Literature." *Job and the Silence of God*. Edited by Christian Duquoc and Casiano Floristán. New York: Seabury Press, 1983: 73-77.

1491. Boice, James M. *Our Sovereign God*. Grand Rapids, MI: Eerdmans, 1977.

1492. Borchert, Gerald L. "The Conduct of Christians in the Face of the 'Fiery Ordeal'." *Review and Expositor* 79 (1982): 451-462. [1 Peter 4:12-5:11.]

1493. Breitbart, Sidney. "Problem of Theodicy." *Dor Le Dor* 15 (1987): 223-233.

1494. Breslauer, S. Daniel. "Power, Compassion and the Servant of the Lord in Second Isaiah." *Encounter* 48 (1987): 163-178.

1495. Brockway, R.W., and P.J. Hordern. "The Devil and Job." *Faith and Freedom* 36 (1982): 41-44.

1496. Bronson, Cor. "A Pastor's Workshop: The Gospel of Mark and Conflicts with Evil Today." *Evangelical Review of Theology* 6 (1982): 275-285.

1497. Brown, Schuyler. "Biblical Imagery and the Experience of Evil." *Union Seminary Quarterly Review* 44 (1990): 151-156.

1498.   Brueggemann, Walter. "From Hurt to Joy, From Death to Life." *Interpretation* 28 (1974): 3-19.

1499.   ———. *The Prophetic Imagination*. Philadelphia, PA: Westminster Press, 1978.

1500.   ———. *Genesis*. Atlanta, GA: John Knox Press, 1982.

1501.   ———. "Biblical Faith as Cosmic Hurt." (Weber Lecture, 1982). *Moravian Theological Seminary Bulletin*, 1977-1985: 83-92.

1502.   ———. *The Message of the Psalms: A Theological Commentary*. Minneapolis, MN: Augsburg Publishing House, 1984.

1503.   ———. "Theodicy in a Social Dimension." *Journal of the Study of the Old Testament* 33 (1985): 3-25.

1504.   ———. "The Costly Loss of Lament (Psalm 39)." *Journal for the Study of the Old Testament* 36 (1986): 57-71.

1505.   ———. *Hopeful Imagination: Prophetic Voices in Exile*. Minneapolis, MN: Augsburg/Fortress Press, 1986.

1506.   ———. *Israel's Praise: Doxology Against Idolatry and Ideology*. Philadelphia, PA: Fortress Press, 1988.

1507.   Bube, Richard. "Response to Evil: A Christian Dilemma." *Perspectives on Science and Christian Faith: Journal of the American Scientific Affiliation* 35 (1983): 225-234.

1508.   Buber, Martin. "A God Who Hides His Face." *The Dimensions of Job*. Edited by Nahum Glatzer. New York: Schocken Books, 1969.

1509.   Buck, Fidelis. "Foreword" to *Sin in the Bible*. [Old Testament section by Albert Gelin; New Testament section by Albert Descamps. Translated by Charles Schaldenbrand. New York: Desclee, 1964. Original French edition published in 1960.]

1510.   Burtness, James H. "Sharing the Suffering of God in the Life of the World: From Text to Sermon on 1 Peter 2:21." *Interpretation* 23 (1969): 277-288.

1511.   Buttrick, George Arthur. *God, Pain and Evil*. Nashville, TN: Abingdon Press, 1966. [Biblical inspiration versus rational theodicies.]

1512.   Byrne, Brendan. "Living Out the Righteousness of God: The Contribution of Romans 6:1-8:13 to an Understanding of Paul's Ethical Presuppositions." *Catholic Biblical Quarterly* 43 (1981): 557-581.

1513.   Camroux, Martin. "The Problem of Suffering (Sermon, 5th Sunday after Easter: Romans 8:26-39)." *Expository Times* 98 (1987): 211-212.

1514.   Carroll, Robert P. "Theodicy and the Community: The Text and Subtext of Jeremiah 5:1-6." *Prophets, Worship and Theodicy*. Edited by J. Barton, R. Carroll, et al. Papers, Joint British-Dutch Old Testament Conference. Leiden: E.J. Brill, 1984: 19-38.

1515.   Carson, D.A. *Divine Sovereignty and Human Responsibility*. Atlanta, GA: John Knox Press, 1981. [See also his more recent, *How Long, O Lord? Reflections on Suffering and Evil*. Grand Rapids, MI: Baker Book House, 1990.]

1516.   ———. "Introduction." *Right With God*. Edited by D.A. Carson. Grand Rapids, MI: Baker Book House, 1991. [Chapters include Edmund Clowney's "The

Biblical Doctrine of Justification by Faith"; Guillermo Mendez's "Justification and Social Justice"; and chapters on justification in Paul, the various Gospels, and in Hinduism, Islam and Buddhism.]

1517. Clarke, Oliver Fielding. *God and Suffering: An Essay in Theodicy*. Derby: Peter Smith Publishers, 1964. [Theodicy in Leibniz, Boehme, Old Testament/Hebrew Bible, and New Testament.]

1518. Clines, David J.A. "False Naivety in the Prologue to Job." *Hebrew Annual Review* 9. Edited by Reuben Ahroni. Columbus, OH: Ohio State University Press, 1985: 127-136.

1519. Coats, George W. "2 Samuel 12:1-7A." *Interpretation* 40 (1986): 170-174.

1520. Cohn, Robert L. "Biblical Responses to Catastrophe." *Judaism* 35 (1986): 263-276.

1521. Cole, Graham A. "Towards a New Metaphysic of the Exodus." *Reformed Theological Review* 42 (1983): 75-84.

1522. Collet, Jean. "From Job to Bergman: Anguish and Challenge." *Job and the Silence of God*. Edited by Christian Duquoc and Casiano Floristán. New York: Seabury Press, 1983: 69-72.

1523. Cott, Jeremy. "The Biblical Problem of Election." *Journal of Ecumenical Studies* 21 (1984): 199-228.

1524. Cox, Claude E. "Elihu's Second Speech According to the Septuagint." *Studies in the Book of Job*. Edited by Walter E. Aufrecht. Waterloo, ON: Wilfred Laurier University Press, 1985: 36-53.

1525. Cox, Dermot. "A Rational Inquiry Into God: *Chapters 4-27* of the Book of Job." *Gregorianum* 67 (1986): 621-658.

1526. ——. *The Triumph of Impotence: Job and the Tradition of the Absurd*. Rome: Universita Gregoriana, 1978.

1527. Crenshaw, James L. "Theodicy." *Supplementary Volume to Interpreter's Dictionary of the Bible*." New York: Abingdon Press, 1972-1976.

1528. ——. "Popular Questioning of the Justice of God in Ancient Israel." *Zeitschrift für die Alttestamentliche Wissenschaft* 82 (1970): 380-395.

1529. ——. *Prophetic Conflict*. Berlin and New York: Walter de Gruyter, 1971.

1530. ——. *Hymnic Affirmation of Divine Justice*. Society of Biblical Literature Dissertation Series, 24. Missoula, MT: Scholars Press, 1975.

1531. ——. "The Problem of Theodicy in Sirach: On Human Bondage." *Journal of Biblical Literature* 94 (1975): 47-64.

1532. ——. "The Human Dilemma and Literature of Dissent." *Tradition and Theology in the Old Testament*. Edited by D.A. Knight. Philadelphia, PA: Fortress Press, 1977: 235-258.

1533. ——. "In Search of the Divine Presence: Some Remarks Preliminary to a Theology of Wisdom." *Review and Expositor* 74 (1977): 353-369.

1534.   ———. "The Shadow of Death in Ecclesiastes." *Israelite Wisdom: Theological and Literary Essays in Honor of Samuel Terrien*. Edited by J.G. Gammie, *et al*. Missoula, MT: Scholars Press, 1978: 205-216.

1535.   ———. "The Birth of Skepticism in Ancient Israel." *The Divine Helmsman*. Edited by James Crenshaw and Samuel Sandmal. New York: KTVA, 1980: 1-19.

1536.   ———. *Old Testament Wisdom: An Introduction*. Atlanta, GA: John Knox Press, 1981.

1537.   ———. *A Whirlwind of Torment*. Philadelphia, PA: Fortress Press, 1984.

1538.   ———. "The High Cost of Preserving God's Honor." *World and I* 2 (1987): 375-382.

1539.   Crook, M.B. *The Cruel God*. Boston, MA: Beacon Press, 1959.

1540.   Crotty, Robert B. "The Suffering Moses of Deutero-Zechariah." *Colloquium* (Australia—New Zealand) 14 (1982): 43-50.

1541.   Culver, Robert D. "The Nature and Origin of Evil." *Bibliotheca Sacra* 129 (1972): 106-115.

1542.   Curtis, John Briggs. "On Job's Response to Yahweh." *Journal of Biblical Literature* 98 (1979): 497-511.

1543.   Davids, Peter H. "Theological Perspectives on the Epistle of James." *Journal of the Evangelical Theological Society* 23 (1980): 97-103.

1544.   De Villiers, J.L. "Joy of Suffering in 1 Peter." *Neotestamenticia* 9 (1975): 64-86. [Also published in *Essays on the General Epistles of the New Testament*. W. Nicol, et al. Ptretria, South Africa: Co-Secretary Publications, 1975, 64-86.]

1545.   Decock, Paul B. "The Understanding of Isaiah 53:7-8 in Acts 8:32-33." *The Relationship Between the Old and New Testament*. C. van der Waal, *et al*. Proceedings of the New Testament Society of South Africa. Bloemfontein: University of the Orange Free State, 1981: 111-133.

1546.   Denton, D.R. "Hope and Perseverance." *Scottish Journal of Theology* 34 (1981): 313-320.

1547.   Dillon, Richard J. "The Psalms of the Suffering Just in the Accounts of Jesus' Passion." *Worship* 61 (1987): 430-444.

1548.   Donahue, John R. "Biblical Perspective on Justice." *Faith That Does Justice*. Edited by John C. Haughey. New York: Paulist Press, 1977: 68-112.

1549.   Donelson, Lewis R. "'Do Not Resist Evil' and the Question of Biblical Authority." *Horizons in Biblical Theology* 10 (1988): 133-146.

1550.   Dowd, Sharon Echols. *Prayer, Power and The Problem of Suffering: Mark 11:22-25 in the Context of Markian Theology*. Atlanta, GA: Scholars Press, 1988. SBL Dissertation Series, 105. [Contains an extensive bibliography. Dowd argues that prayer in Matthew responds to the theodicy issue.]

1551.   Duquoc, Christian. "Demonism and the Unexpectedness of God." *Job and the Silence of God*. Edited by Christian Duquoc and Casiano Floristán. New York: Seabury Press, 1983: 81-87.

1552. Dussell, Enrique D. "The People of El Salvador: the Communal Sufferings of Job." *Job and the Silence of God*. Edited by Christian Duquoc, and Casiano Floristán. New York: Seabury Press, 1983: 61-68.

1553. Eichrodt, Walther. *Theology of the Old Testament*. Evanston, IL: Northwestern University Press, 1967. [See especially pages 167-185. Published also by Philadelphia, PA: Westminster Press, 1961.]

1554. Eldridge, Victor J. "Jeremiah, Prophet of Judgment." *Review and Expositor* 78 (1981): 319-330.

1555. Fitch, William. *God and Evil: Studies in the Mystery of Suffering and Pain*. Grand Rapids, MI: Eerdmans, 1967.

1556. Fitzgerald, John T. *Cracks in an Earthen Vessel: An Examination of the Catalogues of Hardships in the Corinthian Correspondence*. Atlanta, GA: Scholars Press, 1988.

1557. Fitzmyer, Joseph A. *Paul and His Theology: A Brief Sketch*. Englewood Cliffs, NJ: Prentice-Hall, 1988. [First edition published as *Pauline Theology: A Brief Sketch*. Prentice-Hall, 1967.]

1558. Fohr, S.D. *Adam and Eve*. Lanham, MD: University Press of America, 1986.

1559. Forster, Roger, and Paul V. Marston. *God's Strategy in Human History*. Wheaton, IL: Tyndale House, 1973.

1560. Freedman, David Noel. "The Elihu Speeches in the Book of Job." *Harvard Theological Review* 61 (1968): 51-59.

1561. ———. "Is it Possible to Understand the Book of Job?" *Biblical Research* 4 (1988): 26-33.

1562. Friesen, Gary. *Decision Making and the Will of God: A Biblical Alternative to the Traditional View*. Portland, OR: Multnomah Press, 1980.

1563. Frost, Stanley Brice. "The Death of Jonah: A Conspiracy of Silence." *Journal of Biblical Literature* 87 (1968): 369-382.

1564. Frye, Northrup. *The Great Code: The Bible and Literature*. Toronto, ON: Academic Press, 1981.

1565. Gaffin, Richard B. "The Usefulness of the Cross." *Wesleyan Theological Journal* 41 (1979): 228-246. [1 Peter 4:12-13.]

1566. Garland, David E. "Severe Trials, Good Gifts, and Pure Religion: James 1." *Review and Expositor* 83 (1986): 383-394.

1567. Gaston, Lloyd. "Abraham and the Righteousness of God." *Horizons in Biblical Theology* 2 (1980): 39-68.

1568. Geisler, Norman L. *Miracles and the Modern Mind: A Defense of Biblical Miracles*. Grand Rapids, MI: Baker Book House, 1992.

1569. Gerstenberger, Erhard S. "Jeremiah's Complaints." *Journal of Biblical Literature* 82 (1963): 32-45.

1570. ———. "Enemies and Evildoers in the Psalms: A Challenge to Christian Preaching." *Horizons in Biblical Theology* 4 (1982/1983): 61-77.

1571.   Gerstenberger, Erhard S., and Wolfgang Schrage. *Suffering*. Nashville, TN: Abingdon Press, 1977. [Translated by John Steely. Originally published as *Leiden*. Stuttgart: Kohlhammer, 1977. See also Schrage's *The Ethics of the New Testament*. Philadelphia, PA: Westminster Press, 1988; Gerstenberger's more recent publication is a chapter, "'Where Is God?' The Cry of the Psalmists," *Where Is God? A Cry of Human Distress*. Edited by Christian Duquoc and Casiano Floristán. *Concilium*. London: SCM Press, 1992: 11-22. The entire issue is devoted to the theodicy issue, with chapters by Christian Duquoc, "'Who is God?' Becomes 'Where is God?' A Shift in a Question," 1-10; Gregory Baum, "Sickness and the Silence of God," 23-26; etc.]

1572.   Girard, René. *Job, The Victim of his People*. Translated by Yvonne Freccero. Stanford, CA: Stanford University Press, 1987.

1573.   Gisberg, H.L. "Job the Patient and Job the Impatient." *Conservative Judaism* 21 (1969): 88-111.

1574.   Glatzer, Nahum N. "The Book of Job and Its Interpreters." *Biblical Motifs*. Edited by Alexander Altmann. Cambridge, MA: Harvard University Press, 1966: 197-220.

1575.   ———. "'Knowest Thou': Notes on the Book of Job." *Studies in Rationalism, Judaism and Universalism*. Edited by Raphael Loewe. London: Routledge and Kegan Paul, 1966: 73-86.

1576.   Good, Edwin Marshall. *Irony in the Old Testament*. Philadelphia, PA: Westminster Press, 1965. Second edition, Sheffield: Almond Press, 1981. [See also Edwin Marshall Good, *In Times of Tempest: A Reading of Job*. Stanford, CA: Stanford University Press, 1990.]

1577.   Gordis, Robert. *The Book of God and Man: A Study of Job*. Chicago, IL: University of Chicago Press, 1965. [*Chapter 10*, "Job and the Mystery of Suffering," 135-156.]

1578.   ———. "A Cruel God or None: Is There No Other Choice?" *Judaism* 21 (1972): 277-284.

1579.   ———. *The Book of Job: Commentary, New Translation and Special Studies*. New York: Jewish Theological Seminary of America, 1978.

1580.   ———. "Job and Ecology (and the Significance of Job 40:15)." *Hebrew Annual Review* 9 (1985): 189-202.

1581.   Gorringe, Timothy J. "Job and the Pharisees." *Interpretation* 40 (1986): 17-28.

1582.   Gowan, Donald E. *The Triumph of Faith in Habakkuk*. Atlanta, GA: John Knox Press, 1976.

1583.   Gray, John. "The Book of Job in the Context of Near Eastern Literature." *Zeitschrift für die Alttestamentliche Wissenschaft* 82 (1970): 251-169.

1584.   Green, Joel B. "Jesus on the Mount of Olives (Luke 22:39-46): Tradition and Theology." *Journal for the Study of the New Testament* 26 (1986): 29-48.

1585.   Greenfield, Jonas C. *The Book of Job*. Philadelphia, PA: The Jewish Publication Society of America, 1980.

1586.   Gutiérrez, Gustavo. "But Why Lord? On Job and the Suffering of the Innocent." *Other Side* 23 (1987): 18-23.

1587.   ——.*On Job*. New York: Orbis, 1987.

1588.   Habel, Norman C. *The Book of Job: A Commentary*. Philadelphia, PA: Westminster Press, 1985.

1589.   ——. "Gutiérrez on Job: A Review Essay ("On God-Talk and the Suffering of the Innocent"). *Lutheran Theological Journal* 22 (1988): 37-40 [see #1587].

1590.   Hafemann, Scott J. *Suffering and the Spirit*. Philadelphia, PA: Coronet Books, 1986.

1591.   ——. "The Comfort and Power of the Gospel: The Argument of 2 Corinthians 1-3." *Review and Expositor* 86 (1989): 325-344.

1592.   Hall, Randy. "For to This You Have Been Called: The Cross and Suffering in 1 Peter." *Restoration Quarterly* 19 (1976): 137-147.

1593.   Halpern, Baruch. "YHWH's Summary Justice in Job XIV 20." *Vetus Testamentum* 28 (1978): 472-474.

1594.   Hamilton, W.T. "Difficult Texts from Job." *Difficult Texts of the Old Testament Explained*. Edited by Wendel Winkler. Hurst, TX: Winkler Publishing, 1982: 301-310.

1595.   Hammer, Reuven. "Two Approaches to the Problem of Suffering." *Judaism* 35 (1986): 300-305. [Suffering in the Books of Job and Ruth.]

1596.   ——. "The Biblical Perception of the Origin of Evil." *Judaism* 39 (1990): 318-325.

1597.   Hancock, Eugenia Lee. "The Impatience of Job." *Spinning a Sacred Yarn: Women Speak from the Pulpit*. Edited by Ann Greenawalt Abernethy, Carole Carlson, Patricia A. Carque, et al. New York: Pilgrim Press, 1982: 98-106.

1598.   Hanson, Anthony T. "The Theology of Suffering in the Pastoral Epistles and Ignatius of Antioch." *Studia Patristica* 17 (1982): 694-696. [Part 2 of 3. Edited by Elizabeth A. Livingstone. New York: Pergamon Press, 1982.]

1599.   Hanson, Bradley. "School of Suffering." *Dialog* 20 (1981): 39-45. [Paul's theology of suffering.]

1600.   Hanson, Paul D. "Conflict in Ancient Israel and its Resolution." *Understanding the Word*. Edited by J. Butler, E. Conrad, and B. Ollenburger. Sheffield: University of Sheffield Press, 1985: 185-205.

1601.   Hardy, Graham W. "The Mystery of Suffering." *Expository Times* 68 (1957): 215-216. [Job 1:21.]

1602.   Harrelson, Walter J. "Blessings and Curses." *Interpreters Dictionary of the Bible, Volume I*. Edited by George Arthur Buttrick. Nashville, TN: Abingdon Press, 1962: 446-448.

1603.   ——. "Ezra Among the Wicked in 2 Esdras 3-10." *The Divine Helmsman: Studies on God's Control of Human Events, Presented to Lou H. Silberman*. Edited by James L. Crenshaw and Samuel Sandmel. New York: KTVA, 1980.

1604.   Haughery, John C. "Jesus as the Justice of God." *The Faith That Does Justice*. Edited by John C. Haughey. New York: Paulist Press, 1977: 264-290.

1605.   Hendrickx, Herman. *Social Justice in the Bible*. Quezon City, Phillipines: Claretian, 1985.

1606.   Heuschen, J. "Sinner." *Encyclopedic Dictionary of the Bible*. New York: McGraw-Hill, 1963: 2235-2239.

1607.   ———. "Suffering." *Encyclopedic Dictionary of the Bible*. New York: McGraw-Hill, 1963: 2340-2345.

1608.   Hiebert, D. Edmond. "Selected Studies from 1 Peter: Part I: Following Christ's Example: An Exposition of 1 Peter 2:21-25." *Bibliotheca Sacra* 139 (1982): 32-45.

1609.   ———. "Selected Studies from I Peter: Part II: The Suffering and Triumphant Christ: An Exposition of I Peter 3:18-22." *Bibliotheca Sacra* 139 (1982): 146-158.

1610.   Hill, David. "On Suffering and Baptism in 1 Peter." *Novum Testamentum* 18 (1976): 181-189.

1611.   Hodges, Zane C. "Those Who Have Done Good—John 5:28-29." *Bibliotheca Sacra* 136 (1979): 158-166.

1612.   Holdsworth, John. "The Sufferings in 1 Peter and 'Missionary Apocalyptic'." *Studia Biblica*, 1978. Journal for the Study of the New Testament, Supplement Series 3. Edited by Elizabeth A. Livingstone. Sheffield: University of Sheffield Press, 1980: 225-232.

1613.   Holst, Larry. "Biblical Motifs of Suffering." *American Protestant Hospital Association Bulletin* 47 (1983): 1-7.

1614.   Hooker, Morna D. "Interchange and Suffering." *Suffering and Martyrdom in the New Testament*. Edited by William Horbury and Brian McNeil. New York and Cambridge: Cambridge University Press, 1981: 70-83.

1615.   Hora, Robert, and David M. Robinson. "Does the Book of Job Offer an Adequate Pastoral Response to Suffering?" *Church Divinity*. Edited by J. Morgan. Bristol, IN: Wyndham Hall Press, 1981: 67-73.

1616.   Horbury, William. "Suffering and Messianism in Yose Ben Yose." *Suffering and Martyrdom in the New Testament*. Edited by William Horbury and Brian McNeil. New York and Cambridge: Cambridge University Press, 1981: 143-182.

1617.   Hughes, Philip Edgecumbe. *Hope for a Despairing World: The Christian Answer to the Problem of Evil*. Grand Rapids, MI: Baker Book House, 1977. [God is in control: actively, passionately, redemptively.]

1618.   Irwin, William A. "Job and Prometheus." *Journal of Religion* 30 (1950): 90-108.

1619.   Jai Singh, Herbert. "Bible Studies (Matthew 6:13)." *Religion and Society* (1981): 65-74.

1620.   James, Stephen A. "Divine Justice and the Retributive Duty of Civil Government." *Trinity Journal NS* 6 (1985): 199-210.

1621.   Janzen, J. Gerald. *Job*. Atlanta, GA: John Knox Press, 1985.

1622.   ———. "Creation and the Human Predicament in Job." *Ex Auditu* 3 (1987): 45-53.

1623.   ———. "The Place of the Book of Job in the History of Israel's Religion." *Ancient Israelite Religion: Essays in Honor of Frank Moore Cross*. Edited by

Patrick D. Miller, Jr., and Paul D. Hanson. Minneapolis, MN: Augsburg Publishing House, 1987: 523-537.

1624. Johnson, Dennis E. "Fire in God's House: Imagery from Malachi 3 in Peter's Theology of Suffering (1 Peter 4:12-19)." *Journal of the Evangelical Theological Society* 29 (1986): 285-294.

1625. Jones, Edgar. "Suffering in the Psalter: A Study of the Problem of Suffering in the Book of the Psalms." *Congregational Quarterly* 34 (1956): 53-63. [See also his *The Triumph of Job*. London: SCM Press, 1966.]

1626. Jones, E. Stanley. *The Divine Yes*. Nashville, TN: Abingdon Press, 1975. [Jesus as the "divine yes" to the problem of suffering.]

1627. Jones, Peter Rhea. "Preaching from Romans." *Review and Expositor* 73 (1976): 465-476.

1628. Jung, Carl G. *Answer to Job*. Princeton, NJ: Princeton University Press, 1958, 1969, 1973. [Other references to Jung's theodicy are listed in *Appendix D*.]

1629. Kaiser, Walter C. *A Biblical Approach to Personal Suffering*. Chicago, IL: Moody Press, 1982.

1630. Kapelrud, Arvid S. "The Identity of the Suffering Servant." *Near Eastern Studies in Honor of William Foxwell Albright*. Edited by Hans Goedicke. Baltimore, MD: Johns Hopkins University Press, 1971: 307-314.

1631. ———. "Second Isaiah and the Suffering Servant." *Hommages à André Dupont-Sommer*. N. Avigad, et al. Librairie Adrien-Maisoneuve, 1971: 297-303.

1632. ———. "The Main Concern of Second Isaiah." *Vetus Testamentum* 32 (1982): 50-58.

1633. Karff, Samuel E. "Ministry In Judaism: Reflections on Suffering and Caring." *A Biblical Basis for Ministry*. Edited by Earl E. Shelp. Philadelphia, PA: Westminster Press, 1981: 72-100.

1634. Kayalaparamphi, T. "Christian Suffering in 1 Peter." *Biblehashyam* (India) 3 (1977): 7-9.

1635. Keck, Leander E. "Paul and Apocalyptic Theology." *Interpretation* 38 (1984): 229-241.

1636. Kee, Alistair. *From Bad Faith to Good News: Reflections on Good Friday and Easter*. Philadelphia, PA: Trinity Press, 1991.

1637. Kee, Howard Clark. *Medicine, Miracle and Magic in New Testament Times*. Cambridge and New York: Cambridge University Press, 1986.

1638. Kent, H. Harold. *Job, Our Contemporary*. Grand Rapids, MI: Eerdmans, 1967.

1639. Kent, John L. "Latent Compensations." *Expository Times* 61 (1950): 275-277.

1640. ———. "The Call to Endurance." *Expository Times* 68 (1957): 119-120.

1641. Kerr, Hugh T. "Enduring to the End." *Theology Today* 37 (1980): 289-293.

1642. ———. "Lent to be Spent." *Theology Today* 37 (1980): 289-293. [Editorial.]

1643. Kertelege, Karl. "Biblical Revelation about Sin, Conversion, and the Following of Christ." *Moral Theology Today: Certitudes and Doubts*. Edited by Donald

G. McCarthy. St. Louis, MO: The Pope John XXIII Medical-Moral Research and Education Center, 1984: 27-30.

1644. Kinet, Dirk. "The Ambiguity of the Concepts of God and Satan in the Book of Job." Translated by M. Kohl. *Job and the Silence of God*. Edited by Christian Duquoc and Casiano Floristán. New York: Seabury Press, 1983: 30-35.

1645. Kirk, Gordon E. "Endurance in Suffering in 1 Peter." *Bibliotheca Sacra* 138 (1981): 46-56.

1646. Kirschner, Robert. "Apocalyptic and Rabbinic Responses to the Destruction of 70." *Harvard Theological Review* 78 (1985): 27-46.

1647. Klein, Ralph W. *Israel in Exile*. Philadelphia, PA: Fortress Press, 1979.

1648. Kock, Klaus. *The Prophets. Volumes I and II*. Minneapolis, MN: Fortress/Augsburg Press, 1982 and 1984.

1649. ———. "Is There a Doctrine of Retribution in the Old Testament?" *Theodicy in the Old Testament*. Edited by James L. Crenshaw. Philadelphia, PA: Fortress Press, 1983: 57-87.

1650. Kraeling, Emil Gottlieb H. "A Theodicy—and More." *The Dimensions of Job*. Edited by Naham N. Glatzer. New York: Schocken Books, 1969.

1651. Kuhl, Curt. *The Prophets of Israel*. Edinburgh and London: Oliver and Boyd, 1960.

1652. Kysar, Robert. *The Fourth Evangelist and His Gospel: An Examination of Contemporary Scholarship*. Minneapolis, MN: Augsburg Publishing House, 1975. [*Chapter 2*, "The Eschatology of the Gospel," 207-214.]

1653. Labuschagne, C.J. *The Incomparability of Yahweh in the Old Testament*. Leiden: Brill, 1966.

1654. Lacocque, André. "Job and the Symbolism of Evil." *Biblical Research* 24/25 (1979/1980): 7-19.

1655. ———. "Job and the Impotence of Religion and Philosophy." *Semeia* 19 (1981): 33-52.

1656. La Croix, Richard R. "The Paradox of Eden." *International Journal for Philosophy of Religion* 15 (1984): 171-172.

1657. Larue, Gerald A. "The Book of Job on the Futility of Theological Discussion." *Personalist* 45 (1964): 72-79.

1658. Lash, Nicholas. "What Might Martyrdom Mean?" *Ex Auditu* 1 (1985): 14-24.

1659. ———. *Theology on the Way to Emmaus*. London: SCM Press, 1986.

1660. Levenson, Jon D. *Creation and the Persistence of Evil: The Jewish Drama of Divine Omnipotence*. New York: Harper and Row, 1988.

1661. Lewis, Arthur H. *The Dark Side of the Millennium: The Problem of Evil in Revelation 20: 1-10*. Grand Rapids, MI: Baker Book House, 1980.

1662. Lewis, Edwin. "Christian Theodicy: An Exposition of Romans 8:18-39." *Interpretation* 11 (1957): 405-420.

1663. Lind, Millard C. "Monotheism, Power, and Justice: A Study in Isaiah 40-55." *Catholic Biblical Quarterly* 46 (1984): 432-446.

1664. Lindars, Barnabas. "Good Tidings to Zion: Interpreting Deutero-Isaiah Today." *Bulletin of the John Rylands University Library* 68 (1986): 473-497.

1665. Lindström, Fredrick. *God and the Origin of Evil: A Contextual Analysis of Alleged Monistic Evidence in the Old Testament.* Translated by Frederick H. Cryer. Sweden: CWK Gleerup, 1983.

1666. Liptzin, Sol. "Theodicy in the Bible." *Dor Le Dor* 13 (1985): 174-178.

1667. Loader, James A. "Different Reactions of Job and Qoheleth to the Doctrine of Retribution." *OTWSA [Ou-Testamentiese Werkgemeenskap]* 15/16, Studies in Wisdom Literature. Edited by W.E. Van Wyk. 1973: 43-48. [NHW Press, 1981. Papers read at OTWSA meetings at the University of Pretoria, 1972 and the University of South Africa, 1973.]

1668. ———. "Job—Answer or Enigma." *Old Testament Essays.* Edited by James A. Loader and J. Le Roux. University of South Africa Press, 1984: 1-38.

1669. Long, Thomas G. "Job: Second Thoughts in the Land of Uz(il)." *Theology Today* 45 (1988): 5-20.

1670. Longstaff, Thomas R.W. "Crisis and Christology: The Theology of Mark." *New Synoptic Studies.* Edited by William R. Farmer. Macon, GA: Mercer University Press, 1983: 373-392.

1671. Mafico, Temba J. "The Crucial Question Concerning the Justice of God (Gen 18:23-26)." *Journal of Theology for Southern Africa* 42 (1983): 11-16.

1672. Manus, Ch. Ukachuku. "Apostolic Suffering (2 Cor 6:4-10): The Sign of Christian Existence and Identity." *Asia Journal of Theology* 1 (1987): 41-54.

1673. Marcus, Joel. "The Evil Inclination in the Epistle of James." *Catholic Biblical Quarterly* 44 (1982): 606-621.

1674. Marshall, L.H. *The Challenge of New Testament Ethics.* London: Macmillan, 1964. [*Chapter 3*, "Jesus' View of Evil"; *Chapter 4*, "Jesus' View of Good"; *Chapter 9*, "Paul's Ethical Terminology"; Paul's view of evil; Paul's view of good; etc.]

1675. McDermet, William W., III. "Suffering and the Righteousness of God." *Encounter* 40 (1979): 421-429.

1676. McKay, John W. "Elihu: A Proto-Charismatic?" *Expository Times* 90 (1979): 167-171.

1677. McNeil, Brian. "The Odes of Solomon and the Sufferings of Christ." *Symposium Syriacum*, 1976. Edited by A. Voobus. Rome: Pontifical Gregorian University, 1978: 31-38.

1678. ———. "Suffering and Martyrdom in the Odes of Solomon." *Suffering and Martyrdom in the New Testament.* Edited by William Horbury and Brian McNeil. New York and Cambridge: Cambridge University Press, 1981: 136-142.

1679. Migliore, Daniel L. "Barth and Block on Job: A Conflict of Interpretations." *Understanding the Word: Essays in Honour of Bernard Anderson.* Edited by

James T. Butler, Edgar W. Conrad, and Ben C. Ollenburger. Sheffield: University of Sheffield Press, 1985: 265-279.

1680.   Miller, Patrick D. *Sin and Judgment in the Prophets*. Chico, CA: Scholars Press, 1982.

1681.   ———. "Trouble and Woe." *Interpretation* 37 (1983): 32-45.

1682.   Miller, Stewart. "Pain and God's Grace (Sermon, 7th Sunday Before Easter; 2 Cor 12:7)." *Expository Times* 95 (1984): 147-148.

1683.   Mintz, Alan. "The Rhetoric of Lamentations and the Representation of Catastrophe." *Prooftexts* 2 (1982): 10-16.

1684.   ———. *Hurban: Responses to Catastrophe in Hebrew Literature*. New York: Columbia University Press, 1984.

1685.   Miskotte, Kornelis Heiko. *When the Gods are Silent*. New York: Harper and Row, 1966 and London: Collins, 1967.

1686.   Mitchell, Stephen. "The Book of Job." *Tikkun* 1 (1985): 56-64.

1687.   Moore, Michael S. "Human Suffering in Lamentations." *Revue Biblique* 90 (1983): 534-555.

1688.   Mtetwa, C.N. "Suffering and Christian Hope." *Salvation Today for South Africa*. Edited by Hans-Jürgen Becken. Durban, Natal: Lutheran Publishing House, 1974: 46-49.

1689.   Muilenburg, James. "The Terminology of Adversity in Jeremiah." *Translating and Understanding the Old Testament*. Edited by H. Frank and William L. Reed. Nashville, TN: Abingdon Press, 1970: 42-63.

1690.   Murphy, Roland E. "Biblical Insights and Suffering, Pathos and Compassion." *Whither Creativity, Freedom, Suffering?* Edited by Francis A. Eigo. Villanova, PA: Villanova University Press, 1981: 53-75.

1691.   Murray, Gilbert. "Beyond Good and Evil." *Dimensions in Job*. Edited by Nahum Glatzer. New York: Schocken, 1969: 194-197.

1692.   Nelson, Christine. "Job: The Confessions of a Suffering Person." *Spinning a Sacred Yarn: Women Speak from the Pulpit*. Ann Greenawalt Abernethy, Carole Carlson, Patricia A. Carque, et al. New York: Pilgrim Press, 1982: 144-148.

1693.   Nereparampil, Lucius. "Liberation as Salvation: A Johannine Interpretation." *Journal of Dharma* 2 (1977): 68-81.

1694.   Newell, J. Altus. "Preaching in the Context of Crises Sermon: Thy Will Be Done." *Preaching in Today's World*. Compiled by James C. Barry. Nashville, TN: Broadman Press, 1984: 165-178.

1695.   Neyrey, Jerome H. "The Form and Background of the Polemic in 2 Peter." *Journal of Biblical Literature* 99 (1980): 407-431. [Critique of Ernst Käsemann, "An Apologia for Primitive Christian Eschatology." *Essays on New Testament Themes*. London: SCM Press, 1964, 169-195.]

1696.   Nissen, Hans Jorg. "The Problem of Suffering and Ethics in the New Testament." *Studia Biblica* (1978), *Journal for the Study of the New Testament,*

Supplement Series 3. Edited by Elizabeth A. Livingstone. Sheffield: University of Sheffield Press, 1980: 277-287.

1697.   O'Connell, Kevin G. "Habakkuk—Spokesman to God." *Currents in Theology and Mission* 6 (1979): 227-231.

1698.   O'Connor, Daniel John. "Theodicy in the Whirlwind." *Irish Theological Quarterly* 54 (1988): 161-174.

1699.   O'Sullivan, Michael A. "Blood, Sweat and Tears: Suffering for the Kingdom." *Restoring the Kingdom*. Edited by D. Ferme. New York: Rose of Sharon Press, 1984: 101-111.

1700.   Omanson, Roger L. "Suffering for Righteousness Sake." *Review and Expositor* 79 (1982): 439-450. [1 Peter].

1701.   Ortemann, Claude. "How Should Christians Speak of Suffering?" *Lumen Vitae* 38 (1983): 32-45.

1702.   ———. "How Did Jesus React to Suffering?" *SEDOS Bulletin* 3 (1987): 98-101.

1703.   Osborne, Thomas P. "Guide Lines for Christian Suffering: A Source-Critical and Theological Study of 1 Peter 2:21-25." *Biblica* 64 (1983): 381-408.

1704.   Packer, James I. "Sacrifice and Satisfaction." *Our Savior God*. Edited by J. Boice. Grand Rapids, MI: Baker Book House, 1980: 125-137.

1705.   Park, Chang Wan. "One of the Bible Studies (Mark 8:31-9:1)." *Reformed World* 31 (1980): 20-25.

1706.   Patterson, Charles H. *The Philosophy of the Old Testament*. New York: Roland Press, 1953.

1707.   ———. "Concerning Knowledge of Good and Evil." *Personalist* 41 (1960): 459-469.

1708.   Paul, Shalom, M. "Psalm XXVII and the Babylonian Theodicy." *Vetus Testamentum* 32 (1982): 489-492.

1709.   Peake, A.S. *The Problem of Suffering in the Old Testament*. London: Robert Bryant and C.H. Kelly, 1904.

1710.   Penchansky, David. *The Betrayal of God: Ideological Conflict in Job*. Philadelphia, PA: Westminster/John Knox Press, 1989.

1711.   Pierce, Edith Lovejoy. "Meditation on the Problem of Evil." *Brethren Life and Thought* 10 (1965): 41-43. [Luke 13:4.]

1712.   Piper, John. "The Righteousness of God in Romans 3:1-8." *Theologische Zeitschrift* 36 (1980): 3-16.

1713.   ———. "The Demonstration of the Righteousness of God in Romans 3:25, 26." *Journal for the Study of the New Testament* 7 (1980): 2-32.

1714.   ———. *The Justification of God*. Grand Rapids, MI: Baker Book House, 1983.

1715.   Plank, Karl A. *Paul and the Irony of Affliction*. Atlanta, GA: Scholars Press, 1987.

1716.   Pope, Marvin H. *Job: Introduction, Translation and Notes*. Garden City, NY: Doubleday, 1965. [Revised third edition, 1973.]

1717. Price, Robert M. "Illness Theodicies in the New Testament." *Journal of Religion and Health* 25 (1986): 309-315.

1718. Priest, John. "Job and *J.B.*: The Goodness of God or the Godness of Good?" *Horizons, Journal of the College Theology Society* 12 (1985): 265-283. [Dismissing God as a significant factor in human experience, *J.B.* comes closer to the mainstream of canonical tradition than does the Book of Job.]

1719. Proudfoot, Merrill. *Suffering: A Christian Understanding*. Philadelphia, PA: Westminster Press, 1964. [Paul's theology of suffering.]

1720. Raabe, Paul R. "The Effect of Repetition in the Suffering Servant Song." *Journal of Biblical Literature* 103 (1984): 77-81.

1721. ———. "Human Suffering in Biblical Context." *Concordia Journal* 15 (1989): 139-155.

1722. Raitt, Thomas M. *A Theology of Exile: Judgment/Deliverance in Jeremiah and Ezekiel*. Philadelphia, PA: Fortress Press, 1977. [See especially pages 83-105.]

1723. Ramm, Bernard L. *The God Who Makes a Difference*. Waco, TX: Word Books, 1972. [*Chapters 8-10* discuss theodicy.]

1724. Ramsey, Johnny. "Difficult Texts from Genesis." *Difficult Texts of the Old Testament*. Edited by Wendel Winkler. Hurst, TX: Winkler Publications, 1982: 205-213.

1725. Rankin, Oliver Shaw. *Israel's Wisdom Literature: Its Bearing on Theology and the History of Religion*. New York: Schocken, 1969. [Originally published in Edinburgh: T&T Clark, 1936.]

1726. Rao, S. Prabhakara, and M. Prakasa Reddy. "Job and his Satan—Parallels in Indian Scripture." *Zeitschrift für die Alttestamentliche Wissenschaft* 91 (1979): 416-422.

1727. Raphael, David D. "Tragedy and Religion." *Twentieth Century Interpretations of the Book of Job*. Edited by P.S. Sanders. Englewood Cliffs, NJ: Prentice-Hall, 1968: 46-55. [See also David D. Raphael, *The Paradox of Tragedy*. London: Allen and Unwin, 1960.]

1728. Reicke, Bo. "The Knowledge of the Suffering Servant." *Das Ferne und nahe Wort*. [Festschrift, Leonhard Rost.] Berlin: Verlag Alfred Töpelmann, 1967: 186-192.

1729. ———. "Paul's Understanding of Righteousness." *Soli Deo Gloria: New Testament Studies in Honor of William Childs Robinson*. Edited by J. McDowell Richards. Richmond, VA: John Knox Press, 1968: 37-49.

1730. Rembaum, Joel E. "The Development of a Jewish Exegetical Tradition Regarding Isaiah 53." *Harvard Theological Review* 75 (1982): 289-311.

1731. Rendall, Robert. "The Note of Crisis in Biblical History." *Evangelical Quarterly* 22 (1950): 83-94.

1732. Renner, Johannes T.E. "Aspects of Pain and Suffering in the Old Testament." *Colloquium* (Australia—New Zealand) 15 (1982): 32-42.

1733. Reumann, John H.P. "The Justification of the Unjust—Righteousness and Eschatology," and "The Justification of God: Righteousness and The Cross." *Moravian Theological Seminary Bulletin* 1 (1964): 1-15, 16-31.

1734. Revard, Stella P. "The Gospel of John and Paradise Regained: Jesus as 'True Light'." *Milton and Scriptural Tradition*. Edited by James H. Sims and Leland Ryken. Columbia, MO: University of Missouri Press, 1984: 142-159.

1735. Rife, Ronald D. "What To Do About Thorns." *Christianity Today* 19 (1975): 11-15. [Paul's suffering.]

1736. Roffey, John W. "Genesis 3: A Foray into Psychology and Biblical Theology." *Colloquium* (Australia—New Zealand) 20 (1987): 48-56.

1737. Ross, John M. "God's Use of Evil." *Church Quarterly Review* 165 (1964): 472-480.

1738. Roth, Robert Paul. "Christ and the Powers of Darkness: Lessons from Colossians." *Word and World* 6 (1986): 336-344.

1739. Rowlet, Harold Henry. *Job*. London: Thomas Nelson, 1970. [Also published by Grand Rapids, MI: Eerdmans, 1980.]

1740. Ryan, Michael D. "A Midrash on the Job." *Drew Gateway* 48 (1977): 32-40.

1741. Sabourin, Leopold. "Formulations of Christian Beliefs in Recent Exposition on Paul's Epistles to the Romans and Galatians." *Religious Studies Bulletin* 1 (1981): 120-136.

1742. Samuel, Leith. "Spiritual Lift No One is Talking About." *Christianity Today* 21 (1977): 10-12.

1743. Sanders, Ed. P. *Paul and Palestinian Judaism*. Philadelphia, PA: Fortress Press, 1977.

1744. Sanders, James A. *Suffering as Divine Discipline in the Old Testament and Post-Biblical Judaism*. Rochester, NY: Colgate Rochester Divinity School, 1955.

1745. Sandmel, Samuel. "Some Comments on Providence in Philo." *The Divine Helmsman*. Edited by James L. Crenshaw and Samuel Sandmel. New York: KTAV, 1980: 79-85.

1746. Santala, Risto. "The Suffering Messiah and Isaiah 53 in the Light of Rabbinic Literature." *Springfielder* 39 (1976): 177-182.

1747. Scharlemann, Martin H. "Divine Providence: Biblical Perspectives." *The Caring God: Perspectives on Providence*. Edited by Carl S. Meyer and Herbert T. Mayer. St. Louis, MO: Concordia Publishing House, 1973: 19-44.

1748. Scharlemann, Robert P. "The Being of God When God is Not Being God." *Deconstruction and Theology*. Edited by Carl A. Raschke. New York: Crossroad, 1982.

1749. Schimmel, Sol. "Job and the Psychology of Suffering and Doubt." *Journal of Psychology and Judaism* (1987): 239-249.

1750. Schmid, H.H. "Creation, Righteousness and Salvation: 'Creation Theology'." *Creation in the Old Testament*. Edited by Bernard W. Anderson. Philadelphia, PA: Fortress Press, 1984: 102-117.

1751. Schreiner, Susan E. "'Through a Mirror Dimly': Calvin's Sermons on Job." *Calvin Theological Journal* 21 (1986): 175-193. [Contains extensive footnoted references to the writings of Calvin and his interpreters.]

1752. Schulweis, Harold M. "Karl Barth's Job: Morality and Theodicy." *Jewish Quarterly Review* 65 (1975): 156-167. [See Barth's *Church Dogmatics, Volume 4.*]

1753. Seeskin, Kenneth R. "Job and the Problem of Evil." *Philosophy and Literature* 11 (1987): 226-241.

1754. Shapiro, David S. "The Problem of Evil and the Book of Job." *Judaism* 5 (1956): 46-52.

1755. Sheldon, Mark. "Job, Human Suffering and Knowledge: Some Contemporary Jewish Perspectives." *Encounter* 41 (1980): 229-235. [Discusses Solomon B. Freehof, *Book of Job: A Commentary.* New York: Union of American Hebrew Congregations, 1958; Martin Buber, "A God Who Hides His Face," *The Dimensions of Job* [#1508]; and Robert Gordis, *The Book of God and Man* [#1577].]

1756. Shelly, Rubel. "The Origin and Reality of Sin and Suffering and the Existence of a Merciful God." *Difficult Texts of the Old Testament.* Edited by Wendel Winkler. Hurst, TX: Winkler Publications, 1982: 30-39.

1757. Shelp, Earl E., and Ron Sunderland. *AIDS and the Church.* Philadelphia, PA: Westminster Press, 1982.

1758. Sherwin, Byron L. "Portrait of God as a Young Artist: The Flood Revisited." *Judaism* 33 (1984): 469-478. [Calls for a new concept of God, other than one of divine retribution (the flood as punishment); calls for a passionate creator, rather than a statically perfect God.]

1759. Simundson, Daniel J. *Faith Under Fire.* Minneapolis, MN: Augsburg Publishing House, 1980. [Discussion of biblical theodicy, containing an overview of the major perspectives. See also Simundson's *The Message of Job: A Theological Commentary.* Minneapolis, MN: Augsburg Publishing House, 1986.]

1760. ———. *Where Is God in My Suffering? Biblical Responses to Seven Searching Questions.* Minneapolis, MN: Augsburg Publishing House, 1983. [The questions: Do I Deserve This?; My God, Why Hast Thou Forsaken Me?; Can Any Good Come From This?; Why Do Friends Condemn Me?; Why Doesn't God Do Something?; Whose Fault Is It?; Is There Any Hope?]

1761. Skehan, Patrick William. "Job's Final Plea (Job 29-31) and the Lord's Reply (Job 38-41)." *Biblica* 45 (1964): 51-62.

1762. Slater, C. Peter. "Evil and Ultimacy." *Studies in Religion* 4 (1974/1975): 137-146.

1763. Smith, Jonathan Z. "A Pearl of Great Price and a Cargo of Yams: A Study in Social Incongruity." *History of Religions* 16 (1986): 1-19.

1764. Smith, Kenneth A. "Duress in Matthean Catechesis: Stress and the Growth of Faith." *Religious Education* 78 (1983): 108-118.

1765. Snaith, Norman. *The Book of Job: Its Origin and Purpose.* London: SCM Press, 1968.

1766. Snook, Lee E. "Interpreting Luke's Theodicy for Fearful Christians." *Word and World* 3 (1983): 304-311.

1767. Soards, Marion L. "The Silence of Jesus Before Herod: An Interpretative Suggestion." *Australian Biblical Review* 33 (1985): 41-45.

1768. Sobosian, Jeffrey G. "Suffering, Innocence and Love." *Christian Century* 91 (1974): 397-398.

1769. Songer, Harold S. "New Standing Before God: Romans 3:21-5:21." *Review and Expositor* 73 (1976): 415-424.

1770. Spidell, Steven. "Suffering and Salvation: The Tension of Hope." *Restoration Quarterly* 25 (1982): 75-77. [Sermon, Romans 8:18-25.]

1771. Stagg, Frank. "The Plight of the Jew and Gentile in Sin (Romans 1:18-3:20)." *Review and Expositor* 73 (1976): 401-414.

1772. Stedman, Ray C. *Expository Studies in Job*. Waco, TX: Word Books, 1981.

1773. Steimle, Edmund A. "Preaching and the Biblical Story of Good and Evil." *Union Seminary Quarterly Review* 31 (1976): 198-211. [Steimle regards the most satisfying theological response to theodicy to be Reinhold Niebuhr's *The Nature and Destiny of Man*. New York: Charles Scribner's Sons, 1943.]

1774. Steuernagel, Valdir R. "An Exiled Community as a Missionary Community: A Study Based on 1 Peter 2: 9-10." *Evangelical Review of Theology* 10 (1986): 8-18.

1775. Stott, John R.W. "Christian Responses to Good and Evil—A Study of Romans 12:9-13:10." *Perspectives on Peacemaking*. Edited by John A. Bernbaum. Ventura, CA: Regal Books, 1984: 43-56. [Retributive justice (punishment for evil) and formative justice are essential aspects of God's moral governance of the world.]

1776. Stuhlmueller, Carroll. "The Painful Cost of Great Hopes: The Witness of Isaiah 40-55." *Sin, Salvation and the Spirit*. Edited by D. Durken. Collegeville, MN: Liturgical Press, 1979: 146-162.

1777. ———. "Voices of Suffering in Biblical Prophecy and Prayer." *The Meaning of Suffering*. Edited by Flavian Dougherty. New York: Human Sciences Press, 1982: 97-158.

1778. Sutcliffe, Edmund F. *Providence and Suffering in the Old and New Testaments*. New York: Thomas Nelson and Sons, 1953.

1779. Sweet, John Philip McMurdo. "Maintaining the Testimony of Jesus: The Suffering of Christians in the Revelation of John." *Suffering and Martyrdom in the New Testament: Studies Presented to G.M. Styler*. Edited by William Horbury and Brian McNeil. New York and Cambridge: Cambridge University Press, 1981: 101-117.

1780. Terrien, Samuel L. "The Book of Job: Introduction and Exegesis." *Interpreter's Bible* 3. New York: Abingdon Press, 1951-1957: 877-1198.

1781. ———. *Job: Poet of Existence*. Indianapolis, IN: Bobbs-Merrill, 1957.

1782. ———. *The Elusive Presence: The Heart of Biblical Theology*. New York: Harper and Row, 1983.

1783. Thiering, Barbara. "Suffering and Asceticism at Qumran, as Illustrated in the Hodayot." *Revue de Qumran* 8 (1974): 393-405. [The Qumran Psalms of Thanksgiving.]

1784.   Thomas, George. "Transforming the Tragic into the Creative." *Preaching on Suffering and a God of Love*. Edited by Henry J. Young and Nathan A. Scott. Philadelphia, PA: Fortress Press, 1978: 18-21.

1785.   Thompson, Alden Lloyd. *Responsibility for Evil in the Theodicy of IV Ezra*. Society for Biblical Literature Dissertation Series, 29. Missoula, MT: Scholars Press, 1977.

1786.   Tiede, David L. "An Easter Catechesis: The Lessons of 1 Peter." *Word and World* 4 (1984): 192-201.

1787.   Tilley, Terrence. "God and the Silencing of Job." *Modern Theology* 5 (1989): 257-270.

1788.   Towner, W. Sibley. *How God Deals with Evil*. Biblical Perspectives on Current Issues. Philadelphia, PA: Westminster Press, 1978. [Detailed discussion of the biblical theodicy of divine retribution.]

1789.   Travis, Stephen H. "The Value of Apocalyptic." *Tyndale Bulletin* 30 (1979): 53-76.

1790.   Tsevat, Matitiahu. "The Meaning of the Book of Job." *Hebrew Union College: Annual* 37 (1966): 73-106.

1791.   Tuckett, Christopher N. "The Present Son of Man (Mk 2:10,28; Q)." *Journal for the Study of the New Testament* 20 (1982): 58-81.

1792.   Turner, Dale E. "Why Me, O Lord, Why Me?" *Christian Ministry* 37 (1983): 27-28. [Sermon on Job 5:7 and Romans 8:28].

1793.   Urbach, E.E. *The Sages*. Jerusalem: Magnes Press, 1975. [See pages 255-285.]

1794.   Van Daalen, David H. "The Revelation of God's Righteousness in Romans 1:17." *Studia Biblica* (1978): *Journal for the Study of the New Testament, Supplement Series 3*. Edited by Elizabeth A. Livingstone. Sheffield: Sheffield University Press, 1980: 383-389.

1795.   Van de Beek, Abraham. *Why? On Suffering, Guilt, and God*. Translated by John Vriend. Grand Rapids, MI: Eerdmans, 1990.

1796.   Van den Beld, Avande. "Romans 7:14-25 and the Problem of 'Akrasia'." *Religious Studies* 21 (1985): 495-515. [Concerning the "weakness of the will."]

1797.   Van Selm, A. *Job: A Practical Commentary*. Translated by John Vriend. Grand Rapids, MI: Eerdmans, 1985.

1798.   Vawter, Bruce. *Job and Jonah: Questioning the Hidden God*. New York: Paulist Press, 1983.

1799.   Walsh, James P.M. *The Mighty From Their Thrones: Power in the Biblical Tradition*. Minneapolis, MN: Fortress/Augsburg Press, 1987.

1800.   Watson, Nigel M. "Simplifying the Righteousness of God: A Critique of J.C. O'Neill's Romans." *Scottish Journal of Theology* 30 (1977): 453-469. [Critical assessment of J.C. O'Neill's *Paul's Letter to the Romans*. London: Penguin Books, 1975.]

1801.   Weber, Max. *Ancient Judaism*. New York: Free Press, 1952. [See especially 297-335.]

1802. Webster, Douglas D. "Reflections on Suffering." *Crux* 20 (1984): 2-8.

1803. Weiss, Paul. "God, Job and Evil." *Dimensions of Job*. Edited by Nahym N. Glatzer. New York: Schocken Books, 1981: 181-193.

1804. Wenham, John W. *The Goodness of God*. Downers Grove, IL: InterVarsity Press, 1974. [Republished as *The Enigma of Evil: Can We Believe in the Goodness of God?* Grand Rapids, MI: Zondervan, 1985.]

1805. Westermann, Claus. *What Does the Bible Say About God?* Atlanta, GA: John Knox Press, 1979.

1806. ———. *The Structure of the Book of Job: A Form Critical Analysis*. Philadelphia, PA: Fortress Press, 1981.

1807. ———. *Praise and Lament in the Psalms*. Atlanta, GA: John Knox Press, 1981.

1808. ———. "The Two Faces of Job." *Job and the Silence of God*. Edited by Christian Duquoc and Casiano Floristán. New York: Seabury Press, 1983: 15-22.

1809. Whedbee, James William. "The Comedy of Job." *Studies in the Book of Job, Semeia* 7 (1977): 1-39. [See also James Whedbee, *Israel and Wisdom*. New York: Abingdon Press, 1974.]

1810. Wilcox, John T. *The Bitterness of Job: A Philosophical Reading*. Ann Arbor, MI: University of Michigan Press, 1989.

1811. Williams, James G. "'You Have Not Spoken Truth of Me': Mystery and Irony in Job." *Zeitschrift für die Alttestamentliche Wissenschaft* 83 (1971): 231-255.

1812. Williams, Ronald J. "Theodicy in the Ancient Near East." *Canadian Journal of Theology* 2 (1956): 14-26.

1813. Williams, Sam K. *Jesus' Death as Saving Event: The Background and Origin of a Concept*. Harvard Dissertations in Religion. Missoula, MT: Scholars Press for *Harvard Theological Review*, 1975.

1814. ———. "The Righteousness of God in Romans." *Journal of Biblical Literature* 99 (1980): 241-290.

1815. Willmington, Harold L. "The Man Satan Wanted." *Fundamentalist Journal* 5 (1986): 67.

1816. Wolff-Salin, Mary. "Jung Answers Job." *Books in Religion* 14 (1986): 1, 4, 14-15. [Excerpt from Mary Wolff-Salin, *No Other Light: Points of Convergence in Psychology and Spirituality*. New York: Crossroad, 1986. Other references to Carl Jung's theodicy are listed in *Appendix D*.]

1817. Wolowelsky, Joel B. "A Talmudic Discussion on Yissurin Shel Ahavah." *Judaism* 33 (1984): 465-468.

1818. Wright, John H. "Problem of Evil, Mystery of Sin and Suffering." *Communico (International Catholic Review)* 6 (1979): 140-156.

1819. Yancey, Philip. "When the Facts Don't Add Up: A Just, Loving, and Powerful God Should Follow Certain Rules, Shouldn't He?" *Christianity Today* 30 (1986): 19-22. [See also Yancey's "The Bible's 'Feisty Old Men': The Old Testament Prophets," *Christianity Today* 31 (1987), 17-21. Other publications by Yancey are listed in *Appendix D*.]

1820.   Yates, Roy. "The Powers of Evil in the New Testament." *Evangelical Quarterly* 52 (1980): 97-111.

1821.   ——. "Christ and the Powers of Evil in Colossians." *Studia Biblica, 1978. Journal for the Study of the New Testament, Supplement Series 3*. Edited by Elizabeth A. Livingstone. Sheffield: Sheffield University Press, 1980: 461-468.

1822.   Young, Frances M. "Adam and Anthropos: A Study of the Interaction of Science and the Bible in Two Anthropological Treatises of the Fourth Century." *Vigiliae Christianae* 37 (1983): 110-140. [Gregory of Nyssen's *Ad Opificio* and Nemesius of Emesa's *De natura Hominis*.]

1823.   Zeisler, John A. "Salvation Proclaimed." *Expository Times* 93 (1982): 356-359. [Romans 3: 21-26.]

1824.   Zhitlowsky, C. "Job and Faust." *Two Studies in Yiddish Culture*. Edited by Percy Matenko. Leiden: Brill, 1968. [See pages 90-162.]

1825.   Zimmerli, Walther. *Old Testament Theology in Outline*. Atlanta, GA: John Knox Press, 1978.

1826.   Zuck, Roy B. *Job*. Everyman's Bible Commentary. Chicago, IL: Moody Press, 1978. [See also Zuck's edited volume, *Sitting with Job: Selected Studies on the Book of Job*. Grand Rapids, MI: Baker Book House, 1992. See note 22 in the introduction to this chapter for a list of the authors in this anthology.]

1827.   Zuckermann, Bruce Edward. *Job the Silent*. New York and Oxford: Oxford University Press, 1990.

Appendix B

Historical Theodicy

This annotated bibliography has focused on the past thirty years of publications on theodicy, largely (though not exclusively) by analytic theologians and philosophers: publications on the free will defense, best possible world theodicy, natural evil theodicy, and the mass of literature that discusses the logical and evidential versions of the problem of evil, John Hick's Irenaean alternative to the traditional Augustinian theodicy, and the process theodicy inspired by Alfred North Whitehead and Charles Hartshorne. But the traditional Augustinian—Thomistic theodicy, the theodicy that has dominated the western Christian world for several centuries, continues to produce relevant discussions.[1] There are, of course, an abundance of publications on "historical" figures like Leibniz, Kant, Augustine, and others, the relevant references to which have been included in this appendix— "relevant" in the sense of being pertinent to the issues discussed in the annotated chapters. It is somewhat mystifying (to me, at least) that most of the authors of the publications listed in this appendix have not concerned themselves to enter into the "mainstream" dialogue as much as one would have expected. I suspect that those who write from an historical (or certainly from a Thomistic) perspective probably consider themselves writing in the "mainstream," but the sheer weight of publications in the scholarly journals would not bear this out. A line, albeit vague, can be drawn between philosophical theodicy and theological theodicy. The annotated chapters, for example, contain a majority of publications which do not assume a Thomistic (or other denominational) theological bias.

While I have relegated the publications written from the perspective of conservative Protestant theodicy to *Appendix D*, these publications have much in common with the listings in *Appendix B*; both reflect the so-called "Augustinian" theodicy and do not engage in much dialogue with the issues which consume the publications listed in the annotated chapters. I do not presume to suggest why there has been this kind of isolation between those who write on contemporary issues and those who focus more on historical figures. Indeed, the isolation between those who write theologically and denominationally is greater still from those who write philosophically. I suspect theological and denominational biases dictate how one addresses the theodicy issue. The aim of Thomists, for example, seems largely to be that of clarifying and elaborating the writings of Aquinas, rather than that of producing new solutions to the theodicy issue or engaging in more fruitful dialogue with those outside Thomist circles. Much the same holds for conservative fundamentalist theology, which defends versions of the Augustinian theodicy. The latter, in turn, is solidly biblically based. There are exceptions, of course, but the divergence of perspectives and the lack of intense and meaningful dialogue is noticeable.

In what follows, major publications on the theodicies of *Augustine, Leibniz, Hume,* and *Kant,* among other historical figures, are listed. Obviously, the writings of *Thomas Aquinas* have given rise to a massive and often technical, "scholastic" literature. In recognition of this, I have annotated some of the most significant of these publications.

By way of a brief introduction, I note here that there are various theological and philosophical themes that recur in these writings. Among them is the view that evil is the *"privation of good,"* that good, not evil has been created by God, and that evil is not desired by God. The world's evil is parasitic on good, a deprivation of the good created by God. This theory, the "privation of good," appears repeatedly as an aspect of the theodicy solution. Yet it is noteworthy that Augustine seems to have utilized the theory *not* as a theodicy, but as an argument against dualism. Nonetheless, Protestant thinkers as well as Thomists have given this theory a distinguished place in their discussions of the problem of evil. *Paul Tillich* and *Karl Barth,* two of the most influential Protestant thinkers of this century, have defined evil as "non-being." Influential philosophers like *Martin Heidegger* and *Jean-Paul Sartre* hold similar theories, variations on this eminent theme, as it were.

John Hick, among others, has condemned attempts to use the privation account in theodicy as "untenable and dangerous," as "a mistaken hypostatization of language" which is of little use in resolving the theodicy issue.[2] This issue stands in need of attention, since it remains a major aspect of traditional theodicy, despite the growing criticisms of many outside the more traditional framework.

Also figuring prominently in traditional Thomistic and—to a lesser extent—in some versions of conservative Protestant theodicy is the *"principle of plenitude."* This theory holds that God created a universe containing an extensive variety of creatures, creatures which necessarily have varying abilities and qualities. Since divine "goodness," as Aquinas taught, "could not be adequately represented by one creature alone,"[3] a multiplicity of creatures is the result. "The universe would not be perfect if only one grade of goodness were found in things."[4] "It pertains to divine providence that the grades of being which are possible are fulfilled," and some things necessarily will be better than others, since some will have the power to fall from the good.[5] Austin Farrer has employed this principle in his theodicy as a "mutual interference of systems." The species conflict, but the world would be the lesser had God chosen not to create some of the species that were possible.[6]

John Hick, Peter Hare and Edward Madden, among a host of others, have rejected this theory as denying God's voluntary creation and as culminating in the Leibnizian proposal that this is the "best of all possible worlds," a view which many critics find problematic. The "principle of plenitude," I would note, does not necessarily lead to this conclusion, certainly not in Thomism. But if this world were indeed considered to be the "best possible world," resignation and despair might well be the appropriate response.[7]

Another philosophical theme utilized frequently in the traditional theodicies is the time-honored *"aesthetic theory,"* dating back at least as far as Plato. This theory holds that God created a good world, a world which is good as a *whole,* while the individual *parts* may appear to fallible human minds to be evils in themselves. From God's infinite and perfect perspective, however, these evils are either *means to good ends* or *parts of the good whole.* Jacques Maritain writes, accordingly, that "God allows certain evils to happen in order to bring about a greater good therefrom."[8] This has been a predominant aspect of theodicy since the writings of Augustine and—even more so—of Aquinas. Yet it has not gone unchallenged both from outside and within the Thomistic framework. The challenge from without has been to insist that the theory renders illusory the evils in the world, as goods in disguise.[9] From within Thomism, Karl Rahner has rejected one of the implications of the theory used in contemporary discussions, that suffering creatures are a necessary side-effect of an evolving universe. "It is possible," Rahner writes, "to imagine freedom and its dignity existing without suffering in paradisiacal harmony," a point exploited at length by Charles Journet.[10] Rahner insists that the fact that freedom "has produced immense and indescribable suffering that cannot be blamed on material and biological conditions" renders this explanation for evil "unsatisfactory and superficial."[11]

Thomistic and some conservative Protestant discussions on theodicy utilize also the distinction (rejected by Luther, Calvin, and contemporary process thinkers, among others)[12] between God's *permitting* and God's *causing* evil, or some variation of this theme. Charles Journet, for example, has used this principle prominently, and has concluded that since evil is not willed by God directly, the conflicts and hostility among the species are best understood as unavoidable or accidental side-effects of the promotion of some good. For God to do away with the side-effects, as Aquinas had argued centuries before, would mean that God would have to do away with the species themselves.[13] Jacques Maritain explains this by noting that evil is "permitted by God without being in absolutely any way willed or caused by [God]."[14] God is the first cause of all things, yet we ourselves are the cause of our evil acts. Moral evil is possible where God "causes the free agent to tend to a morally good act, but which included ... the possibility of being shattered."[15] The creature is responsible, then, in the sense that God's permissive decree does not cause the evil, but only involves the decision not to prevent it.[16]

Austin Farrer likewise defends the validity of this "double effect" principle. His analysis has been acclaimed by recent commentators as among the most careful and consistent attempts to specify what the concept means and to defend its viability.[17] "Two agents for the same act," Farrer concedes, "would be indeed impossible, were they both agents in the same sense and on the same level." Yet, as he argues, the terms "causality" and "agency" can be used with respect to God only analogically. Farrer defends creaturely free will and appeals both to biblical testimony and Christian experience to seek to resolve the issue of reconciling divine causation with human freedom. He rejects the view that God's primary causation is so all-pervasive that it renders a human free will meaningless: "We know that the action of a man can be the action of God in him; our religious existence is an experimenting with this relation. Both the divine and the human actions remain real and therefore free in the union between them."[18]

It is interesting that Karl Rahner, in his most explicit and direct discussion of the theodicy issue, rejects the use of this concept. The distinction between God's causing and permitting, he insists, is of secondary importance since God is ultimately the sole ground and cause of all things. "Having regard to God's omnipotent freedom, which knows no bounds, causing and permitting seem to us to come so closely together that we can ask quite simply why God allows us to suffer, without having to distinguish *a priori* in this 'allowing' by God between permitting and causing."[19]

Besides these philosophical themes, the traditional Augustinian–Thomistic theodicy employs several theological themes.[20] Traditional theodicy, whether it be Thomistic or conservative Protestantism, still focuses generally upon what John Hick has labelled the "Augustinian" theodicy. I prefer the term Augustinian–Thomistic theodicy, or indeed, one could refer to it as the "Augustinian–Thomistic–Reformation theodicy," since many of its theological features (if not its philosophical features) are utilized by the reformers. The Adamic myth plays a central role in this theodicy. God's goodness is exonerated, since God has created a good creation. It is the "fall" of the angels and the ensuing "fall" of Adam and Eve which has destroyed the goodness created by God. The question as to *why* or *how* a good creation ("perfect" in Augustine's writings) could fall has not been answered to the satisfaction of many, yet the traditional view is that we have inherited the "original sin" of the first human beings and deserve the evil and suffering which have resulted from this inheritance. We are, according to Augustine, in a state of *non posse non peccare*, "not able not to sin," without the grace of Christ. All evil, Augustine believed, is the result of human sin: moral evil is caused by human sin, and physical evil is God's just punishment for that sin. "An evil will is the cause of all evil" and God's "just judgment is the cause of our having to suffer from its consequences."[21] Charles Journet represents much of Thomistic theodicy in his support of this ancient theme. "The evil of sin," he taught, "occasions the evil of punishment," and different sins (original sin, mortal sin, venial sin) call for different punishments.[22] This is one version of the Thomistic principle of "moral balance": God punishes sin in order to maintain the moral balance of the universe.

Countless discussions of traditional theodicy have used the Adamic myth as their theological basis, and have gone on to argue for a *free will defense* to explain the persistence of moral evil. Augustine taught that both God and humans cause what takes place: "We may understand both that we do them and that God makes us do them."[23] Journet reiterates Aquinas's version of this: "It is clear that the initiative" for our acts differs "according to whether the free act is good or evil." "If the free act is morally good, bringing with it positive new values, the first initiative must surely be attributed to God."[24] Sin, on the other hand, "is produced by [hu]man [beings] alone," and while God is the first (primary) cause of everything, sin is not a positive being; "it is a privation introduced into a positive being."[25] Despite the doctrines of original sin, divine predestination, and God as the primary cause of all events (creatures as the secondary causes), traditional theodicy largely has held that human freedom is the cause of moral evil. Luther rejected this outright, noting that there is no freedom in humans, in angels or in beasts, since God is the all-causative force. Yet Luther (as did Calvin and others in the subsequent tradition) held that we are responsible, nonetheless, for our acts. The free will defense, indeed, occurs over and over again in the "traditional," "classical" theodicy—despite internal and external challenges, notably the debates about whether divine power and human free will are compatible or incompatible, and all that this implies.

Karl Rahner, to cite this prominent theologian once again, rejects the free will argument, at least as it has been interpreted as an exclusive explanation for human suffering. Such a view would set up human freedom "as somehow purely and simply absolute and underivable in its decision."[26] Human freedom is not an unconditional but rather "a created freedom, sustained in its existence and nature always and everywhere by God's supreme providence." We are free, Rahner argues, but every decision is "completely embraced solely by God's disposition."[27] David Griffin and other process theists argue, moreover, that the traditional free will defense is flawed by its illogical doctrine of unilateral divine power.[28]

Rahner's conclusion displays the tension within Thomism and conservative Protestant theodicy: human beings are responsible for evil, and yet God's omnipotent causal agency is the ultimate and primary cause of all things. Scholars debate whether God's causative power is unilateral and coercive. The issue has become quite complex and is of great importance to the theodicy question.[29] In light of this tension, it is hardly surprising that many of these writers appeal to the mystery of faith as the final solution to the theodicy puzzle. "The incomprehensibility of suffering," Rahner concludes, "is part of the incomprehensibility of God." Suffering "is the form...in which the incomprehensibility of God himself appears."[30]

Notes

1. See *Appendix E* for some of the most relevant dissertations.

2. John Hick, *Evil and the God of Love* (Second edition, New York: Harper and Row, 1978): 182ff.

3. See Hick, *Evil and the God of Love*, 95. The reference cited is from Thomas Aquinas, *Summa Theologica*, translated by the Fathers of the English Dominican Province (London: R & R Washbourne, Ltd., 1912): Part I, Question xlvii, Art. 1.

4. See Hick, *Evil and the God of Love*, 95. The reference cited is from Thomas Aquinas, *Summa Theologica*, Part I, Question xxv, Article 6.

5. See critical discussions by David Griffin, *God, Power and Evil* (Philadelphia, PA: Westminster Press, 1976 and Lanham, MD: University Press of America, 1990), and John Hick, *Evil and the God of Love*. The text cited is from Aquinas's *Summa Contra Gentiles*. Translated by the Fathers of the English Dominican Province, in *Great Books of the Western World* (Encyclopedia Britannica, Inc., 1952).

6. See Austin Farrer, *Love Almighty and Ills Unlimited* (London: Collins, 1966).

7. See Hick, *Evil and the Process God*, 70-82; and Peter Hare and Edward Madden, *Evil and the Concept of God* (Springfield, IL: C.C. Thomas, 1968): 68-69.

8. Jacques Maritain, *Saint Thomas and the Problem of Evil* (Milwaukee, WI: Marquette University Press, 1942); and Maritain, *God and the Permission of Evil* (Milwaukee, WI: Bruce Publishing Company, 1966). The cited text is from Thomas Aquinas's *Treatise on the Incarnation*.

9. If this were the case, of course, it could be argued that it is a great evil for God to have deceived us so. See Descartes on this and moderns like See David Griffin, *God, Power and Evil, Chapter 7*.

10. Charles Journet, *The Meaning of Evil* (New York: P.J. Kennedy and Sons, 1961): 91, 114-118.

11. Karl Rahner, "Why Does God Allow Us to Suffer?" *Theological Investigations, Volume XIX* (New York: Crossroad, 1983): 198.

12. For references, see David Griffin, *God, Power and Evil*; John Hick, *Evil and the God of Love*; Barry Whitney, *What Are They Saying About God and Evil?* (New York and Mahwah, NJ: Paulist Press, 1989); etc.

13. See Charles Journet, *The Meaning of Evil*, 77-86.

14. Maritain, *God and the Permission of Evil*, 1 (note 2), etc.

15. Maritain, *God and the Permission of Evil*, 37.

16. Maritain, *God and the Permission of Evil*, 63.

17. See, for example, Maurice Wiles, "Farrer's Concept of Double Agency," *Theology* 84 (1981): 243-249.

18. Austin Farrer, *Faith and Speculation* (London: Adam and Charles Black, 1967): 104.

19. Rahner, "Why Does God Allow Us to Suffer?", 196.

20. In distinguishing between the Augustinian theological and philosophical themes, I am following Hick's lead. See his *Evil and the God of Love*.

21. See, for example, Augustine, *On Free Will* III, 48, in *Augustine's Earlier Writings*. Translated by John Burleigh (London: SCM Press, 1953): 200. See also Augustine's *Confessions*, VII (New York: The Modern Library, 1949): 122. For an effective critique of Augustine's theodicy, see Fred Berthold's "Free Will and Theodicy in Augustine: An Exposition and Critique," *Religious Studies* 17 (1981): 525-535. See also the detailed critiques of David Griffin, *God, Power and Evil*, and John Hick, *Evil and the God of Love*.

22. Journet, *The Meaning of Evil*, 184.

23. Augustine, *On the Predestination of the Saints*, XXII, in *Basic Writings of Saint Augustine*, 2 Volumes, edited and with an introduction by Whitney J. Oates (New York: Random House, 1948): 797.

24. Journet, *The Meaning of Evil*, 176-177.

25. Journet, *The Meaning of Evil*, 178.

26.   Rahner, "Why Does God Allow Us to Suffer?", 201.
27.   Rahner, "Why Does God Allow Us to Suffer?", 202.
28.   See the introduction to *Chapter 6*.
29.   One example of the debate is the exchange between David Griffin and David Basinger, as noted in *Chapter 6*. There are countless versions of this debate and while process thinkers are among those who lead the way in rejecting the traditional God of classical Christianity, there is debate even within the process community about the nature and extent of God's non-coercive, non-unilateral coercive power. This has been one of the areas in which I have published and would refer the reader to my *Evil and the Process God* (London, Lewiston, NY, and Toronto, ON: Edwin Mellen Press, 1985).
30.   Rahner, "Why Does God Allow Us to Suffer?", 206. See also Rahner's "The Human Question of Meaning in the Face of the Absolute Mystery of God," *Theological Investigations XVII* (New York: Crossroad, 1983): 89-104.

I   Aquinas and Thomism [Selected Publications]

For some of the relevant writings by Thomas Aquinas (1225-1274), see the following: *Basic Writings of Saint Thomas Aquinas*. Edited by Anton C. Pegis. New York, Random House, 1945; *Summa Contra Gentiles*. Translated by Charles J. O'Neil. Notre Dame, IN: University of Notre Dame Press, 1975; *Summa Theologica*. London: Eyre and Spottiswoode, 1964.

1828.   Anglin, Bill, and Stewart Goetz. "Evil is Privation." *International Journal for Philosophy of Religion* 13 (1982): 3-12. [Refutes Kane's argument ("Evil and Privation" [#1884]) against evil as *privation*. Anglin and Goetz argue that there are reasons for accepting the privation of good theory other than those rejected by Kane. They argue also that God cannot create something inherently evil without compromising the divine goodness. See also Bill Anglin's book-length defense of Thomistic theism, *Free Will and Christian Faith*. Oxford: Clarendon Press, 1990.]

1829.   Ayers, Robert H. "A Viable Theodicy for Christian Apologetics." *Modern Schoolman* 52 (1975): 391-403. [Argues for the necessity of a natural or rational theodicy as a *necessary, though not sufficient condition* for revealed theodicy. Theology must respond to the challenge of analytic philosophy to avoid mere subjective emotionalism. A major problem for theodicy is the inconsistency of Aquinas's view of divine omniscience. Freedom and determinism must be more clearly defined as well. Ayers argues that the content of revelation is coherent with the theodicy of natural theology which he has outlined. Aquinas's view of omnipotence (God can do all things which are within the scope of possibility) is a necessary element in a viable theodicy, but Aquinas's understanding of omniscience is flawed. If God knows all things simultaneously, then either time is unreal or God is not really omniscient. Otherwise, events can be known to be actual before they are actual—an obvious contradiction. Furthermore, there would be no freedom in human beings. Ayers proposes a limitation on omniscience similar to that placed on omnipotence; God is inside time such that temporal experience is as real for God as it is for human experience. (See Teske's response, "Omniscience, Omnipotence, and Divine Transcendence" [#1947]).]

1830.   Balthasar, Hans Urs von. "The Problem of Evil." *Internationale Katholische Zeitschrift* 8 (1979): 193-250.

1831.   Belleggia, Concetta. *God and the Problem of Evil*. Boston, MA: St. Paul Editions, 1980.

1832.   Boyle, Joseph M. "The Principle of Double Effect: Good Actions Entangled in Evil." *Moral Theology Today: Certitudes and Doubts*. Edited by D. McCarthy. Braintree, MA: Pope John Center, 1984: 243-260.

1833.   Burrell, David B. *Aquinas, God and Action*. Notre Dame, IN: University of Notre Dame Press, 1979. [Answers philosophical objections to Aquinas from process philosophers, notably Charles Hartshorne, and the psychological objections from Carl Jung against evil as *privatio boni*. See also Burrell's "Does Process Theology Rest on a Mistake?" *Theological Studies* 43 (1982), 125-135.]

1834.   ———. "Maimonides, Aquinas and Gersonides on Providence and Evil." *Religious Studies* 20 (1984): 335-352.

1835.   ———. "God's Eternity." *Faith and Philosophy* 1 (1984): 389-406.

1836.   Clarke, W. Norris. "A New Look at the Immutability of God." *God: Knowable and Unknowable*. Edited by Robert J. Roth. New York: Fordham University Press, 1973: 43-72. [Thomists have been content to relegate all change and diversity to the creature and, as such, have not explained how God can love creatures and enter into dialogue with us. Process theists have a legitimate grievance against the way Thomists have failed to handle this issue. Clarke accepts God's "real" relation to the world, but suggests also constructive ways in which process philosophy could be rendered more congenial to Thomism. [See Lewis Ford's response, "The Immutable God and Father Clarke"[#995].]

1837.   ———. "Freedom as Value." *Freedom and Value*. Edited by Robert O. Johann. New York: Fordham University Press, 1976: 1-20. [Argues, following St. Thomas, that freedom is not an ultimate or absolute value by itself, but takes on such value only insofar as it is freedom for value, freedom for good, and for the sake of the Infinite Good. Freedom cut off from the good in the Infinite Good sinks into irrational indeterminacy. (The book contains eight other reflections on the mystery of human freedom by members of the Philosophy department at Fordham).]

1838.   ———. *The Philosophical Approach to God: A Contemporary Neo-Thomist Perspective*. Winston-Salem, IL: Wake Forest University Publications, 1979. [Contains revised version of his chapter in *God Knowable and Unknowable*, edited by Robert J. Roth: "A New Look at the Immutability of God" [#1836]. See Lewis Ford's response, "The Immutable God and Father Clarke" [#995]; see also Ford's "Can Freedom Be Created?" *Horizons, Journal of the College Theology Society* 4 (1977), 183-188. Clarke's response to Ford is in "Christian Theism and Whiteheadian Process Philosophy," *Process Theology*. Edited by Ronald H. Nash. Grand Rapids, MI: Baker Book House, 1987, 217-251.]

1839.   Connellan, Colm. *Why Does Evil Exist? A Philosophical Study of the Contemporary Presentation of the Question*. Hicksville, NY: Exposition Press, 1974. [Defence of Aquinas's theodicy, in response to the challenges of the contemporary writers, Antony Flew and Albert Camus.]

1840.   Connery, John R. "Deliver Us From Evil: Venial Sin and the Moral Life." *Principles of Catholic Moral Life*. Edited by W. May. Chicago, IL: Franciscan Herald Press, 1980: 221-235.

1841.   ———. "Catholic Ethics: Has the Norm for Rule-Making Changed?" *Theological Studies* 42 (1981): 232-250.

1842.   ———. "The Basis for Certain Key Exceptionless Moral Norms." *Moral Theology Today: Certitudes and Doubts*. Edited by D. McCarthy. Braintree, MA: Pope John Center, 1984: 182-192.

1843.   Coughlan, Michael. "Essential Aims and Unavoidable Responsibilities: A Response to Anscombe." *Bioethics* 4 (1990): 63-65. [Maintains that Anscombe and other supporters of *the principle of double effect* erroneously assume an agent is not responsible for the evil consequences of good actions.]

1844.   Courteney, William J. "The Dialectic of Omnipotence in the High and Late Middle Ages." *Divine Omniscience and Divine Omnipotence in Medieval Philosophy*. Edited by Tamar Rudavsky. Boston, MA: Reidel, 1985: 243-269.

1845. Cowburn, John. *Shadows and the Dark: The Problems of Suffering and Evil.* London: SCM Press, 1979. [Presents a solution to two of the problems of evil: for the first, concerning suffering which is no one's fault, Cowburn's theodicy relies upon that of Teilhard and process theology, reassessing the traditional conceptions of divine omnipotence, omniscience, and providence. For the second, concerning moral evil and the kinds of physical evils which follow from it, Cowburn draws on literary works (*MacBeth*, *Othello*, and *The Brothers Karamazov*), as well as on Karl Barth and evangelical theologians, arguing that the remedy for moral evil is repentance and forgiveness.]

1846. Craig, William Lane. "Aquinas on God's Knowledge of Future Contingents." *Thomist* 54 (1990): 33-79. [For other Craig publications on omniscience and the middle knowledge debates, see *Chapters 2 and 3*.]

1847. ———. "St. Anselm on Divine Knowledge and Future Contingents." *Laval Théologique et Philosophique* 42 (1986): 93-104. [See critical response to Craig by Theodore J. Kondoleon, "God's Knowledge of Future Contingents Singulars: A Reply" [#1890].]

1848. Curran, Charles E. "The Principle of Double Effect: Some Historical and Contemporary Observations." *L'Agire Morale.* Yves Congar, et al. Atti Del Congresso Internationale Rome and Napels: Edizioni Domenicane Italiane, 1977: 426-449.

1849. D'Arcy, Martin C. *The Pain of this World and the Providence of God.* New York: Longmans, Green and Co., 1935, 1953. [A discussion of the problem of evil in the form of a dialogue between people of various perspectives. D'Arcy presents a Thomistic theodicy. Evil is the *privation* of good. Human freedom, divine causation, and the fact that evil are to be seem in the light of Christ's salvific action on our behalf.]

1849. ———. *The Problem of Evil.* New York: Paulist Press, 1971. [God *permits*, rather than *causes*, evils. D'Arcy rejects false solutions which hold that evil is a positive thing, that God is finite, and that the problem of evil is a logical problem which threatens God's existence. The solution to the theodicy issue is found both in reason (which vindicates God) and revelation (which tells us what God is like and shows us how to live). The fall and original sin show us God's purposes and why sin and evil exist. The cross and redemption show us how sin can be seen as *felix culpa*.]

1851. Davies, Brian. *Thinking About God.* London: Geoffrey Chapman, 1983. *Chapter 8*, "God and Goodness," 200-231. [Presents a Thomist theodicy. Davies rejects Alvin Plantinga's free will defense [see Chapter 2], siding with John Mackie, who holds that God could have created a world where people always act rightly. Davies supports Flew's contention (*The Presumption of Atheism* [#225]) that the free will defense ignores the Christian doctrine of creation: God is the first cause in a nontemporal sequence. Davies rejects the theodicies of John Hick [see Chapter 5] and Richard Swinburne [see Chapter 4] for holding that evil serves a good end: Davies holds that it is not clear that moral goodness could not exist without evils. Hick and Swinburne, and many others, mistakenly assume, moreover, that God is obliged to act morally. This is contradicted by biblical passages and by divine changelessness and the creation "out of nothing": God is the cause of all things, including moral obligations, but is not bound by them. Davies's God wills *only* what is good; evil is the *privation* of this goodness. God has created free creatures who cause moral evil. God is good, according to Davies, because (for example) God causes what is good.]

1852. ————. *An Introduction to the Philosophy of Religion*. Oxford: Oxford University Press, 1982. [See response by Moulder, "In Search of a Theodicy" [#1327] and more recently by Jeff Gordon, "The Doctrine of Conservation and the Free-Will Defense," *Sophia* 31 (1992), 59-64. Gordon refutes Davies's contention that classical theism cannot have a free will defense because its God is involved in every causal process. Gordon argues for compatibilism.]

1853. ————. "The Problem of Evil and Modern Philosophy—I." *New Black friars* 63 (1982): 529-539. [Offers a Thomistic solution to the problem of evil. Davies argues that we should not regard God as a being along side other beings who can interfere with our freedom. God should be seen, rather as the reason there is anything at all.]

1854. ————."The Problem of Evil and Modern Philosophy—II." *New Blackfriars* 64 (1983): 18-28. [Against Hick and Swinburne who argue that God must be good, Davies argues that, as creator, *God is not a being* and, hence, is not an ultimately responsible being. God is good but not in the sense that this term applies to human beings: God is the cause of all that is good.]

1855. ————. "God and Evil: Responses and Questions." *Clergy Review* 68 (1983): 383-390. [A survey of various responses to the problem of evil, with brief reference to Mackie, Hick's Irenaean theodicy, the free will defense and the objections of Mackie (shared by Aquinas and the contemporary Thomist, Herbert McCabe: God could have created free creatures who always use their freedom for good). Davies contends that Dostoevsky's protest against the "higher harmony" cuts across Hick's theodicy and the free will defense. Davies considers also Aquinas's view of evil as the *privation* of good, Moltmann's suffering God, McCloskey's critique, and others. He concludes with a brief annotated bibliography.]

1856. Davis, Douglas P. "Suárez and the Problem of Positive Evil." *American Philosophical Quarterly* 65 (1991): 259-266. [Contends that Francisco Suárez (1548-1617) was unsuccessful in arguing that there can be positive evil and yet retain its *privative* nature. See also Douglas Davis, "The Privation Account of Evil: H.J. McCloskey and Francisco Suárez," *Proceedings of the American Catholic Philosophical Association* 61 (1987), 199-208.]

1857. Dedek, John F. "Intrinsically Evil Act: An Historical Study of the Mind of St. Thomas." *Thomist* 43 (1979): 385-413.

1858. Dodds, Michael J. "Thomas Aquinas, Human Suffering, and the Unchanging Love of God." *Theological Studies* 52 (1991): 330-344. [Defends Aquinas's theodicy versus "suffering of God" theodicy. He maintains that divine compassion is not a *reaction* to suffering but a benevolent *action* on behalf of creatures.]

1859. Doering, Bernard. "Jacques Maritain, George Bernanos and Julien Green on the Mystery of Suffering and Evil." *Religion and Literature* 17 (1985): 37-55. [Discussion of Maritain's *God and the Permission of Evil* [#1899], and the writings of Julien Green (*Léviathan*, Paris: Plon, 1929) and George Bernanos (*Sous le Soleil de Satan*. Edited by William Bush. Paris: Plon, 1982). Maritain's final solution seemed to be that God suffers with us in our suffering: see other references to this theme in *Appendix C*.]

1860.   Donceel, Joseph F. "Second Thoughts on the Nature of God." *Thought* 46 (1971): 346-370. [Advocates a modification of the traditional Thomist God of immutability, following the lead of Hegel and Whitehead. Donceel holds that God must be affected by the world's suffering and (in agreement with Teilhard de Chardin) holds that God cannot create a world in evolution without physical evil.]

1861.   ———. *The Searching Mind: An Introduction to a Philosophy of God*. Notre Dame: Notre Dame University Press, 1979. [In a brief section on theodicy (152-163), Donceel maintains that Teilhard's optimism about having solved the problem of evil was premature: he has not shown that creation without evolution and evolution without the byproducts of evil are impossible or contradictory. Donceel appeals to Maurice Blondel's explanation of natural evil (*L'Action*. Paris: Alcan, 1893) as a condition for moral growth. He appeals also to the unfathomable mystery of an infinite God: there must be an explanation for evil, but it is hidden in the mystery of God.]

1862.   Dupré, Louis. "Themes in Contemporary Philosophy of Religion." *New Scholasticism* 43 (1969): 577-601. [Includes a discussion of Maritain's *God and the Permission of Evil* [#1899]. Maritain liberated the problem of evil from the Molinists and Banesism, yet his own solution is only half-hearted: a God who chooses purposes and realizes them through human free action cannot avoid falling under Maritain's own objections. If we are free, then even redemptive events (the incarnation) cannot be predetermined by God.]

1863.   Felt, James W. "Invitation to a Philosophic Revolution." *New Scholasticism* 45 (1971): 87-109. [Contends that traditional Thomistic metaphysics must be revised to reconcile necessary conclusions of Thomas's system (God is immutable) with known facts of experience (God loves us and responds to us). Felt acknowledges that it is difficult to reconcile the Thomistic necessity of an intrinsic divine indifference with a divine concern for creatures: Aquinas's view that God could have prevented all evils contradicts the revelation of divine love.]

1864.   Flynn, Thomas. "Time Redeemed: Maritain's Christian Philosophy of History." *Understanding Maritain: Philosopher and Friend*. Edited by Deal W. Hudson and M. Mancini. Macon, GA: Mercer University Press, 1988: 307-324.

1865.   Gewirth, Alan. "Natural Law, Human Action, and Morality." *The Georgetown Symposium on Ethics: Essays in Honor of Henry Babcock Veatch*. Edited by Rocco Porreco. Lanham, MD: University Press of America, 1984: 67-90.

1866.   Gleason, Robert W. *The Search for God*. New York: Sheed and Ward, 1964. [Contemporary Thomist defense of God versus various challenges. *Chapter 5*, "Anguish," analyses the concept of anguish in assorted historical figures. Gleason contends that the Catholic solution to the problem of anguish differs from the Protestant solutions and existential solutions. Rather than stoic acceptance, the Catholic solution sees anguish against the background of the cross.]

1867.   Gornall, Thomas. "A Note on the Problem of Evil." *Heythrop Journal* 3 (1962): 241-247. [Presents a Thomistic solution to theodicy. He argues that punishment is never willed by God *per se*, but only *per accidens*. Penalty in this life (arising from God's created world) is intended to restore the creature to good. God did not create a world without moral evil, since without sin we would not know the depth of divine love.]

1868.   Hart, Charles A. *Thomistic Metaphysics: An Inquiry into the Act of Existing.*
         Englewood Cliffs, NJ: Prentice-Hall, 1959. [*Chapter 15*, "The Problem of Evil,"
         discusses (via close scrutiny of primary texts) the nature of evil and its cause in
         the writings of Aquinas. Hart concludes that Aquinas's theodicy is the mean (a
         qualified optimism) between the extremes of the optimism of a Leibniz and the
         pessimism of a Nietzsche or Schopenhauer.]

1869.   Hemmerle, Klaus. "Evil." *Sacramentum Mundi, Volume 2.* Edited by Karl Rahner,
         et al. New York: Herder and Herder, 1968: 279-283. [See also the entry on "theo-
         dicy" [#1886].]

1870.   Higgins, David. "Evil in Maritain and Lonergan: The Emerging Probability of a
         Synthesis." *Jacques Maritain.* Edited by John F.X. Knasas. Notre Dame, IN: Uni-
         versity of Notre Dame Press, 1988: 235-242. [Argues that there is a synthesis of
         themes regarding theodicy in Maritain and Lonergan: Maritain's inverted intuition
         and Lonergan's inverse insights; Maritain's detailed analysis of the role of God and
         the creature in the act of choosing to do evil and Lonergan's notion of basic sin;
         Maritain's initial intuition of being and Lonergan's transcendental precepts; and the
         Name of God as referring to either the first cause or the ultimate solution.]

1871.   Hill, William J. "Does the World Make a Difference to God?" *Thomist* 38 (1974):
         146-164. [Concedes to process philosophers that the concept of God must embrace
         both contingency and temporality. Yet, Hill defends the Thomist tradition by expli-
         cating the Thomistic distinction between the *entitative* and the *intentional* orders,
         hitherto "latent" and undeveloped in the writings of Aquinas. This distinction can
         show both God's absolute immutability and his "changement" in others.]

1872.   ———. "Does God Know the Future? Aquinas and Some Moderns." *Theological
         Studies* 36 (1975): 3-18.

1873.   ———. "Two Gods of Love: Aquinas and Whitehead." *Listening* 14 (1976): 249-264.

1874.   ———. "The Doctrine of God After Vatican II." *Thomist* 51 (1987): 395-418.
         [Much recent theology exploits an anthropomorphic starting point, which historizes
         the deity of God and, among other things, introduces suffering in God. Hill contends
         that such a God would be less than God, whether this suffering were a necessity or
         freely willed by God. (See also the other entries by Hill, which make similar points
         about the immutability of God. Hill argues that the concept of God, as shown by
         Whitehead, must embrace contingency and temporality, attributes which have been
         understood hitherto as non-divine).]

1875.   Hudson, Deal W. "Can Happiness be Saved?" *Jacques Maritain.* Edited by John
         F.X. Knasas. Notre Dame, IN: University of Notre Dame Press, 1988: 257-264.
         [For Maritain, it is no accident that the happy life should contain pain. Yet he
         envisages within pain a "law of creative conflict" that enables persons to move to
         higher forms of active peace and transfiguring integration.]

1876.   Janssens, Louis. "Ontic Evil and Moral Good." *Louvain Studies* 4 (1972): 115-
         156. [Published also in *Readings in Moral Philosophy, I: Moral Norms and Cath-
         olic Tradition.* Edited by Charles C. Curran and Richard A. McCormick. New
         York: Paulist Press, 1979.]

1877. ——. "Norms and Priorities in a Love Ethic." *Louvain Studies* 6 (1977): 207-238.

1878. ——. "St. Thomas Aquinas and the Question of Proportionality." *Louvain Studies* 11 (1982): 26-46.

1879. ——. "A Moral Understanding of Some Arguments of Saint Thomas." *Ephemerides Theologicae Lovanienses* 62 (1987): 354-360.

1880. ——. "Ontic Good and Evil: Premoral Values and Disvalues." *Louvain Studies* 16 (1987): 62-82.

1881. Journet, Charles Cardinal. *The Meaning of Evil*. Translated by Michael Barry. New York: P.J. Kennedy and Sons, 1961. [Defends a contemporary (and often cited) version of Thomistic theodicy. Journet argues that evil is *the privation of good*, that God *permits* evil rather than *causes* evil directly, and that God does so since it is better to draw good from evil than to permit no evil at all. Journet defends the power and goodness of God, and the view that a world with evil may be incomparably better than a world without evil. Animal suffering is the price paid for animal life: to do away with the suffering would be to do away with the animal itself. Animals suffering can be a means to test the faith of human beings. Journet defends, furthermore, the doctrine of hell as a necessary end for human sinners. The faithful alone will be redeemed.]

1882. ——. "Jacques Maritain: Theologian." *New Scholasticism* 46 (1972): 32-50. [Contends that Maritain unlocked the problem of the relations between divine grace and human freedom, a problem which had come to a dead end. The first initiative rests with the sinner alone: God is in no way responsible for evil, yet struggles against it with initiatives of grace, initiatives which we "shatter." Maritain held also that God suffers with us: see the numerous publications on this theme in *Appendix C*.]

1883. Joyce George H. *Principles of Natural Theology*. New York: Longmans, 1972. [Presents and defends a Thomistic theodicy. God has created a good world, but not the "best possible world" (see *Chapter 3* for more on this theme). Physical evils are the natural accompaniment of physical creatures. Divine providence is an effective means in aiding us to secure our ultimate beatitude through such evils. Moral evils, however, are not to be explained merely as the result of misuse of free will, since freedom need not involve the power to choose wrong. Such evils are a probation: we must earn our reward. If, however, *all* of humanity were to attain final beatitude, probation would have little meaning.]

1884. Kane, G. Stanley. "Evil and Privation." *International Journal for Philosophy of Religion* 11 (1980): 43-58. [Clarifies the theory of evil as *the privation of good*. Kane concludes that the theory is mistaken and that the reasons proponents of the theory accepted it are less than cogent. (See the response of Anglin and Goetz, "Evil is Privation" [#1828]).]

1885. Kelly, Anthony. "God: How Near a Relation?" *Thomist* 34 (1970): 191-229. [Argues that the traditional understanding of divine immutability in Thomism needs to be reexamined. A purely external relation of reason is not sufficient; God must be related to the world with a real internal relatedness.]

1886. Kern, Walter, and Jörg Splett. "Theodicy." *Sacramentum Mundi, Volume 6*. Edited by Karl Rahner, et al. New York: Herder and Herder, 1970: 213-218. [Surveys selective historical answers to the theodicy issue. The authors define modern theodicies as either optimistic or pessimistic. The former hold that evil is intrinsic to the world, but this relativizes evil as a means to an end. The *best of all possible worlds* view fails on philosophical and theological grounds: the perfection of the material world always admits of a higher perfection. Pessimists, on the other hand, exaggerate evil, make it an absolute, and in so doing distort the doctrine of God. The cross of Christ, however, as the consequence of sin, renders all metaphysical tragedy-writing anaemic. This statement of the problem is the solution: the sin of humans becomes the mystery (or scandal) of the love of God. Sin was the occasion of the cross and the cross is the inner ground for the permission of evil. The redemption of Christ has replaced the disruption of sin and its consequences.]

1887. King, James T. "Is Relation to God Logically Impossible?" *Proceedings of the American Catholic Philosophical Association* 42 (1968): 126-136. [Contends that much of traditional theodicy is mistaken in that it has ignored the basic fact that God is not related to the world.]

1888. Kitchel, Jean Clare. "The Value of Human Suffering: Pope John Paul II and Karol Wojtyla." *Proceedings of the American Catholic Philosophical Association* 60 (1986): 185-193.

1889. Knasas, John F.X. "Aquinas and Finite Gods." *Proceedings of the American Catholic Philosophical Association* 53 (1979): 88-97.

1890. Kondoleon, Theodore J. "God's Knowledge of Future Contingents Singulars: A Reply." *Thomist* 56 (1992): 117-139. [Response to William Craig, "St. Anselm on Divine Knowledge and Future Contingents" [#1847].]

1891. Kretzmann, Norman. "A Particular Problem of Creation: Why Would God Create This World?" *Being and Goodness*. Edited by Scott MacDonald. Ithaca, NY: Cornell University Press, 1991: 229-249.

1892. Kretzmann, Norman, and Eleonore Stump. "Being and Goodness." *Being and Goodness*. Edited by Scott MacDonald. Ithaca, NY: Cornell University Press, 1991: 98-128. [Reprinted from *Divine and Human Action: Essays in the Metaphysics of Theism* [#1439].]

1893. Küng, Hans. *Does God Exist?* New York: Vintage Books, 1981. [See the response to Küng's brief section on theodicy by David Griffin, "The Rationality of Belief in God: A Response to Hans Küng" [#867].]

1894. Langan, John P. "Sins of Malice in the Moral Psychology of Thomas Aquinas." *Annual of the Society of Christian Ethics*. Edited by David C. Yeager, 1987: 179-198.

1895. Lonergan, Bernard J.F. *Insight*. New York: Philosophical Library, 1958. [Analysis the processes by which we know, and then the structure of what we know. He explores the problem of what we can know of God, the fact of evil, and the possible solution to the theodicy issue. Sin and evil, however, are unintelligible and cannot be explained fully. The question is how to reconcile this fact of human existence [evil] with what we know about God. God ought to have given us a supernatural means to love and in such a way that we could freely accept it and cooperate with God.]

1896. Lubac, Henri De. "Can a Will be Essentially Good?" *The Human Person and the World of Values*. Edited by Balduin V. Schwarz. Bronx, NY: Fordham

University Press, 1960: 121-131. [Affirms that the will is of the moral order inasmuch as it chooses moral goods and that the will is, at the same time, of the natural order in the sense in which the natural order is opposed to the moral order. The latter implies liberty; the former implies an imposed necessity.]

1897. Maritain, Jacques. *Saint Thomas and the Problem of Evil*. Milwaukee, WI: Marquette University Press, 1942. [Defense of Aquinas's theodicy: the *privation* theory, the perfection of the universe as a whole, and evil action as a result of a defect in the agent (a voluntary and free defect). Maritain argues that the defect is itself not an evil. The first initiative of evil permitted by God comes from the creature alone, from our voluntary and free failure. Human beings, not God, are the cause of moral evils.]

1898. ———. *Existence and the Existent*. New York: Doubleday, 1948.

1899. ———. *God and the Permission of Evil*. Milwaukee, WI: Bruce Publishing Co., 1966. [Maintains that the fundamental principle in theodicy discussions is that God is innocent of evil. The evil of nature is not the object of God's willing or permission: it happens indirectly according to the very essence of material reality. Maritain focuses on moral evil, the sin freely chosen by human beings. By distinguishing between God's antecedent and consequent wills, between shatterable and unshatterable notions of the First Cause, and other factors, he seeks to show that moral evil is permitted by God without being willed or caused by God.]

1900. Mascall, Eric L. *He Who Is*. London, New York: Longmour, Green & Co. and Hamden, CT: Archon Books, 1970. [*Chapter 12*, "The Moral Argument and the Problem of Evil" (179-183), argues that suffering is a problem largely because of our limitations of knowledge and imagination. Mascall maintains that if we could see from God's perspective, it would be obvious that present suffering cannot be compared to the glory that will be revealed in us. Sufferings are instrumental to this end. See also Mascall's *Existence and Analogy*. London: Darton, Longman and Todd, 1949; and his *The Openness of Being*. London: Darton, Longman and Todd, 1971.]

1901. May, William E. "Aquinas and Janssens on the Moral Meaning of Human Acts." *Thomist* 48 (1984): 566-606. [Refutes Louis Janssens's interpretation of Aquinas's view of the structure and moral meaning of human acts ("Ontic Evil and Moral Good" [#1876], "Norms and Priorities in a Love Ethic" [#1877], and "St. Thomas Aquinas and the Question of Proportionality" [#1878]).]

1902. McCabe, Herbert. "God: III—Evil." *New Blackfriars* 62 (1981): 4-17. [Defends Thomistic theodicy against modern criticisms. God brings about all that is good and does not directly bring about anything that is evil. McCabe defends the *privation* theory of evil. He explains natural evil as inevitable in a material world (lions fulfil themselves by eating lambs), and moral evil as the result of human freedom. Yet God could have made a world in which no one sinned and everyone was free. Why God permits moral evil is an unfathomable mystery, yet it is not a contradiction.]

1903. McFadden, Thomas M. "Theodicy." *Encyclopedic Dictionary of Religion, III*. Edited by Paul Kevin Meagher, Thomas O'Brian, and Sister Consuelo Maria Aherne. Washington, DC: Corpus Publications, 1979: 3489. [Reference to Augustine and Leibniz.]

1904. Moran, Lawrence. "On Uncaused Events." *Proceedings of the American Catholic Philosophical Association* 40 (1966): 86-93. [For Aristotle and Aquinas, chance and evil events are identical.]

1905. Muller, Richard A. "Incarnation, Immutability, and the Case for Classical Theism." *Westminster Theological Journal* 45 (1983): 22-40.

1906. Mulligan, Dermot. "Moral Evil, St. Thomas and the Thomists." *Philosophical Studies* (Ireland) 9 (1960): 3-26.

1907. Nerney, Gayne. "Aristotle and Aquinas on Indignation: From Nemesis to Theodicy." *Faith and Philosophy* 8 (1991): 81-95. [Aquinas's critique of Aristotle's evaluation of the ethical significance of "indignation."]

1908. O'Brian, Thomas C. "Suffering." *Encyclopedic Dictionary of Religion, II*. Edited by Paul Kevin Meagher, Thomas O'Brian, and Sister Consuelo Maria Aherne. Washington, DC: Corpus Publications, 1979: 3411. [Discusses Aquinas's view of evil as *privation*. O'Brian notes that Aquinas held that every evil is either the evil of sin or the evil of punishment, and that Christ absorbed the evil of punishment redemptively, as expiation and atonement. The mystery of the suffering Christ is the only divinely-given response to suffering. The power communicated by faith in Christ is the only resource that keeps the sufferer from despair and blasphemy.]

1909. ———. "Evil." *Encyclopedic Dictionary of Religion I*. Edited by Paul Kevin Meagher, Thomas O'Brian, and Sister Consuelo Maria Aherne. Washington, DC: Corpus Publications, 1979: 1275. [Defends the view of evil as the *privation* of good. O'Brian maintains also that Christ is the only absolutely sure answer to the problem of evil. The divine response is pardon and reconciliation. See also O'Brian's other entries: "Suffering"; "Guilt and Punishment"; and "Mortal Sin."]

1910. O'Connor, Daniel John. *Aquinas and Natural Law*. London: Macmillan, 1967.

1911. Oesterle, John. "St. Thomas, Moral Evil, and the Devil." *L'Agire Morale*. Edited by Yves Congar, et al. Atti Del Congresso Internationale Rome and Napels: Edizioni Domenicane Italiane, 1977: 510-515.

1912. Owens, Joseph. "Theodicy, Natural Theology, and Metaphysics." *The Modern Schoolman* 28 (1951): 126-137. [See also Joseph Owens, *Saint Thomas Aquinas and the Existence of God: Collected Papers*. Albany, NY: State University of New York Press, 1980.]

1913. Partee, Charles. "Predestination in Aquinas and Calvin." *Reformed Review* 32 (1978): 14-22. [Holds that for both Calvin and Aquinas, there is no genuine human free will.]

1914. Pendergast, Richard. J. *Cosmos*. New York: Fordham University Press, 1973. [*Chapter 7*, "The Problem of Evil," addresses theodicy in the context of the developing cosmos. He argues that evil is the result of the defective symbolizing activity of creatures which fail to complete the original being with which God endows us. Yet physical evil is inevitable in a world in which humans might not have sinned. Sin corrupted the evolutionary process. Pendergast defends an interpretation of original sin against its rejection by modern scientific views. (See Galligan's critical assessment, in his *God and Evil* [#1092]).]

1915.   Petit, François. *The Problem of Evil*. New York: Hawthorn, 1959. [Evil is insoluble apart from the fall, redemption, glorification, and ascetic life. Evil is *privation* which becomes, in the void it creates, an appeal to God and to divine action. Petit surveys various mythic, historical and biblical theories of evil, and the theories of Augustine and Aquinas. With Aquinas, he contends, "Christian thought on the subject of evil reached its full elaboration." He then offers a theodicy, based on Thomistic principles: God works good out of the evil of *privation*, as warnings to prevent more serious evils, as reparation, and as perfecting power. Evil will remain throughout eternity; the damned will remain separated from God forever, yet there is hope of salvation for the faithful.]

1916.   Pontifex, Dom Mark. *The Existence of God*. New York: Longmans, Green and Co., 1947. [*Chapter 7*, "The Problem of Evil," offers a Thomistic theodicy: evil is *privation* of good, divine causative power, etc. Pontifex argues that for a creature to be capable of supreme happiness, the Beatific Vision, it must have freedom. The creature must be built up from imperfection to perfection. Moral evil is the result of free will, despite divine causative power; physical evil is the result of the very nature of our universe. If God had created another universe, we would not have the chance for ultimate happiness. God may have created worlds with less suffering than ours, but it was better for ours to be created than not created.]

1917.   ———. "God and the Mystery of Evil." *Downside Review* 75 (1957/1958): 123-124. [Response to Dom Bruno Webb's "God and the Mystery of Evil" [#1953]. Pontifex disputes various of Webb's points, that the damned suffer eternally, for example. This, claims Pontifex, leaves no place for God's mercy.]

1918.   ———. "The Value of Pain." *Downside Review* 76 (1958): 349-363. [Argues that just punishment is the pain a sinner suffers either as a result of sin or in order to put things right.]

1919.   ———. *Freedom and Providence*. London: Burns & Oates, 1960. [Presents a theodicy based on Thomistic principles. He argues that evil is the *privation* of good; God's power and goodness are ultimate; the whole is good as such, while the parts experience evils; creatures cannot attain perfection without prior frustration (suffering); God has not created a better world with less evil since this is not possible with respect to individual human beings: we would not exist as we are in a different kind of world. Animal suffering is beyond our grasp since we do not know enough about what animals feel. He argues a middle position between the Molinists and extreme Thomists with respect to God's knowledge and creaturely freedom. God permits the creature's failure because this is unavoidable if there is to be supreme happiness possible for the creature. The creature's failure has a negative priority over the intensity of God's causal act upon the creature.]

1920.   ———. "The Question of Evil." *Prospects for Metaphysics*. Edited by Ian Ramsey. New York: Philosophical Library, 1961: 121-137. [Contends that evil, the result of free will, is the unavoidable condition for good. Free will in creatures can be reconciled with divine power only by seeing that creatures can initiate failure (negative causality) but are not the ultimate source of positive action. Creation is a gradual process in which there is a stage of imperfection before perfection is reached.]

1921.   ———. "God's Omnipotence." *Downside Review* 87 (1969): 381-390. [Holds that God's power over creation necessarily is limited: creatures are dependent upon God's causality except for sinning.]

1922.   Quinn, John M. "Triune Self-Giving: One Key to the Problem of Suffering." *Thomist* 44 (1980): 173-218. [Rejects the suffering, finite God proposed by process thinkers, Whitehead and Hartshorne (and by other "finitists," Berdyaev, and Peter Bertocci). Rather than this type of manoeuvre to explain evil (among other things), Quinn supports the more traditional view that God is loving and caring not in spite of being immutable, but because of it. God causes evils which will produce goods and ultimate triumph over suffering.]

1923.   Rahner, Karl. "On the Theology of the Incarnation." *Theological Investigations, Volume 4*. Baltimore: Helicon, 1966: 105-120.

1924.   ———. "Hell." *Sacramentum Mundi, Volume 3*. Edited by Karl Rahner, et al. New York: Herder and Herder, 1969: 7-10.

1925.   ———. "Original Sin." *Sacramentum Mundi, Volume 4*. Edited by Karl Rahner, et al. New York: Herder and Herder, 1969: 328-334.

1926.   ———. "Salvation." *Sacramentum Mundi, Volume 5*. Edited by Karl Rahner, et al. New York: Herder and Herder, 1969: 405-409.

1927.   ———. "Why Does God Allow Us to Suffer?" *Theological Investigations, Volume 19*. New York: Crossroad, 1983: 194-208. [Rejects four prominent traditional theories regarding evil: suffering as a natural side-effect in an evolving world; suffering an effect of creaturely, sinful freedom; suffering as a situation of trial and maturing; and suffering as a pointer to another life, an eternal life. Rahner concludes that suffering is incomprehensible to human minds, just as God is incomprehensible to us.]

1928.   Rahner, Karl, and Herbert Vorgrimler. "Evil, Wickedness." *Theological Dictionary*. New York: Herder and Herder, 1965: 156-157. [Maintains that, in itself, evil has no independent reality. The source of evil is the free choice of the will, in opposition to good, beginning with the rebellion of the Angels who became wicked spirits (Demons). The end of the power of evil has been proclaimed and ushered in by Christ. (See also the entries for "Original Sin," "Sin," "Soteriology," "Suffering," "Theodicy," "Trinity," etc.)]

1929.   Rojas, Jose. "St. Thomas on the Direct/Indirect Distinction." *Ephemerides Theologicae Lovanienses* 63 (1988): 371-392.

1930.   Schillebeeckx, Edward C. "Christian Identity and Human Integrity." *Is Being Human a Criterion for Being Christian?* Edited by Jean-Pierre Jossua and Claude Geffré. Edinburgh: T&T Clark, 1982: 23-31. [Argues that suffering through and for others is an expression of the unconditional validity of a praxis of doing good and of resistance to evil and innocent suffering.]

1931.   Schoonenberg, Piet. "Process or History in God?" *Louvain Studies* 4 (1973): 303-319. [Holds that there is much to learn from process theology about the image of God as being "dipolar" and, more specifically, that God's knowing of the world implies a real change in God. (See *Chapter 6*) for "process theodicy" publications.]

1932.   ———. *Man and Sin*. Notre Dame, IN: University of Notre Dame Press, 1965.

1933.   ———. "Sin." *Sacramentum Mundi, Volume 6.* Edited by Karl Rahner, et al. New York: Herder and Herder, 1970: 87-92.

1934.   Siwek, Paul. *The Philosophy of Evil.* New York: Roland Press, 1950. [Maintains that evil is the *privation* of being. Evil is necessary, a source of good. Evil recalls us to our immortal destiny.]

1935.   ———. "Evil, a Consequence of Sin." *Revue de l'Université d'Ottawa* 25 (1955): 26-52. [Refutes the theories of Charles Secrétain (*La Civilisation et la Croyance.* Paris, 1893) and Charles Renouvier (*Le Personnalisme.* Paris: Alean, 1926). Both held that the origin of evil is explained by the sin of human beings.]

1936.   ———. "The Problem of Evil in the Theory of Dualism." *Laval Théologique et Philosophique* 11 (1955): 67-80. [Rejects Manichean and Zoroastrian dualisms, since they contradict the *privation* of good view of evil and the omnipotence of God.]

1937.   ———. "How Pantheism Resolves the Enigma of Evil." *Laval Théologique et Philosophique* 11 (1955): 213-221. [Contends that there is no evil in a pantheistic monism. Good and evil, according to Spinoza, are mental concepts. Evil is the *privation* of good. Siwek argues that Spinoza's solution to theodicy is superficial and illusory: by denying the reality of evil, Spinoza turned it into tragedy and despair.]

1938.   Smith, Brooke Williams. *Jacques Maritain, Antimodern or Ultramodern: An Historical Analysis of His Critics, His Thought and His Life.* Oxford: Elsevier, 1976.

1939.   Smith, Gerald. *Natural Theology.* New York: Macmillan, 1951, 1959. [*Chapter 16,* "The Providence of God," contains a brief Thomistic theodicy: evil (physical and moral) is the *privation* of good. God has created a plenitude, a variety of creatures to imitate the divine perfection. Contrariety of physical goods must cause physical evils. Moral evils, the result of free will, is the price for the possibility of happiness. God causes free choices. It is incomprehensible how God's causality is reconcilable, ultimately, with free acts of creatures, yet this is because God transcends us so greatly.]

1940.   Stokes, Walter. "Freedom as Perfection: Whitehead, Thomas, and Augustine." *Proceedings of the American Catholic Philosophical Association* 36 (1962): 132-142. [Agrees with Whiteheadian process thought that the traditional Thomist interpretation of God as immutable is "a metaphysical scandal."]

1941.   ———. "God for Today and Tomorrow." *New Scholasticism* 37 (1963): 351-378.

1942.   ———. "Whitehead's Challenge to Theistic Realism." *New Scholasticism* 38 (1964): 1-21.

1943.   ———. "Is God Really Related to this World?" *Proceedings of the American Catholic Philosophical Association* 39 (1965): 145-151.

1944.   ———. "A Whiteheadian Approach to the Problem of God." *Traces of God in a Secular Culture.* Edited by George McLean. Staton Island, NY: Alba House, 1973: 61-84.

1945.   Stump. Eleonore. "Dante's Hell, Aquinas' Moral Theory, and the Love of God." *Canadian Journal of Philosophy* 16 (1986): 181-198. [Noting Aquinas's view of God and Dante's vision of hell, Stump argues that it is possible to claim both that God is good and that some persons are assigned to hell.]

1946.   ———. "Atonement According to Aquinas." *Philosophy and the Christian Faith*. Edited by Thomas V. Morris. Notre Dame, IN: University of Notre Dame Press, 1988: 61-91.

1947.   Teske, Roland J. "Omniscience, Omnipotence, and Divine Transcendence." *New Scholasticism* 53 (1979): 277-294. [Refutation of Ayers's redefinition of divine omniscience ("A Viable Theodicy for Christian Apologetics" [#1829]). Ayers's views of omniscience implies that God's knowledge is caused by human events, and that God is not the omni- potent cause of such contingencies. Teske makes use of Bernard Lonergan's interpretation of Aquinas to argue that Ayers's definition of omniscience is incompatible with human freedom. Lonergan's implicit definition of transcendence shows (contra Ayers) that God's omniscience is not incoherent with human freedom and that there is no denial of the reality of time.]

1948.   Torre, Michael. "The Sin of Man and the Love of God." *Jacques Maritain*. Edited by John F.X. Knasas. Notre Dame, IN: University of Notre Dame Press, 1988: 203-213. [Defends Maritain from the charge of misinterpreting Aquinas via a detailed analysis of relevant Thomistic texts. Torre holds that Maritain's most important contribution, perhaps, is his insistence that God is not responsible in any way for human sin, not even in permitting it. Torre supports also Maritain's insight about God's suffering: see *Appendix C*.]

1949.   Van Zeller, Dom Hubert. *Suffering in Other Worlds*. Springfield, IL: Templegate, 1964. [An interpretation of suffering as God-sent opportunity for spiritual growth. Divine providence implies that there is nothing haphazard about the allocation of human suffering. Suffering is deserved; it punishes and purifies.]

1950.   Vertin, Michael. "Philosophy of God: Theology and the Problems of Evil." *Laval Théologique et Philosophique* 37 (1981): 15-32. [Outlines a response to the problem of evil, based on the writings of Bernard Lonergan. Evil is understood best as the *privation* of good, yet theology can explicate revelation in a way which illuminates how fault and suffering are (at a deeper level) sin and punishment, and how their counterparts are love and redemption. Vertin concludes that we ought to respond to evil by striving to eliminate personal sinning, by accepting suffering as deserved for personal sins (the ethical aspect of suffering), and by accepting suffering which is not perceived to be deserved as the result also of personal sins (the tragic aspect of suffering).]

1951.   Walsh, James, and Patrick G. Walsh, editors. *Divine Providence and Human Suffering*. Wilmington, DE: Michael Glazier, 1985. [An anthology of writings on suffering in the writings of the early church. The Appendix contains the Apostolic Letter of Pope John Paul II, *Salvifici Doloris*, "The Christian Significance of Human Suffering." The Pope maintains that Christ's suffering and death were the price of our redemption, a fulfilment of the Scriptures. With Christ's suffering, all human suffering entered a new environment. Suffering is a test to which all are subjected. To share in Christ's glory is to suffer with Christ, to succumb to God's saving power.]

1952.   Watson, S. Youree. "The Other Face of Evil." *Essays in Morality and Ethics*. The Annual Publication of the College Theology Society. New York/Ramsey: Paulist Press, 1980: 3-28. [Defends and clarifies the *privation* of good theory of evil. Watson argues that God permits evil acts which could have been prevented by

God, since God will draw some good from the evil act. Denies as paradoxical that God can determine acts and that these acts can be free. Physical evils are necessary in an evolving world. There is constant destruction for the sake of higher values, sought by God. Theodicy must be seen from the perspective of eternal life. If not, we may well wonder why God has not intervened more often.]

1953. Webb, Bruno. "God and the Mystery of Evil?" and "Rejoinder to Pontifex." *Downside Review* 75 (1957): 338-358; (1958): 217-219. [Elaborates Aquinas's view of evil as the *privation* of good and the view that all creation is prone to evil (natural and moral) because of its finite nature. The physical evil which predates human beings is due to fallen angels. The origin of evil lies in the first spirit which committed sin. See response by Pontifex, "God and the Mystery of Evil" [#1917].]

1954. Williams, C.J.F. "Is God Really Related to His Creatures?" *Sophia* 8 (1969): 1-10.

1955. Wilson, Patricia. "Human Knowledge of God's Existence in the Theology of Bernard Lonergan." *Thomist* 35 (1971): 260-275.

1956. Wippel, John F. "Divine Knowledge, Divine Power and Human Freedom in Thomas Aquinas and Henry of Ghent." *Divine Omniscience and Divine Omnipotence in Medieval Philosophy*. Edited by Tamar Rudavsky. Boston, MA: Reidel, 1985: 213-242.

1957. Wright, John H. "Divine Knowledge and Human Freedom: The God Who Dialogues." *Theological Studies* 38 (1977): 450-477. [Contends that the traditional Thomist understanding of God as immutable essence does not account for how God is able to respond to a free human response. Wright argues for a third position between process philosophy traditional Thomism (as it is understood by process philosophy): the world's relationship to God does not condition the existence of God, but only its communication.]

1958. ———. "Problem of Evil, Mystery of Sin and Suffering." *Communico* 6 (1979): 140-156. [Maintains that biblical insight reveals that suffering is a sharing in the redemptive suffering of Christ.]

II   Augustine [Selected Publications]

Some of the most relevant of Augustine's writings are his *Confessions* (written in 397-401). New York: Mentor Books, 1963; *On Free Will* (written in 388, *Book I* and 391-395, Books II–III). *Augustine: Earlier Writings*. Edited by John H.S. Burleigh. Philadelphia, PA: Westminster Press, 1953; *The City of God* (written in 413-427). New York: Modern Library, 1950; *Enchiridion* (written in 426-427.)

1959. Andresen, C. *Bibliographia Augustiniana*. Darmstadt, 1973. [Contains a complete bibliography of Augustine's publications.]

1960. Babcock, William S. "Augustine on Sin and Moral Agency." *Journal of Religious Ethics* 16 (1988): 28-55. [Special edition on the "Ethics of Saint Augustine," edited by William S. Babcock.]

1961.   Berthold, Fred. "Free Will and Theodicy in Augustine: An Exposition and Critique." *Religious Studies* 17 (1981): 525-535.

1962.   Bonner, Gerald. *St. Augustine of Hippo—Life and Controversies*. London: SCM Press, 1963.

1963.   Borchert, Donald M. "Beyond Augustine's Answer to Evil." *Canadian Journal of Theology* 8 (1962): 237-248.

1964.   Brown, Robert F. "The First Evil Will Must be Incomprehensible: A Critique of Augustine." *Journal of the American Academy of Religion* 46 (1978): 315-329.

1965.   Burns, J. Patout. "Augustine on the Origin and Progress of Evil." *Journal of Religious Ethics* 16 (1988): 9-27. [Special edition on the "Ethics of Saint Augustine," edited by William S. Babcock.]

1966.   Burrell, David. "Reading the *Confessions* of Augustine: An Exercise in Theological Understanding." *Journal of Religion* 50 (1970): 327-351.

1967.   Burt, Donald X. "To Kill or Let Live: Augustine on Killing the Innocent." *Proceedings of the American Catholic Philosophical Association* 58 (1984): 112-119.

1968.   Cooper, Robert M. "Saint Augustine's Doctrine of Evil." *Scottish Journal of Theology* 16 (1963): 256-276.

1969.   Doull, James A. "Augustinian Trinitarianism and Existential Theology." *Dionysus* 3 (1979): 111-159.

1970.   Evans, Gillian R. *Augustine on Evil*. Cambridge, London, New York: Cambridge University Press, 1982.

1971.   Kaufman, Peter Iver. "Augustine, Evil, and Donatism: Sin and Sanctity Before the Pelagian Controversy." *Theological Studies* 51 (1990): 115-126.

1972.   Kirwan, Christopher. *Augustine*. London: Routledge, 1989.

1973.   Lavere, George J. "The Political Realism of Saint Augustine." *Augustinian Studies* 11 (1980): 135-144.

1974.   Lucas, J.R. "Pelagius and St. Augustine." *Journal of Theological Studies* 22 (1971): 73-85.

1975.   Maker, William A. "Augustine on Evil: The Dilemma of the Philosophers." *International Journal for Philosophy of Religion* 15 (1984): 149-160. [Argues that Augustine's account of evil as *privation of good* is superior to Manicheism and Platonism.]

1976.   McGrath, Alister E. "'The Righteousness of God' from Augustine to Luther." *Studia Theologica: Scandinavian Journal of Theology* 36 (1982): 63-78.

1977.   ———. "Divine Justice and Divine Equity in the Controversy Between Augustine and Julian of Eclanum." *Downside Review* 101 (1983): 312-319.

1978.   O'Brien, William J. "Towards Understanding Original Sin in Augustine's *Confessions*." *Thought* 49 (1974): 436-446.

1979.   O'Meara, John. *The Young Augustine*. London: Longman, 1980.

1980.   Pagels, Elaine. *Adam, Eve and the Serpent*. New York: Random House, 1988.

1981.   Prendiville, John G. "The Development of the Idea of Habit in the Thought of Saint Augustine." *Traditio* 28 (1972): 29-99.

1982.   Ranson, Guy H. "Augustine's Account of the Nature and Origin of Moral Evil." *Review and Expositor* 50 (1953): 309-322.

1983.   Rist, John M. "Plotinus on Matter and Evil." *Phronesis* 6 (1961): 154-166.

1984.   ———. "Augustine on Free Will and Predestination." *Journal of Theological Studies* 20 (1969): 420-447.

1985.   ———. "Plotinus and Augustine on Evil." *Plotino e il Neoplatonismo*. Edited by V. Cilento, et al. Roma: Academia Nasionale Dei Lincei, 1974: 495-508.

1986.   Rohatyn, D.A. "Augustine, Freedom, Evil and the Contemporary Predicament in Philosophy." *Aitia: Philosophy Humanities Magazine* 4/5 (1976/1977): 74-80.

1987.   Rowe, William L. "Augustine on Foreknowledge and Free Will." *Review of Metaphysics* 18 (1964): 356-363.

1988.   Russell, Frederick H. "'Only Something Good Can Be Evil': The Genesis of Augustine's Secular Ambivalence." *Theological Studies* 51 (1990): 698-716.

1989.   Sinnige, T.G. "Gnostic Influences in the Early Works of Plotinus and in Augustine." *Plotinus Amid Gnostics and Christians*. Edited by David T. Runia. Amsterdam: Free University Press, 1984: 73-97. [See Runia's published dissertation, *Philo of Alexandria and the "Timaeus" of Plato*. Amsterdam: Free University Press, 1983 and Leiden, 1986.]

1990.   Stark, Judith C. "The Problem of Evil: Augustine and Ricoeur."*Augustinian Studies* 13 (1982): 111-122. [Comparison of Augustine and Paul Ricoeur, both of whom conceived of evil as *nothingness*, Augustine in the ontological and moral senses; Ricoeur in the symbolic sense.]

1991.   Starnes, Colin. "Saint Augustine on Infancy and Childhood: Commentary on the First Book of Augustine's *Confessions*." *Augustinian Studies* 6 (1975): 15-43.

1992.   ———. "Saint Augustine and the Vision of the Truth: A Commentary on the Seventh Book of Augustine's *Confessions*." *Dionysius* 1 (1977): 85-126.

1993.   Woelfel, James W. *Augustinian Humanism: Studies in Human Bondage and Earthly Grace*. Washington, DC: University Press of America, 1979.

III   Leibniz [Selected Publications]

For some of the relevant publications by G.F.W. Leibniz (1646-1716), see the following: *Theodicy: Essays on the Goodness of God, the Freedom of Man and the Origin of Evil*. Translated by E.M. Huggard. London: Routledge and Kegan Paul, 1952. *The Philosophical Writings of Leibniz*. Translated by Mary Morris. London: Dent, 1934; *New Essays on Human Understanding*. Cambridge: Cambridge University Press, 1981; and *Philosophical Papers and Letters*. Dordrecht and Boston, MA: Reidel, 1970. [See also the discussions on "Best Possible World Theodicy," in *Chapter 3*.]

1994.   Adams, Robert M. "Leibniz's Theory of Contingency." *Leibniz: Critical and Interpretive Essays*. Edited by Michael Hooker. Minneapolis, MN: University of Minnesota Press, 1982: 243-283.

1995.   Allen, Diogenes. "The Theological Relevance of Leibniz's Theodicy." *Studia Leibnitiana Supplementa* 4 (1972): 83-90.

1996.   Brooks, Richard A. *Voltaire and Leibniz*. Geneve: Librairie Droz, 1984.

1997.   Brown, Gregory. "Leibniz's Theodicy and the Confluence of Worldly Goods." *Journal of the History of Philosophy* 26 (1988): 571-591. [Defends Leibniz against critics who dismiss his assumption that a variety of goods must be maximized in the best of all possible worlds: happiness, pleasure, love, perfection, being, power, freedom, harmony, order and beauty. Brown argues that these goods can be simultaneously maximized.]

1998.   Copp, David. "Leibniz's Theory That Not All Possible Worlds Are Compossible." *Studia Leibnitiana* 5 (1973): 26-42.

1999.   Davis, John W. "Leibniz and King." *Studia Leibnitiana Supplementa* 4 (1972): 111-124.

2000.   Howe, Leroy T. "Leibniz on Evil." *Sophia* 10 (1971): 8-17.

2001.   King, William. *Essay on the Origin of Evil*. New York: Garland Publishing, 1978. [Originally published in 1731.]

2002.   Kivy, Peter. "Voltaire, Hume, and the Problem of Evil." *Philosophy and Literature* 3 (1979): 211-224.

2003.   Korsmeyer, Carolyn. "Is Pangloss Leibniz?" *Philosophy and Literature* 1 (1977): 201-208.

2004.   Lloyd, Genevieve. "Leibniz and Possible Individuals and Possible Worlds." *Australasian Journal of Philosophy* 56 (1978): 126-142.

2005.   Mates, Benson. "Leibniz on Possible Worlds." *Leibniz*. Edited by Harry G. Frankfort. Garden City, NY: Doubleday and Company, 1974: 335-364.

2006.   Norton, David L. "Leibniz and Bayle: Manicheism and Dialectic." *Journal of the History of Philosophy* 2 (1964): 23-36.

2007.   Rescher, Nicholas. "Theodicy." *The Philosophy of Leibniz*. Englewood Cliffs, NJ: Prentice-Hall, 1967: 148-160.

2008.   ———. *Leibniz: An Introduction to his Philosophy*. Oxford: Blackwell, 1979.

2009.   Russell, Leonard James. "Possible Worlds in Leibniz." *Studia Leibnitiana* 1 (1969): 161-175.

2010.   Schmidtz, David. "Freedom in the Best of All Possible Worlds." *American Journal of Theology and Philosophy* 9 (1988): 187-193.

IV   Hume [Selected Publications]

For some of the relevant publications by David Hume (1711-1776), see the following: *Dialogues Concerning Natural Religion*. Edited by N. Kemp Smith.

Edinburgh: Nelson, 1947; *An Inquiry Concerning Human Understanding*. Edited by C.W. Hendel. New York: Liberal Arts, 1955. Also published in Indianapolis: Hackett Publishing Co., 1977; *An Enquiry Concerning the Principles of Morals*. La Salle, IL: Open Court, 1966; etc.

2011. Capitan, William Henry. "Part X of Hume's Dialogues." *American Philosophical Quarterly* 3 (1966): 82-85.

2012. Davis, John W. "Going Out the Window: A Comment on Tweyman's 'Hume's Dialogues on Evil'" [#2025]. *Hume Studies* 13 (1987): 86-97.

2013. Dragona-Monachou, Myrto. "Providence and Fate in Stoicism and Prae-Neoplatonism: Calcidius as an Authority on Cleanthes' Theodicy." *Philosophia* 3 (1973): 262-304. [See also Dragona-Monachou's "The Problem of Evil in Philo of Alexandria" (in Greek), *Philosophia* (Athens) 5 (1975/1976), 306-352.]

2014. Flage, Daniel. "Hume's Ethics." *Philosophical Topics* 16 (1985): 71-88.

2015. Gaskin, John C.A. *Hume's Philosophy of Religion*. London: Macmillan and New York: Barnes and Noble, 1978.

2016. Hare, Peter H., and Edward H. Madden. "The Powers That Be." *Dialogue* 10 (1971): 12-31.

2017. Harré, Rom, and Edward Madden. *Causal Powers*. Oxford: Blackwell, 1975. [Rejection of Hume's view of causality and a reconstruction of causal relations along non-Humean lines.]

2018. Jacquette, Dale. "Analogical Inference in Hume's Philosophy of Religion." *Faith and Philosophy* 2 (1985): 287-294.

2019. Merrill, Kenneth R., and Donald G. Wester. "Hume on the Relation of Religion to Morality." *Journal of Religion* 60 (1980): 272-284.

2020. Nathan, George. "Comments on Tweyman's 'Hume's Dialogues on Evil' [#2025] and Davis's "Going Out the Window: A Comment on Tweyman's 'Hume's Dialogues on Evil'" [#2012]. *Hume Studies* 13 (1987): 93-103.

2021. Pakaluk, Michael. "Cleanthes' Case for Theism." *Sophia* 27 (1988): 11-19. [Contends that a much stronger case for theism could have been made by Cleanthes in Hume's *Dialogues*.]

2022. Salmon, Wesley. "Religion and Science: A New Look at Hume's *Dialogues*." *Philosophical Studies* 33 (1978): 143-176.

2023. Solon, T.P.M., and S.K. Wertz. "Hume's Argument from Evil." *Personalist* 50 (1969): 383-392.

2024. Tilley, Terrence W. "Hume on God and Evil: *Dialogues X and XI* as Dramatic Conversation." *Journal of the American Academy of Religion* 56 (1988): 703-726.

2025. Tweyman, Stanley. "Hume's Dialogues on Evil." *Hume Studies* 13 (1987): 74-85. [See responses by Wadia [#2026], Nathan [#2020] and Davis [#2012], following in text. See also Tweyman's *Scepticism and Belief in Hume's 'Dialogues Concerning Natural Religion*.' Dordrecht: Martinus Nijhoff, 1986.]

2026. Wadia, Pheroze S. "Philo Confounded." *McGill Hume Studies* 22. Edited by David Norton, Nicholas Capaldi, and Wade Robinson. Montreal, PQ: McGill University Press, 1979.

2027.   ———. "Comment on Professor Tweyman's 'Hume's Dialogues on Evil'" [#2025]. *Hume Studies* 13 (1987): 104-111.

2028.   Walls, Jerry L. "Hume on Divine Amorality." *Religious Studies* 26 (1990): 256-266. [Rejects Hume's arguments which seek to undermine divine goodness.]

2029.   Wolfe, Julian. "Hume on Evil." *Scottish Journal of Theology* 34 (1981): 63-70.

V   Kant [Selected Publications]

Among the relevant publications by Immanuel Kant (1724-1804) are the following: *Religion Within the Limits of Reason Alone*. Translated by Theodore M. Greene and Hoyt H. Hudson. New York: Harper Torchbooks, 1960; "On the Failure of All Attempted Philosophical Theodicies." *Kant on History and Religion*. Translated by Michel Despland. Montreal, PQ: McGill–Queen's University Press, 1973; *The Metaphysics of Morals*. Indianapolis, IN: Bobbs-Merrill, 1965; *Prolegomena to any Future Metaphysics*. Indianapolis, IN: Hackett Publishing Co, 1977; the three "Critiques"; etc.

2030.   Acton, Harry Burrows. *Kant's Moral Philosophy*. London: Macmillan, 1970.

2031.   Carnois, Bernard. *The Coherence of Kant's Doctrine of Freedom*. Translated by David Booth. Chicago, IL: University of Chicago Press, 1987.

2032.   Despland, Michel. *Kant on History and Religion*. Montreal and London: McGill-Queen's University Press, 1973. [One section deals with "The Rise of the Problem of Evil." See critical response by Ann Loades, "Kant's Concern with Theodicy [#2039].]

2033.   Engstrom, Stephen. "Conditional Autonomy." *Philosophy and Phenomenological Research* 49 (1988): 435-453. [Rejects passages in Kant's writings which suggest a rigoristic distinction between good and evil and the view that all agents are necessarily evil. Neither view is necessitated by Kant's basic conception of morality.]

2034.   Fackenheim, Emil L. "Kant and Radical Evil." *University of Toronto Quarterly* 23 (1954): 339-353.

2035.   Gill, Jerry H. "Kant, Analogy, and Natural Evil." *International Journal for Philosophy of Religion* 15 (1984): 12-28.

2036.   Hill, Thomas E. "Moral Purity and the Lesser Evil." *Monist* 66 (1983): 213-232.

2037.   Korsgaard, Christine M. "The Right to Lie: Kant on Dealing with Evil." *Philosophy and Public Affairs* 15 (1986): 325-349.

2038.   Lichtigfeld, A. "A Kantian Contribution to the Problem of Evil." *Kant Studien* 58 (1967): 54-57.

2039.   Loades, Ann L. "Kant's Concern with Theodicy." *Journal of Theological Studies* 26 (1975): 361-376. [Kant rejects Leibniz's solution but maintains an optimistic faith in God.]

2040. ———. *Kant and Job's Comforters*. Newcastle Upon Tyne, England: Avero, 1985. [Detailed study of Kant's theodicy and its historical context. The book contains an extensive bibliography, 159-174.]

2041. McKenzie, David. "A Kantian Theodicy." *Faith and Philosophy* 1 (1984): 236-247.

2042. Michalson, Gordon E., Jr. "The Inscrutability of Moral Evil in Kant." *Thomist* 51 (1987): 246-269.

2043. ———. "Moral Regeneration and Divine Aid in Kant." *Religious Studies* 25 (1989): 259-270.

2044. ———. *Fallen Freedom: Kant on Radical Evil and Moral Degeneration*. Cambridge: Cambridge University Press, 1991. [Contains extensive bibliography of Kant's writings and secondary references, 162-168.]

2045. Post, Werner. "The Problem of Evil." *Moral Evil under Challenge*. Edited by Johannes B. Metz. London: Burns and Oates, 1970: 105-114.

2046. Quinn, Philip L. "Christian Atonement and Kantian Justification." *Faith and Philosophy* 3 (1986): 440-462.

2047. Rossi, Philip J. "Moral Autonomy, Divine Transcendence and Human Destiny: Kant's Doctrine of Hope as Philosophical Foundation for Christian Ethics." *Thomist* 46 (1982): 441-458.

2048. Stevens, Rex Patrick. "The Impact of Theodicy on Kant's Conception of Moral Practice." *Theoria* 47 (1981): 93-108.

2049. Sullivan, Roger J. *Immanuel Kant's Moral Theory*. Cambridge: Cambridge University Press, 1989.

2050. Treloar, John L. "The Crooked Wood of Humanity: Kant's Struggle with Radical Evil." *Philosophy and Theology* 3 (1989): 335-353.

2051. Wood, Allen W. *Kant's Moral Religion*. Ithaca, NY: Cornell University Press, 1970.

2052. ———. "Kant's Compatibilism." *Self and Nature in Kant's Philosophy*. Edited by Allen W. Wood. Ithaca, NY: Cornell University Press, 1984: 73-101.

VI Related Publications on Historical Theodicy
[Selected Publications]

2053. Agonito, Rosemary. "The Paradox of Pleasure and Pain: A Study of the Concept of Pain in Aristotle." *Personalist* 57 (1976): 105-112.

2054. Aja, Egbeke. "Hobbism and the African Moral Tradition: A Comparative Study." *Indian Philosophical Quarterly, Supplement* 15 (1988): 21-33.

2055. Alluntis, Felix, and Allan B. Wolter. "Duns Scotus on the Omnipotence of God." *Ancients and Moderns, Volume 5*. Edited by John K. Ryan. Washington, DC: Catholic University Press, 1970: 178-222.

2056.   Anderson, C. Anthony. "Divine Omnipotence and Impossible Tasks: An Intentional Analysis." *International Journal for Philosophy of Religion* 15 (1984): 109-124.

2057.   Anderson, Daniel E. "Descartes and Atheism." *Tulane Studies in Philosophy* 29 (1980): 11-24.

2058.   Ansbro, John J. "Kierkegaard's Gospel of Suffering." *Philosophical Studies* (Ireland) 16 (1967): 182-192.

2059.   Bargeliotes, Leonidas. "The Problem of Evil in Pletho." *Diotima* 4 (1976): 116-125.

2060.   Barnhart, Joe E. "An Ontology of Inevitable Moral Evil." *Personalist* 47 (1966): 102-111. [Argues that Karl Barth's doctrine of God allows (implicitly, at least) the possibility of a genuine struggle in God, and an ontological basis of moral evil (in *das Nichtige*). E.S. Brightman developed this theory consciously and explicitly [see #2066 and #2067].]

2061.   Baumgarten, Eduard. "The 'Radical Evil' in Jaspers' Philosophy." *The Philosophy of Karl Jaspers*. Edited by Paul Arthur Schilpp. New York: Tudor Publishing Company, 1957, 1981: 337-367.

2062.   Blanshard, Brand. "Kierkegaard on Faith." *Personalist* 49 (1968): 5-22.

2063.   Boudier, C. Struyker. "Alienation and Liberation: Evil and Redemption in the Thought of Sartre and Marcuse." *Man and World* 6 (1973): 115-142.

2064.   Bouwsma, O.K. "Descartes' Evil Genius." *Philosophical Essays*. Lincoln, NE: University of Nebraska Press, 1982: 85-98.

2065.   Bowmer, John C. "John Wesley's Philosophy of Suffering." *London Quarterly and Holborn Review* 184 (1959): 60-66.

2066.   Brightman, Edgar Sheffield. "The Problem of Good and Evil." *A Philosophy of Religion*. New York: Greenwood Press, 1940: 240-275. [See also Brightman's *The Problem of God*. New York: Abingdon, 1930.]

2067.   ———. "An Empirical Approach to the Nature of God." *Person and Reality: An Introduction to Metaphysics*. Edited by Peter A. Bertocci. New York: Ronald Press, 1958: 322-342.

2068.   Brogan, Walter A. "The Central Significance of Suffering in Nietzsche's Thought." *International Studies in Philosophy* 20 (1988): 53-62. [Argues that the will to power in Nietzsche is understood properly only if the intrinsic relationship between power and suffering is appreciated. See the response by Palmer [#2152].]

2069.   Brown, Delwin. "Grace: A Meditation from Camus." *Iliff Review* 43 (1986): 3-10. [See also *Appendix D*.]

2070.   Brown, Robert F. *The Later Philosophy of Schelling: The Influence of Boehme on the Works of 1809-1815*. Lewisburg, PA: Bucknell University Press, 1977.

2071.   Calvert, Brian. "Descartes and the Problem of Evil." *Canadian Journal of Philosophy* 2 (1972): 117-126. [Descartes rejected the free will defense for much the same reasons as Antony Flew and John Mackie.]

2072.   Čapek, Milič. "Professor Blanshard on Kierkegaard." *Modern Schoolman* 48 (1970): 44-53. [See Blanshard, [#2062].]

2073.   Capobianco, Richard. "Heidegger and the Critique of the Understanding of Evil as *Privatio Boni*." *Philosophy and Theology* 5 (1991): 175-185.

2074.   Carnell, Edward J. *The Burden of Sören Kierkegaard*. Grand Rapids, MI: Eerdmans, 1965.

2075.   Carson, D.A. "Divine Sovereignty and Human Responsibility in Philo." *Novum Testamentum* 23 (1981): 148-164.

2076.   Carter, Charles W. "Evil, the Marrer of God's Creative Purpose and Work." *A Contemporary Wesleyan Theology*, 2 Volumes. Edited by Charles W. Carter. Grand Rapids, MI: Francis Ashbury Press (Zondervan), 1983: Volume I: 237-286.

2077.   Cartwright, David. "Schopenhauer as Moral Philosopher—Towards the Actuality of his Ethics." *Schopenhauer-Jahrbuch* 70 (1989): 54-65.

2078.   Caton, Hiram. "Kennington on Descartes' Evil Genius" [#2118]. *Journal of History of Ideas* 34 (1973): 639-641; and "Rejoinder [to Richard Kennington]: The Cunning of the Evil Demon," 641-643. [See Kennington's response, "Reply to Canton," 643-644.]

2079.   Chisholm, Roderick M. *Brentano and Intrinsic Value*. New York: Cambridge University Press, 1986.

2080.   Clark, David W. "Voluntarism and Rationalism in the Ethics of Ockham." *Franciscan Studies* 31 (1971): 72-87.

2081.   Collins, James. "Josiah Royce: Analyst of Religion as Community." *American Philosophy and the Future*. Edited by Michael Novak. New York: Scribners, 1968: 193-218.

2082.   Costello, Edward B. "Is Plotinus Inconsistent on the Nature of Evil?" *International Philosophical Quarterly* 7 (1967): 483-497.

2083.   Cress, Donald A. "Descartes' Doctrine of Voluntary Infinity." *Southern Journal of Philosophy* 54 (1990): 149-164.

2084.   Cunneen, Sally. "Listening to Illich: Comment on Media/Arts." *Christian Century* 93 (1976): 805-806.

2085.   DeSiano, Frank. "Of God and Man: Consequences of Abelard's Ethic." *Thomist* 35 (1971): 631-660.

2086.   Dewey, Bradley R. "Kierkegaard on Suffering: Promise and Lack of Fulfilment in Life's Stages." *Humanitas* 9 (1972): 21-45.

2087.   Duncan, Robert. "The Problem of Evil: A Comparison of Classical and Biblical Versions." *Christian Scholar's Review* 3 (1973): 25-32.

2088.   Dunning, Stephen N. "Rhetoric and Reality in Kierkegaard's Postscript." *International Journal for Philosophy of Religion* 15 (1984): 125-137.

2089.   Ehrlich, Leonard H. "The Problem of Evil." *Karl Jaspers: Philosophy as Faith*. Amherst, MA: University of Massachusetts Press, 1975: 177-208.

2090.   Elliot, Robert, and Michael Smith. "Descartes, God and the Evil Spirit." *Sophia* 17 (1978): 33-36. [See response by O'Briant [#2149].]

2091.   Elrod, John William. "Climacus, Anti-Climacus, and the Problem of Suffering." *Thought* 55 (1980): 306-319. [Kierkegaard.]

2092.   Ferguson, John. "The Achievement of Clement of Alexander." *Religious Studies* 12 (1976): 59-86.

2093.   Floyd, William E.G. *Clement of Alexander's Treatment of the Problem of Evil.* London: Oxford University Press, 1971.

2094.   Frings, Manfred S. "Is There Room for Evil in Heidegger's Thought or Not?" *Philosophy Today* 32 (1988): 79-92.

2095.   Gatta, Julia. "Julian of Norwich: Theodicy as Pastoral Art." *Anglican Theological Review* 63 (1981): 173-181.

2096.   Gillies, Robert. "A Little Known American." *Expository Times* 97 (1986): 323-328. [Critique of Edgar S. Brightman, 1884-1953.]

2097.   Goedert, G. "The Dionysian Theodicy." *Studies in Nietzsche's Concept of Biblical Religion.* Edited by James C. O'Flaherty, Timothy F. Sellner, and Robert M. Helm. Chapel Hill, NC: University of North Carolina Press, 1976: 319-340.

2098.   Goetz, Ronald. "The Divine Burden." *Christian Century* 95 (1978): 298-302. [Criticism of Anselm's doctrine of the atonement.]

2099.   Grau, Gerd-Günther. "Nietzsche and Kierkegaard." *Studies in Nietzsche.* Edited by James C. O'Flaherty, Timothy F. Sellner, and Robert M. Helm. Chapel Hill, NC: University of North Carolina Press, 1985: 226-251.

2100.   Greene, William C. *Moira: Fate, Good and Evil in Greek Thought.* New York: Harper and Row, 1963. [First published in 1944.]

2101.   Grislis, Egil. "Luther's Understanding of the Wrath of God." *Journal of Religion* 41 (1961): 277-292.

2102.   ————. "Suffering and Hope: Recurrent Ideas Among Latvian Lutherans in Exile." *Lutheran Quarterly* 22 (1970): 298-318. [Examines the views on suffering of five Latvian theologians.]

2103.   Günther, Hans Jurgen H. "The Problem of Evil—Enlightened?" *Indian Journal of Theology* 30 (1981): 81-94. [Argues that the enlightenment failed to understand evil as sin and hence was unable to solve the problem of evil. Günther makes reference to Kant, Leibniz, Ritschl, Nietzsche, and Indian thinkers like Roy, Vivekananda, Tagore, Aurobindo, etc. All presupposed mistakenly that there is one part of human beings—reason which is unaffected by evil.]

2104.   Harper, Ralph. *The Seventh Solitude: Metaphysical Homelessness in Kierkegaard, Dostoevsky, and Nietzsche.* Baltimore, MD: Johns Hopkins University Press, 1965.

2105.   Hasker, William S. "Holiness and Systematic Evil: A Response to Albert Truesdale." *Wesleyan Theological Journal* 19 (1984): 60-62. [Response to Truesdale's "Christian Holiness and the Problem of Systemic Evil" [#2179].]

2106.   Hay, Eldon R. "God and Evil: Zoroaster and Barth." *Dalhousie Review* 49 (1969): 369-376.

2107. Hershbell, Jackson P. "Berkeley and the Problem of Evil." *Journal of the History of Ideas* 31 (1970): 543-554. [See also Denis Hsin-An Tsai's "God and the Problem of Evil in Berkeley," *Philosophical Review* 6 (1983), 125-136.]

2108. Hewsen, Robert H. "Eznik of Kolb and the Problem of Evil." *Eastern Churches Review* 3 (1971): 396-404. [Examines the views of the Greek Fathers on evil. Evil is the result of human freedom which has disobeyed God's will, and is tolerated by God as a demonstration of mercy.]

2109. Heyer, George S. "St. Anselm on the Harmony Between God's Mercy and God's Justice." *The Heritage of Christian Thought*. Edited by Robert E. Cushman and Egil Grislis. New York: Harper and Row, 1965: 31-40.

2110. Hillsheim, James W. "Suffering and Self-Cultivation: The Case of Nietzsche." *Educational Theory* 36 (1986): 171-178.

2111. Hughes, Paul A. "How Did Man Change When Adam Fell?" *Paraclete* 23 (1989): 2-23.

2112. Imlay, Robert A. "Descartes' Two Hypotheses of the Evil Genius." *Studia Leibnitiana* 12 (1980): 205-214.

2113. Jenyns, Soame [1704-1787]. *A Free Inquiry into the Nature and Origin of Evil*. Contemporary edition. New York: Garland Publishing, 1976.

2114. Jette, Celine Rita. *The Philosophy of Nietzsche in the Light of Thomistic Principles*. New York: Pageant Press, 1967.

2115. Jones, Geraint V. "The Concept of Evil in the Philosophy of Karl Jaspers." *The Philosophical Journal* 1 (1964): 102-115.

2116. Kane, G. Stanley. *Anselm's Doctrine of Freedom and Will*. Lewiston, NY, and Toronto, ON: Edwin Mellen Press, 1981.

2117. Kelly, Robert A. "The Suffering Church: A Study of Luther's *Theologia Crucis*." *Concordia Theological Quarterly* 50 (1986): 3-17.

2118. Kennington, Richard. "The Finitude of Descartes' Evil Genius." *Journal of History of Ideas* 34 (1973): 441-446. [See response by Caton [#2078].]

2119. Khan, Abrahim Habibulla (Ivan). "Kierkegaard's Conception of Evil." *Journal of Religion and Health* 14 (1975): 63-66. [Holds that suffering purifies the soul in "the religious stage" of life.]

2120. Kihanski, Alexander Sissel. *An Analytical Interpretation of Martin Buber's 'I and Thou'*. Woodbury, NY: Barron's Education Service, 1974. [Besides Buber's *I and Thou* (New York: Charles Scribner's Sons, 1958, 1970), see also his *Good and Evil*. New York: Charles Scribner's Sons, 1952.]

2121. Kinlaw, Jeffrey C. "Determinism and the Hiddenness of God in Calvin." *Religious Studies* 24 (1988): 497-510.

2122. Klann, Richard. "Human Claims to Freedom and God's Judgment." *Concordia Journal* 11 (1985): 52-61. [Reference to Martin Luther.]

2123. Kornberg, Jacques. *Evil: A Short History*. CBC Sound Recording and Transcript, "Ideas" series. Toronto: CBC Learning Systems, 700, 1971. [References to Schopenhauer, Freud, Marx.]

2124.   Koutsouvilis, A. "Is Suffering Necessary for the Good Man?" *Heythrop Journal* 13 (1972): 44-53. [Discussion of Kierkegaard and Socrates on suffering.]

2125.   Kraut, Richard. *Aristotle on Human Good*. Princeton, NJ: Princeton University Press, 1989.

2126.   Kuderowicz, Zbigniew. "Suffering and the Meaning of History." *Dialectics and Humanism* 2 (1981): 133-144. [References to Hegel, Schopenhauer, Dilthey.]

2127.   Kyle, Richard. "The Divine Attributes in John Knox's Concept of God." *Westminster Theological Journal* 48 (1986): 161-172.

2128.   LaCroix, Wilfred L. "Hegel's System and the Necessity and Intelligibility of Evil." [Parts I and II]. *Idealistic Studies* 1 (1971): 46-64; 102-119.

2128.   Laky, John J. *A Study of George Berkeley's Philosophy in the Light of the Philosophy of St. Thomas Aquinas*. Washington, DC: Catholic University of America Press, 1950.

2130.   LaPorte, Jean B. "Gregory the Great as a Theologian of Suffering." *Patristic and Byzantine Review* 1 (1982): 22-31.

2131.   Lesser, Harry. "Nietzsche and the Pre-Socratic Philosophers." *Journal of the British Society for Phenomenology* 18 (1987): 30-37.

2132.   Lewis, Charles. "Morality and Deity in Nietzsche's Concept of Biblical Religion." *Studies in Nietzsche*. Edited by James C. O'Flaherty, Timothy F. Sellner, and Robert M. Helm. Chapel Hill, NC: University of North Carolina Press, 1985: 69-85.

2133.   Loades, Ann L. "Analogy, and the Indictment of the Deity: Some Interrelated Themes." *Studia Theologica* 33 (1979): 25-43. [Theodicy was overlooked in the controversy following Darwin's *Origin of Species*.]

2134.   Logarbo, Mona. "Salvation Theology in Julian of Norwich: Sin, Forgiveness, and Redemption in the *Revelations*." *Thought* 61 (1986): 369-380.

2135.   Long, A.A. "The Stoic Concept of Evil." *Philosophical Quarterly* 18 (1968): 329-343.

2136.   Longsworth, William M. "Kierkegaard and Pastoral Ministry." *Perkins Journal of Theology* 37 (1983): 1-10.

2137.   McCarthy, Vincent A. "Schelling and Kierkegaard on Freedom and Fall." *The Concept of Anxiety: A Commentary*. Edited by Robert L. Perkins. Macon, GA: Mercer University Press, 1985: 89-109.

2138.   McGrath, Alister E. "Rectitude: The Moral Foundation of Anselm of Canterbury's Soteriology." *Downside Review* 99 (1981): 204-213.

2139.   Minnema, Theodore. "Calvin's Interpretation of Human Suffering." *Exploring the Heritage of John Calvin*. Edited by David E. Holwerda. Grand Rapids, MI: Baker Book House, 1976: 140-162.

2140.   Miri, Sujata. *Suffering*. Simla: Indian Institute of Advanced Study, 1976. [Reference to Schopenhauer, Nietzsche, Kierkegaard, Sartre, Aurobindo, The Buddha, and Sankara.]

2141.   Mohr, Richard. "Plato's Final Thoughts on Evil: *Laws X*, 899-905." *Mind* 87 (1978): 572-575.

2142.   ———. "The Mechanism of Flux in Plato's *Timaeus*." *Apeiron* 14 (1980): 96-114.

2143.   ———. "The Sources of Evil: The Problem of Evil and the ἀρχὴ κινήσεως Doctrine in Plato." *Apeiron* 14 (1980): 41-56.

2144.   Morgan, Michael L. "Martin Buber, Cooperation and Evil." *Journal of the American Academy of Religion* 68 (1990): 99-109.

2145.   Mosshammer, Alden A. "Non-Being and Evil in Gregory of Nyssa." *Vigiliae Christianae* 44 (1990): 136-137.

2146.   Murphry. Lawrence F. "Martin Luther and Gabriel Biel: A Disagreement about Original Sin." *Science et Esprit* 32 (1980): 51-72.

2147.   Nelson, Janet L. "Society, Theodicy and the Origins of Heresy: Towards a Reassessment of the Medieval Evidence." *Schism, Heresy and Religious Protest*. Edited by Derek Baker. Cambridge: Cambridge University Press, 1972: 65-77.

2148.   Nicole, Roger. "John Calvin's Treatment of the Atonement." *Westminster Theological Review* 47 (1985): 197-225.

2149.   O'Briant, Walter H. "Is Descartes' Evil Spirit Finite or Infinite?" *Sophia* 18 (1979): 28-32. [Response to Robert Elliot and Michael Smith, "Descartes, God and the Evil Spirit" [#2090].]

2150.   O'Brien, Denis. "Plotinus on Evil: A Study of Matter and the Soul in Plotinus's Conception of Human Evil." *Le Néoplatonisme*. Edited by C. de Vogel, et al. Paris: Éditions du Centre National de la Recherche Scientifique, 1971: 113-146. [Expanded and slightly corrected version of his "Plotinus on Evil," *Downside Review* 87 (1969), 68-110.]

2151.   Olds, Mason. "Religion After Nietzsche." (2 parts.) *Religious Humanism* 17 (1983): 154-162; (1984): 28-35.

2152.   Palmer, Richard. "Response to Brogan's 'The Central Significance of Suffering in Nietzsche's Thought'" [#2068]. *International Studies in Philosophy* 20 (1988): 63-65.

2153.   Papaioannou, Kostas. "History and Theodicy." *Diogenes* 53 (1966): 38-63.

2154.   Pavkovic, Aleksandar. "Is the Evil Demon a Sceptical Device?" *Contemporary Yugoslav Philosophy*. Edited by Aleksandar Pavkovic. Dordrecht: Kluwer Academic Publishers, 1988: 229-240.

2155.   Radford, Robert. "Aristotle on Doing Evil." *Journal of Thought* 1 (1966): 9-22.

2156.   Reinhardt, Lloyd. "Desire, Evil and Grace." *Philosophy* 53 (1978): 325-333.

2157.   Richardson, Herbert W., and Jasper Hopkins. Translators and editors. *Complete Treatises I-IV* [of St. Anselm]. New York and Toronto, ON: Edwin Mellen Press, 1975. [*Volume II* includes Anselm's "Freedom of Choice"; "The Harmony of the Foreknowledge, the Predestination, and the Grace of God with Free Choice."]

2158.   Ricoeur, Paul. "Two Encounters with Kierkegaard: Kierkegaard and Evil; Doing Philosophy After Kierkegaard." *Kierkegaard's Truth: The Disclosure of the Self*. Edited by Joseph H. Smith. New Haven, CT: Yale University Press, 1981: 313-341.

2159. Rodgers, Symeon. "The Soteriology of Anselm of Canterbury: An Orthodox Perspective." *Greek Orthodox Theological Review* 34 (1989): 19-43.

2160. Royce, Josiah. *Studies of Good and Evil*. Hamden, CT: Archon, 1964. [See the critical study by Joan Collins, "Josiah Royce: Evil in the Absolute." *Idealistic Studies* 13 (1983), 147-165.]

2161. Sabatino, Charles J. "An Interpretation of Significance of Theonomy within Tillich's Theology." *Encounter* 45 (1984): 23-38.

2162. Salamun, Kurt. "Moral Implications of Karl Jaspers' Existentialism." *Philosophy and Phenomenological Research* 49 (1988): 317-323.

2163. Santurri, Edmund N. "Theodicy and Social Policy in Malthus' Thought." *Journal of History of Ideas* 43 (1982): 315-330.

2164. Scaer, David P. "The Concept of Anfechtung in Luther's Thought." *Concordia Theological Quarterly* 47 (1983): 15-30.

2165. Schulweis, Harold M. "Theodicy and the Ground of Being: Paul Tillich." *Philosophy Today* 18 (1974): 338-342.

2166. Scuiry, Daniel E. "The Anthropology of St. Gregory of Nyssa." *Diakonia* 18 (1983): 31-42.

2167. Sefler, George F. "Nietzsche and Dostoevsky on the Meaning of Suffering." *Religious Humanism* 4 (1970): 145-150.

2168. Slater, C. Peter. "Tillich on the Fall and the Temptation of Goodness." *Journal of Religion* 65 (1985): 196-207.

2169. Smith, Joel R. "Creation, Fall and Theodicy in Paul Tillich's *Systematic Theology*." *Kairos and Logos*. Edited by John J. Carney. Macon, GA: Mercer University Press, 1978: 158-187.

2170. Smith, Joseph H. *Kierkegaard's Truth*. New Haven, CT: Yale University Press, 1981.

2171. Soffer, Walter. "Descartes, Rationality, and God." *Thomist* 42 (1978): 666-691.

2172. Sorabji, Richard. *Necessity, Cause, and Blame: Perspectives on Aristotle's Theory*. Ithaca, NY: Cornell University Press, 1980.

2173. Sponheim, Paul. "Kierkegaard and the Suffering of the Christian Man." *Dialog* 3 (1964): 199-206.

2174. Stenson, Sten H. "Evil and Absurdity in Religion" and "Evil and Absurdity in Existential Philosophy." *Sense and Nonsense in Religion*. Nashville, TN: Abingdon, 1969: 24-99, 45-99.

2175. Storms, C. Samuel. "Jonathan Edwards on the Freedom of the Will." *Trinity Journal* 3 (1982): 131-169.

2176. Strozewski, Wladyslaw. "Some Remarks on the Nature and Origin of Good and Evil." *Dialectics and Humanism* 2 (1978): 173-179.

2177. Thulstrup, Marie Mikulová. "Suffering." *Kierkegaard and Human Values*. Edited by Niels Thulstrup and Marie Mikulová Thulstrup. Copenhagen: C.A. Reitzels Boghandel, 1980: 135-162.

2178. Tinder, Galen. "Luther's Theology of Christian Suffering." *Dialog* 25 (1986): 108-113.

2179. Truesdale, Albert L. "Christian Holiness and the Problem of Systemic Evil." *Wesleyan Theological Journal* 19 (1984): 39-59. [See William S. Hasker's response [#2105].]

2180. Tsirpanlis, C.N. "The Concept of Universal Salvation in Saint Gregory of Nyssa." *Studia Patristica* 17 (1982): 1131-1144.

2181. Tyson, John R. "Sin, Self and Society: John Wesley's Hamartiology Reconsidered." *Anglican Theological Journal* 44 (1989): 77-89.

2182. Uhl, Anton. "Suffering from God and Man: Nietzsche and Dostoevsky." *Nietzsche and Christianity*. Edited by Claude Geffré and Jean-Pierre Jossua. New York: Seabury Press, 1981: 32-41.

2183. Urban, Linwood. "William of Ockham's Theological Ethics." *Franciscan Studies* 33 (1973): 310-350.

2184. Wertz, S.K. "Descartes and the Paradox of the Stone." *Sophia* 23 (1984): 19-24.

2185. Williams, Robert R. "Theodicy, Tragedy, and Soteriology: The Legacy of Schleiermacher." *Harvard Theological Review* 77 (1984): 395-412.

2186. Wren, Thomas E. "Is Hope a Necessary Evil? Some Misgivings about Spinoza's Metaphysical Psychology." *Journal of Thought* 7 (1972): 67-76.

2187. Young, Frances M. "Insight or Incoherence? The Greek Fathers on God and Evil." *Journal of Ecclesiastical History* 24 (1973): 113-126.

2188. Young, Julian. "A Schopenhauerian Solution to Schopenhauerian Pessimism." *Schopenhauer-Jahrbuch* 68 (1987): 53-69.

Appendix C

Suffering of God Theodicy

During the past several decades, there has been a growing number of theologians, philosophers and biblical scholars who have become disenchanted with the doctrine of divine impassibility, the doctrine which denies that God can suffer. Since about 1890, English theologians have led the movement in reconstructing the concept of God as a suffering God.[1] In North America, it has been the process philosophers and theologians, influenced by the Englishman founder, *Alfred North Whitehead*, who have advocated a vision of God as a suffering companion, a God who is affected by creaturely actions, decisions, joys and sorrows. There is a massive literature on process theology and philosophy, much of which centers on its revised theism.[2] The attributes of God (as traditionally conceived) as omnipotent, immutable, omniscient, etc., have been challenged and replaced by a revised theism which includes a suffering God. It is the reconsideration of divine immutability or impassibility that is most relevant to the theology of the suffering of God. While this bibliography could list only a portion of the enormous literature on process theism and in particular the debates about divine attributes (see *Chapter 6*), the relevant publications of *Daniel Day Williams* have been included in this section as a major example of process thinking on divine suffering.[3] Williams, an eclectic mix of Whiteheadian–Hartshornean process thought, the empirical theology of the Chicago school, among other influences, suggested three reasons for the rise in popularity of the suffering God: (1) the influence of process theology; (2) the biblical movement which flourished during the Second World War and in which God was seen as an active participant in human history; and (3) contemporary understandings of the atonement: the passion of Christ has been taken more seriously than in the past for the model of God.[4]

There are increasing numbers of influential writers who have been attracted to a consideration and development of the theme of divine suffering. *Abraham Heschel* is a good example, having argued effectively that the prophetic writings contain clear references to divine passion. Heschel contends that the prophets' anthropomorphic depictions of God are central to the entire biblical discussion. He finds in the prophets a very different understanding of God than that of the Greeks. "The most exalted idea applied to God," he argues, "is not infinite wisdom, infinite power," but rather, "concern and involvement."[5] Heschel defines divine pathos as central to the prophetic message, a view which has been seen as revolutionary, and one which challenges "the whole venerable tradition of Jewish and Christian metaphysical theology from Philo and Maimonides, and Thomas Aquinas to Herman Cohen, Étienne Gilson, and Paul Tillich."[6]

Among the earliest and most formidable critics of Heschel has been *Eliezer Berkovits*, who argues that the divine pathos theme is based on a fallacious line of reasoning, based on a literalistic interpretation of biblical texts.[7] One the other hand, one of Heschel's disciples, *Rabbi Harold Kushner*, has utilized some of Heschel's themes (and themes consistent with those in process theology) in his phenomenal best-seller, *When Bad Things Happen to Good People*.[8] The popularity of this book and its theology of a God who suffers with us is not, in itself, a test of the validity of the suffering God. It does, however, reveal a deeply set conviction that the understanding of God must change from the all-powerful, all-causative God, to one of companionship and consolation.

Terrence Fretheim[9] and *Paul Fiddes*,[10] among others, have (like Heschel) published major discussions of the theme of divine pathos. The passion of Christ, like that of the divine suffering theme in the Hebrew prophets, moreover, has been exploited as key evidence for a suffering God. Process philosopher *Lewis S. Ford* has argued persuasively that there is a strong biblical background for divine suffering, despite the overshadowing of this theme by the Hellenistic view of God as impassive and all-determining—a view which was entrenched by the controversy about divine suffering in the third century.[11] *Joseph Hallman's* recent study, *The Descent of God: Divine Suffering in History and Theology*[12] is a masterful study of the divine immutability and impassibility doctrine in historical thinking and also in the more contemporary philosophy of Hegel and Whitehead. By contrast, philosopher *Richard Creel* have provided an impressive defense of the traditional doctrine of a God who is impassible and who does not suffer.[13] Creel's arguments are in dialogue with and in opposition to the challenging view of process philosophers who insist that God is "dipolar," both immutable in some sense and mutable in others. This entire question of the passibility/impassibility of God, the divine immutability, is a most complex and hotly debated issue for which there is a massive literature mounting.[14]

Warren McWilliams has documented the writings of six of the major exponents of the suffering of God theme: *Geddes MacGregor, Jung Young Lee, Daniel Day Williams, James Cone, Jürgen Moltmann, Kazoh Kitamori*—all Protestants, yet from widely divergent backgrounds.[15] McWilliams notes that there is a strong and growing acknowledgement that God is a "suffering companion" (Whitehead), even though there is strong resistance to this revised understanding of God. *Richard Bauckham's* informative analysis of the issue[16] notes that while the idea that "God cannot suffer ... was accepted as axiomatic in Christian theology from the early Greek Fathers until the nineteenth century," the orthodox view "in this century [has] been progressively abandoned." *Ronald Goetz* likewise affirms that the "age-old dogma that God is impassible, immutable, and incapable of suffering is, for many, no longer tenable. The ancient theopaschite heresy that God suffers has, in fact, become the new orthodoxy"[17]—an overstatement perhaps, but an intriguing one. The recent book of Paul Fiddes, *The Creative Suffering of God*,[18] is a particularly thorough examination of recent versions of the suffering of God theme in several of its major exponents. His proposal for a vision of God who has freely chosen to limit the divine freedom and to suffer change, to journey through time and even to suffer death, while yet remaining the living God, is a creative blend of process theism and the insights of Moltmann, Jüngel, and others—Karl Barth in particular.

Paul Schilling,[19] and *Richard Bauckham*,[20] among others,[21] have documented an impressive number of adherents of the divine suffering theology, supplementing the early study (1926) of *J.K. Mozley*.[22] They note that among those who have supported the passibility of God theme are the influential German theologian *Jürgen Moltmann*, the American theologian *Geddes MacGregor*, the black liberationist *James Cone*, the Japanese theologian *Kazoh Kitamori*, the Korean theologian *Jung Young Lee*, among growing numbers of others, including many in the liberation movements—blacks, feminists, and third world liberationists. Others include Catholic writer *Hans Küng*, Russian theologian *Nicholas Berdyaev*, Protestants *Karl Barth, Dietrich Bonhoeffer* and *Emil Brunner*, and many others.

The relationship of the divine suffering theme to theodicy is what interests us here. It is no accident, as Richard Bauckham has pointed out, that the contemporary concern with the question of divine suffering has arisen frequently out of situations in which suffering has been acute.[23] English theologians responded to the devastation of the Second World War, Japan's theologians responded to Hiroshima and Nagasaki, Moltmann responded to his experience as a prisoner of war and developed it into a theology of the holocaust, and liberationists responded to social and economic discrimination and repression. Daniel Day Williams, as noted above, has attributed the rise of the suffering of God theme to these cultural factors, as well as to other factors, including (perhaps, especially) the development of process philosophy.

Notes

1. For pre-1960 references, see Richard Bauckham, "Only the Suffering God Can Help: Divine Passibility in Modern Theology," *Themelios* 9 (1984): 6-12.
2. See the 1976 bibliography, *Alfred North Whitehead: A Primary—Secondary Bibliography*, by Barry Woodbridge (Bowling Green, OH: Philosophy Documentation Center, Bowling Green State University, 1976). The journal I edit, *Process Studies*, continually updates the process bibliography by its abstracts of relevant articles and dissertations.
3. Daniel Day Williams is credited by John Cobb as having written the first systematic process theology: see Williams, *The Spirit and the Forms of Love* (New York: Harper and Row, 1968). Cobb's reference is in his "A Process Systematic Theology," *Journal of Religion* 50 (1970): 175. A bibliography of Williams's publications was published by *Union Seminary Theological Quarterly* 30 (1975): 217-229.
4. Daniel Day Williams, *What Present Day Theologians Are Thinking* (New York: Harper and Row, 1967): 171-172.
5. Abraham Heschel, *The Prophets* (New York: Harper and Row, 1962): 241.
6. Fritz Rothchild, "Architect and Herald of a New Theology, *America* 128 (1973): 211.
7. Eliezer Berkovits, "Dr. A.J. Heschel's Theology of Pathos." *Tradition, A Journal of Orthodox Thought* 6 (1964): 67-104.
8. Harold Kushner, *When Bad Things Happen to Good People* (New York: Schocken, 1981).
9. Terrence Fretheim, *The Suffering God: An Old Testament Perspective* (Philadelphia, PA: Fortress Press, 1984).
10. Paul S. Fiddes, *The Creative Suffering of God* (New York and Oxford: Oxford University Press, 1988).
11. Lewis S. Ford. *The Lure of God: A Biblical Background for Process Theism* (Philadelphia, PA: Fortress Press, 1978). See also the relevant work of David Griffin, *A Process Christology* (Philadelphia, PA: Westminster Press, 1973. Republished by University Press of America, 1990). Griffin's other publications are relevant: see his *God, Power and Evil: A Process Theodicy* (Philadelphia, PA: Westminster Press, 1976. Republished by the State University of New York Press, 1991). His published dissertation is also relevant: *A Process Christology* (Philadelphia, PA: Westminster Press, 1973. Republished in 1990 by University Press of America).
12. Joseph Hallman, *The Descent of God: Divine Suffering in History and Theology*. (Philadelphia, PA: Fortress Press, 1991).
13. Richard Creel, *The Divine Impassibility* (New York and Cambridge: Cambridge University Press, 1986). [A recent critique of Creel's now celebrated book, which has come to my attention as this volume was in the final stages of proofing and printing, is that of George W. Shields, "Hartshorne and Creel on Impassibility," *Process Studies* 21 (1992): 44-59. See the following note.]

14.   The amount of literature on the issue of divine immutability has grown considerably over the past few years. This issue has been the focus of process philosophy, as one of its central criticisms of traditional Thomistic theology. See, for example, Barry L. Whitney, "Divine Immutability in Contemporary Thomism and Process Philosophy," *Horizons, Journal of the College Theology Society* 7 (1980): 49-68. See also Thomas Weinandy, *Does God Change? Mutability and Incarnation*. Still River, MA: St. Bede's Publications, 1985. See also Theodore Kondoleon's "The Immutability of God: Some Recent Challenges," *New Scholasticism* 58 (1984): 293-315; Bruce Ware's "An Exposition and Critique of the Process Doctrines of Divine Mutability and Immutability," *Westminster Theological Journal* 47 (1985): 175-196; the David Burrell—Philip Devenish debate in *Theological Studies* 43 (1982); etc.

15.   Warren WcWilliams, *The Passion of God* (Macon, GA: Mercer University Press, 1985).

16.   Richard Bauckham, "Only the Suffering God Can Help," 6. This article contains numerous bibliographical references to the literature on the suffering of God theme.

17.   Ronald Goetz, "The Suffering God: Rise of a New Orthodoxy." *The Christian Century* 103 (1986): 385-389.

18.   See note 11.

19.   Paul Schilling, *God and Human Anguish* (Nashville, TN: Abingdon Press, 1977).

20.   Richard Bauckham, "Only the Suffering God Can Help" (see above).

21.   See Barry L. Whitney, *What Are They Saying About God and Evil?* (New York/Mahwah, NJ: Paulist Press, 1989).

22.   J.K. Mozley, *The Impassibility of God: A Survey of Christian Thought* (London: Cambridge University Press, 1962).

23.   Bauckham, "Only the Suffering God Can Help," 9.

Suffering of God Theodicy [Selected Publications]

2189. Althaus, Paul. *The Theology of Martin Luther*. Translated by Robert C. Schults. Philadelphia, PA: Fortress Press, 1966.

2190. Altizer, Thomas J.J. *The Gospel of Christian Atheism*. Philadelphia, PA: Westminster Press, 1966. [His radical version of *kenosis* is that the self-emptying of God in Jesus is really the death of God.]

2191. Altizer, Thomas J.J., and William Hamilton. *Radical Theology and the Death of God*. Indianapolis, IN: Bobbs-Merrill, 1966.

2192. Alves, Ruben A. *A Theology of Human Hope*. New York: Corpus Books, 1969.

2193. Baker, John R. "Christological Symbol of God's Suffering." *Religious Experience and Process Theology*. Edited by Harry J. Cargas and Bernard Lee. New York: Paulist Press, 1976: 93-105.

2194. Barnhart, Joe E. "Incarnation and Process Philosophy." *Religious Studies* 11 (1967): 225-232.

2195. Barth, Karl. *Church Dogmatics*. English translation edited by Geoffrey William Bromiley and Thomas F. Torrence. Edinburgh: T&T Clark, 1936-1977. [Four volumes in thirteen parts. For one of the most detailed analyses of Barth's theology as it relates to the suffering of God theme, see Paul Fiddes, *The Creative Suffering of God* [#2229]. Barth's God suffers not merely in the indirect sense that the Son is united with suffering in human form, but directly in the divine being. God suffers in the "form of the servant," while remaining immutable in the "form of glory."]

2196. Bauckham, Richard. "Moltmann's Eschatology of the Cross." *Scottish Journal of Theology* 23 (1970): 304-308. [Contends that Moltmann has a "near-Marcionite" view of God: Moltmann's God becomes love in the process of salvation history. God not only is revealed to us but God is in the process of becoming God.]

2197. ——. "Jürgen Moltmann." *One God in Trinity*. Edited by D. Spiceland. London: Bagster, 1980: 121-124.

2198. ——. "'Only the Suffering God Can Help': Divine Passibility in Modern Theology." *Themelios* 9 (1984): 6-12. [Brief historical survey of the suffering of God theme.]

2199. ——. "Theodicy from Ivan Karamazov to Moltmann." *Modern Theology* 4 (1987): 83-97.

2200. ——. "Moltmann's *Theology of Hope* Revisited." *Scottish Journal of Theology* 42 (1989):199-214.

2201. Baynes, Simon. "The Japanese and the Cross." *Japan Christian Quarterly* 46 (1980): 146-150. [Discusses Kitamori's theodicy.]

2202. Beardslee, William A. *A House for Hope: A Study in Process and Biblical Thought*. Philadelphia, PA: Westminster Press, 1972.

2203. Berdyaev, Nicholas. *Freedom and the Spirit*. Translated by O.F. Clarke. London: Geoffrey Bles, 1935.

2204. ———. *Spirit and Reality*. Translated by G. Reavey. London: Geoffrey Bles, 1946.

2205. ———. *The Destiny of Man*. Translated by N. Duddington. London: Geoffrey Bles, 1955. New York: Harper and Row, 1966. [See also his *Dostoevsky*. Cleveland, OH: Word Publishing, 1962.]

2206. Bhattacharyya, Kalidas. "Does God Suffer?" *Visva Bharati Journal of Philosophy* 7 (1969/1970): 34-47. [Argues that from Hindu and Christian perspecives, God does not suffer.]

2207. Braaten, Carl E. "A Trinitarian Theology of the Cross." *Journal of Religion* 56 (1976): 113-121. [Argues that Moltmann's theology of the cross is too dependent on Paul and is a reductionism of the canon. Moltmann uses the language of suffering but does not present a sustained treatment of patripassianism.]

2208. Brasnett, B.R. *The Suffering of the Impassible God*. London: SPCK Press, 1928.

2209. Burnley, Edward. "Impassibility of God." *Expository Times* 67 (1955): 90-91.

2210. Burt, Donald X. "The Powerlessness of God or the Powerlessness of Man." *The Existence of God*. Proceedings of the American Catholic Philosophical Association, 46 (1972). Edited by George F. McLean. Washington, DC: 142-148. [Surveys the responses of Weil, Camus and Rubenstein to the problem of evil. Burt concludes that the power of God is expressed in the creation of free human beings. God is powerless in face of such freedom in humanity.]

2211. Cauthen, Kenneth. *Science, Secularization and God*. Nashville, TN: Abingdon, 1969: 159-161.

2212. Childs, Brevard S. *Biblical Theology in Crisis*. Philadelphia, PA: Westminster Press, 1970.

2213. Chopp, Rebecca S. *The Praxis of Suffering: An Interpretation of Liberation and Political Theologians*. New York: Orbis Books, 1986. [Chapters on Moltmann: "Language of God as the Language of Suffering"; José Míguez Bonino: "The Conversion to the Word"; Gustavo Gutiérrez: "A Theology for Historical Amnesia"; Johannes Baptist Metz: "The Subject of Suffering"; and others, with a final chapter, "Toward Praxis: A Method for Liberation Theology."]

2214. ———. "Theological Persuasion: Rhetoric, Warrants and Suffering." *World-views and Warrants: Plurality and Authority in Theology*. Edited by William Schweiker and Per M. Anderson. Lanham, MD: University Press of America, 1987: 17-31.

2215. Clark, J.P.H. "*Fiducia* in Julian of Norwich." *Downside Review* 99 (1981): 214-229.

2216. Cone, James. *Black Theology and Black Power*. New York: Seabury Press, 1969. [See the critical responses by Jones, "Theodicy and Methodology in Black Theology: A Critique of Washington, Cone, and Cleage" [#2263], and "Theodicy: The Controlling Category for Black Theology" [#2264]; McWilliams, *The Passion of God: Divine Suffering in Contemporary Protestant Theology* [#2321]; Henry J. Young, "Black Theology and the Work of Henry R. Jones" [#2442]; etc.]

2217. ———. *A Black Theology of Liberation*. Philadelphia, PA: Lippincott, 1970.

2218.   ——. *The Spirituals and the Blues*. New York: Seabury Press, 1972.

2219.   ——. *God of the Oppressed*. New York: Seabury Press, 1975.

2220.   ——. *My Soul Looks Back*. Nashville, TN: Abingdon, 1982.

2221.   Dawe, Donald G. *The Form of a Servant: A Historical Analysis of the Kenotic Motif*. Philadelphia, PA: Westminster, 1963. [An informative historical survey of *kenotic* Christology.]

2222.   DeWitt, Jesse R. "The Power of Suffering Love." *Christian Social Action* 1 (1988): 14.

2223.   Dinsmore, Charles Allen. *Atonement in Literature and Life*. Boston, MA: Houghton Mifflin Co., 1906.

2224.   Duclow, Donald F. "'My Suffering is God': Meister Eckhart's *Book of Divine Consolation*." *Theological Studies* 44 (1983): 570-586.

2225.   Duncan, J. Ligon III. "Divine Passibility and Impassibility in Nineteenth-Century American Confessional Presbyterian Theologians." *Scottish Bulletin of Evangelical Theology* 8 (1990): 1-15.

2226.   Edwards, Rem B. "Is an Existential System Possible?" *International Journal for Philosophy of Religion* 17 (1986): 201-208. [See also Rem Edwards, "The Pagan Doctrine of the Absolute Unchangeableness of God." *Religious Studies* 14 (1978): 305-313.]

2227.   Ellisen, Stanley E. "Long Suffering of God: What Is He Like?" *God: What Is He Like?* Edited by William F. Kerr. Wheaton, IL: Tyndale House, 1977: 85-96.

2228.   Farley, Wendy L. *Tragic Vision and Divine Compassion: A Contemporary Compassion*. Louisville, KY: Westminster/John Knox Press, 1990. [The published version of Farley's 1988 Vanderbilt dissertation. Her theodicy rejects the traditional views of Augustine, Aquinas, Calvin, et al, with respect to divine power and predestination. Farley rejects the Fall–Redemption Christian myth as a justification of evil, and takes exception to the traditional model of power as dominating. (For other feminist views of the rejection of traditional theism's model of divine power and proposals for new understandings of God, see *Appendix D*).]

2229.   Fiddes, Paul S. *The Creative Suffering of God*. Oxford: Oxford University Press, 1988. [Detailed study of the suffering of God theology. Fiddes considers four main trends: the "theology of the cross" (Karl Barth, Jürgen Moltmann, Eberhard Jüngel); American process philosophy (Alfred North Whitehead, Charles Hartshorne, John Cobb, Lewis Ford, Joseph Bracken); the "death of God" theology (Bonhoeffer, Nietzsche, Feuerbach, Paul van Buren, Thomas Altizer); and the rejection of divine impassibility by modern followers of classical theism (Macquarrie, Tillich, Berdyaev, Pannenberg, etc.). Fiddes argues that the insights of process theology can be modified usefully by the theology of Karl Barth, to produce a viable version of the suffering of God theme.]

2230.   Fingarette, Herbert. *The Self in Transformation: Psychoanalysis, Philosophy and the Life of the Spirit*. New York: Harper and Row, 1965.

2231.   Forsyth, Peter Taylor. *The Justification of God: Lectures for War-Time on a Christian Theodicy*. London: Duckworth, 1916. [Republished in London:

Independent Press, 1957. The relevant chapters are *Chapters 7*, "Teleology Acute in a Theodicy," and also *Chapter 8*, "Philosophical Theodicy."]

2232.   ——. *The Person and Place of Jesus Christ*. Grand Rapids, MI: Eerdmans, 1964.

2233.   Franks, Harold. R.S. "Passibility and Impassibility." *Encyclopedia of Religion and Ethics 9*. Edited by James Hastings. New York: Charles Scribner's Sons, 1928.

2234.   Fretheim, Terrence E. "Jonah and Theodicy." *Zeitschrift für die Alttestamentliche Wissenchaft* 90 (1978): 227-237. [God chooses to suffer for Nineveh.]

2235.   ——. *The Suffering of God: An Old Testament Perspective*. Philadelphia, PA: Fortress Press, 1984. [Detailed study of the suffering God in the Hebrew Scriptures. After discussing how God is present, he argues that God suffers in various ways: *because* of Israel for rejecting their God, *with* Israel in their sufferings, and *for* Israel: "God can accomplish the creative act only by a *via dolorosia*." There is some use of process language in this book: God shares the divine power, God's power is "limited," and God's future being is open.]

2236.   ——. "The Repentance of God: A Key to Evaluating Old Testament God-Talk." *Horizons in Biblical Theology* 10 (1988): 57-70.

2237.   ——. "Suffering God and Sovereign God in Exodus: A Collision of Images." *Horizons in Biblical Theology* 11 (1989).

2238.   Gilkey, Langdon. *Reaping the Whirlwind: A Christian Interpretation of History*. New York: Seabury, 1976.

2239.   Goetz, Ronald. "The Divine Burden." *Christian Century* 95 (1978): 298-302.

2240.   ——. "Karl Barth, Jürgen Moltmann and the Theopaschite Revolution." *Festschrift: A Tribute to Dr. William Hordern*. Edited by W. Freitag. Regina, SK: University of Saskatchewan Press, 1985: 17-28.

2241.   ——. "The Suffering God: The Rise of a New Orthodoxy." *Christian Century* 103 (1986): 385-389. [Maintains that the ancient theopaschite heresy that God suffers has become the new orthodoxy, represented by seminal figures like Barth, Berdyaev, Bonhoeffer, Brunner, Cobb, Cone and liberation theology generally, Küng, Moltmann, (Reinhold) Niebuhr, Pannenberg, Ruether and feminist theology generally, Temple, Teilhard, and others. Goetz concludes that the suffering of God does not resolve theodicy, but exacerbates the problem.]

2242.   Goldingay, John E. "Theology and Healing." *Churchman* 92 (1978): 23-33.

2243.   Grant, Colin. "The Abandonment of Atonement." *King's Theological Review* 9 (1986): 1-8.

2244.   ——. "Possibilities for Divine Passibility." *Toronto Journal of Theology* 4 (1988): 3-18. [Citing major figures, classical and contemporary, Grant clarifies the development of the contemporary immanentist conception of God which has replaced the classical, traditional, interventionist understanding of God. Grant argues that it is legitimate to recognize the human dimension in God which requires the acknowledgment that God suffers. The assumption of divine immutability and impassibility obscured the gospel of love by failing to recognize the divine identification with humanity.]

2245.   Griffin, David R. *A Process Christology*. Philadelphia, PA: Westminster Press, 1973. [Republished in Lanham, MD: University Press of America, 1990. Griffin examines the Christologies of major thinkers (Tillich, H. Richard Niebuhr, Bultmann, Schleiermacher, etc.) and proposes an alternative process Christology in which Jesus is God's decisive revelation. See also numerous Griffin entries in *Chapter 6*.]

2246. Gunton, Colin. *Becoming and Being*. Oxford: Oxford University Press, 1978. [Critical comparison of God in Karl Barth and Charles Hartshorne. See the critical response by Fiddes, in his *The Creative Suffering of God*. [#2229].]

2247. Hallman, Joseph M. *The Descent of God: Divine Suffering in History and Theology*. Philadelphia, PA: Fortress Press, 1991. [A defense of the suffering of God in historical and contemporary figures: Philo, Augustine, Tertullian, Lactantious, Gregory of Nyssa, Hilary of Poitiers, Hegel and Whitehead, among some others.]

2248. ———. "Divine Suffering and Change in Origen and *Ad Theopompum*." *Second Century* (1990): 85-98.

2249. Hammer, Robert A. "The God of Suffering." *Center Journal* 31 (1976/1977): 34-41.

2250. Hanson, Geddes. "The Hope: God's Suffering in Man's Struggle." *Reformed World* 36 (1980): 72-79.

2251. Harris, Richard. "Ivan Karamazov's Argument." *Theology* 81 (1978): 104-114.

2252. Harrison, William Pope. "Can the Divine Nature Suffer?" *Methodist Quarterly Review* 25 (1987): 119-121.

2253. Hartshorne, Charles. "Whitehead's Idea of God." *The Philosophy of Alfred North Whitehead*. Edited by Paul A. Schilpp. La Salle, IL: Open Court, 1941: 513-519. [See numerous other listings by Hartshorne in *Chapter 6*, merely a portion of his several hundred publications.]

2254. Heschel, Abraham J. *Man is Not Alone: A Philosophy of Religion*. New York: Farrer, Straus and Giroux, 1951.

2255. ———. "The Divine Pathos: The Basic Category of Prophetic Theology." *Judaism* 2 (1953): 61-67.

2256. ———. *God in Search of Man*. New York: Harper and Row, 1955. New York: Farrer, Straus and Giroux, 1959.

2257. ———. *Between God and Man*. Edited by Fritz A. Rothchild. New York: Free Press, 1959. [See also Rothchild's "Architect and Herald of a New Theology." *America* 128 (1973): 210-212. A discussion of Abraham Heschel's impact.]

2258. ———. *The Prophets*. New York: Harper and Row, 1962.

2259. Hill, David. "Can God be Infinite?" *Journal of the West Virginia Philosophical Society* 3 (1976): 17-20. [Critiques the free will defense as an argument for an infinite God. God is either finite or non-existent.]

2260. Hodgson, Peter C. *Jesus—Word and Presence: An Essay in Christology*. Philadelphia, PA: Fortress Press, 1971. [See David Griffin's response, in *A Process Christology* [#2245].]

2261. House, Francis H. "The Barrier of Impassibility." *Thought* 83 (1980): 409-415. [Critical discussion of divine impassibility in Moltmann and Vanstone [#2417].]

2262. Jantzen, Grace M. "Christian Hope and Jesus' Despair." *King's Theological Review* 5 (1982): 1-7. [Critical analysis of Jürgen Moltmann's seminal book, *The Crucified God* [#2338].]

2263. Jones, William R. "Theodicy and Methodology in Black Theology: A Critique of Washington, Cone, and Cleage." *Harvard Theological Review* 64 (1971): 541-557. [Rejects the traditional God of overruling sovereignty. Argues in favor of a "humanocentric theism."]

2264. ———. "Theodicy: The Controlling Category for Black Theology." *Journal of Religious Thought* (1973): 28-38.

2265. ———. *Is God a White Racist? A Preamble to Black Theology.* Garden City, NY: Anchor Press/Doubleday, 1973.

2266. Jüngel, Eberhard. *Death: The Riddle and the Mystery.* Translated by I. Nicol and U. Nicol. Edinburgh: Saint Andrews Press, 1975.

2267. ———. *The Doctrine of the Trinity: God's Being is in Becoming.* Translated by H. Harris. Grand Rapids, MI: Eerdmans, 1976.

2268. ———. *God as the Mystery of the World: On the Foundation of the Theology of the Crucified One in the Dispute Between Theism and Atheism.* Translated by D.L. Guder. Edinburgh: T&T Clark, 1983.

2269. ———. "The Christian Understanding of Suffering." *Journal of Theology for South Africa* 45 (1988): 3-13.

2270. Kaufman, Peter Iver. "Daniel Day Williams and the Science of Suffering." *Union Seminary Quarterly Review* 36 (1978): 35-46.

2271. Kazantzakes, Nikos. *The Suffering God.* New Rochelle, NY: Caratzas Brothers, 1979.

2272. Kee, Alistair. *The Way of Transcendence: Christian Faith Without Belief in God.* Harmondsworth, Middlesex: Penguin Books, 1971.

2273. Khan, Abraham H. "God Suffers: Sense or Nonsense?" *Indian Journal of Theology* 29 (1979): 91-99.

2274. Kim, Chung Choon. "The Hope: God's Suffering in Man's Struggle (Part 2)." *Reformed World* 36 (1980): 13-19. [Part 1 is by Lochman [#2298].]

2275. Kitamori, Kazoh. "The Theology of the Pain of God." *Japan Christian Quarterly* 19 (1953): 318-210. [See the critique by Warren McWilliams' important book, *The Passion of God: Divine Suffering in Contemporary Protestant Theology* [#2321], among others.]

2276. ———. "The Japanese Mentality and Christianity." *Japan Christian Quarterly* 26 (1960): 170-173.

2277. ———. "Christianity and Other Religions in Japan." *Japan Christian Quarterly* 26 (1960): 230-238.

2278. ———. *Theology of the Pain of God.* Translated by M.E. Bratcher. Richmond, VA: John Knox, 1965. [Original Japanese text published in 1946.]

2279. ———. "Is 'Japanese Theology' Possible?" *Northeastern Journal of Theology* 3 (1969): 83-87.

2280. ———. "The Problem of Pain in Christology." *Christ and the Younger Churches.* Edited by Georg F. Vicedom. London: SPCK Press, 1972: 83-90. [Originally published in German. München: Chr. Kaiser Verlag, 1968.]

2281. Knight, Harold. *The Hebrew Prophetic Consciousness.* London: Lutterworth Press, 1947.

2282. König, Adrio. "The Idea of 'The Crucified God': Some Systematic Questions." *Journal of Theology for Southern Africa* 39 (1982): 55-61.

2283. ———. "A Theology of Comfort." *Journal of Theology for Southern Africa* 41 (1984): 55-57.

2284. Koyama, Kosuke. "The Hand Painfully Open." *Lexington Theological Quarterly* 22 (1987): 33-43.

2285. ———. *Waterbuffalo Theology.* Maryknoll, NY: Orbis Books, 1974.

2286. ———. "Reflections on War and Peace for an Ecumenical Theology 40 Years After Hiroshima." *Mid-Stream* 25 (1986): 141-154.

2287. Kraus, H.J. "The Living God: A Chapter of Biblical Theology." *Theology of the Liberating Word.* Edited by F. Herzog. Nashville, TN: Abingdon, 1971.

2288. Küng, Hans. *On Being a Christian.* Translated by Edward Quinn. New York: Pocket Books, 1978. [See pages 428-436. See also Küng's *Does God Exist?* [#1893]. Küng follows Hegel's view as a "prolegomenon to a future christology": kenosis is the inner life of the trinity; finitude is an inner aspect of the life of God.]

2289. Kuyper, Lester J. "The Suffering and the Repentance of God." *The Reformed Review* 18 (1965): 3-16. [Historical survey of the suffering and repentance of God. Kuyper discusses positively Mozley's six questions about the repentance of God *(The Impassibility of God: A Survey of Christian Thought* [#2351]) and considers historical figures, including Philo, Augustine, Jerome, Calvin, Barth, and others on divine immutability.]

2290. ———. "The Suffering and the Repentance of God." *Scottish Journal of Theology* 22 (1969): 257-277.

2291. ———. "Righteousness and Salvation." *Scottish Journal of Theology* 30 (1977): 233-252.

2292. Laporte, Jean-Marc. "Kenosis: Old and New." *Ecumenist* 12 (1974): 17-21. [Shows how the kenotic theme is present in R.D. Laing and H. Fingarette. Laporte argues that divine *kenosis* is not weakness, but strength.]

2293. Lee, Bernard. "The Helplessness of God." *Encounter* 38 (1977): 325-336.

2294. Lee, Jung Young. *Cosmic Religion.* New York: Harper and Row, 1978. [Original edition, New York: Philosophical Library, 1973].

2295. ———. *God Suffers for Us: A Systematic Inquiry into a Concept of Divine Passibility.* The Hague: Martinus Nijhoff, 1974. [See the critical response by Warren McWilliams, *The Passion of God: Divine Suffering in Contemporary Protestant Theology* [#2321], and Paul Fiddes, *The Creative Suffering of God* [#2229], among others.]

2296. ——. *The Theology of Change: A Christian Concept of God in an Eastern Perspective.* Maryknoll, NY: Orbis Books, 1979.

2297. Levy, Eric P. "The Two Natures of Christ: Suffering Victim and Pitying Witness." *Toronto Journal of Theology* 5 (1989): 57-62.

2298. Lochman, Jan M. "The Hope: God's Suffering in Man's Struggle (Part 1)." *Reformed World* 36 (1980): 5-12. [Part 2 is by Kim [#2274].]

2299. Loeschen, John. "The God Who Becomes." *Thomist* 35 (1971): 405-422.

2300. Löffler, Paul. "The Reign of God Has Come in the Suffering Christ: An Exploration of the Power of the Powerless." *International Review of Mission* 68 (1979): 109-114.

2301. Lossky, William. *The Mystical Theology of the Eastern Church.* London: J. Clarke and Co., 1973.

2302. MacGregor, Geddes. "Does Scripture Limit the Power of God?" *Hibbert Journal* 53 (1955): 382-386. [Maintains that there is not the slightest suggestion of the notion of omnipotence, when considering the biblical texts, as implying the "power to do anything."]

2303. ——. *Introduction to Religious Philosophy.* Boston, MA: Houghton Mifflin Co., 1959.

2304. ——. "The Kenosis." *Anglican Theological Review* 45 (1963): 15-27.

2305. ——. *Philosophical Issues and Religious Thought.* Boston, MA: Houghton Mifflin Company, 1973. [*Chapter 5* of *Part I*, "Evil in Classical Theism"; *Part II*, "God as Kenotic Being."]

2306. ——. *He Who Lets Us Be: A Theology of Love.* New York: Seabury Press, 1975. [Defines and defends kenotic theology and employs it with respect to the theodicy issue. See the critical response by Warren McWilliams, *The Passion of God: Divine Suffering in Contemporary Protestant Theology* [#2321].]

2307. Macquarrie, John. *Principles of Christian Theology.* New York: Charles Scribner's Sons, 1966. [Revised edition, London: SCM Press, 1977.]

2308. ——. "Kenoticism Reconsidered." *Theology* 77 (1974): 115-124.

2309. ——. *The Humility of God.* Philadelphia, PA: Westminster Press, 1978.

2310. ——. *Christian Hope.* London and Oxford: Mowbrays, 1978.

2311. Mauldin, Frank L. "Misplaced Concreteness in the Problem of Evil." *Religious Studies* 11 (1984): 243-255. [Utilizes Alfred North Whitehead's term, the fallacy of misplaced concreteness—taking a partial truth for the entire truth—to define the theodicy issue. The logical version is misguided: it uses abstract terms without considering the redemptive history in Christian experience, experienced through the Trinity.]

2312. McCullagh, C. Behan. "Theology of Atonement." *Other Side* 151 (1987): 26-27.

2313. McGill, Arthur C. "Human Suffering and the Passion of Christ." *The Meaning of Suffering.* Edited by Flavian Dougherty. New York: Human Sciences Press, 1982: 150-194.

2314.   McKenzie, John L. "The Son of Man Must Suffer." *The Mystery of Suffering and Death*. Edited by Michael J. Taylor. Garden City, NY: Image Books, 1973: 31-44. [Reprinted from *The Way* 7 (1967): 6-17.]

2315.   McWilliams, Warren. "The Passion of God and Moltmann's Christology." *Encounter* 40 (1979): 313-326.

2316.   ———. "Theodicy According to James Cone." *Journal of Religious Thought* 36 (1979/1980): 45-54. [Focuses on Cone's *God of the Oppressed* [#2219]. Mc-Williams contends that God's active involvement in history is the central feature of Cone's theodicy and that the cross points to God's own suffering. Cone rejects Hick's theodicy and Augustinian theodicy for focusing on the origin of evil, rather than on political dimensions of suffering.]

2317.   ———. "Divine Suffering in Contemporary Theology." *Scottish Journal of Theology* 33 (1980): 35-53. [See also [#2321].]

2318.   ———. "The Pain of God in the Theology of Kazoh Kitamori." *Religious Studies* 8 (1981): 184-200. [See also [#2321].]

2319.   ———. "A Kenotic God and the Problem of Evil." *Encounter* 42 (1981): 15-27. [Sympathetic, critical analysis of the *"kenotic"* theodicy of Jürgen Moltmann.]

2320.   ———. "Daniel Day Williams' Vulnerable and Invulnerable God." *Encounter* 44 (1983): 73-89. [See also [#2321].]

2321.   ———. *The Passion of God: Divine Suffering in Contemporary Protestant Theology*. Macon, GA: Mercer University Press, 1985. [Detailed analysis of the theology of divine suffering in Jürgen Moltmann, Kazoh Kitamori, Geddes MacGregor, James Cone, Daniel Day Williams, and Jung Young Lee.]

2322.   Meeks, M. Douglas. "The 'Crucified God' and the Power of Liberation." *Philosophy of Religion and Theology*. Compiled by James W. McClendon. American Academy of Religion Annual Proceedings, 1974: 31-42. [Meeks defends divine suffering and assesses its relationship to liberation theology [see #2324].]

2323.   ———. *Origins of the Theology of Hope*. Philadelphia, PA: Fortress Press, 1974.

2324.   ———. "God's Suffering Power and Liberation." *Journal of Religious Thought* 33 (1976): 44-54. [Previously published as "The 'Crucified God' and the Power of Liberation" [#2322].]

2325.   Merkle, John C. "Heschel's Theology of Divine Pathos." *Abraham Joshua Heschel: Exploring his Life and Thought*. Edited by John C. Merkle. New York: Macmillan, 1985: 66-83. [Defense of Heschel's seminal work, *The Prophets* [#2258], versus the most sustained and previously unanswered criticism, that of Eliezer Berkovits, "Dr. A.J. Heschel's Theology of Pathos." *Tradition: A Journal of Orthodox Thought* 6 (1964): 67-104.]

2326.   Metz, Johannes Baptist. "The Future in the Memory of Suffering." *New Questions on God*. Edited by Johannes B. Metz. New York: Herder and Herder, 1972: 9-25.

2327.   Meyer, Richard. "Toward a Japanese Theology: Kitamori's Theology of the Pain of God." *Concordia Theological Monthly* 33 (1962).

2328.   Michalson, Carl. *Japanese Contributions to Christian Theology*. Philadelphia, PA: Westminster Press, 1960. [Discusses Kitamori's theology, among others.]

2329. Migliore, Daniel L. "The Passion of God and the Prophetic Task of Pastoral Ministry." *The Pastor as Prophet*. Edited by Earl E. Shelp and R. Sunderland. New York: Pilgrim Press, 1985: 114-134.

2330. Moltmann, Jürgen. *Theology of Hope: On the Ground and Implications of a Christian Eschatology*. Translated by James W. Leitch. London: SCM, 1967.

2331. ———. *Religion, Revolution, and the Future*. Translated from German by M. Douglas Meeks. New York: Charles Scribner's Sons, 1969.

2332. ———. *The Future of Hope: Theology as Eschatology*. Edited by Frederick Herzog. New York: Herder and Herder, 1970.

2333. ———. *Hope and Planning*. Translated by Margaret Clarkson. New York: Harper and Row and London: SCM Press, 1971.

2334. ———. "'The Crucified God': A Trinitarian Theology of the Cross." *Interpretation* 26 (1972): 278-299. [All suffering in human history is also the suffering of God. This suffering did not start with the cross, but has always been an aspect of God, back to the *creatio ex nihilo*.]

2335. ———. "Response to the Opening Presentations." *Hope and the Future of Man*. Edited by Ewert H. Cousins. Philadelphia, PA: Fortress Press, 1972: 55-59.

2336. ———. *Theology and Joy*. Translated by R. Urlich. London: SCM Press, 1973.

2337. ———. "Resurrection as Hope." *The Mystery of Suffering and Death*. Edited by Michael J. Taylor. Garden City, NY: Image Books, 1973, 199-216.

2338. ———. *The Crucified God: The Cross of Christ as the Foundation and Criticism of Christian Theology*. Translated by R.A. Wilson and John Bowden. New York: Harper and Row, 1974. [Many of the critical responses to this seminal text which, with Moltmann's other publications, constitute one of the most profound explorations of the suffering of God theme, are listed in this appendix. See, for example, the publications of Richard Bauckham, Paul Fiddes, and Warren McWilliams, among others.]

2339. ———. "The Passion of Life." *Currents in Theology and Mission* 1 (1974): 3-9.

2340. ———. "The Crucified God." *Theology Today* 31 (1974): 6-18.

2341. ———. *The Experiment Hope*. Edited by M. Douglas Meeks. Philadelphia, PA: Fortress Press, 1975.

2342. ———. "Ecumenism Beneath the Cross." *African Ecclesiastical Review* 19 (1977): 2-9.

2343. ———. *The Church and the Power of the Spirit: A Contribution to Messianic Ecclesiology*. Translated by Margaret Kohl. New York: Harper and Row, 1977.

2344. ———. *The Future of Creation: Collected Essays*. Translated by Margaret Kohl. London: SCM Press, 1979.

2345. ———. *The Trinity and the Kingdom of God: The Doctrine of God*. Translated by Margaret Kohl. London: SCM Press, 1981. [While God has suffered since the creation, the Trinity is the unique, most densely concentrated suffering God has endured.]

2346.   ———. *The Power of the Powerless*. Translated from German by Margaret Kohl. San Francisco, CA: Harper and Row, 1983.

2347.   ———. "Theodicy." *A New Dictionary of Christian Theology*. London: SCM Press, 1983: 564-566.

2348.   ———. *God in Creation: An Ecological Doctrine of Creation*. London: SCM Press, 1984/1985.

2349.   ———. "God and the Nuclear Catastrophe." *Pacifica* 1 (1988): 157-170.

2350.   Morse, Christopher. *The Logic of Promise in Moltmann's Theology*. Philadelphia, PA: Fortress Press, 1976.

2351.   Mozley, John Kenneth. *The Impassibility of God: A Survey of Christian Thought*. Cambridge: Cambridge University Press, 1926. [Surveys the early history of the divine impassibility doctrine. God suffers because God freely chooses to enter into human experiences of suffering; God does not suffer because God has no choice. See the critical comments by Kuyper, "The Suffering and the Repentance of God" [#2290].]

2352.   Mutoh, Kazuo. "Kitamorian Theology." *Japan Christian Quarterly* 19 (1953): 231-234.

2353.   Northan, Joan. "The Kingdom, the Power and the Glory." *Expository Times* 99 (1988): 300-303.

2354.   Nouwen, Henri J.M. *The Wounded Healer: Ministry in Contemporary Society*. Garden City, NY: Doubleday, 1979. [Maintains that those who minister to the suffering ought to do so by making their own wounds available as a source of healing, as an imitation of Christ.]

2355.   ———. "The Suffering Christ: Peacemaking Across the Americas." *Other Side* 147 (1983): 16-19.

2356.   Nouwen, Henri J.M., and Donald P. McNeill, and Douglas A. Morrison. *Compassion: A Reflection on the Christian Life*. Garden City, NY: Doubleday, 1982.

2357.   Nygren, Anders. *Agape and Eros*. Translated by Philip S. Watson. Chicago, IL: University of Chicago Press, 1982.

2358.   O'Donnell, John. *Trinity and Temporality: The Christian Doctrine of the Cross in the Light of Process Theology and the Theology of Hope*. Oxford: Oxford University Press, 1983: *Chapter 4*.

2359.   O'Hanlon, Gerald F. *The Immutability of God in the Theology of Hans urs von Balthasar*. Cambridge: Cambridge University Press, 1991. [Contains complete Balthasar primary bibliography and an extensive secondary bibliography.]

2360.   Ohlrich, Charles. *The Suffering God*. Downers Grove, IL: InterVarsity Press, 1982.

2361.   Outler, Albert C. *Who Trusts in God: Musings on the Meaning of Providence*. New York: Oxford University Press, 1968.

2362.   ———. "God's Providence and the World's Anguish." *The Mystery of Suffering and Death*. Edited by Michael J. Taylor. Garden City, NY: Image Books, 1973: 3-23. [Excerpt from Outler's *Who Trusts in God?* [#2361].]

2363. Overing, Joanna. "There is No End of Evil: The Guilty Innocents and their Fallible God." *The Anthropology of Evil*. Edited by David Parkin. Oxford: Blackwell, 1985: 244-278.

2364. Owen, Huw Parri. *Concepts of Deity*. New York: Herder and Herder, 1971.

2365. Owen, O.T. "Does God Suffer?" *Church Quarterly Review* 158 (1957): 176-184. [Argues the traditional view that God does *not* suffer; only as such can God's transcendence be safeguarded.]

2366. Page, Ruth. "Human Liberation and Divine Transcendence." *Theology* 85 (1982): 184-190.

2367. Pannenberg, Wolfhart. *Jesus—God and Man*. Translated by L.L. Wilkins and D.A. Priebe. Philadelphia, PA: Westminster Press, 1968.

2368. Perkins, Davis. "The Problem of Suffering: Atheistic Protest and Trinitarian Response." *St. Luke's Journal of Theology* 23 (1979): 14-32. [Uses Moltmann's "crucified God"–theme to argue that the Trinity addresses the problem of suffering: God was *not* present in the Holocaust; the Holocaust, rather, was present *in* God. Suffering is a constituent element of God.]

2369. Phillips, Anthony. "The Servant—Symbol of Divine Powerlessness." *Expository Times* 90 (1979): 370-374.

2370. Plantinga, Cornelius. "A Love So Fierce." *Reformed Journal* 36 (1986): 5-6.

2371. ——. "Dignitas." *Reformed Journal* 39 (1989): 2-4.

2372. Polen, Nehemia. "Divine Weeping: Rabbi Kalonymos Shapiro's Theology of Catastrophe in the Warsaw Ghetto (*Esh Kodesh* or Fire of Holiness)." *Modern Judaism* 7 (1987): 253-269.

2373. Pollard, T. Evan. "The Impassibility of God." *Scottish Journal of Theology* 8 (1955): 353-364. [Rejects the Greek influence in Christianity, in conceiving God as impassible. The view was assumed, rather than argued by the Apostolic Fathers. To continue to accept the traditional view, he argues, would imply that the scriptures would have to be rewritten. It also denies the incarnation and attributes a vague Supreme Being rather than a God of personality.]

2374. Post, Stephen G. "Disinterested Benevolence: An American Debate over the Nature of Christian Love." *Journal of Religious Ethics* 14 (1986): 356-368.

2375. ——. "The Inadequacy of Selflessness: God's Suffering and the Theory of Love." *Journal of the American Academy of Religion* 51 (1988): 213-228.

2376. Power, William. "The Doctrine of the Trinity and Whitehead's Metaphysics." *Encounter* 44 (1983): 287-302.

2377. Prior, David. *Jesus and Power*. Downers Grove, IL: InterVarsity Press, 1987.

2378. Raabe, Paul R. "The Suffering of God." *Concordia Journal* 12 (1986): 147-152. [Review article of Terrence Fretheim's *The Suffering of God: An Old Testament Perspective* [#2235]. Raabe argues that the positive features of Fretheim's book is its "incarnational-sacramental" theology and its "theology of the cross." Negatively, he argues, Fretheim reads the biblical texts too much through the eyes of process theology.]

2379. Relton, H. Maurice. *Studies in Christian Doctrine*. New York: Macmillan, 1960.

2380. Richard, Lucien. "Kenotic Christology in a New Perspective." *Eglise et Théologie* 7 (1976): 5-39. [In a text with copious footnoted references, Richard surveys the past two centuries of "kenotic chris- tology," including Protestants (Karl Barth, Dietrich Bonhoeffer, Thomas Altizer, Jürgen Moltmann), Roman Catholics (Hans Küng, Karl Rahner, Urs von Balthasar), and process theology (Williams Beardslee, John Cobb, David Griffin).]

2381. ———. *A Kenotic Christology: In the Humanity of Jesus the Christ, the Compassion of God*. Lanham, MD: University Press of America, 1982.

2382. Robinson, H. Wheeler. *Suffering, Human and Divine*. New York: Macmillan, 1939. [Argues that God suffers as the Holy Spirit. See also his related book, *Redemption and Revelation*. London: Nisbet, 1942.]

2383. Robinson, John A.T. *The Human Face of God*. Philadelphia, PA: Westminster Press, 1973. [Severely rejects kenotic christologies as fruitless expenditures of theological ingenuity.]

2384. Russell, John M. "Impassibility and Pathos in Barth's Idea of God." *Anglican Theological Review* 70 (1988): 221-232.

2385. Sano, Roy I. "The Asian American Context: Analyzing the International Dimensions Theologically." *South East Asia Journal of Theology* 21 (1980/1981): 121-133.

2386. ———. "Transforming Suffering: Struggle with Life as an Asian American." *Changing Contexts of our Faith*. Edited by L. Russell. Philadelphia, PA: Fortress Press, 1985: 63-79.

2387. Sarot, Marcel. "Patripassianism, Theopaschitism and the Suffering of God." *Religious Studies* 26 (1990): 363-375. [Contains a critique of both Richard Creel's *Divine Impassibility* [#837] and Augustine Shutte's "A New Argument for the Existence of God." *Modern Theology* 3 (1987): 157-177.]

2388. ———. "Auschwitz, Morality and the Suffering of God." *Modern Theology* 7 (1991): 135-152. [See also Sarot's more recent, "Suffering of Christ, Suffering of God?" *Theology* 95 (1992): 113-118.]

2389. Schulweis, Harold M. "Charles Hartshorne and the Defenders of Heschel." *Judaism* 24 (1975): 58-62.

2390. Scott, David A. "Ethics on a Trinitarian Basis: Moltmann's *The Crucified God*." *Anglican Theological Review* 60 (1978): 166-179.

2391. Shoji, Tsutomu. "Sin and Suffering: Japan and the Peoples of Asia." *Japan Christian Quarterly* 47 (1981): 12-19.

2392. Simpson, Theodore. "A Very Present Help in Trouble." *Journal of Theology for Southern Africa* 21 (1987): 43-50. [Follows Moltmann's view that the cross implies a suffering God. God freely enters humanity's suffering in order that alienated humans can recover to wholeness and freedom through the demonstration of God's acceptance of us.]

2393. Slusser, Michael. "The Scope of Patripassianism." *Studia Patristica* 17 (1982): 169-175. [Contends that trustworthy evidence of patripassianism after 250 CE is negligible. The doctrine is also scripturally indefensible.]

2394. Sobrino, Jon. *Christology at the Crossroads: A Latin American Perspective.* Maryknoll, NY: Orbis Books, 1978.

2395. ———. "Liberation from Sin." *Theology Digest* 37 (1990): 141-146. [Originally published in *Sal Terrae* 76 (1988): 15-28]. [The poor in Latin America show us our sin by accepting us as we are, thereby doing what God wants for all sinners: forgiveness–acceptance.]

2396. Soelle, Dorothee. *Christ the Representative: An Essay in Theology after the "Death of God."* Translated by D. Lewis. London: SCM Press, 1967.

2397. ———. *Suffering.* Translated by Everett R. Kalin. London: Darton, Longman and Todd, 1975.

2398. ———. "Blood of the Dragon, Blood of the Lamb." *Other Side* 151 (1987): 26-27.

2399. ———. *Thinking About God: An Introduction to Theology.* Translated by Gott Denkin. Philadelphia, PA: Trinity Press International, 1990. [Chapters on various approaches to theology, creation, sin, feminist liberation theology, grace, black theology, Jesus, the end of theism and the question of God.]

2400. Stockdale, Fairbank Barnes. "Does God Suffer?" *Methodist Review* 81 (1899): 87-92.

2401. Stott, John R.W. "God on the Gallows: How Could I Worship a God Immune to Pain?" *Christianity Today* 122 (1987): 28-30.

2402. Surin, Kenneth. "The Impassibility of God and the Problem of Evil." *Scottish Journal of Theology* 35 (1981): 97-115. [Defends the view that God is passible, versus impassible. Following Moltmann and Soelle, Surin argues that the theodicy problem is resolved by the theology of the cross. God limits the divine omnipotence in identifying with human suffering and through the incarnation. He concludes that kenotic theodicy is a "non-theodicy," a suffering theophany.]

2403. ———. "Christology, Tragedy and 'Ideology'." *Theology* 89 (1986): 285-290. [Response to Philip West, "Christology as 'Ideology'" [#2422].]

2404. ———. "Some Aspects of the 'Grammar' of 'Incarnation' and 'Kenosis': Reflections Prompted by the Writings of Donald MacKinnon." *Christ, Ethics and Tragedy.* Edited by Kenneth Surin. Cambridge: University of Cambridge Press, 1989: 93-116.

2405. Sutherland, Denis. "Impassibility, Asceticism and the Vision of God." *Scottish Bulletin of Evangelical Theology* 5 (1987): 197-210.

2406. Taliaferro, Charles. "The Passibility of God." *Religious Studies* 25 (1989): 217-224.

2407. Tanenzapf, Sol. "Heschel and His Critics." *Judaism* 23 (1974): 133-145.

2408. Taylor, Patty. "Participating in the Sufferings of God." *Theological Students Fellowship (TSF) Bulletin* 5 (1982): 2-5. [Assesses Bonhoeffer's understanding of the suffering of God and "participating in the sufferings of God."]

2409. Telepneff, Gregory. "Theopascite Language in the Soteriology of Saint Gregory the Theologian." *Greek Orthodox Theological Review* 32 (1987): 403-416.

2410. Thomsen, Mark W. "Jesus Crucified and the Mission of the Church." *International Review of Mission* 77 (1988): 247-264.

2411. Tillich, Paul. *Theology of Culture*. Edited by R.C. Kimball. New York: Oxford University Press, 1959.

2412. ———. *The Courage to Be*. London: Collins, 1962.

2413. ———. *Systematic Theology*. Combined Volumes I-III. London: James Nesbit, 1968. [Originally published in 3 volumes by University of Chicago Press, 1951-1963. Combined Volumes I-III, 1967.]

2414. Trethowan, Illtyd. "Christology Again." *Downside Review* 95 (1977): 1-10.

2415. ———. "The Significance of Process Theology." *Religious Studies* 19 (1983): 311-322.

2416. Vanhoutte, Johan. "God as Companion and Fellow-Sufferer: An Image Emerging from Process Thought." *Archivio di Filosofia* 56 (1988): 191-225.

2417. Vanstone, W.H. *Love's Endeavour, Love's Expense*. London: Darton, Longman and Todd, 1977.

2418. ———. *The Risk of Love*. New York: Oxford University Press, 1978.

2419. Vieth, Richard F. *Holy Power, Human Pain*. Bloomington, MN: Meyer Stone Publications, 1985. [Argues against traditional theism, for a more passionate God. Vieth utilizes Whitehead, Moltmann, Heschel, and biblical resources.]

2420. Ware, Bruce A. "An Exposition and Critique of the Process Doctrines of Divine Mutability and Immutability." *Westminster Theological Journal* 47 (1985): 175-196.

2421. Weddle, David L. "God the Redeemer: Sovereignty and Suffering." *Christianity Today* 104 (1969): 12-15. [Sympathetic exposition of the suffering of God portrayed by Nicholas Berdyaev and process philosopher Charles Hartshorne. He differs from Hartshorne by holding that God's power has been self-limited.]

2422. West, Philip. "Christology as Ideology." *Theology* 88 (1985): 428-436.

2423. Westermann, Claus. *Elements in Old Testament Theology*. Translated by Douglas W. Scott. Atlanta, GA: John Knox Press, 1982.

2424. Wild, Robert. *Who I Will Be: Is There Joy and Sorrow in God?* Danville, NJ: Dimension Books, 1976.

2425. Williams, Daniel Day. "The Victory of Good." *Journal of Liberal Religion* 3 (1942): 171-185. [Presents a process theological understanding of God (Whiteheadian, Hartshornean) as involved with and responsive to the world.]

2426. ———. *God's Grace and Man's Hope*. New York: Harper and Row, 1949, 1965.

2427. ———. *What Present Day Theologians are Thinking*. New York: Harper and Row, 1959. Revised third edition, 1967.

2428. ———. "Deity, Monarchy and Metaphysics: Whitehead's Critique of the Theological Tradition." *The Relevance of Whitehead*. Edited by Ivor Leclerc. New York: Macmillan, 1961: 161-180.

2429. ———. "The Vulnerable and Invulnerable God." *Christianity and Crisis* 22 (1962): 27-30. [In distinction to traditional Christianity, Williams defends Alfred North Whitehead's view that God is the "fellow sufferer who understands." In loving, God is vulnerable; yet in this love, God is invulnerable as well, since "the greater the love, the more steady and unalterable its commitment."]

2430.   ———. "How Does God Act? An Essay in Whitehead's Metaphysics." *Process and Divinity*. Edited by Williams L. Reese and Eugene Freeman. La Salle, IL: Open Court, 1964: 161-180.

2431.   ———. *The Spirit and the Forms of Love*. New York: Harper and Row, 1968. [The first systematic process theology. Among the many critical responses to this well-known book is Warren McWilliams, *The Passion of God: Divine Suffering in Contemporary Protestant Theology* [#2321].]

2432.   ———. "Suffering and Being in Empirical Theology." *The Future of Empirical Theology*. Edited by Bernard E. Meland. Chicago, IL: University of Chicago Press, 1969: 175-194.

2433.   Wilson, Bruce. "The God who Suffers: A Re-examination of the Theology of Unjust Suffering." *St. Mark's Review* 140 (1990): 21-31.

2434.   Wimberly, Edward P. "The Suffering God." *Preaching on Suffering and a God of Love*. Edited by Henry J. Young and Nathan A. Scott. Philadelphia, PA: Fortress Press, 1978: 56-62. [Maintains that God suffers but is able to help us find the resources to cope with evil and suffering.]

2435.   Wolfinger, Franz. "Toward a Theology of Suffering." *Theology Digest* 29 (1981): 34-36. [Abstract of the original German publication, "Leiden als theologisches Problem: Versuch einer Problemskizze," *Catholica* 32 (1978), 242-266. Wolfinger argues that the classical view of God needs modification. After discussing traditional views, he supports Moltmann's view of divine suffering as more promising.]

2436.   Wolterstorff, Nicholas. *Reason within the Bounds of Religion*. Grand Rapids, MI: Eerdmans, 1976. [See also Wolterstorff's *Lament for a Son*. Grand Rapids, MI: Eerdmans, 1987.]

2437.   ———."Suffering Love." *Philosophy and the Christian Faith*. Edited by Thomas V. Morris. Notre Dame, IN: University of Notre Dame Press, 1988: 196-237. [Critique of Augustine and Aquinas for their view that God does not suffer.]

2438.   Wondra, Gerald. "The Pathos of God." *Reformed Review* 18 (1964): 28-35.

2439.   Woollcombe, Kenneth J. "The Pain of God." *Scottish Journal of Theology* 20 (1967): 129-148.

2440.   Woznicki, Andrzei. "God's Existence and the Evil of Suffering." *God in Contemporary Thought: A Philosophical Perspective*. Edited by Sebastian Matczak. New York: Learned Publications, 1977: 1021-1041. [Overview of the theodicies of Josiah Royce, Dostoevsky, Kant, Sartre, and Nietzsche. Woznicki concludes that the ontological fallacy of the alleged incongruity between God's existence and the existence of evil in the world consists mainly in recognizing God's immanence and transcendence as consistent with the spatio-temporal order of our human existence. Being both immanently and transcendentally transcendent, God cannot partake in suffering; yet phenomenologically, by creating contingent creatures (rather than perfect creatures) God is the origin of suffering. The evil can be existentially experienced, nevertheless, either positively or negatively. The book also contains a select bibliography.]

2441. Young, Frances. "God Suffered and Died." *Incarnation and Myth: The Debate Continued*. Edited by M.D. Goulder. Grand Rapids, MI: Eerdmans, 1979: 101-103.

2442. Young, Henry James. "Black Theology and the Work of Henry R. Jones." *Religion in Life* 44 (1975): 14-23. [Critical discussion of H.R. Jones, *Is God a White Racist? A Preamble to Black Theology* [#2265].]

2443. ———. "Black Theology: Providence and Evil." *Duke Divinity School Review* 40 (1975): 87-96.

2444. ———. "Does Christianity Proclaim Redemption In and Through or Despite Suffering?—Special Emphasis on the Black Experience." *The Meaning of Suffering*. Edited by Flavian Dougherty. New York: Human Sciences Press, 1982: 299-340.

2445. Zahl, Paul F.M. "The Historical Jesus and Substitutionary Atonement." *St. Luke's Journal of Theology* 26 (1983): 313-332.

2446. Zimany, Roland D. "Moltmann's Crucified God." *Dialog* 16 (1977): 49-57. [Argues that Moltmann neglects the life of Jesus and uses too narrow a basis for his theodicy.]

Appendix D

Miscellaneous Publications

This appendix lists approximately 1,300 publications that address various aspects of the theodicy issue.[1] The lists necessarily are selective, but I have made a conscientious effort to include as many of the pertinent items as possible. The mass of published material that is relevant (in some manner or other) to the main discussions—the items listed in the annotated chapters—is considerable, to say the very least. The relevant material involves no less than a good portion of the incredibly diverse enterprise known as "theology." Theodicy is central to that enterprise. The problem of evil is among the most important theological issues; indeed, it is among the most important human issues.

The items are organized around the following themes: *pain and theodicy, divine providence and theodicy, evil in literature, original sin and theodicy, Jewish and Holocaust theodicy, Satan and theodicy, theodicies other than Judaeo-Christian, women and theodicy,* and a very large section of *miscellaneous publications*. This latter section includes many items on *existential coping* with evil and suffering, the subject of a large and expanding popular literature. I refer to this as "popular" since most of these writings ignore the theological and philosophical debates and focus, choosing rather to focus on the more practical coping techniques in face of personal tragedy, loss, grief, death, and suffering in general. Other items listed deal with some of the *ethical and medical issues* about suffering, and items written by and about important figures whose writings are no longer as central to the "mainstream" discussions as they once were (*C.S. Lewis, Paul Ricoeur, Ernest Becker, Henry Nouwen,* etc.). Some notable exceptions are *Simone Weil* and *Dorothee Soelle,* whose writings and some of the important secondary literature are listed here. These contributions to theodicy are important, although they are peripheral in the defined sense of not addressing the "mainstream" philosophica/theological debates reflected in the annotated chapters. Also listed are some of the most important of the numerous general studies which exist in abundance, and some of the major references to *conservative theological publications* on the theodicy issue. There are, at the very least, a few hundred books on "philosophy of religion" and a good proportion of these books contain chapters on the problem of evil. Not all of them contribute anything original to the issue. Those which do are entered in the bibliography, either in the chapters or appendices. This, at least, was my intent.

The subsection on *pain and theodicy* [i] contains a list of publications that address the nature of pain from a theological perspective. The publications encompass also the area of "medical ethics" and other cross-disciplinary areas—the psychology of pain, the sociology of pain, and related matters. The field of pain research has witnessed a rapid development in recent years, yet the application of this research for theodicy has not been fully explored. It is no mean task to relate the empirical research (which comprises psychological, physiological and clinical data) to the theoretical issue of theodicy. Some work has been done in this regard.

The subsection on *providence and theodicy* [ii] contains publications that address the nature of divine causation and power with respect to the world and, in particular, to the world's suffering. The contemporary world is not as certain of "divine providence" as was the pre-modern-scientific era. Contemporary theologians do not refer to the term, "divine providence," as much as the theologians of the Reformation and those who lived before that seminal event. Contemporary science, represented predominately by evolutionary biology and physics, makes little reference to divine providence. Contemporary theologians refer to the immanence, transcendence and the absoluteness of God, rather than to divine providential guidance—the latter represented in Augustine, Aquinas and Calvin, among the hosts of traditional theologians.[2] The free will—determinism question is as relevant as ever, although cast in somewhat of a different light. Traditional determinism, be it the result of God's causal agency or the result of the physical world, is being challenged by a new indeterminism, represented by contemporary physics and by process thinkers, among others.[3]

The subsection on the *theodicy in literature* [iii] lists many of the relevant writings, acknowledging the fact that all great literature and human creativity in the various visual and musical arts, etc. concerns itself with the fundamental human problem of suffering.[4] Karl Rahner is correct in noting that "Everywhere, everywhen, and everyhow, it seems, this problem [suffering] has been near the heart of the important work of significant writers." The problem of suffering is a problem that no human being can ignore. It is "universal, universally oppressive, and [a problem which] touches our existence at its very roots."[5]

The subsection on *original sin and theodicy* [iv] lists the relevant items that deal with the doctrine of original sin and its role in theodicies. Traditional (conservative) Christian theology (Protestant and Roman Catholic) has attributed the evil and suffering in the world to the "original sin" of the first humans. While liberal theology has "demythologized" the historical and scientific veracity of the Adamic myth of the "fall" into sin, it has held a privileged place in the theology and theodicy of the Christian world.

The subsection on *Jewish and Holocaust theodicy* [v] lists many of the most relevant publications on the Nazi Holocaust, particularly as they relate to the theodicy issue. The brutal and calculated murder of millions of innocent people has become the symbol for evil in our culture. The devastation and overwhelming cruelty displayed in the holocaust has pressed the problem of evil to new awareness and urgency. Jewish and Christian reactions have varied from attributing the evil to God's incomprehensible plan to rejecting belief in the concept of God, as traditionally defined. The 18-volume *Archives of the Holocaust* (Garland, 1991), edited by John Mendelsohn and Donald S. Detwiler, includes an abundance of primary historical sources, and the 13-volume *America and the Holocaust* (Garland, 1991) documents the editor's, David S. Wyman, acclaimed book, *The Abandonment of the Jews: America and the Holocaust, 1941-1945*. Macmillan's 4-volume *Encyclopedia of the Holocaust* (1990) is another noteworthy item among the burgeoning literature on the holocaust. Ellen Fine's book, *Legacy of Night* (State University of New York Press, 1982) contains primary and secondary bibliographical lists of writings by and about Elie Wiesel [in English and French]. See also Molly Abramowitz's book, *Elie Wiesel: An Annotated Bibliography* (Scarecrow Press, 1974), and Irving Abrahamson's "Elie Wiesel: A Selected Bibliography," in *Confronting the Holocaust: The Impact of Elie Wiesel* (Indiana University Press, 1978). Another particularly useful text is the *Bibliography on Holocaust Literature* (Westview Press, 1986), edited by Abraham and Heschel Edelheit. David M. Szonyi's *The Holocaust: An Annotated Bibliography and Resource Guide* (KTAV Publishing House, 1985) is also a recent and useful guide to the literature.

The subsection on *Satan and theodicy* [vi] contains items on demonology and the role of the evil power called Satan in the world's suffering. Traditional Christian theology has attributed the world's evil not only to the fall of Adam and Eve, but to the evil power which goaded them into the sin that forever changed the world. Contemporary liberal scholars have demythologized Satan as an actual being, yet the attribution of evil and suffering to evil powers always has been a dominant Christian explanation for the world's evil. The popularity of movies like *The Exorcist, Rosemary's Baby*, and numerous others which have followed in this genre, has reinforced the traditional conservative belief in satanic powers. The Roman Catholic church, of course, still performs exorcisms, and the conservative (evangelical) branch of Protestantism speaks of the "devil" as a living personal presence. In the past, some theologians and philosophers proposed that the evil power is in God, rather than external to God. Frederick Sontag's argument that there is an evil aspect in God, a view found in past writers like John Stuart Mill, is a contemporary option which has yet to be explored fully. Plato's "External dualism," seeing the evil outside of God, has been exploited by E.S. Brightman, among others.[6]

The subsection on *theodicies other than Judaeo-Christian* [vii] lists the important publications in this area: the theodicy problem is defined differently in eastern religions (Buddhism, Hinduism, Jainism), in the Chinese religions (Confucianism, Taoism, Shinto), and in the tribal religions than in the western monotheistic religions (Judaism, Christianity, Islam). For the latter, the issue has been to reconcile belief in one God, the creator *ex nihilo* of all things. For religions other than the monotheistic religions, the theodicy issue is conceived differently, since (speaking generally) there are evil powers to which evil is attributed. John Bowker's classic book, *Problems of Suffering in Religions of the World* (Cambridge University Press, 1970) and others like Arthur Herman's *The Problem of Evil and Indian Thought* (Motilal Bamarsidass, 1976), and Bruce Reichenbach's recent book, *The Law of Karma* (State University of New York Press, 1990) make important contributions in the theodicy issue in eastern thinking.

The subsection on *women and theodicy* [viii] lists some of the most important of the growing mass of feminist literature. Nel Noddings's *Women and Evil* (University of California Press, 1989), Katherine Keller's *From a Broken Web* (Beacon Press, 1986), are good examples of what is being accomplished in this field. The theodicy issue has not been addressed directly, at least in the sense defined in the annotated chapters, but important feminist writers like *Marjorie Suchocki* and others like *Anna Case-Winters, Sheila Davaney, Nancy Frankenberry* and *Wendy Farley* [see especially *Chapter 6*, since it is process theology that has attracted many feminist writers] have made direct contributions to theodicy. *Dorothee Soelle* and *Simone Weil* are, of course, major feminine voices, and the writings of *Rebecca Chopp*, among growing numbers of others, likewise are making important contributions. I do not accept, however, the recent comment of Alice Laffey, who has been influenced by the critical thought of Terrence Tilley (*The Evils of Theodicy*, Georgetown University Press, 1991) and Kenneth Surin (*Theodicy and the Problem of Evil*, Blackwell, 1986), that "women would not have produced theodicy," that women "would not have abstracted in an effort to explain away human pain," nor "will women support the survival of theodicy" (see her article in the "Review Symposium" on Tilley's *The Evils of Theodicy, Horizons* 18 [1991]). This is yet to be seen. I do anticipate that when more women and feminist writers address the theodicy issue, the issue will be transformed significantly. I expect more emphasis on existential coping than on the traditional theoretical pursuits, and far more emphasis on the nature of and models for divine power (as in process theology).

The subsection, finally, on *miscellaneous publications on theodicy* [ix] covers much ground. The most influential of the existential coping books has been Rabbi Harold Kushner's *When Bad Things Happen to Good People* (Schocken Books, 1981). There have been numerous other books of this kind, the most competent of which are listed in this appendix. Philip Yancey's *Where is God When it Hurts?* (Zondervan, 1977), Burton Cooper's *Why God?* (John Knox, 1988); Wayne and Charles Oates's *People in Pain* (Westminster Press, 1985) are among the most important of these. The recent book by Michael Stoeber, *Evil and the Mystics' God* (University of Toronto Press, 1992) contributes interestingly to the existential aspect of theodicy by relating rational theodicy to the mystics (Dostoevsky, Eckhart, Boehme, etc.) as a resource for its resolution. Reference to evangelical theology, as it relates to the theodicy issue, also is included in this chapter.

Among the items *not* listed here include the mass of published material that discuss the *divine attributes*: omnipotence, omniscience, immutability, providence, sovereignty, etc., and the question of God's relationship to the world. Some of the most relevant of these (the most relevant to the theodicy issue) *have* been listed in the annotated chapters, items on divine omnipotence and omniscience in particular. Other related items that form an enormous literature are those on the *arguments for God's existence*—the theodicy issue is relevant to the proofs, as well as to the theistic arguments against atheism and scepticism, the question of miracles, faith healing, immortality, and mysticism, etc. To have listed these items would have resulted in a book of unmanageable length and complexity, indeed a book that would have taken us too far from the theodicy issue proper, despite the relationship of these items to theodicy.

The question of *miracles (divine intervention)* is perhaps one of the most important of these omitted items.[7] The nature and definition of miracles has been debated seriously since at least *David Hume's* famous rejection of these "violations of natural laws," and the issue has continuing relevance for the theodicy issue, since it addresses the question of *how God acts in the world*. Why does God not intervene with miracles to prevent or eradicate the most hideous evils? Hume and contemporary sceptics have continued to ask this question with specific reference to the theodicy issue. *H.J. McCloskey* and *John Mackie* were among the most persistent and influential philosophers to argue that the lack of miraculous intervention is strong evidence against the existence of the loving and powerful God espoused by western theology. Theistic defenders have argued both that God does perform miracles, without which the world would be much worse, and that God cannot perform miracles without arbitrarily violating divine laws established by God. Like the other sub-sections noted in this appendix, the issue of miracles and its relationship to the theodicy issue is an important and complex issue.[8]

Other groups of publications that are among the most important to theodicy but not listed here include the numerous publications that defend atheism and those that address the *epistemic nature of religious belief, the nature and veridity of mystical experience* (or, more generally, "religious experience"), etc. There is a massive literature on all of these items. The goal of this appendix has been to include as much of the most relevant items as possible within the confines of a single volume.

Notes

1.   *Appendix E* lists the relevant dissertations. The appendix is sub-divided into sections and it is noteworthy that one-quarter of the listings are "theodicy in literature" dissertations. There are many biblical listings, and many historical theodicy listings, as well as many listings relevant to the material discussed in the four annotated chapters, *Chapters 2-7*. There are also a number of "coping" dissertations, medical ethical themes, and others

which correspond to the items listed in *Appendix D*. Some of the many relevant and diverse dissertations listed in *Appendix E* are the following: Peggy L. Day, *Satan in the Hebrew Bible* (Harvard University, 1986); Robert Lee Feldman, *The Problem of Evil in Five Plays by Arthur Miller* (University of Maryland College Park, 1985); Anne T. Field, *Integrating the Shadow: A Contribution of Jungian Psychology to Feminist Theology* (Graduate Theological Union, 1990); José Rafael Garcia, *Liberation and Evil: A Critique of the Thought of Gustavo Gutiérrez and Rubem Alves from the Standpoint of F.R. Tennant's Theodicy* (Claremont Graduate School, 1975); Madeline Walsh Hamblin, *Simone Weil: The Concept of a Self-Emptying God with Special Reference to the Problem of Human Suffering* (University of Southern California, 1976); Abrahim Khan, *The Treatment of the Theme of Suffering in Kierkegaard's Works* (McGill University, 1973); Nancy Anne Marck, *Tragedy and Society: The Novels of George Eliot* (University of Illinois, 1992); Justine Anne McCabe, *The Role of Suffering in the Transformation of Self* (California School of Professional Psychology, Berkeley, 1991); Marlene K. Miner, *The Problem of Evil in the Works of Blake and Shelly* (University of Cincinnati, 1990); Kathleen Mary Sands, *Escape from Paradise: Evil in the Theological Foundations of Rosemary Radford Ruether and Carol P. Christ* (Boston College, 1991); Paul Scatena, *The Epistemic Theory of Pain* (University of Rochester, 1990); Robert C. Sutton, III, *Authentic Responses to Evil in Jesus and Camus* (Drew University, 1988); Graham Brown Walker, Jr., *Elie Wiesel: A Challenge to Contemporary Theology* (Southern Baptist Theological Seminary, 1986); Per Markus Anderson, *Theodicy in a New Key: The Problem of Consent to the Negative in a Technological Culture* (University of Chicago, 1991); James Patterson Browder, III, *Elected Suffering: Toward a Theology for Medicine* (Duke University, 1991); etc.

2. See, for example, the essays in *The Caring God: Perspectives on Providence*. Edited by Carl S. Meyer and Herbert T. Mayer (St. Louis, MO: Concordia, 1973). This text considers not only traditional *biblical* perspectives on providence (Martin H. Scharlemann, and Richard Baepler), but also *philosophical* views (Curtis E. Huber), *sociological* (David Schuller), *psychological* (Ralph Underwager), *historical* (Carl S. Meyer), *literary* (Warren Rubel), and *scientific* (John C. Gienapp) perspectives.

3. The literature on the determinism-free will debates is immense. Much of it is contained in this bibliography, since it has relevance to the theodicy issue. There is, however, much which is peripheral to theodicy, and not listed here.

4. I concur with, and would expand to all of human creativity, Shalom J. Kahn's comment ("The Problem of Evil in Literature," *Journal of Aesthetics and Art Criticism* [1953], 98-110), that all great literature is profoundly moral and that the central problem in literature of all kinds always has been the theme of good and evil.

5. Karl Rahner, "Why Does God Allow Us To Suffer?" *Theological Investigations, XIX* (New York: Crossroad, 1983): 194.

6. On the internal and external dualisms, and their inadequacies as solutions to theodicy, see John Hick's seminal *Evil and the God of Love* (New York: Harper and Row, 1966 and 1977), *Chapter 2*.

7. For some of the most relevant of the recent publications on miracles, see the following: Colin Brown, *That You May Believe: Miracles and Faith Then and Now* (Grand Rapids, MI: Eerdmans, 1985); Colin Brown, *Miracles and the Critical Mind* (Grand Rapids, MI: Eerdmans, 1984); Ralph M. McInery, *Miracles: A Catholic View* (Huntington, IN: Our Sunday Visitor, Inc., 1986); Hubert J. Richards, *The Miracles of Jesus: What Really Happened?* (Mystic, CT: Twenty-Third Publications, 1986); René Latourelle, *The Miracles of Jesus and the Theology of Miracles* (New York/Mahwah: Paulist Press, 1988); Scott D. Rogo, *Miracles: A Parascientific Inquiry into Wondrous Phenomena* (Chicago, IL: Contemporary Books, 1982); David and Randall Basinger, *Philosophy and Miracle: The Contemporary Debate* (New York: Edwin Mellen Press, 1986); Ernst and Marie-Luise Keller, *Miracles in Dispute: A Continuing Debate* (Philadelphia, PA: Fortress Press, 1969; Howard Clark Kee, *Miracles in the Early Christian World: A Study of Sociobiohistorical Method* (New Haven, CT: Yale University Press, 1983); and also Howard Clark Kee's *Medicine, Miracle, and Magic in New Testament Times* (New

York: Cambridge University [Press, 1986); Richard Swinburne, editor, *Miracles* (New York: Macmillan, 1989); Frank Dilley, "Does the 'God Who Acts' Really Act?" *Anglican Theological Review* 47 (1965): 66-80; Norman Geisler, *Miracles and the Modern Mind* (Grand Rapids, MI: Zondervan, 1982); etc. Collin Brown's *That You May Believe* contains a brief annotated bibliography on miracles and healing to 1982. See also William Wainwright's useful *Philosophy of Religion: An Annotated Bibliography* (New York: Garland Publishing, 1976).

8.   See Barry L. Whitney, *Evil and the Process God* (New York and Toronto, ON: Edwin Mellen Press, 1985).

I   Pain and Theodicy [Selected Publications]

2447.   Adams, E.W. "The Problem of Pain as a Doctor Sees It." *Hibbert Journal* 42 (1944): 145-151.

2448.   Ansell, Charles. "Pain and Beyond." *Journal of Pastoral Counselling* 10 (1975): 5-9.

2449.   Boeyink, David E. "Pain and Suffering." *Journal of Religious Ethics* 2 (1974): 85-98.

2450.   Bowers, Margaretta. "Beyond Pain." *Journal of Pastoral Counselling* 10 (1975): 25-28.

2451.   Brand, Paul, and Philip Yancey. "Putting Pain to Work." *Leadership* 5 (1986): 121-125.

2452.   Conwill, William L. "Chronic Pain Conceptualization and Religious Interpretation." *Journal of Religion and Health* 25 (1986): 46-50.

2453.   Fichter, Joseph H. "Religion and Pain." *Theology Today* 38 (1981): 1-4. [Introduction to the journal's special issue on pain. Chapters include Paul W. Pruyser's "The Ambiguities of Religion and Pain Control"; Bernard Spikla, John D. Spangler, and M. Priscilla Rae, "The Role of Theology in Pastoral Care for the Dying"; etc.]

2454.   ———. *Religion and Pain: The Spiritual Dimensions of Health Care.* New York: Crossroad, 1981. [As a sociologist, Fichter seeks a middle course between medical researchers who attempt to relieve pain and theologians who seek to understand it. Fichter argues that theodicies reduce to Job's faith stance. The book investigates the attitudes of health care professionals about religion and how it affects their treatment and comfort of the afflicted. The results, which focus on the wholistic approach, are based on questionnaires to 700 medical practitioners in over 300 health-care facilities.]

2455.   Fischer, Charles N. "Pain as Purgation: The Role of Pathologizing in the Life of the Mystic." *Pastoral Psychology* 27 (1978): 62-70.

2456.   Gardiner, Patrick L. "Pain and Evil. Part II." *Proceedings of the American Aristotelian Society, Supplement* 38 (1964): 107-124. [Part I is Richard M. Hare's "Pain and Evil" [#2462].]

2457.   Gillett, G.R. "The Neurophilosophy of Pain." *Philosophy* 66 (1991): 191-206.

2458.   Grahek, Nikola. "Philosophy and Pain Research." *Contemporary Yugoslav Philosophy: The Analytic Approach.* Edited by Aleksandar Pavkovic. Boston, MA: Kluwer Academic Publishers, 1988.

2459.   Griffin, John Howard. "The Terrain of Physical Pain." *Creative Suffering: The Ripple of Hope.* Edited by Alan Paton, et al. Kansas City, KS: The National Catholic Reporter Publishing Company, 1970: 25-38.

2460.   Haezrahi, Pepita. "Pain and Pleasure: Some Reflections on Susan Stebbing's View that Pain and Pleasure are Moral Values." *Philosophical Studies* 11 (1960): 71-77.

2461.   Hambly, Gordon C. "The Unique Gift of Pain." *The Religious Dimension.* Edited by John Hinchcliff. Auckland: Rep Prep Ltd., 1976: 88-90.

2462. Hare, Richard M. "Pain and Evil." Part I. *Proceedings of the Aristotelian Society. Supplement* 33 (1964): 91-106. [Part II is P.L. Gardiner's "Pain and Evil" [#2456]. See also Hare's "Punishment and Retributive Justice," *Philosophical Topics* 14 (1986): 211-223.]

2463. Kemp, John. "Pain and Evil." *Philosophy* 29 (1954): 13-26.

2464. Leighton, Stephen R. "Unfelt Feelings in Pain and Emotion." *Southern Journal of Philosophy* 24 (1986): 69-79.

2465. Lishman, W.A. "The Psychology of Pain." *From Fear to Faith: Studies of Suffering and Wholeness*. Edited by Norman Autton. London: SPCK and Camelot Press, 1971: 8-22.

2466. Loeser, John D. "What is Chronic Pain?" *Theoretical Medicine* 12 (1991): 213-225.

2467. McConkey, Clarence M. "A Case-Study." *Journal of Pastoral Counselling* 10 (1975): 39-44. [Discussion of the problem of pain.]

2468. McPherson, Robert. "The Chronic Pain Patient: The Role of the Pastor as Helper." *Christian Ministry* 11 (1980): 24-26.

2469. Miller, J. Stewart. "Pain and God's Grace." *Expository Times* 95 (1984): 147-148.

2470. Morris, Herbert. "Guilt and Suffering." *Philosophy East and West* 21 (1971): 419-434. [See response by Edward Harter, "Commentary on 'Guilt and Suffering'." *Philosophy East and West* 21 (1971), 435-441.]

2471. Norton, David L. "'Eudaimonia' and the Pain-Displeasure Contingency Argument." *Ethics* 82 (1972): 314-320.

2472. O'Shaughnessy, R.J. "Enjoying and Suffering." *Analysis* 26 (1966): 153-160.

2473. Opdenaker, Theodore A. "Pain: Its Psychotherapeutic and Spiritual Dimensions." *Journal of Pastoral Counselling* 10 (1975): 29-30.

2474. Patterson, George W. "The Pastoral Care of Persons in Pain." *Journal of Religion and Aging* 1 (1984): 17-30.

2475. Payne, Barbara. "Pain Denial and Ministry to the Elderly." *Theology Today* 38 (1981): 30-36.

2476. Pernick, Martin S. "The Calculus of Suffering in Nineteenth-Century Surgery." *Hastings Center Report* 13 (1983): 26-36. ["To Preserve Life or Relieve Pain?"].

2477. Puccetti, Roland. "Is Pain Necessary?" *Philosophy* 50 (1975): 259-269.

2478. Ropp, Ronald D. "People in Pain." *Journal of Pastoral Care* 40 (1986): 77-85. [Review article of Wayne and Charles Oates, *People in Pain*, 1985 [#3525].]

2479. Sarano, Jacques. *The Hidden Face of Pain*. Translated by Dennis Pardee. Valley Forge, PA: Judsen Press, 1970. [First published as *La Douleur*, 1965.]

2480. Scarry, Elaine. *The Body in Pain: The Making and Unmaking of the World*. New York: Oxford University Press, 1985.

2481. Wall, Patrick D. "The Three Phases of Evil: The Relation of Injury to Pain." *Brain and Mind*. Edited by G. Wolstenholme. Amsterdam: CIBA, 1979. [See also Patrick Wall, *The Challenge of Pain*. Harmondsworth, Middlesex: Penguin, 1982. The original 1973 version was titled *The Puzzle of Pain*.]

2482. Weininger, Benjamin. "Fear of Pain." *Journal of Pastoral Counselling* 10 (1975): 21-24.

2483. Wilder Smith, A.E. *The Paradox of Pain*. Wheaton, IL: Shaw Publishers, 1971.

2484. Yancey, Philip. "Pain: The Tool of the Wounded Surgeon." *Christianity Today* 22 (1978): 12-16.

2485. Zucker, Arnold, et al. "Several Statements on the Topic of Pain." *Journal of Pastoral Counselling* 10 (1975): 73-80.

II Providence and Theodicy [Selected Publications]

2486. Armour, Leslie. "Newman, Arnold and the Problem of Particular Providence." *Religious Studies* 24 (1988): 173-187.

2487. Baepler, Richard. "Providence in Christian Thought." *The Caring God: Perspectives on Providence*. Edited by Carl S. Meyer and Herbert T. Mayer. St. Louis, MO: Concordia Publishing House, 1973: 45-66.

2488. Berkouwer, Gerritt C. *The Providence of God*. Grand Rapids, MI: Eerdmans, 1972.

2489. Boros, Ladislaus. *Pain and Providence*. Baltimore, MD: Helicon, 1966.

2490. Elman, Yaakov. "When Permission is Given: Aspects of Divine Providence." *Tradition* 24 (1989): 24-45.

2491. Flint, Thomas P. "Two Accounts of Providence." *Divine and Human Action*. Edited by Thomas V. Morris. Ithaca, NY: Cornell University Press, 1988: 147-181.

2492. Fulmer, Gilbert. *Providence and Evil*. New York and Cambridge: Cambridge University Press, 1977.

2493. Gienapp, John C. "Providence and Evolutionary Biology." *The Caring God: Perspectives on Providence*. Edited by Carl S. Meyer and Herbert T. Mayer. St. Louis, MO: Concordia Publishing House, 1973: 217-240.

2494. Gilkey, Langdon. "The Concept of Providence in Contemporary Theology." *Journal of Religion* 43 (1963): 171-192.

2495. ———. "Theodicy and Plurality." *Archivio di Filosofia* 56 (1988): 701-720.

2496. Hartt, Julian N. "Creation and Providence." *Christian Theology: An Introduction to its Traditions and Tasks*. Edited by Peter C. Hodgson and Robert H. King. Philadelphia, PA: Fortress Press, 1982: 115-140.

2497. Hesselink, I. John. "The Providence and the Power of God." *Reformed Review* 42 (1988): 97-115.

2498. Hick, John, and Michael Golder. *Why Believe in God?* London: SCM Press, 1983.

2499. Keller, Jack A. "On Providence and Prayer." *Christian Century* 104 (1987): 967-969.

2500.   Langford, Michael. *Providence*. London: SCM Press, 1981.

2501.   Meyer, Carl S. "The Concept of Providence in Modern Historical Thought."
        The Caring God: Perspectives on Providence. Edited by Carl Meyer and Her-
        bert T. Mayer. St. Louis, MO: Concordia Publishing House, 1973: 141-178.

2502.   Meyer, Charles. *Surviving Death: A Practical Guide to Caring for the Dying
        and Bereaved*. Mystic, CT: Twenty-Third Publications, 1988.

2503.   Pole, Nelson. "Living by Sports." *Philosophy in Context* 8 (1979): 64-75. [Ad-
        vocates a myth of meritocracy in place of the traditional Christian myth of provi-
        dence. The implication for the problem of evil is that while the traditional myth
        sees suffering as unjust, for meritocracy, suffering is as just as being rewarded.]

2504.   Rossman, Etta C. "A God of Chance or Providence in the Face of Death and
        Disease?" *Journal of Pastoral Care* 39 (1985): 120-127.

2505.   Schuller, David S. "Sociology's Reluctant Participation in the Dialog Concerning
        Providence." *The Caring God: Perspectives on Providence*. Edited by Carl S.
        Meyer and Herbert T. Mayer. St. Louis, MO: Concordia Publishing House,
        1973: 113-140.

2506.   Shaw, Douglas W.D. "Perspectives on Providence." *New College Bulletin* (1971):
        9-20.

2507.   ———. "Providence and Persuasion." *Duke Divinity School Review* 45 (1980):
        11-22.

2508.   Talbott, Thomas B. "Providence, Freedom, and Human Destiny." *Religious
        Studies* 26 (1990): 227-245. [See also Talbott's "The Doctrine of Everlasting
        Punishment," *Faith and Philosophy* 7 (1990), 19-42. Talbott argues against the
        "moderately conservative theists" who claim that those who freely reject God
        separate themselves from God forever. He establishes his view by considering
        three views of omniscience (including the theory of "middle knowledge": see
        Chapter 3). All of the options render the conservative view invalid.]

2509.   Underwager, Ralph. "Providence and Psychology." *The Caring God: Perspec-
        tives on Providence*. Edited by Carl S. Meyer and Herbert T. Mayer. St. Louis,
        MO: Concordia Publishing House, 1973: 93-112.

2510.   Vieujean, Jean. *Love, Suffering and Providence*. Philadelphia, PA: Westminster
        Press, 1966.

III   Theodicy in Literature [Selected Publications]

2511.   Amstutz, Jakob. "Sickness and Evil in Modern Literature." *Religion and Life*
        34 (1965): 228-298. [Discusses Sartre, Kafka, Goethe, Rilke, and Camus.]

2512.   Archer, Dermot J. "Tolstoy's *God Sees the Truth, But Waits*: A Reflection."
        Religious Studies 21 (1985): 75-90.

2513.   Atkins, Anselm. "Caprice: The Myth of the Fall in Anselm and Dostoevsky."
        Journal of Religion 47 (1967): 295-312.

2514.   Averill, James H. *Wordsworth and the Poetry of Human Suffering*. Ithaca, NY:
        Cornell University Press, 1980.

2515. Babbage, Stuart B. *The Mark of Cain: Studies in Literature and Theology*. Grand Rapids, MI: Eerdmans, 1966.

2516. Bachelder, Robert S. "Real People Struggle with Evil: Piers Paul Read's Characters are not all Squeezed into a Predictable Mold." *Christianity Today* 28 (1984): 53.

2517. Baldwin, Robert C., and James A.S. McPeek. "The Problem of Evil." *Chapter 6* of their *An Introduction to Philosophy Through Literature*. New York: Ronald Press, 1950: 217-260.

2518. Ballard, Edward G. "On Good and Evil in Philosophy of Art and Aesthetic Theory." *Southern Journal of Philosophy* 7 (1969): 273-287. [A Symposium on Aesthetics.]

2519. Barbour, John D. "Tragedy and Ethical Reflection." *Journal of Religion* 63 (1983): 1-25. [Argues that literary tragedies direct attention to certain aspects of moral experience for which particular understandings of ethics fail to account.]

2520. Barr, Browne. "Carol, Christ and the Cake." *Christian Century* 99 (1982): 1286-1287.

2521. Barr, David L. "The Apocalypse as a Symbolic Transformation of the World: A Literary Analysis." *Interpretation* 38 (1984): 39-50.

2522. Basinger, David, and C. Harold Hurley. "Portent in Little: Frost's 'Design' and the Nature of the Creator." *Kerygma and Praxis*. Edited by David Basinger and W. Vanderhoof. Winoma Lake, IN: Light and Life Press, 1984: 133-142.

2523. Bataille, Georges. *Literature and Evil*. Translated by Alastair Hamilton. New York and London: Marion Boyars, 1985.

2524. Bouchard, Larry D. *Tragic Method and Tragic Theology: Evil in Contemporary Drama and Religious Thought*. University Park, PA: Pennsylvania State University, 1989. [Argues that tragedies are symbolic representations of the enigma of evil. Theodicies, however, cannot explain or justify suffering. Bouchard makes reference to Ricoeur, Gadamer, Nietzsche, etc., with respect to the function of tragedy as an art form and as creating the conditions for conversion. He refers also to Augustine, Tillich, and Niebuhr to show the limitations of rational theodicies. Finally, he refers to playwrights, Bochhuth, Lowell, and Shaffer, to show the power of plays to disclose the problematic dimensions of culture and experience.]

2525. Brinker, Menachem. "On the Ironic Use of the Myth of Job in Y.H. Brenner's *Breakdown and Bereavement*." *Biblical Patterns in Modern Literature*. Edited by David H. Hirsch and Nehama Aschkenasy. Chico, CA: Scholars Press, 1984: 115-126.

2526. Brooks, Cleanth. "Faulkner's Vision of Good and Evil." *Religious Perspectives in Faulkner's Fiction: Yoknapatawpha and Beyond*. Edited by J. Robert Barth. Notre Dame, IN: University of Notre Dame Press, 1972: 57-75.

2527. Cole, Douglas. *Suffering and Evil in the Plays of Christopher Marlow*. Princeton, NJ: Princeton University Press, 1962.

2528. Cormier, Ramona. "Process and the Escape from Nihilism." *Tulane Studies in Philosophy* 24 (1975): 1-11. [Discusses Albert Camus.]

2529. Crampton, Georgia Ronan. *The Conditions of Creatures: Suffering and Action in Chaucer and Spencer*. New Haven, CT: Yale University Press, 1974.

2530. Dallby, Anders. *The Anatomy of Evil: A Study of John Webster's "The White Devil."* Lund: CWK Gleerup, 1974.

2531. Danielson, Dennis Richard. *Milton's Good God.* Cambridge and New York: Cambridge University Press, 1981.

2532. Dearlove, J.E. *"J.B.:* The Artistry of Ambiguity." *Christian Century* 93 (1976): 484-487.

2533. Diaconoff, Suellen. *Eros and Power in Les liaisons dangereuses: A Study in Evil.* Geneve: Droz, 1979.

2534. Dryness, William A. *Rouault: A Vision of Suffering and Salvation.* Grand Rapids, MI: Eerdmans, 1971.

2535. Duhourq, Jose L. "The Presentation and Interpretation of Moral Evil in the Contemporary Cinema." *Moral Evil Under Challenge*, Edited by Johannes Baptist Metz. London: Burns and Oates, 1970: 134-142.

2536. Duke, David N. "Giving Voice to Suffering in Worship: A Study in the Theodicies of Hymnody." *Encounter* 52 (1991): 263-272.

2537. Elmen, Paul. "Jerry Kosinski and the Uses of Evil." *Christian Century* 93 (1978): 530-532. [Discusses Kosinski's novels, *Blind Date* and *The Painted Bird*, wherein the world is depicted as a frightening and wicked place.]

2538. Ferlita, Ernest. "Film and the Quest for Meaning." *Religion in Film.* Edited by John May and Michael Bird. Knoxville, TN: University of Tennessee Press, 1982: 115-131.

2539. Fisch, Harold. "Creation in Reverse: *The Book of Job* and *Paradise Lost." Milton and Scriptural Tradition.* Edited by James H. Sims and Leland Ryken. Columbia, MO: University of Missouri Press, 1984: 104-116.

2540. Fisher, Peter F. "Milton's Theodicy." *Journal of the History of Ideas* 17 (1956): 28-53.

2541. Fletcher, John. "Literature and the Problem of Evil: I and II." *Theology* 79 (1976): 274-280; 337-343. [Discusses Charles Dickens, Dostoevsky, Henry James, William Faulkner, and Samuel Beckett.]

2542. Flew, Antony. "Tolstoi and the Meaning of Life." *Ethics* 73 (1963): 110-118.

2543. Franz, Marie Louise von. *Shadow and Evil in Fairy Tales.* Irving, TX: Spring Publications, 1974.

2544. Frodsham, John D. "Conflicting Theodicies: Some Modernist Literary Approaches to the Problem of Evil." *Religious Traditions* 5 (1982): 24-43. [Discusses Dostoevsky and Camus.]

2545. Gordon, Haim. "Dostoevsky and Existentialist Education: Father Zosima as Religious Educator." *Religious Education* 74 (1979): 198-209.

2546. Goss, James. "O'Connor's Redeemed Man: *Christus et/vel Porcus?" Drew Gateway* 44 (1974): 106-119. [Discusses Flannery O'Connor's theodicy. See her *Mystery and Manners.* New York: Farrer, Straus, Giroux, 1969.]

2547. Harcourt, John B. "The Literature of Evil." *Christianity and Literature* 29 (1980): 62-69.

2548. Harries, Richard. "Ivan Karamazov's Argument." *Thought* 81 (1978): 104-111.

2549. Hasker, William S. "MacKay on Being Responsible Mechanism: Freedom in a Clockwork Universe." *Christian Scholar's Review* 8 (1978): 130-140. [See MacKay, "Responsible Mechanism or Responsible Agent? A Response to William Hasker" [#2564].

2550. Howard, Thomas. "On Evil In Art." *Christian Imagination*. Edited by Leland Ryken. Grand Rapids, MI: Baker Book House, 1981: 111-117.

2551. Hunt, John W. "The Theological Complexity of Faulkner's Fiction." *Religious Perspectives in Faulkner's Fiction: Yoknapatawpha and Beyond*. Edited by J. Robert Barth. Notre Dame, IN: University of Notre Dame Press, 1972: 81-87, 141-169.

2552. Idinopulos, Thomas A. "The Mystery of Suffering in the Art of Dostoevsky, Camus, Wiesel, and Grunewald." *Journal of the American Academy of Religion* 43 (1975): 51-61.

2553. ———. "The Gospel of Suffering in Dostoevsky, Camus and Wiesel: Images of Death, Sacrifice, and Hope in Modern Literature." *Ecumenical Institute for Advanced Theological Studies, Yearbook*. Edited by J.V. Allmen, 1973/1974: 63-77.

2554. Jackson, J. "Attic Drama and the Problem of Evil." *Church Quarterly Review* 29 (1957): 339-349. [Discusses the plays of Aeschylus, Sophocles and Euripides.]

2555. Joseph, Sr. Miriam. "Orthodoxy in Paradise Lost." *Laval Théologie et Philosophique* 8 (1952): 243-284. [Discusses the theology of Milton's *Paradise Lost* from the "orthodox" Roman Catholic perspective.]

2556. Kahn, Sholom J. "The Problem of Evil in Literature." *Journal of Aesthetics and Art Criticism* 12 (1953): 98-110. [Maintains that literature has always been concerned with the origin of evil, as well as with the illumination of evil and the sublimation through various patterns of thought, emotion, and art. It has also been concerned with the struggle against evil through revolution, conquest, and faith.]

2557. Kazin, Alfred. "Drama of Good and Evil in American Writing." *An Almost Chosen People*. Edited by Walter Nicgorski. Notre Dame, IN: University of Notre Dame Press, 1976: 51-66.

2558. Kilby, Clyde S. "Mythic and Christian Elements in Tolkien." *Myth, Allegory and Gospel: An Interpretation of J.R.R. Tolkien, C.S. Lewis, G.K. Chesterton, and Charles Williams*. Edited by John W. Montgomery. Minneapolis, MN: Bethany Fellowship, 1976: 119-143.

2559. Kivy, Peter. "Melville's *Billy* and the Secular Problem of Evil: The Worm in the Bud." *Monist* 63 (1980): 480-493. [Maintains that Meville's *Billy Budd* exemplifies the secular problem of evil—the possibility of unmotivated malice. See *Billy Budd, Sailor (An Inside Narrative)*. Edited by Harrison Hayford and Merton M. Sealts, Jr. Chicago, IL: University of Chicago Press, 1962.]

2560. Langer, Lawrence. "The Dominion of Death." *The Holocaust and the Literary Imagination*. Edited by Lawrence Langer. New Haven, CT: Yale University Press, 1975.

2561.   ——. *The Age of Atrocity: Death in Modern Literature*. Boston, MA: Beacon Press, 1978.

2562.   ——. *Versions of Survival: The Holocaust and the Human Spirit*. Albany, NY: State University of New York Press, 1982.

2563.   Larson, Janet K. "The Birth of Evil: Genesis According to Bergman." *Christian Century* 95 (1978): 615 -619.

2564.   MacKay, Donald M. "Responsible Mechanism or Responsible Agent? A Response to William Hasker" [#2549]. *Christian Scholar's Review* 8 (1978): 141-148.

2565.   MacLeish, Archibald. *J.B.* Boston, MA: Houghton Mifflin, 1958. [The well-known verse play about a modern day Job. The play had a run of 364 days on Broadway before it went on tour. Its written version has been acclaimed as among the greatest works of American literature and earned the author a Pulitzer Prize in 1959.]

2566.   Makarushka, Irena. "The Good Mother, The Good Father, and Other Myths About Evil." *Union Seminary Quarterly Review* 44 (1990): 121-136.

2567.   Malone, Peter. *Movie Christs and Anti-Christs*. New York: Crossroad, 1988 and 1990.

2568.   Mauldin, Jane Ellen. "Emerson's Mystical Response to Suffering." *Religious Humanism* 22 (1988): 120-134.

2569.   Mercatante, Anthony S. *God and Evil: Mythology and Folk Lore*. New York: Harper and Row, 1978.

2570.   Merton, Thomas. "Albert Camus' *The Plague*: Introduction and Commentary." *Religious Dimensions in Literature*. Edited by Lee A. Belford. New York: Seabury Press, 1982: 49-88. [Other chapters discuss C.S. Lewis, T.S. Elliot, Charles Williams, and Walker Percy.]

2571.   Metzack, Ronald. *The Puzzle of Pain: Revolution in Theory and Treatment*. New York: Basic Books, 1974.

2572.   ——. "The McGill Pain Questionnaire: Major Properties and Scoring Methods." *Pain* 1 (1975): 277-299.

2573.   Michaelides-Nouaros, Andreas. "Philosophy in Art: The Problem of God in Eugene O'Neill's Play, *Emperor Jones*." *Diotima* 2 (1978): 71-82.

2574.   Mijuskovic, Ben. "Camus and the Problem of Evil." *Sophia* 15 (1976): 11-19. [Argues that Paneloux's speeches in Camus's *The Plague* are the key to Camus's attack on the traditional religious and philosophical justification of evil on the basis of God's transcendent reason.]

2575.   Miller, Justin. "Thomas Traherne: Love and Pain in the Poet of Felicity." *Historical Magazine of the Protestant Episcopal Church* 49 (1980): 209-220.

2576.   Moehle, Natalia. *The Dimensions of Evil and of Transcendence: A Sociological Perspective*. Washington, DC: University Press of America, 1978. [Perspectives on evil in *literature*: D.H. Lawrence, Anton Chekhov, Alexander Solzhenitsyn; in *psychoanalysis*: Sigmund Freud, Erich Fromm; in *social psychology*: Rollo May, Herbert Mead; in *social philosophy*: Hebert Marcuse, Hannah Arendt; and in *sociology*: Moehle's specialty.]

2577. Nelson, Bill. "Evil as Illusion in the Detective Story." *Clues: A Journal of Detection* 1 (1980): 9-14.

2578. O'Brien, Edward, Jr. "Camus and Christianity." *Personalist* 44 (1963): 149-163.

2579. Obuchowski, Peter A. "Emerson, Evolution, and the Problem of Evil." *Harvard Theological Review* 72 (1979): 150-156.

2580. Pachmuss, Temira. "The Metaphysics of Evil." *Chapter 5* of his *F.M. Dostoevsky: Dualism and Synthesis of the Human Soul*. Carbondale, IL: Southern Illinois University Press, 1963: 97-111.

2581. Pielke, Robert G. "Recent Science Fiction and the Problem of Evil." *Philosophy in Context* 11 (1981): 41-50.

2582. Pinkus, Phillip. *Swift's Vision of Evil: A Comparative Study of "A Tale of a Tub" and "Gulliver's Travels."* Victoria, BC: University of Victoria Press, 1975.

2583. Quinn, Philip L. "Tragic Dilemmas, Suffering Love, and Christian Life." *Journal of Religious Ethics* 17 (1989): 151-183.

2584. Radcliff-Umstead, Douglas. *The Mirror of our Anguish: A Study of Luigi Pirandello's Narrative Writings*. Rutherford, NJ: Fairleigh Dickinson University Press, 1978.

2585. Rader, Melvin. "Shelley's Theory of Evil." *Shelley: A Collection of Critical Essays*. Edited by George M. Ridenour. Englewood Cliffs. NJ: Prentice-Hall, 1965: 103-110. [Originally titled, "Shelley's Theory of Evil Misunderstood." *Western Reserve University Bulletin* 23 (1930).]

2586. Rubel, Warren. "Voices of Change: The Arts and Divine Providence." *The Caring God: Perspectives on Providence*. Edited by Carl S. Meyer and Herbert T. Mayer. St. Louis, MO: Concordia Publishing House, 1973: 179-216.

2587. Russell, Kenneth C. "The Devil's Companion and the Miracle Rabbi—Two Novels: Golding's Spire and Wallant's Human Season." *Studia Mystica* 3 (1980): 52-64.

2588. Saez, Richard. *Theodicy in Baroque Literature*. New York: Garland Publishing, Inc., 1985.

2589. Saunders, Thomas. "Religion and Tragedy." *Dalhousie Review* 24 (1968): 283-297. [Considers literary tragedy in fifth century BC Greece (especially Aeschylus) and in Elizabethan England (especially Shakespeare).]

2590. Schillaci, Anthony. "Bergman's Vision of Good and Evil." *Celluloid and Symbols*. Edited by John C. Cooper and Carl Skrade. Philadelphia, PA: Fortress Press, 1970: 75-88. [Other chapters in this volume address further aspects of theology and film: Harvey Cox, "The Purpose of the Grotesque in Fellini's Films"; Robert W. Wagner, "Film, Reality and Religion"; William Hamilton, "Bergman and Polanski on the Death of God"; etc.]

2591. Schilling, S. Paul. "God and Suffering in Christian Hymnody." *Religion in Life* 48 (1979): 323-336. [See also Schilling's *God and Human Anguish* [#1164]].

2592. ———. "Theology in Hymnody." *Reformed Liturgy and Music* 21 (1987): 145-147.

2593. Schwartz, Richard B. *Samuel Johnson and the Problem of Evil*. Madison, WI: University of Wisconsin Press, 1975.

2594. Scott, Nathan A. "The Tragic Vision and the Christian Faith." *Anglican Theological Review* 45 (1963): 23-45.

2595. Sherwood, Terry G. "Conversion Psychology in John Donne's Good Friday Poem." *Harvard Theological Review* 72 (1979): 101-122.

2596. Siegel, Robert H. "The Serpent and the Dove: *Christabel* and the Problem of Evil." *Imagination and the Spirit: Essays in Literature and the Christian Faith Presented to Clyde S. Kilby*. Edited by Charles A. Huttar. Grand Rapids, MI: Eerdmans, 1971: 159-186. [Discusses Coleridge's *Christabel* as the most complete expression of his view of vicarious atonement.]

2597. Simpson, Elizabeth Leonie. "The Dead End: (A Note on) The Social Evolution of Practical Ethics." *Antioch Review* 39 (1981): 357-372.

2598. Smith, C. Michael. "Theology and the Human Story: The Redemptive Passage Through Human Suffering in Dostoevsky's *Crime and Punishment*." *Encounter* 42 (1981): 29-44.

2599. Spivack, Bernard. *Shakespeare and the Allegory of Evil: The History of a Metaphor in Relation to his Major Villains*. New York: Columbia University Press, 1958.

2600. Spivack, Charlotte. *Comedy on Evil in Shakespeare's Stage*. Rutherford, NJ: Fairleigh Dickinson University Press, 1978.

2601. Stern, Jacob. "The Rationality of Evil in Classical Mythology." *Rationality in Thought and Action*. Edited by Martin Tamny. Westport, CT: Greenwood Press, 1986: 209-216.

2602. Stivers, Richard. *Evil In Modern Myth and Ritual*. Athens, GA: University of Georgia Press, 1982. [Discussion of the social construction of evil, the manner in which modern societies create evil as a category of the sacred and how symbols, myths, and rituals of evil are related to this].

2603. Sutherland, Stewart R. *Atheism and the Rejection of God: Contemporary Philosophy and the Brothers Karamazov*. Oxford: Blackwell, 1977.

2604. Tatlow, Anthony T. *The Mask of Evil: Brecht's Response to the Poetry and Thought of China and Japan: A Comparative and Critical Evaluation*. Bern: Peter Lang, 1977.

2605. Thomas, James. *The Speedy Extinction of Evil and Misery: Selected Prose of James Thomas*. Berkeley, CA: University of California Press, 1967.

2606. Thundyil, Zacharias. "Emerson and the Problem of Evil: Paradox and Solution." *Harvard Theological Review* 62 (1969): 51-56.

2607. Tinsley, E. John. "Tragedy and Christian Beliefs." *Theology* 85 (1982): 98-102.

2608. Unrue, Darlene H. "Lawrence's Vision of Evil: The Power-Spirit in *The Rainbow* and *Women in Love*." *Dalhousie Review* 5 (1975/1976): 641-654.

2609. Valliere, Paul. "*The Lady and the Wench*: A Practical Theodicy in Russian Literature." *Union Seminary Quarterly Review* 37 (1981/1982): 69-76.

2610. Vance, Norman. "Corruption and Grace in Graham Greene." *Theology* 86 (1983): 275-283.

2611. Wall, James M. *"The Natural: Evil Battles Good."* *Christian Century* 101 (1984): 563-564. [Discusses Bernard Malamud's 1952 novel, *The Natural*, and the Levinson movie version. See also James Wall's "Biblical Spectators and Secular Man," *Celluloid and Symbols*. Edited by John C. Cooper and Carl Skrade. Philadelphia, PA: Fortress Press, 1970, 51-60.]

2612. Ward, Joseph A. *The Imagination of Disaster: Evil in the Fiction of Henry James*. Lincoln, NE: University of Nebraska Press, 1961.

2613. Wasiolek, Edward. "Dostoevsky, Camus, and Faulkner: Transcendence and Mutilation." *Philosophy and Literature* 1 (1977): 131-146.

2614. Weber, Carl J. "Tragedy and the Good Life." *Dalhousie Review* 25 (1969): 225-233.

2615. Wharton, Robert V. "Evil in an Earthly Paradise: Ivan Karamazov's 'Dialectic' Against God and Zossima's 'Euclidean' Response." *Thomist* 41 (1977): 567-584.

IV Original Sin and Theodicy [Selected Publications]

2616. Allen, E.L. "A Modern View of Sin." *Hibbert Journal* 54 (1956): 235-241.

2617. Ashley, Benedict. "The Development of Doctrine about Sin, Conversion, and the Following of Christ." *Moral Theology Today: Certitudes and Doubts*. Edited by D.G. McCarthy. St. Louis, MO: Pope John Center, 1984: 46-63.

2618. Clarke, D. "Original Sin in the Thought of Teilhard de Chardin." *Laurentianum* 9 (1968): 353-394.

2619. Cohen, Jeremy. "Original Sin as the Evil Inclination—A Polemicist's Appreciation of Human Nature." *Harvard Theological Review* 73 (1980): 495-520.

2620. Connor, James L. "Original Sin: Contemporary Approaches." *Theological Studies* 29 (1968): 215-240.

2621. Cooper, Eugene J. "The Notion of Sin in Light of the Theory of the Fundamental Option: The Fundamental Option Revisited." *Louvain Studies* 9 (1983): 363-382.

2622. Dalferth, Ingolf. "How is the Concept of Sin Related to the Concept of Moral Wrongdoing?" *Religious Studies* 20 (1984): 175-190.

2623. Daly, Gabriel. "Theological Models in the Doctrine of Original Sin." *Heythrop Journal* 13 (1972): 121-142.

2624. Dunfee, Susan Nelson. "The Sin of Hiding: A Feminist Critique of Reinhold Niebuhr's Account of the Sin of Pride." *Soundings* 65 (1982): 316-327.

2625. Duquoc, Christian. "New Approaches to Original Sin." *Cross Currents* 28 (1979): 189-200. [Originally published in *Lumière et Vie* 26 (1977). Translated by Joseph Cunneen.]

2626.   Dyer, George J. "Original Sin: Theological Abstraction or Dark Reality?" *Chicago Studies* 17 (1978): 385-398.

2627.   Foster, Durwood, and Paul Mojzes, editors. *Society and Original Sin: Ecumenical Essays on the Impact of the Fall*. New York: Paragon House, 1985. [Contains chapters by Hans Schwartz, "The Human Prospect in Light of the Fall"; Maurice Boutin, "The Fall: Its Factual Acceptance and Practical Meaning in Contemporary Society"; J. Deotis Roberts, "A Good Thing Spoiled: Reflections on the Personal and Social Dimensions of the Fall and the Problem of Evil" [#2658]; Paul Mojzes, "The Cracked Mirror: Understandings of the Myth of the Fall"; Thomas Walsh, "The Response to Suffering" [#2667]; Lloyd Eby, "Original Sin and Human Value"; M. Darroll Bryant, "Sin and Society"; etc.]

2628.   Fourez, G. "Civil Religion and Original Sin." *New Blackfriars* 63 (1982): 344-348.

2629.   Grant, Brian. *From Sin to Wholeness*. Philadelphia, PA: Westminster Press, 1982.

2630.   Haag, Herbert. "The Original Sin Discussion, 1966-1971." *Journal of Ecumenical Studies* 10 (1973): 259-289.

2631.   Hannah, Vern A. "Original Sin and Sanctification: A Problem for Wesleyans." *Wesleyan Theological Journal* 18 (1983): 47-53.

2632.   Hater, Robert J. "Sin and Reconciliation: Changing Attitudes in the Catholic Church." *Worship* 59 (1985): 18-31.

2633.   Hellwig, Monika K. "Creation, Sin, and the Ambivalence of Power." *Studies in Formative Spirituality* 3 (1982): 215-223.

2634.   Holbrook, Clyde A. "Original Sin and the Enlightenment." *The Heritage of Christian Thought*. Edited by Robert E. Cushman and Egil Grislis. New York: Harper and Row, 1963: 142-165.

2635.   ———. "Jonathan Edwards Addresses Some 'Modern Critics' of Original Sin." *Journal of Religion* 63 (1983): 211-230.

2636.   Hulme, William E. "Sin: Weakness or Defiance?" *Dialogue* 3 (1964): 191-198.

2637.   Kelly, David F. "Aspects of Sin in Today's Theology." *Louvain Studies* 9 (1982): 190-197.

2638.   King-Farlow, John, and David Wesley Hunt. "Perspectives on the Fall of Man." *Scottish Journal of Theology* 35 (1982): 193-204.

2639.   LaPorte, Jean. "Models from Philo in Origen's Teaching on Original Sin." *Laval Théologique et Philosophique* 44 (1988): 191-203.

2640.   Mattam, J. "A Pastoral Approach to Original Sin." *Vidyajyoti* 43 (1979): 377-383.

2641.   McDermott, Brian O. "The Theology of Original Sin: Recent Developments." *Theological Studies* 38 (1977): 478-512.

2642.   ———. "From Symbol to Doctrine: Creation and Original Sin." *Chicago Studies* 19 (1980): 35-50.

2643.   Mendel, Sydney. "Reflections on Original Sin." *Dalhousie Review* 43 (1987): 17-27.

2644. Menninger, Karl. *What Ever Became of Sin?* New York: Hawthorn Books, 1973. [Best-selling "book of the month," inspirational guide about social evils and evil in humans, written by a medical doctor].

2645. Miller-McLemore, Bonnie J. *Death, Sin and the Moral Life: Contemporary Cultural Interpretations of Death.* American Academy of Religion Dissertation Series, 59. Atlanta, GA: Scholars Press, 1988. [Uncovers the assumptions behind the "death and dying movement." Using Augustine, Calvin, Schleiermacher, Niebuhr, Tillich, and others, Miller-McLemore formulates a more theologically adequate understanding of death and illness. The text includes a selected bibliography, 185-196.]

2646. Mitchell, Basil. "How is the Concept of Sin Related to the Concept of Moral Wrongdoing?" *Religious Studies* 20 (1984): 165-174.

2647. O'Connell, Timothy E. "A Theology of Sin." *Chicago Studies* 21 (1982): 277-292. [See also his *Principles of a Catholic Morality*. New York: Seabury, 1978.]

2648. Parker, David. "Original Sin: A Study in Evangelical Theory." *Evangelical Quarterly* 61 (1989): 51-69.

2649. Peat, David. "Creation and Sin." *Ampleforth Journal* 3 (1977): 31-36.

2650. Peter, Carl J. "Original Sin: A Test Case in Theology." *Theology, Exegesis, and Proclamation.* Edited by Roland E. Murphy. New York: Herder and Herder, 1971: 106-112.

2651. Porter, Stanley E. "The Pauline Concept of Original Sin, in Light of Rabbinic Background." *Tyndale Bulletin* 41 (1990): 3-30.

2652. Quinn, Philip L. "Original Sin, Radical Evil and Moral Identity." *Faith and Philosophy* 1 (1984): 188-202. [Examines Kant's theory of radical evil as an attempt to rationalize the doctrine of original sin.]

2653. ———. "In Adam's Fall, We All Sinned." *Philosophical Topics* 16 (1988): 89-117. [Discusses original sin in the writings of Anselm and Kant.]

2654. ———. "Does Anxiety Explain Original Sin?" *Noûs* 24 (1990): 276-284. [Original sin in Kierkegaard.]

2655. Ramm, Bernard L. *Offense to Reason: A Theology of Sin.* New York: Harper and Row, 1985. [Evangelical defense of the Christian doctrine of sin. Ramm argues that the doctrine is the most comprehensive and satisfying solution to theodicy. See also his *The God Who Makes A Difference* [#1723].]

2656. Rigali, Nobert J. "Sin in a Relational World." *Chicago Studies* 23 (1984): 321-332.

2657. Ring, Nancy C. "Sin and Transformation from a Systematic Perspective." *Chicago Studies* 23 (1984): 303-320.

2658. Roberts, J. Deotis. "A Good Thing Spoiled: Reflections on the Personal and Social Dimensions of the Fall and the Problem of Evil." *Society and Sin.* Edited by Durwood Foster and Paul Mojzes. New York: Paragon House, 1985.

2659. Sabourin, Leopold. "Original Sin Again." *Religious Studies Bulletin* 1 (1981): 88-101. [Discussion of M. Flick and Z. Alszeghy, "What Did Trent Teach About Original Sin?" *Theology Digest* 21 (1973), 57-65 (Originally published in *Gregorianum* [1971]), and Flick and Alszeghy's *Il peccato origenale* (Brescila, 1972). Sabourin discusses also H. Rondet, *Original Sin: The Patristic and Theological Background*. New York: Alba House, 1972.]

2660.   Siegel, Seymour. "Sin and Atonement." *Evangelicals and Jews in an Age of Pluralism*. Edited by Marc H. Tanenbaum, Marvin R. Wilson and A. James Rudin. Grand Rapids, MI: Baker Book House, 1984: 163-182.

2661.   Strimple, Robert B. "Bernard Ramm and the Theology of Sin." *Westminster Theological Journal* 49 (1987): 143-152. [Discussion of Ramm's *Offense to Reason* [#2655].]

2662.   Swinburne, Richard. "Original Sinfulness." *Neue Zeitschrift für Systematische Theologie und Religionsphilosophie* 27 (1985): 235-250. [Several other Swinburne publications are listed elsewhere, particularly in *Chapter 4*.]

2663.   Tennant, Frederick Robert. *The Sources of the Doctrines of the Fall and Original Sin*. New York: Schocken Books, 1968, with the 1946 introduction by M.F. Thelan. Originally published in 1903. [See also Tennant's *Concept of Sin*. Cambridge: Cambridge University Press, 1912; *The Origin and Propagation of Sin*. Cambridge: Cambridge University Press, 1902; and his *Philosophical Theology* [see #605].]

2664.   Trigg, Roger H. "Sin and Freedom." *Religious Studies* 20 (1984): 191-202.

2665.   Tsutomu, Shoji. "Sin and Suffering: Japan and the Peoples of Asia." *Japan Christian Quarterly* 47 (1981): 12-19.

2666.   Wainwright, William. "Original Sin." *Philosophy and Christian Faith*. Edited by Thomas V. Morris. Notre Dame, IN: University of Notre Dame Press, 1988.

2667.   Walsh, Thomas. "The Response to Suffering." *Society and Original Sin: Ecumenical Essays on the Impact of the Fall*. Edited by Durwood Foster and Paul Mojzes. New York: Paragon House, 1985.

2668.   Williams, Robert R. "Sin and Evil." *Christian Theology: An Introduction to its Traditions and Tasks*. Edited by Peter C. Hodgson and Robert H. King. Philadelphia, PA: Fortress Press, 1982: 168-195.

2669.   Willimon, William H. *Sighing for Eden: Sin, Evil and the Christian Faith*. Nashville, TN: Abingdon Press, 1985. [Rejects the "false stories" which have attempted to explain evil: capitalism, Marxism and psychology. He maintains that only through the story of Jesus Christ can we see what evil is and how it is defeated.]

2670.   ——. "When Bad Things Happen." *Christian Century* 100 (1989): 198-199.

2671.   Yancey, Philip. "Sin." *Christianity Today* 31 (1987): 30-34.

V   Jewish and Holocaust Theodicy
[Selected Publications]

2672.   Abrahamson, Irving. "Elie Wiesel: A Selected Bibliography." *Confronting the Holocaust: The Impact of Elie Wiesel*. Edited by Alvin H. Rosenfeld and Irving Greenberg. Bloomington, IN: Indiana University Press, 1978.

2673.   Abramowitz, Molly. *Elie Wiesel: An Annotated Bibliography*. Metuchen, NJ: Scarecrow Press, 1974.

2674.   Allen, Diogenes. "Acting Redemptively." *Theology Today* 41 (1984): 265-270.

2675.   Améry, Jean. *At the Mind's Limits: Contemplations by a Survivor on Auschwitz and its Realities*. Translated by Sydney Rosenfeld and Stella P. Rosenfeld. New York: Schocken Books, 1980.

2676.   Arendt, Hannah. *Eichmann in Jerusalem: A Report on the Banality of Evil*. New York: Viking Press, 1963. [See responses by N. Rotenstreich, "Can Evil be Banal?" [#2849] and P. Helm, "Enchantment and the Banality of Evil" [#2789].]

2677.   Aronson, Ronald. "The Holocaust and Human Progress." *Echoes From the Holocaust: Philosophical Reflections on a Dark Time*. Edited by Alan Rosenberg and Gerald E. Meyers. Philadelphia, PA: Temple University Press, 1988: 223-244.

2678.   Avisar, Ilan. "The Evolution of the Israeli Attitude Toward the Holocaust as Reflected in Modern Hebrew Drama." *Hebrew Annual Review* 9. Edited by Reuben Ahroni. Columbus, OH: Ohio State University, 1985: 31-52.

2679.   Bauckham, Richard. "Theology After Hiroshima." *Scottish Journal of Theology* 38 (1985): 583-601.

2680.   Bauer, Yehuda. *The Holocaust in Historical Perspective*. Seattle, WA: University of Washington Press, 1978.

2681.   ———. *American Jewry and the Holocaust*. Detroit, MI: Wayne State University Press, 1981.

2682.   ———. *A History of the Holocaust*. New York: Franklin Watts, 1982.

2683.   Baum, Rainer C. "Holocaust: Moral Indifference as the Form of Modern Evil." *Echoes From the Holocaust: Philosophical Reflections on a Dark Time*. Edited by Alan Rosenberg and Gerald E. Meyers. Philadelphia, PA: Temple University Press, 1988: 53-90.

2684.   Becker, William H. "Questions Out of the Fire: Spiritual Implications of the Holocaust." *Journal of the International Theological Center* 10 (1982/1983): 21-33.

2685.   Ben-David, Eliezer. *Out of the Iron Furnace: The Jewish Redemption from Ancient Egypt and the Delivery from Spiritual Bondage*. Translated by Yaakov Feitman. New York: Shengold, 1975.

2686.   Ben-Yosef, I.A. "Jewish Religious Responses to the Holocaust." *Religion in South Africa* (1987): 15-36.

2687.   Berenbaum, Michael. *The Vision of the Void: Theological Reflections on the Works of Elie Wiesel*. Middletown, CT: Wesleyan University Press, 1979.

2688.   ———. "The Spoken Word and the Temptation of Silence." *America* 159 (1988): 412-413, 420.

2689.   ———. *After Tragedy and Triumph: Modern Jewish Thought and the American Experience*. Cambridge: Cambridge University Press, 1990.

2690.   Berenbaum, Michael, and John K. Roth. "Who, What, When, Where, How." Introduction to their edited volume, *Holocaust: Religious and Philosophical*

Implications. New York: Paragon House, 1989: xiii-xxix. [Contains introductions and excerpts from various texts: Emil Fackenheim's *To Mend the World* [#2756]; André Neher's *The Exile of the Word* [#2829]; Yehuda Bauer's chapter in *Studies in Contemporary Judaism*. Edited by Jonathan Frankel. Bloomington, IN: Indiana University Press, 1984; Gerd Korman's "The Holocaust in American Historcal Writing," *Societas* 2 (1972); David W. Weiss and Michael Berenbaum's "The Holocaust and the Covenant," *Sh'ma* 14 (1984); Michael Berenbaum's "The Uniqueness and Universality of the Holocaust," *American Journal of Theology and Philosophy* 2 (1981); Primo Levi's *The Drowned and the Saved* [#2813]; Yehuda Bauer's *The Jewish Emergence from Powerlessness*. Toronto, ON: University of Toronto Press, 1979; Tadeusz Borowitz's *This Way for the Gas, Ladies and Gentlemen* [#2704]; Jean Améry's *At the Mind's Limits* [#2675]; John Roth's "On Losing Trust in the World," from *Echoes of the Holocaust: Philosophical Reflections on a Dark Time* [#2856]; Elie's Wiesel's *Night* [#2908]; Richard Rubenstein's *After Auschwitz: Radical Theology and Contemporary Judaism* [#2858]; Emil Fackenheim's "Jewish Values in the Post-Holocaust Future: A Symposium," *Judaism* 16 (1967); Berkovits's previously unpublished essay, "In the Beginning Was the Cry"; Irving Greenberg's "Cloud of Smoke, Pillar of Fire" [#2779]; Richard Rubenstein and Elie Wiesel's "An Exchange," *The German Church Struggle and the Holocaust* [see #2861]; and others. Each of the book's chapters contain informative bibliographies.]

2691.   Berkovits, Eliezer. *God, Man and History*. Middle Village, NY: Jonathan David, 1959.

2692.   ———. "Reconstructionist Theology: A Critical Evaluation." *Tradition* 2 (1959/ 1960): 20-66.

2693.   ———. *Faith After the Holocaust*. New York: KTAV Publishing House, 1973.

2694.   ———. *Major Themes in Modern Philosophies of Judaism*. New York: KTAV Publishing House, 1974.

2695.   ———. *With God in Hell*. New York: Sanhedrin Press, 1979.

2696.   ———. *Crisis and Faith*. New York: Sanhedrin Press, 1979.

2697.   ———. "In the Beginning was the Cry." *Holocaust: Religious and Philosophical Implications*. Edited by John Roth and Michael Berenbaum. New York: Paragon House, 1989: 298-301.

2698.   Bertman, Martin A. "The Hebrew Encounter With Evil." *Apeiron* 9 (1975): 43-47.

2699.   Blau, Joseph J. "Evil in Popular Medieval Judaism." *Union Seminary Quarterly Review* 37 (1981/1982): 115-124.

2700.   Blenkinsopp, Joseph. "The Judge of All the Earth: Theodicy in the Midrach on Genesis 18:22-33." *Journal of Jewish Studies* 41 (1990): 1-12.

2701.   Bloesch, Donald G. "Sin, Atonement and Redemption." *Evangelicals and Jews in an Age of Pluralism*. Edited by Marc H. Tannenbaum, Marvin R. Wilson, and A. James Rudin. Grand Rapids, MI: Baker Book House, 1984: 163-195. [Evangelical Christian view of sin and redemption. See also Bloesch's "Process Theology and Reformed Theology," *Process Theology*. Edited by Ronald H. Nash. Grand Rapids, MI: Baker Book House, 1987, 31-56.]

2702. Borowitz, Eugene B. "Covenant Theology—Another Look." *World View* 16 (1973). [See also his *How Can a Jew Speak of Faith Today?* Philadelphia, PA: Westminster Press, 1969.]

2703. ——. "Liberal Jews in Search of an 'Absolute'." *Cross Currents* 29 (1979): 9-14.

2704. Borowitz, Tadeusz. *This Way for the Gas, Ladies and Gentlemen.* Translated by Maria Borowitz. New York: Penguin Books, 1979. [Originally published in 1959.]

2705. Bosmajian, Hamida. *Metaphors of Evil: Contemporary German Literature and the Shadows of Nazism.* Iowa City, IA: University of Iowa Press, 1979.

2706. Breitbart, Sidney. "The Jewish and Christian Covenants and the Holocaust." *Dor Le Dor* 17 (1988/1989: 97-106.

2707. Brenner, Reeve Robert. *The Faith and Doubt of Holocaust Survivors.* New York: Free Press, 1980.

2708. Breslauer, S. Daniel. "Theodicy and Ethics: Post-Holocaust Reflections." *American Journal of Theology and Philosophy* 8 (1987): 137-149. [See also Breslauer, "Towards a New View of Covenant," *Encounter* 45 (1984), 43-51. See response by Ellenson, "The Holocaust, Covenant, and Revelation: Comments on S. Breslauer's 'Towards a New View of Covenant'" [#2746].]

2709. Brown, Robert McAfee. *The Psuedonyms of God.* Philadelphia, PA: Westminster Press, 1972.

2710. ——. "The Holocaust: The Crisis of Indifference." *Conservative Judaism* 31 (1976/1977): 16-20.

2711. ——. "Reflections on the Holocaust." *Union Seminary Quarterly Review* 32 (1977): 131-155.

2712. ——. "The Holocaust as a Problem in Moral Choice." *When God and Man Failed.* Edited by Harry James Cargas. New York: Macmillan, 1981: 81-102.

2713. ——. *Elie Wiesel: Messenger to All Humanity.* Notre Dame, IN: Notre Dame University Press, 1983. [See also his "Wiesel's Case Against God." *Christian Century* 99 (1980), 109-112.]

2714. ——. "'Some are Guilty, All are Responsible': Heschel's Social Ethics." *Abraham Joshua Heschel.* Edited by John C. Merkle. New York: Macmillan, 1985: 123-141.

2715. ——. "Madness, Caprice and Friendship: Elie Wiesel's *Twilight*." *America* 159 (1988): 408-410.

2716. Bulka, Reuven P. "Different Paths, Common Thrust: The Shoalogy of Berkovits and Frankl." *Tradition* 19 (1981): 322-339.

2717. ——. "To Be Good or Evil: Which is More Natural?" *Journal of Psychology and Judaism* 14 (1990): 53-72.

2718. Buser, Michael B. *Auschwitz as Revelation.* Washington, DC: Georgetown University Press, 1974.

2719. Cargas, Harry James. *Harry James Cargas in Conversation with Elie Wiesel.* New York: Paulist Press, 1979.

2720.　——. *A Christian Response to the Holocaust*. Denver, CO: Stonehenge, 1981.

2721.　——. "Holocaust Literature: Today's Burning Bush." *When God and Man Failed: Non-Jewish Views of the Holocaust*. Edited by Harry James Cargas. New York: Macmillan, 1981: 179-183.

2722.　——. "Modern World Literature and the Holocaust." *When God and Man Failed*. Edited by Harry James Cargas. New York: Macmillan, 1981: 196-201.

2723.　——. *The Holocaust: An Annotated Bibliography*. Haverford, PA: The Catholic Library Association, 1977. Second edition, Chicago, IL: American Library Association, 1985.

2724.　——. "Drama Reflecting Madness: The Plays of Elie Wiesel." *America* 159 (1988): 414-415, 421.

2725.　——. *Shadows of Auschwitz: A Christian Response to the Holocaust*. New York: Crossroad/Continuum, 1990.

2726.　Cedars, Marie M. "Silence and Against Silence: The Two Voices of Elie Wiesel." *Cross Currents* 35 (1986): 257-266.

2727.　Charny, Israel W. *How Can We Commit the Unthinkable? Genocide, the Human Cancer*. New York: Hearst Books, 1982.

2728.　Charry, Ellen Z. "Jewish Holocaust Theology: An Assessment." *Journal of Ecumenical Studies* 18 (1981): 128-139.

2729.　Chopp, Rebecca S. "The Interruption of the Forgotten." *The Holocaust as Interruption*. Edited by Elisabeth Schüssler Fiorenza and David Tracy. Edinburgh: T&T Clark, 1984: 19-25.

2730.　Cohen, Arthur A. *The Tremendum: A Theological Interpretation of the Holocaust*. New York: Crossroad, 1981. [See response by Rubenstein, "Naming the Unnamable; Thinking the Unthinkable: A Review Essay of Arthur Cohen's *The Tremendum*" [see #2859].]

2731.　Cohen, Shaye J.D. "The Destruction: From Scripture to Midrash." *Proof-texts* 2 (1982): 18-39.

2732.　Cohn-Sherbok, Dan. "Jewish Theology and the Holocaust." *Theology* 86 (1983): 84-90.

2733.　——. "Jewish Faith and the Holocaust." *Religious Studies* 26 (1990): 277-293.

2734.　Conyers, Abda Johnson. "Teaching the Holocaust: The Role of Theology." *Perspectives in Religious Studies* 8 (1981): 128-142.

2735.　Cuddihy, John M. "The Elephant and the Angels; or The Uncivil Irritatingness of Jewish Theodicy." *Uncivil Religion: The Interreligious Hostility in America*. Edited by Robert Bellah and Frederick E. Greenspahn. New York: Crossroad, 1986: 23-37.

2736.　Culp, Mildred L. "Wiesel's Memoir and God Outside Auschwitz." *Explorations in Ethnic Studies* 4 (1981): 62-74.

2737.　Dedmon, Robert. "Job as Holocaust Survivor." *St. Luke Journal of Theology* 26 (1983): 165-185.

2738. Devenish, Philip E. "Jews and Christians Searching for God." *Christian-Jewish Relations* 17 (1984): 13-19.

2739. Donat, Alexander. *The Holocaust Kingdom*. New York: Holocaust Library, 1978.

2740. Dorff, Elliot N. "God and the Holocaust." *Judaism* 26 (1977): 27-34.

2741. Duclow, Donald F. "Into the Whirlwind of Suffering: Resistance and Transformation." *Second Opinion* 9 (1988): 11-27. [Discusses *Job*, *The Plague* by Albert Camus, and *Devotions* by John Donne.]

2742. Eckardt, A. Roy. "Ha'Shoah as Christian Revolution: Toward the Liberation of the Divine Righteousness." *Quarterly Review* 2 (1982): 52-67.

2743. Eckardt, A. Roy, and Alice L. Eckardt. "Studying the Holocaust's Impact Today: Some Dilemmas of Language and Method." *Echoes of the Holocaust: Philosophical Reflections on a Dark Time*. Edited by Alan Rosenberg and Gerald E. Meyers. Philadelphia, PA: Temple University Press, 1988: 432-442. [See also their collaboration, "The Holocaust and the Enigma of Uniqueness: A Philosophical Effort at Practical Clarification," *Annals of the American Academy of Political and Social Science* 450 (1980), 165-178. Also relevant is their "How German Thinkers View the Holocaust," *Christian Century* 93 (1976). See also Alice L. Eckardt's "The Holocaust: Christian and Jewish Relations," *Journal of the American Academy of Religion* 42 (1974), 467-469.]

2744. ———. *Long Night's Journey into Day: Life and Death After the Holocaust*. Detroit, MI: Wayne State University Press, 1982.

2745. Edelheit, Abraham J., and Hershel Edelheit. Editors. *Bibliography on Holocaust Literature*. Boulder, CO: Westview Press, 1986.

2746. Ellenson, David. "The Holocaust, Covenant, and Revelation: Comments on S. Daniel Breslauer's 'Towards a New View of Covenant'" [see #2708], *Encounter* 45 (1984): 53-59.

2747. Englander, Lawrence. "Revelation from a Limited God: A Re-Evaluation of Torah as Blueprint." *Journal of Reform Judaism* 35 (1988): 65-75.

2748. Estess, Ted L. *Elie Wiesel*. New York: Frederick Ungar, 1980.

2749. Evans, John X. "After the Holocaust: What Then Are We To Do?" *Center Journal* 4 (1984): 75-98.

2750. Everett, Robert A. "The Impact of the Holocaust on Christian Theology." *Christian Jewish Relations* 15 (1982): 3-11.

2751. Ezrahi, Sidra. "The Holocaust Writer and the Lamentation Tradition: Responses to Catastrophe in Jewish Literature." *Confronting the Holocaust: The Impact of Elie Wiesel*. Edited by Alvin H. Rosenfeld and Irving Greenberg. Bloomington, IN: Indiana University Press, 1978: 133-149.

2752. Fackenheim, Emil L. *Quest for Past and Future: Essays in Jewish Theology*. Bloomington, IN: University of Indiana Press, 1968.

2753. ———. *God's Presence in History: Jewish Affirmations and Philosophical Reflections*. New York: Harper and Row, 1972.

2754. ———. *Encounters Between Judaism and Modern Philosophy*. New York: Basic Books, 1973.

2755.   ———. *The Jewish Return into History: Reflections in the Age of Auschwitz and a New Jerusalem*. New York: Schocken Books, 1978.

2756.   ———. *To Mend the World: Foundations of Future Jewish Thought*. New York: Schocken Books, 1982.

2757.   ———. "The Holocaust and Philosophy." *Journal of Philosophy* 82 (1985): 505-514.

2758.   ———. "The Holocaust and Philosophy: Reflections on the Banality of Evil." *Independent Journal of Philosophy* 6 (1988): 63-69.

2759.   ———. *The Jewish Bible After the Holocaust*. Bloomington, IN: Indiana University Press, 1991.

2760.   Fasching, Darrell J. "Can Christian Faith Survive Auschwitz?" *Horizons, Journal of the College Theology Society* 12 (1985): 7-26.

2761.   Feuer, Lewis S. "The Reasoning of Holocaust Theology." *This World* 35 (1986): 70-82.

2762.   Fine, Ellen S. *Legacy of Night: The Literary Universe of Elie Wiesel*. Albany, NY: State University of New York Press, 1982. [Contains primary and secondary bibliography of Elie Wiesel.]

2763.   Fischer, John. "God After the Holocaust: An Attempted Reconciliation." *Judaism* 32 (1983): 309-320.

2764.   Flannery, Edward H. *The Anguish of the Jews: Twenty-Three Centuries of Anti-Semitism*. New York: Macmillan, 1976.

2765.   Fleischner, Eva Marie. "The Christian and the Holocaust: An Attempted Reconciliation." *Journal of Ecumenical Studies* 7 (1970): 331-333.

2766.   ———. "The Crucial Importance of the Holocaust for Christians." *Engage/Social Action* (December, 1976): 26-33.

2767.   Frey, Robert Seitz. "Issues in Post-Holocaust Christian Theology." *Dialog* 22 (1983): 227-235.

2768.   ———. "Post-Holocaust Theodicy: Images of Deity, History, and Humanity." *Bridges* 3 (1991): 9-32.

2769.   Frey, Robert Seitz, and Nancy Thompson-Frey. *The Imperative of Response: The Holocaust in Human Context*. Lanham, MD: University Press of America, 1985.

2770.   Friedman, Maurice S. "The Dialogue with the Absurd: The Latter Camus and Franz Kafka, Elie Wiesel and the Modern Job." *To Deny Our Nothingness: Contemporary Images of Man*. Edited by Maurice S. Friedman. New York: Dell, 1974. [See also Friedman's earlier, *Martin Buber: The Life of Dialogue*. London: Routledge and Kegan Paul, 1954. *Part Four*, "The Nature and Redemption of Evil."]

2771.   Friedman, Mosheh Y'chiail. "Thoughts on the Nature of Man." *Jewish Observer* 16 (1983): 6-9.

2772.   Garrison, Jim. "The Darkness of God: Theology After Hiroshima." *Human Survival and Consciousness Evolution*. Edited by Stanislav Grof and Marjorie Livingston Valier. Albany, NY: State University of New York Press, 1988: 151-176. [See also Garrison's book-length study, *The Darkness of God* [#854].]

2773. Glatt, Melvin Jay. "God the Mourner—Israel's Companion in Tragedy." *Judaism* 28 (1979): 72-79. [See also Glatt's "Midrash: The Defender of God." *Judaism* 35 (1986): 87-97.]

2774. Goldman, Norman Saul. "Maimonides on the Pathology of Evil: Moses Maimonides and Pastoral Psychology." *Journal of Pastoral Counselling* 11 (1976/1977): 3-13. [See Moses Maimonides (1135-1204), *Guide for the Perplexed*. Translated by Michael Friedlander. Dover Edition, 1956. Chicago, IL: University of Chicago, 1963.]

2775. ——. "Mythology of Evil in Judaism." *Journal of Religion and Health* 15 (1976): 230-240.

2776. Goodman, Lenn E. "Saadiah Gaon on the Human Condition." *Jewish Quarterly Review* 67 (1976): 23-29. [*The Book of Beliefs and Opinions.*]

2777. Gottschalk, Stephen. "Theodicy After Auschwitz and the Reality of God." *Union Seminary Quarterly Review* 41 (1987): 77-91.

2778. Greenberg, Irving. "Judaism and Christianity After the Holocaust." *Journal of Ecumenical Studies* 12 (1975): 521-551.

2779. ——."Cloud of Smoke, Pillar of Fire: Judaism, Christianity, and Modernity After the Holocaust." *Auschwitz: Beginning of a New Era?* Edited by Eva Fleischner. New York: KTAV Publishing House, 1977: 7-55. [The responses by Alan T. Davies ("Response to Irving Greenberg") and Alfred Kazin ("The Heart of the World") follow in the text, 57-64 and 65-72.]

2780. ——. "The New Spirit in Christian-Jewish Relations." *Journal of Ecumenical Studies* 16 (1979): 249-267. [Also published in *Christian Jewish Relations* 15 (1980), 20-39.]

2781. Halberstam, Joshua. "Philosophy and the Holocaust." *Metaphilosophy* 12 (1981): 227-283.

2782. Hamburgh, Max. "Is the Holocaust Relevant to Sociobiology?" *Journal of Religion and Health* 19 (1980): 320-325.

2783. Hare, Peter H. "The Abuse of Holocaust Studies: Mercy Killing and the Slippery Slope." *Echoes of the Holocaust: Philosophical Reflections on a Dark Time*. Edited by Alan Rosenberg and Gerald E. Meters. Philadelphia, PA: Temple University Press, 1988: 412-420.

2784. Harries, Richard B. "Power and Powerlessness in Judaism and Christianity." *Christian Jewish Relations* 21 (1988): 37-39.

2785. Hauerwas, Stanley. "Jews and Christians Among the Nations: The Social Significance of the Holocaust." *Cross Currents* 31 (1981): 15-34.

2786. Hayman, A. Peter. "Rabbinic Judaism and the Problem of Evil." *Scottish Journal of Theology* 29 (1976): 461-476.

2787. ——. "Theodicy in Rabbinic Judaism." *Transactions, Glasgow University Oriental Society* 26 (1975/1976). Glasgow University. Edited by Robert P. Carroll, 1979: 28-43.

2788. ——. "The Fall, Free Will and Human Responsibility in Rabbinic Judaism." *Scottish Journal of Theology* 37 (1984): 13-22.

2789. Helm, Thomas E. "Enchantment and the Banality of Evil." *Religion in Life* 49 (1980): 81-95. [Response to Arendt's *Eichmann in Jerusalem: A Report on the Banality of Evil* [#2676].]

2790. Heschel, Susannah. "Something Holy in a Profane Place: Germans and Jews in Suffering and Prayer." *Christianity and Crisis* 46 (1986): 338-342.

2791. Horkheimer, Max. *Eclipse of Reason.* New York: Seabury, 1974.

2792. Humphreys, W. Lee. *The Tragic Vision and the Hebrew Tradition.* Philadelphia, PA: Fortress, 1985.

2793. Idinopulos, Thomas A. "The Holocaust in the Stories of Elie Wiesel." *Soundings* 55 (1972): 202.

2794. ——."Christianity and the Holocaust." *Cross Currents* 26 (1977): 407- 415.

2795. ——. "Art and the Inhuman: A Reflection on the Holocaust." *When God and Man Failed: Non-Jewish Views of the Holocaust.* Edited by Harry James Cargas. New York: Macmillan, 1981: 184-195. [Originally published in *Christian Century* 91 (1974). See also Idinopulos, "The Mystery of Suffering in the Art of Dostoevsky, Camus, Wiesel and Grunewald" [#2552].]

2796. Jacobs, Lewis."The Problem of Evil in Our Time." *Judaism* 17 (1968): 347-351.

2797. Jakobovits, Immanuel. "Jewish Views on Infanticide." *Infanticide and the Value of Life.* Edited by Marvin Kohl. Buffalo, NY: Prometheus Books, 1978: 23-31.

2798. Jocz, Jakob. "Israel After Auschwitz." *The Witness of the Jews to God.* Edited by David W. Torrance. Edinburgh: Handsel Press, 1982: 58-70.

2799. Jonas, Hans. "The Concept of God after Auschwitz: A Jewish View." *Journal of Religion* 67 (1987): 1-13. [Also published in *Echoes of the Holocaust: Philosophical Reflections on a Dark Time.* Edited by Alan Rosenberg and Gerald E. Meyers. Philadelphia, PA: Temple University Press, 1988, 292-305.]

2800. Katz, Jacob. *From Prejudice to Destruction: Anti-Semitism, 1700-1933.* Cambridge, MA: Harvard University Press, 1980.

2801. Katz, Steven T. *Post-Holocaust Dialogues: Critical Studies in Modern Jewish Thought.* New York: New York University Press, 1983.

2802. Katzenelson, Yitzak. *The Song of the Murdered Jewish People.* Translated by Noah H. Rosenbloom. Tel Aviv, Isreal: Hakibbutz Hameuchad 1980.

2803. Knopp, Josephine Z. "The Holocaust: Elie Wiesel." *The Trials of Judaism in Contemporary Jewish Writings.* Edited by Josephine Knopp. Urbana, IL: University of Illinois Press, 1975.

2804. Kobelski, Paul J. *Melchizedek and Melchiresac.* Washington, DC: Catholic Biblical Association of America, 1987. [Detailed, critical discussion of good and evil in Judaism.]

2805. Kren, George M. "The Holocaust: Moral Theory and Immoral Acts." *Echoes of the Holocaust: Philosophical Reflections on a Dark Time.* Edited by Alan Rosenberg and Gerald E. Meyers. Philadelphia, PA: Temple University Press, 1988: 245-261.

2806. Kren, George M., and Leon Rappoport. *The Holocaust and the Crisis of Human Behavior.* New York: Holmes and Meier, 1980.

2807. Lackey, Douglas. "Extraordinary Evil or Common Malevolence: Evaluating the Jewish Holocaust." *Journal of Applied Philosophy* 3 (1986): 167-181.

2808. Lang, Berel. "Tolerance and Evil: Teaching the Holocaust." *Teaching Philosophy* 7 (1984): 199-204.

2809. Langer, Lawrence L. "Beyond Theodicy: Jewish Victims and the Holocaust." *Religious Education* 84 (1989): 48-54.

2810. Levi, Primo. *The Periodic Table*. Translated by Raymond Rosenthal. New York: Schocken Books, 1984.

2811. ———. *The Reawakening*. Translated by Stuart Woolf. New York: Summit Books, 1985.

2812. ———. *Survival in Auschwitz: The Nazi Assault on Humanity*. Translated by Stuart Woolf. New York: Collier, 1971.

2813. ———. *The Drowned and the Saved*. Translated by Raymond Rosenthal. New York: Summit Books, 1986.

2814. ———. *Moments of Reprieve*. Translated by Ruth Feldman. New York: Summit Books, 1986.

2815. Levinas, Emmanual. "Useless Suffering." Translated by Richard Cohen. *The Provocation of Levinas*. Edited by Robert Bernasconti. London: Routledge, 1988: 157-167.

2816. Lincoln, Timothy D. "Two Philosophies of Jewish History After the Holocaust." *Judaism* 25 (1976): 150-157. [Discusses Rubenstein's *After Auschwitz* [#2858] and Berkovits's *Faith After the Holocaust* [#2693].]

2817. Littell, Franklin H. *The Crucifixion of the Jews*. New York: Harper and Row, 1975.

2818. ———. "Ethics After Auschwitz." *When God and Man Failed: Non-Jewish Views of the Holocaust*. Edited by Harry James Cargas. New York: Macmillan, 1981: 38-50.

2819. Luban, Marvin. "Kaddish: Man's Reply to the Problem of Evil." *Studies in Torah Judaism*. Edited by Leon D. Stitskin. New York: Yeshiva University Press, 1969: 191-234.

2820. Lubarsky, Sandra D. "Ethics and Theodicy: Tensions in Emil Fackenheim's Thought." *Encounter* 44 (1983): 59-72.

2821. Lustiger, Cardinal Jean-Marie. "The Absence of God? The Presence of God? A Meditation on Three Parts on *Night*." *America* 159 (1988): 402-406.

2822. Magurshak, Dan. "The 'Incomprehensibility' of the Holocaust: Tightening Up Some Loose Usage." *Echoes of the Holocaust: Philosophical Reflections on a Dark Time*. Edited by Alan Rosenberg and Gerald E. Meyers. Philadelphia, PA: Temple University Press, 1988: 421-431.

2823. Maybaum, Ignaz. *The Face of God after Auschwitz*. Amsterdam: Polak and Van Gennep. 1965.

2824. McGarry, Michael B. *Christianity After Auschwitz*. New York: Paulist Press, 1977.

2825.   ——. "Emil Fackenheim and Christianity After the Holocaust." *American Journal of Theology and Philosophy* 9 (1988): 117-136.

2826.   McRobert, Laurie. "Emil L. Fackenheim and Radical Evil: Transcendent, Unsurpassable, Absolute." *Journal of the American Academy of Religion* 57 (1989): 325-340.

2827.   Metz, Johannes Baptist. "Facing the Jews: Christian Theology after Auschwitz." *The Holocaust as Interpretation*. Edited by Elisabeth Schüssler Fiorenza and David Tracy. Edinburgh: T&T Clark, 1984: 26-33.

2828.   Morgan, Michael L. "Jewish Ethics After the Holocaust." *Journal of Religious Ethics* 12 (1984): 256-277.

2829.   Neher, André. *The Exile of the Word, From the Silence of the Bible to the Silence of Auschwitz*. Philadelphia, PA: Jewish Publication Society of America, 1981. [First published in 1970 as *L'Exil de la parole*. Translated by David Maisel].

2830.   ——. "*Shaddai*: The God of the Broken Arch (A Theological Approach to the Holocaust)." *Confronting the Holocaust: The Impact of Elie Wiesel*. Edited by Alvin H. Rosenfeld and Irving Greenberg. Bloomington, IN: Indiana University Press, 1978: 150-158.

2831.   Och, Bernard. "Judaism as Tragic Religion." *Judaism* 35 (1986): 487-494.

2832.   Pattison, E. Mansell. "The Holocaust as Sin: Requirements in Psychoanalytic Theory for Human Evil and Mature Morality." *Psychoanalytic Reflections on the Holocaust*. Edited by Steven A. Luel and Paul Marcus. New York: KTAV Publishing House, 1984: 71-91.

2833.   Pawlikowski, John T. *The Challenge of the Holocaust for Christian Theology*. New York: ADL, 1978.

2834.   Peck, Abraham J., editor. *Jews and Christians After the Holocaust*. Philadelphia, PA: Fortress Press, 1982. [Foreword by Elie Wiesel. Chapters by various authors: David Tracy, "Religious Values After the Holocaust: A Catholic View"; Irving Greenberg, "Religious Values After the Holocaust: A Jewish View"; Allan R. Brockway, "Religious Values After the Holocaust: A Protestant View"; Alfred Gottschalk, "Introduction: Religion in a Post-Holocaust World"; etc.]

2835.   Phillips, Anthony. "Forgiveness Reconsidered." *Christian Jewish Relations* 19 (1986): 14-21.

2836.   Polish, Daniel. "A Painful Legacy: Jews and Catholics Struggle to Understand Edith Stein and Auschwitz." *Ecumenical Trends* 16 (1987): 153-155.

2837.   Rittner, Carol. "An Interview with Elie Wiesel." *America* 159 (1988): 395-400.

2838.   Robbins, Jerry K. "The Negative Theodicy of Elie Wiesel." *Dialog* 26 (1987): 131-133.

2839.   Rosenbaum, Irving J. *The Holocaust and Halakhah*. New York: KTAV Publishing House, 1976.

2840.   ——. "Holocaust and Halakhah." *Contemporary Jewish Ethics*. Edited by Menachem Marc Keller. New York: Sanherdrin Press, 1978: 402-419.

2841.   Rosenberg, Alan. "The Philosophical Implications of the Holocaust." *Perspectives on the Holocaust*. Edited by Randolph L. Braham. Boston, MA: Kluwer-Nijhoff, 1983: 1-18.

2842.   ———. The Crisis in Knowing and Understanding the Holocaust." *Echoes of the Holocaust: Philosophical Reflections on a Dark Time*. Edited by Alan Rosenberg and Gerald E. Meyers. Philadelphia, PA: Temple University Press, 1988: 379-395.

2843.   Rosenberg, Alan, and Paul Marcus. "The Holocaust as a Test of Philosophy." *Echoes of the Holocaust: Philosophical Reflections on a Dark Time*. Edited by Alan Rosenberg and Gerald E. Meyers. Philadelphia, PA: Temple University Press, 1988: 201-222.

2844.   Rosenfeld, Alvin H. "The Problematics of Holocaust Literature." *Confronting the Holocaust: The Impact of Elie Wiesel*. Edited by Alvin H. Rosenfeld and Irving Greenberg. Bloomington, IN: Indiana University Press, 1978: 1-30.

2845.   ———. *A Double Dying: Reflections on Holocaust Literature*. Bloomington, IN: Indiana University Press, 1980.

2846.   Rosenthal, Abigail. *A Good Look at Evil*. Philadelphia, PA: Temple University Press, 1987.

2847.   ———. "The Right Way to Act: Indicting the Victims." *Echoes of the Holocaust: Philosophical Reflections on a Dark Time*. Edited by Alan Rosenberg and Gerald E. Meyers. Philadelphia, PA: Temple University Press, 1988: 149-162.

2848.   Roskies, David G. *Against the Apocalypse: Responses to Catastrophe in Modern Jewish Culture*. Cambridge, MA: Harvard University Press, 1984.

2849.   Rotenstreich, Nathan. "Can Evil be Banal?" *The Philosophical Forum* 16 (1984-1985): 50-62. [Response to Arendt's *Eichmann in Jerusalem: A Report on the Banality of Evil* [#2676].]

2850.   Roth, John K. "Telling a Tale That Cannot Be Told: Reflections on the Authorship of Elie Wiesel." *Confronting the Holocaust: The Impact of Elie Wiesel*. Edited by Alvin H. Rosenfeld and Irving Greenberg. Bloomington, IN: Indiana University Press, 1978: 58-79. [See also Roth's "William James and Contemporary Religious Thought: The Problem of Evil," *The Philosophy of William James*. Edited by W.R. Conti. Hamburg: Felix Meiner, 1976.]

2851.   ———. *A Consuming Fire: Encounters with Elie Wiesel and the Holocaust*. Atlanta, GA: John Knox Press, 1979.

2852.   ———. "A Theology of Protest." *When God and Man Failed: Non-Jewish Views of the Holocaust*. Edited by Harry James Cargas. New York: Macmillan, 1981: 51-73.

2853.   ———. "The Silence of God." *Faith and Philosophy* 1 (1984): 407-420.

2854.   ———. "Philosophy, the Holocaust, and the Advance of Civilization." *Encounter* 46 (1985): 99-105.

2855.   ———. "On the Impossibility and Necessity of Being a Christian: Reflections on Mending the World." *American Journal of Theology and Philosophy* 9 (1988): 75-98.

2856. ——. "On Losing Trust in the World." *Echoes of the Holocaust: Philosophical Reflections on a Dark Time*. Edited by Alan Rosenberg and Gerald E. Meyers. Philadelphia, PA: Temple University Press, 1988: 163-180.

2857. ——. "Shall We Repeat the Evil? Reflection on the Threat of Nuclear War in the 1980s." *Philosophical Essays*. Edited by Yeager Hudson. New York and Toronto, ON: Edwin Mellen Press, 1988: 277-285.

2858. Rubenstein, Richard L. *After Auschwitz: Radical Theology and Contemporary Judaism*. Indianapolis, IN: Bobbs-Merrill, 1966. [A now classic text, containing many papers published previously, including *Chapter 4*, "Reconstructionism and the Problem of Evil, which first appeared in *The Reconstructionist* (January 23, 1959). He argues that the covenant God is obliged to punish evil, and that this punishment supposedly is just and deserved. Yet, since this view implies that the Jews must bear responsibility for the holocaust, Rubenstein rejects the God of the death camps. He rejects the God of absolute power as inconsistent with a world which has become so vicious and absurd.]

2859. ——. "Job and Auschwitz." *Union Seminary Quarterly Review* 25 (1970): 421-437. [Maintains that the holocaust was a unique evil which demands a new understanding of God. Job's God is no longer adequate. See also Rubenstein's review article of Cohen, "Naming the Unnameable; Thinking the Unthinkable: A Review Essay of Arthur Cohen's *The Tremendum*" [#2730], *Journal of Reform Judaism* 31 (1984), 43-45.]

2860. ——. *Morality and Eros*. New York: McGraw-Hill, 1970.

2861. ——. "Some Perspectives on Religious Faith After the Holocaust." *The German Church Struggle and the Holocaust*. Edited by Franklin H. Littell and Hubert G. Locke. Detroit, MI: Wayne State University Press, 1974: 256-268. [See also the exchange between Richard Rubenstein and Elie Wiesel in this text.]

2862. ——. *The Cunning of History: The Holocaust and the American Future*. New York: Harper and Row, 1978.

2863. Rubenstein, Richard L., and John K. Roth. *Approaches to Auschwitz: The Holocaust and Its Legacy*. Atlanta, GA: Westminster/John Knox Press, 1987. [Contains select bibliography: 389-406. Most of the items have not been listed in this present bibliography since they do not bear directly on the perspective of analytic theodicy; yet for those interested in the holocaust as the main perspective by which to approach theodicy, this and other more extensive bibliographies are available: see the introductory notes for *Appendix D* and various entries in this section.]

2864. Rubinoff, Lionel. "Auschwitz and the Pathology of Jew-Hatred." *Auschwitz: Beginning of a New Era?* Edited by Eva Fleischner. New York: KTAV Publishing Company, 1977: 347-371.

2865. Ruether, Rosemary Radford. *Faith and Fratricide: The Theological Roots of Anti-Semitism*. New York, Seabury Press, 1974.

2866. Rumscheidt, H. Martin. "Dying is the Inmate's Highest Duty." *Studies in Religion* 14 (1985): 487-496.

2867. Samuelson, Norbert M. "Revealed Morality and Modern Thought." *Contemporary Jewish Ethics*. Edited by Menachem M. Kellner. New York: Sanhedran Press, 1978: 84-99.

2868. ———. "Solutions to Theodicy Out of the Sources of Judaism." *Religious Education* 84 (1989): 55-67.

2869. Schecter, Nathan. "Pain and the Jewish Patient." *Journal of Psychology and Judaism* 1 (1976): 35-43. [Argues that individual reactions to pain take into account cultural factors. He focuses upon Jewish patients.]

2870. Scheller, Max. "The Meaning of Suffering." *Max Scheller*. Edited by Manfred S. Frings. The Hague: Martinus Nijhof, 1974: 121-163.

2871. Schindler, Pesach. *Hasidic Responses to the Holocaust in Light of Hasidic Thought*. New York: KTAV Publishing House, 1990.

2872. Schulweis, Harold M. "Suffering and Evil." *Great Jewish Ideas*. Edited by Abraham Ezra Millgram. New York: B'nai B'rith Department of Adult Education, 1964. [See also H.M. Schulweis, *Evil and the Morality of God* [#1166].]

2873. Schwartz, Matthew B. "The Meaning of Suffering: A Talmudic Response to Theodicy." *Judaism* 32 (1983): 444-451.

2874. Schweid, Ellezer. "The Holocaust as a Challenge to Jewish Thoughts on Ultimate Reality and Meaning." *Ultimate Reality and Meaning* 14 (1991): 185-209.

2875. Seeskin, Kenneth R. "The Reality of Radical Evil." *Judaism* 29 (1980): 440-453. [Rejects the *privation* account of evil, and contends that evil is caused by human beings, rather than by divine providence.]

2876. ———. "The Perfection of God and the Presence of Evil." *Judaism* 31 (1982): 202-210. [Argues that it is mistaken to seek divine sanction for human suffering. We are responsible for the evil and free to turn from it.]

2877. ———. "What Philosophy Can and Cannot Say about Evil." *Echoes of the Holocaust: Philosophical Reflections on a Dark Time*. Edited by Alan Rosenberg and Gerald E. Meyers. Philadelphia, PA: Temple University Press, 1988: 91-104. [See also Seeskin's *Jewish Philosophy in a Secular Age*. Albany, NY: State University of New York Press, 1990.]

2878. Sereny, Gitta. *Into That Darkness: An Examination of Conscience*. New York: Vintage Books, 1983.

2879. Shapiro, Susan E. "Failing Speech: Post-Holocaust Writing and the Discourse of Postmodernism." *Semeia* 40 (1987): 65-91.

2880. Sheldon, Mark. "Job, Human Suffering and Knowledge: Some Contemporary Jewish Perspectives." *Encounter* 41 (1980): 229-235.

2881. Sherman, Franklin. "Speaking of God After Auschwitz." *Worldview* 17 (1974): 26-30. [See also Sherman's "The Problem of Evil in the Public Sphere," *Dialog* 25 (1986): 97-100].

2882. Sherwin, Byron L. "Theodicy: Reason and Mystery." *Central Conference of American Rabbis Journal* (1971). [See also Sherwin's "The Impotence of Explanation and the European Holocaust," *Tradition* (1972); and his "Wiesel's Midrash, in *Confronting the Holocaust* Edited Alvin H. Rosenfeld and Irving Green- berg. Bloomington, IN: Indiana University Press, 1978.]

2883. Sidorsky, David. "Secular Theodicy and Historical Evidence." *Holocaust and Genocide Studies* 1 (1986): 265-277.

2884. Silverman, David W. "The Holocaust: A Living Force." *Union Seminary Quarterly Review* 32 (1977): 136-139. [Originally published in *Conservative Judaism* 31 (1976/1977), 21-25.]

2885. ———. "The Holocaust and the Reality of Evil." *Evangelicals and Jews in an Age of Pluralism*. Edited by Marc H. Tanenbaum, Marvin R. Wilson, and A. James Rudin. Grand Rapids, MI: Baker Book House, 1984: 268-274.

2886. Simon, Ulrich E. *A Theology of Auschwitz: The Christian Faith and the Problem of Evil*. Atlanta, GA: John Knox Press, 1967.

2887. Singer, Aaron M. "Human Responses to Suffering in Rabbinic Teaching." *Dialogue Alliance* 3 (1980): 49-63.

2888. Slonimsky, Henry. "The Philosophy in the Midrash." *Hebrew Union College Annual* 27 (1956): 235-290.

2889. Sokoloff, Naomi B. "Holocaust Poems in Dan Pagis' Gilgul." *Hebrew Annual Review* 8 (1984): 215-240.

2890. Sontag, Frederick E. "The Holocaust God." *Encounter* 42 (1981): 163-167. [See his more recent, "The Future of God." *Dialogue and Alliance* 5 (1991), 14-16. Several other Sontag references are listed in *Chapter 7*.]

2891. Startzman, L. Eugene. "Elie Wiesel Poses Hard Questions from the Holocaust." *Christianity Today* 27 (1983): 96-99.

2892. Steckel, Charles W. "God and the Holocaust." *Judaism* 20 (1971): 279-285.

2893. Steiner, George. *In Bluebeard's Castle: Some Notes Towards the Redefinition of Culture*. New Haven, CT: Yale University Press, 1971.

2894. ———. *Language and Silence: Essays on Language, Literature, and the Inhuman*. New York: Atheneum, 1972.

2895. Stern, Leonard W. "Contemporary Jewish Views on Suffering and God." *God in Contemporary Thought: A Philosophical Perspective*. Edited by Sebastian Matczak. New York: Rose of Sharon Press, 1977: 1053-1085.

2896. Szonyi, David M. *The Holocaust: An Annotated Bibliography and Resource Guide*. New York: KTAV Publishing House, 1985.

2897. Thomas, Laurence. "Liberalism and the Holocaust: An Essay on Trust and the Black-Jewish Relationship." *Echoes of the Holocaust: Philosophical Reflections on a Dark Time*. Edited by Alan Rosenberg and Gerald E. Meyers. Philadelphia, PA: Temple University Press, 1988: 105-117.

2898. Thompson, Warren K.A. "Ethics, Evil and the Final Solution." *Echoes of the Holocaust: Philosophical Reflections on a Dark Time*. Edited by Alan Rosenberg and Gerald E. Meyers. Philadelphia, PA: Temple University Press, 1988: 181-197.

2899. Tiefel, Hans O. "Holocaust Interpretations and Religious Assumptions." *Judaism* 25 (1976): 135-149. [Proposes four interpretations of the holocaust: Richard Rubenstein, A. Roy Eckardt, Martin Buber, and Emil Fackenheim.]

2900. Troster, Lawrence. "The Definition of Evil in Post-Holocaust Theology." *Conservative Judaism* 39 (1986): 81-98.

2901. ———. "Asymmetry, Negative Entropy and the Problem of Evil." *Judaism* 34 (1985): 453-461.

2902. ———. "The Love of God and the Anthropic Principle." *Conservative Judaism* 40 (1987/1988): 43-51.

2903. Tushnet, Leonard. *The Pavement of Hell*. New York: St. Martin's Press, 1972.

2904. Van Buren, Paul M. *Discerning the Way: Part One of a Theology of the Jewish Christian Reality*. New York: Seabury Press, 1980.

2905. ———. *A Christian Theology of the People Israel: Part Two of a Theology of the Christian Reality*. New York: Seabury Press, 1983.

2906. Waite, Robert G. *The Psychopathic God: Adolph Hitler*. New York: Basic Books, 1977.

2907. Weborg, John. "Abraham Joshua Heschel: A Study in Anthropodicy." *Anglican Theological Review* 61 (1979): 483-497.

2908. Wiesel, Elie. *Night*. New York: Hill and Wang, 1960; New York: Avon, 1969.

2909. ———. *Dawn*. New York: Hill and Wang, 1961; New York: Avon, 1970.

2910. ———. *The Accident*. New York: Hill and Wang, 1962; New York: Avon, 1970.

2911. ———. *The Town Beyond the Wall*. New York: Holt, Reinhart, and Winston, 1964; New York: Avon, 1972.

2912. ———. *The Jews of Silence*. New York: Holt, Reinhart, and Winston, 1966; New York: New American Library, 1967.

2913. ———. *The Gates of the Forest*. New York: Holt, Reinhart, and Winston, 1967; New York: Avon, 1967.

2914. ———. *Messengers of God: Biblical Portraits and Legends*. New York: Random House, 1967; New York: Pocket Books, 1977.

2915. ———. *Legends of Our Time*. New York: Holt, Reinhart, and Winston, 1968; New York: Avon, 1970.

2916. ———. *A Beggar in Jerusalem*. New York: Random House, 1970; New York: Avon, 1971.

2917. ———. *One Generation After*. New York: Random House, 1970; New York: Avon, 1972.

2918. ———. *The Oath*. New York: Random House, 1973; New York: Avon, 1974.

2919. ———. *Souls on Fire: Portraits and Legends of Hasidic Masters*. New York: Random House, 1973.

2920. ———. *Zalmen, or the Madness of God*. New York: Random House, 1974.

2921. ———. *Four Hasidic Masters and their Struggle Against Melancholy*. Notre Dame, IN: University of Notre Dame Press, 1978.

2922. ———. *A Jew Today*. New York: Random House, 1978.

2923. ———. "A Personal Statement from Elie Wiesel: Why I Write." *Confronting the Holocaust: The Impact of Elie Wiesel*. Edited by Alvin H. Rosenfeld and Irving Greenberg. Bloomington, IN: Indiana University Press, 1978: 200-206.

2924.   ——. *The Trial of God: A Play in Three Acts*. New York: Random House, 1979.

2925.   ——. "Myth and History." *Myth, Symbol, and Reality*. Edited by Alan Olson. Notre Dame, IN: University of Notre Dame Press, 1980: 20-30.

2926.   ——. *Five Biblical Portraits*. Notre Dame, IN: University of Notre Dame Press, 1981.

2927.   ——. *The Testament*. New York: Summit Books, 1981.

2928.   Wiesel, Elie, and Philippe de Saint-Cheron. *Evil and Exile*. Notre Dame, IN: University of Notre Dame Press, 1990.

2929.   Willis, Robert E. "Christian Theology After Auschwitz." *Journal of Ecumenical Studies* 12 (1975): 493-519.

2930.   ——. "Bonhoeffer and Barth on Jewish Suffering: Reflections on the Relationship between Theology and Moral Sensibility." *Journal of Ecumenical Studies* 24 (1987): 598-615.

2931.   Wyschogrod, Michael. "Faith and the Holocaust: A Review Essay of Emil Fackenheim's *God's Presence in History*" [#2753]. *Judaism* 20 (1970): 286-294.

2932.   ——. "Auschwitz: Beginning of a New Era: Reflections on the Holocaust." *Tradition* 16 (1977): 63-79.

2933.   Zahn, Gordon C. "Catholic Responses to the Holocaust." *Thought* 56 (1981): 153-162.

VI   Satan and Theodicy [Selected Publications]

2934.   Anshen, Ruth N. *The Reality of the Devil: Evil in Man*. New York: Harper and Row, 1972.

2935.   Avens, Robert. "Image of the Devil in C.G. Jung's Psychology." *Journal of Religion and Health* 16 (1977): 196-222.

2936.   Baskin, Wade. "The Devils of Loudon." *Exorcism Through the Ages*. Edited by Elmo Nauman. Secaucus, NJ: Citadel Press, 1974: 15-20. [Discusses exorcism in the Bible, in Catholic faith, in Greek Orthodoxy, in Medieval Germany, in Hebrew literature and thought, as well as other aspects of exorcism and satanic powers.]

2937.   Bass, Clarence B. "Satan and Demonology in Eschatological Perspective." *Demon Possession*. Edited by John W. Montgomery. Minneapolis, MN: Bethany Fellowship, 1976: 364-371. [This book contains several articles on demonology: demonology in the Bible, in history and law, in literature, in psychiatry, in pastoral care, in theology, etc.]

2938.   Beguin, Albert. "Balzac and the 'End of Satan'." *Soundings in Satanism*. Edited by F. Sheed. New York: Sheed and Ward, 1972: 179-181.

2939.   Benoit, Pierre. "Pauline Angelology and Demonology: Reflections on the Designations of the Heavenly Powers and on the Origin of Angelic Evil According to Paul." *Religious Studies Bulletin* 3 (1983): 1-18.

2940. Berger, Peter L. *A Rumor of Angels: Modern Society and the Rediscovery of the Supernatural*. Garden City, NY: Doubleday, 1969.

2941. Boyd, James W. *Satan and Mara: Christian and Buddhist Symbols of Evil*. Leiden: E.J. Brill, 1975.

2942. Bryson, John. *Evil Angels*. New York: Bantam Books, 1985, 1988.

2943. Carus, Paul. *The History of the Devil and the Idea of Evil*. New York: Bell Publishing Co., 1974.

2944. Coomaraswamy, Amanda Kentish. "Who is Satan and Where is Hell?" *Disguises of the Demonic*. Edited by A. Olson. New York: Association Press, 1975: 57-68.

2945. De Blois, Kees F. "How to Deal with Satan?" *The Bible Translator* 37 (1986): 301-309. [Particular reference to the Book of Job. The article also contains a history of the conceptualization of Satan. For another and much older historical overview, see Daniel Curry, "The Scriptural Doctrine of the Devil," *Methodist Quarterly Review* 66 (1884), 300-315.]

2946. Dickason, C. Fred. *Angels, Elect and Evil*. Chicago, IL: Moody Press, 1975.

2947. Dow, Graham G. "The Case for the Existence of Demons." *Churchman* 94 (1980): 199-208.

2948. Eisenhower, William D. "Your Devil is Too Small (Taking Satan Seriously)." *Christianity Today* 32 (1988): 24-26.

2949. Fortin, Ernest L. "In Defence of Satan: Christian Perspectives on the Problem of Evil." *This World* 25 (1989): 50-58.

2950. Gammie, John G. "The Angelology and Demonology in the Septuagint and the Book of Job." *Hebrew Union College Annual* 56 (1985): 1-19.

2951. Goetz, Joseph W. "Satan and the Occult in Contemporary Society." *Dialogue* 12 (1973): 272-278.

2952. Gonzalez, Gonzalo. "God and the Devil: Conquest of Dualism." *Theology Digest* 26 (1978): 19-23. [Originally published in *Ciencia Tomista* 105 (1977): 279-301.]

2953. Grant, C.K. "The Ontological Disproof of the Devil." *Analysis* 17 (1957): 71-72.

2954. Greeley, Andrew M. *The Devil, You Say!* Garden City, NY: Doubleday, 1974.

2955. Green, Anthony. "Beneficent Spirits and Malevolent Demons: The Iconography of Good and Evil in Ancient Assyria and Babylonia." *Popular Religion*. Edited by Hans Kippenberg, L. Bosch, et al. Leiden: E.J. Brill, 1984: 80-105.

2956. Guthrie, Ellis G. "Satan: Real or Fictitious?" *Brethren Life and Thought* 14 (1969): 160-167.

2957. Haight, David. "Devils." *International Journal for Philosophy of Religion* 5 (1974): 152-156.

2958. Haight, David, and Marjorie Haight. "An Ontological Argument for the Devil." *Monist* 54 (1970): 218-220.

2959. Jennings, F.C. *Satan: His Person, Work, Place and Destiny*. Neptune, NJ: Loizeaux Brothers, 1975.

2960. Johnson, Oliver A. "God and St. Anselm." *Journal of Religion* 45 (1965): 326-334.

2961. Johnston, Jerry. *The Edge of Evil: The Rise of Satanism in North America.* Dallas, TX: Word Publishing, 1989.

2962. Kane, Richard C. *Iris Murdock, Murial Spark, and John Fowles: Didactic Demons in Modern Literature.* Rutherford, NJ: Fairleigh Dickinson University Press, 1980.

2963. Kellenberger, James. "Belief in God and Belief in the Devil." *Sophia* 20 (1981): 3-15.

2964. Kelly, Henry A. *The Devil at Baptism: Ritual Theology and Drama.* Ithaca, NY: Cornell University Press, 1985.

2965. ——. "The Devil at Large." *Journal of Religion* 67 (1987): 518-528.

2966. Key, David Martin. "The Life and Death of the Devil." *Religion in Life* 21 (1951/1952): 73-82. [Brief account of the origin of "the devil" and the demise of such belief in Christianity.]

2967. Kim, Young Oon. "Satan: Reality or Symbol?" *Society and Original Sin: Ecumenical Essays on the Impact of the Fall.* Edited by Durwood Foster and Paul Mojzes. New York: Paragon House, 1985: 21-36.

2968. King, Albion Roy. "The Christian Devil." *Religion in Life* 20 (1950/1951): 61-71.

2969. Kinlaw, Dennis F. "Demythologization of the Demonic in the Old Testament." *Demon Possession.* Edited by John W. Montgomery. Minneapolis, MN: Bethany Fellowship, 1976: 29-35.

2970. Kluger, Rivkah Scharf. *Satan in the Old Testament.* Translated by Hildegard Nigel. Evanston, IL: Northwestern University Press, 1967.

2971. Kriegisch, Rudy. "Do You Give Up the Glamour of Evil?" *African Ecclesiastical Review* 22 (1980): 22-28, and 91-97.

2972. Lussier, E. "Satan." *Chicago Studies* 13 (1974): 3-19.

2973. Madaule, Jacques. "The Devil in Gogol and Dostoevski." *Soundings in Satanism.* Edited by F. Sheed. New York: Sheed and Ward, 1972: 182-202.

2974. Mason, Perry C. "The Devil and St. Anselm." *International Journal for Philosophy of Religion* 9 (1978): 1-15.

2975. Mayer, C.R. "Speak of the Devil." *Chicago Studies* 14 (1975): 7-18.

2976. McDermott, Timothy. "The Devil and his Angels." *New Blackfriars* 48 (1966): 16-25.

2977. Nelis, J.T. "Serpent in Paradise." *Encyclopedic Dictionary of the Bible.* New York: McGraw-Hill, 1963: 2174-2180. [History of Satan in biblical texts.]

2978. Newport, John P. "Satan and Demons: A Theological Perspective." *Demon Possession.* Edited by John W. Montgomery. Minneapolis, MN: Bethany Fellowship, 1976: 325-345.

2979. Nunn, Clyde Z. "The Rising Credibility of the Devil in America." *Heterodoxy: Mystical Experience.* Edited by Richard Woods. River Forest, IL: Listening Press, 1975: 84-100.

2980.   Oberman, Heiko A. "Luther Against the Devil." *Christian Century* 107 (1990): 75-79.

2981.   Palms, Roger C. "Demonolgy Today." *Demon Possession*. Edited by John W. Montgomery. Minneapolis, MN: Bethany Fellowship, 1976: 311-319.

2982.   Peck, Morgan Scott. *People of the Lie: The Hope for Healing Human Evil*. New York: Simon and Schuster, 1983. [Companion volume to his former inspirational book, *The Road Less Travelled: A New Psychology of Love*. Both books are written from its author's psychological/Christian perspective.]

2983.   Perry, Michael. "Taking Satan Seriously." *Expository Times* 101 (1990): 105-112.

2984.   Peters, Ted. "Sin, Sex, and Satan at the Bookstore." *Dialog* 28 (1989): 42-51. [Reference to Becker, Ricoeur, Peck, Russell, and others.]

2985.   Quay, Paul M. "Angels and Demons in the New *Missale Romanum*." *Ephemerides Liturgicae* 94 (1980): 401-410.

2985.   ———. "Angels and Demons: The Teaching of IV Lateran." *Theological Studies* 42 (1981): 20-45.

2987.   Reisz, H. Frederick. "The Demonic as a Principle in Tillich's Doctrine of God." *Theonomy and Autonomy*. Edited by J. Carey. Macon, GA: Mercer University Press, 1984: 135-156.

2988.   Reville, Albert. "History of the Devil." *Exorcism Through The Ages*. Edited by Elmo Nauman. Secaucus, NJ: Citadel Press, 1974: 217-258.

2989.   Richman, Robert. "The Ontological Proof for the Devil." *Philosophical Studies* 9 (1958): 63-64. [See also his response, "The Devil and Mr. Waldman, *Philosophical Studies* 11 (1960), 78-80, to Theordore Waldman's "A Comment Upon the Ontological Proof of the Devil," *Philosophical Studies* 10 (1959), 49-50.]

2990.   Ross, John M. "The Decline of the Devil." *Expository Times* 66 (1954): 58-61.

2991.   Russell, Jeffery Burton. "The Experience of Evil." *Heterodoxy, Mystical Experience, Dissent and the Occult*. Edited by Richard Woods. River Forrest, IL: Listening Press, 1975: 71-83.

2992.   ———. *The Devil: Perceptions of Evil from Antiquity to Primitive Christianity*. Ithaca, NY: Cornell University Press, 1978.

2993.   ———. *Satan: The Early Christian Tradition*. Ithaca, NY: Cornell University Press, 1981.

2994.   ———. *Lucifer, the Devil in the Middle Ages*. Ithaca, NY: Cornell University Press, 1984. [See also his more recent, *The Prince of Darkness: Radical Evil and the Power of Good in History*. London: Thames Hudson, 1989.]

2995.   Rusterholtz, Wallace P. "God and (D)Evil." *Religious Humanism* 17 (1983): 82-87.

2996.   Sanford, John A. *Evil: The Shadow Side of Reality*. New York: Crossroad, 1981. [Discusses biblical healing and healing in the psychology of Carl G. Jung.]

2997.   Scanian, Michael. *Deliverance from Evil Spirits: A Weapon for Spiritual Warfare*. Ann Arbor, MI: Servant Books, 1980.

2998. Showers, R.E. *What on Earth is God Doing? Satan's Conflict with God*. Neptuen, NJ: Loizeaux Brothers, 1973.

2999. Stein, Gordon. *An Anthology of Atheism and Rationalism*. Compiled, edited and introduced by Gordon Stein. Buffalo, NY: Prometheus Books, 1980. [*Chapter 5*, "The Devil, Evil, and Morality," contains a critique of theodicy, belief in the devil, and theistic morality, followed by a selections of essays.]

3000. Sundberg, Walter. "The Demonic in Christian Thought." *Lutheran Quarterly* 39 (1987): 413-437.

3001. Sweet, John Philip McMurdo. "'Taking Satan Seriously': A Reply [to Perry [#2983]]." *Egilse et Théologie* 101 (1990): 266-267.

3002. Tatford, Frederick A. *Satan: The Prince of Darkness*. Grand Rapids, MI: Kregel Publications, 1975.

3003. Tischler, Nancy M. "Taking Satan Seriously: Until We See Evil We Cannot Know the Full Glory and Power of God." *Christianity Today* 23 (1978): 29-30.

3004. Valensin, Auguste. "The Devil in Dante." *Soundings in Satanism*. Edited by F. Sheed. New York: Sheed and Ward, 1972: 138-149.

3005. Wink, Walter. *The Powers*. Three Volumes. [Volume I: *Naming the Powers*; Volume II: *Unmasking the Powers: The Invisible Forces that Determine Human Existence*; Volume III: *Engaging the Powers*]. Philadelphia, PA: Fortress Press, 1986.]

3006. Woods, Richard J. "The Devil, Evil and Christian Experience." *Listening* 12 (1977): 21-42.

VII   Theodices Other than Judaeo-Christian
[Selected Publications]

3007. Abe, Masao. "The Problem of Evil in Christianity and Buddhism." *Buddhist Christian Dialogue*. Edited by Paul O. Ingram and Frederick Streng. Honolulu, HI: University of Hawaii Press, 1986. [Also published in *Person and Society*. Edited by George F. McLean and Hugo Meynell. Lanham, MD: University Press of America, 1985, 125-142.]

3008. ——. "The Problem of Self-Centeredness as the Root of Human Suffering." *Japanese Religions* 15 (1989): 15-25.

3009. Abe, Masao, and Francis H. Cook. "Responses to Langdon Gilkey." *Buddhist Christian Studies* 5 (1985): 67-100. [Gilkey participates in this dialogue [see #1098].]

3010. Amore, Roy C. "The Karmic, Theistic, and Mechanistic Explanations of the Problem of Evil." *Drew Gateway* 42 (1971): 102-111.

3011. Awn, Peter J. "The Ethical Concerns of Classical Sufism." *Journal of Religious Ethics* 11 (1983): 240-263.

3012. ——. "Giving and Harming: Buddhist Symbols of Good and Evil." *Developments in Buddhist Thought*. Edited by Roy C. Amore. Waterloo, ON: Wilfred Laurier University Press, 1979: 93-103.

3013. Ayoub, Mahmoud Mustafa. "The Problem of Suffering in Islam." *Journal of Dharma* 2 (1977): 267-294.

3014. ———. *Redemptive Suffering in Islam: A Study of the Devotional Aspects of 'Ashura in Twelver Shi'ism*. The Hague: Mouton, 1978.

3015. ———. "The Idea of Redemption in Christianity and Islam." *Mormons and Muslims*. Edited by S. Palmer. Salt Lake City, UT: Bookcraft, Inc., 1983: 105-116.

3016. Bareau, André. "The Experience of Suffering and the Human Condition in Buddhism." *Buddhism and Christianity*. Edited by Claude Geffré and Dhavmony Mariasusai. New York: Seabury Press, 1979: 3-10.

3017. Berndt, Ronald M. "A Profile of Good and Bad in Australian Aboriginal Religion." *Colloquium* 12 (1979/1980): 17-32.

3018. Berry, Thomas. "The Problem of Moral Evil and Guilt in Early Buddhism." *Moral Evil under Challenge*. Edited by Johannes Baptist Metz. London: Burns and Oates, 1970: 126-133.

3019. Betty, L. Stafford. "Aurobindo's Concept of Lila and the Problem of Evil." *International Philosophical Quarterly* 16 (1976): 315-329.

3020. Bousfield, John. "Good, Evil and Spiritual Power: Reflections on Sufi Teachings." *The Anthropology of Evil*. Edited by David Parkin. Oxford: Blackwell, 1985: 194-208.

3021. Bowker, John. "The Problem of Suffering in the Qur'an." *Religious Studies* 4 (1969): 183-202.

3022. ———. *Problems of Suffering in Religions of the World*. Cambridge: Cambridge University Press, 1970.

3023. ———. "Suffering as a Problem in Religions." *The Meaning of Suffering*. Edited by Flavian Dougherty. New York: Human Sciences Press, 1982: 15-54.

3024. Boyd, James W. "The Path of Liberation from Suffering in Buddhism." *Buddhism and Christianity*. Edited by Claude Geffré and Mariasuai Dhavmony. New York: Seabury, 1979: 11-21.

3025. Clooney, Francis X. "Evil, Divine Omnipotence, and Human Freedom: Vedanta's Theology of Karma." *Journal of Religion* 69 (1989): 530-548.

3026. Eberhard, Wolfram. *Guilt and Sin in Traditional China*. Berkeley, CA: University of California Press, 1967.

3027. Eby, Lloyd. "The Unification Understanding of God." *Hermeneutics and Horizons*. Edited by F. Flinn. New York: Rose of Sharon Press, 1982: 159-169.

3028. Ess, Josef Van. "Wrongdoing and Divine Omnipotence in the Theology of Abu Ishaq An-Nazzam." *Divine Omniscience and Omnipotence*. Edited by Tamar Rudavsky. Boston, MA: Reidel, 1985: 53-67.

3029. Fingarette, Herbert. "Action and Suffering in the *Bhagavad Gita*." *Philosophy East and West* 34 (1984): 357-370.

3030. Goswami, Chitta R. "Suffering in the Indian Consciousness." *Ohio Journal of Religious Studies* 3 (1975): 19-28.

3031.   Gregory, Peter N. "The Problem of Theodicy in the *Awakening of Faith.*" *Religious Studies* 22 (1986): 63-78. [A major Chinese Buddhist text.]

3032.   Herman, Arthur L. "Indian Theodicy: Samkara and Ramanuja on *Brahma Sutra II.*" *Philosophy East and West* 21 (1971): 165-181.

3033.   ———. *The Problem of Evil and Indian Thought.* Delhi: Motilal Banarsidass, 1976. [See also Herman's "God, Evil and Annie Besant," *Philosophica* 11/14 (1982/1985), 80-95.]

3034.   Hobart, Mark. "Is God Evil?" *The Anthropology of Evil.* Edited by David Parkin. Oxford: Blackwell, 1985: 165-193. [Argues that the Balinese society's solution to the trilemma (God as omnipotent, omnibenevolent and evil exists) is to elaborate the second premise; in allowing human beings to discriminate, God allows the existence of badness.]

3035.   Hodgson, Marshall G.S. "A Comparison of Islam and Christianity as Framework for Religious Life." *Diogenes* 32 (1960): 49-74.

3036.   Hsu, Sung-Peng. "Lao Tzu's Conception of Evil." *Philosophy East and West* 26 (1976): 301-316.

3037.   Inden, Ronald. "Hindu Evil as Unconquered Lower Self." *The Anthropology of Evil.* Edited by David Parkin. Oxford: Blackwell, 1985: 142-164.

3038.   Jaini, Padmanabh S. "Samskara-Duhkhata and the Jain Concept of Suffering." *Revelation in Indian Thought: A Festschrift in Honour of Professor T.R.V. Murti.* Edited by Harold Coward and Krishna Sivarama. Dharma Publications, 1977: 153-157.

3039.   James, G. "The Unification Doctrine of the Fall and the Problem of Evil." *Society and Original Sin.* Edited by Durwood Foster and Paul Mojzes. New York: Paragon House, 1985: 86-99.

3040.   Jhingran, Saral. "The Problem of Suffering: Some Religio-Metaphysical Perspectives." *Indian Philosophical Quarterly* 12 (1985): 403-413.

3041.   Kalupahana, David J. "The Notion of Suffering in Early Buddhism Compared with Some Reflections of Early Wittgenstein." *Philosophy East and West* 27 (1977): 423-431. [Argues that for both Buddhism and Wittgenstein, suffering is dependent upon the inner will.]

3042.   Kenney, J. Frank. "The Concept of Suffering in Classical Samkhya." *Journal of Dharma* 2 (1977): 295-301.

3043.   Kondo, Akihisa. "Illusion and Human Suffering: A Brief Comparison of Horney's Ideas with Buddhistic Understanding of Mind." *Buddhist and Western Psychology.* Edited by N. Katz. Boulder, CO: Prajna Press, 1983: 139-148.

3044.   La Combe, Oliver. "Buddhist Pessimism?" *Buddhist Studies in Honour of W. Rahula.* Edited by Somaratna Balasooriya. London: Gordon Fraser Gallery Ltd., 1980: 113-117.

3045.   Lai, Whalen W. "Symbolism of Evil in China: The K'ung-Chia Myth Analyzed." *History of Religions* 23 (1984): 316-343.

3046.   Larson, Gerald James. "The Relation Between 'Action' and 'Suffering' in Asian Philosophy." *Philosophy East and West* 34 (1984): 351-356.

3047.   Lindgren, A. Bruce. "Sin and Redemption in the Book of Mormon." *Restoration Studies II: A Collection of Essays About the History, Beliefs and Practices of the Reorganized Church of Latter Day Saints*. Edited by Maurice L. Draper. Independence, MO: Temple School, 1983: 201-206.

3048.   Ling, Trevor Oswald. *Buddhism and the Mythology of Evil: A Study in Theravada Buddhism*. London: Allen and Unwin, 1962.

3049.   Malhotra, M.K. "Karl Jaspers and Indian Philosophy." *Philosophy Today* 6 (1962): 52-59.

3050.   Malkani, Ghanshamdas Rattanmal. "The Problem of Evil." *Philosophical Quarterly India* 35 (1962): 167-178.

3051.   ———. Some Criticisms of the Karmic Law by Professor Warren E. Steinkraus Answered." *Philosophical Quarterly India* 38 (1966): 155-162. [Response to Steinkraus, "Some Problems in Karma" [#3080].]

3052.   Masih, Yakub. "The Concept of Suffering." *Visva Bharati Journal of Philosophy* 6 (1969/1970): 7-10.

3053.   ———. *Introduction to Religious Philosophy*. Delhi: Motilal Banarsidass, 1971.

3054.   Mathur, Dinesh Chandra. "J. Krishnamurti on Choiceless Awareness, Creative Emptiness and Ultimate Freedom." *Diogenes* 126 (1984): 91-103.

3055.   Mehta, Mahesh M."The Concept of Suffering in Indian Thought." *Bharata Manisha Quarterly* 2 (1976): 73-81.

3056.   Mellor, Philip A. "Self and Suffering: Deconstruction and Reflexive Definition in Buddhism and Christianity." *Religious Studies* 27 (1991): 49-63.

3057.   Miller, J. Stewart. "Buddhism and Wieman on Suffering and Joy." *Buddhism and American Thinkers*. Edited by Kenneth K. Inada and Nolan P. Jacobson. Albany, NY: State University of New York Press, 1984: 89-110.

3058.   Mischke, James A. "Evil, Society, and Navajo Culture." *Anima* 8 (1981): 33-36.

3059.   Misra, Ram S. "Some Notes on the Concept of Suffering." *Visva Bharati Journal of Philosophy* 6 (1969/1970): 11-15.

3060.   Murti, T.R.V. "The Concept of Freedom as Redemption." *Types of Redemption*. Edited by Raphael J.Z. Werblowsky. Leiden: E.J. Brill, 1970: 213-222.

3061.   Nayak, G.C. *Evil, Karma, and Reincarnation*. Santiniketan, West Bengal: Center of Advanced Study in Philosophy, Visva Bharati, 1973.

3062.   Nyang, Sulayman S. "The Islamic Concept of Sin." *Society and Original Sin*. Edited by Durwood Foster and Paul Mojzes. New York: Paragon House, 1985: 52-61.

3063.   O'Flaherty, Wendy Doniger. *The Origins of Evil in Hindu Mythology*. Berkeley, CA: University of California Press, 1976.

3064.   Obeyseekere, Ranjini, and Gananath Obeyseekere. "The Tale of the Demon Kali: A Discourse on Evil." *History of Religions* 29 (1990): 318-334.

3065.   Ogden, Schubert M., and David Lochhead. "Responses to Gishin Tokiwa." *Buddhist Christian Studies* 5 (1985): 131-155. [Response to Tokiwa's "Chan (Zen) View of Suffering" [#3083].]

3066. Ormsby, Eric L. *Theodicy in Islamic Thought: The Dispute Over Al-Ghazali's "Best of All Possible Worlds."* Princeton, NJ: Princeton University Press, 1984.

3067. Perrett, Roy W. "Karma and the Problem of Suffering." *Sophia* 24 (1985): 4-10. [Refutation of the claim of John Hick, that karma provides an answer to the problem of suffering, claiming that the theory involves an infinite regress.]

3068. Pruett, Gordon E. *The Meaning and End of Suffering for Freud and the Buddhist Tradition.* Lanham, MD: University Press of America, 1987.

3069. Ratman, Ram Kumar. "Duhka: Advaitic Perspective." *Indian Philosophical Quarterly* 15 (1988): 13-24.

3070. Reichenbach, Bruce R. *The Law of Karma: A Philosophical Study.* Honolulu, HI: University of Hawaii Press, 1990. [For an earlier treatment of this much-discussed theme in Indian thought, see A.R. Wadia. "Philosophical Implications of the Doctrine of Karma." *Philosophy East and West* 15 (1965), 145-152.]

3071. Saher, P.J. *The Conquest of Suffering: An Enlarged Anthology of George Grimm's Works on Buddhist Philosophy and Metaphysics.* Delhi, India: Motilal Banarsidass, 1977.

3072. Saraswati, Swami Brahmanandendra. "Searchlight on Ramanuja's System of the Embodied God." *Brahmavadin* 11 (1976): 100-125.

3073. Saxena, S. Kiran. "Fabric of Self-Suffering: A Study in Gandhi." *Religious Studies* 12 (1976): 239-247.

3074. Schloegl, Irmgard. "Suffering in Zen Buddhism." *Theoria to Theory* 11 (1977): 217-227.

3075. Sharma, Arvind. *A Hindu Perspective on the Philosophy of Religion.* New York: St. Martin's Press, 1990.

3076. Sharma, Ram Prakash. "The Problem of Evil in Buddhism." *Journal of Dharma* 2 (1977): 307-311.

3077. Smart, Ninian. "Action and Suffering in the Theravadian Tradition." *Philosophy East and West* 34 (1984): 371-378.

3078. Sonneborn, John A. "God, Suffering and Hope: A Unification View." *Unity in Diversity.* Edited by Henry O. Thompson. *Unity in Diversity: Essays in Religion by Members of the Faculty of the Unification Theological Seminary.* New York: Rose of Sharon Press, 1984: 163-239.

3079. Southwood, Martin. "Buddhism and Evil." *The Anthropology of Evil.* Edited by David Parkin. Oxford: Blackwell, 1985: 128-141.

3080. Steinkraus, Warren E. "Some Problems in Karma." *Philosophical Quarterly India* 38 (1966): 145-154. [See response by Malkani [#3051].]

3081. Stuart, Albert C. "The Ground of Evil in Buddhism." *Listening* 18 (1983): 73-82.

3082. Tiwari, Kapil N. "Suffering: Indian Perspectives." *MLBD Newsletter* 8 (1986): 1-5. [Contains short articles by several authors on various aspects of suffering in Hinduism, Buddhism and Jainism.]

3083. Tokiwa, Gishin. "Chan (Zen) View of Suffering." *Buddhist Christian Studies* 5 (1985): 103-129. [See various responses by Schubert Ogden [#3065], David

Lockhead, and others in "Responses to Gishin Tokiwa." *Buddhist Christian Studies* 5 (1985), 131-155.]

3084.   Tripathi, Bashihtha N. *Indian View of Spiritual Bondage*. Varansi (India): Aradhana Prakashan, 1987.

3085.   Varma, Ved Prakash. "Monotheism and the Problem of Evil." *Indian Philosophical Quarterly* 2 (1975): 341-352.

3086.   Verdu, A. *Early Buddhist Philosophy in Light of the Four Noble Truths*. Washington, DC: University Press of America, 1979.

3087.   Weeraratne, Amarasiri. "Buddhism and the Problem of Suffering." *Buddhist Annual*. Edited by E.H. de Alwis, 1970: 52-55.

3088.   Wei-Ming, Tu. "Pain and Suffering in Confucian Self-Cultivation." *Philosophy East and West* 34 (1984): 329-338.

3089.   Yearley, Lee H. "Toward a Typology of Religious Thought: A Chinese Example." *Journal of Religion* 55 (1975): 426-443.

3090.   Younger, Paul. "Buddhism and the Indian Religious Tradition." *Developments in Buddhist Thought*. Edited by Roy C. Amore. Waterloo, ON: Wilfred Laurier University Press, 1979: 104-112.

VIII Women and Theodicy [Selected Publications]

3091.   Carson, Anne. *Feminist Spirituality and the Feminine Divine: An Annotated Bibliography*. Trumansburg, NY: Crossing Press, 1986.

3092.   Cooey, Paula. "Suffering and Power: An Anatomy of Transformation." *Anima* 15 (1988): 128-136.

3093.   Daly, Mary. *Beyond God the Father: Toward a Philosophy of Women's Liberation*. Boston, MA: Beacon Press, 1973.

3094.   ——. *Pure Lust: Elemental Feminist Philosophy*. Boston, MA: Beacon, 1984.

3095.   Douglas, Jane Dempsey. *Women, Freedom and Calvin*. Louisville, KY: John Knox/Westminster Press, 1991.

3096.   Eickwort, Kathy. "Litany of Women in Pain." *Women's Spirit Bonding*. Edited by Janet Kalven and Mary Buckley. New York: Pilgrim Press, 1984: 65-66.

3097.   Englesman, Joan Chamberlain. *The Feminine Dimension of the Divine*. Philadelphia, PA: Westminster Press, 1979.

3098.   Fiorenza, Francis P. "Joy and Pain as Paradigmatic for Language about God." *Theology of Joy*. Edited by Johannes Baptist Metz and Jean-Pierre Jossua. New York: Herder and Herder, 1974: 67-80. [Critique of process theology, Moltmann, and Kitamori regarding *the suffering of God* theme: see *Appendix C* for other listings.]

3099.   Garside, Christine. "Good and Evil: A Study of the Eve-Mary Polarity and its Significance for Women." *Women and Religion*. American Academy of Religion

Papers for Women and Religion Group. Missoula, MT: University of Montana Press, 1973: 104-127.

3100. Gross, Rita M. "Suffering, Feminist Theory, and Images of Goddess." *Anima* 13 (1986): 39-46.

3101. Gundersdorf von Jess, Wilma. "Suffering, the Scapegoat Syndrome, and Prophetic Activism." Symposium: Toward a Theology of Feminism? *Horizons, Journal of the College Theology Society* 2 (1975): 115-117. [Response to Daly's *Beyond God the Father* [#3093]].

3102. Hays, Hoffman Reynolds. *The Dangerous Sex: The Myth of Feminine Evil*. New York: Putnam, 1964.

3103. Heyward, Isabel Carter. *The Redemption of God: A Theology of Mutual Relation*. Lanham, MD: University Press of America, 1982. [Discusses Elie Wiesel's theodicy, the justification of God in Augustinian and Irenaean theodicy, concluding with a section on Wiesel's writings on the redemption of God. Also contains several appendices on the relevance of Schleiermacher, Gustavo Gutiérrez, a feminist critique, etc.]

3104. ———. *Our Passion for Justice: Images of Power, Sexuality, and Liberation*. New York: Pilgrim Press, 1984.

3105. Johnson, Elizabeth A. "The Incomprehensibility of God and the Image of God as Male and Female." *Theological Studies* 45 (1984): 441-465.

3106. Kaiser, Barbara Bakke. "Poet as 'Female Impersonator': The Image of Daughter Zion as Speaker in Biblical Poems of Suffering." *Journal of Religion* 67 (1987): 164-182.

3107. Keller, Katherine. *From a Broken Web: Separation, Sexism, and Self*. Boston, MA: Beacon Press, 1986. [Feminist critique of western philosophy and theology and psychology, proposing reconciled male/female interrelatedness versus traditional patriarchal dominance.]

3108. Kwok, Pui Lan. "God Weeps with our Pain." *East Asia Journal of Theology* 2 (1984): 228-232. [Feminist theology in Asia.]

3109. Maguire, Daniel. "The Feminization of God and Ethics." *Christianity and Crisis* 42 (1982): 59-67.

3110. McDonagh, Edna. "Man and Woman Are in the Image of God and We Are All Brothers and Sisters in Christ." *The Dignity of the Despised*. Edited by Jacques Marie Pohier. New York: Seabury Press, 1979: 115-124.

3111. McFague, Sallie. *Metaphorical Theology: Models of God in Religious Language*. Philadelphia, PA: Fortress Press, 1982.

3112. ———. *Models of God: A Theology for an Ecological, Nuclear Age*. Philadelphia, PA: Fortress Press, 1967.

3113. Mollenkott, Virginia Ramsey. *The Divine Feminine: The Biblical Imagery of God as Female*. New York: Crossroad, 1983.

3114. Moore, Rick D. "Personification of the Seduction of Evil: 'The Wiles of the Wicked Woman'." *Restoration Quarterly* 10 (1981): 505-519. [See John M. Allegro, *"'The Wiles of the Wicked Woman'*: A Sapiential Work of Qumran's

Fourth Cave." *Palestinian Exploration Quarterly* (1964), 53-55. More complete text published in Allegro's *Discourses in the Judaean Desert of Jordon, V* (Oxford: Oxford University Press, 1968), 82-85.]

3115.   Noddings, Nel. *Caring: A Feminine Approach to Ethics and Moral Education.* Berkeley and Los Angeles, CA: University of California Press, 1984.

3116.   ——. "Do We Really Want to Produce Good People?" *Journal of Moral Education* 17 (1987): 177-188.

3116.   ——. *Women and Evil.* Berkeley, CA: University of California Press, 1989. [Examination of several theological, psychological, and philosophical associations of women with evil; she proposes a counter-definition of evil, from the perspective of women's experience. The text contains a select bibliography, 265-272.]

3118.   O'Connor, June. "Two Critical Questions." Symposium: Toward a Theology of Feminism?" *Horizons, Journal of the College Theology Society* 2 (1975): 114-115. [Response to Mary Daly's *Beyond God the Father* [#3093].]

3119.   Ochshorn, Judith. *The Feminine Experience and the Nature of the Divine.* Bloomington, IN: Indiana University Press, 1981.

3120.   Palmer, Sally. "The Wounded Healer." *Spinning a Sacred Yarn: Women Speak from the Pulpit.* Edited by Ann Greenawalt Abernethy, Carole Carlson, Patricia A. Carque; et al. New York: Pilgrim Press, 1982: 149-152.

3121.   Phillips, John A. *Eve: The History of an Idea.* San Francisco, CA: Harper and Row, 1984.

3122.   Plaskow, Judith. *Sin, Sex and Grace: Women's Experience and the Theologies of Reinhold Niebuhr and Paul Tillich.* Lanham, MD: University Press of America, 1980. [Critical study of sin and grace in Tillich and Niebuhr, from the perspective of women's experience.]

3123.   Prusak, Bernard P. "Woman: Seductive Siren and Source of Sin? Pseudepigraphical Myth and Christian Origins." *Religion and Sexism.* Edited by Rosemary R. Ruether. New York: Simon and Schuster, 1974: 89-116.

3124.   Psorulla, Elvira M. "Consecrated Women: Ministers of Faith to a Suffering World." *The Religious Woman.* Edited by Jean Daniélou, et. al. Boston, MA: Daughters of St. Paul, 1974: 149-171.

3125.   Ruether, Rosemary Radford. "Misogynism and Virginal Feminism." *Religion and Sexism.* Edited by Rosemary Radford Ruether. New York: Simon and Schuster, 1974.

3126.   ——. *Sexism and God-Talk: Toward a Feminist Theology.* Boston, MA: Beacon Press, 1983.

3127.   Russell, Letty M. *Household of Freedom: Authority in Feminist Theology.* Philadelphia, PA: Westminster Press, 1987.

3128.   Sagan, Eli. *Freud, Women and Morality: The Psychology of Good and Evil.* New York: Basic Books, 1988.

3129.   Saiving-Goldstein, Valerie. "The Human Situation: A Feminine View." *Woman Spirit Rising: A Reader in Feminist Theology*. Edited by Carol Christ and Judith Plaskow. New York: Harper and Row, 1979 [see #769].

3130.   Sanderson, Lilian Passmore. *Against the Mutilation of Women: The Struggle to End Unnecessary Suffering*. London: Ithaca Press, 1981.

3131.   Schaper, Donna. "The Movement of Suffering." *Spinning a Sacred Yarn: Women Speak from the Pulpit*. Edited by Ann Greenawalt Abernethy, Carole Carlson, Patricia A. Carque; et al. New York: Pilgrim Press, 1982: 192-198.

3132.   Schonsheck, Jonathan. "Human Nature, Innateness and Violence Against Women." *Philosophical Essays on the Ideas of a Good Society*. Edited by Yeager Hudson and Creighton Peden. Lewiston, NY and Queenston, ON: Edwin Mellen, 1988: 187-197.

3133.   Schüssler, Elisabeth Fiorenza. *In Memory of Her: A Feminist Theological Reconstruction of Christian Origins*. New York: Crossroad, 1983.

3134.   Soelle, Dorothee. *The Strength of the Weak: Toward a Christian Feminist Identity*. Translated by Robert and Rita Kimber. Philadelphia, PA: Westminster Press, 1984.

3135.   Tennis, Diane. "Suffering." *Spinning a Sacred Yarn: Women Speak from the Pulpit*. Edited by Ann Greenawalt Abernethy, Carole Carlson, Patricia A. Carque, et al. New York, Pilgrim Press, 1982: 203-207.

3136.   Trible, Phyllis. *God and the Rhetoric of Sexuality*. Philadelphia, PA: Fortress Press, 1978.

3137.   ———. *Texts of Terror: Literary-Feminist Readings of Biblical Narratives*. Philadelphia, PA: Fortress Press, 1984. [Hagar, Tamar, etc.]

3138.   Walker, Curtis T. "A Christian Perspective of God and Suffering Particularly in Family Violence/Spouse Abuse." *AME Zion Quarterly Review* (1987): 22-37.

3139.   Watkins, Renée Neu. "Two Women Visionaries and Death: Catherine of Siena and Julian of Norwich." *Numen* 30 (1983): 174-198.

3140.   Welch, Sharon D. *A Feminist Ethic of Risk*. Minneapolis, MN: Fortress Press, 1990.

IX   Miscellaneous Publications on Theodicy [Selected]

3141.   Abelson, Raziel. "To Do or Let Happen." *American Philosophical Quarterly* 19 (1982): 219-229. [Discussion of euthanasia].

3142.   Aichele, George, Jr. "The Slaughter of Innocents." *Christian Century* 95 (1978): 1262-1263. [Discussion of the dark side of the birth of Christ: the slaughter of innocent male infants.]

3143.   Albano, Peter J. "Ricoeur's Contribution to Fundamental Theology." *Thomist* 46 (1982): 573-592.

3144.   Alexander, Laurence L. "Ricoeur's *Symbolism of Evil* and Cross-Cultural Comparison: The Representation of Evil in Maya Indian Culture." *Journal of the American Academy of Religion* 44 (1976): 705-714.

3145. Allen, Diogenes. "Restoration of Conscience." *Princeton Seminary Bulletin* 67 (1975): 75-81.

3146. ———. *Three Outsiders: Pascal, Kierkegaard, Simone Weil*. Cambridge: Cowley, 1983.

3147. ———. "Simone Weil on Suffering and 'Reading.'" *Communio* 7 (1984): 297-304. [Discusses the religious understanding of nature by Weil.]

3148. Allik, Tina. "Matthew Fox: On the Goodness of Creation and Finitude." *Listening* 24 (1989): 54-72. [Comparison of the Irenaean and Augustinian theodicies. See also Allik's "Narrative Approaches to Human Personhood: Agency, Grace and Innocent Suffering," *Philosophy and Theology* 1 (1987), 305-333. Discusses Ricoeur's theodicy, etc.]

3149. Allison, C. FitzSimmons. *Guilt, Anger and God: The Pattern of our Discontent*. Wilton, CT: Morehouse-Barlow, 1972. [Critiques non-Christian view of discontent (anger, "disesteem," guilt, and death) in Freud, D.H. Lawrence, Marcuse, and others. He then examines the Christian Gospel's message about these problems.]

3150. Amato, Joseph A. *Victims and Values: A History and a Theory of Suffering*. New York: Greenwood Press, 1990.

3151. Anderson, Herbert, and Kenneth R. Mitchell. *All our Loses, All our Griefs: Resources for Pastoral Care*. Philadelphia, PA: Westminster Press, 1983. [Analysis of the process and dynamics of grief and a theology of grieving.]

3152. Andic, Martin. "Simone Weil and Kierkegaard." *Modern Theology* 2 (1985): 20-41. [Explores the influence of Kierkegaard on Weil.]

3153. Antarkar, S.S. "Wickedness: Its Possibilities and Analysis." *Indian Philosophical Quarterly* 9 (1981): 65-75. [Critique of Patrick Nowell-Smith's view of wickedness, in *Ethics*. London: Penguin Books, 1954.]

3154. Arapura, John G. *Religion as Anxiety and Tranquillity*. Paris: Mouton, 1973.

3155. Atkinson, David J. "Conscience." *Free to Be Different*. Edited by M. Jeeves, R. Berry and D. Atkinson. Grand Rapids, MI: Eerdmans, 1984: 129-150.

3156. Auer, Johannes A.C. Fagginger, and Julian Hartt. *Humanism and Theism*. Ames, IA: Iowa State University Press, 1981. [Updates the Humanism–Theism Controversy. See also Auer's *Humanism States its Case*. Boston, MA: Beacon Press, 1933. Reprinted by Ann Arbor, MI: University Microfilms, 1967.]

3157. Baier, Kurt. "The Meaning of Life." *The Meaning of Life*. Edited by Steven Sanders and David R. Cheney. Englewood Cliffs, NJ: Prentice-Hall, 1980.

3158. Bailey, Jack S. *Let Not Your Heart Be Troubled*. Bountiful, UT: Horizon Publishers, 1977.

3159. Bakan, David. *Disease, Pain, Sacrifice: Toward a Psychology of Suffering*. Boston, MA: Beacon Press, 1968.

3160. Barlow, Sally. "A Response and More Questions." *Blueprints for Living: Perspectives for Latter-Day Saint Women*. Edited by M. Mouritsen. Salt Lake City, UT: Brigham Young University Press, 1980: 107-111.

3161. Barnhart, Joe E. *Religion and the Challenge of Philosophy*. Totowa, NJ: Little-field, Adams, 1975.

3162. Baylis, Charles A.C. "C.I. Lewis's Theory of Value and Ethics." *Journal of Philosophy* 61 (1964): 559-566.

3163. Bayly, Joseph. "The Suffering of Children." *The Spiritual Needs of Children: A Guide for Nurses, Parents, Teachers*. Edited by Judith Allen Shelly. Downers Grove, IL: InterVarsity Press, 1982: 109-115.

3164. Beattie, Paul H. "The Tragic View of Life." Three Parts. *Religious Humanism* 19 (1985): 54-61; 111-121; and 166-173.

3165. Becker, Ernest. *The Structure of Evil: An Essay on the Unification of the Science of Man*. New York: Free Press, 1968 and 1976. [This classic work presents a unified vision of human beings from the perspectives of psychology, sociology, history, and philosophy.]

3166. ———. *The Denial of Death*. New York: Free Press, 1973. [The fear of death drives human beings to attempt to overcome it through culturally standardized hero-systems and symbols which provide the promise of infinity.]

3167. ———. *Escape from Evil*. London: Macmillan, 1975. [Contains chapters on "The Basic Dynamic of Human Evil," "The Nature of Social Evil," etc.]

3168. Beirnaert, Louis. "Psychoanalytical Theory and Moral Evil." *Moral Evil Under Challenge*. Edited by Johannes Baptist Metz. London: Burns and Oates, 1970: 45-55.

3169. Bell, Richard H. "Theology as Grammar: Is God an Object of Understanding?" *Religious Studies* 11 (1975): 307-317.

3170. Benn, Stanley I. "Wickedness." *Ethics* 95 (1985): 795-810.

3171. Benson, John E. "Ernest Becker: A New Enlightenment View of Evil?" *Dialog* 25 (1986): 101-107. [Outlines Becker's approach to the problem of human destructiveness. Becker's later work addressed the problem of evil and the vicious nature of human beings. One of the failures of the social sciences was its failure to deal with this problem, a problem which challenges the Enlightenment's understanding of the science of human beings. Becker's theories merged Freudian and Marxist thought.]

3172. Berger, Peter L. *The Sacred Canopy: Elements of a Sociological Theory of Religion*. New York: Anchor/Doubleday and Company, 1967. Reprinted, 1969.

3173. Berkhof, Hendrikus. *Christ and the Powers*. Scottdale, PA: Herald Press, 1962.

3174. Bertocci, Peter A. *Is God for Real?* New York: Thomas Nelson Inc., 1971.

3175. ———. "Idealistic Temporalistic Personalism and Good-And-Evil." *Proceedings of the Catholic Philosophical Association* 51 (1977): 56-65. [Argues, following his teacher, E.S. Brightman, that evil cannot exist by itself: it is always a parasite on the good. God's power may be finite, not by self-limitation only, but because of some impediment which is co-eternal within the divine being.]

3176. ———. *The Goodness of God*. Washington, DC: University Press of America, 1981. [Maintains that experiential data, including religious experience, can be formulated into a more adequate view of God than that of traditional theism and humanistic naturalism.]

3177.   ———. "A Theist Explanation of Evil." *The Challenge of Religion: Contemporary Readings in Philosophy of Religion*. Edited by Frederick Ferré, Joseph J. Kockelmans, and John E. Smith. New York: Seabury Press, 1982: 330-344. [Bertocci's essay was published first in his *Introduction to the Philosophy of Religion*. Englewood Cliffs, NJ: Prentice-Hall, 1951, 389-441. He rejects the argument of traditional theists, that nondisciplinary evil is a necessary part of "the best compossible world." This vision is not grounded adequately in human experience (the criterion of truth). Following E.S. Brightman, Bertocci argues that *God is finite*, that there is a Given aspect of God (not external to God) which God cannot control completely.]

3178.   Beversluis, J. *C.S. Lewis and the Search for Rational Religion*. Grand Rapids, MI: Eerdmans, 1985. [Contains updated bibliography of Lewis's critics and supporters, and the first book-length philosophical analysis of Lewis's defense of Christianity. A recent critical response to this book is found in Hugo Meynell's "An Attack on C.S. Lewis," *Faith and Philosophy* 8 (1991), 305-316.]

3179.   Bishop, John. "The Broken Things of Life." *Expository Times* 95 (1984): 214-215.

3180.   Bloom, Anthony [Metropolitan of Surozh]. "The Theology of Suffering." *From Fear to Faith*. Edited by Norman Autton. London: SPCK Press, 1971: 23-34.

3181.   ———. "Suffering and Death of Children." *Eastern Churches Review* 8 (1976): 107-112.

3182.   Blum, Alan F. "The Collective Representation of Affliction: Some Reflections on Disability and Disease as Social Facts." *Theoretical Medicine* 6 (1985): 221-232.

3183.   Bly, Stephen A. *God's Angry Side*. Chicago, IL: Moody Press, 1982.

3184.   Boas, George. "Warfare in the Cosmos." *Diogenes* 78 (1972): 38-51.

3185.   Bonar, Horatius. *When God's Children Suffer*. New Canaan, CT: Keats Publishing, 1981.

3186.   Bosch, David J. "The Problem of Evil in Africa: A Survey of African Views on Witchcraft and of the Response of the Christian Church." *Like a Roaring Lion: Essays on the Bible, Church and Demonic Powers*. Edited by P. deVilliers. Pretoria: University of South Africa Press, 1987: 38-62.

3187.   Bosley, Richard. *On Good and Bad: Whether Happiness is the Highest Good*. Lanham, MD: University Press of America, 1988.

3188.   Bourgeois, Patrick L. and Frank Schalow. "The Integrity and Fallenness of Human Existence." *Southern Journal of Philosophy* 25 (1987): 123-132. [Heidegger, Ricoeur.]

3189.   Braaten, Carl E. "Evil." *Dialogue* 25 (1986): 87-113.

3190.   Brandt, David. *Is That All There Is? Overcoming Disappointment in an Age of Diminished Expectations*. New York: Pocket Books, 1983.

3191.   Breckenridge, James. "Religion and the Problem of Death." *Journal of Dharma* 4 (1979): 217-227. [Discusses the Zen Buddhist view of death as monism; the Christian view of consolation in death through the suffering of Jesus; and the ways in which the subject of death strains Zen-Christian dialogue: Christian craving for a life after death is rejected as an illusory view since there is a soul or self which experiences salvation. Our true nature is "Buddha-nature," and this does not require salvation.]

3192.   Breton, Stanislas. "Human Suffering and Transcendence." *The Meaning of Suffering*. Edited by Flavian Dougherty. New York: Human Sciences Press, 1982: 55-94.

3193.   Brittain, John N. "Theological Foundations for Spiritual Care." *Journal of Religion and Health* 25 (1986): 107-121.

3194.   Brody, Howard. *Stories of Illness*. New Haven, CT: Yale University Press, 1987.

3195.   Broughton, Walter. "Religiosity and Opposition to Church Social Action: A Test of a Weberian Hypothesis." *Review of Religious Research* 19 (1978): 154-166. [Shows that "discompassionate theodicies" are associated with opposition to efforts of the church to ameliorate social problems.]

3196.   Brown, David. "The Problem of Pain." *The Religion of the Incarnation: Anglican Essays in Commemoration of Lux Mundi*. Edited by Robert Morgan. Bristol: Bristol Classical Press, 1989.

3197.   Brown, Douglas E. "When Suffering Eclipses God: Reflections on the Struggle of an ICU Nurse." *Journal of Religious Ethics* 17 (1989): 87-98.

3198.   Brown, Frank Burch. "Sin and Bad Taste: Aesthetic Criteria in the Realm of Religion." *Soundings* 70 (1987): 65-80.

3199.   Bulman, R. Janoff, and Camille B. Wortman. "Attributions of Blame and Coping in the 'Real World': Severe Accident Victims React to their Lot." *Journal of Personality and Social Psychology* 35 (1977): 351-361.

3200.   Burhoe, Ralph Wendell. "Five Steps in the Evolution of Man's Knowledge of Good and Evil." *Zygon, Journal of Religion and Science* 2 (1967): 77-96.

3201.   Bussell, Harold, Mark Erikson, Earl Palmer, and Timothy Warner. "Facing the Wreckage of Evil." *Leadership* 7 (1986): 132-140. [Interviews.]

3202.   Cahill, Lisa Sowle. "Consent in Time of Affliction: The Ethics of a Circumspect Theist." *Journal of Religious Ethics* 13 (1985): 22-36. [Argues that the problem of evil is an important point of departure for Gustafson's position and that it has important consequences for his theological method and his doctrine of God.]

3203.   Cain, David. "Way of God's Theodicy: Honesty, Presence, Adventure." *Journal of Pastoral Care* 32 (1978): 239-250. [Maintains that the presence of God is the only theodicy. Christian theodicy, at best, can only bear witness to God's self-justification.]

3204.   Campola, Anthony. *The Power Delusion*. Wheaton, IL: Victor Books, 1983.

3205.   Capitan, William H. *Philosophy of Religion: An Introduction*. Indianapolis, IN: Pegasus, 1972.

3206.   Caplan, Lionel. "The Popular Culture of Evil in Urban South India." *The Anthropology of Evil*. Edited by David Parkin. Oxford: Blackwell, 1985: 165-193.

3207.   Capon, Robert Farrar. *The Third Peacock*. Garden City, NY: Doubleday, 1971.

3208.   Carnell, Edward J. *Introduction to Christian Apologetics*. Grand Rapids, MI: Eerdmans, 1948. [Argues against a finite God as a resolution of theodicy.]

3209. Carney, Frederick S. "On McCormick and Teleological Morality." *Journal of Religious Ethics* 6 (1978): 81-107.

3210. Carretto, Carlo. *Why O Lord? The Inner Meaning of Suffering*. Maryknoll, NY: Orbis Books, 1986.

3211. Casey, Joseph. *From Why to Yes: Pain Uncovers the Meaningful Life to a Philosopher*. New York: University Press of America, 1982.

3212. Caskin, J.C.A. *The Question of Eternity: An Outline of the Philosophy of Religion*. New York: Penguin Books, 1984. [*Chapter 6*, "Arguments Against Belief in God," contains critical sections on evil, freedom, and miracles.]

3213. Caspar, Ruth. "A Time to Work; A Time to Play." *Listening* 16 (1981): 18-30. [Maintains that physical, moral and metaphysical evils call forth a response for action (work).]

3214. Cassell, Eric J. "The Nature of Suffering and the Goals of Medicine." *New England Journal of Medicine* 306 (1982): 639-645.

3215. ———. *The Nature of Suffering*. New York: Oxford University Press, 1991. [See also his *The Healer's Art*. Philadelphia, PA: Lippincott, 1976.]

3216 ———. "Recognizing Suffering." *Hastings Center Report* 21 (1991): 24-31.

3217. Cavendish, Richard. *The Powers of Evil in Western Religion, Magic, and Folk Belief*. New York: Putman, 1975.

3218. Chao, Jonathan. "Witness of a Suffering Church: The Chinese Experience." *Evangelical Review of Theology* 8 (1984): 73-89.

3219. Childress, Marianne. "Good As Indefinable." *Wisdom in Depth: Essays for H. Renard*. Edited by Vincent F. Daves, Henri Renard, Maurice R. Holloway, and Leo Sweeney. Milwaukee, WI: Bruce Publishing Co., 1966: 8-29.

3220. Chittister, Joan D. "Presentation of the Data: Will the Lord Find Faith?" *Faith and Ferment: An Interdisciplinary Study of Christian Beliefs and Practices*. Edited by Robert Bilheimer. Minneapolis, MN: Augsburg Publishing House, 1983.

3221. Christopher, Joe R., and Joan K. Ostling. *C.S. Lewis: An Annotated Checklist of Writings About Him and His Works*. Kent, OH: Kent State University Press, 1974.

3222. Clark, J. Michael. "Aids, Death and God: Gay Liberational Theology and the Problem of Suffering." *Journal of Pastoral Counselling* 21 (1986): 40-54.

3223. Clark, Malcolm. "Suffering." *Invitations to Thinking: A Philosophical Workbook*. Dubuque, IA and Toronto, ON: Kendall/Hunt Publishing Company, 1981: 115-130.

3224. Clarkson, Margaret. *Destined for Glory: The Meaning of Suffering*. Grand Rapids, MI: Eerdmans, 1983.

3225. Claypool, John. *Tracks of a Fellow Struggler*. New York: Pillar Books, 1976.

3226. Clendenin, Daniel B. "Security But No Certainty: Toward a Christian Theodicy." *Journal of the Evangelical Theological Society* 31 (1988): 321-328.

3227. Cliff, Michelle. "Sister/Outsider: Some Thoughts on Simone Weil." *Between Women: Biographers, Novelists, Critics, Teachers and Artists Write About their*

Work on Women. Edited by Carol Ascher, Louise de Salvo, and Sara Ruddick. Boston, MA: Beacon Press, 1984.

3228.　Cohen, Albert K. *The Elasticity of Evil: Changes in the Social Definition of Deviance*. Oxford: Oxford University Press, 1974. [Discusses the "elasticity" of evil, its expansion and contraction. Cohen's concern is not with social evils generally, but with the species of evil we call "deviance"—the failure of human conduct to meet the standards and rules we ourselves set.]

3229.　Cohen, Sara Kay. *Whoever Said Life is Fair? A Guide to Growing Through Life's Injustices*. New York: Berkeley Books, 1977. [Inspirational guide for the suffering person.]

3230.　Coles, Robert. "Simone Weil: The Mystery of Her Life." *Yale Review* 73 (1984): 309-320. [See also his brief "Preface" to Eric Springsted's *Simone Weil and the Suffering of Love* [#3642].]

3231.　Collingwood, Robin George. *Faith and Reason: Essays in the Philosophy of Religion*. Chicago, IL: Quadrangle Books, 1968. [Contains his "What is the Problem of Evil?" *Theology* 25 (1922).]

3232.　Collins, Oral E. "Suffering Saints." *God's Prophetic Calendar*. Edited by M. Griswold. Advent Christian General Conference of America, 1983: 51-59.

3233.　Cone, Cecil Wayne. "Why Do the Righteous Suffer?" *Preaching on Suffering and a God of Love*. Edited by Henry J. Young. Philadelphia, PA: Fortress, 1978.

3234.　Cook, Judith A., and Dale W. Wimberly. "If I Should Die Before I Wake: Religious Commitment and Adjustment to the Death of a Child." *Journal for the Scientific Study of Religion* 22 (1983): 222-238.

3235.　Cooper, Burton Z. "Why, God? A Tale of Two Sufferers." *Theology Today* 42 (1986): 423-434. [Excerpt from his book *Why God?* [#3236]. Cooper maintains that the Book of Job makes no sense until we turn away from the monarchical image of God and toward an image of God as vulnerable. Cooper applies this view of Job to the suffering of *New York Times* writer, Russell Baker. (See *Appendix C* for more on the "suffering of God" theodicy).]

3236.　——. *Why God?* Atlanta, GA: John Knox Press, 1988. [A biblically grounded, popularized theodicy, exploring a new vision of God. Referred to by process theologian David Griffin as the best book of its kind: see Griffin's *Evil Revisited* [#873], 230.]

3237.　——. "Education for Suffering and the Shifting of the Catena." *Religious Education* 84 (1989): 26-36. [See also Cooper's "When Modern Consciousness Happens to Good People: Harold Kushner Revisited," *Theology Today* 48 (1991); and his "The Disabled God," *Theology Today* 49 (1992), 173-182.]

3238.　Cosby, Gordon. "A Prayer of a Chance: Taking Evil Seriously." *Sojourners* 15 (1986): 15-19 (Part I).

3239.　——. "To the Limits of Vision: Preaching to a Community of Faith." *Sojourners* 15 (1986): 32-35 (Part II).

3240.　——. "The Call to Community: Depending on God's Grace." *Sojourners* 15 (1986): 36-39 (Part III).

3241.   ———. "Spirituality and Community: Reflections on Evil and Grace (Interview)." *The Rise of Christian Conscience*. Edited by Jim Wallis. San Francisco, CA: Harper and Row, 1977: 154-173.

3242.   Couch, Beatriz Melano. "Religious Symbols and Philosophical Reflection." *Studies in the Philosophy of Paul Ricoeur*. Edited by Charles E. Reagan. Athens, OH: Ohio University Press (1978): 115-132.

3243.   Cox, Charles H., and Jean W. Cox. "The Mystical Experience, With an Emphasis on Wittgenstein and Zen." *Religious Studies* 12 (1976): 483-492.

3244.   Cox, Harvey G. *God's Revolution and Man's Responsibility*. Valley Forge, PA: Judson Press, 1965.

3245.   Cross, R. Nicol. "Shall We Reason with God?" *Hibbert Journal* 46 (1948): 125-128.

3246.   Cross, Wilford O. "The Problem of Human Evil." *Anglican Theological Review* 45 (1963): 1-23.

3247.   Cruise, P.E. "The Problem of Being Simone Weil." *Judaism* 35 (1986): 98-106. [Biographical sketch of Weil's personal suffering and chronic ill-health, culminating in unemployment and death by starvation and tuberculosis at thirty-four years of age.]

3248.   Cunradi, Charles. *The Phenomenon of Evil: Its Scientific Exposition and Realistic Deterrent*. London: Mitre Press, 1966.

3249.   Custance, Arthur C. "The Problem of Evil." *Chapter 4* of *The Flood: Local or Global?* Grand Rapids, MI: Zondervan Publishing House, 1979.

3250.   Daane, James. *The Freedom of God*. Grand Rapids, MI: Eerdmans, 1973.

3251.   Dalton, Peter C. "Death and Evil." *Philosophical Forum* 11 (1979): 193-211.

3252.   Davidson, Glen. *Understanding Mourning: A Guide for Those Who Grieve*. Minneapolis, MN: Augsburg Publishing House, 1984. [See also Glen Davidson's *Living with Dying*. Minneapolis, MN: Augsburg Publishing House, 1975.]

3253.   Davies, Gaius. "The Hands of the Healer: Has Faith a Place?" *Journal of Medical Ethics* 6 (1980): 185-189.

3254.   Davis, Charles. "The Inhumanity of Evil." *Body as Spirit: The Nature of Religious Feeling*. New York: Seabury Press, 1976: 109-124.

3255.   Davis, Stephen T. "Why Did This Happen to Me?—The Patient as a Philosopher." *Princeton Seminary Bulletin* 65 (1972): 61-67. [See also Stephen Davis, "Assurance of Victory," *Pulpit Digest* 41 (1981), 65-69.]

3256.   Davitz, Joel R. *Inferences of Patients' Pain and Psychological Distress: Studies in Nursing Behaviors*. New York: Springer Publishing, 1981.

3257.   Davitz, Lois Jean. *Nurses' Responses to Patients' Suffering*. New York: Springer Publishing, 1980.

3258.   De Beausobre, Iulia. "Creative Suffering." *Theoria to Theory* 12 (1978): 111-121.

3259.   De Schrijver, Georges. "Wholeness in Society—A Contemporary Understanding of the Question of Theodicy." *Tijdschr voor de Studie can de Verlichtling en van*

Het Vrije Denken 12 (1984): 377-394. [Argues that theodicy is transformed into "humanodicy" by some writers.]

3260.　De Villiers, Pieter. "Prisoners of Hope: Disinvestment, Human Suffering and Christianity." *Disinvestment and Human Suffering*. Edited by Pieter de Villiers. Pretoria: CUM Books, C.B. Bible Centre, University of South Africa, 1985: 6-8.

3261.　DeVries, Mark E. "Power and Love Reframed: Theodicy and Therapy." *Journal of Psychology and Christianity* 9 (1990): 18-26.

3262.　DeVries, Peter. *The Blood of the Lamb*. Boston, MA: Little, Brown & Co., 1969.

3263.　Deyneka, Anita, and Peter Deyneka. "A Salvation of Suffering: The Church in the Soviet Union." *Christianity Today* 26 (1982): 19-21.

3264.　Dobson, Edward G. "Suffering and Sickness: Why does God Allow Them?" *Fundamentalist Journal* 6 (1987): 16-17.

3265.　Doherty, Catherine De Huek. "The Meaning of Suffering—A Personal Witness." *The Meaning of Suffering*. Edited by Flavian Dougherty. New York: Human Sciences Press, 1982: 341-349.

3266.　Doob, Leonard William. *Panorama of Evil*. Westport, CT: Greenwood Press, 1978.

3267.　Doran, Robert M. *Subject and Psyche: Ricoeur, Jung, and the Search for Foundations*. Washington, DC: University Press of America, 1977.

3268.　——. "Psyche, Evil and Grace." *Communio* (US) 6 (1979): 192-211. [References to theologian Bernard Lonergan and psychologist Carl Jung.]

3269.　Dotts, Ted. "Six Points in a Theology of Suffering." *Quarterly Review* 6 (1986): 59-63.

3270.　Draison, Marc. *Love, Sin and Suffering*. New York: Macmillan, 1964.

3271.　Drane, James F. *The Possibility of God*. Totawa, NJ: Littlefield, Adams and Co., 1976.

3272.　Dunaway, John M. *Simone Weil*. Boston, MA: Twayne Publishers, 1984.

3273.　Dunne, Carrin. "Between Two Thieves: A Response to Jung's Critique of the Christian Notions of Good and Evil." *Jung's Challenge to Contemporary Religion*. Edited by M. Stein and R. Moore. Wilmette, IL: Chiron Publications, 1989: 15-26.

3274.　Dunning, Stephen N. "History and Phenomenology: Dialectical Structure in Ricoeur's *The Symbolism of Evil*." *Harvard Theological Review* 76 (1983): 343-363.

3275.　Dupré, Louis. "Wounded Self: The Religious Meaning of Mental Suffering." *Christian Century* 93 (1976): 328-331.

3276.　Durfee, Harold A. "Philosophical Idealism: The Irrational and the Personal." *Idealistic Studies* 11 (1981): 263-274.

3277.　Edwards, Charles Thomas. *God is Good*. New York: Exposition, 1974.

3278.　Edwards, James R. "When Bad Things Happen." *Christianity Today* 33 (1989): 30-32.

3279. Eigen, Michael. "On Demonized Aspects of the Self." *Evil, Self and Culture*. Edited by M. Nelson and M. Eigen. New York: Humanities Press, 1984: 91-123.

3280. Eisenbud, Jule. "Freud, the Death Wish, and the Problem of Evil." *Evil, Self and Culture*. Edited by Marie Coleman Nelson and Michael Eigen. New York: Human Sciences Press, 1984: 227-238.

3281. Ekechukwu, Alexander. "The Problem of Suffering in Igbo Traditional Religion." (2 Parts). *African Ecclesiastical Review* 24 (1982): 81-89; 156-163.

3282. ———. "The Problem of Suffering in Igbo Traditional Religion." *Bulletin de Théologie Africaine* 5 (1983): 51-64.

3283. Ellens, J. Harold. "The Problem of Evil." *The Orb: A Journal of Religious Affairs* (1974).

3284. ———. *God's Grace and Human Health*. Nashville, TN: Abingdon Press, 1982.

3285. Ellul, Jacques. *Hope in Time of Abandonment*. New York: Seabury, 1977.

3286. Elshtain, Jean Bethke. "The Vexation of Weil." *Telos* 58 (1983/1984): 195-203.

3287. Engelhardt, H. Tristram. "Ideology and Etiology." *Journal of Medicine and Philosophy* 1 (1976): 256-268. [Discussion of various concepts of disease.]

3288. ———. "Illnesses, Diseases, and Sicknesses." *The Humanity of the Ill*. Edited by Victor Kestenbaum. Knoxville, TN: University of Tennessee Press, 1982: 142-156.

3289. Erickson, Richard C. "Reconciling Christian Views of Sin and Human Growth with Humanistic Psychology." *Christian Scholar's Review* 8 (1978): 114-25.

3290. Evans, C. Stephen. "The Blessings of Mental Anguish." *Christianity Today* 30 (1986): 26-27, 29. [Conservative view that physical and psychological illness may be the result of divine providence.]

3291. ———. *Philosophy of Religion: Thinking About Faith*. Downers Grove, IL: Inter-Varsity Press, 1985. [*Chapter 6*, "Objections to Theism: Modernity, Science and Evil," 121-140.]

3292. Evans, Donald. "Toward a Philosophy of Openness." *Analytic Philosophy of Religion in Canada*. Edited by Mostafa Faghfoury. Ottawa, ON: University of Ottawa Press, 1982. [Maintains that evil is not only a self-inflation which denies our finitude, but also a self-deflation which denies our freedom.]

3293. ———. "On the Nature and Origin of Good and Evil In Human Beings." *Revue de L'Université d'Ottawa/University of Ottawa Quarterly* 55 (1985): 193-207.

3294. Everly, Louis. *Suffering: Reflections on the Mystery of Human Pain and Suffering*. Translated by Marie-Claude Thompson. New York: Herder and Herder, 1967.

3295. Ewing, Alfred C. *The Definition of Good*. New York: Humanities Press, 1966.

3296. Fackre, Gabriel. "Sober Hope: Some Themes in Protestant Theology Today." *Christian Century* 31 (1987): 790-792.

3297. Faley, Roland James. *The Cup of Grief*. New York: Alba House, 1977.

3298. Farley, Edward. *God and Evil: Interpreting a Human Condition*. Philadelphia, PA: Fortress Press, 1990. [Farley presents a theological anthropology, reconstructing the Christian themes of sin and redemption.]

3299.   Fauteux, Kevin. "Good/Bad Splitting in the Religious Experience." *Journal of Pastoral Counseling* 14 (1979): 60-65.

3300.   Feagin, Susan L. "The Pleasures of Tragedy." *American Philosophical Quarterly* 20 (1983): 95-104.

3301.   Fingarette, Herbert. "Punishment and Suffering." *Proceedings of the American Philosophical Association* 50 (1977): 499-525. [Expounds retributive punishment, showing why the law must punish lawbreakers and must make them suffer in a way which fits the crime.]

3302.   ———. "Feeling Guilty." *American Philosophical Quarterly* 16 (1979): 159-164. [Presented as a paper to American Philosophical Association, 1979. See also Fingarette's "The Meaning of Law in the Book of Job," *Revisions: Changing Perspectives in Moral Philosophy*. Edited by Stanley Hauerwas and Alasdair MacIntyre. Notre Dame, IN: University of Notre Dame Press, 1983, 249-286. First published in *Hastings Law Journal* 29 (1978), 1581-1617.]

3303.   Fitch, Robert E. *Of Love and Suffering: Preface to Christian Ethics for Heathen Philosophers*. Philadelphia, PA: Westminster Press, 1970.

3304.   Fleming, James R. "Restoration Through Indemnity and the Problem of Suffering." *Restoring the Kingdom*. Edited by Deane William Ferm. New York: Rose of Sharon Press, 1984: 33-43. [This book contains several articles about the Unification doctrine of indemnity.]

3305.   Foley, Daniel Patrick. "Eleven Interpretations of Personal Suffering." *Journal of Religion and Health* 27 (1988): 321-328.

3306.   Ford, S. Dennis. "The Electronic Church's Aesthetic of Evil." *Christian Century* 98 (1981): 1095-1097. [See also his *Sins of Omission: A Primer of Moral Indifference*. Minneapolis, MN: Fortress Press, 1990.]

3307.   Fossion, André. "The Adventure of Human Suffering: An Anthropological and Theological Reflection." *Lumen Vitae* 30 (1983): 9-31.

3308.   Foster, Daniel W. "Religion and Medicine: The Physician's Perspective." *Health-Medicine and the Faith Traditions*. Edited by Martin Marty and Kenneth L. Vaux. Philadelphia, PA: Fortress Press, 1982: 245-270.

3309.   Foster, Richard. *Celebration as Discipline*. San Francisco, CA: Harper and Row, 1978.

3310.   Fotion, Nicholas. "Wickedness." *Philosophical Quarterly* 11 (1961): 323-327. [See also Nicholas Fotion's *Moral Situations*. Yellow Springs, OH: Antioch Press, 1968.]

3311.   Franck, F. "Victories and Defeats on Paper." *Creative Suffering: The Ripple of Hope*. Edited by James F. Andrews. Kansas City, MO: The National Catholic Reporter Publishing Company 1970: 39-56.

3312.   Frankl, Viktor E. *Man's Search for Himself*. New York: Washington Square Press, 1963.

3313.   ———. *The Doctor and the Soul*. London: Souvenir Press, 1969.

3314.   Fraser, Alexander Campbell. *Philosophy of Theism*. New York: AMS Press, 1979.

3315. Freund, Ernest Hans. *The Ground of Evil-Doing*. North Quincy, MA: Christopher Publishing House, 1971.

3316. Friedman, Barry W. "Spiritual Growth Through Care of the Dying." *Journal of Religion and Health* 22 (1983): 268-277. [Exposition of Kushner's theodicy, as expounded in his *When Bad Things Happen to Good People* [#1132].]

3317. Friedman, Jerome. "Christ's Descent into Hell and Redemption Through Evil: A Radical Reformation Perspective." *Archiv für Reformationsgeschichte* 76 (1985): 217-230.

3318. Fromm, Eric. *The Anatomy of Human Destructiveness*. New York: Holt, Rinehart and Winston, 1973.

3319. Furfey, Paul H. *The Respectable Murderers: Social Evil and Christian Conscience*. New York: Herder and Herder, 1966.

3320. Garbarino, James, and John K. Hershberger. "The Perspective of Evil in Understanding and Treating Child Abuse." *Journal of Religion and Health* 20 (1981): 208-217.

3321. Gaskin, John Charles Addison. *The Quest for Eternity*. New York: Penguin Books, 1984.

3322. Geisler, Norman L. *Christian Apologetics*. Grand Rapids, MI: Baker Book House, 1976. [One of the more than 30 books written by Geisler, a conservative Christian theist. One of his most recent books defends Aquinas against the unfounded current prejudice toward Thomism in evangelical thought; he also defends Aquinas against the criticisms of contemporary process theology: see his *Thomas Aquinas: An Evangelical Appraisal*. Grand Rapids, MI: Baker Book House, 1992.]

3323. Gelvin, Michael L. "The Meanings of Evil." *Philosophy Today* 27 (1983): 201-221.

3324. Gentles, Ian. *Care for the Dying and Bereaved*. Toronto, ON: Anglican Book Centre, 1982.

3325. Gibbs, John C. "Three Perspectives on Tragedy and Suffering: The Relevance of Near-Death Experience Research." *Journal of Psychology and Theology* 16 (1988): 21-33.

3326. Gibbs, Lee W. "The Mystery of Evil." *Academic Study of Religion, 1974 Proceedings*. Edited by Anne Carr. Missoula, MT: University of Montana: Scholars Press, 1974: 34-44. [Presents an overview of the theodicy problem by outlining the methodology and content of a course the author teaches on theodicy.]

3327. Gibson, A. Boyce. "Suffering and its Conquest." *World Perspectives in Philosophy, Religion and Culture*. Patna, India: Bharati Bhawan, 1968: 157-165.

3328. ———. *The Religion of Dostoevsky*. London: SCM Press, 1973.

3329. Giesbrecht, Penny. *Where is God When a Child Suffers?* Hannibal, MO: Hannibal Books, 1988.

3330. Gilbert, Paul. *Human Nature and Suffering*. Hillsdale, NJ: L. Erlbaum Associates, 1989.

3331.   Ginever, G.J. "A Perspective of Evil in Recent Religious Writings." *The Religious Dimension*. Edited by J.C. Hinchclif. Auckland: Rep Prep Ltd., 1976: 76-79.

3332.   Gooch, Paul W. "Religious Perspectives on Suffering and Evil and Peace-Experience." *Journal of Dharma* 11 (1986): 124-146. [Compares various views about suffering (resignation, return, retribution, reincarnation, and resurrection) in the religions of the world.]

3333.   Graham, James. *The Wrath of God*. New York: Dell, 1974.

3334.   Gray, Wallace. "An Encounter with Naturalism in Theology." *Communico Viatorum* 27 (1984): 47-58.

3335.   Griffin, G.A. Elmer. "Analytical Psychology and Dynamics of Human Evil: A Problematic Case in the Integration of Psychology and Theology." *Journal of Psychology and Theology* 14 (1986): 269-277. [Critiques as theoretically inadequate Jung's proposed alternative to traditional Christian theodicy.]

3336.   Grotstein, James S. "Forgery of the Soul: Psychogenesis of Evil." *Evil, Self and Culture*. Edited by Marie Coleman Nelson and Michael Eigen. New York: Human Sciences Press, 1984: 203-226.

3337.   Gruen, A. "On Evil, Psychosis and Conscience." *Review of Existential Psychology and Psychiatry* 13 (1974): 88-97.

3338.   Gunnemann, Jon. *The Moral Meaning of Revolution*. New Haven, CT: Yale University Press, 1979.

3339.   Habgood, J.S. "Medical Ethics—A Christian View." *Journal of Medical Ethics* 11 (1985): 12-13. [Conservative view that theodicy reduces to God as the great healer.]

3340.   Hagerty, Cornelius. *The Problem of Evil*. North Quincy, MA: Christopher Publishing House, 1978. [Originally published, Washington, DC: CUP, 1911.]

3341.   Hampton, Jean. "The Nature of Immorality." *Social Philosophy and Policy* 7 (1989): 22-44.

3342.   Harries, Richard. *C.S. Lewis: The Man and his God*. London: Collins/Fount, 1987.

3343.   Harrity, M. *Thoughts on Suffering, Sorrow and Death*. Huntington, IN: Our Sunday Visitor, Inc., 1973.

3344.   Harsanyi, John C. "Problems with Act-Utilitarianism and with Malevolent Preferences." *Hare and Critics*. Edited by Douglas Seanor. New York: Clarendon/Oxford, 1988: 89-99.

3345.   Hastings, Rashdall. *The Theory of Good and Evil: A Treatise of Moral Philosophy*. London: Oxford University Press, 1924. New York: Kraus, 1971.

3346.   Haught, John F. *Nature and Purpose*. Washington, DC: University Press of America, 1980.

3347.   ——. *The Cosmic Adventure: Science, Religion and the Quest for Purpose*. Ramsey, NJ: Paulist Press, 1984. [See also his *What is God? How to Think About the Divine*. New York/Mahwah, NJ: Paulist Press, 1986.]

3348. ———. "The Informed Universe and the Existence of God." *Existence of God.* Edited by John R. Jacobson and Robert Lloyd Mitchell. New York and Toronto, ON: Edwin Mellen Press, 1988: 223-244.

3349. Hayden, Robert. "Theory of Evil." *World Order* 73 (1978/1979): 23. [Poem.]

3350. Heath, Thomas R. *In Face of Anguish.* New York: Sheed and Ward, 1966.

3351. Hebblethwaite, Brian. *Evil, Suffering and Religion.* New York: Hawthorn Books, 1976. [The focus is on world religions, including the various techniques in world religions for coping with evil, both practically and theoretically.]

3352. Hefner, Philip J. "Purpose, Belonging, and Evil: Pivots of Meaning." *Belief and Ethics.* Edited by W. Widick Schroeder and Gibson Winter. Chicago, IL: Center for the Scientific Study of Religion, 1978: 57-68.

3353. Hellman, John. *Simone Weil: An Introduction to Her Thought.* Waterloo, ON: Wilfred Laurier University Press, 1982.

3354. Hempelmann, Dean L. "Is the Jungian Approach Christian? An Analysis." *Concordia Journal* 12 (1986): 161-166.

3355. Hendry, George S. "Judge Not: A Critical Test of Faith." *Theology Today* 40 (1983): 113-129.

3356. Henry, Carl F.H. *God, Revelation and Authority.* Six Volumes. Waco, TX: Word Books, 1982/1983. [One of numerous books by Carl Henry, one of evangelicalism's most prolific and influential writers.]

3357. ———. "The Stunted God of Process Theology." *Process Theology.* Edited by Ronald H. Nash. Grand Rapids, MI: Baker Book House, 1987: 359-376. Excerpt from his *God, Revelation and Authority* [#3356].]

3358. Hepburn, Ronald W. *Christianity and Paradox: Critical Studies in Twentieth Century Theology.* New York: Pegasus, 1968. [Originally published in 1958.]

3359. Herhold, Robert M. *The Promise Beyond the Pain.* Nashville, TN: Abingdon Press, 1979. [Inspirational discourse: God's sustaining love "takes care of each one of us."]

3360. Hessert, Paul. "Is 'The Living God' a Theological Category?" *The Living God.* Edited by Dow Kirkpatrick. Nashville, TN: Abingdon Press, 1971: 76-95.

3361. Hestevold, H. Scott. "Disjunctive Desert." *American Philosophical Quarterly* 20 (1983): 357-363. [Seeks to resolve the problem of justice and mercy by the doctrine of "disjunctive desert." See following entry.]

3362. ———. "Justice to Mercy." *Philosophy and Phenomenological Research* 47 (1985): 281-291.

3363. Heyns, Johan. "Disinvestment and Human Suffering: A Response [to de Villiers]." *Disinvestment and Human Suffering.* Edited by Pieter de Villiers. Pretoria: CUM Books, C.B. Bible Centre, University of South Africa, 1985.

3364. Hibbert, Christopher. *The Roots of Evil: A Social History of Crime and Punishment.* New York: Minerva, 1963, 1968.

3365. Hocutt, Max. "Must Relativists Tolerate Evil?" *Philosophy Forum* 17 (1986): 188-200. [In response to the question as to whether a relativist can condemn society's basic moral and legal standards, Hocutt argues that there is nothing to prevent a relativist from condemning as contrary to reason and contrary to personal preferences actions acknowledged to be in accord with conventional morality and law.]

3366.   Hoffman, Norbert. "The Crucified Christ and the World's Evil: Reflections on Theodicy in the Light of Atonement." Translated by Michael Waldstein. *Communio, International Catholic Review* 17 (1990): 58-67.

3367.   Holdren, Shirley, and Susan Holdren, with Candace E. Hartzler. *Why God Gave Me Pain.* Chicago, IL: Loyola University Press, 1984.

3368.   Hollon, Ellis W. "Pain, Suffering, and Christian Theodicy." *Perspectives in Religious Studies* 15 (1979): 24-32.

3369.   Hori, Ichiro. "Three Types of Redemption in Japanese Folk Religion." *Types of Redemption.* Edited by Raphael J. Zwi Werblowsky and Claas Jouco Bleeker. Leiden: E.J. Brill, 1970: 105-119.

3370.   Horrigan, James E. *Chance or Design?* New York: Philosophical Library, 1979.

3371.   Howard, Thomas. *The Achievement of C.S. Lewis.* Wheaton, IL: Harold Shaw, 1980.

3372.   Hughes, Richard A. "Bereavement and Pareschatology." *Encounter* 43 (1982): 361-375.

3373.   Hunter, James D. "Subjectivization and the New Evangelical Theodicy." *Journal for the Scientific Study of Religion* 21 (1982): 39-47.

3374.   Hyers, Conrad. "The Universe as 'Controlled Accident'." *Existence of God.* Edited by John R. Jacobson and Robert Lloyd Mitchell. New York and Toronto, ON: Edwin Mellen Press, 1988: 199-211. [See also Hyers's *The Meaning of Creation: Genesis and Modern Science.* Atlanta, GA: John Knox Press, 1984.]

3375.   Ihde, Don, and Richard M. Zaner. *Dialogues in Phenomenology.* The Hague: Nijhoff, 1975.

3376.   Israel, Martin. *The Pain That Heals.* New York: Crossroad, 1982.

3377.   Jackson, Edgar N. *The Role of Faith in the Process of Healing.* Minneapolis, MN: Winston Press, 1981.

3378.   Jaffe, Raymond. "Conservatism and the Praise of Suffering." *Ethics* 77 (1967): 254-267.

3379.   James, Susan. "The Duty to Relieve Suffering." *Ethics* 93 (1982): 4-21.

3380.   Jandv, Arthur. *Prisoners of Pain: Unlocking the Power of the Mind to End Suffering.* Garden City, NY: Anchor/Doubleday, 1980.

3381.   Jenkins, David Edward. "The Anguish of Man, the Praise of God and the Repentance of the Church." *Study Encounter* 10 (1974): 1-8.

3382.   Joad, Cyril E.M. *God and Evil.* New York: Harper and Brothers, 1943.

3383.   Johnson, B.C. *The Atheist Debater's Handbook.* Buffalo, NY: Prometheus Books, 1983. [See also Johnson's "God and the Problem of Evil," *Philosophy and Contemporary Issues.* New York: Macmillan, 1988: 135-140.]

3384. Kahler, Erich. *The True, the Good, and the Beautiful*. Columbus, OH: Ohio State University Press, 1960.

3385. Kaiser, Otto. "Living and Suffering: An Attempt at Assessing the Present Day Position of the Church." *Theologia Evangelica* 17 (1984): 12-17.

3386. Kateb, George. *Hannah Arendt, Politics, Conscience, Evil*. Totowa, NJ: Rowman and Allanheld, 1984.

3387. Katz, Jack. *Seductions of Crime: Moral and Sensual Attractions in Doing Evil*. New York: Basic Books, 1988.

3388. Kaufman, Gordon D. *The Faith of a Heretic*. Garden City, NY: Doubleday, 1961.

3389. ———. "On the Meaning of 'Act of God'." *Harvard Theological Review* 61 (1968): 175-201. [Reprinted in Kaufman's *God: The Problem*, 119-147 [#3390].]

3390. ———. "God and Evil," *Chapter 8* of his *God: The Problem*. Cambridge, MA: Harvard University Press, 1972: 171-200.

3391. ———. "Evil and Salvation: An Anthropological Approach." *Chapter 6* of *The Theological Imagination: Constructing the Concept of God*. Philadelphia, PA: Westminster Press, 1981: 157-171.

3392. ———. "Evidentialism: A Theologian's Response." *Faith and Philosophy* 6 (1989): 35-46.

3393. Kaufmann, Walter. *Critique of Religion and Philosophy*. Garden City, NY: Doubleday, 1961.

3394. Kavolis, Vytautas. "Logics of Evil as Secular Moralities." *Soundings* 68 (1985): 189-211. [In this and other essays, Kavolis distinguishes various logics of evil operative in modern secular society: the liberal, the therapeutic, the naturalistic, the technocratic, and the relational.]

3395. ———. "Civilizational Models of Evil." *Evil, Self and Culture*. Edited by Marie Coleman Nelson and Michael Eigen. New York: Human Sciences Press, 1984: 17-35.

3396. ———. "Models of Rebellion: An Essay in Civilization Analysis." *Morality of Terrorism*. Edited by David C. Rapport and Yonah Alexander. New York: Pergamon Press, 1982: 43-61. [Originally published in *Comparative Civilizations Review* 3 (1979), 13-39.]

3397. Kelly, Derek A. "The Twilight of Reason: A Critical Study of Taylor's *Good and Evil: A New Direction*" [#3658]. *Abraxas* 1 (1977): 297-303.

3398. Kelsey, Morton T. "Reply to Analytical Psychology and Human Evil." *Journal of Psychology and Theology* 14 (1986): 282-284. [Maintains that Carl Jung's work aids in understanding the Bible, God and sin.]

3399. ———. *Healing and Christianity [In Ancient Thought and Modern Times]*. New York: Harper and Row, 1973.

3400. ———. *Discernment: A Study of Ecstasy and Evil*. New York: Paulist Press, 1978.

3401. ———. *Caring: How Can We Love One Another?* New York/Ramsey: Paulist Press, 1981.

3402. ———. *Christo-Psychology*. New York: Crossroad, 1984.

3403.   Kennedy, Eugene. *The Pain of Being Human*. Chicago, IL: Thomas Moore Association, 1972. New York: Doubleday Image Books, 1974.

3404.   Kerenyi, Carl [and others]. *Evil*. Evanston, IL: Northwestern University Press, 1967.

3405.   Kim, Chung Choon. "Suffering and Hope in the Asian Context." *East Asia Journal of Theology* 18/19 (1977): 27-32.

3406.   Kim, Young Oon. "God is Now Closer." *God: The Contemporary Discussion*. Edited by Frederick Sontag and M. Darrol Bryant. New York: Rose of Sharon Press, 1982: 313-331.

3407.   Kingston, Michael J. "Suffering." *Expository Times* 94 (1983): 144-145. [Sermon on 1 Col:24-29 and Lk 9: 18-27.]

3408.   Kleinman, Arthur. *The Illness Narratives: Suffering, Healing and the Human Condition*. New York: Basic Books, 1988.

3409.   Klink, Thomas W. "How Can We Believe in a Good God in Such a World as This?" *Journal of Pastoral Care* 13 (1959): 106-109.

3410.   Klotz, John W. "The Quality of Life." *Concordia Journal* 10 (1984): 94-96. [The biblical message is that only in heaven will we attain the quality of life God intends for us.]

3411.   Kluger, Rivkah Schärf and H. Yehezkel Kluger. "Evil in Dreams: A Jungian View." *Evil: Self and Culture*. Edited by Marie Coleman Nelson and Michael Eigen. New York: Human Sciences Press, 1984: 162-169.

3412.   Kohák, Erazim. "The Person in a Personal World: An Inquiry into the Metaphysical Significance of the Tragic Sense of Life." *Independent Journal of Philosophy* (Austria) 1 (1977): 51-64. [Argues the Personalist position that we can most adequately conceive the world as personal.]

3413.   Kohn, Jacob. *Evolution as Revelation*. New York: Philosophical Library, 1963. [See also Kohn, "God and the Reality of Evil," *Personalist* 33 (1952), 117-130.]

3414.   Kolenda, Konstantin. *Religion Without God*. Buffalo, NY: Prometheus Books, 1976.

3415.   Kolenkow, Anitra Bingham. "Beyond Miracles, Suffering, and Eschatology." *Society of Biblical Literature*, 1973 Seminar Papers. Edited by George W. MacRae. New York: Pergamon Press, 1982: 155-202. [Focuses on the Gospel of Mark.]

3416.   Kollar, Nathan R. *Songs of Suffering*. Minneapolis, MN: Winston Press, 1982. [Inspirational guide for sufferers. See also Kollar's chapter, "Death, Suffering and Religion," *Selected Proceedings on the National Conference: Forum for Death Education and Counselling*. Edited by E. Zimmer and S. Steele. Lexington, MA: Ginn Publishing, 1979, 119-127.]

3417.   Kolnai, Aurel. "The Thematic Primacy of Moral Evil." *Philosophy Quarterly* 6 (1956): 27-42.

3418.   Kosicki, George W. *The Good News of Suffering*. Collegeville, MN: Liturgical Press, 1981.

3419. Kozielecki, Józef. "Suffering and Human Values." *Dialectics and Humanism* 4 (1978): 115-127.

3420. Krauss, Pesach, and Morrie Goldfischer. *Why Me? Coping with Grief, Loss, and Change.* New York: Bantam Books, 1988.

3421. Lacomara, A. *The Language of the Cross.* Chicago, IL: Franciscan Herald Press, 1977.

3422. Lal Pandit, M. "What is Evil?" *The Living Word* 81 (1975): 451-465, and *The Living Word* 82 (1976): 33-56.

3423. Lambert, Frank L. "The Ontology of Evil." *Zygon, Journal of Religion and Science* 3 (1968): 116-128. [As a professional chemist, Lambert describes the natural equilbrium of the world which, when upset, results in evil. Basic statistical thermodydamics describes the natural properties of ordering and disordering in all inanimate arrangements of matter and energy. Organic life seeks to maintain a "metastablic" equilibrium, a state of tension between randomness and order. Evil results in the tipping of the scales of this precarious unstable balance.]

3424. Lamont, Corliss. *The Philosophy of Humanism.* New York: Ungar, 1982.

3425. Lansing, John S. *Evil in the Morning of the World: Phenomenological Approaches to a Balinese Community.* Ann Arbor, MI: University of Michigan Press, 1974.

3426. Lantero, Erminie Huntress. "The Problem of Suffering." *Pastoral Psychology* 3 (1953): 32-38.

3427. Lavelle, Louis. *Evil and Suffering.* New York: Macmillan, 1963.

3428. Lee, Patrick. "Permanence of the Ten Commandments." *Theological Studies* 42 (1981): 422-443.

3429. Legargneur, François-H. "Sickness in a Christian Anthropology." *The Mystery of Suffering and Death.* Edited by Michael J. Taylor. Garden City, NY: Image Books, 1974: 91-100. [Excerpt from his *Lord of the Absurd.* New York: Herder and Herder, 1966, 149-157.]

3430. Lerner, Melvin J. *The Belief in a Just World.* New York: Plenum Press, 1980.

3431. Leslie, John. *Universes.* New York: Routledge, 1989.

3432. Lester, Andrew D. "Ministry with Children in Crisis." *When Children Suffer.* Edited by Andrew D. Webster. Philadelphia, PA: Westminster Press, 1987. [The book contains 18 chapters on various aspects of the problem of the suffering of children: the bereaved child, the terminally ill child, the chronically ill child, the abused child, the disabled child, etc.]

3433. Levine, Hillel. "On the Debanalization of Evil." *Sociology and Human Destiny.* Edited by Gregory Baum. New York: Seabury, 1980: 1-26.

3434. Lewis, Clive Staples. *The Great Divorce.* New York: Macmillan, 1946, 1963. [Originally published in 1945].

3435. ———. *The Problem of Pain.* New York: Macmillan, 1943, 1977. [Lewis's major statement on theodicy, in conjunction with *A Grief Observed*, the latter however, written after the death of his wife, Joy, and contains a reassessment of his views on theodicy.]

3436. ———. *Miracles: A Preliminary Study.* New York: Macmillan, 1947, 1960.

3437. ———. *Mere Christianity.* New York: Macmillan, 1952. [Revised and enlarged edition of three of his books: *The Case for Christianity*, 1942; *Christian Behaviour*, 1943; and *Beyond Personality*, 1944.]

3438. ———. *A Grief Observed.* New York: Bantam Books, 1963. [Published under the pseudonym of N.W. Clerk in 1961.]

3439. ———. *Christian Reflections.* Edited by Walter Hooper. Grand Rapids, MI: Eerdmans, 1967.

3440. ———. *God of the Docks: Essays in Theology and Ethics.* Originally published as *Undeceptions.* Edited by Walter Hooper. Grand Rapids, MI: Eerdmans, 1970.

3441. Lewis, Edwin. "Creative Conflict." *Religion in Life* 21 (1952): 390-400.

3442. Liderbach, Daniel. *The Theology of Grace.* New York and Toronto, ON: Edwin Mellen Press, 1983.

3443. ———. *The Numinous Universe.* New York/Mahwah, NJ: Paulist Press, 1989.

3444. ———. *Why Do We Suffer? New Ways of Understanding.* New York/Mahwah, NJ: Paulist Press, 1992.

3445. Linders, Robert H. "Theodicy: Dogma and Experience." *Theology Today* 35 (1978): 196-201. [Follow-up of his D.Min.Thesis. He explores the theoretical dimensions of theodicy and relates it to the psychological and homiletical dimensions of pastoral ministry. His conclusion is that the theoretical teachings of the church are reflected in ordinary people. Dogma reflects experience, and *vice versa.*]

3446. Little, Patricia. *Simone Weil.* London: Cutler and Grant, 1973. Supplement, 1980. [Contains a complete bibliography of the publications of Simone Weil and secondary literature to 1980.]

3447. Loades, Ann L. "Sacrifice: A Problem for Theology." *Images of Belief.* Edited by D. Jasper. London: Macmillan, and New York: St. Martin's Press, 1984.

3448. ———. "Eucharistic Sacrifice: Simone Weil's Use of a Liturgical Metaphor." *Religion and Literature* 17 (1985).

3449. Loewy, Erich H. "Suffering, Moral Worth, and Medical Ethics: A New Beginning." *Bridges* 1 (1989): 103-117.

3450. ———. "Obligations, Communities, and Suffering: Problems of Community Seen in a New Light." *Bridges* 2 (1990): 1-16.

3451. Lowe, Walter James. "Evil and the Unconscious: A Freudian Exploration." *Soundings* 63 (1980): 7-35.

3452. ———. "Psychoanalysis as an Archaeology of the History of Suffering." *The Challenge of Psychology of Faith.* Edited by Steven Kepnes and David Tracy. Edinburgh: T&T Clark, 1982: 3-9.

3453. ———. "Innocence and Experience." *Evil, Self and Culture.* Edited by Marie Coleman Nelson and Michael Eigen. New York: Human Sciences Press, 1984: 239-267.

3454. ———. "Dangerous Supplement/Dangerous Memory: Sketches for a History of the Postmodern." *Thought* 61 (1986): 34-55.

3455. Luetkehoelter, Gottlieb. "Hope for the Suffering." *Lwf Documentation* 14 (1984): 40-44.

3456. Luke, Helen. "Suffering." *Parabola* 8 (1983): 66-70. [Reference to Carl Jung. Luke argues that suffering breaks through the personal and exposes us to pain and darkness of life. Yet, it opens the way to the ultimate state of passion beyond all passion, the state of being filled by the wholeness of God.]

3457. Lull, Timothy F. "God and Suffering: A Fragment." *Dialog* 25 (1986): 93-96. [Recommends a renewed understanding of Christianity, rather than reformulating our doctrine of God to resolve the theodicy issue.]

3458. Lunman, Reginald S. "Belief in God and the Problem of Suffering." *Evangelical Quarterly* 57 (1985): 327-348.

3459. Lynch, Joe. "A Legacy of Suffering and Hope: The Victims of the Hiroshima and Nagasakai Bomb- ings." *Sojourners* 11 (1982): 35-37.

3460. MacFarlane, Alan. "The Root of All Evil." *The Anthropology of Evil.* Edited by David Parkin. Oxford: Blackwell, 1985: 57-76.

3461. MacNutt, Francis. *Healing.* Indianapolis, IN: Ave Maria Press, 1974.

3462. Maes, John L. *Suffering. A Caregiver's Guide.* Nashville, TN: Abingdon Press, 1990. [Psychologically informed, anecdotal and inspirational guide to surviving suffering by healing grace and growth.]

3463. Mallow, Vernon R. *The Demonic: A Selected Theological Study: An Examination into the Theology of Edwin Lewis, Karl Barth, and Paul Tillich.* Lanham, MD: University Press of America, 1983.

3464. Manning, Clare. "Faith as a Challenge: Personal Reflections." *African Ecclesiastical Review* 24 (1982): 41-44.

3465. Martin, James Alfred. *Fact, Fiction, and Faith.* Oxford: Oxford University Press, 1960.

3466. ———. *Suffering Man, Loving God.* Glasgow: Saint Andrew's Press, 1969. [Revised edition, London: Fount Paperbacks, 1979.]

3467. Marty, William R. "The Search for Realism in Politics and Ethics: Reflections by a Political Scientist on a Christian Perspective." *Logos* 1 (1980): 93-124.

3468. Masani, P.R. "The Thermodynamic and Phylogenetic Foundations of Human Wickedness." *Zygon, Journal of Religion and Science* 20 (1985): 283-320. [Explicates the theological concept, "sinful," in thermodynamic and phylogenic terms in order to establish the proposition that "Homo sapiens is a sinful species." The theological concept of the "fall of man" likewise is shown to be an amalgam of two of thermodynamics and phylogenetics: *Fall I* affects all life; *Fall II*, "original sin," affects only humans.]

3469.   Matsuo, Mikizō. "Recollection of Christian Suffering During the National Crisis." Translated by D. Drummond. *Japan Christian Quarterly* 49 (1983): 134-137.

3470.   Mauriac, François. *Anguish and Joy of the Christian Life*. Wilkes-Barre, PA: Dimension Books, 1964.

3471.   May, William F. *The Patients' Ordeal*. Bloomington, IN: Indiana University Press, 1991.

3472.   McCandless, J. Baradarah. "Role of Theological Understandings in the Pursuit of Pain." *Journal of Pastoral Counselling* 10 (1975): 5-20.

3473.   ——. "Dealing Creatively with Suffering: The Living Death." *Journal of Religion and Health* 17 (1978): 19-30.

3474.   McCarthy, E. Doyle. "The Sources of Human Destructiveness: Ernest Becker's Theory of Human Nature." *Thought* 56 (1981): 44-57.

3475.   McCloskey, Pat. *When You are Angry at God*. New York/Mahwah, NJ: Paulist Press, 1987.

3476.   McCormick, Richard A. *Ambiguity in Moral Choice*. Milwaukee, WI: Marquette University Press, 1973.

3477.   ——. *Doing Evil to Achieve Good*. Chicago, IL: Loyola University Press, 1978.

3478.   ——. "Notes on Moral Theology: 1982." *Theological Studies* 44 (1983): 71-122.

3479.   McCurdy, David B. "Helping Parishioners Confront Suffering." *Christian Ministry* 17 (1986): 23-25.

3480.   McFarland, Dorothy T. *Simone Weil*. New York: Frederick Ungar Publishing Co., 1983.

3481.   McGill, Arthur C. "Structures of Inhumanity." *Disguises of the Demonic*. Edited by A. Olson. New York: Association Press, 1975: 116-133.

3482.   ——. "The Religious Aspects of Medicine." *Medicine and Religion: Strategies of Care*. Edited by Donald W. Shriver, Jr. Pittsburgh, PA: University of Pittsburgh Press, 1980: 148-153.

3483.   McGlynn, James V., and Paul Mary Farley. *A Metaphysics of Being and God*. Englewood Cliffs, NJ: Prentice-Hall, 1966.

3484.   Mechling, Jay. "Myth and Mediation: Peter Berger's and John Neuhaus' Theodicy for Modern America." *Soundings* 62 (1979): 338-368. [Contains Peter Berger's bibliography.]

3485.   Meier, Levi. "Guilt, Suffering and Death: The Impact and the Challenge." *Journal of Psychology and Judaism* 11 (1987): 72-137.

3486.   Melchert, Charles F. "Learning from Suffering, Silence, and Death." *Religious Education* 84 (1989): 37-47.

3487.   Michalson, Carl. "Faith for the Crisis of Suffering." *Religion in Life* 27 (1958): 401-413. [*Chapter 6* of his *Faith for Personal Crises*. New York: Charles Scribner's Sons, 1958.]

3488.   Mickelson, Alvera. "Why Did God Let it Happen? As I Began to Recover, I Pondered the Obsession of Visitors with this Question." *Christianity Today* 28

(1984): 22-24. [Rejects the view that God permits evil for the possibility of greater goods. Much of traditional theodicy impedes our openness to God's healing power.]

3489. Micklem, Nathaniel. *Christian Thinking Today*. London: Duckworth, 1967. [See also his *The Doctrine of Our Redemption*. Nashville, TN: Abingdon-Cokesbury Press, 1948; and *Religion*. Westport, CT: Greenwood Press, 1973.]

3490. ———. *Faith and Reason*. London: Duckworth, 1963. [The chapter on providence, *Chapter 8*, proposes a theodicy which supports the traditional *"privation of good"* theory.]

3491. Migliore, Daniel L. *The Power of God*. Philadelphia, PA: Westminster Press, 1983.

3492. Miller, Eddie L. *God and Reason*. New York: Macmillan, 1972.

3493. Miller, Randolph C. "The Problem of Evil and Religious Education." *Religious Education* 84 (1989): 5-15.

3492. Mindrum, Craig. "Over the Border: The Risks of Understanding Evil." *Criterion* 29 (1990): 21-25.

3495. Mitchell, Basil. "The University Discussion." *New Essays in Philosophical Theology*. Edited by Antony Flew and Alasdair MacIntyre. New York: Macmillan, 1955.

3496. Modahl, Bruce K. "All Things Good and Bad." *Currents in Theology and Missions* 14 (1987): 446-449.

3497. Moede, Gerald F. "God's Power and Our Weakness." *God's Power and our Weakness*. Edited by the Task Force of Persons with Disabilities. Princeton, NJ: Consultation on Church Union, 1982. [In response to a severe case of polio, Moede "discovered" that God does not will particular events such as this, but works through evils for good ends.]

3498. Moore, Barrington. *Reflections on the Causes of Human Misery and Upon Certain Proposals to Eliminate Them*. Boston, MA: Beacon Press, 1969.

3499. Moreno, Antonio. *Jung, Gods, and Modern Man*. London: University of Notre Dame Press, 1970. [Contains bibliography of relevant items by Freud, Jung, Frankl, Fromm, etc.]

3500. Morgan, Barbara Spofford. *Skeptic's Search for God*. New York: Harper and Brothers, 1947. [Introduction by Paul Tillich. Relevant chapters include "The Love of God and Suffering," "Deep Sorrow and Deep Joy," and etc. Morgan argues that fellowship with a suffering God is the answer to the mystery of human suffering.]

3501. Moss, David M. "Judicial Trauma-Juridical Travesty: A Personal Encounter with Evil." *Evil, Self and Culture*. Edited by Marie Coleman Nelson and Michael Eigen. New York: Human Sciences Press, 1984: 181-199.

3502. Mott, Stephen C. "Biblical Faith and the Reality of Social Evil." *Christian Scholar's Review* 10 (1980): 225-240.

3503.   Mowrer, O. Hobart. "A Psychologist's View of Good and Evil and the Church of the Future." *Science and Human Values in the 21st Century*. Edited by Ralph W. Burhoe. Philadelphia, PA: Westminster Press, 1971: 99-115. [See also his earlier, "Sin, the Lesser of Two Evils," *American Psychologist* 15 (1961), 301-304; and his *The Crisis in Psychiatry and Religion*. Princeton, NJ: Van Nostrand, 1962; also his *Morality and Mental Health*. Chicago, IL: Rand-McNally, 1967.]

3504.   ——. "The Problem of Good and Evil Empirically Considered, with Reference to Psychological and Social Adjustment." *Zygon, Journal of Religion and Science* 4 (1969): 301-314. [Human beings inherit good and evil tendencies and we need small support groups to help us in the pursuit of good.]

3505.   Mueller, Gustav E. "Religious Dialectic." *Hibbert Journal* 64 (1966): 65-67.

3506.   Mullen, Peter. "Facing Up to Evil." *Modern Churchman* 22 (1978/1979): 32-37.

3507.   ——. "Religion Without Excuses." *Modern Churchman* 24 (1981): 72-83.

3508.   Murdock, Iris. "On 'God' and 'Good'." *Revisions: Changing Perspectives in Moral Philosophy*. Edited by Stanley Hauerwas and Alasdair MacIntyre. Notre Dame, IN: University of Notre Dame Press, 1983: 68-91.

3509.   Murphree, Jon Tal. *When God Says You're OK*. Downers Grove, IN: Inter-Varsity Press, 1976.

3510.   ——. *A Loving God and a Suffering World: A New Look at an Old Problem*. Downers Grove, IN: InterVarsity Press, 1981. [See also the brief version of this: "A Loving God and a Suffering World: A New Look at an Old Problem." *Reformed Review* 40 (1986), 140.]

3511.   Muto, Susan. "Reading the Symbolic Text: Some Reflections on Interpretation." *Humanitas* 8 (1972): 169-191. [Discussion of Paul Ricoeur's hermeneutics in *Symbolism of Evil* [#3577].]

3512.   Myers, David G. "A Psychology of Evil: Since Sin is Collective as Well as Personal, It Requires a Collective as Well as a Personal Response." *Other Side* 127 (1982): 28-30.

3513.   Nagel, Thomas. "Death." *Noûs* 4 (1970): 73-80.

3514.   Nash, Ronald H. *The Concept of God*. Grand Rapids, MI: Eerdmans, 1983.

3515.   Neuleib, Janice Witherspoon. "The Empty Face of Evil: The Refiner's Fire Myth." *Christianity Today* 19 (1975): 14-16. [Discussion of C.S. Lewis's retelling of the myth of Cupid and Psyche in *Till We Have Faces*, focusing on the face of evil—its definition and habituation.]

3516.   Neville, Mary Gemma. "Thy Will Be Done." *Preaching in Today's World*. Compiled by James C. Barry. Nashville, TN: Broadman Press, 1984: 172-178.

3517.   Neville, Robert C. "Suffering, Guilt and Responsibility." *Journal of Dharma* 2 (1977): 248-259. [Comparison of suffering in Christianity and Hinduism and Buddhism.]

3518.   Newing, Edward. "Sermon Preached in Trinity Theological College Chapel: 'Transformation Through Suffering'." *East Asian Journal of Theology* 1 (1983): 89-94.

3519. Noel, Claude. "The Church Faces a Suffering World." *Serving Our Generation*. Edited by Waldron Scott. Colorado Springs, CO: World Evangelical Fellowship, 1980: 175-185.

3520. Novak, Michael. *The Experience of Nothingness*. New York: Harper and Row, 1971.

3521. ———. *Ascent of the Mountain: Flight of the Dove*. New York: Harper and Row, 1971.

3522. O'Keefe, Mark. *What Are They Saying About Social Sin?* New York/Mahwah, NJ: Paulist Press, 1990.

3523. Oakes, Robert. "The Wrath of God." *International Journal for Philosophy of Religion* 21 (1990): 129-140. [Rejects the dominant theological view which denies wrath in God.]

3524. Oates, Wayne E. "Forms of Grief—Diagnosis, Meaning, and Treatment." *The Meaning of Suffering*. Edited by Flavian Dougherty. New York: Human Sciences Press, 1982: 196-231.

3525. Oates, Wayne E., and Charles Oates. *People in Pain: Guidelines for Pastoral Care*. Philadelphia, PA: Westminster Press, 1985. [Discussion of the spiritual and physical nature of pain, the anatomy and neurochemistry of pain, and the treatment of pain. The authors, a pastor and a neurologist, also discuss the psychological dimension of pain and strategies for its overcoming. See the review article by Ronald R. Ropp, "People in Pain" [#2478].]

3526. Ollenburger, Ben C. "Suffering and Hope: The Story Behind the Book." *Theology Today* 44 (1987): 350-359. [Critical discussion of Johan Christiaan Beker's *Suffering and Hope* [#1482].]

3527. Olson, Mark. "Horrors to Heaven." *Other Side* 23 (1987): 34-37.

3528. Omoregbe, Joseph. "The Problem of Evil in the World." *West African Religions* 19 (1980): 37-45. [Discusses philosophical solutions to theodicy: Stoicism, Plotinus and Augustine, Leibniz and Spinoza, and Teilhard de Chardin. He discusses also religious explanations: Hinduism, Buddhism, Islam and Traditional African Religion, Judaism and Christianity.]

3529. Ophir, Adi. "Beyond Good-Evil: A Plea for a Hermeneutic Ethics." *Philosophical Forum* 21 (1989-1990): 94-121.

3530. Otey, W. Rush. "A Preacher's Problems with the Problem of Evil." *Journal for Preachers* 12 (1989): 19-26.

3531. Packer, James I. *Knowing God*. London: Hodder and Stoughton, 1973.

3532. ———. "Poor Health May Be the Best Remedy: But if You've Got a Headache, Thank God for Aspirin." *Christianity Today* 26 (1982): 14-16. [Conservative theological response to theodicy.]

3533. Pailin, David. *Groundwork for Philosophy of Religion*. London: Epworth Press, 1986. [*Chapter 10* contains a brief discussion of divine goodness and the problem of evil.]

3534. ———. *God and the Processes of Reality: Foundations for a Credible Theism*. London: Routledge, 1989.

3535.   Palmer, George H. *The Nature of Goodness*. Boston, MA: Houghton, 1903. Reprinted by Ann Arbor, MI: University Microfilms, 1967.

3536.   Paluch, Stanley. "A Cosmomorphic Utopia." *Personalist* 54 (1973): 89-91.

3537.   Panken, Shirley. *The Joy of Suffering: Psychoanalytic Theory and Therapy of Masochism*. New York: J. Aronson, 1973.

3538.   Pargament, Kenneth I., and June Hahn. "God and the Just World: Causal and Coping Attributions to God in Health Situations." *Journal for the Scientific Study of Religion* 25 (1986): 193-207. [One of many studies about the relevance of faith for a person's health and for coping with evil and suffering.]

3539.   Parkin, David. "Introduction." *The Anthropology of Evil*. Edited by David Parkin. Oxford: Blackwell, 1985: 1-25. [Contains several essays on various anthropological understandings of evil in different cultures. Some of the more relevant chapters have been listed in this present bibliography.]

3540.   Paton, Alan. "Why Suffering?" *Creative Suffering: The Ripple of Hope*. Edited by James F. Andrews. Kansas City, MO: The National Catholic Reporter Publishing Company, 1970: 13-24.

3541.   Pattison, E. Mansell. "Psychoanalysis and the Concept of Evil." *Evil, Self and Culture*. Edited by Marie Coleman Nelson and Michael Eigen. New York: Human Sciences Press, 1984: 61-88.

3542.   Pechauer, Patricia. "What Does God Require?" *International Review of Missions* 73 (1984): 324-327.

3543.   Peel, Robert. *Spiritual Healing in a Scientific Age*. New York: Harper and Row, 1987.

3544.   Peeters, Guido. "Good and Evil as Softwares of the Brain: On Psychological 'Immediates' Underlying the Metaphysical 'Ultimates'." *Ultimate Reality* 9 (1986): 210-231.

3545.   Pellauer, David. "The Significance of the Text in Ricoeur's Hermeneutic Theory." *Studies in the Philosophy of Paul Ricoeur*. Edited by Charles E. Reagan. Athens, OH: Ohio University Press: 97-114.

3546.   Pelletier, Kenneth R. *Mind as Healer, Mind as Slayer: A Holistic Approach to Preventing Stress Disorders*. New York: Delacarte Press, 1977.

3547.   Peterfreund, Stuart. "Criticism and Metahistory." *Journal of Thought* 17 (1982): 68-84. [Argues that there is a "latent theodicy" which is more basic than intellectual constructs. Critical thought, whether it be scientific or literary, possesses a metahistorical dimension that exists prior to any such structuring device.]

3548.   Peters, Karl E. "Evolutionary Biology and the Problem of Evil." *Zygon, Journal of Religion and Science* 23 (1988): 383-479.

3549.   Petrie, Asenath. *Individuality in Pain and Suffering*. Chicago, IL: University of Chicago Press, 1978.

3550.   Phifer, Kenneth. "Why Me? Why Now?" *Religious Humanism* 19 (1985): 40-45. [See also his "Postscript," *Reason and Religion*. Edited by Stuart Brown. Ithaca, NY: Cornell University Press, 1977, 134-139. Phifer presents a humanistic perspective on suffering: we must forge meaning out of suffering and chaos by cultivating laughter and love.]

3551. Phillips, Leon B., Jr. "Simone Weil and the Concept of Suffering." *Encounter* 39 (1978): 33-38. [Discusses Weil's stoic approach to suffering, maintaining hope that God will reappear, as in the case of Job.]

3552. ———. "Simone Weil: A Stranger Among Her Own." *Encounter* 43 (1982): 205-217.

3553. Philp, H.L. *Jung and the Problem of Evil*. London: Rockcliff, 1958. [The book was written in close contact with Jung, and includes various questions to and answers from Jung.]

3554. Pickering, W.S.F. "Theodicy and Social Theory: An Exploration of the Limits of Collaboration between Sociologist and Theologian." *Sociology and Theology: Alliance and Conflict*. Edited by David Martin, John Orme Mills, and W.S.F. Pickering. New York: St. Martin's Press, 1980: 59-79.

3555. Pink, Arthur. *The Sovereignty of God*. London: Banner of Truth Trust, 1960.

3556. Piper, Otto. "Power of Evil." *Christianity Today* 3 (1959): 3-6.

3557. Piscitelli, Emil J. "Paul Ricoeur's Philosophy of Religious Symbol: A Critique and Dialectical Transposition." *Ultimate Reality and Meaning* 3 (1980): 275-313.

3558. Pocock, David. "Unruly Evil." *The Anthropology of Evil*. Edited by David Parkin. Oxford; Blackwell, 1985: 42-56.

3559. Pojman, Louis P. *Philosophy of Religion*. Belmont, CA: Wadsworth, 1987.

3560. Polkinghorne, John. "Evil." [*Chapter 4* of his *Science and Providence: God's Interaction with the World*. Boston, MA: New Science Library, 1989.]

3561. Poulose, Mar Poulose. "Witnessing to Life in the Midst of Death—A Reluctant Critique on the Life of the Church." *Indian Journal of Theology* 31 (1982): 96-102.

3562. Powell, Jouett Lynn. "The Problem of Evil: Introduction to Formal and Material Elements in the Study of Religion." *Academic Study of Religion: 1974 Proceedings*. Edited by Anne Carr. University of Montana, MT: Scholars Press, 1974: 2-14.

3563. Prasad, Rajendra. "Suffering, Morality and Society." *Indian Philosophical Quarterly* 10 (1983): 161-171. [Argues that in a societal context, all suffering is not evil, as is too often assumed. There are, for examples, reasons which morally justify suffering.]

3564. ———. "Man and Man's God: A Timeless Dialogue." *Indian Philosophical Quarterly* 12 (1985): 113-142.

3565. Prest, A. Patrick L., Jr. "May I Knock on the Door of Heaven?" *St. Luke's Journal of Theology* 19 (1975): 51-66. [Interviews with dying patients about their desire for death to end their pain.]

3566. Priebbenow, C.R. "God's Corrective Use of Evil." *Lutheran Theological Journal* 15 (1981): 45-52.

3567. Proctor, Samuel D. "How to Believe if the Worst Should Come." *Journal of Religious Thought* 40 (1983): 34-44.

3568. Purtill, Richard L. *Reason to Believe*. Grand Rapids, MI: Eerdmans, 1974.

3569.   ——. *Thinking About Religion*. Englewood Cliffs, NJ: Prentice-Hall, 1978.

3570.   ——. *C.S. Lewis's Case for the Christian Faith*. New York: Harper and Row, 1981. [Contains extensive bibliography of the 40 C.S. Lewis books still in print, and a selected list of secondary writings. See also Purtill's *Lord of the Elves and Eldils: Fantasy and Philosophy in C.S. Lewis and J.R.R. Tolkien*. Grand Rapids, MI: Zondervan, 1974.]

3571.   Putman, Caroline Canfield. "The Mode of Existence of Beauty: A Thomistic or a Kantian Interpretation?" *Ancients and Moderns*. Edited by John K. Ryan. Washington, DC: The Catholic University of America Press, 1970: 223-241.

3572.   Rayan, Samuel. "The Justice of God." *Living Theology in Asia*. Edited by J. England. Maryknoll, NY: Orbis Books, 1981: 211-220.

3573.   Reich, Warren T. "Speaking of Suffering: A Moral Account of Compassion." *Soundings* 72 (1989): 83-108.

3574.   Rheubottom, David. "The Seed of Evil Within." *The Anthropology of Evil*. Edited by David Parkin. Oxford: Blackwell, 1985: 77-91.

3575.   Richardson, Herbert W. "Varieties of Suffering." *Creative Suffering: The Ripple of Hope*. Edited by James F. Andrews. Kansas City, MO: The National Catholic Reporter Publishing Company, 1970: 107-122.

3576.   Richmond, Kent D. *Preaching to Sufferers: God and the Problem of Pain*. Nashville, TN: Abingdon Press, 1988.

3577.   Ricoeur, Paul. "The Hermeneutics of Symbols and Philosophical Reflection." *International Philosophical Quarterly* 2 (1962): 191-218. [Summary of Ricoeur's *Symbolism of Evil*. (Ricoeur's *magnum opus*, *Philosophie de la volonté*, has been published in English by three different publishers, using three different translators: the English volumes are *The Voluntary and the Involuntary*. Evanston, IL: Northwestern University Press, 1966; *Fallible Man*. Chicago, IL: Renery, 1965; and *Symbolism of Evil*. New York: Harper and Row, 1967).]

3578.   ——. "From Existentialism to the Philosophy of Language." *Philosophy Today* 17 (1973): 88-96.

3579.   ——. *The Conflict of Interpretations*. Evanston, IL: Northwestern University Press, 1974. [Argues against the classical Augustinian theodicy. He maintains that it fails because of its view of the world as ethically ordered. Yet Hick's alternative theodicy fails as an ethical vision of the world.]

3580.   ——. "Evil, A Challenge to Philosophy and Theology." *Journal of the American Academy of Religion* 53 (1985): 635-648.

3581.   Riddle, Oscar. "The Emergence of Good and Evil." *Zygon, Journal of Religion and Science* 2 (1967): 34-42.

3582.   Riordan, Brendan P. "Anger at God." *Anger*. Edited by Brendan P. Riordan. Whitinsville, MA: Affirmation Books, 1985: 100-115. [Tenth Psychotheological Symposium of the House of Ministry, International Therapeutic Center for Clergy and Religious in Boston, MA.]

3583.   Ro, Chung Hyun. "Suffering and Hope: An Evaluation of the Seoul Theological Consultation, 1979." *Reformed World* 31 (1980): 30-36.

3584. Robbins, Jerry K. "God, Our Efforts, and Evil." *Currents in Theology and Mission* 16 (1989): 85-94. [Reviews the theodicies of C.S. Lewis, Harod Kushner, and Elie Wiesel. He argues that evil is being overcome by good.]

3585. ———. "A Pastoral Approach to Evil." *Theology Today* 45 (1988): 488-495. [Argues that actions ("compassionate support") on behalf of the sufferer are appropriate both for the practical and theoretical problems of evil.]

3586. Roberts, David E. *The Grandeur and Misery of Man.* New York: Oxford University Press, 1955. [*Chapter 4*, "Freedom and Evil," 85-103.]

3587. Roberts, J. Deotis. "A Christian Response to Evil and Suffering." *Religious Education* 84 (1989): 68-76. [Maintains that Christian humanism holds the view that we can transform the evil in the world.]

3588. ———. "Faith in God Confronts Collective Evils." *The Search for Faith and Justice in the Twentieth Century.* Edited by G. James. New York: Paragon House, 1987: 15-27.

3589. Roberts, Robert C. "Compassion." *The Christian Century* 100 (1983): 14-16.

3590. Rodd, Cyril. "The Problem of Suffering—A Dialogue." *Expository Times* 83 (1972): 342-344.

3591. Roderey, Nicholas. *The Way of Power.* New York: Philosophical Library, 1969. [The section on suffering maintains that all suffering has its root in the lack of power, the three faces of which are *pain, grief and failure.* There are three remedies: *power, contention and purpose.*]

3592. Rodgers, Jack L. "Is God a Teddy Bear? Images of God." *The Spiritual Needs of Children.* Edited by Judith Allen Shelly. Downers Grove, IL: InterVarsity Press, 1982: 99-107. [See also Judith Allen Shelly's *Spiritual Dimensions of Health Care.* Downers Grove, IL: InterVarstity Press, 1983.]

3593. Romanell, Patrick. "Some Sobering Reflections on the Human Situation." *Humanitas* (Mexico) 21 (1980): 41-50. [Lists 90 short propositions, ranging in length from a sentence to several sentences. He includes reference to "the problem of good."]

3594. Rosik, Christopher H. "The Psychohermeneutics of Life: Contemplative Reflections on Suffering and Psychotherapy." *Journal of Psychology and Christianity* 9 (1990): 27-36.

3595. Rule, Andrew. "Providence and Preservation." *Basic Christian Doctrines: Contemporary Evangelical Thought.* Edited by Carl F.H. Henry. New York: Holt, Rinehart and Winston, 1962.

3596. Ruse, Michael. "Response to Williams: Selfishness is Not Enough." *Zygon, Journal of Religion and Science* 23 (1988): 413-416. [Response to George Williams, "Huxley's Evolution and Ethics in Sociobiological Perspective" [#3718].]

3597. Rust, Eric Charles. *Religion, Revelation and Reason.* Macon, GA: Mercer University Press, 1981.

3598. Sanders, Steven, and David Cheney. *The Meaning of Life: Questions, Answers and Analysis.* Englewood Cliffs, NJ: Prentice-Hall, 1980.

3599. Sapp, Stephen. "... As the Sparks Fly Upward." *Journal of Religion and Health* 16 (1977): 44-51. [Argues that life is a continuum of suffering and struggle.]

3600. Saylor, Dennis E. "Suffering Saints: the Problem of Evil Re-Examined." *American Protestant Hospital Association Bulletin* 44 (1980): 74-77. [Argues the conservative view that suffering is the result of "the fall," and that God will either intervene miraculously to end our suffering or give us the means to cope with it.]

3601. Schaeffer, Edith. *Affliction*. Old Tappan, NJ: F.H. Revell Co., 1978.

3602. Schemmer, Kenneth E. *Between Faith and Tears*. Nashville, TN: Thomas Nelson Publishers, 1981.

3603. Schiffers, Norbert. "Guilt and Moral Evil in Light of the Study of Behavior." *Moral Evil Under Challenge*. Edited by Johannes Baptist Metz. New York: Herder and Herder, 1970: 56-80.

3604. ———. "Suffering in History." *New Questions on God*. Edited by Johannes Baptist Metz. New York: Herder and Herder, 1972: 38-47.

3605. Schilling, Harold. *The New Consciousness in Science and Religion*. Philadelphia, PA: Pilgrim Press, 1973.

3606. Schmidt, Stephen A. "The Sufferer's Experience: A Journey Through Illness." *Second Option* 13 (1990): 91-108.

3607. Schmitt, Raymond F. "Suffering and Faith." *Journal of Religion and Health* 18 (1979): 263-275.

3608. ———. "Suffering and Wisdom." *Journal of Religion and Health* 20 (1981): 108-123.

3609. Schnackenberg, G. "The Heavenly Feast (Simone Weil: 1909-1943)." *The New Yorker* (September 17, 1984).

3610. Schuchardt, Erika. *Why is This Happening to Me? Guidance and Hope for Those Who Suffer*. Philadelphia, PA: Fortress Press, 1989.

3611. Schwarz, Hans. *Our Cosmic Journey*. Minneapolis, MN: Augsburg Publishing House, 1979. [Contains chapters on theodicy, providence and miracles.]

3612. Schweiker, William, and Per M. Anderson. *Worldviews and Warrants: Plurality and Authority in Theology*. Lanham, MD: University Press of America, 1987.

3613. Seaborg, Glenn T. "The Pain of Having Unused Answers." *Creative Suffering: The Ripple of Hope*. Edited by James F. Andrews. Kansas City, MO: The National Catholic Reporter Publishing Company, 1970: 57-70.

3614. Segal, Robert A. "A Jungian View of Evil." *Zygon, Journal of Religion and Science* 20 (1985): 83-89. [Critical analysis of John Sanford's critique and use of Carl Jung in understanding evil and the theodicy issue. See Sanford's *Evil: The Shadow Side of Reality* [#2996]. Segal argues that both Jung and Sanford focus on moral evils, ignoring physical evils. Yet even moral evils exceed the bounds of psychology: as social scientists, Sanford and Jung can evaluate humans only functionally, not morally.]

3615. Seifert, Henry. *Conquest of Suffering: The Process and Prospects of Non-Violent Resistance*. Philadelphia, PA: Westminster Press, 1965.

3616. Sellers, James Earl. *When Trouble Comes*. Chicago, IL: Franciscan Herald Press, 1976.

3617. Sheed, F.J. "The Tragedy of Contemporary Theology." *Creative Suffering: The Ripple of Hope*. Edited by James F. Andrews. Kansas City, MO: The National Catholic Reporter Publishing Company, 1970: 97-106.

3618. Shepherd, John J. *Experience, Inference, and God*. New York: Barnes and Noble, 1975.

3619. Shideler, Emerson W. "The Place of Faith in a World of Fact." *Zygon, Journal of Religion and Science* 20 (1985): 243-263. [Examines the inter relationship between the worlds of science and religion by discussing key concepts: order, disorder, entropy, evil, freedom, creation, and resurrection. Faith is the power of freedom which makes creativity possible.]

3620. Shinn, Roger L. "Baffling Mix of Confusion and Guilt." *Union Seminary Quarterly Review* 31 (1976): 126-136.

3621. Shriver, Donald W. "The Pain and Promises of Pluralism." *Christian Century* 97 (1980): 345-350.

3622. Shuster, Marguerite. *Power, Paradox, and Pathology*. Grand Rapids, MI: Zondervan, 1987.

3623. Silverstein, Harry S. "The Evil of Death." *Journal of Philosophy* 77 (1980): 401-423. [Contends that the Epicurean view, that death cannot be claimed to be an evil for those who die or are dying, is false. This resolves the Epicurean dilemma, the conflict between the Epicurean view and common sense.]

3624. Simmons, Henry C. *Valuing Suffering as a Christian: Some Psychological Perspectives*. Chicago, IL: Franciscan Herald Press, 1976. [Relies on psychologist Erich Fromm and the elaboration of relevant documents of Vatican II.]

3625. Sinha, Ajit. "The Concept of Suffering: An Existential Approach." *Visva-Bharati Journal of Philosophy* 6 (1969/1970): 16-27.

3626. Slater, C. Peter. *The Dynamics of Religion*. New York: Harper and Row, 1978. [Discussion of various religions, including solutions to theodicy.]

3627. Slater, Darius. "Mysticism in American Wesleyanism: Thomas Upham." *Wesleyan Theological Journal* 20 (1985): 94-107.

3628. Small, R. Leonard. "The Discipline of Suffering (Sermon, Second Sunday After Easter, Job 1:21)." *Expository Times* 67 (1956): 187-188.

3629. ———. "Facing the Tests of Life (Sermon, 1st Sunday in Lent, Hebrews 2:18)." *Expository Times* 68 (1957): 152-154.

3630. Smedes, Lewis B. *How Can it be All Right When Everything is All Wrong?* New York: Harper and Row, 1982. [Book-length discussion of the role of divine grace in overcoming suffering.]

3631. Smith, Roy S. "Mourning Becomes Existence: Martin Buber's 'Melancholy' Ontology." *Journal of Religion* 69 (1989): 326-343.

3632. Smyth, Phyllis. "Palliative Care: A Current Embodiment of New Testament Theology." *Spirit Within Structure: Essays in Honor of George Johnston on the*

Occasion of his Seventieth Birthday. Edited by E. Furcha. Monteray, CA: Pickwick, 1983: 161-180.

3633. Sogani, K.C. "Some Comments on the Active and the Contemplative Values." *Philosophy and Phenomenological Research* 32 (1971): 264-266.

3634. Song, Choan-Seng. "Asia in Suffering and Hope." *Asian Theological Reflections On Suffering*. Edited by Yap Kim Hao. Christian Conference of Asia, 1977: 50-59.

3635. Sontag, Frederick E. *The Return of the Gods: A Philosophical/Theological Reappraisal of the Writings of Ernest Becker*. New York: Peter Lang, 1989. [See also Sontag's "Anthropodicy or Theodicy? A Discussion with Becker's *The Structure of Evil*" [#3165], *Journal of the American Academy of Religion* 49 (1981), 267-274. Sontag argues that while the social sciences have replaced theodicy with anthropodicy, Becker's writings on evil have not shown that God can be removed from consideration: evil demands an explanation beyond the temporal world.]

3636. Sontag, Susan. *Illness as Metaphor*. New York: Farrer, Strauss, and Giroux, 1977.

3637. Sparks, Jack N. "When Christians Suffer." *Sourozh* 31 (1988): 30-34.

3638. Spiro, Melford E. *Burmese Supernaturalism: A Study in the Explanation and Reduction of Suffering*. Englewood Cliffs, NJ: Prentice-Hall, 1967.

3639. Springsted, Eric O. "The Works of Simone Weil." *Theology Today* 38 (1981).

3640. ———. *Christus Mediator: Platonic Meditation on the Thought of Simone Weil*. Chico, CA: Scholars Press, 1983.

3641. ———. "Contradiction, Mystery and the Use of Words in Simone Weil." *Religion and Literature* 17 (1985).

3642. ———. *Simone Weil and the Suffering of Love*. Cambridge, MA: Cowley Publications, 1986. [Contains full bibliographical list of Simone Weil's publications in English and a selected secondary bibliography, mostly English publications of the 1980s, including papers delivered to the American Weil Society, 1981-1985.]

3643. Stackhouse, John G. "There is an Answer to Evil: Something More Reasonable than Rationalistic Solutions to the Problem." *Christianity Today* 28 (1984): 40. [See also Reginald Stackhouse's recent book, *How Can I Believe When I Live in a World Like This?* Toronto, ON: Harper-Collins, 1990. Both authors argue the conservative position that Christ is the answer to suffering, as found in the Christian scriptures.]

3644. Staub, Ervis. *The Roots of Evil: The Origins of Genocide and Other Group Violence*. Cambridge and New York: Cambridge University Press, 1989.

3645. Stellway, Richard J. "Turning the World Rightside Up." *Christianity Today* 30 (1986): 20-22.

3646. Stevens, Richard J. "An Orientation to Black Theology as a Hermeneutic of Suffering." *Scriptura* 21 (1988): 17-26.

3647. Stewart, Edward C.P. "The Primordial Roots of Being." *Zygon, Journal of Religion and Science* 22 (1987): 87-107.

3648. Stewart, John David. "Paul Ricoeur's Phenomenology of Evil." *International Philosophical Quarterly* 9 (1969): 572-589.

3649. Stock, Michael. "'Meaning' in Mental and Emotional Suffering." *Communio* 6 (1979): 325-328.

3650. Story, Peter. "Disinvestment and Human Suffering: A Response [to Pieter de Villiers]." *Disinvestment and Human Suffering*. Edited by Pieter de Villiers. Pretoria: CUM Books, C.B. Bible Centre, University of South Africa, 1985: 20-27.

3651. Strong, Augustus. *Systematic Theology*. Old Tappan, NJ: Flemming Revell Co., 1976.

3652. Stuermann, Walter E. *The Divine Destroyer: A Theology of Good and Evil.* Philadelphia, PA: Fortress Press, 1967.

3653. Sutherland, Stewart R. *God, Jesus and Belief.* Oxford: Oxford University Press, 1984.

3654. ——. "Optimism and Pessimism." *Religious Studies* 17 (1981): 537-548. [Contends that the difference between optimism and pessimism is that the former regards goodness as a human possibility, while the latter does not. Optimism sees the distinction between good and evil as intelligible and a real distinction, and that it is conceivable that goodness might incarnate itself in particular form. It is manifested but not established in Jesus of Nazareth.]

3655. Szczepaski, Jan. "Individuality and the Elimination of Evil." *Dialectics and Humanism* (The Polish Philosophical Quarterly) 2/3 (1986): 23-39.

3656. Talbott, Thomas B. "C.S. Lewis and the Problem of Evil." *Christian Scholar's Review* 17 (1987): 36-51. [Argues that Christianity is a religion of hope and consolation, grounded in belief in God.]

3657. Tangwa, Godfrey. "God and the Problem of Evil." *Thought and Practice* 4 (1982): 79-85.

3658. Taylor, Richard. *Good and Evil: A New Direction.* New York: Macmillan, 1970. [Contends that good and evil are functions of feelings and needs, rather than functions of reason. He rejects rationalistic ethics. See response by Derek Kelly, "The Twilight of Reason" [#3397].]

3659. Terrell, Burnham. "Reflections on War and the Problem of Evil." *Humanist* 27 (1967): 5-8. [Argues that war poses the problem of evil for the humanist. War cannot be justified.]

3660. Teuber, Andreas. "Simone Weil: Equality as Compassion." *Philosophy and Phenomenological Research* 30 (1982): 221-238.

3661. Thielicke, Helmut. "Deliver Us from Evil." *Christianity Today* 28 (1984): 30-35.

3662. Thomas, J.L.H. "Why Did It Happen to Me?" *Religious Studies* 26 (1990): 323-334.

3663. Thomas, J.M. Lloyd. "The Problem of Pain." *Hibbert Journal* 39 (1941): 287-290.

3664. Thompson, Melvyn. *Cancer and the God of Love.* London: SCM Press, 1976.

3665. Thompson, Warren K.A. "Reinhold Niebuhr on Ethics." *Hibbert Journal* 64 (1966): 99-105.

3666.   Thompson, William Irwin. *Evil and World Order*. New York: Harper and Row, 1976.

3667.   Tournier, Paul. *Escape from Loneliness*. Philadelphia, PA: Westminster Press, 1962.

3668.   ——. *Guilt and Grace*. New York: Harper and Row, 1962.

3669.   ——. *The Strong and the Weak*. Philadelphia, PA: Westminster Press, 1963.

3670.   ——. *Creative Suffering*. London: SCM Press, 1982.

3671.   Towne, Edgar A. "Henry Nelson Wieman: Theologian of Hope." *Iliff Review* 27 (1970): 13-24.

3672.   Tracy, Thomas F. *God, Action, and Embodiment*. Grand Rapids, MI: Eerdmans, 1984.

3673.   Tripathi, R.K. "Two Approaches to the Problems of Evil." *Journal of Dharma* 2 (1977): 312-317. [Discusses two approaches to theism: the religious and the reflective approach. There are two kinds of reflective or philosophical approaches to the problem of evil: naturalism and idealism. For both, the problem of evil is not a problem if it is appreciated that evil is not real, but merely an illusion.]

3674.   Turner, Dean. *Commitment to Care: An Integrated Philosophy of Science, Education and Religion*. Old Greenwich, CT: Devin-Adair, 1978.

3675.   Tutu, Desmond Mpilo. *Hope and Suffering: Sermons and Speeches*. Grand Rapids, MI: Eerdmans, 1984. [Originally published in Johannesburg by Skota-ville Publishers, 1983.]

3676.   Tyman, Stephen. "The Problem of Evil in Proto-Ethical Idealism: J.W. Miller's Ethics in Historical Context." *The Philosophy of John William Miller*. Edited by Joseph P. Fell. Lewisburg, PA: Bucknell University Press, 1990: 96-110.

3677.   Tyrrell, Bernard J. *Christo-Therapy: Healing Through Enlightenment*. New York: Seabury, 1975. [See also his *Christo-Therapy II: A New Horizons for Counsellors, Spiritual Directors and Seekers of Healing and Growth in Christ*. Ramsey, NJ: Paulist Press, 1982.]

3678.   Van Den Bogaerde. "Disinvestment and Human Suffering: A Response [to de Villiers]. *Disinvestment and Human Suffering* Edited by Pieter de Villiers. Pretoria: CUM Books, C.B. Bible Centre, University of South Africa, 1985: 16-19.

3679.   Van der Hoeven, J. "The Problem of Evil—Crucible for the Authenticity and Modesty of Philosophizing: In Discussion with Paul Ricoeur." *South African Journal of Philosophy* 5 (1986): 44-52.

3680.   Van der Ven, Johannes A. "Theodicy or Cosmodicy: A False Dilemma?" *Journal of Empirical Theology* 2 (1989): 5-27. [Survey of Catholics in the Netherlands].

3681.   Van Heukelem, Judith F. "Weep With Those Who Weep: Understanding and Helping the Crying Person." *Journal of Psychology and Theology* 7 (1979): 83-91. [Maintains that crying, in response to pain, is a God-given, therapeutic gift.]

3682.   Van Leeuwen, T.M. *The Surplus of Meaning: Ontology and Eschatology in the Philosophy of Paul Ricoeur*. Amsterdam: Rodopi, 1981.

3683. Vanauken, Sheldon. *A Severe Mercy*. San Francisco, CA: Harper and Row, 1977. [Discussion of C.S. Lewis's theodicy.]

3684. ———. "God's Will: Reflections on the Problem of Pain." *The Intellectuals Speak Out About God*. Edited by R. Varghese. Washington, DC: Regnery Gateway, 1984: 355-362.

3685. Vande Kemp, Hendrika. "Character Amor or the Armor of Faith? Reflections on Psychologies of Suffering." *Journal of Psychology and Christianity* 9 (1990): 5-17.

3686. Veto, Miklos J. "Simone Weil and Suffering." *Thought* 40 (1965): 275-286. [Discusses Weil's view of expiatory suffering.]

3687. Vines, Maxwell L. "The Theological Struggle of Woodbine Willie." *Foundations* 22 (1979): 261-272.

3688. Vivian, Frederick. *Human Freedom and Responsibility*. London: Chatto and Windus, 1964.

3689. Wachterhauser, Brice R. "The Problem of Evil and Moral Scepticism." *International Journal for Philosophy of Religion* 17 (1985): 167-174.

3690. Walhout, Donald. *The Good and the Realm of Values*. Notre Dame, IN: University of Notre Dame Press, 1978.

3691. Wall, Robert Walter. "The Problem of Observed Pain: A Study of C.S. Lewis on Suffering." *Journal of the Evangelical Theological Society* 26 (1983): 443-451.

3692. Wallis, Jim. "Waging Peace: Christians' Strongest Weapon Against Spiritual Evil." *Sojourners* 7 (1978): 19-21.

3693. ———. "Staying Hungry." *Sojourners* 10 (1981): 3-4.

3694. ———. "A Prayer of a Chance: Taking Evil Seriously." *Sojourners* 15 (1986): 14-19. [Two-part interview of Gordon Cosby. The second part follows in the succeeding issue of *Sojourners* 15 (1986).]

3695. Walls, Jerry. *Hell: The Logic of Damnation*. Notre Dame, IN: University of Notre Dame Press, 1992.

3696. Walsch, Chad. *C.S. Lewis: Apostle to the Sceptics*. New York: Macmillan, 1977.

3697. ———. *The Literacy Legacy of C.S. Lewis*. New York: Harcourt, 1980.

3698. Walter, Edward. "Are Actualities Prior to Possibilities?" *New Scholasticism* 46 (1972): 202-209.

3699. Walter, E. Wiest. "God's Punishment for Sin?" *Religious Education* 83 (1988): 243-250.

3700. Watson, John. "Martyria." *Coptic Church Review* 4 (1983): 9-13.

3701. Weatherhead, Leslie D. *Why Do Men Suffer?* London: SCM Press, 1935.

3702. ———. *Psychology, Religion, and Healing*. Nashville, TN: Abingdon Press, 1952.

3703. ———. *Salute to a Sufferer*. New York and Nashville, TN: Abingdon Press, 1962.

3704.   Webster, Alexander F.C. "Typologies for an Orthodox Pastoral Theology of Physical Suffering." *Diakonia* 15 (1980): 134-158.

3705.   Weil, Simone. *Gravity and Grace*. New York: Putman, 1952. [Republished by New York: Octagon, 1979.]

3706.   ———. *Waiting on God*. London: Collins, 1959.

3707.   ———. *On Science, Necessity, and the Love of God*. Oxford and New York: Oxford University Press, 1960. [Collected Essays.]

3708.   ———. *Selected Essays, 1934-1943*. London: Oxford University Press, 1962.

3709.   ———. *Seventy Letters*. London: Oxford University Press, 1965.

3710.   ———. *Gateway to God*. Edited by David Raper, with Malcolm Muggeridge and Vernon Sproxton. New York: Crossroad, 1982. [Contains Weil's essay, "The Gate," and "Selected Pensées of Simone Weil."]

3711.   Wells, Donald A. *God, Man and Thinker: Philosophies of Religion*. New York: Random House, 1962.

3712.   Werblowsky, Raphael J. Zwi. "Types of Redemption: A Summary." *Types of Redemption*. Edited by Raphael J.Z. Werblowsky and Claas Jouco Bleeker. Leiden: E.J. Brill, 1970: 243-248. [Summary of the several articles on redemption in this book, from the perspective of various religions.]

3713.   White, George A. *Simone Weil: Interpretation of a Life*. Amherst, MA: University of Massachusetts Press, 1981. [Contains bibliography on Weil in English prior to 1980: see pages 181-194.]

3714.   Whitelaw, David P. "A Theology of Anguish." *Theologia Evangelica* 15 (1982): 38-48.

3715.   Whyte, Susan Reynolds. "Men, Women and Misfortune in Bunyole." *Women's Religious Experience*. Edited by Pat Holden. Totawa, NJ: Barnes and Noble, 1983: 175-192.

3716.   Wicken, Jeffrey S. "The Cosmic Breath: Reflections on the Thermodynamics of Creation." *Zygon, Journal of Religion and Science* 19 (1984): 487-506.

3717.   Williams, Clifford. "When Mercy Hurts." *Christianity Today* 33 (1989): 16-19.

3718.   Williams, George. "Huxley's Evolution and Ethics in Sociobiological Perspective." *Zygon, Journal of Religion and Science* 23 (1988): 388-407. [See response by Ruse [#3596].]

3719.   Willis, Roy. "Do the Fipa Have a Word for It?" *The Anthropology of Evil*. Edited by David Parkin. Oxford: Blackwell, 1985: 209-223.

3720.   Wilson, David D. *Many Waters Cannot Quench: A Study of Pain and Suffering of Eighteenth Century Methodism and the Significance for John Wesley and the First Methodists*. London: Epworth, 1969.

3721.   Winiarz, Mordechai. "Is Religion for the Happy-Minded? A Response to Harold Kushner." *Tradition* 22 (1986): 54-65.

3722.   Woelfel, James W. "Death of God: A Belated Personal Postscript." *Christian Century* 93 (1976): 1175-1178.

3723. Woodfin, Yandall. *With All Your Mind: A Christian Philosophy.* Nashville, TN: Abingdon Press, 1980.

3724. Woods, B.W. *Understanding Suffering.* Grand Rapids, MI: Baker Book House, 1974.

3725. Wuthnow, Robert, Kevin Christiano, and John Kuzlowski. "Religion and Bereavement: A Conceptual Framework." *Journal for the Scientific Study of Religion* 19 (1980): 408-422.

3726. Yancey, Philip. *Where is God When It Hurts?* Grand Rapids, MI: Zondervan Publishing House, 1977. [Biblically based inspirational exploration of the problem of evil.]

3727. ———. "When Bad Things Happen to Good People: The Author of *Where Is God When It Hurts?* Responds." *Christianity Today* 27 (1983): 22-23.

3728. ———. "Helping Those in Pain." *Leadership* 5 (1984): 90-97. [Suffering can never ultimately be meaningless because God has shared it.]

3729. ———. "A Wrestling Match with the Almighty: John Donne Asked the Questions that Face Everyone who Suffers." *Christianity Today* 33 (1989): 22-26.

3730. Yates, John. "Survival as Replication." *Sophia* 28 (1988): 2-9.

3731. Yeager, D.M. "On Making the Tree Good: An Apology for Dispositional Ethics." *Journal of Religious Ethics* 10 (1982): 103-120. [H. Richard Niebuhr.]

3732. Zaidi, Qaiser Sultan. "The Problem of Good and Evil." *Pakistan Philosophical Congress* 12 (1965): 331-336.

Appendix E

Dissertations

The following pages list over 500 of the most relevant dissertations on theodicy[1] and related issues. The items have been divided into two sections: those which are relevant to the annotated chapters, *Chapters 2-7*, and those which are relevant to the other four appendixes, *Appendixes A-D*.[2] This index lists dissertations from as early as 1885 through to the end of 1991. It is not surprising that the number of dissertations each year has escalated significantly. The items listed for the pre-1950s era total about three dozen; there are about 90 listings for the 1950s and 1960s; there are more than 130 for the 1970s, over 170 for the 1980s and about 80 dissertations in the first two years of the 1990s. (As this 1998 publication of this biography is being completed, there is every indication that the number of dissertations on theodicy has continued to escalate significantly during the 1990s.) This burgeoning interest in theodicy is reflected also in the number of items in the annotated chapters and other appendixes (which also have continued to rise dramatically through the 1990s).[3]

Some of the items have been published as books and these have been listed in the appropriate chapters. Not all of the items may be considered "publishable," yet dissertations are a good indication of what is being taught and discussed in graduate seminars, and an indication of the issues considered important by the rising generation of scholars in the field. The bibliographical information, moreover, contained in these dissertations often is helpful.[4]

Approximately one-quarter of the entries could be classified as "theodicy in literature,"[5] ranging from dissertations about the theodicy issue in poets, playwrights, noveliists, film producers, and the like: Wordsworth, Tennyson, Coleridge, Blake, Shelly, Shakes- peare, Charles Williams, Bergman, Joseph Conrad, Hermann Hesse, Christopher Marlow, Camus, Sartre, Milton, Tolkien, Browning, Arthur Miller, Thomas Wolfe, Jane Austen, Victor Hugo, Hawthorne, Golding, Yeats, C.S. Lewis, among others. Another one-quarter of the items are relevant to the issues discussed in the six annotated chapters, *(Chapters 2-7)*: philosophical, analytic themes. The remaining items, approximately half of the total, focus on the issues discussed in the appendixes: studies on biblical theodicy *(Appendix A)*, historical theodicy *(Appendix B)*, suffering of God theodicy *(Appendix C)*, and the diverse issues covered in *Appendix D*: the psychology of evil, existential coping, medical–ethical issues, feministic themes, non-Christian themes, pain, Satan, Jewish and holocaust studies, black theodicy, and others.

I am indebted, of course, to University Microfilms International for their dissertation data base and the hard cover version, *Dissertation Abstracts International* and *Masters Theses*.[6] Most of the dissertations listed here are available from University Microfilms

International in printed form. The data lists of "recent dissertations" in the such periodicals as *Religious Studies Review*, *Review of Metaphysics*, and *Process Studies* also have been helpful in locating relevant dissertations.

Notes

1. Interspersed with the dissertations are a select number of relevant Th.D. and Ed.D. dissertations, as well as some important D.Min., M.A. Theses, and others.
2. As was the case with respect to the material listed in the preceding seven chapters and four appendixes, many of the items could have been listed in more than one section. Yet cross-listing, however desirable, would have made this book double or triple its current length.
3. I have not made exact counts of the items, but the general trend toward an escalation of writings on this issue over the past three decades is obvious.
4. As the Editor (1996–) and Dissertations Abstracts Editor (1990–) for *Process Studies* scholarly journal, I have the opportunity to read scores of dissertations each year. I find this task highly rewarding and informative and an important research resource.
5. To say the least, it seems disproportionate that items in one of the areas of *Appendix D* should total about the same number of listings as those which correspond to the themes covered in *Chapters 2-7*. This may reflect a problem with the bibliographical data bases, but I suspect that it is more the case that the "theodicy and literature" theme has been a prevalent theme. Theodicy, indeed, is a pervasive aspect of literature and the arts, and not the sole terrain of philosophy and theology. While the latter address the issue in a more systematic and structured manner, the existential reality of suffering has always been a major aspect of drama, novels, poetry, and other forms of humanity's creative expression.
6. University Microfilms Inc., the publisher of *Dissertation Abstracts International*, supplies on request, for a reasonable fee, photocopied versions of most of the dissertations listed here and most of the dissertations written in North America.

Dissertations in Theodicy

(Unless otherwise noted, the following items are Ph.D. dissertations.)

I   Items Related to Chapters 2-7

3733.   Adler, Ira N. *Evil and Theism: An Analytic Approach.* New York University 1975.

3734.   Arnold, Steve Richard. *Scientific Research Programs and the Nature of Theology: An Analogy of Lakatos' Model of the Nature of Science and the Nature of Theology in John Hick.* Golden Gate Baptist Theological Seminary, 1987.

3735.   Austin, David Brian. *Regularity and Randomness as Elements of Theodicy.* Southern Baptist Theological Seminary, 1989.

3736.   Baldwin, Dalton DeVere. *A Whiteheadian Solution to the Problem of Evil.* The Claremont Graduate School, 1975.

3737.   Banner, Michael C. *The Justification of Science and the Rationality of Religious Belief* [D.Phil.]. University of Oxford, 1986.

3738.   Barciauskas, Rosemary Curran. *"Redemption Through Suffering": The Task of Human Freedom in the Writings of A.N. Whitehead and Paul Ricoeur and the Implications for a Christian Soteriology.* Fordham University, 1983.

3739.   Barineau, R. Maurice. *Ethical Theodicy and Alfred North Whitehead.* Florida State University, 1989.

3740.   Basinger, Randall G. *Divine Providence: A Comparison of Classical and Process Theism.* Northwestern University, Garrett-Evangelical Seminary, 1978.

3741.   Bavier, Richard Briggs. *The Justification of Evil in Teleological Theodicy.* Brown University, 1974.

3742.   Beaty, Michael Douglas. *The Univocity Thesis and the Moral Goodness of God.* University of Notre Dame, 1986.

3743.   Besancon, Richard. *The Problem of God and Evil in the Thought of Representative Contemporary Philosophers.* Northern Baptist Theological Seminary, 1960.

3744.   Burke, Thomas John, Jr. *Plantinga and the Rationality of Theism.* Michigan State University, 1989.

3745.   Buss, Sarah. *The Conditions of Free Agency.* Yale University, 1989.

3746.   Case-Winters, Anna Lou. *The Problem of Omnipotence: A Theological Exploration of the Meaning of Power.* Vanderbilt University, 1988.

3747.   Cavanagh, Robert R. *Toward a Contemporary Construct of Providence: An Analysis of the Construct of Providence in the Systematic Theology of Paul Tillich and the Neoclassical Metaphysics of Charles Hartshorne.* Graduate Theological Union, 1968.

3748.   Christlieb, Terry Joe. *Theism and Evil: Consistency, Evidence, and Completeness.* Syracuse University, 1988.

3749. Clarke, Randolph K. *An Agent—Causal View of Free Will*. Princeton University, 1990.

3750. Collins, Marvin Allen. *God and Evil in the Process Thought of A.N. Whitehead, Charles Hartshorne and David Griffin: A Question of Theological Coherence*. Fuller Theological Seminary, School of Theology, 1986.

3751. Cook, Robert Richard. *A Representative Survey and Critical Analysis of Theo- logical and Philosophical Discussions of Divine Foreknowledge in the English Speaking World from 1970 to 1989*. Council for National Academic Awards, United Kingdom, 1990.

3752. Davis, Paul. *The Cheap Trick of Compatibilism and Why the Problem of Free Will Won't Go Away*. University of Edinburgh, 1989.

3753. Dees, J. Gregory. *Coercive Offers: A Study of the Nature and Ethics of Coercion*. Johns Hopkins University, 1986.

3754. Demoss, David J. *Compatibilism, Practical Wisdom and the Narrative Self: Or If I Had Had My Act Together, I Could Have Done Otherwise*. University of Virginia, 1987.

3755. Detrixhe, Wylene Rae Wisby. *God and Evil: The Theistic Dilemma*. Vanderbilt University, 1973. [Discussion of Hick, Pike, Plantinga, Mavrodes, Dore, etc.]

3756. Devenish, Philip Edward. *Evil and Theism: An Analytical-Constructive Resolution of the So-Called Problem of Evil*. Southern Methodist University, 1977.

3757. Diehl, David W. *Divine Omniscience in the Thought of Charles Hartshorne and Cornelius Van Til: A Systematic Comparative Study*. Hartford Seminary Foundation, 1978.

3758. Draper, Paul Robert. *The Evidential Problem of Evil*. University of California, Irvine, 1985. [Theism, Natural Theology, Hume]

3759. Durham, Ronald Oatis. *Process Thought and Theodicy: A Critique*. Rice University, 1975.

3760. Ellis, R. *Can God Act in History? A Whiteheadian Perspective*. Oxford University, 1984.

3761. Elmore, Joe Earl. *The Theme of the Suffering of God in the Thought of Nicholas Berdyaev, Charles Hartshorne, and Reinhold Niebuhr*. Columbia University, 1963.

3762. Faber, David Scott. *The Problem of Omnipotence and God's Ability to Sin*. University of Massachusetts, 1989.

3763. Feinberg, John Samuel. *Theologies and Evil*. University of Chicago, 1978.

3764. Fink, Charles K. *Conditionals*. University of Miami, 1988.

3765. Flint, Thomas P. *Divine Freedom*. University of Notre Dame, 1980.

3766. Fox, Mary Johann. *The Meaning of the Notion of Divine Power in the Neoclassical Theism of Charles Hartshorne*. Fordham University, 1977.

3767. Frierson, William Manton. *The Problem of Evil: A Metaphysical and Theological Inquiry*. Emory University, 1977.

3768. Garcia, Jose Rafael. *Liberation and Evil: A Critique of the Thought of Gustavo Gutiérrez and Rubem Alves from the Standpoint of F.R. Tennant's Theodicy*. The Claremont Graduate School, 1975.

3769. Geivett, R. Douglas. *A Critical Evaluation of John Hick's Theodicy in Defense of the Augustinian Tradition* [M.A.]. Gonzaga University, 1985. [See also his dissertation, *The Logic of the Problem of Evil*. University of Southern California, 1991.]

3770. Gerwin, Martin Edgar. *Causality, Agency, Explanation: A Perspective on Free Will and the Problem of Evil*. Princeton University, 1985.

3771. Gordon, Bobby Joe. *The Role of Process Theology in the Christologies of W.N. Pittenger and Wolfhart Pannenberg: An Analysis of the Doctrine of the Person of Christ*. Southwestern Baptist Theological Seminary, 1989.

3772. Grange, Joseph. *Tragic Vision in the Thought of A.N. Whitehead*. Fordham University, 1970.

3773. Greenfield, Stephen Albert. *A Whiteheadian Perspective of the Problem of Evil: Whitehead's Understanding of Evil and Christian Theodicy*. Fordham University, 1973.

3774. Griffin, David R. *Jesus, Revelation, and Truth: A Whiteheadian Essay on Christology*. The Claremont Graduate School, 1970.

3775. Hagerty, Cornelius J. *Problems of Evil*. Catholic University of America, 1911.

3776. Hanson, James Eli. *Evil and Optimism in the Thought of Teilhard de Chardin*. Fordham University, 1975.

3777. Holden, Dennis James. *Ockhamism and the Divine Foreknowledge Problem*. University of California at Irvine, 1988.

3778. Horban, Peter Timothy. *God, Evil, and the Metaphysics of Freedom: An Evaluation of the Free Will Defense of Alvin Plantinga*. University of Western Ontario, London, 1979.

3779. Howell, Chesley T. *A Critique of Theories of Good and Evil in Contemporary Thought*. University of Chicago, 1938.

3780. Iozzio, Mary Jo. *Self-Determination and the Moral Act: A Study of the Contributions of Odon Lottin, O.S.B.* Fordham University, 1990.

3781. Jadlos, Jane. *The Logic of Responsibility: Martin Buber and H. Richard Niebuhr on Religious Experience and Moral Agency*. University of Chicago Divinity School, 1991.

3782. Jooharigian, Robert Badrik. *Evil and the Existence of God*. University of Wisconsin at Madison, 1977.

3783. Joseph, Stephen Gary. *The Problem of Evil—An Examination of Classical and Contemporary Attempts at Philosophical Theodicy—With Special Reference and Attention to the Free-Will Defense*. University of Pennsylvania, 1979.

3784. Keller, James A. *The Concept of Divine Action*. Yale University, 1969.

3785. Lau, Daniel Shing-Ip. *A Theological Analysis of the Problem of Evil*. Brandeis University, 1979.

3786.   Lodahl, Michael Eugene. *A Process Pneumatology Founded in Jewish-Christian Conversation.* Emory University, 1988.

3787.   Loughran, Thomas J. *Theological Compatibilism.* University of Notre Dame, 1986. [Focuses on Aquinas.]

3788.   Mackie, Myra Beth. *John Hick's Theodicy.* Duke University, 1980.

3789.   Mason, David R. *A Study of Time in the Philosophies of Alfred North Whitehead and Martin Heidegger with Implications for a Doctrine of Providence.* University of Chicago, 1973.

3790.   Meierding, Loren Edward. *The Argument From Evil.* University of Texas at Austin, 1978.

3791.   Menssen, Sandra Lee. *Foundations of Theodicy: Is There a Criterion of Goodness for Worlds?* University of Minnesota, 1984.

3792.   Mesle, C. Robert. *Power and Value in Process Philosophy and Theology.* Northwestern University, Garrett-Evangelical Theological Seminary, 1980.

3793.   Meyers, Alan G. The Divine Incompleteness: Two Alternative Theisms. Union Theological Seminary in Virginia, 1987. [Discussion of Cobb and Pannenberg.]

3794.   Milazzo, Gaetano (Tom) Edward-John. *The Protest and the Silence: Suffering and Death as a Theological Problem.* Emory University, 1988.

3795.   Miller, John Edward. *A Process Hermeneutic for Examining Experimental and Biblical Resources Pertaining to the Theological Problem of Evil.* Union Theological Seminary in Virginia, 1982.

3796.   Morgan, Darold H. *Traditional Supernaturalism and the Problem of Evil.* Southwestern Baptist Theological Seminary, 1953.

3797.   Morley, Brian Keith. *Swinburne's Inductive Argument for Theism.* The Claremont Graduate School, 1991.

3798.   Moskup, John. *Divine Omniscience and Human Freedom in Thomas Aquinas and Charles Hartshorne.* University of Texas at Austin, 1979.

3799.   Muray, Leslie A. *A Comparison of the Concept of Freedom in the Thought of Roger Garaudy and Daniel Day Williams.* The Claremont Graduate School, 1982.

3800.   Myers, Michael Warren. *Confessions of a Free-Will Defender: An Analytic Theodicy* [M.A.]. Gonzaga University, 1981.

3801.   Nasser, Alan George. *The Ontological Argument and the Problem of Evil.* Indiana University, 1972.

3802.   Nowlin, Ben Gary. *The Reasonableness of Faith as a Response to Evil.* University of Oklahoma, 1981.

3803.   O'Hanlon, Gerard Francis. *Does God Change? The Immutability of God in the Theology of Hans Urs Von Balthasar.* Queen's University of Belfast (Northern Ireland), 1987.

3804.   Olson, Ronald D. *The Immutability of God: The Study of a Contemporary Theological Dispute in Light of the Phenomenon of Faith.* Vanderbilt University, 1991.

3805. Pauling, Chandler F. *The Problem of Evil in Contemporary Theology*. Aquinas Institute, 1971.

3806. Pederson, Anne Milliken. *An Intimate Correlation Between God and the World: A Comparison Between John Cobb's and Martin Luther's Theology* [Th.D.]. Lutheran School of Theology at Chicago, 1990.

3807. Putney, David Paul. *The Nature and Practice of Freedom: A Dialogue on Freedom and Determinism in Buddhism and Western Philosophy*. University of Hawaii, 1990.

3808. Rainwater, Robert Eugene, Jr. *The Theodicy of John Hick: A Critical Analysis*. Southern Baptist Theological Seminary, 1980.

3809. Ramberan, Osmond George. *Faith, Language and the Problem of Evil in Recent Analytic Philosophy*. McMaster University, 1974.

3810. Ricciardelli, Angela Rose. *A Comparison of Wilfrid Desan's and Pierre Teilhard de Chardin's Thinking with Regard to the Nature of Man's Survival in a United World*. Georgetown University, 1986.

3811. Richardson, W. Mark. *Human Action and the Making of a Theist: A Study of Austin Farrer's Gifford Lectures*. Graduate Theological Union, 1991.

3812. Robison, Jay P. *Personal Eschatology: An Analysis of Contemporary Christian Interpretations*. Southern Baptist Theological Seminary, 1990. [Discussion of Brunner, Boros, Cullmann, Hick, Ferré].

3813. Rodd, Rosemary Anne. *Biology, Ethics and Animals*. Open University (Great Britain), 1987.

3814. Ross, Floyd Hiatt. *Personalism and the Problem of Natural Evil*. Yale University, 1935.

3815. Sauer, Paul Alan. *The Incompatibility of Foreknowledge and Freedom and Some Consequences Stemming Therefrom if Moral Responsibility is Assumed*. Syracuse University, 1991.

3816. Schuttler, Charles. *The Place of Evil in a Moral System*. Boston University Graduate School, 1914.

3817. Scott, Mark Alan. *Theodicy: Failure and Promise within the Thought of Karl Barth, David R. Griffin, and Jürgen Moltmann*. Southern Baptist Theological Seminary, 1987.

3818. Sennett, James Fulton. *Modality, Probability and Rationality: A Critical Examination of Alvin Plantinga's Philosophy*. University of Nebraska at Lincoln, 1990.

3819. Sia, Santiago. *A Study of Charles Hartshorne's Conceptualization of the Religious Term God*. Trinity College, Dublin, 1980.

3820. Stalcup, Bobby Lee. *Evil and Sin in the Process Theology of Pierre Teilhard de Chardin*. Southwestern Baptist Theological Seminary, 1974.

3821. Stoeber, Michael Francis. *Evil and the Mystics' God: Towards a Mystical Theodicy*. University of Toronto, 1990.

3822. Storms, William Claude. *The Problem of Evil for Process Thought: An Examination from the Perspective of Christian Theism.* Southern Baptist Theological Seminary, 1978.

3823. Suchocki, Marjorie Hewitt. *The Correlation Between God and Evil.* The Claremont Graduate School, 1974.

3824. Tarleton, Edward Dee, Jr. Petitionary Prayer and the Logical Coherence of Theism. Southern Baptist Theological Seminary, 1990. [Discusses Aquinas, Swinburne, Brummer].

3825. Thanavelil Kurian, Joseph. *Language, Faith and Meaning: A Critical Study of John Hick's Philosophy of Religion. Towards a Metaphysical Approach to Philosophical Theology.* Pontificia Universitas Gregoriana, 1990.

3826. Underhill, Lee. *The Problem of Evil in the Philosophy of Alfred North Whitehead.* Drew University, 1957.

3827. Vriend, David John. *Causation, Reliability, and God's Foreknowledge.* University of California, Los Angeles, 1987.

3828. Warren, Thomas Bratton. *God and Evil: Does Judeo–Christian Theism Involve a Logical Contradiction?* Vanderbilt University, 1969.

3829. Weisberger, Andrea M. *A Defense of the Argument from Evil: A Critique of Pure Theism.* Vanderbilt University, 1990.

3830. White, Terence Henry. *God and Evil: A Study on the Problem of Evil.* New York University, 1979.

3831. Whitney, Barry L. *The Question of Theodicy in the Neoclassical Metaphysics of Charles Hartshorne.* McMaster University, 1977.

3832. Whitten, Mark W. *An Affirmation of the Ockhamist Explanation of the Compatibility of Divine Foreknowledge and Human Freedom.* Baylor University, 1989.

3833. Wilson, Patrick A. *The Anthropic Cosmological Principle.* University of Notre Dame, 1989.

3834. Wilson, Paul Eddy. *The Bearing of Process Thought on the Problem of Theodicy.* University of Tennessee, 1989.

3835. Young, Henry James. *Two Models of the Human Future: A Study in the Process Theism of Teilhard and Whitehead.* Hartford Seminary Foundation, 1974.

II   Items Relevant to Appendices A-D

[a] Biblical Theodicy

3836. Adams, David Robert. *The Suffering of Paul and the Dynamics of Luke—Acts.* Yale University, 1979.

3837. Anderson, Susan. *Creation in Eschatological Tension: A Premise of Pauline Theodicy* [M.A.]. Oral Roberts University, 1980.

3838. Bechtler, Steven Richard. *Following in His Steps: Christology and Suffering in 1 Peter.* Princeton Theological Seminary, 1991.

3839. Becker, Warren Elton. *Paul the Suffering Apostle: The Place of Suffering in his Life and Theology.* Fuller Theological Seminary, School of Theology, 1982.

3840. Bertoluci, Jose Maria. *The Son of the Morning and the Guardian Cherub in the Context of the Controversy Between Good and Evil* [Th.D.]. Andrews University, 1985. [Satan, Isaiah, Ezekiel.]

3841. Bode, William. *The Book of Job and the Solution of the Problem of Suffering"* [S.T.D.]. Temple University, 1913.

3842. Carmack, Samuel Williams. *Paul's Affirmation of Suffering in Light of his Christology.* Southwestern Baptist Theological Seminary, 1985.

3843. Clinard, H. Gordon. *An Evangelical Critique of the Use of the Classic Biblical Solutions to the Problem of Suffering by Representative Contemporary Preachers.* Southwestern Baptist Theological Seminary, 1958.

3844. Creelman, Harlan. *The Problem of Well-Being and Suffering in the Old Testament.* Yale University, 1894.

3845. Crouch, James Arthur. *The Scope and Significance of Deliverance from the Present Evil Age in Galatians.* New Orleans Baptist Theological Seminary, 1991.

3846. Day, Peggy Lynne. *"Satan" in the Hebrew Bible.* Harvard University, 1986.

3847. Dowd, Sharon Echols. *"Whatever You Ask in Prayer, Believe" (Mark 11:22-25): The Theological Function of Prayer and the Problem of Theodicy in Mark.* Emory University, 1986.

3848. Dumke, James Arthur. *The Suffering of the Righteous in Jewish Apocryphal Literature.* Duke University, 1980.

3849. Gladson, J.A. *Retributive Paradoxes in Proverbs 10-29.* Vanderbilt University, 1978.

3850. Gustafson, Henry A. *The New Testament's Interpretations of Christian Suffering.* University of Chicago, 1967.

3851. Han, Jin Hee. *Yahweh Replies to Job: Yahweh's Speeches in the Book of Job, A Case of Assumptive Rhetoric.* Princeton Theological Seminary, 1988.

3852. Holert, M. Louise. *Extrinsic Evil Powers in the Old Testament* [Th.M.]. Fuller Theological Seminary, School of World Mission, 1985.

3853. Jones-Haldeman, Madelynn. *The Function of Christ's Suffering in First Peter 2:21* [Th.D.]. Andrews University, 1988.

3854. Jones, Arthur H. *Enoch and the Fall of the Watchers: 1 Enoch 1-36.* Vanderbilt University, 1989.

3855. Jones, Benny Joseph. *A Study of the Son of Man in Revelation, With Special Reference to the Suffering Servant Motif.* New Orleans Baptist Theological Seminary, 1990.

3856. Lester, Elwyn Russell. *An Exegetical Approach to the New Testament Concept of Suffering Persecution as a Christian.* Southwestern Baptist Theological Seminary, 1959.

3857. Ludwig, Theodore Mark. *The Suffering Love of God: The Tension Between Judgment and Grace in the Pre-Exilic Prophets.* Concordia Seminary, 1963.

3858. Macky, Peter Wallace. *The Importance of the Teaching on God, Evil and Eschatology for the Dating of the Testaments of the Twelve Patriarchs.* Princeton Theological Seminary, 1969.

3859. Mastag, Horst Dieter. *The Transformations of Job in Modern German Literature.* University of British Columbia, 1990.

3860. Meador, Marion Frank. *The Motif of God as Judge in the Old Testament.* Southwestern Baptist Theological Seminary, 1986.

3861. Melius, Stephen T. *From Hopelessness to Trust: An Eight-Week Adult Bible Study on the Book of Job* [D.Min.]. Boston University School of Theology, 1983.

3862. Moore, Ralph Kelvin. *An Investigation of the Motif of Suffering in the Psalms of Lamentation* [Th.D.]. New Orleans Baptist Theological Seminary, 1988.

3863. Osborne, Thomas P. *Christian Suffering in the First Epistle of Peter.* Catholic University of Louvain, 1981.

3864. Owens, Pamela. *Suffering from "Aleph to Taw": Images of Suffering in the Book of Lamentations in the Context of Other Lament Poetry of the Ancient Near East.* University of Chicago Divinity School, 1991.

3865. Parsons, Ian Ross McKenzie. *Evil Speaking in the Psalms of Lament.* Drew University, 1969.

3866. Pedersen, David Birger. *Torah, Discipleship and Suffering: An Historical Study of the Development of Interrelated Themes in the Old Testament, Post-Biblical Judaism, and the Synoptic Gospels* [Th.D.]. Union Theological Seminary in Virginia, 1971.

3867. Phillips, Mickey Arnold. *A Theological Analysis of Suffering as a Christian Lifestyle in the New Testament.* Southern Baptist Theological Seminary, 1978.

3868. Pipes, Buddy Rogers. *Christian Response to Human Suffering: A Lay Theological Response to the Book of Job* [D.Min.]. Drew University, 1981.

3869. Power, W.J.A. *A Study of Irony in the Book of Job.* University of Toronto, 1961.

3870. Proudfoot, Charles Merrill. *The Apostle Paul's Understanding of Christian Suffering.* Yale University, 1956.

3871. Roseberry, Q. Gerald. *Terminal Anxiety and Psalms of Lament* [D.Min.]. Princeton Theological Seminary, 1988.

3872. Russell, David Michael. *The "New Heavens and New Earth": Hope for the Creation in Jewish Apocalyptic and the New Testament.* Southwestern Baptist Theological Seminary, 1991.

3873. Sanders, Jim A. *Suffering as Divine Discipline in the Old Testament and Post-Biblical Judaism.* Hebrew Union College–Jewish Institute of Religion, 1955.

3874. Seemuth, David P. *Adam the Sinner and Christ the Righteous One: The Theological and Exegetical Substructure of Romans 5:12-21.* Marquette University, 1989.

3875. Shank, Harold. *The Sin Theology of the Cain and Abel Story: An Analysis of Narrative Themes within the Context of Genesis 1-11.* Marquette University, 1988.

3876. Variyamattom, Mathew. *The Language of Suffering in the Book of Jeremiah—A Semantical-Theological Study* [Th.D.]. Pontificia Universitas Gregoriana (Vatican City), 1988.

3877. Vellenga, Jacob John. *The Christian Rationale of Human Suffering Based on the Teachings of the New Testament.* Southern Baptist Theological Seminary, 1942.

3878. Welch, Thomas J. *A Historical-Exegetical Interpretation of the Terms Used for Moral Evil in the Pauline Writings.* Southwestern Baptist Theological Seminary, 1954.

3879. White, Ransom Kelley. *The Problem of Suffering and Its Biblical Solution.* Southern Baptist Theological Seminary, 1922.

3880. Will, James Edward. *Passion as Tragedy: The Problem of Redemptive Suffering in the Passion.* The Claremont Graduate School, 1986.

[b] Theodicy in Literature

3881. Anderson, David Robert. *Thomson's Heavenly Musing: "The Seasons" as Theodicy.* Boston College, 1978.

3882. Anderson, Harry Sheldon. *The Vice: The Structure of Evil in the English Morality Play.* Temple University, 1972.

3883. Averill, James Halsey, Jr. *"Thoughts that Spring out of Suffering": Tragic Response in the Poetry of William Wordsworth.* Cornell University, 1976.

3884. Ayers, Margaret Rose. *An Exposition and Appraisal of C.S. Lewis and his Theo- logy of Suffering: A Roman Catholic Perspective.* Duquesne University, 1991.

3885. Baird, John D. *Suffering in the Life and Works of Georges Duhamel.* University of Washington, 1953.

3886. Bandy, Melanie Flossie. *The Idea of Evil in the Poetry of Blake and Shelley: A Comparative Study.* University of New Mexico, 1971.

3887. Becker, James Earl. *The Poetics of Good and Evil: A Study of Plot and Character in the Later Plays of Charles Williams.* University of Washington, 1979.

3888. Black, Forrest Edward, Jr. *The Nature of Evil in the Tragedies of John Shirley.* Bowling Green State University, 1975.

3889. Bouchard, Larry Drennen. *Tragic Method and Tragic Theology: An Inquiry into Evil and the Drama of Robert Lowell and Peter Shaffer.* University of Chicago, 1984.

3890. Brown, William Clyde. *Anti-theodicy and Human Love in the Films of Ingmar Bergman.* University of Chicago, 1976.

3891. Bruecher, Werner. *The Discovery and Integration of Evil in the Fiction of Joseph Conrad and Hermann Hesse.* University of Arizona, 1972.

3892. Bull, Vivien Seaton. *The Problem of Evil: The Interaction of Philosophy and Fiction (1661-1715).* University of New Mexico, 1977.

3893. Burn, Charlotte Edmonds. *The Control of Evil in Ben Jonson's Masques* [M.A.]. American University, 1972.

3894. Busby, Mark Bayless. *Innocence, Suffering and Release: The Merging Adam-Christ Figure in Contemporary American Fiction.* University of Colorado, 1977.

3895. Case, Anne Merritt. *Pursuit of Wisdom: A Study of the Knowledge of Good and Evil in "Piers Plowman."* Yale University, 1968.

3896. Cole, Douglas. *Suffering and Evil in the Plays of Christopher Marlowe.* Princeton University, 1961.

3897. Cooper, Clara Bomanji. *Willa Cather: The Nature of Evil and its Purgation.* Florida State University, 1969.

3898. Coroneou, Marianthi. *Suffering as Part of the Human Condition in the Fiction of Graham Greene, Albert Camus, and Nikos Kazantzakis.* University of Kentucky, 1967.

3899. Coyle, James John. *The Problem of Evil in the Major Novels of Charles Brockden Brown.* University of Michigan, 1961.

3900. Craft, Commodore., Jr. *A Study of the Interaction of Good and Evil in the Four Major Novel of Charles Brockden Brown* [Ed.D.]. Ball State University, 1976.

3901. Cummings, Richard James. *The Role of Suffering in the Work of J.K. Huysmans.* Stanford University, 1964.

3902. Danielson, Dennis Richard. *Milton and the Problem of Evil: An Essay in Literary Theodicy.* Stanford University, 1979.

3903. Davies, James William. *The Vision of Evil: An Inquiry into the Dialogue Between Emerson, Melville, and Hawthorne and the Nineteenth Century.* Union Theological Seminary, 1958.

3904. Davis, Larry Elton. *A Christian Philosophical Examination of the Picture of Evil in the Writings of J.R.R. Tolkien.* Southwestern Baptist Theological Seminary, 1983.

3905. Diaconoff, Suellen. *Eros and Power in "Les liaisons dangereuses": A Study in Evil.* Indiana University, 1978.

3906. Doane, Margaret Susan. *The Continuation of Romantic Concepts of Innocence and Evil in Robert Browning's "The Ring and the Book."* University of Oregon, 1976.

3907. Donovan, Richard Austin. *Shakespeare and the Game of Evil: A Study of Role-Playing Villains.* University of Minnesota, 1968.

3908. Faulds, Joseph Merkle. *The Son and Satan in "Paradise Lost": An Inquiry into the Poetic Theodicy of John Milton in the Western Tradition.* University of Dallas, 1986.

3909. Feldman, Robert Lee. *The Problem of Evil in Five Plays by Arthur Miller.* University of Maryland College Park, 1985.

3910. Finney, Frank Florer, Jr. *A Critical Examination of the Transition from a Psychological Vision of Life to an Increasingly Christian Awareness of Evil in the Fiction of Thomas Wolfe.* University of Oklahoma, 1961.

3911. Finnigan, David Francis. *Dark Designs: The Presentation of Evil in "Paradise Lost."* University of Oregon, 1970.

3912. Fiondella, Maris Germaine. *Structural Images of Sin and Evil in Book I of "The Fairy Queen."* Fordham University, 1978.

3913. Fleurant, Kenneth John. *Jacques Cazotte and the Supernatural World: Polemics of Good and Evil.* Princeton University, 1973.

3914. Forrest, James French. *The Evil Thought in the Blameless Mind: A Study in the History of a Moral Idea, its Literary Representation, and its Particular Relationship to the Works of John Milton.* Cornell University, 1960.

3915. Fulton, Karen Uitvlugt. *Illusions of Innocence: The Character of Evil in Jane Austen's Novels.* Case Western Reserve University, 1976.

3916. Geare, Jill O'Hora. *The Representation of Suffering in Six of Shakespeare's Tragedies.* University of Toronto, 1983.

3917. Gerstman, Galya. *The Impotent Creator: Art as a Doomed and Dooming Enterprise in the Novels of Victor Hugo.* Columbia University, 1991.

3918. Glazier, Lyle E. *Spenser's Imagery: Imagery of Good and Evil in "The Faerie Queene."* Harvard University, 1950.

3919. Godfrey, Sondra. *The Changing Vision of Evil in Hawthorne's Fiction.* City University of New York, 1976.

3920. Hanenkrat, Frank Thomas. *An Investigation of Hawthorne's Psychology: The Themes of Evil and Love in Selected Short Stories.* Emory University 1971.

3921. Heath, James Roy. *The Approach of Representative Men in Contemporary Literature to Evil and Suffering from the Perspective of the Biblical World View.* Southern Baptist Theological Seminary, 1971.

3922. Honeyford, Bruce N.M. *Problems of Good and Evil in Jacobean Tragedy.* University of Toronto, 1952.

3923. Hood, Gwenyth Elise. *The Lidless Eye and the Long Burden: The Struggle Between Good and Evil in Tolkien's "The Lord of the Rings."* University of Michigan, 1984.

3924. Hoskins, John S., III. *The Problem of Good and Evil in the Novels of Andrew Nelson Lytle* [M.A.]. Vanderbilt University, 1947.

3925. Hume, Beverly Ann. *The Framing of Evil: Romantic Visions and Revisions in American Literature.* University of California, Davis, 1983.

3926. Hunter, Parks Cladwell, Jr. *The Autumn of Strange Suffering: An Interpretation and Criticism of Shelley's "Alastor."* University of Texas at Austin, 1958.

3927. Hutchinson, Mary Anne. *The Devil's Gateway: The Evil Enchantress in Aristo, Tasso, Spenser, and Milton.* Syracuse University, 1975.

3928. Hutchinson, William Henry. *Demonology in Melville's Vocabulary of Evil*. Northwestern University, 1966.

3929. Jacobs, Barry Douglas. *Strindberg and the Problem of Suffering*. Harvard University, 1964.

3930. Janda, Klaus. *Thorns and Crowns: Suffering and Sin in Five of the "Twentieth Century Novels" of William Golding: "Pincher Martin," "Free Fall," "The Pyramid," "Darkness Visible," "The Paper Men."* University of Aberdeen, 1991.

3931. Juris, Albert Stuart. *Satire and the Problem of Evil in Jacobean Drama*. University of Wisconsin at Madison, 1972.

3932. Karrfalt, David Herbert. *Suffering and Theodicy in Wordsworth's Major Poetry*. Southern Illinois University, 1978.

3933. Kilborn, Judith Margaret. *Presence and Absence: Goodness and Evil in "Paradise Lost."* Purdue University, 1985.

3934. Kinnamon, Michael Kurt. *The Cry of the Cuckoo: Literature and Evil in the Contemporary Age*. University of Chicago, 1980.

3935. Kohák, Erazim Vaclav. *Evil and the Christian Symbol of Salvation*. Yale University, 1958.

3936. Kruegel, Fred August. *Suffering and the Sacrificial Ethos in the Dramatic Works of Franz Werfel*. University of Minnesota, 1959.

3937. Labzda, Carol Senftner. *An In-Depth Study on the Role of Suffering in Antoine de Saint-Exupery's "Terre des Hommes"* [M.A.]. Florida Atlantic University, 1977.

3938. Lanham, Jon Alan. *A Critical Edition of "Ideas of Good and Evil" by W.B. Yeats, with Complete Collation, Notes, and Commentary*. University of Toronto, 1976.

3939. Leppe, Suzanne June. *The Devil's Music: A Literary Study of Evil and Music*. University of California, Riverside, 1978.

3940. Levy, Alfred Jacob. *Nathaniel Hawthorne's Attitude Toward Total Depravity and Evil*. University of Wisconsin at Madison, 1957.

3941. Lewin, Lois Symons. *The Theme of Suffering in the Work of Bernard Malamud and Saul Bellow*. University of Pittsburgh, 1967.

3942. Longley, John Lewis, Jr. *The Problem of Evil in Three Novels of William Faulkner*. University of Tennessee, 1949.

3943. Lorch, Lavinia Edgarda. *Tragedy and Remedy: The Lyrics of Euripides'* "Alcestis," "Iphigenia in Tauris," *and* "Helen." Columbia University, 1990.

3944. Lowrie, Joyce Oliver. *Suffering as Punishment and Expiation in Four Nineteenth Century Novelists*. Yale University, 1966.

3945. Mallory, Thomas Oliver, Jr. *The Devil and Thomas Hardy: A Study of the Manifestations of Supernatural Evil in Hardy's Fiction*. University of Illinois at Urbana–Champaign, 1957.

3946. Malone, Gloria Snodgrass. *The Nature and Causes of Suffering in the Fiction of Paule Marshall, Kristin Hunter, Toni Morrison, and Alice Walker*. Kent State University, 1979.

3947. Maltman, Sister Nicholas. *The Study of the Evil Characters in the English Corpus Christi Cycles*. University of California at Berkeley, 1957.

3948. Mao, Nathan Kwok-Kuen. *William Dean Howells on Evil*. University of Wisconsin at Madison, 1966.

3949. Marck, Nancy Anne. *Tragedy and Society: The Novels of George Eliot*. University of Illinois at Urbana–Champaign, 1992

3950. Mauldin, Jane Ellen. *"On That Shaded Day": Ralph Waldo Emerson's Response to Suffering* [D.Min.]. Meadville/Lombard Theological School, 1981.

3951. Mayo, Ada. *Treatment of Death and Eternity in the Prose Fiction of Chingiz Aitmatov*. Bryn Mawr College, 1991. [Russian novelist.]

3952. McCloskey, William Edwards. *"Macbeth": A Birthing from Chaos to Peace*. University of Toledo, 1990.

3953. McMillan, Grant Edgar. *"Nature's Dark Side": Herman Melville and the Problem of Evil*. Syracuse University, 1973.

3954. Mielke, Robert Erven. *"The Riddle of the Painful Earth": W.D. Howells' Explorations of Suffering in his Major Writings of the Early 1890's*. Duke University, 1986.

3955. Miller, Sara. *Evil and Fairy Tales: The Witch as Symbol of Evil in Fairy Tales*. California Institute of Integral Studies, 1984.

3956. Miner, Marlene Renee. *The Problem of Evil in the Works of Blake and Shelley*. University of Cincinnati, 1990.

3957. Moore, Robert Risk. *Faulkner's "Sanctuary": Radical Evil and Religious Vision*. University of Virginia, 1978.

3958. Morton, John Gilliespie. *Aspects of Evil and Death in Eight Plays by Tirso de Molina*. Vanderbilt University, 1972.

3959. Muto, Susan Annette. *The Symbolism of Evil: A Hermeneutic Approach to Milton's "Paradise Lost."* University of Pittsburg, 1970.

3960. Neuleib, Janice Witherspoon. *The Concept of Evil in the Fiction of C.S. Lewis*. University of Illinois at Urbana–Champaign, 1974.

3961. Nordstrom, Louis Douglas. *Sartre and Evil: A Study of "Saint Genet: Actor and Martyr."* Columbia University, 1973.

3962. North, John Stanley. *Tennyson of Knowledge, Evil, and History*. University of Alberta, 1969.

3963. Otto, Linda McHenry. *A Study of Evil and Insanity in Tieck's Early Works*. Northwestern University, 1973.

3964. Painter, Mark Andrew. *The Word and Tragedy: The Revelation of Divine Mystery in the Portrayal of Man as Language* [M.A.]. University of North Texas, 1988. [Discussion of Genesis, Job, Oedipus, King Lear.]

3965. Papper, Emanuel Martin. *Pain, Suffering and Anesthesia in the Romantic Period*. University of Miami, 1990.

3966. Parks, John Gordon. *The Possibility of Evil: The Fiction of Shirley Jackson*. University of New Mexico, 1973.

3967. Paulits, F. Joseph. *Emerson's Concept of Good and Evil*. University of Pittsburgh, 1955.

3968. Ploplis, William Richard. *The Great Name of God: A Study of the Element of Kabbalah in Samuel Taylor Coleridge's Theogony and its Influence on the Theodicy and Cosmology of his Major Poetry*. Loyola University, 1981.

3969. Price, John Sergeant, Jr. *The Humanized Poet: Suffering and Consolation in Wordsworth's Poetry, 1793-1806*. University of Virginia, 1976.

3970. Pustejovsky, John Stephen. *Religious Economy and Social Reality: Structural Responses to Suffering in Two Eighteenth Century Novels*. University of Texas at Austin, 1983.

3971. Ratliff, Gerald Lee. *An Examination of the Parabolic Nature of "Suffering" in Selected Plays by Eugene O'Neill, 1913-1923*. Bowling Green State University, 1975.

3972. Reddin, Chitra Pershad. *Forms of Evil in the Gothic Novel*. Dalhousie University, 1978.

3973. Rhodes, Rodman Dunbar. *Samuel Johnson and the Problem of Evil*. Harvard University, 1963.

3974. Ringler, Ellin Jane. *The Problem of Evil: A Correlative Study of the Novels of Nathaniel Hawthorne and George Eliot*. University of Illinois, Urbana–Champaign, 1967.

3975. Rivers, Julius Edwin, Jr. *Cruelty and Suffering in the Works of Proust*. University of Oregon, 1970.

3976. Rosa, Adrian Wayne. *Elves, the Righteous Ringmakers: Taking Tolkien Seriously* [M.A.]. Florida Atlantic University, 1990.

3977. Rosenbaum, Eric. *The Function of Evil in Schiller's Dramas*. University of Pennsylvania, 1951.

3978. Rosenberg, James L. *Cyril Tourneur: The Anatomy of Evil*. University of Denver, 1955.

3979. Ruesch, Alfred R. *Francis Stuart: The Language of Suffering*. New York University, 1975.

3980. Ruff, Felicia J. *Suffering Angels: Images of Children in Nineteenth Century Drama*. City University of New York, 1991.

3981. Ruprecht, Louis A., Jr. *The Tragic Posture in the Modern Age: An Essay on Tragedy—Classical, Christian and Modern*. Emory University, 1990.

3982. Saez, Richard. *The Redemptive Circle: Illusion and the Beneficence of Evil in Tasso, Milton and Calderon*. Yale University, 1967.

3983. Saposnik, Irving Seymour. *Aspects of Evil in the Works of Robert Louis Stevenson*. University of California at Berkeley, 1965.

3984. Sarot, Ellin. *Snarled in an Evil Time: Responses to War in the Work of W.B. Yeats, Wilfred Owen, and Sylvia Plath*. Columbia University, 1979.

3985.   Schwab, Gweneth Boge. *Theological Implications of Suffering Children in Teaching Four Novels by Dostoevsky, Camus, Golding, Greene* [D.A.]. Illinois State University, 1982.

3986.   Sears, Lloyd C. *Shakespeare and the Problem of Evil.* University of Chicago, 1936.

3987.   Senelick, Lawrence Philip. *The Prestige of Evil: The Murderer as Romantic Hero from Sade to Lacenaire.* Harvard University, 1972.

3988.   Shabetai, Karen. *Blake's Perception of Evil.* University of California at San Diego, 1984.

3989.   Shaw, Brian Arthur. *Aspects of Evil in Five Metrical Old English Saints' Lives.* University of Western Ontario, 1978.

3990.   Siegel, Robert Harold. *The Serpent and the Dove: The Problem of Evil in Coleridge's Poetry.* Harvard University, 1968.

3991.   Smernoff, Richard Alan. *The Nature of Evil in the "Contes et Romans" of Voltaire.* Princeton University, 1969.

3992.   Smith, Gordon Ross. *Good and Evil in Shakespearean Tragedy.* Pennsylvania State University, 1956.

3993.   Spivack, Bernard. *Allegory of Evil.* Columbia University, 1953.

3994.   St. John, Barbara Ann. *The Portrayal of Evil in Selected Children's Books, 1945-1972* [Ed.D.]. University of Toledo, 1973.

3995.   Startzman, Louis Eugene. *Images of Evil in the Formal Verse Satire of Joseph Hall, John Marston, John Donne, and Alexander Pope.* Ohio State University, 1970.

3996.   Steinman, Clayton M. *Hollywood Dialectic: "Force of Evil" and the Frankfurt School's Critique of the Culture Industry.* New York University, 1979.

3997.   Stengel, Wayne Brennan. *Hammer and Nailles: The Problem of "Good" and "Evil" in Six Short Stories of John Cheever* [M.A.]. University of Louisville, 1971.

3999.   Swann, George Rogers. *Philosophical Parallelisms in Six English Novelists: The Conception of Good, Evil and Human Nature.* University of Pennsylvania, 1929.

4000.   Terrill, Carol Jean. *The Conflict Between Good and Evil as a Structural Influence in Medieval French Drama.* University of Kansas, 1973.

4001.   Teunissen, John James. *Of Patience and Heroic Martyrdom: The Book of Job and Milton's Conception of Patient Suffering in "Paradise Regained" and "Samson Agonistes."* University of Rochester, 1967.

4002.   Thompson, Sharon Kay. *The Historical Basis of Satire in Quevedo's "Suenos": The Social Construction of Evil.* University of Minnesota, 1985.

4003.   Topolewski, Nancy E. *The Doctrine of Atonement in the Novels and Theological Works of Charles Williams.* Drew University, 1990.

4004.   Truesdale, Barbara L. *The Problem of Suffering: The Question of Job in "King Lear," "Moby Dick," and "The Sound and the Fury."* Ohio State University, 1991.

4005.   Vasquez, Penelope Rainey. *Literary Convention in Scenes of Madness and Suffering in Greek Tragedy*. Columbia University, 1972.

4006.   Vliet, Rodney Meryl. *The Concept of Evil in the Novels of Robert Penn Warren*. Michigan State University, 1973.

4007.   Wadsworth, Celina. *Symbolism in the Short Stories of Katherine Mansfield: An Epiphany of her Sensitivity to Suffering*. University of Ottawa. 1969.

4008.   Wainer, Alex Myer, Jr. *Tube of Horror: The Cinematic Vision of Television as a Purveyor of Evil* [M.A.]. Regent University, 1990.

4009.   Ward, Joseph Anthony. *Evil in the Fiction of Henry James*. Tulane University, 1957.

4010.   Ward, Joseph Thomas. *Hermin Melville: The Forms and Forces of Evil*. University of Notre Dame, 1959.

4011.   Weiskopf, Dasha Dana. *The Presence of Evil in Three Selected French Novels: André Malrauz, "La Condition Humaine"; Georges Bernanos, "Journal D'un Curé de Campagne"; Albert Camus, "La Peste."* Florida State University, 1985.

4012.   Wildermuth, M. Catherine Turman. *Innocence, Suffering, and Sensibility: The Narrative Function of the Pathetic in Chaucer's Tales of the Clerk, Prioress, and Physician*. Rice University, 1984.

4013.   Williams, Anne. *The Background of Wordsworth's Theodicy of the Landscape*. Cornell University, 1973.

4014.   Williams, Richard H. *The Expression of Common Value Attitudes Towards Suffering in the Symbolism of Mediaeval Art*. Harvard University, 1938.

4015.   Wilson, Miriam. *The Theme of Suffering in Wordsworth's Poetry*. Florida State University, 1963.

4016.   Wilson, Rhonda S. *Levels in William Faulkner's Concept of Suffering* [M.A.]. Florida Atlantic University, 1977.

4017.   Winkler, Frances R. *Significant Characterizations of Incarnate Evil in Narrative English Fiction*. University of Southern California, 1952.

4018.   Wiseman, Richard Wallace. *Music and the Problem of Evil: Condemnation and Affirmation in the Works of Thomas Mann and Hermann Hesse*. University of California at Berkeley, 1961.

4019.   Wolf, Jack Clifford. *Hart Crane's Harp of Evil: A Study of Satanism in "The Bridge."* State University of New York at Buffalo, 1972.

4020.   Wortz, Melinda Farris. *Radical Emptiness: The Spiritual Experience in Contemporary Art*. Graduate Theological Union, 1990.

4021.   Wyant, Jerome Lee. *The Theme of Moral Growth through Suffering in the Poetry and Novels of George Meredith*. University of Nebraska at Lincoln, 1972.

4022.   Wyss, Hal. *Involuntary Evil in the Fiction of Brown, Cooper, Poe, Hawthorne, and Melville*. Ohio State University, 1971.

4023.   Yaco, Rosemary Morris. *Suffering Women: Feminine Masochism in Novels by American Women*. University of Michigan, 1975.

4024. Zimmermann, Edward J. *Light out of Darkness: A Study of the Growth and Structure of Evil in Milton's "Paradise Lost."* State University of New York at Buffalo, 1970.

[c] Historical Theodicy

4025. Aiken, David W. *Sharp Compassion: Kierkegaard on the Problem of Sin.* Boston College, 1990.

4026. Akrong, Abraham Ako. *An Akan Christian View of Salvation from the Perspective of John Calvin's Soteriology.* Lutheran School of Theology at Chicago, 1991.

4027. Anderson-Gold, Sharon Rae. *Teleology and Radical Evil: An Interpretation of the Concept of Species Character in Kant's Philosophy of History.* New School for Social Research, 1980.

4028. Arnold, Winston J. *The Problem of Collective Suffering in the Early Fifth Century According to the "De Civitate Dei": The Pagan-Christian Dialogue on the Question of Responsibility.* University of Montreal, 1964.

4029. Bolton, Frederick John. *Theodicy, A Study of the Thought of Some British Theologians of the Twentieth Century with Reference to the Problem of Evil.* Princeton Theological Seminary, 1964.

4030. Bracken, W. Jerome. *Why Suffering in Redemption? A New Interpretation of the Theology of the Passion in the Summa Theologica, 3. 46-49, by Thomas Aquinas.* Fordham University, 1978.

4031. Brockway, George Max. *Leibniz, Hume, Kant and their Contemporaries on the Problem of Evil.* University of Wisconsin, 1973.

4032. Brooks, Richard A. *Voltaire, Leibniz and the Problem of Theodicy: From "Oedipe" to "Candide."* Columbia University, 1959.

4033. Callewaert, Janet M. *The Role of a Creation Theology in the Contemporary Soteriology of Edward Schillibeeckx.* Catholic University of America, 1988.

4034. Chase, Christopher Loring. *Romantic Piety in the Heroic Church: The Suffering Christ in the Art, Liturgy, and Literature of the First Millennium.* Harvard University, 1978.

4035. Chiang, Chin-Tai. *The Problem of Evil: Bayle to Voltaire, 1688-1778.* Washington University, 1977.

4036. Chitwood, Garret Clayton. *Love and Guilt: A Study of Suffering in Selected Medieval Works.* Case Western Reserve University, 1970.

4037. Christie, Dolores L. *The Moral Methodology of Louis Janssens.* Duquesne University, 1988.

4038. Cook, Edward McLean. *The Deficient Cause of Moral Evil According to St. Thomas.* Catholic University of America, 1962.

4039. Costello, Edward B. *An Analysis and Evaluation of Some Theories of Evil: Plotinus, Aquinas, and Leibniz.* Northwestern University, 1959.

4040.   Cushman, Robert Earl. *Non-Being and the Problem of Evil in Plato*. Yale University, 1942.

4041.   De Coursey, M. Edwin, Sister. *The Theory of Evil in the Metaphysics of St. Thomas and its Contemporary Significance*. Catholic University of America, 1949.

4042.   Desjardins, Michel Robert. *Sin in Valentinianism*. University of Toronto, 1987.

4043.   Edmunds, Bruce T. *The Fall of Man as Temporal and Ontological Discontinuity in the Writings of Blaise Pascal*. Stanford University, 1989.

4044.   Ehrlich, Edith. *Suffering in Nietzsche: Motive and Mask*. University of Massachusetts, 1976.

4045.   Eudaly, Thomas D. *A Kantian Critique of David Lewis's Modal Realism*. University of Illinois at Urbana–Champaign, 1989.

4045.   Fabbro, Ronald. *Cooperation in Evil: A Consideration of the Traditional Doctrine from the Point of View of the Contemporary Discussion about the Moral Act* [Th.D.]. Pontificia Universitas Gregorina (Vatican), 1988.

4047.   Feltz, Lawrence Michael. *The Enigmatic Character of Moral Evil in the Thought of Augustine*. Duquesne University, 1991.

4048.   Freeman, Donald Dale. *Radical Evil and Original Sin: Kant's Doctrine of Freedom in Existential Perspective*. Drew University, 1969.

4049.   Fuller, Benjamin Apthorp Gould. *The Problem of Evil in Plotinus*. Harvard University, 1906.

4050.   Gallagher, David M. *Thomas Aquinas on the Causes of Human Choice*. Catholic University of America, 1989.

4051.   Haden, Norris Karl. *Sufferings of Inwardness: An Analysis of Religious Belief and Existence in the Thought of Kierkegaard and Wittgenstein*. University of Georgia, 1991.

4052.   Hall, Christopher Alan. *John Chrysostom's "On Providence": A Translation and Theological Interpretation*. Drew University, 1991.

4053.   Heaney-Hunter, Jo Ann Catherine. *The Links Between Sexuality and Original Sin in the Writings of John Chrysostom and Augustine*. Fordham University, 1988.

4054.   Hoppmann, William Henry. *The Role of the "Body" in the Philosophy of Friedrich Nietzsche as Artistic-Physician*. Duquesne University, 1986.

4055.   Hughes, Samuel David. *The Problem of Evil as Discussed in the Gifford Lectures from 1889-1986*. Baylor University, 1989.

4056.   Ihejiofor, Thaddeus N. *Freedom and the Natural Inclination of the Will According to St. Thomas Aquinas*. Leuven, Belgium: Katholieke University, 1980.

4057.   Jefferson, Howard Bonar. *The Problem of Evil in the Philosophy of Josiah Royce*. Yale University, 1929.

4058.   Kevern, John. *The Role of Divine Incomprehensibility in the Theologies of Karl Rahner and Hans Urs von Balthasar*. University of Chicago Divinity School, 1991.

4059. Khan, Abrahim Habibulla. *The Treatment of the Theme of Suffering in Kierkegaard's Works.* McGill University, 1973.

4060. Klauder, Francis J. *The Intrinsic Nature of Good and Evil According to St. Bonaventure.* Fordham University, 1953.

4061. Krantz, Susan Lufkin. *Brentano's Theodicy.* Brown University, 1980.

4062. La Delfa, Rosario, *The Suffering of Christ and its Relationship to the Individual According to Newman* [Th.D.]. Pontifica Universitas Gregoriana (Vatican), 1988.

4063. Larson, Curtis W. R. *A Comparison of the Views of Paul and Kierkegaard on Christian Suffering.* Yale University, 1953.

4064. Lorizio, Giuseppe. *Eschaton and History in the Thought of Antony Rosmini: Origin and Analysis of "Theodicy" in Theological Perspective* [Th.D.]. Pontificia Universitas Gregoriana (Vatican), 1988.

4065. Mattson, Pamela K. Grande. *The Ruling Act: An Examination of Friedrich Nietzsche's "Beyond Good and Evil" and "On the Genealogy of Morals."* University of Chicago, 1972.

4066. McCully, George Elliott, Jr. *Juan Luis Vives (1493-1540) and the Problem of Evil in his Time.* Columbia University, 1967.

4067. McKenna, Joseph. *Evil and the Possibility of Social Sin.* Fordham University, 1991.

4068. Nuth, Joan Marie. *Love's Meaning: The Theology of Julian of Norwich.* Boston College and Andover Newton Theological School, 1988.

4069. Oslon, Ronald Dean. *The Immutability of God: The Study of a Contemporary Theological Dispute in Light of the Phenomenon of Faith.* Vanderbilt University, 1991.

4070. Pentz, Rebecca D. *A Defense of the Formal Adequacy of St. Thomas Aquinas' Analysis of Omnipotence.* University of California at Irvine, 1980.

4071. Phillips, Erin. *The Place of Sin in the Theological Anthropology of Karl Rahner.* McMaster University, 1991.

4072. Powell, Thomas Francis. *Royce and the Problem of Evil.* Syracuse University, 1964.

4073. Praetorius, Hugh Michael. *Escape From the Evil Demon: A Discourse of the Cartesianism of Phenomenology.* The Claremont Graduate School, 1969.

4074. Sa, Mija. *A Kierkegaardian Perspective on Suffering.* Drew University, 1983.

4075. Sabom, Claire D. *Pathos, Tragic Wisdom, and "The World as a Human Being": Nietzsche's View of the Mastery of Knowledge Drive in Presocratic Philosophy and in "Thus Spoke Zarathustra."* Emory University, 1989.

4076. Sanders, Theresa. *Karl Rahner and the God of Love.* Syracuse University, 1991.

4077. Shaffer, Deane Leslie. *The Theodicy of Edwin Lewis.* Southern Baptist Theological Seminary, 1960.

4078. Sheedy, Patrick D. *Justice and Human Need: An Investigation of Scriptural and Roman Catholic Sources.* Marquette University, 1989.

4079.   Shelly, Thomas Rubel. *Theodicy in Plato's "Timaeus."* Vanderbilt University, 1981.

4080.   Simon, Richard Keller. *Comedy, Suffering, and Human Existence: The Search for a Comic Strategy of Survival from Sören Kierkegaard to Kenneth Burke.* Stanford University, 1977.

4081.   Skelton, Eugene L. *The Problem of Evil in the Words of William Temple.* Southwestern Baptist Theological Seminary, 1951.

4082.   Skerrett, Katheen. *H.R. Niebuhr: Pain and the Faithful Self.* Harvard University, 1991.

4083.   Slater, Christopher Peter Robert Lawson. *The Question of Evil in Marcel: Some Philosophical Analysis and Saint Augustine.* Harvard University, 1964.

4084.   Smith, Helen Rosalind. *Man's "Conquest of Liberty" and the Problem of Evil: A Study of the Meaning of Salvation in the Writings of Jacques Maritain.* Catholic University of America, 1979.

4085.   Stashwick, Tad Sergei. *Wittgenstein and Theology: "Philosophical Investigations" II, XI and The Problem of Evil.* Yale University, 1983.

4086.   Storms, Charles Samuel. *Jonathan Edwards and John Taylor on Human Nature: A Study of the Encounter Between New England Puritanism and the Enlightenment.* University of Texas at Dallas, 1985. [Original Sin, Free Will, Determinism, Theodicy, etc.]

4087.   Swanson, Severin Alfred. *The Problem of Evil as Reflected in Pulpit Oratory of the Eighteenth Century in France.* University of Wisconsin, 1981.

4088.   Treacy, Charles Jeremiah. *Plato's Doctrine of Evil.* University of Toronto, 1941.

4089.   Velkley, Richard Lee. *Kant as Philosopher of Theodicy.* Pennsylvania State University, 1978.

4090.   Waddle, Sharon Hels. *Dubious Praise: The Form and Context of the Participial Hymns in Job 4-14.* Vanderbilt University, 1987.

4091.   Weithman, Paul J. *Justice, Charity and Property: The Centrality of Sin to the Political Thought of Thomas Aquinas.* Harvard University, 1988.

4092.   Yetzer, Bernard E. *Holiness and Sin in the Church: An Examination of "Lumen Gentium" and "Unitatis Redintegratio" of the Second Vatican Council* [S.T.D.]. Catholic University of America, 1988.

4093.   Zimmerman, Charles Edwin. *Trampling the Serpent's Head: Discipline and Theodicy in Tertullian's Use of Indulgentia Dei.* Emory University, 1984.

[d] Other Relevant Dissertations

4094.   Abbott, Daniel Phillips. *Divine Participation and Eschatology in the Theodicies of Paul Tillich and Jürgen Moltmann.* University of Virginia, 1987.

4095.   Anderson, Per Markus. *Theodicy in a New Key: The Problem of Consent to the Negative in a Technological Culture.* University of Chicago, 1991.

4096. Arathuzik, Mary Diane. *The Cognitive and Affective Appraisal of Suffering Due to Physical Pain and the Coping Strategies and Behaviors of Metastatic Breast Cancer Patients.* [D.N.Sc.]. Catholic University of America, 1986.

4097. Au, Peter Ying-Yuk. *An Evangelical Response to the Theological Method of Jürgen Moltmann's Theology of Hope.* Dallas Theological Seminary, 1990.

4098. Ayoub, Mahmoud Mustafa. *Redemptive Suffering in Islam: A Study of the Devotional Aspects of 'Ashura in Twelver Shi'ism in the Middle Ages.* Harvard University, 1975.

4099. Barnesm, Linda. *Practices of Chinese Medicine in Boston: A Study in Meanings of Healing.* Harvard University, 1991.

4100. Barnhart, Joe Edward. *The Religious Epistemology and Theodicy of Edward John Carnell and Edgar Sheffield Brightman: A Study in Contrasts."* Boston University Graduate School, 1964.

4101. Beeson, Robert J. *Theism and Theodicy: A Project-Thesis on the Problem of Evil* [Th.D.]. Wesley Theological Seminary, 1982.

4102. Bentley, Robert A. *The Work of God Through Suffering Arising from Egocentricity.* University of Chicago, 1952.

4103. Bennett, Ronald Eugene. *A Pastoral Understanding of and Response to the Issue of Human Suffering."* Vanderbilt University Divinity School, 1969.

4104. Berke, Matthew B. *Political Philosophy and the Tragic Sense of Life: A Study of Reinhold Niebuhr.* Yale University, 1990.

4105. Bernard, Joel Charles. *From Theodicy to Ideology: The Origins of the American Temperance Movement.* Yale University, 1983.

4106. Boyd, James Waldemar. *Satan and Maraä: A Comparative Study of the Symbols of Evil in Early Greek Christian and Early Indian Buddhist Traditions.* Northwestern University, 1970.

4107. Brame, Grace Adolphsen. *Divine Grace and Human Will in the Writings of Evelyn Underhill.* Temple University, 1988.

4108. Brock, Rita. *A Christology of Erotic Power: Journeys By Heart.* The Claremont Graduate School, 1988.

4109. Brotherston, Bruce Wallace. *Moral Evil and the Social Conscience.* Harvard University, 1923.

4110. Browder, James Patterston, III. *Elected Suffering: Toward a Theology for Medicine.* Duke University, 1991.

4111. Burrow, Rufus, Jr. *A Critique of E.S. Brightman's Conception of God, with Special Reference to Excess Evil.* Boston University Graduate School, 1983.

4112. Bush, Theodore Andrew. *Human Suffering in the Theology of Wayne E. Oates.* Aquinas Institute, 1980.

4113. Buhrer, James Daniel. *Evil, Moral and Physical, in Experience, History and Philosophy.* American University, 1918.

4114. Camacho, Haroldo Samuel. *A Synthesis of Moltmann's Christology with Jung's God-Image Archetypal: A Theological Psychology for Pastoral Counselling and Psychotherapy*. The School of Theology at Claremont, 1991.

4115. Carter, Ronald Lee. *An Examination of the Logic of Borden Parker Bowne's Response to the Problem of Good and Evil*. Boston University, 1985.

4116. Casey, Barry L. *Hope, Suffering, and Solidarity: The Power of the Sabbath Experience*. The Claremont Graduate School, 1988.

4117. Chopp, Rebecca Sue. *The Interruption of Interpretation: The Function and Claims of Suffering in Liberation and Political Theologies*. University of Chicago, 1983.

4118. Crews, Rowan D., Jr. *The Praise of God and the Problem of Evil: A Doxological Approach to the Problem of Evil and Suffering*. Duke University, 1989.

4119. Daley, John B. *The Christian Explanation of the Problem of Suffering*. Niagara University, 1936.

4120. Davis, Douglas Paul. *Is Evil a Relation? A Study in the Metaphysics of Value*. State University of New York at Buffalo, 1986. [Discussion of Francisco Suaréz, A.C. Ewing, Ralph Barton Perry.]

4121. Descoteaux, Carol Jane. *Chronic Suffering: A Theological and Ethical Reflection on Brazil's Basic Ecclesial Communities and Jean Vanier's L'Arche*. University of Notre Dame, 1985.

4122. Dickinson, John Mervyn. *Aggression and the Status of Evil in Man: A Critical Analysis of Sigmund Freud's Assumptions from the Theological Perspective of Reinhold Niebuhr*. Boston University Graduate School, 1964.

4123. Dubina, Virginia Wallace. *The Problem of Theodicy in the Mystical Writings of William Law*. University of Miami, 1971.

4124. Dunaway, Lloyd Philip. *Evil as God's Own Problem: A Study of the Theodicies of Karl Barth and E.S. Brightman*. Baylor University, 1979.

4125. Farley, Wendy Lee. *Tragic Vision and Divine Compassion: A Paradigm of God's Relationship to Ruptured Existence*. Vanderbilt University, 1988.

4126. Field, Anne Therese. *Integrating the Shadow: A Contribution of Jungian Psychology to Feminist Theology*. Graduate Theological Union, 1990.

4127. Fogarty, Harry Wells. *Approaches to the Process of Personal Transformation: The Spiritual Exercises of Ignatius Loyola and Jung's Method of Active Imagination*. Union Theological Seminary in the City of New York, 1987.

4128. Foreman, Willie James. *The Problem of God and Evil and Its Implications for Christian Education in the Black Church*. The School of Theology at Claremont, 1972.

4129. Friedman, Maurice S. *Martin Buber, Mystic, Existentialist, and Social Prophet: A Study in the Redemption of Evil*. University of Chicago, 1950.

4130. Front, Henri Elias. *The Problem of Evil in the Midrash Rabba*. Hebrew Union College–Jewish Institute of Religion (Ohio), 1963.

4131. Futterman, Michael David. *Judaism, Hinduism and Theodicy: A Comparative Study of the Judaic and Hindu Treatment of the Problem of Evil.* New York University, 1977.

4132. Gammache, Richard James, III. *Suffering Adult Development: Learning How to Suffer as the Means to Full Human Maturity and Self-Realization—Lessons from Eminent Christian Mystics.* University of Illinois at Urbana–Champaign, 1985.

4133. Garcia, Alberto Lazaro. *Theology of the Cross: A Critical Study of Leonardo Boff's and Jon Sobrino's Theology of the Cross in Light of Martin Luther's Theology of the Cross as Interpreted by Contemporary Luther Scholars* [Th.D.]. Lutheran School of Theology at Chicago, 1987.

4134. Giles, T. Edward. *A Series of Sermons and Feed Back Sessions Addressing Some of the Issues Related to Pain and Suffering* [D.Min.]. Drew University, 1982.

4135. Gindes, Stephanie. *The Psychology of Evil.* United States International University, 1976.

4136. Glancy, Jennifer Ann. *Satan in the Synoptic Gospels.* Columbia University, 1990.

4137. Gokey, Francis X. *The Terminology for the Devil and Evil Spirits in the Apostolic Fathers.* Catholic University of America, 1961.

4138. Goldsmith, Robin Squier. *Comparative Analysis of the Social Ethics of Reinhold Niebuhr and Martin Buber.* Northwestern University, 1986.

4139. Gray, Cornelius Alex. *The Biblical and Ethical Elements in the Preaching of Martin Luther King: A Theology of Black Hope.* The School of Theology at Claremont, 1988.

4140. Hageman, Louise. *Suffering and its Significance for Personal and Spiritual Life.* Duquesne University, 1972.

4141. Hall, Douglas John. *The Suffering of the Church: A Doctrinal Study of an Aspect of the Nature and Destiny of the Christian Church.* Union Theological Seminary, 1963.

4142. Hamblin, Madeline Walsh. *Simone Weil: Concept of a Self-Emptying God with Special Reference to the Problem of Human Suffering.* University of Southern California, 1976.

4143. Harvey, Louis-Charles. *Action-Ful Faith: A Theological Response to Black Suffering.* Union Theological Seminary, New York, 1978.

4144. Heffner, Blake Richard. *A Catechism for Kenotic Spirituality: The Book of Spiritual Poverty in Analysis and Reflection.* Princeton Theological Seminary, 1986. [Eickhart, Mysticism, Rheinland School.]

4145. Herman, Arthur Ludwig. *The Problem of Evil and Indian Thought.* University of Minnesota, 1970.

4146. Highfield, Ronald Curtis. *The Doctrine of Sin in Ecumenical Perspective: A Comparison of Karl Barth and Karl Rahner.* Rice University, 1988.

4147. Huckabay, Harry Hunter, Jr. *Pastoral Care and the Issue of Theodicy.* [D.Min.]. University of the South, 1984.

4148. Inati, Shams C. *An Examination of Ibn Sina's Solution for the Problem of Evil*. State University of New York at Buffalo, 1979.

4149. Isenberg, Elliott. *The Experience of Evil: A Phenomenological Approach*. California Institute of Integral Studies, 1983.

4150. Ish-Horowicz, Moshe. *Theodicy as Evidenced by Early Rabbinic Discussions of the Flood*. Victoria University of Manchester, 1987.

4151. Ives, Christopher A. *A Zen Buddhist Social Ethic*. The Claremont Graduate School, 1988.

4152. Jackson, Gregory D. *The Understanding of Sin in the Theology of Wolfhart Pannenberg*. Southern Baptist Theological Seminary, 1988.

4153. Jones, H. Kimball. *Toward an Ethic of the Whole Person: A Study of C.G. Jung's Theory of Shadow and Evil and its Implications for Christian Ethics*. Union Theological Seminary, New York, 1981.

4154. Kalinowski, Anthony Gerald. *Chronic Pain and Suffering*. University of Chicago, 1982.

4155. Kim, Young Ae. *Han: From Brokenness to Wholeness: A Theoretical Analysis of Korean Women's Han and a Contextualized Healing Methodology*. The School of Theology at Claremont, 1991.

4156. Kreidler, Mary Helen Cole. *Meaning in Suffering: A Nursing Dilemma* [Ed.D.]. Columbia University Teacher's College, 1978.

4157. Kremer, William Richard. *Toward a Modern Doctrine of Judgment: A Study in the Theology of Karl Barth and Paul Tillich*. Southern Baptist Theological Seminary, 1986.

4158. Kuehnert, Philip Rudolph. *In Defense of the Indefensible: Theodicy in Pastoral Counselling* [S.T.D.]. Dissertation. Emory University, 1987.

4159. Lambert, George Everett. *The Prior Suffering of God as a Tool in Pastoral Care of Trauma and Traumatic Loss"* [D.Min.]. Trinity Lutheran Seminary, 1986.

4160. Lammers, Ann Conrad. *A Study of the Relation Between Theology and Psychology: Victor White and C.G. Jung*. Yale University, 1987.

4161. Lamore, George Edward, Jr. *Theories of Natural Evil in the Thought of Henry Nelson Wieman, Edwin Lewis, and Paul Tillich*. Boston University School of Theology, 1959.

4162. Lawson, Jonathan Mark. *The Contextualization of Suffering in American Society: A Theological Response to Apathy*. Southern Baptist Theological Seminary, 1990.

4163. Lee, Chung Young. *The Suffering of God: A Systematic Inquiry into a Concept of Divine Passibility*. Boston University, 1968.

4164. Lee, Ronald Glenn. *Exploded Graces: Providence and the Confederate Israel in Evangelical Southern Sermons, 1861-1865* [M.A.]. Rice University, 1990.

4165. Le Guin, Katherine Wesley. *Disease as Suffering: An Interpretation*. Emory University, 1981.

4166. Levan, Christopher. *Dialogue with Dispensation: Doctrines of Providence, God, and Eschatology*. McGill University, 1991.

4167. Liderbach, Daniel. *Martin Luther's Theology of Suffering in Modern Translation: A Comparative Study in the Roots of Dietrich Bonhoeffer's Theology of Suffering*. University of St. Michael's College, Toronto, 1979.

4168. Lysaught, Mary Therese. *To Suffer Patiently: The Structure and Significance of Suffering in Discourse in Medical Ethics*. Duke University, 1990.

4169. Macke, Beth A. *A Comparative Study of Two Roman Catholic Healing Rituals* [M.A.]. University of South Alabama, 1988.

4170. Magagna, Richard. *A Study of the Relationship of Sin, Evil, Finitude, and Value in "Nature, Man and God" by William Temple*. Drew University, 1968.

4171. Majors, Clyde Rolston. *The Contemporary Emphasis on Transformation: Its Relation to a Christian Approach to the Problem of Suffering* [Th.D.]. Southwestern Baptist Theological Seminary, 1973.

4172. Malmberg, Susan Frieda. *Muslim Religious Beliefs and the Provision of Grief Therapy*. M.S. California State University, 1990.

4173. Marziz, Cecelia Loreto. *Religion and Coping with Poverty in Brazil*. Boston University, 1989.

4174. Mason, George A., Jr. *God's Freedom as Faithfulness: A Critique of Jürgen Moltmann's Social Trinitarianism*. Southwestern Baptist Theological Seminary, 1987.

4175. Mathew, Thomson Kuzhivelil. *A Clinical Model of Pastoral Ministry in Chronic Pain* [D.Min.]. Oral Roberts University, 1986.

4176. McCabe, Justine Ann. *The Role of Suffering in the Transformation of Self*. California School of Professional Psychology, Berkeley, 1991.

4177. McFarlane, Adrian Anthony. *Toward a Grammar of Fear: A Phenomenological Analysis of the Experience and the Interpretation of Fear as a Propaedeutic to the Study of the Problem of Evil."* Drew University, 1985.

4178. McGee, Ellen Flanagan. *An American Approach to the Problem of Evil: A Study of the History of its Development and its Articulation as a Philosophy by William James*. Fordham University, 1969.

4179. McGill, William Marcus. *Reason, Faith, and the Problem of Evil in the Thought of Edgar S. Brightman and Nels F.S. Ferré*. Boston University, 1974.

4180. McReynolds, Sally Ann. *Eschatology and Social Action in the Work of Paul Ricoeur*. Catholic University of America, 1988.

4181. Meier, Levi. *Chronic Pain, Suffering, and Spirituality: The Relationship Between Chronic Pain, Suffering, and Different Religious Approaches*. University of Southern California, 1981.

4182. Miller, Arlene. *Becoming Good: Psychosocial Conflict or Submission to the Good? A Dialogue Between Erik Erikson and Stanley Hauerwas*. Temple University, 1991.

4183.   Minton, Frank D. *Providence and Evil: A Study Based on the Thought of Friedrich Schleiermacher and Paul Tillich.* University of Chicago, 1969.

4184.   Miyake-Stoner, Nobuko. *Hiroshima: The Suffering and the Hope as a Resource for the Church's Peace Ministry* [D.Min.]. The School of Theology at Claremont, 1986.

4185.   Moore, Karen Dayle. *Rape and Worship: Toward a Feminist Theodicy* [D.Min.]. The School of Theology at Claremont, 1989.

4186.   Morrison, Robert L. *Process Thought and the Doctrine of Divine Immutability.* Boston University, 1991.

4187.   Muhima, Edward Bakaitwako. *"The Fellowship of Suffering": A Theological Interpretation of Christian Suffering Under Idi Amin.* Northwestern University, 1981.

4188.   Neville, Mary Gemma. *Redemptive Meaning of Suffering and Death* [D.Min.]. Andover Newton Theological Seminary, 1986.

4189.   Newman, Randall. *The Will in Bondage: An Analysis of the Doctrine of Original Sin in the Thought of Reinhold Niebuhr and Paul Tillich.* University of Chicago Divinity School, 1991.

4190.   Norman, Ralph Vernon, Jr. *Theodicy and the Form of Redemption.* Yale University, 1961.

4191.   Nyomi, Setriakor Kobla. *A Pastoral Perspective on Ministry to Persons Dealing with Loss Due to Natural Disasters in Ghana.* Princeton Theological Seminary, 1991.

4192.   Oberholzer, Felicidad. *The Transformation of Evil into Sin and Sin into Sorrow and Forgiveness: Lessons from Analytic Psychology and Theology.* Graduate Theological Union, 1984.

4193.   Ormsby, Eric Linn. *An Islamic Version of Theodicy: The Dispute over Al-Ghazali's "Best of All Possible Worlds."* Princeton University, 1981.

4194.   Otto, Randall E. *The God of Hope: The Trinitarian Vision of Jürgen Moltmann.* Westminster Theological Seminary, 1990.

4195.   Outwater, Dennis L. *The Problem of Evil: A Comparison of Theological and Depth-Psychological Perspectives.* University of Chicago, 1972.

4196.   Rennie, Robert Melvin. *The Christian and the Continuing Problems of Human Life: Ways in Which Beliefs in the Power of God Help the People of First Baptist to Cope with Death, Suffering and Injustice* [D.Min.]. Drew University, 1976.

4197.   Roumm, Phyllis G. *Portraits of Suffering Womanhood in Representative Nineteenth-Century American Novels: The Contribution of Kate Chopin.* Kent State University, 1977.

4198.   Rubenstein, Richard Lowell. *Psychoanalysis and the Image of Evil in Rabbinic Literature: An Examination of the Freudian Interpretation of Religion in the Light of Rabbinic Legend.* Harvard University, 1960.

4199.   Sameshima, Yasuko. *A Cross-Cultural Comparison of Nurses' Inferences of Suffering* [Ed.D.]. Columbia University Teacher's College, 1975.

4200. Sands, Kathleen Mary. *Escape from Paradise: Evil in the Theological Foundations of Rosemary Radford Ruether and Carol P. Christ.* Boston College, 1991.

4201. Scatena, Paul. *An Epistemic Theory of Pain.* University of Rochester, 1990.

4202. Schermerhorn, Richard Alonzo. *The Problem of Evil in the Philosophy of James Ward.* Yale University, 1931.

4203. Schimel, Ruth Mara. *Becoming Courageous: A Search for Process.* George Wasington University, 1990.

4204. Seif, Nancy Gordon. *Otto Rank: On Human Evil.* Yeshiva University, 1980.

4205. Sevensky, Robert Leo. *Toward a Philosophy of Evil: The Role of the Myth of the Fall in the Thought of Paul Tillich and Paul Ricoeur.* Boston College, 1977.

4206. Shippey, Robert Clifford, Jr. *The Suffering of God in Karl Barth's Doctrines of Election and Reconciliation.* Southern Baptist Theological Seminary, 1991.

4207. Shorish-Shamley, Zieba Nisa. *The Self and Other in Afghan Cosmology: Concepts of Health and Illness Among the Afghan Refugees.* University of Wisconsin, 1991.

4208. Slavin, Malcolm Owen. *The Theme of Feminine Evil: The Image of Woman in Male Fantasy and its Effect on Attitudes and Behavior.* Harvard University, 1972.

4209. Smith, Adam Herbert. *The Problem of Theodicy in the Thought of Paul Tillich.* The Claremont Graduate School, 1973.

4210. Southern, Lonnie Steven. *A Christian Analysis of Suffering* [D.Min.]. The School of Theology at Claremont, 1977.

4211. Stevens, Richard John. *Suffering as the Key to Political and Social Transformation in South Africa.* Princeton Theological Seminary, 1985.

4212. Stewart, John David. *Paul Ricoeur's Phenomenology of Evil.* Rice University, 1965.

4213. Sugnet, Charles Joseph. *Social Evil and Private Virtue in the British Novel.* University of Virginia, 1970.

4214. Sutton, Robert Chester, III. *Authentic Responses to Evil in Jesus and Albert Camus.* Drew University, 1988.

4215. Szeto, Paul Cheuk-Ching. *Suffering in the Experience in the Protestant Church in China (1911-1980): A Chinese Perspective* [D.Miss.]. Fuller Theological Seminary, 1980.

4216. Terry, David Jonathan. *Martin Luther on the Suffering of the Christian.* Boston University, 1990.

4217. Terry, Ronald Franklin. *The Problem of Evil in the Theologies of Paul Tillich and Henry Nelson Wieman.* Iliff School of Theology, 1962.

4218. Thompson, Charles B. *The Problem of Good-and-Evil in Theistic Personalism, with Special Attention to E.S. Brightman.* New Orleans Baptist Theological Seminary, 1964.

4219. Thornton, Sharon Garred. *Pastoral Care and the Reality of Suffering: Pastoral Theology from the Perspective of Theology of the Cross.* Graduate Theological Union, 1991.

4220.   Tolaas, Gregory R. *"Telling the Story": A Dialectic of Hope and Healing for the Suffering, the Dying and the Living* [D.Min.]. Luther Northwestern Theological Seminary, 1990.

4221.   Toolan, David S. *The Problem of Evil and the Mystic's Way to God: A Study of William Ernest Hocking.* Southern Methodist University, 1974.

4222.   Toombs, S. Kay E. *The Meaning of Illness: A Phenomenological Approach to the Patient-Physician Relationship.* Rice University, 1990.

4223.   Tsambassis, Alexander Nicholas. *Evil and the "Abysmal Nature" of God in the Thought of Brightman, Berdyaev, and Tillich.* Northwestern University, 1957.

4224.   Udoff, Alan Lawrence. *Evil, History and Faith.* Georgetown University, 1982.

4225.   Van Beek, Aart Martin. *Grief and Theodicy: An Attempt to Determine the Usefulness of a Rational Approach Following Personal Loss* [D.Min.]. The School of Theology at Claremont, 1980.

4226.   Van Wyk, Ignatius William Charles. *The Theodicy Problem as Focus Point of the Church Political and Theological Issues: A Discussion with Jürgen Moltmann* [D.D.]. University of Pretoria (South Africa), 1987.

4227.   Vaughn, Stanley Bruce. *Intersubjectivity as the Ground of Hope: Psychoanalytical and Theological Perspectives.* Vanderbilt University, 1991. [Terminal illness and pastoral counselling.]

4228.   Vaught, Laud Oswald. *A Study of the Ontology of Evil in the Educational Philosophy of Martin Buber.* University of North Dakota, 1974.

4229.   Visser, Petrus Johannes. *Compensation and Satisfaction in Terms of the Action for Pain and Suffering* [L.L.D.]. University of South Africa, 1980 [Afrikaans.]

4230.   Walker, Graham Brown, Jr. *Elie Wiesel: A Challenge to Contemporary Theology.* Southern Baptist Theological Seminary, 1986.

4231.   Walls, Jerry L. *The Logic of Damnation: A Defense of the Traditional Doctrine of Hell.* University of Notre Dame, 1989.

4232.   Waschenfelder, Jacob Ludwig. *J.B. Metz's Critique of Religious Apathy.* McMaster University, 1990.

4233.   Wiesner, Naphtali A. *Faith and Suffering: A Study of the Impact of Concentration Camp Experiences on Moral and Religious Attitudes.* New School for Social Research, 1951.

4234.   Williamson, Arthur Harold. *Anti-Christ's Career in Scotland: The Imagery of Evil and the Search for a Scottish Past.* Washington University, 1974.

4235.   Wortham, Carol Barbee. *An Investigation of the Influence of Religiosity on the Ease with which Nurses Respond to Death and Dying Situations.* Emory University, 1989.

4236.   Wright, Willie Lee. *Theodicy: Black Suffering* [D.Min.]. The School of Theology at Claremont, 1976.

4237.   Younger, Paul. *The Birth of the Indian Religious Tradition or Studies in the Indian Concept of Duhkha.* Princeton University, 1965.

Index I

Chapters 2–7

Numbers in this index refer to the entry numbers. Numbers in square brackets indicate an author is cited within the annotation of another author and that the former's publication has not been assigned a separate item number. This has been kept to a minimum and used only when it was especially relevant. Note also that some annotations contain more than one publication by a single author. In these cases, only one item number has been assigned. Note, finally, that this index does not cite references to authors/publications within annotations which have been assigned their own numbers.

Index II

Appendices A–E

Numbers in this index refer to the entry numbers. Numbers in square brackets indicate an author is cited within the annotation of another author and that the former's publication has not been assigned a separate item number. This has been kept to a minimum and used only when it was especially relevant. Note also that some annotations contain more than one publication by a single author. In these cases, only one item number has been assigned. Note, finally, that this index does not cite references to authors/ publications within annotations which have been assigned their own numbers.

Anglin, B. 1828
Ansbro, J.J. 2058
Ansell, C. 2448
Anshen, R.N. 2934
Antarkar, S.S. 3153
Arapura, J.G. 3154
Arathuzik, M.D. 4096
Archer, D.J. 2512
Archer, G. 1468
Arendt, H. 2676
Armour, L. 2486
Armstrong D.R. 1469
Arnold, S.R. 3734
Arnold, W.J. 4028
Aronson, R. 2677
Ashley, B. 2617
Atkins, A. 2513
Atkinson, D.J. 3155
Au, P.Y. 4097
Auer, J.A. 3156
Austin, D.B. 3735
Avens, R. 2935
Averill, J.H. 2514, 3883
Avisar, I. 2678
Awn, P.J. 3011, 3012
Ayers, M.R. 3884
Ayers, R.H. 1829
Ayoub, M.M. 3013, 3014, 3015, 4098

B

Babbage, S.B. 2515
Babcock, W.S. 1960
Bachelder, R.S. 2516
Baepler, R. 2487
Baier, K. 3157
Bailey, J.S. 3158
Baird, J.D. 3885
Bakan, D. 3159
Baker, J.R. 2193
Baldwin, D.D. 3736
Baldwin, R.C. 2517
Balentine, S.E. 1470
Ballard, E.G. 2518
Balthasar, H.U. von 1830
Bandy, M.F. 3886
Banner, M. 3737
Barbour, J.D. 2519
Barciauskas, R. 3738

Bareau, A. 3016
Bargeliotes, L. 2059
Barineau, R.M. 3739
Barlow, S. 3160
Barnesm, L. 4099
Barnhart, J.E. 2060, 2194, 3161, 4100
Barr, B. 2520
Barr, D.L. 2521
Barr, J. 1471, 1472, 1473, 1474
Barraclough, R. 1475
Barth, K. 2195
Barton, J. 1476
Barton, S. 1477
Basinger, D. 2522
Basinger, R.G. 3740
Baskin, W. 2936
Bass, C.B. 2937
Bataille, G. 2523
Bauckham, R. 2196, 2197, 2198, 2199, 2200, 2679
Bauer, Y. 2680, 2681, 2682, [#2690]
Baum, G. [#1571]
Baum, R.C. 2683
Baumgarten, E. 2061
Bavier, R. 3741
Baylis, C.A.C. 3162
Bayly, J. 3163
Baynes, S. 2201
Beardslee, W.A. 2202
Beasley-Murray, G.R. 1478
Beattie, P.H. 3164
Beaty, M.D. 3742
Bechtler, S.R. 3838
Becker, E. 3165, 3166, 3167
Becker, J.E. 3887
Becker, W.E. 3839
Becker, W.H. 2684
Beeson, R.J. 4101
Beguin, A. 2938
Beirnaert, L. 3168
Beker, J.C. 1479, 1480, 1481, 1482
Bell, R.H. 3169
Belleggia, C. 1831
Ben-David, E. 2685
Ben-Yosef, I.A. 2686
Benn, S.I. 3170
Bennett, G. 1483
Bennett, R.A. 1484

Brown, Robert F. 1964, 2070
Brown, Robert M. 2709, 2710, 2711,
    2712, 2713, 2714, 2715
Brown, S. 1497
Brown, W.C. 3890
Bruecher, W. 3891
Brueggemann, W. 1498, 1499, 1500,
    1501, 1502, 1503, 1504, 1505, 1506
Bryant, M.D. [#2627]
Bryson, J. 2942
Bube, R. 1507
Buber, M. 1508 [#2120]
Buck, F. 1509
Buhrer, J.D. 4111
Bulka, R.P. 2716, 2717
Bull, V.S. 3892
Bulman, R.J. 3199
Burhoe, R.W. 3200
Burke, T. 3744
Burn, C.E. 3893
Burns, J.P. 1965
Burnley, E. 2209
Burrell, D.B. 1833, 1834, 1835, 1966
Burrow, R. 4112
Burt, D.X. 1967, 2210
Burtness, J.H. 1510
Busby, M.B. 3894
Buser, M.B. 2718
Bush, T.A. 4113
Buss, S. 3745
Bussell, H. 3201
Buttrick, G.A. 1511
Byrne, B. 1512

C

Cahill, L.S. 3202
Cain, D. 3203
Callewaert, J.M. 4033
Calvert, B. 2071
Camacho, H.S. 4114
Campola, A. 3204
Camroux, M. 1513
Čapek, M. 2072
Capitan, W.H. 2011, 3205
Capobianco, R. 2073
Caplan, L. 3206
Capon, R.F. 3207

Cargas, H.J. 2719, 2720, 2721, 2722,
    2723, 2724, 2725
Carmack, S.W. 3842
Carnell, E.J. 2074, 3208
Carney, F.S. 3209
Carnois, B. 2031
Carretto, C. 3210
Carroll, R.P. 1476, 1514
Carson, A. 3091
Carson, D.A. 1515, 1516, 2075
Carter, C.W. 2076
Carter, R.L. 4115
Cartwright, D. 2077
Carus, P. 2943
Case, A.M. 3895
Case-Winters, A.L. 3746
Casey, B.L. 4116
Casey, J. 3211
Caskin, J.C.A. 3212
Caspar, R. 3213
Cassell, E.J. 3214, 3215, 3216
Caton, H. 2078
Cauthen, K. 2211
Cavanagh, R.R. 3747
Cavendish, R. 3217
Cedars, M.M. 2726
Chao, J. 3218
Charny, I.W. 2727
Charry, E.Z. 2728
Chase, C.L. 4034
Cheney, D. 3598
Chiang, C. 4035
Childress, M. 3219
Childs, B.S. 2212
Chisholm, R.M. 2079
Chittister, J.D. 3220
Chitwood, G.C. 4036
Chopp, R.S. 2213, 2214, 2729, 4117
Christiano, K. 3725
Christie, D.L. 4037
Christlieb, T.J. 3748
Christopher, J.R. 3221
Clark, D.W. 2080
Clark, J.M. 3222
Clark, J.P.H. 2215
Clark, M. 3223
Clarke, D. 2618
Clarke, O.F. 1517

E

Paulits, F.J. 3967
Pavkovic, A. 2154
Pawlikowski, J.T. 2833
Payne, B. 2475
Peake, A.S. 1709
Peat, D. 2649
Pechauer, P. 3542
Peck, A.J. 2834
Peck, M.S. 2982
Pedersen, D.B. 3866
Pederson, A.M. 3806
Peel, R. 3543
Peeters, G. 3544
Pellauer, D. 3545
Pelletier, K.R. 3546
Penchansky, D. 1710
Pendergast, R.J. 1914
Pentz, R.D. 4070
Perkins, D. 2368
Pernick, M.S. 2476
Perrett, R.W. 3067
Perry, M. 2983
Peter, C.J. 2650
Peterfreund, S. 3547
Peters, T. 2984
Peters, K.E. 3548
Petit, F. 1915
Petrie, A. 3549
Phifer, K. 3550
Phillips, A. 2369, 2835
Phillips, E. 4071
Phillips, J.A. 3121
Phillips, L.B. 3551, 3552
Phillips, M.A. 3867
Philp, H.L. 3553
Pickering, W.S. 3554
Pielke, R.G, 2581
Pierce, E.L. 1711
Pink, A. 3555
Pinkus, P. 2582
Piper, J. 1712, 1713, 1714
Piper, O. 3556
Pipes, B.R. 3868
Piscitelli, E.J. 3557
Plank, K.A. 1715
Plantinga, C. 2370, 2371
Plaskow, J. 3122
Ploplis, W.R. 3968

Pocock, D. 3558
Pojman, L.P. 3559
Pole, N. 2503
Polen, N. 2372
Polish, D. 2836
Polkinghorne, J. 3560
Pollard, T.E. 2373
Pontifex, M. 1916, 1917, 1918, 1919,
    1920, 1921
Pope, M.H. 1716
Porter, S.E. 2651
Post, W. 2045
Post, S.G. 2374, 2375
Poulose, M.P. 3561
Powell, J.L. 3562
Powell, T.F. 4072
Power, W. 2376
Power, W.J.A. 3869
Praetorius, H.M. 4073
Prasad, R. 3563, 3564
Prendiville, J.G. 1981
Prest, A.P. 3565
Price, J.S. 3969
Price, R.M. 1717
Priebbenow, C.R. 3566
Priest, J. 1718
Prior, D. 2377
Proctor, S.D. 3567
Proudfoot, C.M. 3870
Proudfoot, M. 1719
Pruett, G.E. 3068
Prusak, B.P. 3123
Pruyser, P.W. [#2453]
Psorulla, E.M. 3124
Puccetti, R. 2477
Purtill, R.L. 3568, 3569, 3570
Pustejovsky, J.S. 3970
Putman, C.C. 3571
Putney, D.P. 3807

Q

Quay, P.M. 2985, 2986
Quinn, J.M. 1922
Quinn, P.L. 2046, 2583, 2652, 2653,
    2654

R

Raabe, P.R. 1720, 1721, 2378

Smyth, P. 3632
Snaith, N. 1765
Snook, L.E. 1766
Soards, M.L. 1767
Sobosian, J.G. 1768
Sobrino, J. 2394, 2395
Soelle, D. 2396, 2397, 2398, 2399, 3134
Soffer, W. 2171
Sogani, K.C. 3633
Sokoloff, N.B. 2889
Solon, T.P.M. 2023
Song, Choan-Seng. 3634
Songer, H.S. 1769
Sonneborn, J.A. 3078
Sontag, F. 2890, 3635
Sontag, S. 3636
Sorabji, R. 2172
Southern, L.S. 4210
Southwood, M. 3079
Spangler, J.D. [#2453]
Sparks, J.N. 3637
Spidell, S. 1770
Spikla, B. [#2453]
Spiro, M.E. 3638
Spivack, B. 2599
Spivack, C. 2600, 3993
Splett, J. 1886
Sponheim, P. 2173
Springsted, E.O. 3639, 3640, 3641, 3642
St. John, B.A. 3995
Stackhouse, J.G. 3643
Stackhouse, R. [#3643]
Stagg, F. 1771
Stalcup, B.L. 3820
Stark, J.C. 1990
Starnes, C. 1991, 1992
Startzman, L.E. 2891, 3995
Stashwick, T.S. 4085
Staub, E. 3644
Steckel, C.W. 2892
Stedman, R.C. 1772
Steimle, E.A. 1773
Stein, G. 2999
Steinman, C.M. 3996
Steiner, G. 2893, 2894
Steinkraus, W.E. 3080
Stellway, R.J. 3645

Stengel, W.B. 3997
Stenson, S.H. 2174
Stern, L.W. 2895
Stern, J. 2601
Steuernagel, V.R. 1774
Stevens, Rex P. 2048
Stevens, Richard J. 3646, 4211
Stewart, E.C.P. 3647
Stewart, J.D. 3648, 4212
Stivers, R. 2602
Stock, M. 3649
Stockdale, F.B. 2400
Stoeber, M.F. 3821
Stokes, W. 1940, 1941, 1942, 1943, 1944
Storms, C.S. 2175, 4086
Storms, W.C. 3822
Story, P. 3650
Stott, J.R.W. 1775, 2401
Strimple, R.B. 2661
Strong, A. 3651
Strozewski, W. 2176
Stuart, A.C. 3081
Stuermann, W.E. 3652
Stuhlmueller, C. 1776, 1777
Stump, E. 1892, 1945, 1946
Suchocki, M.H. 3823
Sugnet, C.J. 4213
Sullivan, R.J. 2049
Sundberg, W. 3000
Sunderland, R. 1757
Surin, K. 2402, 2403, 2404
Sutcliffe, E.F. 1778
Sutherland, D. 2405
Sutherland, S.R. 2603, 3653, 3654
Sutton, R.C. 4214
Swann, G.R. 3999
Swanson, S.A. 4087
Sweet, J.P. 1779, 3001
Swinburne, R. 2662
Szczepański, J. 3655
Szeto, P. 4215
Szonyi, D.M. 2896

T

Talbott, T.B. 2508, 3656
Taliaferro, C. 2406
Tanenzapf, S. 2407

Van Buren, P.M. 2904, 2905
Van Daalen, D.H. 1794
Van Den Bogaerde. 3678
Van der Hoeven, J. 3679
Van der Ven, J.A. 3680
Van Heukelem, J.F. 3681
Van Leeuwen, T.M. 3682
Van Selm, A. 1797
Van Wyk, I.W. 4226
Van Zeller, D.H. 1949
Vanauken, S. 3683, 3684
Vance, N. 2610
Vande Kemp, H. 3685
Vanhoutte, J. 2416
Vanstone, W.H. 2417, 2418
Variyamattom, M. 3876
Varma, V.P. 3085
Vasquez, P.R. 4005
Vaughn, S.B. 4227
Vaught, L.O. 4228
Vawter, B. 1798
Velkley, R.L. 4089
Vellenga, J.J. 3877
Verdu, A. 3086
Vertin, M. 1950
Veto, M.J. 3686
Vieth, R.F. 2419
Vieujean, J. 2510
Vines, M.L. 3687
Visser, P.J. 4229
Vivian, F. 3688
Vliet, R.M. 4006
Vorgrimler, H. 1928
Vriend, D.J. 3827

W

Wachterhauser, B.R. 3689
Waddle, S.H. 4090
Wadia, A.R. [#3070]
Wadia, P.S. 2026, 2027
Wadsworth, C. 4007
Wagner, R.W. [#2590]
Wainer, A.M. 4008
Wainwright, W. 2666
Waite, R.G. 2906
Waldman, T. [#2989]
Walhout, D. 3690
Walker, C.T. 3138

Walker, G.B. 4230
Wall, James M. 2611
Wall, P. 2481
Wall, R.W. 3691
Wallis, J. 3692, 3693, 3694
Walls, J.L. 2028, 3695, 4231
Walsch, C. 3696, 3697
Walsh, J.P.M. 1799
Walsh, J. 1951
Walsh, P.G. 1951
Walsh, T. 2667
Walter, E. 3698
Walter, E.W. 3699
Ward, J.A. 2612, 4009
Ward, J.T. 4010
Ware, B.A. 2420
Warner, T. 3201
Warren, T.B. 3828
Waschenfelder, J.L. 4232
Wasiolek, E. 2613
Watkins, R.N. 3139
Watson, J. 3700
Watson, N.M. 1800
Watson, S.Y. 1952
Weatherhead, L.D. 3701, 3702, 3703
Webb, B. 1953
Weber, M. 1801
Weber, C.J. 2614
Weborg, J. 2907
Webster, A.F.C. 3704
Webster, D.D. 1802
Webster, D.G. 2019
Weddle, D.L. 2421
Weeraratne, A. 3087
Wei-Ming, T. 3088
Weil, S. 3705, 3706, 3707, 3708, 3709, 3710
Weininger, B. 2482
Weisberger, A.M. 3829
Weiskopf, D.D. 4011
Weisner, N.A. 4233
Weiss, D.W. [#2690]
Weiss, P. 1803
Weithman, P.J. 4091
Welch, T.J. 3878
Welch, S.D. 3140
Wells, D.A. 3711
Wenham, J.W. 1804

Z

Zahl, P.F.M. 2445
Zahn, G.C. 2933
Zaidi, Q.S. 3732
Zaner, R.M. 3375
Zeisler, J.A. 1823
Zhitlowsky, C. 1824
Zimany, R.D. 2446
Zimmerli, W. 1825
Zimmerman, C.E. 4093
Zimmermann, E.J. 4024
Zuck, R.B. 1826
Zucker, A. 2485
Zuckermann, B.E. 1827

Afterword

As the first bibliography on the vastly complex and increasingly important *theodicy* issue, this book was long overdue when it first was published in 1993. I am confident that in the few years since its publication, it has become an essential research tool for scholars and students working in the field and that it will remain so for many years to come. The present state of computer data bases available is a chaos of information which takes almost as much time to sort as to use. My purpose was to organize the material in a useful manner so that those who work in this field will be able to locate the main publications on any particular aspect of the vast theodicy literature. My annotations seek to be objective summaries of the main publications, noting the main arguments and theses in the items listed.

I suggested this project to Garland Publishing in February, 1987. The next six years were consumed largely by this task, although there were various interruptions which delayed this work. In early 1988, I was elected for a three-year term as Head of my department during a very difficult time in the department's history. With the permission of the University of Windsor's Vice-President–Academic, I reluctantly resigned this administrative work after one year, in order to devote more time to this research project. I was able to complete and publish a little book, an overview of theodicy, for Paulist Press *(What Are They Saying About God and Evil?)* and continued work on various other research projects related to theodicy and to process thought. As other professional academics will understand, my "day job" as a university professor is consumed by teaching, administrative and assorted public duties. Research time is a hard-found luxury.

This project, however, was aided significantly by the generosity of the University of Windsor in awarding me its "Academic Development Fund Grant," a six-month administrative leave (1989), a six-month sabbatical leave (1990), a University Research Professorship (1992/1993), and a six-month sabbatical leave (1998), all of which released me from some teaching and administrative obligations. The Canadian government supported this project with a major "Social Sciences and Humanities Research Grant" with which I was able to purchase most of the recent books on theodicy and to hire research assistants to aid me in collecting and photocopying the hundreds of items which are entered in this bibliography. The result of this work has given me a privileged awareness of most of the publications and dissertations (as well as the book reviews, not listed in this bibliography) that have been written on the theodicy issue during the past 30-35 years.

A final word of explanation is in order about the nature of the entries and the selection process. I have made a concerted effort to include all that is *relevant*. Some limitations, of course, had to be imposed on the work since there are many thousands of *relevant* items. My decision was to focus on the analytic philosophical and theological debates in the academic journals and books since the late 1950s, the time when current interest in the theodicy question reemerged in the theological and philosophical literature. The items relegated to the five appendices are no less important than those listed in the six chapters. The appendices are meant to supplement the chapters' items, rather than omit them as not directly appropriate for inclusion in the six chapters. I have attempted to provide annotations which are accurate and useful to researchers and I have tried not to mangle the names of the authors, many of whom previously had been unfamiliar to me. I trust that those who are in the Thomist tradition are not offended by the relegation of the items in *Appendix B* to an appendix, and that those who are traditional conservative Protestants are not offended by the relegation of the major publications from this perspective to an appendix, *Appendix D*. I have sought to annotate as many of the major publications in the four appendices as time permitted, and included an appendix on dissertations to acknowledge their important contributions.

Finally, despite long months checking and rechecking the volume numbers, page references, and the like, there will be the inevitable omissions and annoying typos. I have done all I can to eliminate such problems. For those whose relevant work may not have been included in this bibliography, my apologies and also an offer of token consolation: I have made an effort to include everything that was relevant to the issues. There may be items missing, nonetheless. I invite submissions (at the address below) from authors whose relevant works may have been missed. I have amassed an enviable library of theodicy publications and look forward to updating the data periodically and to contributing companion volumes of critical essays on this most important of theological and philosophical pursuits.

Barry L. Whitney
University of Windsor
Windsor, Ontario, Canada N9B3P4
8 May 1998

AUTHOR VITAE

Barry Whitney (1947–) earned his Honours B.A. in English, Religion, and Philosophy from Carleton University in Ottawa (1967-1971), and his Ph.D. in Philosophy of Religion from McMaster University in Hamilton, Ontario (1971-1976). He studied briefly at the University of Texas in Austin with philosopher Charles Hartshorne, and at the University of Western Ontario in London with philosopher A.H. Johnson. His dissertation constructed a theodicy based on Hartshorne's prolific publications.

Dr. Whitney is Professor of Philosophy of Religion at the University of Windsor, and has published several books and dozens of journal articles and reviews on process philosophy and on the problem of evil. He is also editor of the scholarly journal, *Process Studies*.